Digital Learning
Resources

*Of the People,
A History of the
United States*
Volume II: Since 1865,
with Sources
FOURTH EDITION

Michael McGerr, Jan Ellen
Lewis, James Oakes, Nick
Cullather, Jeanne Boydston,
Mark Summers, Camilla
Townsend, Karen M. Dunak

Carefully scratch off the silver
coating to see your personal
redemption code.

Oxford Insight Study
Guide and
Additional Digital
Course Materials

Of the People comes with a
wealth of powerful tools to help
you succeed in your course.

**Follow these steps to access your
resources:**

Visit oup.com/he/oakes-mcgerr4e

Select the edition you are using, then select
student resources for that edition

Follow the on-screen instructions, entering
your personal redemption code when
prompted

For assistance with code redemption or
registration, please contact customer support at
learninglinkdirect.support@oup.com.
or 855-281-8749.

OXFORD
UNIVERSITY PRESS

P9-CJN-278

Of the People

Of the People

A HISTORY OF THE UNITED STATES *Fourth Edition*
WITH SOURCES

VOLUME II Since 1865

Michael McGerr

Jan Ellen Lewis

James Oakes

Nick Cullather

Mark Summers

Camilla Townsend

Karen M. Dunak

New York   Oxford
Oxford University Press

Oxford University Press is a department of the University of Oxford.
It furthers the University's objective of excellence in research, scholarship,
and education by publishing worldwide. Oxford is a registered trademark of
Oxford University Press in the UK and certain other countries.

Published in the United States of America by Oxford University Press
198 Madison Avenue, New York, NY 10016, United States of America.

© 2019, 2017, 2013, and 2011 by Oxford University Press

ISBN: 978-0-19-090997-0

9 8 7 6 5 4 3
Printed by LSC Communications, United States of America

Jeanne Boydston
1944–2008
Historian, Teacher, Friend

Brief Contents

Contents

CHAPTER 16 The Triumph of Industrial Capitalism, 1850–1890   496

CHAPTER 17 The Culture and Politics of Industrial America, 1870–1892   524

CHAPTER 19 A United Body of Action, 1900-1916   588

CHAPTER 20   A Global Power, 1914–1919   618

CHAPTER 22 A Great Depression and a New Deal, 1929–1940   678

CHAPTER 24 The Cold War, 1945–1954   742

CHAPTER 26 "The Table of Democracy," 1960–1968   804

CHAPTER 27 Living with Less, 1968–1980   836

CHAPTER 28 The Triumph of Conservatism, 1980–1991   868

CHAPTER 30 "A Nation Transformed," The Twenty-First Century 934

Appendices

Maps

Features

AMERICA AND THE WORLD

STRUGGLES FOR DEMOCRACY

Preface

At Gettysburg, Pennsylvania, on November 19, 1863, President Abraham Lincoln dedicated a memorial to the more than 3,000 Union soldiers who had died turning back a Confederate invasion in the first days of July. There were at least a few ways that the president could have justified the sad loss of life in the third year of a brutal war dividing North and South. He could have said it was necessary to destroy the Confederacy's cherished institution of slavery, to punish southerners for seceding from the United States, or to preserve the nation intact. Instead, at this crucial moment in American history, Lincoln gave a short, stunning speech about democracy. The president did not use the word, but he offered its essence. The term *democracy* came from the ancient Greek word *demos*—for "the people." To honor the dead of Gettysburg, Lincoln called on northerners to ensure "that government of the people, by the people, for the people, shall not perish from the earth."

With these words, Lincoln put democracy at the center of the Civil War and at the center of American history. The authors of this book share his belief in the centrality of democracy; his words, "of the people," give our book its title and its main theme. We see American history as a story "of the people," of their struggles to shape their lives and their land.

Our choice of theme does not mean we believe that America has always been a democracy. Clearly, it has not. As Lincoln gave the Gettysburg Address, most African Americans still lived in slavery. American women, North and South, lacked rights that many men enjoyed; for all their disagreements, white southerners and northerners viewed Native Americans as enemies. Neither do we believe that there is only a single definition of democracy, either in the narrow sense of a particular form of government or in the larger one of a society whose members participate equally in its creation. Although Lincoln defined the northern cause as a struggle for democracy, southerners believed it was anything but democratic to force them to remain in the Union at gunpoint. As bloody draft riots in New York City in July 1863 made clear, many northern men thought it was anything but democratic to force them to fight in Lincoln's armies. Such disagreements have been typical of American history. For more than 500 years, people have struggled over whose vision of life in the New World would prevail.

It is precisely such struggles that offer the best angle of vision for seeing and understanding the most important developments in the nation's history. In particular, the democratic theme concentrates attention on the most fundamental concerns of history: people and power.

Lincoln's words serve as a reminder of the basic truth that history is about people. Across the 30 chapters of this book, we write extensively about complex events. But we also write in the awareness that these developments are only abstractions unless they are grounded in the lives of people. The test of a historical narrative, we believe, is whether its characters are fully rounded, believable human beings.

The choice of Lincoln's words also reflects our belief that history is about power. To ask whether America was democratic at some point in the past is to ask how much power various groups of people had to make their lives and their nation. Such questions of power necessarily take us to political processes, to the ways in which people work separately and collectively to enforce their will. We define politics quite broadly in this book. With the feminists of the 1960s, we believe that "the personal is the political," that power relations shape people's lives in private as well as in public. *Of the People* looks for democracy in the living room as well as the legislature, and in the bedroom as well as the business office.

Focusing on democracy, people, and power, we have necessarily written as wide-ranging a history as possible. In the features and in the main text, *Of the People* conveys both the unity and the great diversity of the American people across time and place. We chronicle the racial and ethnic groups who have shaped America, differences of religious and regional identity, the changing nature of social classes, and the different ways that gender identities have been constructed over the centuries.

While treating different groups in their distinctiveness, we have integrated them into the broader narrative as much as possible. A true history "of the people" means not only acknowledging their individuality and diversity but also showing their interrelationships and their roles in the larger narrative. More integrated coverage of Native Americans, African Americans, Latinos, and other minority groups appears throughout the fourth edition.

Of the People also offers comprehensive coverage of the different spheres of human life—cultural as well as governmental, social as well as economic, environmental as well as military. This commitment to comprehensiveness is a reflection of our belief that all aspects of human existence are the stuff of history. It is also an expression of the fundamental theme of the book: the focus on democracy leads naturally to the study of people's struggles for power in every dimension of their lives. Moreover, the democratic approach emphasizes the interconnections between the different aspects of Americans' lives; we cannot understand politics and government without tracing their connection to economics, religion, culture, art, sexuality, and so on.

The economic connection is especially important. *Of the People* devotes much attention to economic life, to the ways in which Americans have worked and saved and spent. Economic power, the authors believe, is basic to democracy. Americans' power to shape their lives and their country has been greatly affected by whether they were farmers or hunters, plantation owners or slaves, wage workers or capitalists, domestic servants or bureaucrats. The authors do not see economics as an impersonal, all-conquering force; instead, we try to show how the values and actions of ordinary people, as well as the laws and regulations of government, have made economic life.

We have also tried especially to place America in a global context. The history of America, or any nation, cannot be adequately explained without understanding its relationship to transnational events and global developments. That is true for the first chapter of the book, which shows how America began to emerge from the collision of Native Americans, West Africans, and Europeans in the fifteenth and sixteenth centuries. It is just as true for the last chapters of the book, which demonstrate how globalization and the war on terror transformed the United States at the turn of the twenty-first century. In the chapters in between, we detail how the world has changed America and how America has changed the world. Reflecting the concerns of the rest of the book, we focus particularly on the movement of people, the evolution of power, and the attempt to spread democracy abroad.

Abraham Lincoln wanted to sell a war, of course. But he also truly believed that his audience would see democracy as quintessentially American. Whether he was right is the burden of this book.

New to the Fourth Edition

We are grateful that the first, second, and third editions of *Of the People* have been welcomed by instructors and students as a useful instructional aid. In preparing the fourth edition, our primary goal has been to maintain the text's overarching focus on the evolution of American democracy, people, and power; its strong portrayal of political and social history; and its clear, compelling narrative voice. To that end, the broad representation of Native Americans, African Americans, and other minority groups in this text shows the full diversity of the American people. One of the text's strengths is its critical-thinking pedagogy because the study of history entails careful analysis, not mere memorization of names and dates.

History continues, and the writing of history is never finished. For the fourth edition, we have updated the following elements based on the most recent scholarship:

Number of Chapters

The book has been condensed from 30 chapters and an epilogue to 30 chapters: the number of Gilded Age chapters has been reduced from three (formerly Chapters 16, 17, and 18 in the third edition) to two (Chapters 16 and 17 in the fourth edition) to streamline the narrative flow and more evenly balance the distribution of chapters to allow for more coverage of recent history. The chapter content has been redistributed as follows to accommodate this restructuring.

Chapter 15: Reconstructing a Nation, 1865–1877
- Includes a new section titled "A Reconstructed West," which is comprised of the following sections from the third edition's Chapter 16:
  - The Overland Trail
  - The Origins of Indian Reservations
  - The Destruction of Indian Subsistence
- The chapter-ending section "The End of Reconstruction" now concludes with "Sharecropping Becomes Wage Labor" from the third edition's Chapter 16.

Chapter 16: The Triumph of Industrial Capitalism, 1850–1890
- Includes the section "Social Darwinism and the Growth of Scientific Racism" from the third edition's Chapter 17
- Includes "Struggles for Democracy: 'The Chinese Must Go'" from the third edition's Chapter 17
- Includes the section "The Knights of Labor and the Haymarket Disaster" from the third edition's Chapter 18

Chapter 17: The Culture and Politics of Industrial America, 1870–1892
- Formerly Chapter 18 in the third edition
- Includes the section "The Elusive Boundaries of Male and Female," which is comprised of the following sections from the third edition's Chapter 17:
  - The Victorian Construction of Male and Female
  - Victorians Who Questioned Traditional Sexual Boundaries

- Content from the third edition's Chapter 17 "American Portrait: Anthony Comstock's Crusade Against Vice" is incorporated into the discussion "The Victorian Crusade for Morality."
- Includes the section "The Varieties of Urban Culture" from the third edition's Chapter 17, now simply titled "Urban Culture."
- Includes the section "A New Cultural Order: New Americans Stir Old Fears," which is comprised of the following sections from the third edition's Chapter 17:
  - Josiah Strong Attacks Immigration
  - From Immigrants to Ethnic Americans
  - The Catholic Church and Its Limits in Immigrant Culture
  - Immigrant Cultures
- Includes the section "The Rise and Fall of the National Labor Union" from the third edition's Chapter 15

Chapter 30: "A Nation Transformed," The Twenty-First Century

Formerly the Epilogue, this chapter has been revised and significantly expanded to cover the span of years since 2001.

- Revised discussion of Obama's second term in office
- New discussions on:
  - Climate change
  - The rise of the Islamic State
  - Diversity, division, and discrimination in the United States, with emphasis on the justice system's treatment of African Americans and Deferred Action for Childhood Arrivals (DACA)
  - Expanded discussion of LGBTQ rights
  - Shifting religious beliefs and practices in the United States
  - The implications of deindustrialization, digitization, and globalization on jobs and growth
  - The growing income inequality gap
  - How economic change has impacted the status of women, men, baby boomers, and millennials, as well as increased the divide between urban and rural areas
  - How growing wealth inequality has intensified the problem of money in politics
  - The emergence of four contending political approaches
  - The Presidential Election of 2016

New Additions to American Portrait, American Landscape, America and the World, and Struggles for Democracy Features

These popular features from the third edition have been updated with eight new American Portraits, four new American Landscapes, eight new America and the World features, and three new Struggles for Democracy.

Photos

Approximately one-third of the photos have been revised throughout the chapters and sources.

Primary Sources

A version of the text is available with end-of-chapter primary source documents, both textual and visual, designed to reinforce students' understanding of the material by drawing connections among topics and thinking critically. Nearly all chapters include at least one new source document:

- Source 2.3 Father Pierre Cholonec, Life of Kateri (1715)
- Source 3.1 Edward Waterhouse's Report on the Uprising of 1622
- Source 5.4 George Whitefield, Account of a Visit to Georgia (1738)
- Source 6.5 The Stamp Act Riots: The Destruction of Thomas Hutchinson's House (1765)
- Source 7.2 Alexander Hamilton Recommends Arming Slaves and George Washington Rejects the Idea (1779)
- Source 8.2 Thomas Jefferson's Letter to Philip Mazzei (1796)
- Source 9.5 Elder David Purviance's Description of the Cane Ridge Revival (1801)
- Source 10.5 Frances Kemble's Journal (1838–1839)
- Source 11.2 Angelina Grimké, Excerpt from *An Appeal to the Women of the Nominally Free States* (1838)
- Source 12.5 María Amparo Ruiz, *The Squatter and the Don* (1885)
- Source 13.4 Abraham Lincoln, Speech at Springfield, Illinois (1857)
- Source 14.1 John Sherman, A Letter on the Crisis to Philadelphians (1860)
- Source 14.3 Cornelia Hancock, Letter to Her Sister (1863)
- Source 14.4 John Beauchamp Jones Observes the Deterioration on the Confederate Home Front (1863–1864)
- Source 15.5 A Southern Unionist Judge's Daughter Writes the President for Help (1874)
- Source 15.6 Red Cloud Pleads the Plains Indians' Point of View at Cooper Union (1870)
- Source 16.6 James Baird Weaver, *A Call to Action* (1892)
- Source 17.5 Visual Documents: "Gift for the Grangers" (1873) and the Jorns Family of Dry Valley, Custer County, Nebraska (1886)
- Source 18.1 Frederick Winslow Taylor, Excerpts from *The Principles of Scientific Management* (1911)
- Source 20.1 World War I–Era Music: "I Didn't Raise My Boy to Be a Solider" (1915) and "Over There" (1917)
- Source 21.1 Hiram Wesley Evans, Excerpts from "The Klan: Defender of American-ism" (1925)
- Source 22.4 Remembering the Great Depression, Excerpts from Studs Terkel's *Hard Times* (1970)
- Source 23.2 Charles Lindbergh, America First Committee Address (1941)
- Source 24.2 High School and College Graduates in the Cold War (1948–1950)
- Source 25.1 Gael Greene, "The Battle of Levittown" (1957)
- Source 25.3 Visual Documents: Automobile Advertisements (1953–1955)
- Source 26.5 John Wilcock, "The Human Be-In" and "San Francisco" (1967)
- Source 27.2 Nixon Decides on the Christmas Bombing (1972)
- Source 28.1 Visual Document: US Centers for Disease Control, AIDS Awareness Poster (1980s)

- Source 29.3 Visual Document: Aziz + Cucher, "Man with Computer" (1992)
- Source 30.2 Barack Obama, Keynote Address, Democratic Party Convention (2004)
- Source 30.3 Debate in the House of Representatives on a Resolution "That Symbols and Traditions of Christmas Should Be Protected" (2005)
- Source 30.4 Harry M. Reid, "The Koch Brothers" (2015)
- Source 30.5 Steve A. King, "Illegal Immigration," House of Representatives (2007)
- Source 30.6 Donald Trump, Extract of Remarks at a "Make America Great Again" Rally in Harrisburg, Pennsylvania (2017)

Hallmark Features

- Each chapter opens with an **American Portrait** feature, a story of someone whose life in one way or another embodies the basic theme of the pages to follow.
- Select chapters include an **American Landscape** feature, a particular place in time where issues of power appeared in especially sharp relief.
- To underscore the fundamental importance of global relationships, select chapters include a feature on **America and the World**.
- Each chapter includes a **Struggles for Democracy** feature, focusing on moments of debate and public conversation surrounding events that have contributed to the changing ideas of democracy, as well as the sometimes constricting but overall gradually widening opportunities that evolved for the American people as a result.
- **Common Threads** focus questions at chapter openings.
- **Time Lines** in every chapter.
- A list of chapter-ending key terms, **Who, What, Where**, helps students recall the important people, events, and places of that chapter.
- All chapters end with both **Review Questions**, which test students' memory and understanding of chapter content, and **Critical-Thinking Questions**, which ask students to analyze and interpret chapter content.

Learning Resources for *Of the People*

Oxford University Press offers instructors and students a comprehensive ancillary package for qualified adopters.

Ancillary Resource Center (ARC)

This online resource center, available to adopters of *Of the People*, includes the following:

- Instructor's Resource Manual: Includes, for each chapter, a detailed chapter outline, suggested lecture topics, and learning objectives, as well as approximately 40 multiple-choice, short-answer, true-or-false, fill-in-the-blank, and 10 essay questions for each chapter
- A Computerized Test Bank that includes all of the test items from the Instructor's Resource Manual
- PowerPoints and Computerized Test Bank: Includes PowerPoint slides and JPEG and PDF files for all the maps and photos in the text, and approximately 1,000 additional PowerPoint-based slides from OUP's US History Image Library, organized by themes and periods in American history.

- The US History Video Library, Produced by Oxford University Press: Each 3- to 5-minute video covers a key topic in US history, from Squanto to John Brown, from Mother Jones to the "disco wars" of the late 1970s/early 1980s. Combining motion pictures, stills, audio clips, and narration, these videos are ideal for both classroom discussion or as online assignments.

Oxford First Source

This database includes hundreds of primary source documents in US history. The documents cover a broad variety of political, economic, social, and cultural topics and represent a cross section of American voices. Special effort was made to include as many previously disenfranchised voices as possible. The documents are indexed by date, author, title, and subject. Short documents (one or two pages) are presented in their entirety while longer documents have been carefully edited to highlight significant content. Each document is introduced with a short explanatory paragraph and accompanied with study questions.

A complete **Course Management cartridge** is also available to qualified adopters. Instructor's resources are also available for download directly to your computer through a secure connection via the instructor's side of the companion website. Contact your Oxford University Press sales representative for more information.

Student Companion Website at www.oup.com/us/oakes-mcgerr

The open-access Online Study Center designed for *Of the People: A History of the United States*, Fourth Edition helps students to review what they have learned from the textbook as well as explore other resources online.

Sources for *Of the People: A History of the United States, Volume I to 1877* (ISBN 978019091014) and *Of the People: A History of the United States, Volume II Since 1865* (ISBN 9780190910150)

Edited by Maxwell Johnson, and organized to match the table of contents of *Of the People*, this two-volume sourcebook includes five to six primary sources per chapter, both textual and visual. Chapter introductions, document headnotes, and study questions provide learning support. Each volume of the sourcebook is only $5.00 when bundled with *Of the People*.

Mapping and Coloring Book of US History

This two-volume workbook includes approximately 80 outline maps that provide opportunities for students to deepen their understanding of geography through quizzes, coloring exercises, and other activities. *The Mapping and Coloring Book of US History* is free when bundled with *Of the People*.

E-Books

Digital versions of *Of the People* are available at many popular distributors, including Chegg, RedShelf, and VitalSource.

Other Oxford Titles of Interest for the US History Classroom

Oxford University Press publishes a vast array of titles in American history. The following list is just a small selection of books that pair particularly well with *Of the People: A History of the United States*, Fourth Edition. Any of these books can be packaged with *Of the People* at a significant discount to students. Please contact your Oxford University Press sales representative for specific pricing information or for additional packaging suggestions. Please visit www.oup.com/us for a full listing of Oxford titles.

Writing History: A Guide for Students, **Fifth Edition, by William Kelleher Storey, Professor of History at Millsaps College**

Bringing together practical methods from both history and composition, *Writing History* provides a wealth of tips and advice to help students research and write essays for history classes. The book covers all aspects of writing about history, including **finding topics and researching** them, **interpreting source materials, drawing inferences from sources, and constructing arguments.** It concludes with three chapters that discuss writing effective sentences, using precise wording, and revising. Using numerous examples from the works of cultural, political, and social historians, *Writing History* serves as an ideal supplement to history courses that require students to conduct research. The fifth edition includes expanded sections on peer editing and topic selection, as well as new sections on searching and using the Internet. *Writing History* can be packaged with *Of the People: A History of the United States*, Fourth Edition. Contact your Oxford University Press sales representative for more information.

The Information-Literate Historian: A Guide to Research for History Students, **Third Edition, by Jenny Presnell, Information Services Library and History, American Studies, and Women's Studies Bibliographer, Miami University of Ohio**

This is the only book specifically designed to teach today's history student how to most successfully select and use sources—primary, secondary, and electronic—to carry out and present their research. Written by a college librarian, *The Information-Literate Historian* is an indispensable reference for historians, students, and other readers doing history research. *The Information-Literate Historian* can be packaged with *Of the People: A History of the United States*, Fourth Edition. Contact your Oxford University Press sales representative for more information.

Acknowledgments

We are grateful to our families, friends, and colleagues who encouraged us during the planning and writing of this book. We would like once again to thank Bruce Nichols for helping launch this book years ago. We are grateful to the editors and staff at Oxford University Press, especially our acquisitions editor, Charles Cavaliere, and our development editor, Maegan Sherlock. Charles's commitment made this text possible and Maegan deftly guided the development of the fourth edition. Thanks also to our talented production team, Barbara Mathieu, senior production editor, and Michele Laseau, art director, who helped to fulfill the book's vision. And special thanks go to Leslie Anglin, our copyeditor; to Rowan Wixted, assistant editor; and to the many other people behind the scenes at Oxford for helping this complex project happen.

The authors and editors would also like to thank the following people, whose time and insights have contributed to the first, second, third, and fourth editions.

Expert Reviewers of the Fourth Edition

Daniel Anderson
Cincinnati State University

Tramaine Anderson
Tarrant County College

Matthew Campbell
Lone Star College–Cypress Fairbanks

Gregg S. Clemmer
Carroll Community College

John Patrick Daly
College at Brockport, State University of New York

Maureen Elgersman Lee
Hampton University

Michael Frawley
University of Texas of the Permian Basin

Robert Genter
Nassau Community College

Sakina M. Hughes
University of Southern Indiana

Katrina Lacher
University of Central Oklahoma

Robert Lee
St. Louis Community College–Meramec

Matthew Oyos
Radford University

Stephen Todd Pfeffer
Columbus State Community College

Brenden Rensink
Brigham Young University

Marie Stango
California State University, Bakersfield

Expert Reviewers of the Third Edition

Greg Hall
Western Illinois University

Ross A. Kennedy
Illinois State University

Randall M. Miller
Saint Joseph's University

David W. Morris
Santa Barbara City College

Adam Pratt
University of Scranton

Judith Ridner
Mississippi State University

Robert A. Smith
Pittsburg State University

Timothy B. Smith
University of Tennessee at Martin

Linda D. Tomlinson
Fayetteville State University

Gerald Wilson
Eastern Washington University

Expert Reviewers of the Second Edition

Marjorie Berman
Red Rocks Community College–Lakewood

Will Carter
South Texas Community College

Jonathan Chu
University of Massachusetts, Boston

Sara Combs
Virginia Highlands Community College

Mark Elliott
University of North Carolina–Greensboro

David Hamilton
University of Kentucky

James Harvey
Houston Community College

Courtney Joiner
East Georgia College

Timothy Mahoney
University of Nebraska–Lincoln

Abigail Markwyn
Carroll University

Brian Maxson
Eastern Tennessee State University

Matthew Oyos
Radford University

John Pinheiro
Aquinas College

James Pula
Purdue University–North Central

John Rosinbum
Arizona State University

Christopher Thrasher
Texas Tech University

Jeffrey Trask
University of Massachusetts–Amherst

Michael Ward
California State University–Northridge

Bridgette Williams-Searle
The College of Saint Rose

Expert Reviewers of the First Edition

Thomas L. Altherr
Metropolitan State College of Denver

Luis Alvarez
University of California–San Diego

Adam Arenson
University of Texas–El Paso

Melissa Estes Blair
University of Georgia

Lawrence Bowdish
Ohio State University

Susan Roth Breitzer
Fayetteville State University

Margaret Lynn Brown
Brevard College

W. Fitzhugh Brundage
University of North Carolina–Chapel Hill

Gregory Bush
University of Miami

Brian Casserly
University of Washington

Ann Chirhart
Indiana State University

Bradley R. Clampitt
East Central University

William W. Cobb Jr.
Utah Valley University

Cheryll Ann Cody
Houston Community College

Sondra Cosgrove
College of Southern Nevada

Thomas H. Cox
Sam Houston State University

Carl Creasman
Valencia Community College

Christine Daniels
Michigan State University

Brian J. Daugherity
Virginia Commonwealth University

Mark Elliott
University of North Carolina–Greensboro

Katherine Carté Enge
Texas A&M University

Michael Faubion
University of Texas–Pan American

John Fea
Messiah College

Anne L. Foster
Indiana State University

Matthew Garrett
Arizona State University

Tim Garvin
California State University–Long Beach

Suzanne Cooper Guasco
Queens University of Charlotte

Lloyd Ray Gunn
University of Utah

Richard Hall
Columbus State University

Marsha Hamilton
University of South Alabama

Mark Hanna
University of California–San Diego

Joseph M. Hawes
University of Memphis

Melissa Hovsepian
University of Houston–Downtown

Jorge Iber
Texas Tech University

David K. Johnson
University of South Florida

Lloyd Johnson
Campbell University

Catherine O'Donnell Kaplan
Arizona State University

Rebecca M. Kluchin
California State University–Sacramento

Michael Kramer
Northwestern University

Louis M. Kyriakoudes
University of Southern Mississippi

Jason S. Lantzer
Butler University

Shelly Lemons
St. Louis Community College

Charlie Levine
Mesa Community College

Denise Lynn
University of Southern Indiana

Lillian Marrujo-Duck
City College of San Francisco

Michael McCoy
Orange County Community College

Noeleen McIlvenna
Wright State University

Elizabeth Brand Monroe
Indiana University–Purdue University Indianapolis

Kevin C. Motl
Ouachita Baptist University

Todd Moye
University of North Texas

Charlotte Negrete
Mt. San Antonio College

Julie Nicoletta
University of Washington–Tacoma

David M. Parker
California State University–Northridge

Jason Parker
Texas A&M University

Burton W. Peretti
Western Connecticut State University

Jim Piecuch
Kennesaw State University

John Putman
San Diego State University

R. J. Rockefeller
Loyola College of Maryland

Herbert Sloan
Barnard College, Columbia University

Vincent L. Toscano
Nova Southeastern University

William E. Weeks
San Diego State University

Timothy L. Wood
Southwest Baptist University

Jason Young
SUNY–Buffalo

Expert Reviewers of the Concise Second Edition

Hedrick Alixopulos
Santa Rosa Junior College

Guy Alain Aronoff
Humboldt State University

Melissa Estes Blair
Warren Wilson College

Amanda Bruce
Nassau Community College

Jonathan Chu
University of Massachusetts–Boston

Paul G. E. Clemens
Rutgers University

Martha Anne Fielder
Cedar Valley College

Tim Hacsi
University of Massachusetts–Boston

Matthew Isham
Pennsylvania State University

Ross A. Kennedy
Illinois State University

Eve Kornfeld
San Diego State University

Peggy Lambert
Lone Star College–Kingwood

Shelly L. Lemons
St. Louis Community College

Carolyn Herbst Lewis
Louisiana State University

Catherine M. Lewis
Kennesaw State University

Daniel K. Lewis
California State Polytechnic University

Scott P. Marler
University of Memphis

Laura McCall
Metropolitan State College of Denver

Stephen P. McGrath
Central Connecticut State University

Vincent P. Mikkelsen
Florida State University

Julie Nicoletta
University of Washington Tacoma

Caitlin Stewart
Eastern Connecticut State University

Thomas Summerhill
Michigan State University

David Tegeder
Santa Fe College

Eric H. Walther
University of Houston

William E. Weeks
University of San Diego

Kenneth B. White
Modesto Junior College

Julie Winch
University of Massachusetts–Boston

Mary Montgomery Wolf
University of Georgia

Kyle F. Zelner
University of Southern Mississippi

Expert Reviewers of the Concise First Edition

Hedrick Alixopulos
Santa Rosa Junior College

Guy Alain Aronoff
Humboldt State University

Melissa Estes Blair
Warren Wilson College

Amanda Bruce
Nassau Community College

Jonathan Chu
University of Massachusetts–Boston

Paul G. E. Clemens
Rutgers University

Martha Anne Fielder
Cedar Valley College

Tim Hacsi
University of Massachusetts–Boston

Matthew Isham
Pennsylvania State University

Ross A. Kennedy
Illinois State University

Eve Kornfeld
San Diego State University

Peggy Lambert
Lone Star College–Kingwood

Shelly L. Lemons
St. Louis Community College

Carolyn Herbst Lewis
Louisiana State University

Catherine M. Lewis
Kennesaw State University

Daniel K. Lewis
California State Polytechnic University

Scott P. Marler
University of Memphis

Laura McCall
Metropolitan State College of Denver

Stephen P. McGrath
Central Connecticut State University

Vincent P. Mikkelsen
Florida State University

Julie Nicoletta
University of Washington Tacoma

Caitlin Stewart
Eastern Connecticut State University

Thomas Summerhill
Michigan State University

David Tegeder
Santa Fe College

Eric H. Walther
University of Houston

William E. Weeks
University of San Diego

Kenneth B. White
Modesto Junior College

Julie Winch
University of Massachusetts–Boston

Mary Montgomery Wolf
University of Georgia

Kyle F. Zelner
University of Southern Mississippi

About the Authors

Michael McGerr is the Paul V. McNutt Professor of History at Indiana University–Bloomington. He is the author of *The Decline of Popular Politics: The American North, 1865–1928* (1986) and *A Fierce Discontent: The Rise and Fall of the Progressive Movement, 1870–1920* (2003), both from Oxford University Press. He is writing "*The Public Be Damned*": *The Kingdom and the Dream of the Vanderbilts*. The recipient of a fellowship from the National Endowment for the Humanities, Professor McGerr has won numerous teaching awards at Indiana, where his courses include the US Survey; War in Modern American History; Rock, Hip Hop, and Revolution; Big Business; The Sixties; and American Pleasure. He has previously taught at Yale University and the Massachusetts Institute of Technology. He received his BA, MA, and PhD from Yale.

Jan Ellen Lewis is Professor of History and Dean of the Faculty of Arts and Sciences, Rutgers University–Newark. She also teaches in the history PhD program at Rutgers, New Brunswick, and was a visiting professor of history at Princeton. A specialist in colonial and early national history, she is the author of *The Pursuit of Happiness: Family and Values in Jefferson's Virginia* (1983) as well as numerous articles and reviews. She has coedited *An Emotional History of the United States* (1998), *Sally Hemings and Thomas Jefferson: History, Memory, and Civic Culture* (1999), and *The Revolution of 1800: Democracy, Race, and the New Republic* (2002). She has served as president of the Society of Historians of the Early American Republic, as chair of the New Jersey Historical Commission, and on the editorial board of the *American Historical Review*. She is an elected member of the Society of American Historians and the American Antiquarian Society. She received her AB from Bryn Mawr College and MAs and PhD from the University of Michigan.

James Oakes has published several books and numerous articles on slavery and antislavery in the nineteenth century, including *The Radical and the Republican: Frederick Douglass, Abraham Lincoln, and the Triumph of Antislavery Politics* (2007), winner of the Lincoln Prize in 2008. Professor Oakes is Distinguished Professor of History and Graduate School Humanities Professor at the City University of New York Graduate Center. In 2008, he was a fellow at the Cullman Center at the New York Public Library. His new book is *Freedom National: The Destruction of Slavery in the United States* (February 2013).

Nick Cullather is a historian of US foreign relations at Indiana University–Bloomington. He is author of three books on nation building: *The Hungry World* (2010), a story of foreign aid, development, and science; *Illusions of Influence* (1994), on US–Philippines relations; and *Secret History* (1999 and 2006), a history of the CIA's overthrow of the Guatemalan government in 1954. He received his PhD from the University of Virginia.

Mark Summers is the Thomas D. Clark Professor of History at the University of Kentucky–Lexington. In addition to various articles, he has written *Railroads, Reconstruction, and the Gospel of Prosperity* (1984), *The Plundering Generation* (1988), *The Era of Good Stealings*

(1993), *The Press Gang* (1994), *The Gilded Age; or, The Hazard of New Functions* (1997), *Rum, Romanism and Rebellion* (2000), *Party Games* (2004), and *A Dangerous Stir* (2009). At present, he has just completed a book about a Tammany politician, *Big Tim and the Tiger.* He is now writing a survey of Reconstruction and a book about 1868. He teaches the American history survey (both halves), the Gilded Age, the Progressive Era, the Age of Jackson, Civil War and Reconstruction, the British Empire (both halves), the Old West (both halves), a history of political cartooning, and various graduate courses. He earned his BA from Yale and his PhD from the University of California–Berkeley.

Camilla Townsend is Professor of History at Rutgers University–New Brunswick. She is the author of five books, among them *Annals of Native America* (2016), *Malintzin's Choices: An Indian Woman in the Conquest of Mexico* (2006), and *Pocahontas and the Powhatan Dilemma* (2004), and she is the editor of *American Indian History: A Documentary Reader* (2010). The recipient of fellowships from the National Endowment for the Humanities and the John Simon Guggenheim Memorial Foundation, she has also won awards at Rutgers and at Colgate, where she used to teach. Her courses at the graduate and undergraduate level cover the colonial history of the Americas, as well as Native American history, early and modern. She received her BA from Bryn Mawr and her PhD from Rutgers.

Karen M. Dunak is Associate Professor of History at Muskingum University in New Concord, Ohio. She is the author of *As Long as We Both Shall Love: The White Wedding in Postwar America* (2013), published by New York University Press. She currently is working on a book about media representations of and responses to Jacqueline Kennedy Onassis. Her courses include the US Survey, Women in US History, Gender and Sexuality in US History, and various topics related to modern US history. She earned her BA from American University and her PhD from Indiana University.

Jeanne Boydston was Robinson-Edwards Professor of American History at the University of Wisconsin–Madison. A specialist in the histories of gender and labor, she was the author of *Home and Work: Housework, Wages, and the Ideology of Labor in the Early American Republic* (1990); coauthor of *The Limits of Sisterhood: The Beecher Sisters on Women's Rights and Woman's Sphere* (1988); and coeditor of *Root of Bitterness: Documents in the Social History of American Women*, second edition (1996). The recipient of numerous teaching awards, she gave courses in women's and gender history, the United States before the Civil War, and global and comparative history. Her BA and MA were from the University of Tennessee, and her PhD was from Yale University.

Of the People

Reconstructing a Nation

1865–1877

< **Terror in the South**

459

AMERICAN PORTRAIT

John Dennett Visits a Freedmen's Bureau Court

John Richard Dennett arrived in Liberty, Virginia, on August 17, 1865, on a tour of the South reporting for the magazine *The Nation*. The editors wanted accurate weekly accounts of conditions in the recently defeated Confederate states, and Dennett was the kind of man they could trust: a Harvard graduate, a firm believer in the sanctity of the Union, and a member of the class of elite Yankees who thought of themselves as the "best men" the country had to offer.

At Liberty, Dennett was accompanied by a Freedmen's Bureau agent. The Freedmen's Bureau was a branch of the US Army established by Congress to assist the freed people. Dennett and the agent went to the courthouse because one of the Freedmen's Bureau's functions was to adjudicate disputes between the freed people and southern whites.

The first case was that of an old white farmer who complained that two blacks who worked on his farm were "roamin' about and refusin' to work." He wanted the agent to help find the men and bring them back. Both men had wives and children living on his farm and eating his corn, the old man complained. "Have you been paying any wages?" the Freedmen's Bureau agent asked. "Well, they get what the other niggers get," the farmer answered. "I a'n't payin' great wages this year." There was not much the agent could do, but one of his soldiers volunteered to go and tell the blacks that "they ought to be at home supporting their wives and children."

A well-to-do planter came in to see if he could fire the blacks who had been working on his plantation since the beginning of the year. Warned not to beat his workers the way he would slaves, the planter complained that they were unmanageable without what he considered proper punishment. Under the circumstances, the planter wondered, "Will the Government take them off our hands?" The agent suspected that the planter was looking for a way to dismiss his workforce unpaid at the end of the growing season. "If they've worked on your crops all the year so far," the agent told the planter, "I guess they've got a claim on you to keep them a while longer."

Next came a "good-looking mulatto man" representing a number of African Americans worried that they would be forced into five-year contracts with their employers. "No, it a'n't true," the agent said. Could they rent or buy land to work themselves? "Yes, rent or buy," the agent said. But with no horses, mules, or plows, the former slaves wanted to see "if the Government would help us out after we get the land." All that the agent could offer was a note from the bureau authorizing them to acquire farms of their own.

The last case involved a field hand whose master had beaten him with a stick. The agent sent the field hand back to work. "Don't be sassy, don't be lazy when you've got work to do; and I guess he won't trouble you." A minute later, the worker returned to procure a letter to his master "enjoining him to keep the peace, as he feared the man would shoot him, he having on two or three occasions threatened to do so."

Most of the cases Dennett witnessed centered on labor relations, which often spilled over into other matters, including the family lives of former slaves, their civil rights, and their ability to buy land. The freed people preferred to work their own land but lacked the resources to rent or buy farms. Black workers and white owners who negotiated wage contracts had trouble figuring out each other's rights and responsibilities. The former masters clung to all their old authority that they could. Freed people wanted as free a hand as possible.

The Freedmen's Bureau was in the middle of these conflicts. Generally, agents tried to see to it that freed people had written contracts guaranteeing their essential right to work as free laborers, uncoerced by whip, club, or gun. Southern whites resented any intrusion with people they still saw as essentially property, and they let civil authorities know it. The Freedmen's Bureau became a lightning rod for the political conflicts of the Reconstruction period.

Conditions in the South elicited sharply different responses from lawmakers in Washington. At one extreme was President Andrew Johnson, who believed in small government and a speedy readmission of the southern states and looked on the Freedmen's Bureau with suspicion. At the other extreme were radical Republicans calling on the federal government to redistribute confiscated land to former slaves, give African American men the vote, and take it away from whites who were not loyal to the United States during the war. In between, there were moderate Republicans who at first tried to work with the president and were content simply to guarantee African Americans' basic civil rights. But as reports of violence and the abusive treatment of the freed people reached Washington, Republicans shifted in more radical directions.

Back and forth it went: events in the South triggered policy decisions in Washington, which in turn shaped events in the South. What John Dennett saw in Liberty, Virginia, was a good example of this. Policies set in Washington shaped what the Freedmen's Bureau agent could do for former masters and slaves. However, those policies shifted when the Bureau's reports and those of journalists, like Dennett, exposed just how troubled southern conditions were. From this interaction the politics of Reconstruction, and with it a "New South," slowly emerged.

Wartime Reconstruction

Even as emancipation began, the US government began experimenting with reconstructing the Union. The two goals merged: by creating new, loyal southern states and making their abolition of slavery a condition for reunion, Lincoln could enact emancipation there without court challenge. Through a generous policy of pardons, he could encourage Confederates to make their peace with the Union, speeding the war's end.

Despite the chorus of cries for hanging Jefferson Davis from a sour-apple tree, few northerners wanted to pursue bloody punishments for the million Confederate soldiers who were technically guilty of treason. In the end, Confederate generals went home unharmed to become lawyers, businessmen, and planters; General Robert E. Lee became a college president. No civil leader was hanged for treason, not even Jefferson Davis. Two years after his arrest, he walked out of prison, thanks to bail put up by northerners like editor Horace Greeley. In later years, former Confederates became senators, governors, and federal judges. Months before the war ended, northerners were raising money to rebuild the southern economy and feed its destitute people. What the North wanted was not vengeance, but guarantees of lasting loyalty and a meaningful freedom. Questions arose with no easy answers: What did it take to reunite America? Should it be restored, or reconstructed, and if the latter, how drastically? How far could yesterday's enemies be trusted? What did freedom mean, and what rights should the "freed people" enjoy? In reconstructing society, how far did the government's power go?

Lincoln's Ten Percent Plan Versus the Wade-Davis Bill

Lincoln moved to shape a postwar South based on free labor and to replace military control, Banks's included, with new civil governments. However, wartime Reconstruction had to take Confederate resistance into account. Any terms the president set would need to attract as much white southern support as it could and hold out an inducement to those at war with the United States to return to their old loyalties. In December 1863, Lincoln issued a Proclamation of Amnesty and Reconstruction, offering a full pardon and the restoration of civil rights to all those who swore loyalty to the Union, excluding only a few high-ranking Confederate military and political leaders. When the number of loyal whites in a former Confederate state reached 10 percent of the 1860 voting population, they could organize a new state constitution and government. But Lincoln's "Ten Per Cent Plan" also required that the state abolish slavery, just as Congress had demanded before admitting West Virginia to the Union earlier in the year. Attempts to establish a loyal government foundered, but circumstances in Louisiana proved more promising. Under General Banks's guidance, Free State whites met in New Orleans in 1864 and produced a new state constitution abolishing slavery.

By that time, however, radical Unionists were expecting more. Propertied and well educated, the free black community in New Orleans pleaded that without equal rights to education and the vote, mere freedom would not be enough. Impressed by their argument, Lincoln hinted to Louisiana authorities that he would welcome steps opening the vote for at least some blacks. The hints were ignored.

Black spokesmen found a friendlier audience among radical Republicans in Congress, among them Thaddeus Stevens of Pennsylvania and Charles Sumner of Massachusetts. Believing that justice required giving at least some blacks the vote and setting a more rigorous standard of loyalty for white southerners than Lincoln's plan offered, they shared a much wider concern that any new government must rest on statutory law, not presidential proclamations and military commanders' decrees. They were not at all prepared to treat Lincoln's "loyal" states as fit to return to Congress—not when so much of Louisiana and Arkansas remained in Confederate hands and was excluded from the new constitution-making—not when a speckling of enclaves pretended to speak for the state of Virginia.

As doubts grew about Louisiana's Reconstruction, Congress edged away from Lincoln's program. In mid-1864, Senator Benjamin F. Wade of Ohio and Congressman Henry Winter Davis of Maryland proposed a different plan, requiring a majority of a state's white voters to swear allegiance to the Union before Reconstruction could begin. Slavery must also be abolished and full equality before the law must be granted to African Americans. Lincoln pocket-vetoed the Wade-Davis bill to protect the governments that were already under way toward reform. However, he could not make Congress admit a single one of his newly reconstructed states.

The Meaning of Freedom

"We was glad to be set free," a former slave remembered years afterward. "I didn't know what it would be like. It was just like opening the door and lettin' the bird fly out. He might starve, or freeze, or be killed pretty soon but he just felt good because he was free." Blacks' departure came as a terrible shock to masters lulled into believing that their "servants" appreciated their treatment. Some former slave owners persuaded themselves that they were the real gainers of slavery's abolition. "I was glad and thankful—on my own account—when slavery ended and I ceased to belong, body and soul, to my negroes," a Virginia woman later insisted. Forced to do their own cooking or washing, other mistresses fumed at blacks' ingratitude. In fact, many African Americans left, not out of unkindness, but simply to prove that they could get along on their own. White fears that blacks, once free, would murder their masters proved groundless.

Leaving the plantation was the first step in a long journey for African Americans. Many took to the roads, some of them returning to their old homes near the coasts, from which masters had evacuated as Union armies approached. Others went searching for family members, separated from them during slavery. For 20 years, black newspapers carried advertisements, appealing for news of a husband or wife long since lost. Those who had not been separated went out of their way to have their marriages secured by law. That way, their children could be made legitimate and their vows made permanent. Once married, men sought sharecropping contracts that allowed their families to live with them on plantations. Because black women across the South had become what the law called "domestic dependents," husbands could refuse employers their wives' services and keep them home. In fact, freedwomen were likelier to work outside the home than white women. They tended the family garden, raised children, hired out as domestics, and, as cotton prices fell, shared the work of hoeing and picking in the fields just so the family could make ends meet.

The end of slavery meant many things to freed people. It meant that they could move about their neighborhoods without passes, and that they did not have to step aside to let whites pass them on the street. They could own dogs or carry canes, which had always been the master's exclusive privilege. They could dress as they pleased or choose their own names, including, for the first time, a surname.

Freedom liberated African Americans from the white minister's take on Christianity. No longer were large portions of the Bible closed off to them. Most southern blacks withdrew from white churches and established their own congregations, particularly in the Methodist and Baptist faith. In time, the church emerged as a central institution in the southern black community, the meeting place, social center, and source of comfort that larger society denied them. A dozen years after the war, South Carolina had a thousand ministers of the African Methodist Episcopal Church alone.

To read the Gospel, however, freed people needed schooling. One former slave remembered his master's parting words on this matter: "Charles, you is a free man they say, but Ah tells you now, you is still a slave and if you lives to be a hundred you'll STILL be a slave, 'cause you got no education, and education is what makes a man free!" Even before the war ended, northern teachers poured into the South to set up schools. When the fighting stopped, the US Army helped recruit and organize thousands of northern women as teachers, but they could never send enough. Old and young spared what time they had from work, paying teachers in eggs or produce when coin was scarce. Black classes met wherever they could: in mule stables and cotton houses, even the slave pen in New Orleans, where the old auction block became a globe stand. Due to a lack of school-books, they read dictionaries and almanacs. On meager resources, hundreds of thousands of southern blacks learned to read and write over the course of the next generation. The first black colleges would be founded in the postwar years, including Hampton Institute in Virginia and Howard University in Washington, DC. The American Missionary Associa-tion established seven, among them Atlanta and Fisk Universities.

Finally, freedom allowed freed people to congregate, to celebrate the Fourth of July or Emancipation Day, or to petition for equal rights before the law. Memorial Day may have begun with blacks gathering to honor the Union dead whose sacrifices had helped make them free.

Experiments with Free Labor

Many whites insisted that blacks would never work in freedom and foresaw a South ruined forever. Freed people proved just the opposite though. When Union troops landed on the Sea Islands off South Carolina in November 1861, the slaveholders fled, leaving behind between 5,000 and 10,000 slaves. Within months the abandoned plantations of the Sea Islands were being reorganized. Eventually black families were given small plots of their own land to cultivate, and in return for their labor they received a "share" of the year's crop. When the masters returned after the war to reclaim their lands, the labor system had already proven itself. Much modified, it would form the basis for the arrange-ment known as "sharecropping."

The sugar and cotton plantations around New Orleans provided another opportunity to shape the future of free labor. When the Union army came to occupy New Orleans in 1862, the tens of thousands of field hands on these plantations were no longer slaves, but the landowners still held possession of the land. Unlike the Sea Islands, these plantations could not be broken up. And sugar plantations could not be effectively organized into small sharecropping units.

Hoping to stem the flow of black refugees to Union lines and cut the loss of black lives in the contraband camps, Union general Nathaniel Banks issued stringent regulations to put the freed people back to work quickly in Louisiana. At the time, Banks was the com-mander of the Department of the Gulf during the occupation of New Orleans and his policy, known as the Banks Plan, required freed people to sign yearlong contracts to work on their former plantations. Workers would be paid either 5 percent of the proceeds of the crop or three dollars per month. The former masters would provide food and shelter, and African American workers were forbidden to leave the plantations without permission. Established planters welcomed the plan, but many critics protested that Banks had simply replaced one form of slavery with another; however, most freed people knew the differ-ence and accepted the work conditions. The Banks Plan became the model for plantations throughout the lower Mississippi Valley.

Understandably, freed people wanted land of their own. Only then could they avoid working for their old masters on any terms. "The labor of these people had for two hun-dred years cleared away the forests and produced crops that brought millions of dollars annually," H. C. Bruce explained. "It does seem to me that a Christian Nation would, at least, have given them one year's support, 40 acres of land and a mule each." As the war ended, many African Americans expected the government's help in becoming landowners. Union general William Tecumseh Sherman heard an appeal from freed people on the Sea Islands. "The way we can best take care of ourselves is to have land," they argued, "and turn it out and till it by our own labor." Convinced, Sherman issued Special Field Order No. 15 granting captured land to the freed people. By June, 400,000 acres had been distributed to 40,000 former slaves.

Congress did not leave matters there. In March 1865, the Republicans established the Bureau of Refugees, Freedmen, and Abandoned Lands, commonly known as the Freedmen's Bureau. In the area of labor relations, the Bureau sometimes sided with landowners against the interests of the freed people. But it also provided immediate relief for thousands of people of both races. Indeed, of more than 18 million rations distributed over three years, more than 5 million went to whites in need. The Bureau joined with northern religious groups in creating some 4,000 black schools. It ran charity hospitals and provided medical services. Freed people came to Bureau agents for justice when white-dominated courts denied it and took counsel when labor contracts were to be negotiated. Some agents sided instinctively with the former masters. Most courted white hostility by protecting freed people from violence, settling their complaints, advising them on labor contracts, and seeing that employers paid as promised.

The Freedmen's Bureau also became involved in the politics of land redistribution and controlled the disposition of 850,000 acres of confiscated and abandoned Confederate lands. In July 1865, General Oliver Otis Howard, the head of the Bureau, directed his agents to rent the land to the freed people in 40-acre plots that they could eventually purchase. Many agents believed that to reeducate them in the values of thrift and hard work, the freed people should be encouraged to save money and buy land for themselves. A Freedman's Savings Bank helped many do just that.

Moderate and radical Republicans alike were determined to press for more than a nominal freedom for blacks. Equally important, Congress made it clear that it would insist on being consulted in any Reconstruction policy.

Presidential Reconstruction, 1865–1867

Andrew Johnson took office in April 1865 as a great unknown. Born in a log cabin and too poor to attend school, he began his career on a tailor's bench where he had shown grit and enterprise. In time he had risen to moderate wealth in the eastern Tennessee hill country, enough to own slaves, but he never forgot his humble beginnings. Before the war, he had defended slavery and the common man, called for taxpayer-supported public schools, and free homesteads. A courageous Union Democrat in wartime, he had run roughshod over Tennessee Confederates as military governor. He hated treason and the rich planters that he blamed for the war. Johnson deserved much of the credit for Tennessee abolishing slavery; however, he alarmed some radicals along the way who found more pardons than penalties in his policies. Convinced that a lasting reunion of the states could only come by earning white southerners' good will and determined to see the Thirteenth Amendment ratified quickly, the president started Reconstruction six months before Congress convened and left it entirely in white hands. In doing so, he offended not only the radicals favoring a color-blind suffrage but also the moderates who believed that Reconstruction must be done by law and not executive order.

The Political Economy of Contract Labor

Presidential Reconstruction began in late May 1865, when President Johnson offered amnesty and the restoration of property to white southerners who swore loyalty to the Union, excluding only high-ranking Confederate military and political leaders and very rich planters. He named provisional governors in seven seceded states and told them to organize constitutional conventions. For readmission to the Union and restoration of their full privileges, conventions must adopt the Thirteenth Amendment, void their secession ordinances, and repudiate their Confederate war debt. Most of the constitutional conventions met the president's conditions, though with grumbling and legal quibbling. Many made clear that they still thought the South had been right all along. They only bowed to military force. "We have for breakfast salt-fish, fried potatoes, and treason," a lodger at a Virginia boarding house wrote. "Fried potatoes, treason, and salt-fish for dinner. At supper the fare is slightly varied, and we have treason, salt-fish, fried potatoes, and a little more treason."

Elections under these new constitutions would then choose civil governments to replace provisional authority. Only white men covered by the amnesty proclamation or subsequent pardons could vote, but by September Johnson was signing pardons wholesale. Secessionists flocked to the elections that followed the conventions. Freshly pardoned Confederates won some of the most prominent offices, former Confederate vice president Alexander Stephens among them.

White southerners welcomed Johnson's leniency. Once pardoned, they petitioned for restoration of their confiscated or abandoned properties. In September 1865, Johnson ordered the Freedmen's Bureau to return the lands to their former owners. By late 1865, former slaves were being forced off the 40-acre plots that the government agency had given them.

No sooner did conservative legislatures meet than they fashioned "Black Codes" defining, or rather confining, blacks' new freedom. Some states ordered different punishments: fines for whites and whipping or sale for black offenders. Elsewhere, lawmakers forbade freed people from renting land, owning guns, or buying liquor. Vagrancy laws gave police wide discretion to collar any black and subject him or her to forced labor, sometimes for an old master. Apprenticeship statutes let the courts take away black children without parents' consent and bind them out to years of unpaid labor. Blacks were allowed to testify only in certain cases. They were taxed to pay for white schools, but the Johnsonian state governments provided them with none of their own.

Landowners gave their black employees as little as they could. With the legal machinery backing them up, they forced them into labor contracts that stipulated what they could do with their private time. One planter required his black workers to "go by his direction the same as in slavery time." Other landowners denied them the right to leave the plantation without their "master's" consent. Some arrangements allotted as little as a tenth of the crop in wages, and many employers found an excuse to turn their field hands off unpaid as soon as the crop was in. It was no wonder that many freedmen saw contract labor as slavery under a new name, or that thousands refused to sign any terms at the year's end.

Resistance to Presidential Reconstruction

An undercurrent of violence underlay conservative control. In North Carolina, a resident wrote, the Negro was "sneered at by all and informed daily yes hourly that he is incompetent to care for himself—that his race is now doomed to perish from off the face of the Earth—that he will not work—that he is a thief by nature[,] that he lies more easily and naturally than an honest man breathes." Blacks were assaulted for not showing proper deference to whites, for disputing the terms of labor contracts, or for failing to meet the standards that white employers demanded. Black churches were burned, rebuilt, and burned again. A Freedmen's Bureau agent in Kentucky classified the incidents in just a few counties: twenty-three "cases of severe and inhuman beating and whipping of men; four of beating and shooting; two of robbing and shooting; three of robbing; five men shot and killed; two shot and wounded; four beaten to death; one beaten and roasted; three women assaulted and ravished; four women beaten, two women tied up and whipped until insensible; two men and their families beaten and driven from their homes, and their property destroyed; two instances of burning of dwellings and one of the inmates shot." White witnesses refused to acknowledge what they knew to be true, white judges dismissed cases involving black defendants, and white juries invariably acquitted the offenders. If Johnson expressed content with the speedy restoration of loyalty in the South, a growing chorus of complaints from freed people and Unionists down South told a different story.

Congress Clashes with the President

Troubled by presidential Reconstruction's failings, a Republican Congress refused to readmit former Confederate states without investigation. A Joint Committee on Reconstruction was formed to examine their loyalty and the safety of white and black Unionists' rights. At the same time, moderate Republicans also wanted to establish a program for readmission that Johnson would support. By expanding the power of the Freedmen's Bureau and proposing a Civil Rights bill, they thought they had the makings of a compromise.

The first extended the Bureau's life, strengthened its powers, and permitted it to set up courts that allowed black testimony. The second overturned the Dred Scott decision by granting United States citizenship to American men regardless of race. This marked the first time that the federal government intervened in states' rights to guarantee due process and basic civil rights.

To Republicans' amazement, Johnson vetoed both bills and in terms that made no compromise possible. Hinting that Congress had no right to reconstruct until the southern states were readmitted and doubting blacks' fitness to enjoy the same civil rights as whites, the president declared Reconstruction completed. Unable to override the Freedmen's Bureau bill veto, Congress did pass the Civil Rights bill, which served as the foundation for section one of the Fourteenth Amendment, and later that summer a new Freedmen's Bureau bill.

Origins of the Fourteenth Amendment

During the spring of 1866, the Joint Committee on Reconstruction proposed a Fourteenth Amendment to the Constitution, outlining the conditions that Republicans thought were essential for a just and lasting peace. Provisions guaranteed payment of the national debt and prevented payment of the Confederate one. Confederates who had held public office before the war were barred from office until Congress removed

Anti-Freedmen's Bureau Poster Led by President Andrew Johnson, attacks on the Freedmen's Bureau became more and more openly racist in late 1865 and 1866. This Democratic Party broadside was circulated during the 1866 election.

their disabilities. Replacing the Constitution's three-fifths clause, which allowed slaves to be counted as three-fifths of a human being for the purpose of taxation and representation, representation in Congress would now be based on a state's voting population. If freed blacks entitled southern states to additional House seats, that representation entitled blacks to the right to vote (see Table 15–1). "Happy will our disappointment be if this dry stalk shall bud and blossom into Impartial Suffrage," one radical wrote, doubtfully. Even if it did not, the South would return to Congress weaker in strength than it had left. But the crucial provision wrote civil rights guarantees into fundamental law, guaranteeing citizenship to all males born in the United States. Few of its authors could foresee how, over the century to come, its promise would expand the national commitment to furthering equality, not just for men but for women and other disadvantaged groups; nor could they see how far it could be used to expand the government's authority to set things right.

Deserted by the party that had elected him, Johnson fought on. He launched the National Union movement, a bipartisan coalition of conservatives whose goal was to defeat Republicans at the midterm elections. A railroad tour from Chicago and back to Washington allowed him to make his case to the American people. However, the National Union movement fizzled; hardly any Republican thought the proposed Amendment presented

Table 15-1 Reconstruction Amendments, 1865–1870

Amendment	Main Provisions	Congressional Passage (two-thirds majority in each house required)	Ratification Process (three-quarters of all states including ex-Confederate states required)
13	Slavery prohibited in the United States	January 1865	December 1865 (27 states, including 8 southern states)
14	1. National citizenship for all men and women born in the United States	June 1866	Rejected by 12 southern and border states, February 1867
	2. State representation in Congress reduced proportionally to number of voters disenfranchised		Radicals make readmission of southern states hinge on ratification
	3. Former high-ranking Confederates denied right to hold office until Congress removes disabilities		Ratified July 1868
	4. Confederate debt repudiated		
15	Denial of franchise because of race, color, or past servitude explicitly prohibited	February 1869	Ratification required for readmission of Virginia, Texas, Mississippi, and Georgia; ratified March 1870

unfair terms for a defeated South. Johnson's "Swing Around the Circle" tour ended in crowds trading insults with the president.

Two incidents confirmed northern fears that presidential Reconstruction had left southern Unionists defenseless. On May 1, 1866, after two drivers—one black, one white—had a traffic accident, Memphis police arrested the black one. A group of black veterans tried to prevent the arrest and, as a result, a white crowd gathered. A riot broke out. Over the next three days, white mobs burned hundreds of homes, destroyed churches, and attacked black schools. Five black women were raped; nearly fifty people, all but two of them black, were killed.

Three months later, violence of an explicitly political dimension broke out in New Orleans. Alarmed at former Confederates' return to power in Louisiana, "Free Staters" sought to recall the state's 1864 constitutional convention. They may have meant to open voting rights to some blacks or cut "rebels" out, but they never got the chance. On July 30, 1866, when a few dozen delegates assembled at Mechanics Institute, white mobs set on the convention's supporters, who were mostly black. Led by police and firemen, many of them Confederate veterans, rioters opened fire on a black parade and broke into the convention hall. "The floor was covered with blood," one victim remembered, "and in walking downstairs the blood splashed under the soles of my boots." Blacks trying to surrender were gunned down. By the time the attackers dispersed, 34 blacks and 3 white supporters had been killed, and another 100 had been injured.

Congressional Reconstruction

The elections of 1866 became a referendum on whether Johnson's policies had gone far enough to assure the permanent safety of the Union. But they also posed competing visions of what American democracy should mean. For President Johnson, "democracy" meant government by local majorities, which often meant white supremacy. For African Americans and a growing number of Republicans in Congress, genuine democracy demanded a firm foundation of equal civil and political rights. The sweep that followed brought in an even more solidly Republican Congress than before and doomed presidential Reconstruction. Congressional Reconstruction would be far different. It was an extraordinary series of events, second only to emancipation in its impact on the history of the United States.

The South Remade

Republicans had agreed on the Fourteenth Amendment's provisions as a final settlement of the war's issues. Southern states that ratified it would be readmitted, whether they enfranchised blacks or not. Tennessee ratified the amendment and was readmitted to Congress immediately. But in the remaining southern states, conservatives rejected the amendment by wide margins, and with the president's encouragement. As unpunished assaults on Unionists and freed people continued, Congress lost patience. In the short run, the army could keep order, but a long-term solution was needed. Moderate Republicans came to agree with radicals: only by putting loyal men, regardless of race, in charge could a loyal, just South come into being. The only other alternative would be an open-ended national commitment to rule the South by force.

Although they were far from what radical Republicans had hoped for, in March 1867, Congress passed two Reconstruction Acts. Leaving the Johnsonian state governments in office, the acts declared them provisional and their officeholders subject to removal if they hamstrung the Reconstruction process. Ten ex-Confederate states were divided into five military districts and placed under army supervision (see Map 15–1). The army would register voters, both white and black, except for the comparatively small number disqualified by the not-yet-ratified Fourteenth Amendment. To regain congressional representation, each state must call a constitutional convention and draw up a new constitution providing for equal civil and political rights. Voters then must ratify it, and the newly elected governments must adopt the Fourteenth Amendment. Military oversight would end as civil authority replaced it. Thus, most white southern men had a say in constructing the new political order, and when those states were readmitted, they were granted the same rights as others. For all the laws' limits, remaking state governments and requiring a broader male suffrage promised a Radical Reconstruction indeed.

The Impeachment and Trial of Andrew Johnson

Johnson could not stop congressional Reconstruction. But he could temper it. Battling now to protect the executive's powers, Johnson shared Democrats' fears that Congress had veered far from the Constitution, placing military authority above civil authority and overturning what he saw as the natural order of society, where blacks were kept in subordination.

In vain, radical Republicans called for Johnson's impeachment. Instead, Congress tried to restrain him by law. The Tenure of Office Act kept the president from removing

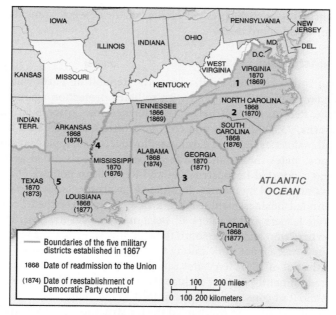

Map 15-1   Reconstruction and Redemption By 1870, Congress had readmitted every southern state to the Union. In most cases the Republican Party retained control of the "reconstructed" state governments for only a few years.

officials who had been appointed in his administration with Senate confirmation. Another law required that every presidential order to the military pass through General Ulysses S. Grant. Johnson could still dismiss district commanders (and did when they interpreted their powers differently than he did), but as long as Grant headed the army and Edwin M. Stanton the War Department, Republicans felt that they had safeguarded the Reconstruction Acts against a potential coup.

Provoked by these challenges to his authority, Johnson issued interpretations of the Reconstruction Acts to permit wider conservative registration, forcing Congress into special session to revise the law with a Third Reconstruction Act. He issued broader amnesty proclamations for former Confederates, forced the dismissal of Republican officers, and, abiding by the Tenure of Office Act, suspended Stanton in August 1867. When the Senate reinstated him the following winter, Johnson ordered him ejected. "What good did your moderation do you?" radical Republican Thaddeus Stevens taunted moderates. "If you don't kill the beast, he will kill you." With the law seemingly broken, the House impeached Johnson.

The expected removal never happened. Rejecting Stevens's argument that presidential obstruction was enough for conviction, senators required an intentional violation of law. The Tenure of Office Act's wording was so unclear that it may not have applied to Stanton. When the president promised to restrain himself and selected a successor to Stanton that moderates trusted, the impeachment process lost momentum. In May, the Senate fell one vote short of the two-thirds needed to convict. Within a month, Congress had readmitted seven southern states, thus limiting Johnson's power to thwart Reconstruction in those states; with Grant's election to the presidency that fall, the new governments had whatever support the army could afford them.

Radical Reconstruction in the South

With the help of Union Leagues, auxiliaries of the Republican Party whose goal was to mobilize and educate black voters, and with military protection against conservative violence in place, Radical Reconstruction transformed the Cotton South dramatically. Within six months, 735,000 blacks and 635,000 whites had registered to vote. Blacks formed electoral majorities in South Carolina, Florida, Mississippi, Alabama, and Louisiana and in most states they found white support in the so-called scalawags, white Southerners who supported Reconstruction and Republican policies. Wartime Unionists, hill farmers neglected by planter-dominated governments, debtors seeking relief, development-minded businessmen seeking a new, more diversified South, and even some Confederate leaders and planters all welcomed Radical Reconstruction. Carpetbaggers, northerners who had come south to farm, invest, preach, or teach, were few in numbers, but they took a front rank among the leaders in black-majority states.

Starting in the fall of 1867, ten states called constitutional conventions, heavily Republican and predominantly, but not exclusively, white. The results of these conventions, so-called Black and Tan constitutions, guaranteed a color-blind right to suffrage, mandated public school systems, and overhauled the tax structure. They also included a right to bear arms in their bills of rights. Only a few states shut any Confederates out of the vote, and most of those that did removed the electoral disabilities before a year was out.

Achievements and Failures of Radical Government

Later caricatured as a dire era of "bayonet" and "negro rule," Radical Reconstruction was neither. The Republican governments won in fairer elections and with greater turnouts than any that the South had known up until that time. Republican leadership remained overwhelmingly white and, for the most part, southern born. While some 700 blacks served in state legislatures, only in South Carolina and possibly Louisiana did they ever outnumber whites. No state elected a black governor, while only 16 blacks served in Congress, 2 of whom were senators. Still, the contrast between what had been and what would follow as a result of Reconstruction was revolutionary. These Reconstruction legislatures were more representative of their constituents than most legislatures in nineteenth-century America (see Figure 15–1). While some African American officeholders were indeed

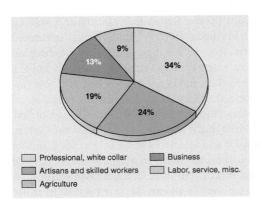

Professional, white collar
Artisans and skilled workers
Agriculture
Business
Labor, service, misc.

Figure 15-1 Occupations of African American Officeholders During Reconstruction Although former slaves were underrepresented among black officeholders, the Reconstruction governments were among the most broadly representative legislatures in US history.

illiterate, former slaves who did not own land, a disproportionate number came from the tiny prewar free African American elite of ministers, teachers, and small business owners. Freed people also filled hundreds of county offices. They served as sheriffs, bailiffs, judges, and jurors, offering the promise, at least, of a fair hearing in court for black defendants and litigants. Sharing power locally meant a greater chance for black communities to share in the benefits of public expenditures.

Republican rule delivered on its promises. The whipping post and debtor's prison vanished. The new governments funded insane asylums, roads, and prisons. Homestead exemptions protected debtors' real estate, and lien laws gave tenant farmers more control over the crops they grew and awarded artisans a first right to their employer's assets. The right of married women to hold property in their own name was expanded. Across the Deep South, laws took on racial discrimination on streetcars and railroad lines, mandating equal treatment. Most important, most Reconstruction governments built or extended access to the free public school system to African Americans. Underfunded and segregated, those schools nonetheless boosted literacy rates, especially among freed people.

Radical Members One of the greatest achievements of congressional Reconstruction was the election of a significant number of African Americans to public office.

The Political Economy of Sharecropping

Radical Reconstruction made it easier for the former slaves to negotiate the terms of their labor contracts. Workers with grievances had a better chance of securing justice, as southern Republicans became sheriffs, justices of the peace, and county clerks, and as southern courts allowed blacks to serve as witnesses and sit on juries.

The strongest card in the hands of the freed people was a shortage of agricultural workers in the South. After emancipation, thousands of blacks sought opportunities in towns and cities or in the North. Though most blacks remained in the South as farmers, they reduced their working hours in several ways. Black women still worked the fields but spent more time nursing their infants and caring for their children. And the children went to school when they were able. The resulting labor shortage forced white landlords to renegotiate their labor arrangements with the freed people.

The contract labor system that had developed during the war and under presidential Reconstruction was replaced with a variety of regional arrangements. On the Louisiana sugar plantations, the freed people became wage laborers. But in tobacco and cotton regions, where most freed people lived, a new system of labor, sharecropping, developed. Under this system, an agricultural worker and his family typically agreed to work for one year on a particular plot of land, with the landowner providing the tools, seed, and work animals. At the end of the year, the crop was split, perhaps one-third going to the sharecropper and two-thirds to the owner.

Sharecropping shaped the economy of the postwar South by transforming the production and marketing of cash crops. Landowners broke up their plantations into family-sized plots, worked by sharecroppers in family units with no direct supervision. Each sharecropping family established its own relationship with local merchants to sell crops and buy supplies. Merchants became crucial to the southern credit system, because most southern banks could not meet the banking standards established by Congress during the Civil War. Storekeepers, usually the only people who could extend credit to sharecroppers, provided sharecroppers with food, fertilizer, animal feed, and other provisions during the year until the crop was harvested.

These developments had important consequences for white small farmers. More merchants fanned out into up-country areas inhabited mostly by ordinary whites, areas now served by railroads sponsored by the Reconstruction legislatures. With merchants offering credit and railroads offering transportation, small farmers started to produce cash crops. Thus, Reconstruction sped the process by which southern yeomen abandoned self-sufficient farming for cash crops.

Sharecropping spread quickly among black farmers in the Cotton South. By 1880, 80 percent of cotton farms had fewer than 50 acres, and the majority of those farms were operated by sharecroppers (see Maps 15–2 and 15–3). Sharecropping had several advantages for landlords. It reduced their risk when cotton prices were low and encouraged workers to increase production without costly supervision. Further, if sharecroppers changed jobs before the crop was harvested, they lost a whole year's pay. But there were also advantages for the workers. For freed people with no hope of owning their own farms, sharecropping at least rewarded their hard work. The bigger the crop, the more they earned. It gave them more independence than contract labor.

Sharecropping also allowed the freed people to work in families rather than in gangs. Freedom alone had rearranged the powers of men, women, and children within the families

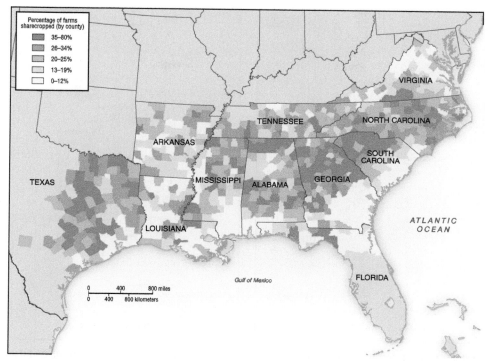

Map 15-2 **Sharecropping** By 1880, the sharecropping system had spread across the South. It was most common in the inland areas, where primarily cotton and tobacco plantations existed before the Civil War.

of former slaves. Parents gained new control over their children. They could send sons and daughters to school or put them to work. Successful parents could give their children an important head start in life. Similarly, African American husbands gained new powers.

The marriage laws of the mid-nineteenth century that defined the husband as the head of the household were irrelevant to slaves, because their marriages had no legal standing. With emancipation, these patriarchal assumptions of American family law shaped the lives of freed men and women. Once married, women often found that their property belonged to their husbands. The sharecropping system further assumed that as head of the household the husband made the economic decisions for the entire family. Men signed most labor contracts, and most contracts assumed that the husband would take his family to work with him.

Sharecropping shaped the social system of the postwar South. It influenced the balance of power between men and women. It established the balance of power between landowners and sharecroppers. It tied the southern economy to agriculture, in particular to cotton production, impeding the region's overall economic development.

The Gospel of Prosperity

Only a diversified economy could break the planters' hold over a black labor force; railroads could lower farmers' shipping costs and tap the South's coal and iron resources.

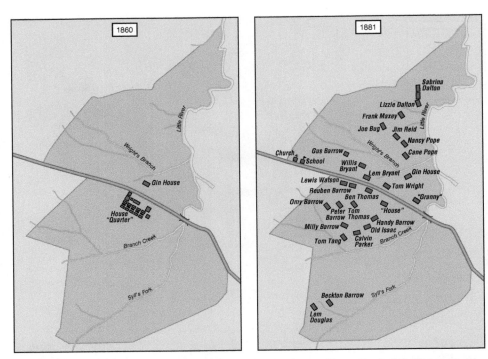

Map 15-3   The Effect of Sharecropping in the South: The Barrow Plantation in Oglethorpe County, Georgia Sharecropping cut large estates into small landholdings worked by sharecroppers and tenants, changing the landscape of the South.

Economic development might even give the South an independence worth having: it was no longer required to look north for its investment capital or finished goods. A program that made all classes prosper seemed ready-made to recruit more whites for a party and push racial issues into the background. Republicans preached a "gospel of prosperity" that would use government aid to build a richer South and benefit ordinary white southerners. Reconstruction governments committed the states' credit and funds to building its industrial base.

The strategy had big drawbacks. Diverting scarce resources to railroads and corporations left less for black constituencies' needs, especially school systems. Investors hesitated to invest in bonds issued by governments at risk of violent overthrow. Hungry corporations hounded the legislature for favors and made bribery their clinching argument. State-owned railroads were sold to private firms for a song—and a payoff. States already spending heavily to repair the damage of the war and to build new state services on a much-reduced tax base obligated themselves for millions more. As taxes soared, white farmers became increasingly receptive to Democratic claims that they were being robbed, their money wasted by swag-grabbing outsiders and ignorant black upstarts in office. The passage of civil rights bills, ending discrimination in public transportation, only alienated former scalawags further and stirred conservatives to bring the stay-at-homes to the polls. Everywhere, Republicans were split over how far to trust former Confederates. That division lost Virginia and Tennessee to the "Redeemers," conservative white Democrats, in 1869. In Arkansas, two Republicans claimed the governorship in 1872, and two years later they raised armies to fight it out. The "Brooks-Baxter war" ended with the Democrat-backed contestant winning and a new constitution that put both Republicans out for good.

A Counterrevolution of Terrorism and Economic Pressure

Republicans' policy failures alone did not destroy them. Terrorism and economic pressure did. Everywhere planters used their power to keep black tenants from voting. White radicals found themselves shunned by society. They were denied credit or employment unless they left politics. As early as 1867, secret organizations were arising, bent on Reconstruction's overthrow and the restoration of white dominance, which, effectively, meant bringing Democrats into power by threats, beatings, and killings. From the Carolinas to Texas, the Ku-Klux Klan and similar organizations shot Republican lawmakers and burned black schools and churches, often in broad daylight. Black landowners and renters were targeted. African American employees or tenants who complained about being cheated faced flogging or assassination for "insolence." Teachers, party organizers, and white wartime Unionists all fell victim. Politically active blacks were threatened, driven from their homes, whipped, or shot. Their wives were raped and their homes plundered while Democratic newspapers defamed the victims. In a single year, authorities counted well over 500 killings in Georgia alone—and just about no arrests, much less indictments. Witnesses refused to testify, intimidated juries dared not convict, and sheriffs dared not arrest. In Arkansas, Texas, and Tennessee, Republican governors mustered a white militia and broke the terrorist movement. Elsewhere they found themselves powerless or outgunned. Terrorism carried North Carolina, Alabama, and Georgia for the Democrats in 1870, crippling Reconstruction in the first state and effectively ending it in the other two. By 1872, Redeemers had regained control of the whole upper and border South. After that, they rigged the election laws to curb the black vote and put any Republican comeback out of reach.

Reconstruction had not been meant to work that way. Instead of being able to defend themselves, Reconstruction governments found themselves desperately dependent on national support. But that support had been dissipating ever since the passage of the Reconstruction Acts.

As terrorism mounted, Congress legislated to protect a free, fair vote. The most important, the 1871 "Ku Klux" Act, gave the US government the power to suppress the Klan, even suspending the writ of habeas corpus. President Grant moved cautiously, however, because the newly created Justice Department lacked both funds and personnel. When the time limit on the law's most effective provisions expired, Congress did not renew them and did nothing to expand the government's ability to cope with violence when it broke out again, a few years later. Still, thousands of arrests and hundreds of convictions ended the Klan, restoring peace in time for the 1872 presidential elections.

Reconstructing America's Foreign Policy

As the Civil War approached, slavery's expansionists tainted manifest destiny for everyone but Democrats. Republicans had no intention of spreading an empire of the unfree—nor of letting any European power do so. In Mexico, the French emperor had installed a puppet state headed by Maximilian, the Austrian archduke. The Johnson administration helped force France to withdraw its troops. Unbacked, Maximilian's regime collapsed. Spreading the republic's bounds would only spread liberty. It might even give black southerners a place free of race prejudice where they could fulfill their potential. Secretary of State William Seward dreamed of all North America, perhaps even most of the Caribbean, as one vast federation; Senator Charles Sumner suggested that the United States ease Canada into the Union.

Nothing of the kind happened. Seward's biggest success came in 1867, in purchasing Alaska from Russia. A few months later, however, the Senate rejected a treaty buying the Virgin Islands from Denmark and held off on leasing a naval base in Santo Domingo. A treaty with Colombia giving the United States exclusive rights to build a canal across the Isthmus of Panama came to nothing. Canadians showed no interest in joining the Union and instead forged a union of their own separate provinces.

Not all the wealth of the West Indies could carry the United States beyond trade to the taking of territory. Slavery's end killed most of the zest for annexing Cuba; the fact that its people were Catholics and racially diverse alarmed even some Republicans. When a rebellion broke out there in 1868, Congress did nothing about it. Similar inhibitions thwarted Grant's plan to annex Santo Domingo in 1870. As head of the Senate Foreign Relations Committee, Sumner's opposition doomed the treaty and, ironically, himself; as a result, Grant and Fish forced the Senate to depose him from his chairmanship.

A Reconstructed West

Events out west may have contributed to the nation's declining interest in southern affairs. The lands beyond the Missouri River were being reconstructed just as dramatically, and, when it came to their original inhabitants, far more brutally. In the West, most troops occupied states and territories and kept the peace. Here, too, the Gospel of Prosperity promised a new civilization, based on outsiders settling and bringing their eastern values and eastern capital with them. Passed during the Civil War, the Homestead Act was meant to populate the West with independent small farmers. Millions came in the 40 years that followed and continued to take out titles until 1934; millions more bought land at nominal prices under supplementary laws. Their movement has become the stuff of legend. But these hardy individuals did not settle an empty prairie. Native people held it already.

The Overland Trail

In popular images, the West was a haven for rugged men who struck out on their own, but most migrants went in family groups, and the families were mostly middle class. Few poor people could afford the journey and still hope to buy land and set up a farm.

The journey across the Overland Trail (see Map 15–4) had become safer over the years. The US government built forts to supply migrants and protect the trail from (rare) Indian attacks. Mormon settlers in Utah had built Salt Lake City into a major stopping point and the heart of a thriving economy. On May 10, 1869, two railroads, the Central Pacific, building from California, and the Union Pacific, building from the Missouri River, joined at Promontory Point, Utah. This first transcontinental railroad line effectively replaced the five-month journey of covered wagons with a trip of a little less than a week. Four more transcontinentals would reach the Pacific over the next generation. Out from them radiated branch lines and side spurs, to tie the West into eastern markets. Where the companies set down depots, towns sprang up, unlike in the East, where the towns came first and the railroads afterward. Irresponsibly and sometimes crookedly financed, subsidized by all levels of government, their construction almost guaranteeing an eventual wreck (actual and financial), railroads became the symbol for the age. They represented to many Americans the enterprising spirit, the intrepid nature, and the arrogance of industrial capitalism. They turned Minnesota's Red River valley into a sea of wheat and dominated California's government. They also gave the army an unprecedented mobility that it would very much need. By the time the railroad presidents drove the golden spike at Promontory Point, the government had become occupied by the growing problem of Native American–white relations in the West.

Map 15-4   The Overland Trail No transcontinental railroad existed until 1869. Even thereafter, most settlers moved west on a series of well-developed overland trails.

Chinese Laborers Building Railroad This 1877 picture of a Southern Pacific Railroad trestle shows the crude construction methods used to build the first line across the Sierra Nevada.

The Origins of Indian Reservations

In 1851, more than 10,000 Native Americans from across the Great Plains converged on Fort Laramie in Wyoming Territory. All the major Indian peoples were represented: Sioux, Cheyenne, Arapaho, Crow, and many others. They came to meet with government officials who hoped to develop a lasting means of avoiding Indian–white conflict. Since the discovery of gold a few years earlier, white migrants had been crossing through Indian territory on their way to California, most of them already prejudiced against the Indians. US officials wanted to prevent outbreaks of violence between whites and Indians as well as between Indian nations. They proposed creating a separate territory for each Indian tribe, with government subsidies to entice the Indians to stay within their territories. This was the beginning of the reservation system, and for the rest of the century the US government struggled to force the Indians to accept it.

The government had good reason to advocate for reservations. At their worst, both whites and Indians behaved ferociously. Civilians in one territory raised $5,000 for Indian scalps, promising $25 for any "with ears on." At Sand Creek, Colorado, militia slaughtered and scalped over 100 friendly Indians, two-thirds of them women and children. Fingers were cut off for the rings, body parts for souvenirs. In the northern Rockies, warriors led by the Northern Plains Indian leader Red Cloud lured forces from Fort Phil Kearny, killed them all, and stripped and mutilated the bodies. But Red Cloud could also say truthfully, "When the white man comes in my country, he leaves a trail of blood behind him." The reservation system was corrupt and badly handled. Agents for the Bureau of Indian Affairs cheated Indians and the government alike, sometimes reaping huge profits. But the reservations failed mostly because not all Indians agreed to stay within their designated territories, leading to armed confrontations and reprisals. "The more we can kill this year, the less will have to be killed the next war," General William Tecumseh Sherman declared.

Instead of extermination, the government opted for a more comprehensive reservation policy. Two treaties divided the Great Plains into two vast Indian territories. The Medicine Lodge Treaty, signed in Kansas in 1867, organized thousands of Indians across the southern plains. In return for government supplies, most of the southern plains peoples agreed to restrict themselves to the reservation. The Northern Plains Indians did not agree so readily. Inspired by Red Cloud, some insisted that the United States abandon forts along the Bozeman Trail. When the government agreed, Red Cloud signed the Fort Laramie Treaty in 1868. (It was one of the last. Starting in 1871, the government stopped treating the tribes as separate nations. They were subject peoples, nothing more.)

Red Cloud abided by the treaties for the rest of his life. They failed all the same. Not all the tribes approved of the treaties, and on the southern plains, raiding parties gave the army all the excuse it needed for payback. On Thanksgiving Day, 1868, the Seventh Cavalry, led by Lieutenant-Colonel George Armstrong Custer, massacred Cheyennes at Washita Creek, Oklahoma. Among the fallen was Black Kettle, who had survived the Sand Creek massacre in Colorado and whose influence had brought other tribes to make peace at Medicine Lodge. President Grant's "Peace Policy" had replaced selfish politicians with high-minded ministers as its go-betweens to the tribes and emphasized negotiation and assimilation over war and expulsion. However, there was no peace out West; not for the Comanches, Navajos, Modocs, or Lakota Sioux. And those last, in one general's opinion, were the greatest light cavalry in history.

The Lakota had a chance to prove their skill in battle. In Dakota Territory the discovery of gold in the Black Hills in 1874 brought thousands of whites onto Indian territory. When the Lakota refused to cede their lands to the miners, the government sent in the army, led by the charismatic, headstrong Lieutenant-Colonel Custer. In June 1876, Custer made two critical mistakes: he split his forces, and he failed to keep them in communication with each other. He and hundreds of his men were slaughtered at Little Bighorn, Montana, by 2,000 Indian warriors led by Crazy Horse.

"Custer's Last Stand" was the stuff of legends, but the real story came afterward. The Lakota could win battles, but not the war. Significantly, Crow warriors died with Custer. As in most other struggles, Native Americans served as US scouts, adjuncts, and allies. There was never a united Indian resistance, because, as far as Native Americans were concerned, there were no such things as Indians. There were Blackfoots, Nez Percés, Arapahoes, and Comanches. They could be broken and beaten one by one, or turned against one another—and they were. The longer a war went on, the more tribes gave up or switched sides. The army had learned to adapt to a different kind of fighting. It hit the enemy in winter, when its forces were pinned down as they had been at Washita Creek. It destroyed not only Indian soldiers but also villages and crops to starve them into submission. In the Southwest, it used Apaches to hunt down other Apaches and adopted mule trains in place of slow, cumbersome supply wagons.

The Destruction of Indian Subsistence

At the same time as the discovery of gold in the Black Hills, the demand for hides brought a different kind of gold rush to the plains: the mass slaughter of buffalo herds. Profit and sport drove the hunt, but cattlemen had no objection to opening up the range for their own stock. The army saw a bonus in anything wiping out subsistence for Indians off the reservation. "Kill every buffalo you can," a colonel urged one hunter. "Every buffalo dead is an Indian gone." Railroads joined in, sponsoring mass kills from slow-moving trains on the prairies. Some 13 million bison in 1850 dwindled by 1880 to a few hundred. The only buffalo a westerner was likely to see by 1920 was the one on the back of the nickel.

In the Northwest in 1877, the Nez Percés, fleeing from Union troops, began a dramatic trek across the mountains in an attempt to reach Canada. The Nez Percés eluded the troops and nearly made it over the Canadian border. However, hunger and the elements forced Chief Joseph and his exhausted people to agree to go to their reservations.

Pursued and deprived of allies one by one, Chief Sitting Bull and his last few warriors gave up in 1881. By then, most Indian wars were like jail breakouts: small, sporadic, and ugly. The ugliest came at Wounded Knee, South Dakota, in 1890. Fearing that the Ghost Dance religious revival movement would stir up rebellion, soldiers gunned down over 200 Native American men, women, and children. Sitting Bull did not live to see it. He had been shot resisting arrest days before.

Indian Village Routed, Geronimo Fleeing from Camp Oil on canvas by Frederic Remington, 1896.

Sharing none of the settlers' fear of and less of their contempt for Indians, reformers hoped that reservations would function not just as holding pens, but as schools and civilizers. Lincoln's commissioner of Indian Affairs, William P. Dole, believed that "Indians are capable of attaining a high degree of civilization." Like other reformers, Dole equated civilization with a belief in individual property rather than communal holdings, Christian values rather than native religions, and the discipline of the regular hours that farmers and workers, rather than hunters, observed. Accordingly, reformers set out, as one of them put it, to destroy the Indian and save the person. They introduced government schools on reservations to teach the virtues of private property, individual achievement, and social mobility.

The reformers' influence peaked in 1887 when Congress passed the Dawes Severalty Act, the most important Indian legislation of the century, and the very kind of confiscation never done on freed peoples' behalf. Reservation land was broken up into separate plots and distributed among individual families. The goal was to force Indians to live like white farmers. But the lands allotted were generally so poor, and the plots so small, that their owners quickly sold them. Large tracts were kept in trust by the government and gradually sold off, purportedly to pay for uplifting and assimilating the Indians. By the early twentieth century only a few, sharply diminished reservations remained outside the desert Southwest. Native American cultures endured, but many Native Americans did not. Poverty, overcrowding, and epidemic disease brought their population to its lowest point. For many eastern onlookers, those conditions only proved how unworthy the race was to compete in the struggle for life—a conclusion all too many had drawn about African Americans from Reconstruction's downfall.

The Retreat from Republican Radicalism

A series of makeshift laws and improvisations, congressional Reconstruction had stirred misgivings among moderate Republicans who were fearful of stretching the Constitution too far and uneasy with using the expanded authority that war had given them in peacetime. New steps, such as confiscating planters' property, say, or a nationally funded school system, were out of the question. Even the Freedmen's Bureau was cut back and, except for education, closed down completely when reconstructed states were readmitted to Congress. Public backlash against radicalism gave Democrats heavy gains in the 1867 elections. In order to survive, Reconstruction had to consolidate its gains and leave the new state governments to fulfill its promises.

Republicans Become the Party of Moderation

By then, the 1868 presidential campaign was under way. Running the war hero General Ulysses S. Grant for president, Republicans could offer a candidate who was above politics. His slogan, "Let us have peace," emphasized that the party meant to restore the Union, rather than advance radicalism. The platform endorsed congressional Reconstruction and defended black voting in the South, but it insisted that states not covered by Reconstruction should decide the issue of suffrage for themselves. Positioning themselves as protectors of the war's accomplishments came all the more easily after Democrats nominated former New York governor Horatio Seymour on a platform declaring the Reconstruction Acts as illegal, null and void. Their fiercest spokesmen swore that if Democrats won, they would overturn the newly elected southern governments and install white conservative ones. Voiding those governments would invalidate the Fourteenth Amendment, ratified by southern legislatures; some partisans even argued that every measure passed since southern congressmen walked out in 1861 had no legal force. Bondholders, fearful that Democrats would turn their national securities into waste paper or pay them in depreciated "greenbacks," thought Grant the safer choice, even without Republicans' shouting that Seymour's election would reward traitors and bring on civil war again.

Northern voters got a taste of what Democratic rule would mean in an epidemic of violence across the South. Riots and massacres in Louisiana and Georgia kept Republicans from voting and carried both states for Seymour. In the North, the outrages may have been decisive in electing Grant. Carrying the electoral college by a huge margin, he won the popular vote more narrowly with just 53 percent, and then only because of a heavy black turnout in his favor.

Reconstructing the North

Although Reconstruction was aimed primarily at the South, the North was affected as well, especially by the struggle over the black vote. The transformation of the North was an important chapter in the history of Reconstruction.

The Fifteenth Amendment and Nationwide African American Suffrage

Segregated into separate facilities or excluded entirely, denied the right to vote in nearly every state outside of New England, blacks in wartime fought to end discrimination in the North. Biracial efforts chipped away at many states' discriminatory "Black Laws" and the Fourteenth Amendment eliminated the rest nationwide. Streetcar lines in some cities stopped running separate cars, black testimony was admitted on the same terms as white, and in a few northern communities, black children began attending white schools. Ending the color bar on voting and jury service proved to be more difficult: when impartial suffrage went on the ballot, most northern states voted against it (though most Republicans favored it and Congress mandated it in the territories and the District of Columbia).

The shocking electoral violence of 1868 persuaded Republicans that equal suffrage in the South needed permanent protection. In 1869, Congress added a Fifteenth Amendment to the Constitution forbidding the use of "race, color, or previous condition of servitude" as a bar to suffrage in the North as well as the South. For those states not yet readmitted to the Union (Virginia, Mississippi, and Texas), it made ratification of the amendment an additional condition. On March 30, 1870, the Fifteenth Amendment became part of the Constitution.

Revolutionary as it was, the Fifteenth Amendment had serious limitations that would weaken its impact later. As the Supreme Court would note, it did not confer a right to vote on anybody. It simply limited the grounds on which it could be denied. States could impose property or taxpaying qualifications or a literacy test if they pleased, as long as the restrictions made no distinction on the basis of race. They could set up residency require-ments or limit the vote to naturalized citizens, or to men.

Women and Suffrage

The issue of black voting added to tensions among northern radicals. Feminists and abolitionists had worked together in the struggle for emancipation, but signs of trouble appeared as early as May 1863 at the convention of the Woman's National Loyal League in New York City. The League had been organized to assist in defeating the slave South. One of the convention's resolutions declared that "there never can be a true peace in this Republic until the civil and political rights of all citizens of African descent and all women are practically established." For some delegates, this went too far. They argued that it was inappropriate to inject the issue of women's rights into the struggle to restore the Union.

With the war's end, the radical crusade for black suffrage intensified debate among reformers. Elizabeth Cady Stanton and others pointed out the injustice of letting "Patrick and Sambo and Hans and Yung Tung" vote while propertied, educated women were denied suffrage. The Fourteenth Amendment, by privileging male inhabitants' right to vote explicitly, appalled Stanton, and the Fifteenth Amendment's failure to address gender discrimination at the polls only confirmed her suspicion that what one abolitionist called "the Negro's hour" would never give way to one for women. Friendly to women's suffrage though they were, abolitionists like Frederick Douglass and suffragists like Lucy Stone argued that the critical issue was the protection of the freed people. "When women, because they are women, are dragged from their homes and hung upon lamp-posts," Douglass reminded an audience, "when their children are torn from their arms and their brains dashed to the pavement; when they are the objects of insult and outrage at every turn; when they are in danger of having their homes burnt down over their heads; when their children are not allowed to enter schools; then they will have an urgency to obtain the ballot." In 1869, radical and abolitionist allies parted ways. The women's suffrage movement divided into rival organizations, Stanton's National Woman Suffrage Association and Stone's American Woman Suffrage Association.

Some radicals, Charles Sumner among them, favored women's suffrage, but most Republicans did not. The territories of Wyoming and Utah enfranchised women. Elsewhere, lawmakers let women participate in school-board elections, but voting reform went no further. Most states refused even to put the issue on the ballot. When they did so, it was voted down. Denying women's appeal that as citizens they were entitled to vote, the Supreme Court declared that the Fourteenth Amendment's right of citizenship did not carry that right with it.

The End of Reconstruction

Events outside the South helped speed Reconstruction's collapse. Reform-oriented Republicans felt alarm at the spread of political corruption after the war. Convinced, too, that full reconciliation must come, now that the war's goals had been met, they broke with the party and abandoned their support for federal intervention in southern affairs. Additionally, a depression took voters' minds off Reconstruction issues. By 1876, "Redemption" had carried white Democrats to power in all but a few southern states. Yet a hotly disputed presidential election and divided power would doom even those.

Corruption Is the Fashion

Never before had corruption loomed so large in the United States. With more money to spend, more favors to give, and more functions to perform, both state and federal governments found themselves besieged by supplicants, and officeholders found opportunities to turn a dishonest penny where none had existed before. In New York City, infamous state senator William M. Tweed used the Tammany Hall political machine to steal tens of millions of dollars. Senators bought their seats in Kansas and South Carolina, while Tennessee congressmen sold appointments to West Point. The Standard Oil Company allegedly controlled Pennsylvania's legislature. As Henry Clay Warmoth, the governor of Louisiana put it, corruption was "the fashion." He, incidentally, was very fashionable himself.

With an honest but credulous chief executive, Grant's administration became notoriously corrupt. Customs collectors shook down merchants and used their employees to manage party conventions. With help from administration insiders, the notorious speculators Jay Gould and Jim Fisk tried to corner the nation's gold supply and brought on a brief, ruinous panic on Wall Street. Grant's private secretary was even exposed as a member of the "Whiskey Ring," a group of distillers and revenue agents who cheated the government out of millions of dollars in taxes. Charges of making money by swindling the Indians forced the Secretary of Interior out of office. Months later, the Secretary of War quit when investigators traced kickbacks to his wife. Having overcharged the government for supplies while building the Union Pacific Railroad, the fraudulent Credit Mobilier contracting firm shared mammoth profits with nearly a dozen top congressmen. The Republican platform, one critic snarled, was just a conjugation of the verb "to steal."

Southern corruption reflected national patterns. In the worst states, both parties stole, bribed, and profited. But in the South, Democrats blamed such action on ignorant black voters and nonlandowning white Republicans. Shifting the issue from equal rights to honest government, they insisted that clean, cheap government, run by society's natural leaders (white and well-heeled), would benefit all races. Every scandal discredited Republican rule further, including the many

President Grant as a Strong Man Despite solid accomplishments and his own honesty, Ulysses S. Grant would be remembered for scandals in just about every department. Here he upholds various corrupt "rings" and the thieves and hacks that mulcted the War and Navy Departments, the government of the District of Columbia, and the custom-house service.

upright and talented leaders, both black and white, that fought against corruption. This helped galvanize the opposition, destroying Republican hopes of attracting white voters and weakening support for Reconstruction. By 1875, northerners assumed the worst of any carpetbagger, even one fighting to cut taxes and block cheats.

Liberal Republicans Revolt

Voicing widely held concerns, a small, influential group of northern Republican intellectuals, editors, and activists challenged a political system that, in their view, rested on greed, selfishness, partisanship, and politicians' keeping war hatreds alive. Known as "liberal Republicans," they viewed bosses and political machines, which were out to loot the Treasury, and special interests as detrimental to good government. They were weary of railroads receiving land grants, of steamship lines receiving subsidies, and government clerkships that were given to cronies. Decrying corruption and disenchanted with Reconstruction, they called for reform: a lower tariff, a stable currency system based on gold, a merit-based civil service system for appointments to office, and full, universal amnesty for former Confederates.

When Democrats announced a "New Departure," accepting the three constitutional amendments, liberal Republicans took them at their word. Despairing of preventing Grant's renomination, they nominated the eccentric, reform-minded editor Horace Greeley for president in 1872. The platform promised to end all political disabilities and reconcile North and South, in essence by ending all federal intervention on black southerners' behalf. Desperate to win, Democrats endorsed the editor, their lifelong enemy, but thousands stayed home on election day rather than vote for him. Having cut the tariff and restored the office-holding rights of all but a handful of ex-Confederates, Republicans won many reformers back. Greeley lost in a landslide and died in a sanitarium less than a month later.

Grant's reelection bought Reconstruction time, but it could not do more than that. Northerners, even Republican ones, became increasingly alarmed every time the national government used its power to act on behalf of Reconstruction governments and deal with issues that should be handled by local authorities. As a result, the president found it increasingly hard to justify intervening on the behalf of black voters.

"Redeeming" the South

In September 1873, America's premier financial institution, Jay Cooke & Company, went bankrupt after overextending itself on investments in the Northern Pacific Railroad. Within weeks, hundreds of banks and thousands of businesses failed. The country sank into a depression that lasted five years. Unemployment rose to 14 percent as corporations slashed wages. Bitter strikes in textile plants, coal fields, and on the railroad lines ended in failure and violence. As America turned its attention to issues of corruption, labor unrest, and economic depression, Reconstruction took a backseat.

Between the corruption scandals buffeting the Grant administration and the economic crisis, northern voters' interest in Reconstruction plummeted. Those who had favored government intervention to keep "Rebels" from coming to power no longer saw the need. Former Confederates stood by the flag as earnestly as Unionists. In the 1874 elections, Democrats made a dramatic comeback. For the first time since 1859, they carried the House, guaranteeing a deadlocked Congress. Outgoing Republicans

STRUGGLES FOR DEMOCRACY

An Incident at Coushatta, August 1874

If biracial democracy had a chance anywhere in Reconstruction Louisiana, it was upstate in Red River parish. With African Americans outnumbering whites more than two to one, majority rule meant Republican government. As in so many other black counties, whites held the choicest offices: sheriff, tax collector, and mayor of the parish seat in Coushatta. A Vermont-born Union veteran, Marshall Harvey Twitchell, represented Red River in the state senate. Most of the wealth and nearly all the property stayed in native white hands, just as it had before the war. Blacks continued to raise and harvest the cotton on other people's land.

Nevertheless, Reconstruction made a difference for African Americans. They elected members of their own race to the police jury that did most of the parish's day-to-day governing. Several justices of the peace who handled minor civil cases were black. Farmers, field hands, and day laborers performed jury duty. What freed people wanted most, however, was what white conservatives had long denied

them, a functioning public school system. Twitchell saw that they got one, with separate schools for whites and blacks. So prosperous was Red River under "Negro rule," Twitchell bragged, that it was evident to "the most perfect stranger."

Having the most votes was not enough, however. All the influential newspapers and nearly all the property and firepower in Red River parish remained with the Democrats. When hard times hit, Republicans' enemies organized rifle clubs and a White League, which acted as the military arm of the Democratic Party. Unlike the Ku Klux Klan, it operated in the open and without disguises. By mid-1874, death threats against Republican officials were being posted on the streets of Coushatta. "Your fate is sealed," one letter warned judges. "Nothing but your blood will appease us." Alarmed, the police jury resigned and white Republicans left the parish.

That August, White Leaguers pretended to have uncovered a black plot to slaughter white residents. On that excuse, they arrested several dozen black Republican

made one last advance, passing Charles Sumner's civil rights bill, which outlawed discrimination in public places. The law left segregated schools and cemeteries alone, and most southern establishments ignored even those provisions that did pass. But with Congress's adjournment in March 1875, Republicans no longer had any chance of bolstering Reconstruction with legislation, or even funding an army big enough to protect a fair vote at the polls.

Supreme Court rulings made implementing Reconstruction legislation harder still. In the 1873 *Slaughterhouse* cases, a majority decided that the Fourteenth Amendment's protection of equal rights under the law covered only those rights associated with national citizenship. Rights affiliated with state citizenship—for example, the right to butcher cattle

Terror in the South Thomas Nast's 1874 cartoon depicts a White League member and a Klan member joining hands over a terrorized black family. Nast's point was not that emancipation had been a mistake, but that without national protection, freed people's fate was worse than slavery.

leaders and all the white parish officers. To save their lives, the officials resigned. The vigilantes promised them an armed escort out of the parish, but instead, it led them into an ambush. Mounted gunmen from the neighboring parish killed six prisoners. Later they rode into Coushatta and hanged two of the captured blacks as well. Absent on political business, Twitchell alone survived. When he returned in 1876, an unknown gunman shot him, costing him both arms. From then on, Republican majorities counted for nothing. Democrats did the voting and governing and thus radical Reconstruction's gains melted away.

Coushatta's fate was Louisiana's. White Leaguers overthrew the governor in September 1874. Federal intervention restored him, but it could not save local Republican governments like Red River's. "The State government has no power outside of the United States Army . . . no power at all," an officer confessed. "The White League is the only power in the State."

when a Louisiana state law gave a monopoly to one particular firm—could only be upheld by the state. In 1876, the justices whittled down the national government's power to protect black voters from intimidation and violence or even their right to bear arms and hold public meetings. In *United States v. Cruikshank*, the Court took up a horrific massacre of some 150 black state militiamen at Colfax, Louisiana, on Easter Sunday, 1873; it decided that the equal protection clause applied only to state governments' actions, not that of the paramilitaries responsible. In *Hall v. DeCuir* (1878), the Supreme Court invalidated a Louisiana law prohibiting racial segregation on public transportation. In the Civil Rights Cases of 1883, the Supreme Court declared that the Fourteenth Amendment did not cover discriminatory practices by private persons.

Even before the 1874 elections, southern Reconstruction was collapsing. As the number of white Republicans fell, the number of black Republicans holding office in the South increased. But the persistence of black officeholders only reinforced the Democrats' determination to "redeem" their states from Republican rule. Blaming hard times on "carpetbagger" corruption and high taxes, conservatives formed taxpayers' leagues and armed themselves in White Leagues, paramilitary groups whose goal was to remove Republicans from office and prevent freedmen from voting. Crude appeals to white supremacy and harsh economic pressure forced most scalawags to drop out of politics, making it easier to draw a sharp color line. Paramilitaries then applied violence and intimidation to keep blacks from the polls. By the fall of 1874, they were overthrowing local governments in Mississippi and Louisiana. White Leagues took over the streets in New Orleans and briefly ousted the governor. Terrorism helped "redeem" Alabama that November, among other places.

That left two securely Republican states, both with considerable black majorities: South Carolina and Mississippi. In 1875, Democrats in the latter mounted the most blatant show of force yet. Governor Adelbert Ames begged for federal help and was told to look to his own resources first. The election that followed was as quiet as White League shotguns could make it. In the end, enough blacks were disfranchised and enough scalawags voted their racial prejudices to hand power to the Democrats. Within months they forced Ames's resignation. In 1876, South Carolina whites adopted the "Mississippi Plan" with an even more open commitment to violent overthrow of the Republican majority. Mounted, armed men broke up Republican rallies. In Hamburg, white paramilitaries besieged the local black militia and, after their surrender, killed seven of them. "We write to tell you that our people are being shot down like dogs, and no matter what democrats may say," one South Carolinian wrote the president, "unless you help us our folks will not dare go to the polls." In Louisiana, Redeemer violence may have been worse still.

The Twice-Stolen Election of 1876

Amid a serious economic depression, and with an electorate tired of Reconstruction, the Democrats stood a good chance of winning the presidency in 1876. The Democratic candidate, New York governor Samuel J. Tilden, had won a reputation for fighting thieves in his own party. On election night, Tilden won 250,000 more votes than his Republican opponent, Ohio governor Rutherford B. Hayes (see Map 15–5). But Republican "returning boards" in three southern states—Florida, South Carolina, and Louisiana—counted Hayes in and gave him a one-electoral vote victory.

Democrats swore that they had been cheated out of the presidency, though even without white violence and manipulation, Hayes probably would have won not just in the three disputed states but elsewhere in the South. Both houses of Congress deadlocked on counting the electoral votes. Cries of "Tilden or Blood" rang through the air. In the end, both sides compromised by choosing a special electoral commission to settle the matter. In an eight-to-seven vote, it awarded Hayes every disputed state. House Democrats could not stop "His Fraudulency" from being sworn in, but their southern members, cutting the best deal they could, agreed to drop their obstruction in return for assurances that Hayes would not aid in the survival of the last two Reconstruction governments. A month after taking office, Hayes withdrew the regiments guarding Republican statehouses in South Carolina and Louisiana; by that time Redeemer Democrats had full control of the states

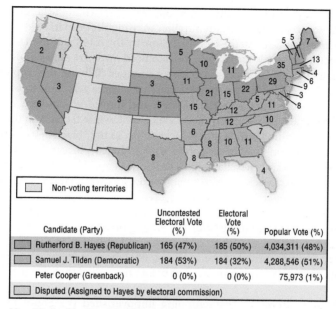

Map 15-5   **The Presidential Election, 1876**   In 1876, the Democratic presidential candidate, Samuel Tilden, won what popular vote white southern Democrats permitted to be cast, but he was denied the presidency because Republicans claimed that a fair count gave Louisiana, South Carolina, Oregon, and Florida to their candidate, Rutherford B. Hayes.

anyway. This order marked Reconstruction's symbolic end. Hereafter, the president would emphasize goodwill between the North and South and trust Redeemers' promises to protect black rights—a trust that was speedily betrayed, and nowhere more so than on the farms where most freed people worked for a white landowner.

Sharecropping Becomes Wage Labor

As the southern economy recovered from the devastation of the Civil War, many observers predicted a bright future for the region. Optimists saw a wealth of opportunities from untapped natural and human resources, a South freed from the inefficient slave labor system and ripe for investment.

Americans were building railroads at an exuberant clip, but southerners built them faster—with northern money. By 1890, steel mills lit the night skies of Birmingham, Alabama. Textile mills dotted the Piedmont Plateau (along the eastern foothills of the Appalachian Mountains from Virginia to Georgia). Southerners were migrating from the countryside to the towns, expanding cotton production into new areas, like the rich Mississippi delta soil. Yet ordinary southerners, especially African Americans, did not share in the New South's prosperity.

Redemption shifted the terms of the new labor relationship between landlords and sharecroppers in landowners' direction. The most important question was who owned the cotton crop at the end of the year: the sharecropper who raised it, the landlord who owned the farm, or the merchant who lent the supplies to bring the crop in.

Legal resolution in favor of the landlord came by the middle of the 1880s. The courts defined a sharecropper as a wage laborer. The landlord owned the crop and paid his workers a share of it as a wage. Landlords also won a stronger claim on the crop than the merchant creditors. Under the circumstances, merchants were reluctant to advance money to sharecroppers. Many left plantation districts and moved up-country, doing business with white yeomen farmers. Trapped in a cycle of debt, white farmers in the 1880s began losing their land and falling into tenancy. Meanwhile, in the "black belt" (where most African Americans lived and most of the cotton was produced), successful landlords became merchants while successful merchants purchased land and hired sharecroppers of their own. By the mid-1880s, black sharecroppers worked as wage laborers for the landlord-merchant class across much of the South.

Sharecropping differed in two critical ways from the wage work of industrial America. First, sharecropping was family labor, depending on a husband and father who signed the contract and delivered the labor of his wife and children to the landlord. Second, because sharecropping contracts were yearlong, the labor market was restricted to a few weeks at the end of each year. If croppers left before the end of the year, they risked losing everything.

The political economy of sharecropping impoverished the South by binding the region to cotton, a crop that steadily depleted the soil even as prices fell. Yet most southern blacks found few alternatives. In time a few black farmers purchased their own land, but their farms were generally tiny and the soil poor. The skilled black artisans who had worked on plantations before the Civil War moved to southern cities, where they took unskilled, low-paying jobs. Northern factories were segregated, as were the steel mills of Birmingham, Alabama, and the Piedmont textile mills. Black women worked as domestic

Time Line

▼**1851**
Fort Laramie Treaty establishes Indian reservations

▼**1862**
Passage of Homestead Act

▼**1863**
Lincoln's Proclamation of Amnesty and Reconstruction

▼**1864**
Wade-Davis Bill

▼**1865**
Thirteenth Amendment adopted and ratified

Freedmen's Bureau established
Confederate armies surrender
Lincoln assassinated; Andrew Johnson becomes president
Johnson creates provisional governments in the South; new civil governments begin
Joint Committee on Reconstruction established by Congress

▼**1866**
Congress renews Freedmen's Bureau; Johnson vetoes it
Civil Rights Act vetoed by Johnson; Congress overrides veto

Congress passes Fourteenth Amendment
New Orleans and Memphis massacres
Republicans sweep midterm elections

▼**1867**
First, Second, and Third Reconstruction Acts passed
Tenure of Office Act
Medicine Lodge Treaty

▼**1868**
Second Fort Laramie Treaty
Washita Massacre

servants to supplement their husbands' meager incomes. Wage labor transformed southern blacks' lives, but it brought no prosperity.

The "New South" of industry and diversified agriculture opened southern forests to northern timber companies and dotted southern rivers with textile mills, but it did not break the stranglehold that cash crops and plantations had over the economy. It made the region more dependent on northern capital and finished goods than ever. Most of all, for the freed people outside a few large cities, it did not prove new at all. They found themselves excluded from juries and unprotected from white harassment and attack. White judges, white police, and white sheriffs guaranteed a white justice that treated every black witness's testimony as suspect and turned petty larceny into an excuse for jail time and permanent disfranchisement. Black convicts stood more chance of serving on the chain gang, often hired out as cheap labor to employers who paid the state pennies a day for the work done. In the Deep South, lynchings became almost an everyday occurrence, and, to judge from the souvenir sellers and excursion trains bringing in viewers, a kind of obscene spectator sport. Prejudice closed the door to blacks seeking to become professionals or craftsmen and guaranteed the skimpiest of funding for their schools. In a few states, the whipping post made a comeback. With the laws and the lawless working together to keep most blacks from voting, freedom meant much less than it had in Reconstruction days. But now, there were few northerners willing to listen when black southerners appealed for help.

Hoping to escape poverty and discrimination, some former slaves moved west. One group, the Exodusters, moved to the Kansas prairie during the mid-1870s. By 1880, more than 6,000 blacks had joined them, searching for cheap land for independent farms. Like white farmers, the Exodusters fought with cattlemen. Blacks who settled in cow towns such as Dodge City and Topeka found the same discrimination they had known in the South. Still, some of the Exodusters did buy land and build farms.

Johnson fires Secretary of War Stanton
House of Representatives impeaches Johnson
Senate trial of Johnson ends in acquittal
Fourteenth Amendment ratified
Waves of Klan violence sweep Cotton South
Ulysses S. Grant elected president

▼1869
Congress passes Fifteenth Amendment

▼1870
Fifteenth Amendment ratified

▼1872
"Liberal Republican" revolt
Grant reelected

▼1873
Financial "panic" sets off depression

▼1875
"Mississippi Plan" succeeds
Civil Rights Act enacted

▼1876
Disputed presidential election of Rutherford B. Hayes and Samuel J. Tilden
Custer's Last Stand at Little Bighorn

▼1877
Electoral commission names Rutherford B. Hayes president
Last Reconstruction governments collapse

▼1887
Dawes Severalty Act

Conclusion

Inspired by a vision of society based on equal rights and free labor, Republicans expected emancipation to transform the South. Freed from the shackles of the slave power, the region might yet become a shining example of democracy and prosperity. Twenty years later, events seemed to mock that promise. The South was scarcely more industrial than before the war and, as far as former slaves were concerned, far from completely free. Cotton, sugar, rice, and tobacco still defined the South's economy far more than the hoped-for mines and mills. Only a small fraction of freed people had become landowners, and most of them would never escape poverty and dependence on propertied whites. After the Panic of 1873, sharecropping eliminated most blacks' hope of real economic independence. As fears of a new rebellion dimmed, Republicans lost their zeal for federal intervention in the South. Republican state authorities could not save themselves, much less their black constituents. Chastened by Reconstruction's defects, Americans began to turn their attention to the new problems of urban, industrial America and to the epic success story, as they saw it, of the "winning of the West."

Even so, the achievements of Reconstruction were monumental. In the West, it settled vast multitudes of people—and unsettled multitudes more. Over two generations, it created as many states as had gone into rebellion in 1861. Across the South, African Americans carved out a space in which their families could live more freely than before. Black and white men elected to office some of the most democratic state legislatures of the nineteenth century. Thousands of black workers had escaped a stifling contract-labor system for the comparatively wider autonomy of sharecropping. Hundreds of thousands of former slaves learned to read and write and were able to worship in churches of their own making. Most important, Reconstruction added three important amendments to the Constitution that transformed civil rights and electoral laws throughout the nation. For the first time, the protections in the Bill of Rights would apply not just against national encroachment but that of the states as well. As a result of those changes in fundamental law, Reconstruction, then, was not so much a promise broken as one waiting to be fulfilled.

Who, What, Where

Review Questions

1. What made congressional Reconstruction "radical"?
2. How did conditions for the readmission of states into the Union change over time?
3. How did Reconstruction change the South?
4. How did western Indians respond to westward expansion?
5. How did Reconstruction change the North?
6. What were the major factors that brought Reconstruction to an end?

Critical-Thinking Questions

1. Compare and contrast wartime Reconstruction, presidential Reconstruction, and congressional (radical) Reconstruction. What were the key differences between the three phases?
2. How critical was the failure of land redistribution for blacks? Was sharecropping an acceptable substitute for achieving economic freedom? Why or why not?
3. How did terrorism and economic pressure both hinder and help the Reconstruction of the South?

Suggested Readings

Foner, Eric. *Reconstruction: America's Unfinished Revolution, 1863–1877*. New York: HarperCollins, 2014.

Hahn, Steven. *A Nation Under Our Feet: Black Political Struggles in the Rural South from Slavery to the Great Migration*. Cambridge, MA: Harvard University Press, 2003.

Litwack, Leon. *Been in the Storm So Long: The Aftermath of Slavery*. New York: Oxford University Press, 1979.

Summers, Mark Wahlgren. *The Ordeal of the Reunion: A New History of Reconstruction*. Chapel Hill: University of North Carolina Press, 2014.

For further review materials and resource information, please visit www.oup.com/us/oakes-mcgerr

CHAPTER 15: RECONSTRUCTING A NATION, 1865–1877
Primary Sources

15.1 PETROLEUM V. NASBY [DAVID ROSS LOCKE], *A PLATFORM FOR NORTHERN DEMOCRATS* (1865)

David Ross Locke, the editor of the *Toledo Blade,* made his fortune under another name: Petroleum V. Nasby, a fictional postmaster and sometimes pastor, whose letters gave a Republican spoof of what Copperhead Democrats believed. Bad spelling was a common way of signaling to readers that a piece was meant to be humorous, though Locke also meant to show that Nasby's ideas were not only vicious and absurd but founded on a virtually illiterate ignorance.

Saint's Rest (wich is in the Stait uv Noo Jersey), June the 23d, 1865

These is the dark days uv the dimokrasy. The misforchoons that befell our armies in front uv Richmond, the fall uv our capital, follered by the surrender uv our armies to Grant and Sherman, hez hurt us. Our leaders are either pinin in loathsome dunguns, incarseratid by the hevin-defyin, man-destroyin, tyrannical edix uv our late lamented President, or are baskin in the free air uv Italy and Canady. We hev no way uv keepin our voters together. Opposin the war won't do no good, for before the next elecshun the heft uv our voters will hev diskiverd that the war is over. The fear uv drafts may do suthin in some parts uv Pennsylvany and suthern Illinoy, for sum time yuit, but that can't be depended on.

But we hev wun resource for a ishoo—ther will alluz be a dimokrasy so long as ther's a nigger.

Ther is a uncompromising dislike to the nigger in the mind uv a ginooine dimekrat. The Spanish bullfighter, when he wants to inflame the bull to extra cavortin, waves a red flag afore him. When yoo desire a dimekrat to froth at the mouth, yoo will find a black face will anser the purpose. Therefore, the nigger is, today, our best and only holt. Let us use him.

For the guidance uv the faithful, I shel lay down a few plain rools to be observed, in order to make the most uv the capital we hev:

(1) Alluz assert that the nigger will never be able to take care uv hisself, but will alluz be a public burden. He may, possibly, give us the lie by goin to work. In sich a emergency, the dooty uv every dimekrat is plane. He must not be allowed to work. Associashens must be organized, pledged to neither give him employment, to work with him, to work for anyone who will give him work, or patronize any wun who duz. (I wood sejest that sich uv us ez hev bin forchoonit enuff to git credit, pay a trifle on account, so ez to make our patronage worth suthin.) This course, rigidly and persistently follered, will drive the best uv em to stealin, and the balance to the poorhouses, provin wat we hev alluz claimed, that they are a idle and vishus race. Think, my brethren, wat a inspirin effeck our poorhouses and jails full uv niggers wood hev on the people! My sole expands ez I contemplate the deliteful vision.

(2) Likewise assert that the nigger will come North, and take all the good places, throwin all our skilled mechanics out uv work by underbiddin uv em. This mite be open to two objecshuns, to-wit: It crosses slitely rool the 1, and white men mite say, ef there's jist enuff labor for wat's here, why not perhibit furriners from comin? I anser: It's the biznis uv the voter to reconcile the contraicshun—he may believe either or both. Ez to the second objeckshun, wher is the Dimekrat who coodent be underbid, and stand it even to starvashen, ef the underbiddin wux dun by a man uv the proud Caukashen race? And wher is the Dimekrat so lost to manhjood ez not to drink blood, ef the same underbiddin is dun by a nigger? The starving for work ain't the question—it's the color uv the cause uv the starvashen that makes the difference.

Nigger equality may be worked agin to advantage. All men, without distincshun uv sex, are fond uv flatrin theirselves that somebody's lower down in the scale uv humanity than they is. Ef 'twan't for niggers, what wood the dimokrasy do for sumbody to look down upon? It's also shoor to enlist wun style uv wimmen on our sides. In times gone by, I've notist gushin virgins uv forty-five, full sixteen hands high and tough ez wire, holdin aloft banners onto which wuz inscribd—"Save us from Nigger Equality." Yoo see it soothed em to hev a chase uv advertising, 1st, That they wuz frail, helplis critters; and, 2d, That, anshent and tough ez they wuz, some wun wuz still goin for em.

Ef ther ain't no niggers, central commities must furnish em. A half dozen will do for a ordinary county, ef they're hustled along with energy. Ef they won't steal, the central commities must do it theirselves. Show yer niggers in a township in the morning, an the same nite rob the clothes-lines and hen-roosts. Ever willin to sacrifice myself for the cause, I volunteer to do this latter dooty in six populous counties.

These ijees, ef follered, will, no doubt, keep us together until our enemies split, when we will reap the reward uv our constancy and fidelity. May the Lord hasten the day.

Petroleum V. Nasby
Lait Paster uv the Church uv the Noo Dispensashun

Source: David Ross Locke/Petroleum V. Nasby, *A Platform for Northern Democrats*, from Locke, *The Struggles, Social, Financial and Political of Petroleum V. Nasby* (Boston, 1888), quoted in William Benton, publ., *The Annals of America. Volume 9, 1858–1865: The Crisis of the Union* (Chicago: Encyclopedia Britannica, Inc., 1968), pp. 597–598.

15.2 MISSISSIPPI BLACK CODE (1865)

Faced with the speedy emancipation of nearly half of Mississippi's population, the first all-white postwar legislature set out to define what rights blacks should enjoy in freedom. Some of the most basic were guaranteed, including the right to marry and hold property, and to testify under certain limited circumstances. Others were denied, among them the right to vote, sit on juries, hold office, or intermarry with whites. Most controversially, the Apprentice and Vagrancy Laws created a structure, color-blind in its outward workings, that effectively allowed white authorities to commandeer blacks and force them into involuntary labor or even to sell their labor to white bidders at auction.

Apprentice Law

Section 1. *Be it enacted by the legislature of the state of Mississippi*, that it shall be the duty of all sheriffs, justices of the peace, and other civil officers of the several counties in this state to report to the Probate courts of their respective counties semiannually, at the January and July terms of said courts, all freedmen, free Negroes, and mulattoes under the age of eighteen within their respective counties, beats, or districts who are orphans, or whose parent or parents have not the means, or who refuse to provide for and support said minors; and thereupon it shall be the duty of said Probate Court to order the clerk of said court to apprentice said minors to some competent and suitable person, on such terms as the court my direct, having a particular care to the interest of said minors:

Provided, that the former owner of said minors shall have the preference when, in the opinion of the court, he or she shall be a suitable person for that purpose.

Section 2. *Be it further enacted*, that the said court shall be fully satisfied that the person or persons to whom said minor shall be apprenticed shall be a suitable person to have the charge and care of said minor and fully to protect the interest of said minor. The said court shall require the said master or mistress to execute bond and security, payable to the state of Mississippi, conditioned that he or she shall furnish said minor with sufficient food and clothing; to treat said minor humanely; furnish medical attention in case of sickness; teach or cause to be taught him or her to read and write, if under fifteen years old; and will conform to any law that may be hereafter passed for the regulation of the duties and relation of master and apprentice:

Provided, that said apprentice shall be bound by indenture, in case of males until they are twenty-one years old, and in case of females until they are eighteen years old.

Section 3. *Be it further enacted*, that in the management and control of said apprentices, said master or mistress shall have power to inflict such moderate corporeal chastisement as a father or guardian is allowed to inflict on his or her child or ward in common law:

Provided, that in no case shall cruel or inhuman punishment be inflicted.

Section 4. *Be it further enacted*, that if any apprentice shall leave the employment of his or her master or mistress without his or her consent, said master or mistress may pursue and recapture said apprentice and bring him or her before any justice of the peace of the county, whose duty it shall be to remand said apprentice to the service of his or her master or mistress; and in the event of a refusal on the part of said apprentice so to return, then said justice shall commit said apprentice to the jail of said county, on failure to give bond, until the next term of the country court; and it shall be the duty of said court, at the first term thereafter, to investigate said case; and if the court shall be of opinion that said apprentice left the employment of his or her master or mistress without good cause, to order him or her to be punished, as provided for the punishment of hired freedmen, as may be from time to time provided for by law, for desertion, until he or she shall agree to return to his or her master or mistress:

Provided, that the court may grant continuances, as in other cases; and provided, further, that if the court shall believe that said apprentice had good cause to quit his said master or mistress, the court shall discharge said apprentice from said indenture and also enter a judgment against the master or mistress for not more than $100, for the use and benefit of said apprentice, to be collected on execution, as in other cases.

Section 5. *Be it further enacted*, that if any person entice away any apprentice from his or her master or mistress, or shall knowingly employ an apprentice, or furnish him or her food or clothing, without the written consent of his or her master or mistress, or shall sell or give said apprentice ardent spirits, without such consent, said person so offending shall be deemed guilty of a high misdemeanor, and shall, on conviction thereof before the county court, be punished as provided for the punishment of persons enticing from their employer hired freedmen, free Negroes, or mulattoes.

. . . Section 10. *Be it further enacted,* that in all cases where the age of the freedman, free Negro, or mulatto cannot be ascertained by record testimony, the judge of the county court shall fix the age.

Vagrancy Law

Section 2. *Be it further enacted,* that all freedmen, free Negroes, and mulattoes in this state over the age of eighteen years found on the second Monday in January 1966, or thereafter, with no lawful employment or business, or found unlawfully assembling themselves together either in the day or nighttime, and all white persons so assembling with freedmen, free Negroes, or mulattoes, or usually associating with freedmen, free Negroes, or mulattoes on terms of equality, or living in adultery or fornication with a freedwoman, free Negro, or mulatto, shall be deemed vagrants; and, on conviction thereof, shall be fined in the sum of not exceeding, in the case of a freedman, free Negro, or mulatto, $50, and a white man, $200, and imprisoned at the discretion of the court, the free Negro not exceeding ten days, and the white man not exceeding six months.

Section 3. *Be it further enacted,* that all justices of the peace, mayors, and aldermen of incorporated towns and cities of the several counties in this state shall have jurisdiction to try all questions of vagrancy in their respective towns, counties, and cities; and it is hereby made their duty, whenever they shall ascertain that any person or persons in their respective towns, counties, and cities are violating any of the provisions of this act, to have said party or parties arrested and brought before them and immediately investigate said charge; and, on conviction, punish said party or parties as provided for herein. . . .

Section 5. *Be it further enacted,* that all fines and forfeitures collected under the provisions of this act shall be paid into the county treasury for general county purposes; and in case any freedman, free Negro, or mulatto shall fail for five days after the imposition of any fine or forfeiture upon him or her for violation of any of the provisions of this act to pay the same, that it shall be, and is hereby made, the duty of the sheriff of the proper county to hire out said freedman, free Negro, or mulatto to any person who will, for the shortest period of service, pay said fine or forfeiture and all costs:

Provided, a preference shall be given to the employer, if there be one, in which case the employer shall be entitled to deduct and retain the amount so paid from the wages of such freedman, free Negro, or mulatto then due or to become due; and in case such freedman, free Negro, or mulatto cannot be hired out he or she may be dealt with as a pauper.

Section 6. *Be it further enacted,* that the same duties and liabilities existing among white persons of this state shall attach to freedmen, free Negroes, and mulattoes to support their indigent families and all colored paupers; and that, in order to secure a support for such indigent freedmen, free Negroes, and mulattoes, it shall be lawful, and it is hereby made the duty of the boards of county police of each county in this state, to levy a poll or capitation tax on each and every freedman, free Negro, or mulatto, between the ages of eighteen and sixty years, not to exceed the sum of $1 annually, to each person so taxed, which tax, when collected, shall be paid into the county treasurer's hands and constitute a fund to be called the Freedman's Pauper Fund, which shall be applied by the commissioners of the poor for the maintenance of the poor of the freedmen, free Negroes and mulattoes of this state, under such regulations as may be established by the boards of county police, in the respective counties of this state.

Section 7. *Be it further enacted,* that if any freedman, free Negro, or mulatto shall fail or refuse to pay any tax levied according to the provisions of the 6th Section of this act, it shall be prima facie evidence of vagrancy, and it shall be the duty of the sheriff to arrest such freedman, free Negro, or mulatto, or such person refusing or neglecting to pay such tax, and proceed at once to hire, for the shortest time, such delinquent taxpayer to anyone who will pay the said tax, with accruing costs, giving preference to the employer, if there be one.

Section 8. *Be it further enacted,* that any person feeling himself or herself aggrieved by the judgment of any justice of the peace, mayor, or alderman in cases arising under this act may, within five days, appeal to the next term of the county court of the proper county, upon giving bond and security in a sum not less than $25 nor more than $150, conditioned to appear and prosecute said appeal, and abide by the judgment of the county court, and said appeal shall be tried *de novo* in the county court, and the decision of said court shall be final.

Source: Mississippi Black Code, 1865, from *Laws of the State of Mississippi, Passed at a Regular Session of the Mississippi Legislature* (Jackson, 1866), pp. 82–93, 165–167, quoted in William Benton, publ., *The Annals of America. Volume 9, 1858–1865: The Crisis of the Union* (Chicago: Encyclopedia Britannica, Inc., 1968), pp. 628–634.

15.3 SHARECROPPING CONTRACT BETWEEN ALONZO T. MIAL AND FENNER POWELL (1886)

For Republicans, the essence of "free labor" was the *contract*, the notion that either a governing figure and his people, or a wealthy man and those who labored for him, both had to subscribe voluntarily to an explicit agreement outlining their mutual responsibilities in order for their relationship to be binding. Unfortunately, after the war, southern blacks freed from slavery but without land sometimes had little choice but to sign stringent labor contracts with landlords, who were often former slave owners. A system emerged known as sharecropping. The tenant, or "cropper," would sign an annual contract to work a plot of land in return for a share of the crop. The following is a sharecropping contract from 1886, between a landlord named A. T. Mial and a sharecropper named Fenner Powell.

This contract made and entered into between A. T. Mial of one part and Fenner Powell of the other part both of the County of Wake and state of North Carolina—

Witnesseth—That the Said Fenner Powell hath bargaded and agreed with the Said Mial to work as a cropper for the year 1886 on Said Mial's land on the land now occupied by Said Powell on the west Side of Poplar Creek and a point on the east Side of Said Creek and both South and North of the Mial road, leading to Raleigh, That the said Fenner Powell agrees to work faithfully and diligently without any unnecessary loss of time, to do all manner of work on Said farm as may be directed by Said Mial, And to be respectful in manners and deportment to Said Mial.

And the Said Mial agrees on his part to furnish mule and feed for the same and all plantation tools and Seed to plant the crop free of charge, and to give the said Powell One half of all crops raised and housed by Said Powell on Said land except the cotton seed. The Said Mial agrees to advance as provisions to Said Powell fifty pound of bacon and two sacks of meal per month and occasionally some flour to be paid out of his the Said Powell's part of the crop or from any other advance that may be made to Said Powell by Said Mial. As witness our hands and seals this the 16th day of January A.D. 1886.

Source: Contract between Alonzo T. Mial and Fenner Powell, January 1886, in Roger Ransom and Richard Sutch, *One Kind of Freedom: The Economic Consequences of Emancipation* (New York: Cambridge University Press, 1977), p. 91.

15.4 JOSEPH FARLEY, AN ACCOUNT OF RECONSTRUCTION

Joseph Farley, born in 1843 in Virginia, ran away and joined the Union army. Later he was given a pension. "At that time I never thought about dying," he remembers. "I never thought about anybody shooting me; I just thought about shooting them." Interviewed in 1930 by a black student from Fisk University, he gave a rambling account, from which the postwar material has been excerpted. As with all distant recollections, Farley's may have been affected by the lapse of time and the person conducting the interview.

It was a long, long time before everything got quiet after the war. On Franklin Street here I saw once 100 Ku Klux Klans, with long robes and faces covered. You don't know anything of them. They were going down here a piece to hang a man. There were about 600 of us soldiers, so we followed them to protect the man. The Klan knew this, and passed on by the house and went on back to town and never did bother the man.

One time a colored soldier married a white woman over here at Fort Bruce. The man belonged to my company. His name was Sergeant Cook. About twenty of the soldiers went to the wedding, and they had about five or six white men who said he couldn't marry this woman. Old Dr. Taylor . . . came over to marry them. He stood near me and I told him to go on and marry this couple or else someone here would die. He looked around and saw all these soldiers and he knew about us and that we meant for him to do as he had been told. He married them and we guarded our hack over to the war boat on the Cumberland. They went over to Nashville and lived there. They had a daughter whose name was Mrs. Gnatt. When they married was in 1866. Mrs. Gnatt could tell you her father was named Cyrus Cook. Guess you know you can't do that now, no sir; you just can't do that now. At one time a colored man could ride anywhere he wanted to, but now he can't do it. I am one of the first voters of Montgomery County. They told me at one time that I was not to come to the polls or I would be met by 600 men on horses. So about six or eight hundred of us armed and went to the polls with our bayonets. That man that had told me that did not show up. So we voted, and voted for whom we wanted. At that time the Rebels who rebelled against this country could not vote and they said that these Negroes shouldn't vote but we showed them. Of course, they came down and stood and looked at us but they didn't bother us. We went there armed and prepared for fighting so that if they started anything, there would be trouble. When they mustered me out from the army, I brought my gun from Nashville right here to Clarksville and kept it twenty-five years. Finally I let an old soldier have it.

When I first came here we had no teachers here but white teachers. They would call the roll same as calling the roll for soldiers. They taught school in the churches before they had school houses. They used to go to school at night and work all day. Clarence C. White's father, Will White, was the first teacher or principal of the school here in Clarksville.

. . . .

When the War was over some of the colored returned to their white folks, but I didn't want to be under the white folks again. I was glad to get out. Once, for fifteen years here, I run a saloon and livery stable. One time I worked on a boat. When I was on my first boat, one time I went to vote. A white man told me that if I voted Republican he would fire me, so I told him to fire me then. I just told him he could fire me right now for I didn't want to work anyway. I went on and voted the Republican ticket, and they told me they liked my principle and I could go on and go to work.

I still got my discharge from way back in 1866. I keeps it and I mean to keep it as long as I live. I am proud of it.

Source: George P. Rawick, ed. *The American Slave: A Composite Autobiography. Volume 18. Unwritten History of Slavery* (Fisk University) (Westport, CT: Greenwood, 1972), pp. 121–128.

15.5 A SOUTHERN UNIONIST JUDGE'S DAUGHTER WRITES THE PRESIDENT FOR HELP (1874)

Mrs. S. A. Wayne was the daughter of an Alabama Unionist, Judge James A. Abrahams. As the 1874 political campaign grew more violent, she wrote begging President Grant to send protection to Republicans like herself. Soon after the letter was sent, Abrahams was shot by persons unknown. Shortly after that, Grant sent troops to Livingston County. It was not enough to give black and white voters the security they needed; Democratic "Redeemers" swept the election.

I feel more like addressing you as my dear Father & Friend for such you have proven to me & mine—but—Oh, my God! you have no conception of the trouble we are in—War is declared in our midst and though the U. S. troops are here the Ku Klux are worse than before they came—And who are they fighting? The poor defenseless negroes—Why? For voting or rather expressing their determination to vote the Republican ticket—This evening the lives of my husband—father & brother were threatened—with the intention of making them renounce their principles—God only knows what the end will be—I have seen the Capt & Lt stationed at this place—& they say the only hope is Martial law—& that is the only remedy—Since I last wrote you some four or five negroes have been killed in this County—& the Ku Klux are now at Belmont 16 miles from this place in force & will probably murder as many more—They are exasperated against the three white Republicans in this place because they refused to go with them on one of their raids last weeks—hence the threats against their lives—My Father left this evening & I pray God he may not return until Martial law is declared—Oh my dear Sir *you can save* the country—oh protect the Union loving men against those who despise it & are doing all to overthrow it—I write you this not thinking my enlisting in the cause will help it, but because I feel it my duty to let you know how great our trouble is—No excuse can be given by these murderers—for since the assassination of Mr Billings not one single

Republican meeting has been held in this county—And this is what the Democrats are fighting for—Unless Martial law is declared hundreds of the poor negroes will be killed—even now they do not sleep in their houses & are hunted down like wild beasts by the Democracy because they will not vote their ticket—Oh! My dear Sir act & be our friends. God knows the innocent only suffer—& the blush of shame mantles my cheek when I read the pitiable excuses in the Democratic papers—apologizing for their cowardly deeds—No brave man is afraid of a few of them in open daylight but a hundred or two banded together; making night hideous with their demoniac yells is enough to make the stoutest heart quail—I have written you hurriedly—There is no security in the mails & I send this by a U.S. Paymaster who arrived here this afternoon & leaves to night—Again I beg you to help us in this dreadful emergency—No U.S. Marshall has been here & if they were to come they could not punish these murderers immediately—& they ought to be dealt with severely & immediately—This is private & I write as to my own dear Father & confide to you our troubles—We have lived in the midst of it since the war & it is more terrible now than ever—Every Union man will be killed if active steps are not taken by the Government to stop it—I am ever your true & loving Union woman.

Source: S. A. Wayne to Ulysses S. Grant, September 18, 1874, quoted in John Y. Simon, ed., *The Papers of Ulysses S. Grant: Volume 25: 1874* (Carbondale: Southern Illinois University Press, 2003), pp. 195–196.

15.6 RED CLOUD PLEADS THE PLAINS INDIANS' POINT OF VIEW AT COOPER UNION (1870)

As one of the foremost leaders of the Teton Sioux, Red Cloud had kept the US Army at bay for several years. The war, as his speech pointed out, had never been his own doing. He, like many other Indians, sought a fair peace; like them, he found that all the power to define what peace meant and how it would be enforced lay in the hands of the indifferent, the ill-informed, and the insatiable.

My brethren and my friends who are here before me this day, God Almighty has made us all, and He is here to bless what I have to say to you today. The Good Spirit made us both. He gave you lands and He gave us lands; He gave us these lands; you came in here, and we respected you as brothers. God Almighty made you but made you all white and clothed you; when He made us He made us with red skins and poor; now you have come.

When you first came we were very many, and you were few; now you are many, and we are getting very few, and we are poor. You do not know who appears before you today to speak. I am a representative of the original American race, the first people of this continent. We are good and not bad. The reports that you hear concerning us are all on one side. We are always well-disposed to them. You are here told that we are traders and thieves, and it is not so. We have given you nearly all our lands, and if we had any more land to give we would be very glad to give it. We have nothing more. We are driven into a very little land, and we want you now, as our dear friends, to help us with the government of the United States.

The Great Father made us poor and ignorant—made you rich and wise and more skillful in these things that we know nothing about. The Great Father, the Good Father in Heaven, made you all to eat tame food—made us to eat wild food—gives us the wild food. You ask anybody who has gone through our country to California; ask those who have settled there and in Utah, and you will find that we have treated them always well. You have children; we have children. You want to raise your children and make them happy and prosperous; we want to raise and make them happy and prosperous. We ask you to help us to do it.

At the mouth of the Horse Creek, in 1852, the Great Father made a treaty with us by which we agreed to let all that country open for fifty-five years for the transit of those who were going through. We kept this treaty; we never treated any man wrong; we never committed any murder or depredation until afterward the troops were sent into that country, and the troops killed our people and ill-treated them, and thus war and trouble arose; but before the troops were sent there we were quiet and peaceable, and there was no disturbance. Since that time there have been various goods sent from time to time to us, the only ones that ever reached us, and then after they reached us (very soon after) the government took them away. You, as good men, ought to help us to these goods.

Colonel Fitzpatrick of the government said we must all go to farm, and some of the people went to Fort Laramie and were badly treated. I only want to do that which is peaceful, and the Great Fathers know it, and also the Great Father who made us both. I came to Washington to see the Great Father in order to have peace and in order to have peace continue. That is all we want, and that is the reason why we are here now.

In 1868 men came out and brought papers. We are ignorant and do not read papers, and they did not tell us right what was in these papers. We wanted them to take away their forts, leave our country, would not make war, and give our traders something. They said we had bound ourselves to trade on the Missouri, and we said, no, we did not want that. The interpreters deceived us. When I went to Washington I saw the Great Father. The Great Father showed me what the treaties were; he showed me all these points and showed me that the interpreters had deceived me and did not let me know what the right side of the treaty was. All I want is right and justice. . . . I represent the Sioux Nation; they will be governed by what I say and what I represent. . . .

Look at me. I am poor and naked, but I am the Chief of the Nation. We do not want riches, we do not ask for riches, but we want our children properly trained and brought up. We look to you for your sympathy. Our riches will . . . do us no good; we cannot take away into the other world anything we have—we want to have love and peace. . . . We would like to know why commissioners are sent out there to do nothing but rob [us] and get the riches of this world away from us?

I was brought up among the traders and those who came out there in those early times. I had a good time for they treated us nicely and well. They taught me how to wear clothes and use tobacco, and to use firearms and ammunition, and all went on very well until the Great Father sent out another kind of men—men who drank whisky. He sent out whisky-men, men who drank and quarreled, men who were so bad that he could not keep them at home, and so he sent them out there. I have sent a great many words to the Great Father, but I don't know that they ever reach the Great Father. They were drowned on the way, therefore I was a little offended with it. The words I told the Great Father lately would never come to him, so I thought I would come and tell you myself.

And I am going to leave you today, and I am going back to my home. I want to tell the people that we cannot trust his agents and superintendents. I don't want strange people that we know nothing about. I am very glad that you belong to us. I am very glad that we have come here and found you and that we can understand one another. I don't want any more such men sent out there, who are so poor that when they come out there their first thoughts are how they can fill their own pockets.

We want preserves in our reserves. We want honest men, and we want you to help to keep us in the lands that belong to us so that we may not be a prey to those who are viciously disposed. I am going back home. I am very glad that you have listened to me, and I wish you good-bye and give you an affectionate farewell.

Source: *New York Times*, July 17, 1870, cited in William Benton, publ., *Annals of America, Volume 10: Reconstruction and Industrialization* (Chicago: Encyclopedia Britannica, Inc., 1968), 242–244.

The Triumph of Industrial Capitalism

1850-1890

COMMON THREADS

In what ways were the problems of Reconstruction and the problems of industrialization similar?

What made "big business" different from earlier enterprises?

How did the new social order of the late nineteenth century resemble what came before it, and how was it different later?

< The Eads Bridge

AMERICAN PORTRAIT

Rosa Cassettari

In 1884, Rosa Cassettari left an Italian village near Milan and joined the stream of migrants from all across Europe bound for America. Others went full of dreams. "The country where everyone would find work! Where wages were so high that no one had to go hungry! Where all men were free and equal and where even the poor could own land!" But Rosa left behind her son to rejoin her brutal, abusive husband, Santino, an iron miner in Missouri. Unable to read or write, she expected the worst, and rightly. "All us poor people had to go down through a hole to the bottom of the ship," she remembered. Crowded in darkness, sleeping on wooden shelves, feeding from tin plates, Rosa felt no relief to see land. Cheated in New York and forced to make her way to Missouri with nothing to eat, she arrived in a shabby cluster of tents and shanties, where she added to Santino's wages by cooking for a dozen miners. With no doctors or midwives available, Rosa gave birth to a premature child alone on the floor of her cabin. The last straw came when Santino used his savings to open a house of prostitution. Rosa fled for her life, and friends helped her move to Chicago. Was this the Promised Land?

Rosa thought so. She worked hard all her life, knew hunger in bad times, and just got by in good ones. But she always found friends to help her and religious faith to comfort her. In time she found work at Chicago Commons, a settlement house founded to help immigrants get by in a strange, often bewildering city. She discovered a strength and courage she had never known at home. When she went back to Italy to bring over her son, villagers gaped. She was wearing a hat and new shoes and "they thought I was something wonderful." When she told them that poor people in America ate meat every day, they could not believe it. And she lived to see her children doing better than she had—not rich, but not in want.

Rosa was one of millions of people uprooting themselves worldwide in the late nineteenth century. They moved from the countryside to the city or from town to town. They shifted from less developed regions to places where industrialization was well under way. The magnet for most of the movement was a core of industrial capitalist societies, and the United States was just one destination among many.

Common laborers moved from place to place because jobs were unsteady, or they moved when work was finished. Hired hands plodded the roads in autumn following the harvest, spent winters working in Washington's lumber camps, and toiled by summer along the Erie Canal. African American sharecroppers in the South moved at year's end, eventually into cotton-growing districts, into towns and cities, or out of the South. White tenant farmers found new homes and better living conditions in company-owned coal- and textile-mill towns. Native Americans, their domains already in flux for centuries, now lost most of their lands to white settlement and were herded onto reservations. And all across America, the children of farmers traded the charm and endless labor of rural life for the bright-lit, squalid metropolises of the East.

They went seeking work, and that meant working for somebody else, on terms that the employer set. It meant working with new, complicated machines, with foul air, dirty rivers, or ravaged land. Working people had been freed from the things that once tied them to the land, such as feudal dues and slavery. But wage labor often compelled men and women to shift from country to country, and finally from continent to continent. To watch Rosa Cassettari as she traveled from Italy to Chicago is to witness one small part of a process set in motion by global needs and once-unimaginable aspirations.

The Political Economy of Global Capitalism

The economic history of the late nineteenth century was sandwiched between two great financial panics in 1873 and 1893. Both were followed by prolonged periods of high joblessness and labor strife. Between the two panics, prices dropped. Farmers with crops selling for less felt the crushing weight of money borrowed when prices were high. Manufacturers cut costs by increasing production, by replacing skilled labor with technology, and by drawing on the international labor market for a cheaper workforce. Still, amid bouts of hard times, the American economy transformed dramatically and, for consumers and many workers, for the better.

The "Great Depression" of the Late Nineteenth Century

On July 16, 1877, workers for the Baltimore and Ohio Railroad struck at Martinsburg, West Virginia, over one wage cut too many. Within days, the strike spread to the Pennsylvania Railroad, the New York Central, the Great Western, and the Texas Pacific. Governors ordered the strikers to disperse. They asked for federal troops and got them. Soldiers fired on protestors in Pittsburgh, and for a while, confrontations between workers and armed forces fanned the flames of insurrection. "Other workingmen followed the example of the railroad employees," explained Henry Demarest Lloyd, a prominent social critic. "At Zanesville, Ohio, fifty manufactories stopped work. Baltimore ceased to export petroleum. The rolling mills, foundries, and refineries of Cleveland were closed. . . . Merchants could not sell, manufacturers could not work, banks could not lend. The country went to the verge of a panic." The strike was broken, though a hundred lives were lost by that time. Alarmed state authorities went on an armory-building binge and recruited a National Guard to keep order or break strikes in the future. Between 1875 and 1910, state troops were called out nearly 500 times.

The "Great Railroad Strike" of 1877 was fueled by an economic depression that began with the Panic of 1873 (see Chapter 15) and spread throughout the developed world. Immigrant arrivals in New York—200,000 every year between 1865 and 1873—fell to less than 65,000 in 1877. Although employment (and immigration) recovered in the 1880s, prices and wages continued to fall. Then, in 1893, another panic struck. Major railroads went bankrupt, including four of the five transcontinentals. Over 500 banks and 15,000 businesses shut down.

The world was shrinking. In 1866, Cyrus Field's telegraph cable was laid under the Atlantic Ocean. Now Americans could read Europe's latest news the next morning. They could cluster at the depot to hear the latest box score, sent by telegraph even as the game went on. Railroads carried Pillsbury's flour from Minneapolis mills to Massachusetts; refrigerated cars carried Chicago's "dressed beef" carcasses to California; and the catalog brought the goods of a nation to every farm on the high plains so efficiently that consumers swore "by God, the Ten Commandments, and Sears, Roebuck." Thanks to the steamship, midwestern wheat fed customers in Russia, and boards cut from the forests of the Cascades turned into flooring for plantations in Malaya. In Pittsburgh's steel mills, Slavic languages and Hungarian were as common as German and Russian in Lower East Side New York's needle trades. Capitalism, not just transportation, had mingled peoples together.

An industrializing and liberalizing Europe had cut families free from their traditional ties to the land. Many migrated to better themselves: some within Europe, some to South America or Canada, and many to America (see Map 16–1). In many Irish families,

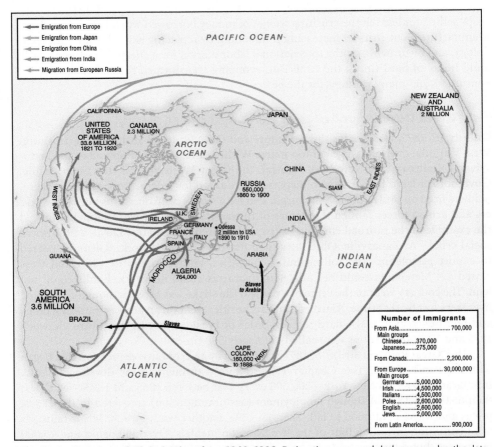

Map 16-1   Patterns of Global Migration, 1840–1900 Emigration was a global process by the late nineteenth century. But more immigrants went to the United States than to all other nations combined. *Source:* London Times Atlas.

AMERICA AND THE WORLD

The Global Migration of Labor

Nineteenth-century migrants tended to leave areas already in the grip of social and economic change. Rosa Cassettari, for example, had worked in a silk-weaving factory in Italy. At first, the largest numbers emigrated from the most developed nations, such as Great Britain and Germany. Later in the century, as industrial or agricultural revolution spread, growing numbers of immigrants came from Scandinavia, Russia, Italy, and Hungary (see Map 16-1). As capitalism developed in these areas, small farmers were forced to produce for a highly competitive international market. The resulting upheaval sent millions of rural folk into the worldwide migratory stream.

Improvements in transportation and communication made migration easier. In 1856, more than 95 percent of immigrants came to America aboard sailing vessels. By the end of the century, more than 95 percent came in steamships. The Atlantic crossing took one to three months under sail, but only 10 days by steam. Beginning in the 1880s, fierce competition among steamship lines lowered the cost of a transatlantic ticket. But the great migrations were also related to economic and political turmoil. After 1890, immigration from northern and western Europe fell off sharply, as industrial growth soaked up surplus labor. At the same time, agrarian crises drove out peasants from eastern and southern Europe. Southern Italy could barely compete with Florida and California's lemons and oranges and found the American protective tariff closing off its biggest overseas wine market. Straitened Italian farmers started coming to the United States.

Jewish immigration was propelled by different impulses. In the Russian empire, pogroms, anti-Jewish riots, erupted in 1881–1882, 1891, and 1905–1906. Many Jews were killed. Anti-Semitic laws confined Russian Jews to the so-called Pale of Settlement along the empire's western and southern borders. The May Laws of 1882 severely restricted their religious and economic life. Starting in the 1880s, anti-Semitic riots brought fire and murder into the Jewish ghettoes. Sometimes the police looked on; sometimes they joined the rioters. The government not only encouraged the persecution; at times, it provoked it. By 1890, Russian Jews were making new homes for themselves in America. Swanky hotels snubbed them, clubs blackballed them, but here they could publish newspapers in Yiddish or Hebrew, worship freely, hope for schooling, even a college education, for their children, and make a living. A few went to Congress. One later became the prime minister of Israel.

Most immigrants, though, just came to America looking for work. Many planned to make money and then return home, as thousands of Italians and Slovaks did. (Some, discovering to their surprise that they had become more American than they expected, came back to stay.) Some came with education and skills, most with little more than their ability to work. They usually found their jobs through families, friends, and fellow immigrants. Letters from America told of high wages and steady employment. Communities of immigrant workers provided the support that newcomers like Rosa Cassettari needed. Some immigrants settled directly on farms, but the overwhelming mass lived in cities.

sending sons and daughters abroad meant money packets sent home to allow the rest to stay behind. Italians and eastern Europeans, known as "birds of passage," often came west only to earn money and return. But their cheap labor and that of millions who came to stay built the railroads and forged the steel. They slaughtered sheep and cattle in Chicago's stockyard district, "Packingtown," for Philip Armour and Gustavus Swift. Others worked as domestic servants, served behind store sales counters, or ran the sewing machines that met a national demand for ready-made clothing.

The Economic Transformation of the West

For novelists, the West seemed like a separate world from the industrial transformation of the East: a land where the old-fashioned manly virtues of the cowboy, the trapper, the prospector, and the homesteader carved a destiny out of the wilderness. In fact, the economic revolution may have changed the West more than anywhere else. Lawless violence and wild speculation were part of the western experience, but so were the struggling families, start-up companies, and hard-working immigrants that remade Cleveland and Chicago. By 1900, thanks to the revolution that eastern-run railroads made, the West provided Americans with the meat and bread for their dinner tables, the wood that built their homes, and the gold and silver that backed up their currency. The West was being drawn into the political economy of global capitalism. As much as any eastern city, it had become diverse and ethnically and economically complex well before the director of the US Census declared the frontier "closed" in 1890. And when it came to savage labor strife, there was nothing Pittsburgh's victims could have told the miners in Cripple Creek or Leadville, Colorado.

Cattlemen: From Drovers to Ranchers

The cowboy is the mythic figure of the American West: a rugged loner who scorned society for the freedom of the trail. In fact, cowboys were usually single men. They worked hard and played harder, spending their earnings on a shave, a new suit of clothes, and a few good nights in town. Civil War veterans, former slaves, displaced Indians, and Mexicans all became cowboys. Their pay was low, their work dangerous and unsteady, and their chances of reaching real independence were slim.

Longhorn cattle were as much a part of western legend as the cowboys who drove them. With the westward spread of the railroads, Texas ranchers began driving huge herds of Texas longhorns up the Chisholm Trail north onto the Great Plains. They brought the herds to railroad towns from which the cattle could be shipped, such as Abilene, Wichita, or Dodge City, Kansas. Cattlemen sold half of their stock to eastern markets and the other half in the West, some to the government for feeding soldiers and reservation Indians.

But the Texas longhorn had several drawbacks: it was tough and rangy, it produced more bone and sinew than meat, it carried a tick that devastated many of the other grazing animals, and it took a long time to fatten up. Investors began to breed hybrid cattle that were less hardy but beefier and of higher quality. By the early 1880s, investors were pouring capital into mammoth cattle-herding companies. The Great Plains became seriously overstocked. The depleted grazing lands left the cattle weak from malnutrition, and in the late 1880s several devastating winters wiped out whole herds. It was said that a person could walk across Kansas and never touch ground, just stepping from carcass to carcass.

Open-range herding became so environmentally destructive that it was no longer economically feasible. Long drives became increasingly difficult as farmers fenced in the plains, but they also became less necessary because railroads could pick up cattle just about everywhere. By the 1890s, huge cattle companies were giving way to smaller ranches that raised hybrid cattle. Cowboys became ranch hands with regular wages, like miners and factory workers.

In the mid-1880s, more than 7 million head of cattle roamed the Great Plains, but as their numbers declined, sheep replaced them. Although sheep proved even more ecologically destructive than cattle, by 1900 sheepherding had largely taken the place of the cattle industry in Wyoming and Montana and was spreading to Nevada. Sheepherding had the advantage of not interfering with small farmers as much as cattle driving did.

Commercial Farmers Remake the Plains

Between 1860 and 1900, the number of farms in America nearly tripled, thanks largely to the economic development of the West. On the Great Plains and in the desert Southwest, farmers took up former Indian lands. In California, white settlers poached on the estates of Spanish-speaking landlords, stripping them of their natural resources and undermining their profitability. Over time, Hispanic ranchers gave way to European American farmers. The Hispanic population of Los Angeles fell from 82 percent in 1850 to 19 percent in 1880. A similar pattern occurred in New Mexico and Texas.

This ethnic shift signaled profound changes in the ecology and political economy of the West, driven by the exploding global demand for western products. Cattle ranchers were feeding eastern cities. Lumber from the Pacific Northwest found its way to Asia and South America. By 1890, western farmers produced half of the wheat grown in the United States, and they shipped it across the globe.

But farming in the arid West was unlike eastern farming. The 160-acre homesteads that lawmakers proposed in the original Homestead Act proved too small for guaranteeing a viable living on the parched prairies, though hundreds of thousands staked claims—and kept on doing so until 1934. Farmers needed costly equipment and extensive irrigation to produce wheat and corn for international markets. To make these capital investments, they mortgaged their lands. For mechanized, commercial agriculture to succeed on mortgaged land, western farms had to be much bigger than 160 acres.

Government homesteads made up only a fraction of all the lands sold. Speculators may have bought up as much as 350 million acres from state or federal governments or from Indian reservations. Railroads were granted another 200 million acres by the federal government. They sold much of it at bargain rates. The more farmers the railroads could settle on their lands, the more customers they would have, and the more farm produce there would be to ship. Railroads set up immigration bureaus and offered settlers cheap transportation, credit, and agricultural aid. The Great Plains filled with settlers from the East Coast and from Ireland, Germany, and Scandinavia.

Changes in the Land

No Garden of Eden welcomed prairie farmers. "All Montana needs is rain," a promoter was said to have told one settler—who agreed: but that was also all that Hell needed. Rain fell rarely and in sparse amounts on the Great Plains and the desert Southwest.

Mining Camps in the West

Rosa Cassettari's mining camp experience had none of the glamour that mythology lends those farther West. The greatest strike came in 1848 when James Marshall found gold at John Sutter's mill site in the California foothills. Prospectors poured in by the thousands, creating boomtowns like Ophir and You-Be-Damned overnight—and ghost towns just as quickly, when the lode gave out. Findings actually peaked years after the Forty-Niners' gold rush. New discoveries pulled prospectors eastward, into Colorado in 1859, Idaho in 1862, and Montana in 1864. In Nevada, prospectors hit the largest vein of all, the Comstock Lode. It would yield $350 million worth of gold and silver over 20 years.

Western mining camps were raw, violent, male-dominated, and diverse. New England Yankees mingled with Australians, Mexicans, Chinese, and African Americans. Alone or in small groups, they panned for gold, squatting in icy stream beds. Once the surface gold had been captured, miners shoveled dirt into boxes or sluices to capture ore by running water over it. A few miners struck it rich. The biggest winners may have been the storekeepers who sold blasting powder, shovels, and groceries. Four became partners and built the western half of America's first transcontinental railroad. They had such a stranglehold on California's transit system that locals called their company "the Octopus." Levi Strauss, a German immigrant, came to sell canvas tents and made a fortune turning them into pants—and Levis, as they came to be called, sell worldwide today.

Penniless Irish-born Marcus Daly did even better. Pooling resources, he and some San Francisco investors dug for silver in Montana and hit one of the world's largest veins of copper. The Anaconda mine made Daly millions. Its high-grade copper entered worldwide markets, wherever cities and industries needed copper wire to harness electricity's power. Partly due to

Howling blizzards, blistering summers that warped railroad track out of alignment, sky-blackening clouds of locusts, and loneliness meant ruin for some, despair for others. Yet settlers came, worked, endured, and improvised. With little wood or stone available, many farmers built sod houses—even sod schoolhouses. Joseph Glidden's invention, barbed wire, provided them fencing. Strong steel plows cut a sod so knotted with grass roots that hoes bounced off it like paving. Windmills rose from the prairie to pump water from hundreds of feet below ground and over time drain much of it dry. Mennonite settlers from Russia brought durum wheat, ideal for the harsh climate. Everywhere, families built schools, churches, and communities alongside the now-ubiquitous railroad stations.

The western environment was newly made. Wolves, elk, and bears were exterminated as farmers brought in pigs, cattle, and sheep. Tulare Lake, covering hundreds of square miles of California's Central Valley, was sucked dry by 1900. Mines sent tons of earth and

Chinese and Anglo Miners near Sacramento, California, 1852 Digging for gold paid off mostly in aches, misery, and loneliness. The so-called Forty-Niners included immigrants from across the Pacific and from Latin America, but just about no women.

Anaconda, by 1883 the United States led the world in producing copper.

Daly's venture represented the future. By the 1870s, gold veins ran too deep for lone prospectors to reach; heavy, costly machines were needed. Minerals like zinc and copper required a heavier initial investment that would take much longer to be repaid. Mine shafts needed timber supports in a treeless land, as well as blowers to cool the 130-degree temperatures deep underground. Deep mines needed constant pumping: 2 million gallons of water seeped into the Comstock every day. Copper or silver took smelting. Thus, corporations alone could tap most of the West's mineral wealth. Engineers and wage laborers, managed from boardrooms miles away, extracted, smelted, and shipped the ore. Even Comstock's 750 miles of tunnels 3,000 feet underground were corporation run. Companies built the railroads to carry ore to market and to the towns where miners lived. These were shabby, utilitarian places without libraries, parks, schools—or the chance to strike it rich on one's own. The Comstocks had given way to the Cassettaris.

rock down the rivers of the Sierra Nevada, threatening entire cities with flooding. The skies above Butte, Montana, turned gray from pollutants released by copper-smelting plants. Sheepherding destroyed the vegetation on the eastern slopes of the Rocky Mountains and the Sierra Nevada. But the West was also dotted with communities and railroad depots. California oranges found a market in New England, and Washington apple orchards filled the stalls in eastern markets.

By the turn of the century, states and reservations stood where the Cheyenne, Dakota, and Comanche nations had commanded vast domains. Settlers of many ethnicities—Swedish, Finnish, Hispanic, and others—experienced the bounty and hardship of what had once been Indian land. Corporate enterprises and mechanized farms now shared the West with the homesteaders and storekeepers. Farmers had connected to world markets. They were clothed and supplied by cities' industries. They owed eastern railroad corporations their access to the world, and they owed nearly everything else to eastern mortgage holders. Mining and lumber corporations employed tens of thousands of wage laborers. Thanks to the gold rush, San Francisco rose from 5,000 inhabitants midcentury to 150,000 twenty years later. Denver was incorporated in 1861 with a population just below 5,000. By 1870, it had grown twentyfold.

America Moves to the City

Between 1850 and 1900, the map of the United States was redrawn, thanks to the appearance of dozens of new cities (see Figure 16–1). In 1850, the largest city in the United States was New York, with a population of just over half a million. By 1900, New York, Philadelphia, and Chicago each had more than a million residents.

The industrial city was different from its predecessors. By the middle of the nineteenth century the modern "downtown" was born, a place where people shopped and worked but did not necessarily live. Residential neighborhoods separated city dwellers from the downtown districts and separated the classes from one another. Streetcars and commuter railroads brought middle-class clerks and professionals from their homes to their jobs and back, but the fares were beyond the means of the working class. The rich built their mansions uptown, but workers had to stay within walking distance of their jobs.

Cities became more crowded, unsanitary, and unsafe. Yellow fever and cholera epidemics were frequent. Fires periodically wiped out entire neighborhoods. In October 1871, much of Chicago went up in flames. Immigrant slums sprang up in most major cities of America, as well as in mill towns and mining camps. In 1890, Jacob Riis published *How the Other Half Lives*, exposing conditions in downtown New York, the breeding grounds of vice, crime, and despair. He described a dark three-room apartment that six people shared. The two bedrooms were tiny, the beds nothing more than boxes filled with "foul straw." Such conditions were a common feature of urban poverty in the late nineteenth century.

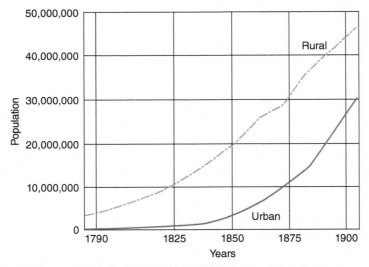

Figure 16–1   Proportion of Population Living in Cities, 1790–1900 While a growing proportion of Americans lived in cities, city dwellers would outnumber rural Americans only in the twentieth century.

Yet during these same years urban reformers and technology made city life less dangerous and more comfortable. Professional fire and police departments protected cities from fire outbreaks and violence. Boards of health and quarantine laws brought epidemics under control. By the century's end, city dwellers could count on clean drinking water, efficient transportation, great museums, public libraries, parks, and a variety of entertainment unimaginable in the countryside.

By 1900, travelers walking down New York City's Bowery at midnight could feel safer, basking in the blaze of electric lights. Thomas Alva Edison's invention of the commercially viable incandescent light bulb in 1879 was only one invention among many to dispel that darkness. He and other inventors created the dynamo to generate electricity, as well as alternating current to transmit power more efficiently. City dwellers would be the first to light their homes with electricity, the first to install telephones, and those most likely to receive mail every day, Sundays included. They would also be the ones most likely to eat fruits and vegetables out of season. Thanks to mass production, Gilded Age manufacturers would introduce canned foods into American diets. For those with money to spare, nothing could compare with the new, gigantic department stores, able to sell an endless variety of goods at the lowest prices because they dealt in such tremendous volume. Where else but Philadelphia would have Wanamaker's, with three acres of selling area and 129 counters, stretching two-thirds of a mile? Where else but New York would have a Heinz food sign six stories high, requiring 1,200 light bulbs? Cities showed off industrial capitalism's riches at their best, as well as its victims at their worst.

Nobody represented both sides of capitalism as well as a young Scots immigrant who came with his parents to

Wanamaker's Grand Depot Department Store, 1876 "Big business" in the late nineteenth century not only mass-produced goods but also sold them in large quantities at low prices. John Wanamaker's Philadelphia department store was among the most famous of these large, new retailers and funded Wanamaker's political activity against corrupt city officials.

Pittsburgh and started out in a textile mill for $1.20 a week. Fifty years later, Andrew Carnegie sold his steel mills to J. Pierpont Morgan for $480 million.

The Rise of Big Business

Before the Civil War the only enterprises in the United States that could be called "big businesses" were the railroads (see Map 16–2). Indeed, railroads became the model for a new kind of business—big business—that emerged during the 1880s. Big businesses had massive bureaucracies managed by professionals rather than owners and were financed through a national banking system centered on Wall Street. They marketed their goods and services across the world and generated wealth in staggering concentrations, giving rise to a class of men whose names—Carnegie, Rockefeller, Morgan, and Vanderbilt— became synonymous with American capitalism.

The Rise of Andrew Carnegie

Andrew Carnegie was an immigrant, whereas most businessmen were native born. His childhood in Scotland was marked by poverty, whereas most of America's leading men of business were raised in comfort. Nevertheless, Andrew Carnegie was the perfect reflection of the rise of big business. In the course of his career, Carnegie mastered the telegraph, railroad, petroleum, iron, and steel industries and set the example for modern management techniques and strict accounting procedures in manufacturing. Other great industrialists and financiers made their mark in the last half of the nineteenth century. Canadian-born James J. Hill's railroad empire filled the grain elevators with wheat

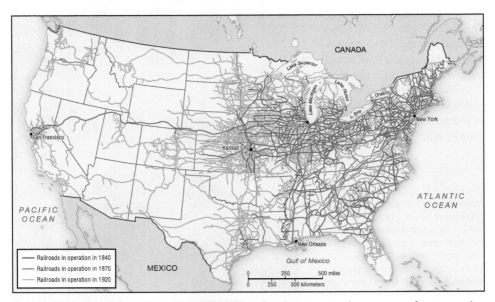

Map 16-2   The Growth of Railroads, 1850–1890 Railroads were more than a means of transportation; they were also America's first "big business." They set the model for running huge industrial corporations, and the growth of railroads fostered the iron and steel industries.

that made Minneapolis the country's great flour-making center; his money built copper smelters in Montana and an apple-growing industry in Washington. German-born Friederich Weyerhäuser's timber company logged the West and furnished the boards that homesteaders on the treeless prairie needed so desperately. However, none had lives that took on the mythic proportions of that of the Scottish lad who came to America at the age of 12 and ended up the world's richest man.

Not content with his job at a textile mill, Carnegie enrolled in a night course to study accounting, and a year later he got a job as a messenger boy in a telegraph office. So astute and hard-working was Andrew that by 1851 he was promoted to telegraph operator. There he displayed a rare talent for leadership. He recruited bright, hard-working men and organized them with such stunning efficiency that the Pennsylvania Railroad offered Carnegie a job, first as a private secretary and later in management.

Carnegie came to the firm at a time when rail construction was soaring. Petroleum refiners shipped their kerosene by rail. Mining corporations needed railroads to ship their coal and iron. By the mid-1850s, the largest factory in the country, the Pepperell Mills in Biddeford, Maine, employed 800 workers, whereas the Pennsylvania Railroad then had more than 4,000 employees. If an engineer arrived late, or if a fireman came to work drunk, trains were wrecked, lives were lost, and business failed. The railroads thus borrowed the disciplinary methods and bureaucratic structure of the military to ensure that the trains ran safely and on time. J. Edgar Thomson, the Pennsylvania's president, established an elaborate bookkeeping system providing detailed knowledge of every aspect of the Pennsylvania's operations. Based on that data, the company could reward managers who improved the company's profits and eliminate those who failed.

Carnegie succeeded. As superintendent of the western division, he helped make the Pennsylvania a model of efficiency. By 1865, with 30,000 employees and lines stretching east to New York City and west to Chicago, it was the largest private company in the world. It was also necessarily one of the most financially intricate. Railroads dwarfed all previous business enterprises in the amount of investment capital they required and in the complexity of their financial arrangements. A major line might require over a hundred separate kinds of account books. Railroads were the first corporations to issue stocks through sophisticated trading mechanisms that attracted investors from around the world. To organize the market in such vast numbers of securities, the modern investment house was developed.

Carnegie Dominates the Steel Industry

By 1872, Carnegie had taken on other interests as well. His Keystone Bridge Company built the first steel arch bridge over the Mississippi. Acquiring a controlling interest in the Union Iron Company, Carnegie had overhauled it, adapting the Pennsylvania's managerial techniques and accounting practices. He also integrated operations: unlike other firms, his would not just melt iron ore into pig iron, but make bars of it, and turn those bars into beams and plates. Eliminating middlemen meant savings, and savings let him sell for less. As Carnegie put it, "Watch the costs and the profits will take care of themselves."

More important, his railroad experience taught him that steel, not iron, was the future. Under the loads of larger, heavier trains, iron rails simply could not hold up for long. Though prohibitively expensive at first, steel rails lasted 20 years, whereas iron ones

The Eads Bridge The steel arches of the Eads Bridge across the Mississippi River at St. Louis were both an engineering marvel and a triumph of Andrew Carnegie's managerial skills.

needed replacement at 5. Steel also proved better for making locomotives, boilers, and railroad cars. In the 1860s, two developments cleared the path for the transition from iron to steel. First, Henry Bessemer's patented process for turning iron into steel became available to American manufacturers. Second, iron ore began flowing from deposits in northern Michigan. With access to investment capital and Thomson for his partner, Carnegie opened a steel plant in 1873. Despite a worldwide depression, it turned a profit immediately.

Big Business Consolidates

In the late nineteenth century, every great industry conjured up the name of a magnate: Carnegie in steel, Gustavus Swift or Philip Armour in meatpacking, John D. Rockefeller in oil refining, James J. Hill or Collis P. Huntington in railroads, and J. P. Morgan in financing (see Map 16–3). Actually, no single individual or family could own most big businesses because they required too much capital (financial resources). They were run by professionally trained managers. The highest profits went to companies with the most efficient bureaucracies. Because the businesses were so big and their equipment so expensive, they had to operate continuously. In an economic slowdown, an average factory could close its doors for a while, but big businesses could not.

With railroads and telegraph lines opening up national markets and new technology allowing mass production at lower costs, industries faced unprecedented competition. They met this challenge of competition and the need for a regular source of supply by adopting *vertical integration*. This was the attempt to control as many aspects of a business

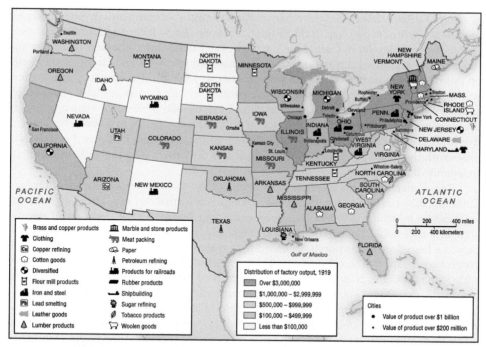

Map 16-3   Major American Industries, ca. 1890 An industrial map of late nineteenth-century America shows regions increasingly defined not by what they grew but by what they made.

as possible, from the production of raw materials to the sale of the finished product. Carnegie did not just manufacture steel; he owned the iron mines and handled the marketing of finished steel. He also grasped two profit-making strategies that other firms, from breweries to makers of canned goods, had learned: economies of scale and *continuous flow*. Bigger furnaces could produce steel more cheaply. Running them 24 hours a day, seven days a week, made every minute count. And with the help of the Jones Mixer, a container keeping pig iron molten, the biggest component in steel would be ready for immediate use. Rails poured into molds did not even wait in the plant to cool. Flatcars carried them outside, while others lined up to be filled. By such means over 15 years, Carnegie cut steel prices in half. Without these innovations, the gridwork of steel railroad lines would never have been—nor that new, lighter superstructure of girders that allowed the first skyscrapers to tower above Chicago and New York.

The same commitment to continuous flow made Philip D. Armour and Gustavus Swift into the nation's premier meatpackers. Instead of the local slaughterhouse, firms in Chicago's "Packingtown" had assembly lines carrying a steady stream of carcasses, with each employee assigned one task in the disassembling of pigs and cattle. To save on freight rates for live cattle, the packers built refrigerator cars to carry the "dressed beef" alone to distant markets. Armour also realized that by making money off the rest of the animal, he could lower the price for which he sold his meat. By 1900, the fat, bones, blood, and bristles were turned into hairbrushes, fertilizer, soap, and even the stuffing for automobile cushions—and Armour could sell his beef at four cents a pound.

John D. Rockefeller tried the other solution to cutthroat competition, *horizontal consolidation*: control of one step in the industrial process. Rockefeller had founded Standard Oil in 1867 in Cleveland, Ohio. Like Carnegie, Rockefeller hired the best managers and financiers to build and run the most efficient modern refineries and cut his dependence on railroad transport by investing in pipelines to carry the oil. However, he was also more willing than Carnegie to wipe out his competitors by any means available. Rockefeller squeezed from the railroads preferential shipping rates and rebates, the return of part of the standard price charged to other refiners—a critical advantage in a savagely competitive business. As president of the National Refiners' Association, he formed cartels, alliances with the major operators in other states. But the cartels were too weak to eliminate independent refiners.

Rockefeller found his solution in merging all the major companies under Standard Oil leadership. In 1882, the Standard Oil combine was formalized as a "trust," an elaborate legal device by which different producers came together under the umbrella of a single company that could police competition internally. In 1889, the New Jersey legislature passed a law allowing corporations based in that state to form "holding companies" that controlled companies in other states. Thus, the trust gave way to the holding company, with Standard Oil of New Jersey its most prominent example. Within a decade, holding companies dominated some of America's largest industries.

Standard Oil became a notorious example of how big business had changed the American economy—and, some thought, for the worse. Rockefeller's many charities never buried his reputation as a "robber baron," a term thrown at the titans of industry, transport, and finance. Exceptional in an age when most firms remained small and most industries stayed competitive (railroads mercilessly so), these "captains of industry" were admired and feared in equal measure.

A New Social Order

Americans took pride in having no such rigid class system as in Europe. Anyone could rise, and, as Rosa Cassettari noticed, the poor need not doff their caps before the rich. But class divisions ran deep all the same. One could see that clearly, just by comparing Carnegie's Scottish castle with Painters' Row, where his unskilled workers lived in unventilated wooden houses without running water and with privies for all perched up the hill.

Lifestyles of the Very Rich

Between 1850 and 1890, the proportion of the nation's wealth owned by the 4,000 richest families nearly tripled. At the top of the social pyramid clustered some 200 families worth more than $20 million each. Concentrated in the Northeast, New York especially, these families flaunted their opulence. Spread more evenly across America were the several thousand millionaires made rich by cattle ranching, agricultural equipment, mining, commerce, and real estate. Most of America's millionaires traced their ancestry to Great Britain. Usually they were Protestant, mostly Episcopalians, Presbyterians, or Congregationalists. By the standards of their day they were unusually well educated and, more often than not, voted Republican. (Southerners remained firmly Democratic.)

The upper classes lived in mammoth houses. Some addresses became celebrated for their wealth: Fifth Avenue in Manhattan, Nob Hill in San Francisco, and Boston's Back Bay. Wealthy suburbs (Brooklyn Heights, Philadelphia's Main Line, and Brookline, Massachusetts) became privileged retreats. The richest families also built country estates that rivaled the stately homes of England and the chateaus of France, such as the palace-sized "cottages" along the Newport, Rhode Island, shoreline. The leading figures in New York's high society competed to stage the most lavish balls and dinner parties, in one case with hundred-dollar bills as party favors. It was left to the new middle class to display the traditional virtues of thrift and self-denial.

The Consolidation of the New Middle Class

In 1889, the *Century Dictionary* introduced the phrase "middle class" in the United States. The new term reflected a fresh awareness that American society had distinct gradations. Professionals were the backbone of the new middle class of the nineteenth century. All professions organized themselves into associations—some 200 between 1870 and 1890 alone—that set educational and ethical standards for admission and practice. Corporations needed professional managers, not swashbuckling gamblers. Business schools arose, teaching the science of accounting and the art of management. By 1920, 1,700 schools trained nurses, nearly all of them women. (At the same time, doctors' associations used their power over licensing to get rid of midwives; Rosa Cassettari was not the only one to do without.) Educators even gave a professional veneer to housekeeping by inventing "home economics" courses. States had a vested interest in professionalism, too. By 1900, most required association-drafted bar exams for lawyers and medical exams for doctors.

Behind the new professional managers marched an expanding white-collar army of cashiers, clerks, and government employees, mostly men. Their annual incomes far outpaced independent craftsmen and factory workers. They also had a better chance to rise. A beginning clerk might make only $100 a year, but within five years his salary could approach $1,000. At a time when a skilled Philadelphia factory hand made under $600, over 80 percent of the male clerks in the Treasury Department earned twice that.

Improved roads and mass-transit systems allowed middle-class families to escape the city's clamor and crowdedness, though suburbs, like city neighborhoods, were made for every income. The invention of oil-based house paints in the 1870s allowed owners to give the outside any color they pleased. Thanks to the mass-produced "Excelsior" mower and romantic associations with the Old South, the normal middle-class residence had a front porch and a lawn; but the crabgrass got blamed on eastern European immigrants, who supposedly brought it with them.

Only the most successful craftsmen matched the incomes and suburban lifestyles of white-collar clerks. Butchers might earn more than $1,600 annually, for example, but shoemakers averaged little more than $500. But while a shoemaker earned little more than a skilled factory worker, if he owned his own shop, he enjoyed an independence that middle-class Americans cherished. A cigar maker working on high-priced "seed and Havanas" had skills that gave him far more say in his work than the unskilled employees making two-cent "stogies" with a cigar mold. Pride and power, not just pay, defined job satisfaction. In carpentry and in the coal mines, specialized skills made workers hard to replace. But around them, labor-saving machinery was increasing a far more dependent industrial working class made up of people like Rosa Cassettari.

The Industrial Working Class Comes of Age

"When I first went to learn the trade," John Morrison told a congressional committee in 1883, "a machinist considered himself more than the average workingman; in fact, he did not like to be called a workingman. He liked to be called a mechanic." Morrison identified one of the great changes in nineteenth-century America. "Today," Morrison lamented, the mechanic "is simply a laborer." Technological innovations replaced artisans with semiskilled or unskilled factory laborers. For traditional mechanics, this felt like downward mobility.

Because most factory workers and common laborers were migrants (or children of migrants) from small towns, farms, or abroad, few experienced factory work as a degradation of their traditional skills, as Morrison did. They had a chance to move upward from unskilled to skilled positions. Shop foremen might become storekeepers. Working-class families took comfort that their children had a still better chance of moving into the middle class. But industrial labor was a harsh existence for all factory operatives, who toiled long hours in difficult conditions performing repetitive tasks with little job security. Most luckless and hardest pressed were the common laborers, earning their keep by physical exertion. Their numbers grew throughout the century until by 1900 unskilled labor made up a third of the industrial workforce.

In 1900, women accounted for nearly one of every five Americans gainfully employed, mostly in unskilled or semiskilled labor. In northern middle-class homes, young Irish women worked as domestics, jobs held in the South by African American women. Jewish women sewed garments for as little as three dollars for a six-day week, and Italians worked on lace and paper flowers in their tenements. A smaller proportion of women held white-collar jobs, as teachers, nurses, or low-paid clerical workers and salesclerks behind department store counters.

The same hierarchy that favored men in the white-collar and professional labor force existed in the factories and sweatshops. In the clothing industry, for example, units dominated by male workers were higher up the chain of command than those dominated by women. Indeed, as the textile industry became a big business, the proportion of women working in textile mills steadily declined. The reverse trend affected white-collar workers. As department stores expanded in the 1870s and 1880s, they hired women, often Irish immigrants, for jobs with low wages and none of the prospects for promotion men still had. White-collar work did not confer middle-class status upon women as it did upon men in the late nineteenth century.

Few working-class wives and mothers took jobs outside the home, but many took in boarders or did laundry. The poorer working-class families survived by sending their children to work. The rich sent their daughters to finishing schools and their sons to boarding schools; middle-class parents sent their children to public schools; anything beyond grade school ranked as a luxury among those less well off than that. Ten-year-olds could be found tending the cotton spindles or picking shale off the conveyor belts coming up from the coal mines. They ran barefoot through New York's streets hawking newspapers and lugged red-hot, newly cast bottles from the furnaces in glass factories. Only in Horatio Alger novels did "Mark the Match-Boy" strike it rich.

Division of labor allowed more goods to be made for much lower per-unit labor costs. The introduction of the sewing machine in the 1850s, for example, gave rise to sweatshops where work was subdivided into simple, repetitive tasks. One group produced collars for men's shirts, another produced sleeves, and another stitched the parts together. Division of labor saved employers on training, and in industries where turnover was high, it kept the machinery running. Factory work was at best insecure, subject to swings in the business cycle. But unskilled workers also lacked the leverage to improve their own conditions. If Carnegie's workers, blinded or crippled on the job, got nothing more than the privilege of begging at the mill gates—if lung diseases were as common in textile factories as the "mill child's cough" and gangrene of the jaw among boys making matches—workers had no options beyond leaving and being fired.

Workmen's compensation was rare, and retirement pensions were unknown. Helplessness and the pool of surplus labor made organizing unions a challenge among the unskilled. Men laying railroad track or digging subway tunnels were always moving on, with common labor often seasonal and factory turnover high. In some meatpacking houses, turnover came close to 100 percent annually. A strike depleted workers' savings

Cannery in Sunnyvale, California The mass production of food involved a large female labor force, as this picture shows. Quite possibly, employers hired so readily not just because they could pay women less, but because anything involving the preparation of food fit in with the stereotype of "woman's work."

quickly. Exceptionally mobile and easily replaceable, immigrants increasingly came from places unfamiliar with the idea of organized labor and from cultures where religion defined identity more than class. Employers knew that by using them or, better still, black Americans as strikebreakers, they could turn race against race, native against foreigner. "Scabs," as those taking strikers' places were called, faced insult and threat. Some were beaten, others killed. Some firms built private armies to enforce control, but they could usually count on the police and state militia to help them win a strike.

Social Darwinism and the Growth of Scientific Racism

As ethnicity identification developed in the late nineteenth century, class divisions were increasingly difficult to isolate from cultural distinctions. The middle class, for example, was overwhelmingly native born, white, Anglo-Saxon, and Protestant. By contrast, the working class came largely from racial and religious minorities, many of them foreign born (see Figure 16–2). By 1900, 75 percent of manufacturing workers were immigrants or their children, and in large cities, nearer 85 percent. The South's laborers were overwhelmingly black sharecroppers. As educated elites defined high culture, they drew on

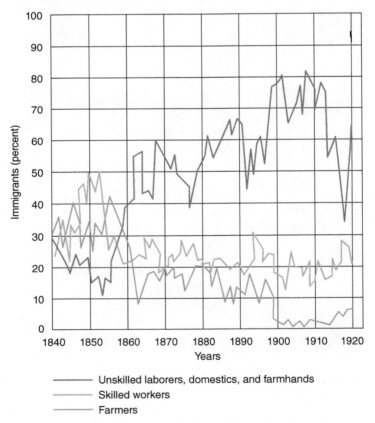

Figure 16-2   **Working-Class Immigration, 1840-1920** *Source*: US Bureau of Census.

traditions and tastes formed by the propertied classes of a less culturally diverse America, one increasingly under challenge.

Pundits and professors argued that this form of society, stratified by class, race, ethnicity, and gender, was not only how things had to be, but how natural law required them to be. In 1859, Charles Darwin published his masterpiece of evolutionary theory, *On the Origin of Species*. Several scientists had already suggested that life had evolved over a long period of time, but Darwin offered the first persuasive explanation of how this had taken place. He argued that a process of "natural selection" favored those biological changes that were most suited to the surrounding environment. American scientists took readily to Darwinism. Asa Gray at Harvard and Joseph LeConte at the University of California spread the evolutionary word in their influential textbooks on botany and geology. By 1900, virtually all American high school science textbooks embraced evolution.

Darwin's influence did not stop with the natural sciences. Social scientists applied the theory of natural selection to social evolution. This combination of social theory with evolutionary science was known as Social Darwinism. Social Darwinists argued that human inequality was the outcome of a struggle for survival in which the fittest rose to the top. This theory made the rich seem more fit than the poor and blacks seem less fit than whites. To Social Darwinists, inequality was the natural order of things. In this way, Darwin's theory was hijacked to defend the new social order of industrial capitalism.

Natural selection was also invoked to show an inherent African racial inferiority (and that of Indians as well). Racists had argued that without slavery, freed blacks could not compete—or even survive. After the war, newspapers predicted the disappearance of African Americans by century's end and of Indians within a generation or two more. The 1890 census seemed to show a declining African American population, and racial theorists published influential studies "proving" that competition with whites was killing blacks off. Their only salvation, biologist Joseph LeConte argued, would come through permanent subordination. Only white overlordship could save blacks from their natural fate.

Far more influential than LeConte was statistician Frederick L. Hoffman's full-length treatise *Race Traits and Tendencies of the American Negro*, published in 1896. The book's many tables and figures gave the authoritative air of social science to Hoffman's conclusion: ever since leaving the shelter of slavery, blacks had been degenerating morally. Evolutionary theory doomed them to poverty and social inferiority.

Social Darwinism had plenty of defenders, notably Professor William Graham Sumner of Yale University. "Before the tribunal of nature," he asserted, "a man has no more right to life than a rattlesnake." Any government intervention to help the unfortunate interfered with natural selection. It would be useless in the long run and a harmful interference with the rigid economic laws of supply and demand in the short run. But the Sumners of the world found themselves under increasing challenge well before the century ended. Ministers, who saw man as a moral, rather than an economic, animal, rejected the concept of a natural selection process based on selfishness and scramble. Economist Richard T. Ely argued that even in economic decisions, self-interest did not play the all-controlling role that Social Darwinism presumed. Success, a younger generation of economists and social scientists argued, depended not just on a person's natural gifts but also on the surrounding conditions. Change the conditions—replace a slum with clean and healthy apartments, an alley with a playground or a park, a pittance with a living wage—and the man or woman with abilities might have the chance to use them to rise.

STRUGGLES FOR DEMOCRACY

"The Chinese Must Go"

For the Chinese, immigrating to America proved a disastrous success. With no other group did the promise of a new beginning suffer so badly in the translation.

In the mid-nineteenth century, the Chinese fled the convulsions of the Taiping Rebellion, a massive civil war that left 20 million dead. Some immigrants found work in the California gold fields; others dug the mines or laid track on the transcontinental railroad. Contractors swore by them: they did the hardest work at the lowest wage and never complained. Mines in Idaho and Montana imported Chinese labor. In California's inland valley, they earned a dollar a day digging the irrigation ditches for the great farms. As tourist hotels opened in southern California, they welcomed the Chinese as cooks and help. Along the Pacific coast, their vessels hauled in shoals of fish, ready to be dried, salted, and barreled for sale in China. Others dove

for abalone; well-polished, the shells sold by the hundreds of thousands in Europe. They planted the vineyards north of San Francisco Bay and harvested the orchards south of it. The Bing cherry was developed by a Chinese horticulturist in Oregon, the frost-resistant orange by a Chinese immigrant in Florida. Saving their money, the thriftier Chinese opened up laundries and retail shops. Every major city had its "Chinatown," colorful, congested, and overwhelmingly male: the first generations of Chinese were sojourners, meaning to prosper and return home. They rented rather than bought homes and left their families behind. Those who died in America, if they could afford it, had their remains shipped back to their native soil for burial.

Hard-working, resourceful, sober, willing, and almost obsessive about paying what they owed, the Chinese were the very personification of the Horatio Alger

In that sense, the modern university reflected the inequalities of the age—and the promise. Leading scholars in the new "social sciences" of sociology, anthropology, and political science gave authority to Social Darwinism's conjectures, by dividing the world into great and inferior nations. At the top were the so-called Teutonic nations of Western Europe and North America. This hierarchy, far from reflecting the biases of its creators, was grounded in the objective methods of pure science—or so anthropologists, sociologists, and professional economists claimed. However, a vocal minority, just as well trained abroad, came back to apply objective standards to Social Darwinism and expose its fallacies.

Colleges thus helped reinforce elite power while opening the door a crack to those wanting to enter that elite realm. Only a tiny fraction of Americans attended college, mostly native-born and well-to-do males. Nevertheless, it was a larger fraction than ever before. One reason was that the first Morrill Land Grant Act of 1862 had endowed the states with great tracts to fund institutions teaching "agriculture and the mechanic ideal for success. That, however, was just the problem. White workers resented their cheap labor and the corporations that used them as strikebreakers. Keeping apart and failing to assimilate, Chinese immigrants remained alien, closed off by differences in language and religion from their neighbors. It was widely believed that the Chinese ate birds' nests, rats, squirrels, and, worst of all, abalone. Ignorance only kindled fantasies among whites, of a Chinatown crowded with opium dens, racketeers, and prostitution rings—all of which did exist—and not much else. Alarmist writers forecast a race war, where the "Celestials" conquered the world for their emperor.

Even as other immigrants became voters, the Chinese found themselves isolated and imperiled. Courts refused Chinese testimony because of the race's supposed habit of lying. Trade unions refused to admit them. Rioters in Los Angeles tore through the Asian community, beating up and killing whomever they could find and looting every store; a city councilman led the mob, and the chief of police sealed Chinatown off so that the victims could not escape.

Vigilantes burned down Chinatowns across the West. Farmers employing Chinese laborers had their barns and fields torched. By 1877, anger against the Chinese and railroad barons had become a political uprising, with the cry, "The Chinese must go!" California's new constitution barred them from public schools and taxed them out of the mining and fishing industries. National laws over the next 20 years would close the doors to new immigration and make it harder for residents to visit home and return to the United States.

Closing the doors to their home country had an unexpected effect. Cut off from their Old World communities, forced to make a lifetime commitment to their new homeland, the survivors learned English, brought their families over, and remade themselves as Chinese Americans. They adopted Western clothing; their sons and daughters went to Sunday school, joined the Boy Scouts, and organized chapters of the YMCA and YWCA. All the same, full assimilation would not come in their lifetimes, nor their grandchildren's. In more than a mere physical sense, the Statue of Liberty faced away from the newcomers of the Pacific Rim.

arts." Seventy "land grant" institutions were founded, including the major state university systems of New York, Illinois, Michigan, and California. Those in the Midwest admitted women as well as men. Women's colleges also opened their doors: six of the "Seven Sisters" began after the Civil War. By 1910, two in five college students were women. If blacks found themselves largely shut out of the elite schools (which also set quotas limiting Jewish admissions), they, too, had new opportunities in land grant institutions as well as in black colleges like Fisk University in Tennessee or Booker T. Washington's Tuskegee Institute in Alabama.

Social scientists such as Ely and Hoffman prided themselves on their commitment to the truth as facts and statistics revealed it. Like advocates of high culture, sociologists and anthropologists claimed to have isolated the definitive truths of human society. But not all "realists" sought solace in statistics. Some of America's best artists responded to the realities of a diverse, urban, industrial America. They could see what it took no advanced degree to grasp: that a many-cultured society was being enriched and reshaped by those very people that Social Darwinists had dismissed as the losers in humankind's struggle to advance.

The Knights of Labor and the Haymarket Disaster

Workers had known that all along, their share fell far behind what their labor deserved. Between 1860 and 1890, wages overall grew by 50 percent, but elite skilled and semi-skilled workers in a handful of industries, such as printing and metalworking, got the lion's share of the gains. The vast majority of workers suffered directly from deflation and economic instability. By 1880, 40 percent of industrial workers lived at or below the poverty line, and the average worker was unemployed for 15 to 20 percent of the year. To relieve their plight, American workers sought political solutions to economic problems.

Inspired by the radicalism of the Civil War and Reconstruction, industrial workers across the North organized dozens of craft unions, Eight-Hour Leagues, and working-men's associations, all designed to protect northern workers who were overworked and underpaid. They called strikes, initiated consumer boycotts, and formed consumer coop-eratives. In 1867 and 1868, workers in New York and Massachusetts campaigned for laws restricting the workday to eight hours. Soon, workers began electing their own candidates to state legislatures.

Before the Gilded Age, labor organizations had never drawn many workers. The tradition of individuals lifting themselves up bred a distrust of collective solutions. Founded in 1866, the National Labor Union (NLU) was the first significant postwar effort to organize all "working people" into a national union. William Sylvis, an iron molder, founded the NLU and became its president in 1868. He denied any "harmony of interests" between workers and capitalists. On the contrary, every wage earner was at war with every capitalist, whose "profits" robbed working people of the fruits of their labor.

Under Sylvis's direction, the NLU advocated a wide range of political reforms, not just bread-and-butter issues. Sylvis believed that through organization American workers could take the "first step toward competence and independence." He argued for a doubling of the average worker's wages. He supported voting rights for blacks and women. Nevertheless, after a miserable showing in the elections of 1872, the NLU fell apart.

Despite the collapse of the NLU, a more successful alternative had already begun. In 1869, some Philadelphia garment makers formed the Noble and Holy Order of the

Time Line

▼**1848**
Andrew Carnegie emigrates to the United States

▼**1857**
Henry Bessemer develops process for making steel

▼**1859**
Oil discovered in western Pennsylvania and the petroleum boom begins

▼**1862**
Homestead Act

▼**1866**
First successful transatlantic telegraph cable begins operation

▼**1869**
Opening of the first transcontinental railroad

Knights of Labor. The Knights were inspired by the producers' ideology and admitted everyone from self-employed farmers to unskilled factory workers. Stressing the need for uplift and temperance, the Knights advocated a host of reforms, including the eight-hour day, equal pay for men and women, the abolition of child and prison labor, inflation of the currency to counteract the deflationary spiral, and a national income tax.

Only a strong national organization able to hold various locals together and provide necessary funds would give the Knights credibility among potential recruits. In the late 1870s, a new constitution required all members to pay dues and let the national organization support local boycotts. Open to women as well as men, skilled and unskilled, black and white (but not Chinese), the Knights grew rapidly, from 19,000 members in 1881 to 111,000 in 1885. Terence Powderly, leader of this largely working-class movement, believed in neither socialism nor the notion that there was any necessary conflict between labor and capital. Wage earners were "producers," and he meant to overthrow "wage slavery," not capitalism itself. Powderly favored arbitration and conciliation over confrontation, and the consumer boycott over the strike. Local assemblies struck anyhow. They even forced a settlement out of the railroads of the Southwest, including those of the notorious Jay Gould, who had bragged that he "could hire one half of the working class to kill the other half." The Knights' lobbying helped put through the Chinese Exclusion Act in 1882 and a federal law against imported contract labor three years later. By 1886, membership swelled to nearly a quarter of a million. Labor parties elected mayors and city councilmen; only vote fraud kept them from making Henry George mayor of New York. They even talked of fielding a presidential ticket.

But the more the Knights of Labor grew, the more the strains among its members showed. Shopkeepers and small-factory owners had very different interests from wage laborers, especially when it came to strikes. By 1886, work stoppages were twice what they had been the year before. The "Great Upheaval" had begun. The more Knights there were, the more militant they sounded. The culmination came when trade unions called for a nationwide strike for the eight-hour day. On May 1, 1886, workers across the country walked off their jobs in one of the largest labor walkouts in American history. In Chicago 80,000 workers went out on strike. The Chicago strike was largely peaceful until May 4, when, at an anarchist rally at Haymarket Square, someone from the crowd tossed a bomb into a line of police. Eight policemen were killed. Police shot into the crowd. Four people died. Many more were wounded. The bomb thrower was never identified.

▼1871
Great Chicago Fire

▼1872
Andrew Carnegie's steel works open near Pittsburgh

▼1873
Financial panic, followed by depression

▼1877
The "Great Railroad Strike"

▼1882
John D. Rockefeller forms Standard Oil trust
Thomas Edison develops the first commercially viable incandescent electric light

▼1890
Jacob Riis publishes How the Other Half Lives
Director of US Census declares frontier "closed"

▼1893
Financial panic, followed by depression

Haymarket Riot The Haymarket "riot," as it was misnamed, set off a wave of middle-class hysteria against foreigners, radicals, and labor unions. This image correctly shows police firing into the crowd. Inaccurately, it shows members of the crowd firing back, the orator apparently urging them on. It also leaves out the women and children who attended.

Anarchists—who questioned the legitimacy of all government power—had little influence on the labor movement, but their fiery rhetoric invoking the use of violence made them conspicuous. In a blatantly unfair trial with perjured testimony, eight of them were found guilty of inciting the "Haymarket riot." Four were hanged, one committed suicide, and the others went to prison. (In 1893, Governor John Peter Altgeld pardoned the survivors. He knew it would doom him politically; it did.) Haymarket was a turning point in American labor politics. A wave of revulsion against labor agitation swept the country, and state anti-labor laws sprinkled the statute books. The Knights never recovered from the Haymarket disaster. Instead, the labor movement found its new leadership in Samuel Gompers's American Federation of Labor, which concentrated on organizing skilled workers and making demands that could be met immediately, without waiting for political reforms: "bread-and-butter unionism," as some called it.

Conclusion

Rosa Cassettari and Andrew Carnegie—two immigrants whom the new global economy of industrial capitalism helped draw overseas—met wholly different destinies. Not just their origins, but gender roles, opportunity, and good luck explained how they ended up. Yet both shared the same striving spirit that held out at least the chance for them to better themselves (as Cassettari did, however modestly) and their adopted country. Cassettari's experience with failure impelled her to search for something better. Carnegie's success made him yearn for more than money. By 1900, having thrown his energies into getting, Carnegie threw them all into giving. He set up endowments, funded universities, and founded an institute for peace. He had helped create an industrial nation. Now he set out to re-create American culture. Ironically, the Rosa Cassettaris of the world had beaten him to it.

Who, What, Where

Review Questions

1. Define "industrial capitalism." How was industrial capitalism a global phenomenon in the late nineteenth century?

2. What were the differences in lifestyle and in opportunities for those in America's upper, middle, and lower classes, and how did those differences widen or narrow during the late nineteenth century?

3. How was the West absorbed into the national and international markets?

Critical-Thinking Questions

1. How and why did the effects of industrial capitalism differ in the South, West, and North?

2. Historians often refer to this period as the "Gilded Age." "Gilded" refers to something of base or common substance coated with a thin layer of gold, so that it seems far brighter and more valuable than it is. In view of America's industrial development at this time, do you think the term "Gilded Age" is appropriate? Why or why not?

3. Aside from the expansion of industrial capitalism, what factors affected American development during this period? How important are those factors in comparison to capitalism's growth?

Suggested Readings

Chandler, Alfred D. *The Visible Hand: The Managerial Revolution in American Business.* Cambridge, MA: Harvard University Press, 1977.

Cronon, William. *Nature's Metropolis: Chicago and the Great West.* New York: W. W. Norton, 1991.

White, Richard. *The Republic for Which It Stands: The United States During Reconstruction and the Gilded Age, 1865–1896.* New York: Oxford University Press, 2016.

For further review materials and resource information, please visit www. oup.com/us/oakes-mcgerr

CHAPTER 16: THE TRIUMPH OF INDUSTRIAL CAPITALISM, 1850–1890
Primary Sources

16.1 RUSSELL H. CONWELL, "ACRES OF DIAMONDS" (1860s–1920s)

A Baptist pastor from Philadelphia, Russell H. Conwell's most widely known work was his sermon "Acres of Diamonds," first prepared in 1861 when he was 18, and added to and improved upon years later. Over a half century, he would deliver it more than 6,000 times, earning some $8 million from lecture fees. It expressed the faith of the age that any enterprising person could succeed and that individual effort was sure to be rewarded.

You and I know there are some things more valuable than money; of course, we do. Ah, yes! By a heart made unspeakably sad by a grave on which the autumn leaves now fall, I know there are some things higher and grander and sublimer than money. Well does the man know, who has suffered, that there are some things sweeter and holier and more sacred than gold. Nevertheless, the man of common sense also knows that there is not any one of those things that is not greatly enhanced by the use of money. Money is power.

Love is the grandest thing on God's earth, but fortunate the lover who has plenty of money. Money is power: money has powers; and for a man to say, "I do not want money," is to say, "I do not wish to do any good to my fellowmen." It is absurd thus to talk. It is absurd to disconnect them. This is a wonderfully great life, and you ought to spend your time getting money, because of the power there is in money. And yet this religious prejudice is so great that some people think it is a great honor to be one of God's poor. I am looking in the faces of people who think just that way.

I heard a man once say in a prayer-meeting that he was thankful that he was one of God's poor, and then I silently wondered what his wife would say to that speech, as she took in washing to support the man while he sat and smoked on the veranda. I don't want to see any more of that kind of God's poor. Now, when a man could have been rich just as well, and he is now weak because he is poor, he has done some great wrong; he has been untruthful to himself; he has been unkind to his fellowmen. We ought to get rich if we can by honorable and Christian methods, and these are the only methods that sweep us quickly toward the goal of riches.

. . . A young man came to me the other day and said, "If Mr. Rockefeller, as you think, is a good man, why is it that everybody says so much against him?" It is because he has gotten ahead of us; that is the whole of it—just gotten ahead of us. Why is it Mr. Carnegie is criticized so sharply by an envious world! Because he has gotten more than we have. If a man knows more than I know, don't I incline to criticize somewhat his learning? Let a man stand in a pulpit and preach to thousands, and if I have fifteen people in my church, and they're all asleep, don't I criticize him? We always do that to the man who gets ahead of us. Why, the man you are criticizing has one hundred millions, and you have fifty cents, and both of you have just what you are worth.

. . . If you have no capital, I am glad of it. You don't need capital; you need common sense, not copper cents.

A. T. Stewart, the great princely merchant of New York, the richest man in America in his time, was a poor boy; he had a dollar and a half and went into the mercantile business. But he lost eighty-seven and a half cents of his first dollar and a half because he bought some needles and thread and buttons to sell, which people didn't want.

Are you poor? It is because you are not wanted and are left on your own hands. There was the great lesson. Apply it whichever way you will it comes to every single person's life, young or old. He did not know what people needed, and consequently bought something they didn't want, and had the goods left on his hands a dead loss. A. T. Stewart learned there the great lesson of his mercantile life and said "I will never buy anything more until I first learn what the people want; then I'll make the purchase." He went around to the doors and asked them what they did want, and when he found out what they wanted, he invested his sixty-two and a half cents and began to supply a "known demand." I care not what your profession or occupation in life may be; I care not whether you are a lawyer, a doctor, a housekeeper, teacher or whatever else, the principle is precisely the same. We must know what the world needs first and then invest ourselves to supply that need, and success is almost certain.

. . . In our city especially, there are great opportunities for manufacturing, and the time has come when the line is drawn very sharply between the stockholders of the factory and their employees. Now, friends, there has also come a discouraging gloom upon this country and the laboring men are beginning to feel that they are being held down by a crust over their heads through which they find it impossible to break, and the aristocratic money-owner himself is so far above that he will never descend to their assistance. That is the thought that is in the minds of our people. But, friends, never in the history of our country was there an opportunity so great for the poor man to get rich as there is now and in the city of Philadelphia. The very fact that they get discouraged is what prevents them from getting rich. That is all there is to it. The road is open, and let us keep it open between the poor and the rich.

Source: Russell H. Conwell, *Acres of Diamonds,* foreword by Russell F. Weigley (Philadelphia: Temple University Press, 2002), pp. 23–42.

16.2 VISUAL DOCUMENT: ALFRED R. WAUD, "BESSEMER STEEL MANUFACTURE" (1876)

The manufacture of steel began in the Middle Ages in Europe and Asia, but industrialization enabled the manufacture of high-quality steel in massive quantities. The transformation of iron ore into steel was an intensive process. The arrival of huge converters in enormous steel mills caused some observers to consider both the wondrousness of the new technology and the hell-like conditions that employed it. While the United States benefited from large quantities of steel for railroads, construction, and equipment, steel workers labored under harsh conditions. The forges poured liquid hot metal; workers were exposed to air pollution; and wages provided little to no income for long hours and an extensive workweek with no substantial breaks.

Source: Alfred R. Waud, 1828–1891, artist. "Bessemer Steel Manufacture" (1876).
Library of Congress Prints and Photographs Division, Washington, DC.

16.3 GEORGE STEEVENS, EXCERPT FROM *THE LAND OF THE DOLLAR* (1897)

George Steevens, a British journalist, came across the Atlantic in 1896 to collect material for *The Land of the Dollar*. While visiting Philadelphia, he went to one of the most celebrated department stores in the country, Wanamaker's. His guess that the owner had been a "rattling good" Cabinet officer was half right. In terms of efficiency, Wanamaker proved excellent; as a partisan Republican, he willingly saw to the discharge of as many Democratic postmasters as he could manage, and his readiness to forbid mailing materials that he considered indecent stirred outrage among authors.

In Philadelphia everybody goes to Wanamaker's. Mr. [John] Wanamaker was once Postmaster-General of the Republic, and I should think he was a rattling good one. His store was already the largest retail drapery and hosiery and haberdashery, and all that sort of business, in the world, when by the recent purchase of a giant establishment in New York he made it more largest still. Now the working of Wanamaker's, as I am informed, is this. It is no use going there to get what you want. You must go to get what Mr. Wanamaker wants to sell. He tells you each morning in the newspapers what he has got today, and if you want it you had better go and get it; the chances are it will be gone tomorrow. The head of each department is entrusted with a certain amount of capital, and buys his goods at his own discretion. But woe unto him if he does not turn over his capital quickly. There is a rule that no stock may be in the house more than, I think, three months; after that off it must go at any sacrifice.

"You can always tell when Mr. Wanamaker's in town," said a shopwalker, "because there's always some change being made." And then he added, in a half-voice of awestricken worship, "I believe Mr. Wanamaker loves change for its own sake." For the sake of custom, I should say; for this formula of change for change's sake is one of the master-keys of American character. Mr. Wanamaker keeps a picture-gallery, with some really fine modern paintings, to beguile his patrons. To-day he will have an orchestrion playing, tomorrow a costume exhibition of spinning—girls from all the lands of the earth,—every day something new. One day, by moving a table six feet, so that people had to walk round it instead of past it, he increased the sales of an article from three shillings to hundreds of pounds. If that is not genius, tell me what is.

But the really Napoleonic—I was going to say daemonic—feature of the Wanamaker system is the unerring skill with which it reaps its profits out of the necessities of others. Fixing his price according to the economic doctrine of final utility—taking no account, that is, of the cost of production, but only of the price at which most people will find it worth their while to buy—Mr. Wanamaker realizes 10 per cent for himself, and an enormous saving for the consumers. A cargo of rose-trees had been consigned from Holland to a firm of florists, which failed while the plants were in mid-ocean. They went a-begging till Mr. Wanamaker bought them up and put them on the market at about half the rate current in Philadelphia. In ten days not one of the twenty thousand was left. A firm which manufactured hundred-dollar bicycles found itself without cash to meet its liabilities. Mr. Wanamaker bought up the stock and altered the maker's label as well as one peculiarity of the gear. Then he broke the price to sixty-six dollars, and subsequently to thirty-three. They all went off in a week or so. He bought the plates of a huge edition of the hundred-dollar Century Dictionary, altered the title-page, bound them for himself, and put the article on the market at fifty-one dollars and a half. In six weeks he had sold two thousand. A firm in California, which manufactures an excellent kind of blanket, was in difficulties. Mr. Wanamaker bought up the stock, and sold it at a third of the normal price in three days.

All this is magnificent for the customer, and apparently not unprofitable to Mr. Wanamaker. But plainly somebody has to pay, and who? The small trader. After the rose-tree deal nobody wanted to buy roses of the florists of Philadelphia. The city is stocked with bicycles and Century Dictionaries, and nobody within a radius of miles will want to buy a pair of blankets for a generation. Mr. Wanamaker sends out three hundred and sixty-five thousand parcels to his customers in the slackest month of the year, and turns over thirteen million dollars annually. The small people, it is presumed, are ground to powder against the wall.

Source: George Steevens, *The Land of the Dollar* (New York, 1897), quoted in David Colbert, ed., *Eyewitness to America: 500 Years of America in the Words of Those Who Saw It Happen* (New York: Pantheon Books, 1997), pp. 305–306.

16.4 EMMA LAZARUS, "THE NEW COLOSSUS" (1883)

Emma Lazarus became a prominent writer against anti-Semitism, particularly the Russian empire's pogroms against Jewish people. As an organizer of relief agencies, she was deeply involved in the struggle to keep America's doors open to immigration. Her sonnet, titled "The New Colossus," was inscribed on the pedestal of the Statue of Liberty, which was dedicated in late 1886.

Not like the brazen giant of Greek fame,
With conquering limbs astride from land to land;
Here at our sea-washed, sunset gates shall stand
A mighty woman with a torch, whose flame
Is the imprisoned lightning, and her name
Mother of Exiles. From her beacon-hand
Glows world-wide welcome; her mild eyes command
The air-bridged harbor that twin cities frame.
"Keep, ancient lands, your storied pomp!" cries she
With silent lips. "Give me your tired, your poor,
Your huddled masses yearning to breathe free,
The wretched refuse of your teeming shore.
Send these, the homeless, tempest-tost to me,
I lift my lamp beside the golden door!"

Source: Emma Lazarus, "The New Colossus," quoted in William Benton, publ., *The Annals of America. Volume 11, 1884–1894: Agrarianism and Urbanization* (Chicago: Encyclopedia Britannica, Inc., 1968), p. 107.

16.5 JOSIAH STRONG, EXCERPTS FROM "THE SUPERIORITY OF THE ANGLO-SAXON RACE" (1885)

As the new secretary to the Congregational Home Missionary Society, Josiah Strong began with a revision of the society's manual and ended up publishing a book, combining his notions of social Darwinism and his fears that a white America stood imperiled by what he felt were inferior races: not just African Americans and Chinese immigrants, but the Irish, the Italians, the Slavs, and those of the Jewish faith. Strong's *Our Country* was first published in 1885.

It is not necessary to argue to those for whom I write that the two great needs of mankind, that all men may be lifted up into the light of the highest Christian civilization, are, first, a pure, spiritual Christianity, and second, civil liberty. Without controversy, these are the forces which, in the past, have contributed most to the elevation of the human race, and they must continue to be, in the future, the most efficient ministers to its progress. It follows, then, that the Anglo-Saxon, as the great representative of these two ideas, the despositary of these two greatest blessings, sustains peculiar relations to the world's future, is divinely commissioned to be, in a peculiar sense, his brother's keeper. Add to this the fact of his rapidly increasing strength in modern times, and we have well-nigh a demonstration of his destiny. . . . In one century the United States has increased its territory ten-fold, while the enormous acquisition of foreign territory by Great Britain—and chiefly within the last hundred years—is wholly unparalleled in history. This mighty Anglo-Saxon race, though comprising only one-thirteenth part of mankind, now rules more than one-third of the earth's surface, and more than one-fourth of its people. And if this race, while growing from 6,000,000 to 120,000,000, thus gained possession of a third portion of the earth, is it to be supposed that when it numbers 1,000,000,000, it will lose the disposition, or lack the power to extend its sway? . . .

America is to have the great preponderance of numbers and of wealth, and by the logic of events will follow the scepter of controlling influence. This will be but the consummation of a movement as old as civilization—a result to which men have looked forward for centuries. John Adams records that nothing was "more ancient in his memory than the observation that arts, sciences and empire had traveled westward; and in conversation it was always added that their next leap would be over the Atlantic into America." He recalled a couplet that had been inscribed or rather drilled, into a rock on the shore of Monument Bay in our old colony of Plymouth:

The Eastern nations sink, their glory ends,
And empire rises where the sun descends . . .

. . . Looking at the distant future, I do not think that the Rev. Mr. Zincke takes an exaggerated view when he says: 'All other series of events—as that which resulted in the culture of mind in Greece, and that which resulted in the Empire of Rome—only appear to have purpose and value when viewed in connection with, or rather as subsidiary to, the great stream of Anglo-Saxon emigration to the West.'"

There is abundant reason to believe that the Anglo-Saxon race is to be, is, indeed, already becoming, more effective here than in the mother country. The marked superiority of this race is due, in large measure, to its highly mixed origin. Says Rawlinson: "It is a general rule, now almost universally admitted by ethnologists, that the mixed races of mankind are superior to the pure ones"; and adds: "Even the Jews, who are so often cited as an example of a race at once pure and strong, may, with more reason, be adduced on the opposite side of the argument." The ancient Egyptians, the Greeks, and the Romans, were all mixed races. Among modern races, the most conspicuous example is afforded by the Anglo Saxons. . . . There is here a new commingling of races; and, while the largest injections of foreign blood are substantially the same elements that constituted the original Anglo-Saxon admixture, so that we may infer the general type will be preserved, there are strains of other bloods being added, which, if Mr. Emerson's remark is true, that "the best nations are those most widely related," may be expected to improve the stock, and aid it to a higher destiny. If the dangers of immigration, which have been pointed out, can be successfully met for the next few years, until it has passed its climax, it may be expected to add value to the amalgam which will constitute the new Anglo-Saxon race of the New World. . . .

It may be easily shown, and is of no small significance, that the two great ideas of which the Anglo-Saxon is the exponent are having a fuller development in the United States than in Great Britain. There the union of Church and State tends strongly to paralyze some of the members of the body of Christ. Here there is no such influence to destroy spiritual life and power. Here, also, has been evolved the form of government consistent with the largest possible civil liberty. Furthermore, it is significant that the marked characteristics of this race are being here emphasized most. Among the most striking features of the Anglo-Saxon is his moneymaking power—a power of increasing importance in the widening commerce of the world's future. We have seen . . . that, although England is by far the richest nation of Europe, we have already outstripped her in the race after wealth, and we have only begun the development of our vast resources.

Again, another marked characteristic of the Anglo-Saxon is what may be called an instinct or genius for colonizing. His unequaled energy, his indomitable perseverance, and his personal independence, made him a pioneer. He excels all others in pushing his way into new countries. It was those in whom this tendency was strongest that came to America, and this inherited tendency has been further developed by the westward sweep of successive generations across the continent. So noticeable has this characteristic become that English visitors remark it. Charles Dickens once said that the typical American would hesitate to enter heaven unless assured that he could go farther west.

What is the significance of such facts? These tendencies infold the future; they are the mighty alphabet with which God writes his prophecies. May we not, by a careful laying together of the letters, spell out something of his meaning? It seems to me that God, with infinite wisdom and skill, is training the Anglo-Saxon race for an hour sure to come in the world's future. Heretofore there has always been in the history of the world a comparatively unoccupied land westward, into which the crowded countries of the East have poured their surplus populations. But the widening waves of migration, which millenniums ago rolled east and west from the valley of the Euphrates, meet today on our Pacific coast. There are no more new worlds. The unoccupied arable lands of the earth are limited, and will soon be taken. The time is coming when the pressure of population on the means of subsistence will be felt here as it is now felt in Europe and Asia. Then will the world enter upon a new stage of its history—the *final competition of races, for which the Anglo-Saxon is being schooled.* Long before the thousand millions are here, the mighty *centrifugal* tendency, inherent in this stock and strengthened in the United States, will assert itself. Then this race of unequaled energy, with all the majesty of numbers and the might of wealth behind it—the representative, let us hope, of the largest liberty, the purest Christianity, the highest civilization—having developed peculiarly aggressive traits calculated to impress its institutions upon mankind, will spread itself over the earth. If I read not amiss, this powerful race will move down upon Mexico, down upon Central and South America, out upon the islands of the sea, over upon Africa and beyond. And can any one doubt that the results of this competition of races will be the "survival of the fittest?" "Any people," says Dr. Bushnell, "that is physiologically advanced in culture, though it be only in a degree beyond another which is mingled with it on strictly equal terms, is sure to live down and finally live out its inferior. Nothing can save the inferior race but a ready and pliant assimilation. Whether the feebler and more abject races are going to be regenerated and raised up, is already, very much of a question. What if it should be God's plan to people the world with better and finer material?"

Source: Josiah Strong, "The Superiority of the Anglo-Saxon Race," quoted in William Benton, publ., *The Annals of America. Volume 11, 1884–1894: Agrarianism and Urbanization* (Chicago: Encyclopedia Britannica, Inc., 1968), pp. 72–76.

16.6 JAMES BAIRD WEAVER, *A CALL TO ACTION* (1892)

A Union officer and later an insurgent Iowa Republican, James B. Weaver moved first into the Greenback Party and then joined the Populists. As their presidential candidate in

1892, he issued *A Call to Action*, exposing the gap between the lifestyles of the rich and the conditions of the underprivileged.

If the master builders of our civilization one hundred years ago had been told that at the end of a single century, American society would present such melancholy contrasts of wealth and poverty, of individual happiness and widespread infelicity as are to be found to-day throughout the Republic, the person making the unwelcome prediction would have been looked upon as a misanthropist, and his loyalty to Democratic institutions would have been seriously called in question. Our federal machine, with its delicate inter-lace work of National, State and municipal supervision, each intended to secure perfect individual equality, was expected to captivate the world by its operation and insure domestic contentment and personal security to a degree never before realized by mankind.

But there is a vast difference between the generation which made the heroic struggle for Self-government in colonial days, and the third generation which is now engaged in a mad rush for wealth. The first took its stand upon the inalienable rights of man and made a fight which shook the world. But the leading spirits of the latter are entrenched behind class laws and revel in special privileges. It will require another revolution to overthrow them. That revolution is upon us even now.

Two representative characters—Dives and Lazarus—always make their appearance side by side in disturbing contrast just before the tragic stage of revolution is reached. They were present at the overthrow of ancient civilizations; the hungry multitude stood outside the gates when Belshazzar's impious feast was spread; they were both at the cave of Adullam when the scepter was about to depart from the tyrant Saul to the hands of the youthful David; they stood side by side when Alaric thundered at the gates of Rome; they confronted one another in the fiery tempest of the French revolution and they are sullenly face to face in our own country to-day. . . .

The Banker's Banquet

The following editorial appeared in the *Kansas City Times*, August 30, 1889:

"The contract for serving the banquet for the convention of the American Bankers' Association was yesterday awarded to C.M. Hill, of the Midland Hotel. There were sixty competitors. The price is such as to insure one of the finest banquets ever served in this country. No expense will be spared to make the affair a grand success, even aside from the menu. The banquet will be given in the Priests of Pallas' Temple, at Seventh and Lydia. It will be necessary to build and furnish an annex, where the cooking can be done for 1,500 covers. The preparations seem to take into contemplation a great flow of wine, as there will be six thousand wine glasses and about forty wine servers. There will be in all nearly three hundred waiters. It is estimated that the entire cost of the banquet will be from $15,000 to $20,000. Mr. Hill anticipates some difficulty in securing efficient waiters, and with this particular object in view, will make a trip to New York and Chicago."

This impious feast which took place in the very heart of the mortgage-ridden and debt-cursed West, was the most shocking and brazen exhibition of wanton extravagance and bad morals combined, which the laboring millions of America were ever called upon to behold. What a travesty upon common sense and the ordinary instinct of self-preservation to intrust the finances of a great Nation and the welfare of labor to the hands of such men.

This carousal was but history repeating itself. It is not necessary in our day that an armless hand shall come out of the darkness and write the decree of Heaven upon the wall of the palace while the drunken carousal is being held, as in the time of Belshazzar; nor does it now require an expert Hebrew prophet, like Daniel, to disclose to the King that the sword is about to enter, and that a greater than Darius is thundering at the gates of Babylon, commissioned from on high to restore the stolen treasures of the temple, and to transfer the kingdom to another." . . .

At the Rich Man's Gate

About the time these princely entertainments were given, and in the same year with some of them, one of the metropolitan journals caused a careful canvass to be made of the unemployed of that city. The number was found to be one hundred and fifty thousand persons who were daily unsuccessfully seeking work within the city limits of New York. Another one hundred and fifty thousand earn less than sixty cents per day. Thousands of these are poor girls who work from eleven to sixteen hours per day.

In the year 1890, over twenty-three thousand families, numbering about one hundred thousand people, were forcibly evicted in New York City owing to their inability to pay rent, and one-tenth, of all who died in that city during the year were buried in the Potters Field.

In the *Arena* for June, 1891, will be found a description of tenement house horrors, by Mr. B.O. Flower. He has done a valuable service to humanity by laying before the world the result of his investigations. After describing a family whose head was unable to find work, Mr. Flower says:

"This poor woman supports her husband, her two children and herself, by making pants at twelve cents a pair. No rest, no surcease, a perpetual grind from early dawn, often till far into the night; and what is more appalling, outraged nature has rebelled; the long months of semi-starvation and lack of sleep have brought on rheumatism, which has settled in the joints of her fingers, so that every stitch means a throb of pain. The afternoon we called she was completing an enormous pair of custom-made pants of very fine blue cloth, for one of the largest clothing houses in the city. The suit would probably bring sixty or sixty-five dollars, yet her employer graciously informed his poor white slave that as the garment was so large he would give her an extra cent. Thirteen cents for fine custom-made pants, manufactured for a wealthy firm, which repeatedly asserts that its clothing is not made in tenement houses! Thus with one of the most painful diseases enthroned in that part of the body which must move incessantly from dawn till midnight, with two small dependent children and a husband powerless to help her, this poor woman struggles bravely, confronted ever by a nameless dread of impending misfortune. Eviction, sickness, starvation—such are the ever present spectres, while every year marks the steady encroachment of disease and the lowering of the register of vitality. Moreover, from the window of her soul falls the light of no star athwart the pathway of life.

"In another tenement Mr. Flower found a poor widow with three children, making pants at twelve cents a pair. One of the children had been engaged, since she was two and one-half years old in overcasting the long seams of the garments, made by her mother! In the attic of another tenement a widow was found weeping and working by the side of a cradle where lay a sick child, whose large luminous eyes shone with almost phosphorescent brilliancy from great cavernous sockets, as they wandered from one to another, with a wistful, soul-querying gaze. Its forehead was large and prominent, so much so that looking at the upper part of the head one would little imagine the terrible emaciation of the body, which was little more than skin and hones, and the sight of which spoke more eloquently than words of the ravages of slow starvation and wasting disease. The woman was weeping because she had been notified that if one week's rent was not paid on Saturday she would be evicted, which meant death to her child who was suffering from a rupture, and for whom she was unable to purchase a truss.

"The making at home of clothing, cigars, etc., in New York and Brooklyn is paid at prices on which no women could live were there not other workers in the family. Some of their occupations involved great risks to girls, such as the loss of joints, of fingers, of the hand, or sometimes of the whole arm." . . .

Source: James Baird Weaver, *A Call to Action: An Interpretation of the Great Uprising, Its Sources and Causes* (Des Moines: Iowa Printing Company, 1892), 362–363, 367–370.

The Culture and Politics of Industrial America

1870-1892

< Protestors Outside an Ohio Saloon

AMERICAN PORTRAIT

Luna Kellie and the Farmers' Alliance

As a girl, Luna Kellie dreamed of raising a family on her own farm. Her father, a railroad worker on the Northern Pacific line, did try to make a go of farming in Minnesota but when the farm failed, he moved the family to St. Louis, Missouri. There Luna met and married James T. Kellie. At the age of 18, Luna moved with her husband and their infant to a homestead near Hastings, Nebraska.

Life on the prairie fell far short of her dreams. The Kellies lived in an 8-by-12-foot sod house dug into a hillside. She gave birth to 12 children. Two died. Weakened by the strain of childbirth and constant toil, Luna dreamed of a brighter future, a holiday to Yellowstone's geysers. "Our trip never materialized," she recalled years later, "but we put in some happiest hours of life planning it."

The life of sturdy independence that farmers supposedly enjoyed turned out to be a pinched, isolated existence. Luna tried to connect with friends and neighbors, but there was not much choice. Her family attended a Methodist church until James quarreled with the pastor. Schools were even scarcer than churches, but Luna went out of her way to become active in the school district, where she took part in discussions over whether women should have the right to vote.

Like many rural women, Luna shared the responsibility for managing the farm. She kept a garden, which helped feed the family and brought in extra income from the sale of chickens and eggs. Luna also learned how to tend livestock and grow fruit trees. Her husband tried to grow spring wheat, but between falling prices and high interest rates, their work never freed them from debt. After seven years, the Kellies lost the farm. They struggled to survive by raising chickens, sheep, and livestock.

Like so many prairie farmers just barely scraping by, Luna Kellie turned to the Farmers' Alliance, the largest and most powerful association that coped with agricultural woes. She was not alone: 250,000 women joined the Alliance, making it the largest women's organization in the United States.

For Kellie, the Alliance held out the hope of realizing the dreams of her youth. Its program could break down the isolation of rural life, bringing farmers together in cooperative enterprises while giving them the advantages that the "money power" had taken away. In 1892, when the Nebraska Farmers' Alliance affiliated with the National Farmers' Alliance and Industrial Union, Kellie was elected state secretary. She worked as tirelessly on Alliance business as she had on her own farm, writing countless letters. She edited and set the type for articles for the Alliance newspaper.

Without setting foot outside her home, Luna Kellie found herself at the center of a vast network of farmers who learned from each other by discussing key issues. Starting in efforts to improve rural Americans' lives, the movement quickly advanced into broader questions of political reform. By 1892, the Farmers' Alliance had fostered the most important political insurgency of the late nineteenth century, the Populist Party.

The Elusive Boundaries of Male and Female

Luna Kellie's involvement in politics was a sign that the old assumptions about a "woman's place" in society were shifting, along with notions of how to preserve the independence, opportunity, and equal voice that the republic once had promised to ordinary people. In fact, the political economy of industrial capitalism and the triumph of wage labor helped men and women rethink traditional concepts of masculinity and femininity. As they did so, new cities and newfound leisure time offered unprecedented opportunities to test the conventional boundaries of sexual identity.

The Victorian Construction of Male and Female

Until the mid-1700s, most European doctors believed that there was only one sex: females were simply inferior, insufficiently developed males. Sometime after 1750, however, scientists and intellectuals began to argue that males and females were fundamentally different, that they were "opposite" sexes. For the first time it was possible to argue that women were naturally less interested in sex than men or that men were "active" whereas women were "passive." Nature itself seemed to justify the infamous double standard that condoned sexual activity by men but punished it in women.

Nineteenth-century society drew even more extreme differences between men and women. Taking its name from the long reign of Britain's Queen Victoria, the Victorian era is often stereotyped as an age of sexual repression and cultural conservatism, and it was, up to a point. Boys reading moralistic stories of heroes who overcame their fears prepared for the competitive worlds of business and politics, both largely male preserves. To be a "man" in industrial America was to work in the rough-and-tumble world of the capitalist market. Men proved themselves by their success at making a living and thereby at taking care of a wife and children.

Victorian men defined themselves as rational creatures threatened by insistent sexual drives. Physical exertion was an important device for controlling a man's powerful sexual urges, just as masturbation was deemed an unacceptable outlet for these drives. Men were urged to channel their sexual energies into strenuous activities such as sports and, conveniently enough, wage labor.

Where masculinity became a more rigid concept, femininity became less certain. Women's schools established their own sports programs. Affluent women took up bicycling, tennis, swimming, and croquet. Yet the stereotype persisted that women were too frail for the hurly-burly of business and enterprise. Lacking the competitive instinct of the male, the female was best fitted to become a wife and mother within the protective confines of the home. Just as men joined social clubs and sports teams, a "female world of love and ritual" developed. Middle-class women often displayed among themselves a passionate affection that was often expressed in nearly erotic terms. But genuinely passionate female sexuality disturbed the Victorians. Evidence of sexual passion among women was increasingly diagnosed, mostly by male doctors, as a symptom of a new disorder called "neurasthenia."

Over time, the differences between men and women were defined in increasingly medical terms. Victorian doctors redefined homosexuality as a medical abnormality, a perversion, and urged the passage of laws outlawing homosexual relations. The new science of gynecology powerfully reinforced popular assumptions about gender differences.

Leading male physicians argued that the energy women expended in reproduction left them unable to withstand the rigors of higher education. In extreme cases, physicians would excise a woman's clitoris to thwart masturbation or remove her ovaries to cure neurasthenia.

On the assumption that motherhood was a female's natural destiny, doctors pressed to restrict women's access to contraception and to prohibit abortion. Before the Civil War, many Americans tolerated abortion in the first three months of pregnancy, though they did not necessarily approve of it. This began to change as the medical profession laid claim to the regulation of female reproduction. The American Medical Association (AMA, founded in 1847) campaigned to suppress abortionists and criminalize abortion. The AMA also supported passage of the Comstock Law, which in addition to being the first federal law to ban the production, distribution, and public display of obscenity, outlawed the sale of contraceptive devices. "Our Heavenly Father never sends more mouths than He can feed," one doctor explained. To hear an advocate of the law tell it, the only naysayers were "long-haired men and short-haired women"—the unmanly and unfeminine.

To bolster traditional marriage, states passed laws raising the age of consent, forbidding common-law and interracial marriage, punishing polygamists, and tightening restrictions on divorce. Only in the West did authorities allow incompatibility grounds for ending a marriage. Many places set up family courts to handle desertion and juvenile delinquency. Congress passed several antipolygamy laws to protect Mormon wives and, as a fringe benefit, to take the vote away from a religious group known to lean Democratic.

The Victorian Crusade for Morality

In the Victorian era, reformers saw the city as a place where traditional morality broke down, particularly standards of sexual propriety. With corrupt police lackadaisical about enforcing morality, reformers established private organizations to smite smut with prosecutions and citizens' arrests. Moral crusader Anthony Comstock's New York Society for the Suppression of Vice (SSV) inspired many others. It deputized itself to enforce laws "for the suppression of the trade in, and circulation of, obscene literature and illustrations, advertisements, and articles of indecent or immoral use." Comstock's chief concern was the protection of children. In his book *Traps for the Young* (1883), he warned that obscenity was luring American youngsters into deviant ways by stoking youthful wants and passions until they had "a well-nigh irresistible mastery over their victim." As head of the society, Comstock acted as a special post office agent. "You must hunt these men as you hunt rats," Comstock declared, "without mercy." In many cases, that meant without respecting the rights of due process. Reformers entrapped perpetrators by enticing and then arresting them. Comstock caught America's most notorious abortionist that way. He felt no remorse when she cut her throat rather than go to trial.

Such efforts, however, could not reverse the underlying trends. Illegal contraceptive devices were widely known and used. In major cities, abortionists charged $10 for their services. As for the divorce rate, it increased 15 times over. By 1915, the United States had the highest divorce rate in the world, affecting one marriage in seven. In a new economy based on wage labor, single young men found the city ideal for cutting

Anthony Comstock Crediting himself with 4,000 arrests and destroying 400,000 pictures, New York's most notorious vice crusader showed how governments could take action, in the so-called era of laissez-faire, against views that middle-class moralists found objectionable. This 1906 illustration shows Comstock as a monk thwarting shameless displays of flesh, whether that of women, horses, or dogs.

loose at comparatively little risk. Workers had more leisure and white-collar employees more still. Those looking for prostitutes found them readily available (see Map 17–1). In many towns, they had their own neighborhood, the "red-light district," and sometimes the "sporting trade" published guidebooks detailing different houses' specialties. The relative anonymity of urban life and the cash value set on everything made sin pay better than ever before and perpetrators less fearful of being shamed for it. With prostitutes renting their bodies for as little as 50 cents a trick and with saloon keepers doubling as brothel keepers (or tripling as aldermen), the SSV might win battles, but never the war.

Urban Culture

Cities reflected the diversity and vitality of a changing America, far from the rhythms of Luna Kellie's world and the cherished ideal of the self-sufficient farmer. Urban centers crystallized Americans' larger ambivalence about the social changes of the era. Boasting of how up-to-date their country was, Americans longed for a reassuring past. Tenement kids cheered Buffalo Bill Cody's romanticized re-creations of the plains wars and loved the chance to see Sitting Bull himself. (Sitting Bull liked "Buffalo Bill" more than he liked white civilization. He puzzled at how a society so rich could leave homeless children begging in the streets.) Yankees paid good money for tickets to minstrel shows about happy plantation life down South, and everybody read Joel Chandler Harris's "Uncle Remus" stories, recasting African folk tales with a kindly old slave as their narrator.

At the same time, city culture took on a life all its own. From the 1880s on, it meant bright lights: electricity, in place of dimmer gaslight, and a vigorous "night life." Electric trolleys and

Map 17-1 Houses of Prostitution, 1850–1859 and 1900–1909 One measure of the sexual freedom characteristic of city life was the explosive increase in prostitution. As the demand for prostitution rose, so did attempts to suppress it.
Source: Timothy J. *Gilfoyle, City of Eros* (New York: W. W. Norton, 1992), p. 33.

suburban rail networks drew tens of thousands downtown (see Figure 17–1), to department stores, firms, and factories by day and to theaters, music halls, and concert saloons by night.

One did not have to venture far in the biggest cities to find shows flouting Victorian standards of propriety by using sexual titillation to entertain audiences. Can-can girls, off-color jokes, and comedy skits focusing on the war of the sexes played well in working-class districts. Even among the "respectable classes," both men's and women's clothing became simpler, looser, and more comfortable. Within limits, popular culture idealized the sensuous human body, while for the first time male sports heroes were openly admired for their physiques. Police cracked down on homosexual conduct more severely than before, but the old rules still applied: private and consensual behavior involved relatively little risk.

While reformers like Comstock saw the cities' vice and corruption, linking both to immigrant slums, some of America's best artists created art that reflected the gritty truths of everyday life and celebrated the cities' vitality. If Comstock's admirers defined "culture" as limited to only the great works in the Western European tradition (even suppressing some, such as those by Voltaire, Walt Whitman, Aristophanes, and Ovid), city dwellers embraced a wider array of influences. Out of "Storyville," the red-light district in New Orleans, came the beginnings of jazz; out of the honky-tonks came the first great composers

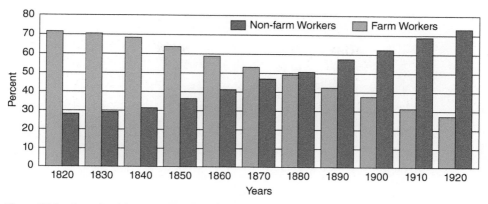

Figure 17-1   Growth of the Nonfarm Sector Underpinning the rise of urban culture was the emergence of a wage-earning labor force. Concentrated in cities, wage earners had cash at their disposal to spend on the amusements cities had to offer.

of ragtime. And a canny publicity agent knew how to sell a faintly risqué painting, *September Morn*: he got Comstock to arrest the gallery owner for indecency. Firms running off copies of it could not keep up with the demand.

A New Cultural Order: New Americans Stir Old Fears

When novelist Henry James returned to the United States in 1907 after a quarter of a century in Europe, he was appalled by the pervasive presence of immigrants in New York City. On the streetcars, he confronted "a row of faces, up and down, testifying, without exception, to alienism unmistakable, alienism undisguised and unashamed." James was one of the many native-born Americans who assumed that their culture was Protestant, democratic, and English speaking. They saw a threat in vast numbers of immigrants who were none of those things and in the roots that ethnic subcultures were setting down in the cities. Yet among immigrants and their children, an ethnic identity was often traded for a broader assimilation into American culture.

Josiah Strong Attacks Immigration

"Every race which has deeply impressed itself on the human family has been the representative of some great idea," clergyman Josiah Strong wrote in *Our Country*. Greek civilization was famed for its beauty, he explained; the Romans for their law; and the Hebrews for their purity. The Anglo-Saxons claimed two great ideas: the love of liberty and "pure spiritual Christianity." Strong was optimistic that as representatives of "the largest liberty, the purest Christianity, the highest civilization," the Anglo-Saxon race would "spread itself over the earth." Published in 1885, Strong's best-selling book went through many editions and was serialized in newspapers across America. Like him, many native-born Americans saw themselves as the defenders of Anglo-Saxon culture.

But there was a problem. Strong and his followers saw the arrival of millions of immigrants as a challenge to Anglo-Saxon America. By 1900, more than 10 million Americans

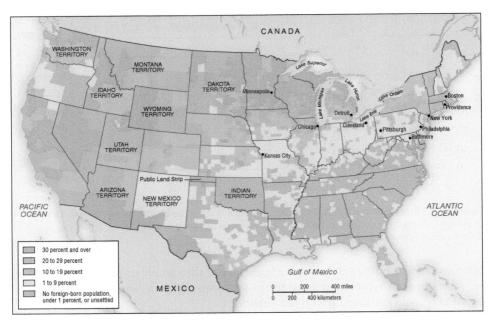

Map 17-2   Population of Foreign Birth by Region, 1880
Source: Clifford L. Lord and Elizabeth H. Lord, *Historical Atlas of the United States* (New York: Holt, 1953).

were foreign born. The typical immigrant, he warned, was not a freedom-loving Anglo-Saxon Protestant but a narrow-minded "European peasant" whose "moral and religious training has been meager or false." Immigrants brought crime to America's cities and, voting in blocs, undermined the nation's politics. "[T]here is no more serious menace to our civilization," Strong warned, "than our rabble-ruled cities."

For Strong, the problem was that immigrants were coming in such huge numbers that assimilation was becoming impossible (see Map 17–2). Worst of all—in Strong's view—the Catholic Church held millions of immigrants in its grip, filling their heads with superstition rather than "pure Christianity." Through its parochial schools, the Catholic Church was training new generations to love tyranny rather than liberty.

Strong and his readers need not have worried (and to be fair, Strong himself saw the real solution in what came to be called the Social Gospel, the active involvement of Protestants in helping those less well off than themselves). Indeed, they misread their own evidence. By cultivating the German vote or the Irish vote, for example, politicians brought immigrants into American culture. Nor were immigrants as slavishly subservient to the Catholic Church as Strong thought.

From Immigrants to Ethnic Americans

In the middle of the nineteenth century, most immigrants came with loyalties to their regions and villages, not to a nationality. German-speaking immigrants thought of themselves primarily as Bavarian or Prussian rather than German, just as Rosa Cassettari thought of herself as Tuscanese and did not count Sicilians as Italians at all. For many Slavs, identification went no further than the parish whose church bells they heard on Sunday morning.

Regional differences faded, an ocean away from home, but they would have done so anyhow. Nationalism as a self-identifying concept was spreading throughout the Western world. It was reflected in a unifying Italy, a consolidated German Reich, the czar's "Russification" program that laid the whip on Jewish backs and made Russian, not French, the language of the St. Petersburg elite. The patriotic fervor that the Civil War unleashed in the United States, liberal revolutions did in Paris and Berlin. Immigrants brought an increasingly robust sense of their ethnic identities with them. At the same time, in the United States secular fraternal organizations and mutual aid societies, designed to help newcomers find jobs and housing, forged wider ethnic identities. In 1893, mine workers formed the Pennsylvania Slovak Catholic Union to help cover burial expenses for those killed in the mines. Most often, however, middle-class immigrants or local priests took the lead in forming fraternal organizations, which eventually counted about half of all immigrants as members.

Some immigrant businessmen led the drive toward larger ethnic definitions. Because regional loyalties among his workers hindered efficiency, Marco Fontana, who ran the Del Monte Company in California, encouraged the growth of an "Italian" identity.

The Catholic Church and Its Limits in Immigrant Culture

The Roman Catholic Church played a complicated role in the development of ethnic immigrant cultures. Many ethnic communities collected donations to build churches to preserve their Old World traditions. But the church also eased the transition into American life. Polish churches in Chicago and German parishes in Milwaukee used their women's groups and youth clubs as mutual aid societies for newcomers.

The church sometimes unintentionally sped the development of ethnic identities. The Irish became more devout in America as they came to rely on the church for help resisting an overwhelmingly Protestant culture. Through the church, Germans also overcame their regional differences. But the more they came to equate their German identity with Catholicism, the more they resented Irish domination of the church hierarchy. German Catholics worked to establish their own churches, with sermons preached in German. By contrast, the Italians distrusted and distanced themselves from the official church. Ethnic diversity made it all the more important for Catholic leaders to find some middle ground. Bishops across North America worked on standardizing Catholic rituals and ceremonies into a uniquely American blend. They published uniform catechisms, established powerful bureaucracies, and discouraged the folk rituals that Italians, Irish, and Slavs had carried with them.

Unlike in Europe, the church had to struggle just to share in the education of immigrant children; controlling it lay wholly beyond their power. Public schools were heavily Protestant. Shifting the focus away from the classics and toward "practical" education and language training, reformers hoped to shape reliable workers and patriotic citizens. But immigrants balked at "Americanization" efforts beyond providing them with skills they could use to get ahead, and the bulwark of their resistance was the church.

During the second half of the nineteenth century, both the Catholic and Lutheran Churches established parochial school systems to give immigrant children an alternative to the biases of public education. In most states and cities, tax revenues went for public schools only, and Germans set up their own parish schools. Even so, parochial education did its part toward eventual assimilation to the New World. Schools in Irish Catholic or German Lutheran parishes fostered distinctly American ethnic identities, as well as a Catholicism and Lutheranism that diverged from Old World norms.

Immigrant Cultures

Newcomers adjusted to American culture on their own terms. Some changed their names to English equivalents: Piccolo became Little, Wahlgren became Green, and Schmidt became Smith. Even those who did not set out to assimilate found that the longer they stayed, the more their customs diverged from those of the Old World. Irish Americans fused together songs from various parts of Ireland and added piano accompaniment. Polish immigrant bands expanded beyond the traditional violin by adding accordions, clarinets, and trumpets. Hundreds of immigrant theaters offered productions that adjusted traditional plot lines to the New World. Jewish plays told of humble peddlers who outwitted their prosperous patrons. Italian folktales celebrated the importance of the family. In these ways, distinctive ethnic identities adapted to urban and industrial America.

At a time when middle-class families had only two or three children, immigrant families remained large. At the turn of the century, Italian mothers in Buffalo, New York, had an average of 11 children. Among Polish wives, the average was closer to 8. In Pennsylvania's coal-mining district, working-class immigrant women had 45 percent more children than native-born women. They had sound economic reasons: families often needed

Immigrants Immigrants often crowded into "tenements," a new form of apartment building that actually improved living conditions for many of America's poor city dwellers.

children's income to get by. However, the death rate among immigrant children was also high. In 1900, one out of three Polish and Italian mothers had seen one of their children die before his or her first birthday.

The Enemy at the Gates

Culture was contested ground, as much a part of urbanization as class conflict and political upheaval. Rural Americans were drawn by urban culture's freedom but troubled by its licentiousness. Native-born Protestants, often truly concerned with helping immigrants, were also suspicious of immigrant folkways. Victorian moralists assailed the collapse of traditional gender distinctions. All these struggles reflected the efforts of Americans to cope with dramatic social transformations. There were no clear winners—unless diversity and a wide array of choices made everyone a winner.

Big-city life stirred images of an alarming diversity: "Chinatowns" in San Francisco and Los Angeles, Polish athletics clubs and German *schutzenvereine* (shooting clubs), pushcart peddlers haggling in Yiddish, Irish Americans demanding that New York's City Hall fly the Irish flag on St. Patrick's Day, Catholics expecting a day off from school on Good Friday. Native-born Protestants fretted that "E Pluribus Unum" might no longer apply: How could we become one, out of so many?

Political opposition to immigration, known as nativism, had enjoyed a brief success in the 1850s. Even foreign-born workers resented low-paid Chinese labor, and in 1882, Congress passed the first Chinese exclusion act. Not the least of the Tammany Hall political machine's sins, in New York reformers' eyes, was how Irish it was, and how public funds endowed Catholic schools there. Especially in the Midwest, anti-Catholicism drew on Protestant nightmares of the Inquisition and beliefs that the church's leaders combined

As the Number of Immigrants to America Swelled, So Did Opposition to Them This 1891 cartoon blames immigration for causing a host of social and political evils.

religious intolerance with a hatred of free government. In the 1890s, the American Protective Association (APA) threw its weight behind candidates favoring Protestant interests.

As immigration increased, nativist rhetoric grew more racist and drew on the dubious sociology of Social Darwinism (see Chapter 16). The threat was no longer merely from radicals and Catholics but also from darker-skinned peoples from Italy, Russia, and eastern Europe. Experts proclaimed the inherent intellectual inferiority of such peoples, giving the imprimatur of science to the most vicious stereotypes. Italians were said to be genetically predisposed to organized violence, Jews to thievery and manipulation. Anti-immigrant societies appeared across America. Mob violence sacked Chinese neighborhoods in Los Angeles in 1871, and 11 Italians were lynched by a New Orleans mob, on charges of having murdered the police chief.

But Protestant cultural politics failed to shut out immigration from southern and eastern Europe; the United States would not even require immigrants to pass a literacy test until 1917. The APA died quickly when politicians recognized that they did better by appealing to immigrant voters. They passed resolutions favoring Irish "home rule" (rather than English occupation), denounced the Russian czar's persecution of Jews, and made Columbus Day a holiday. The real cultural fights came at the state level over issues like outlawing boxing, charging prohibitively high licenses on working-class saloons, making Jewish stores close on the Protestant Sabbath, requiring Protestant Bible reading in public schools, and forcing parochial schools to use Protestant state-mandated textbooks.

Two Political Styles

In a multicultural America, politics did more to assimilate newcomers than to make them feel unwelcome. With only two major parties vying for power, neither could afford to alienate all immigrant groups; however, some Republicans scapegoated the Catholic and Irish ones. Each organization welcomed the foreign-born into its ranks and adjusted its policies at the state and local level to keep their loyalty.

Politics came in two flavors in the Gilded Age: the male-dominated partisanship of voters, political operatives, and officeholders; and the voluntarism of those who put cause above party, from reform societies and women's organizations to labor unions and farmers' groups. The politicians had every advantage on their side. Because the "spoils system" let them appoint every official down to janitor when they took power, they could extort a share of government employees' wages to fund a campaign. They chose the candidates and counted the returns. In close elections, they had "soap" (payoffs to voters) to buy a winning margin. Most of the newspapers framed the news in one party's way. Political organizations became more sophisticated and much more centralized. In this age, people began to speak of "bosses" and "political machines" in which, supposedly, the leader rallied his party followers like an army to carry every election and fill every office: the Democratic hordes in New York City that the Tammany Hall machine mobilized, for example. But time and again, politicians—even Tammany's—found themselves forced to accommodate outside pressures, and by the 1890s, those pressures had remade the very basis of the political game.

The Triumph of Party Politics

Ever since Lincoln's day, most Americans had voted the straight party line every time. Political parties printed and passed out their own ballots for loyalists to drop in the right box. Nobody needed to be literate to make his choice (no state gave women the vote until Wyoming's admission in 1890). Partisans could remove candidates' names from these ballots, and organizers often bribed voters. Intimidation also played a role. In much of the South, passing out Republican ballots was nearly as fatal as yellow fever. "Resurrectionists" voted in dead men's names, "colonizers" crossed state lines to vote in crucial elections, and political agents might even march their purchased public to vote in "blocks of five," as one Indiana Republican advised in 1888. But most voters cast honest ballots and cared so strongly that if they could have voted a dozen times they would have—as, in big cities, some did!

From the 1840s through the 1860s, an average of 69 percent of those eligible voted in presidential elections. During the final quarter of the century, the average rose to 77 percent (see Figure 17–2). Southern figures lagged slightly: between 1876 and 1892, nearly two out of three southern men voted in presidential elections, compared with 82 percent of northern ones. The gap would widen as Democrats perfected the tools for keeping African Americans from casting a ballot or southern Republicans from having the least hope of a free vote and a fair count.

Newspapers played a critical role in maintaining this level of political participation. Much of the press acted as cheerleaders and opinion makers. Most papers survived with the help of party and government advertisements as well as contracts to print ballots and campaign documents. Papers slanted stories their party's way, and proudly. "Republican in everything, independent in nothing," the *Chicago Inter Ocean* boasted.

Campaign hoopla offered voters unrivaled spectacle. Political clubs and military companies paraded. Marchers rang bells, flew banners, and escorted floats with pretty girls representing Liberty, Columbia, or the various states. A good mass meeting combined barbecue, rousing oratory, band music, and fireworks. Together, they made politics America's most popular participatory sport.

Figure 17-2   Percent of Eligible Voters Casting Ballots Between 1840 and 1896, a huge proportion—often 80 percent—of those eligible to vote did so in presidential elections. In the twentieth century, turnout dropped substantially.

However, politics was more than sport. Civil War veterans were reminded, "Vote as you shot!" Roused by the Union veterans' organization, the Grand Army of the Republic, and speeches that used the memory of the war to inflame sectional grievances, Union veterans typically backed the Republican Party. Black Americans also usually supported the party that had ended slavery. Confederates mostly voted Democratic. Democrats spoke for states' rights, small government, and white supremacy. In their eyes, Republicanism meant state and local laws telling people what to drink and how to use their Sundays. As Democrats saw it, "the party of moral ideas" protected the national banker, the railroad tycoon, and the upstart Negro. To Republicans, Democrats were the party of "rum, Romanism, and rebellion," of Catholics, saloon keepers, violence, and vice. They themselves spoke for the northern middle class, especially the better-educated ones. Government, local and national, had a duty to make Americans better off. As the Republicans told it, their party's symbol was the schoolhouse while the Democrats' was the whipping post of slavery. And each side knew that the republic's fate depended on its winning.

Masculine Partisanship and Feminine Voluntarism

The public sphere of campaigns and voting was a man's world; the private sphere of home and family was widely celebrated as a woman's. In practice, though, women shared in popular politics. They decorated the meeting halls, prepared the food, watched and sometimes joined the parades. By the end of the 1880s, both parties pitched part of their appeals to wives and families. Nevertheless, politically active women opted for a different style of politics.

A stereotype that had previously limited female political activity now gave women their chance to enter public debate. Seen as the special protectors of the family's values, women found that their views on marriage, morality, and the need to protect America's children would get a respectful hearing from lawmakers. Women's supposed superior virtue gave them a privileged position in moral reform movements. These included anti-alcohol temperance societies and campaigns for laws to keep the Christian Sabbath holy—by keeping barbershops, museums, and baseball parks closed on Sunday. To protect the private sphere, many women claimed the right to enter the public one.

Women could pursue politics only as representatives of voluntary associations dedicated to specific reforms. Voluntarism mostly recruited members from the educated middle class, who brought their class biases with them.

Sometimes women's associations copied the style of partisan politics, staging mass marches and rallies. But the marching, chanting, military flavor of mass politics did not sit well with society's image of women's traditional role. So activists were likely to concentrate less on rousing voters than on educating them and lobbying elected officials. Men also joined voluntary associations, but they were dismissed by mainstream politicians as "namby-pamby, goody-goody gentlemen." In the late nineteenth century, voluntarism was associated with feminine politics, and party politics was associated with masculinity.

The Women's Christian Temperance Union

Still, voluntarism could do wonders, and over time, the boundaries of the women's sphere became increasingly unclear. One of the most prominent female-backed political movements, the Women's Christian Temperance Union (WCTU), emerged in 1874 to battle the ravages of alcohol. Led by Frances Willard from 1879 until her death in 1898, the WCTU built itself on women's calling as protectors of the home. A decentralized structure allowed groups to tailor their activities to local needs. Women found in the WCTU a source of camaraderie as well as political activism. They made it among the largest women's political organizations in the late nineteenth century, with 150,000 adult members. (The National American Woman Suffrage Association had only 13,000.) The WCTU convened huge rallies with none of the masculine rowdiness of party conventions. Willard and her associates gave speeches, wrote articles, published books and newspaper columns on the evils of drink, organized petition campaigns, and lobbied officeholders.

Under Willard, the crusade against alcohol broadened to tackle the problems of a new industrial society. The WCTU endorsed women's suffrage and formed an alliance with the country's largest labor union. Willard supported laws restricting the workday to eight hours and prohibiting child labor. By the 1890s Willard was treating drunkenness as a public health issue rather than a personal sin, a social problem rather than an individual failure. Temperance advocates supported reforms designed to relieve poverty, improve public health, raise literacy, alleviate the conditions of workers, reform prisons, suppress public immorality, and preserve peace.

In the cities, especially up north, temperance remained a middle-class reform movement, with little appeal in immigrant neighborhoods. The WCTU's strongly evangelical Protestant identity and its association of saloons with aliens and Catholics spoke louder than its official policy of religious toleration. Irish Catholics and German Lutherans resented a campaign aimed to replace altar wine with grape juice in Christian services.

The Critics of Popular Politics

The mix of partisanship and voluntarism made American politics more "popular" than ever before, attracting women and men, blacks and whites, immigrants and the native born, working class and middle class. But some Americans saw behind the spectacle to the games professional politicians played. After the Civil War, a small but influential group known as Liberals (and later as Mugwumps) challenged the party-run state. Alarmed at its selfishness, corruption, and incompetence, they called for government by professionals and independent agencies. Though some agreed with Charles Francis Adams that "[u]niversal suffrage can only mean in plain English the government of ignorance and vice," most believed that with a cleaner politics and "campaigns of education," the people would see where their true interests lay. A merit system must reward ability in the public service; a government-issued official (Australian) ballot distributed only at polling places must give every voter the chance to choose, in privacy, among all the possibilities. Tasks like setting a fair railroad rate or tariff duty, running a park system, or policing a great city should no longer be left to vote-getters. Education and expertise, not political pull, must drive policy.

Thanks to Liberals, the nonpartisan secret ballot was adopted everywhere. In 1881, supporters of good government organized the National Civil Service Reform League to prevent political parties from filling government positions. Victory came two years later with the establishment of a Civil Service Commission that would assign federal jobs on the basis of merit rather than patronage. Some states followed suit. But regarding the problems of rapid industrialization, Liberals' solutions fell short.

Most Americans approached their politics looking backward to the issues of the Civil War and Reconstruction. Every president but one between 1869 and 1901 had

STRUGGLES FOR DEMOCRACY

The "Crusade" Against Alcohol

Just before Christmas in 1873, Dr. Diocletian Lewis arrived in Hillsboro, Ohio, to speak on the evils of alcohol. He had given the speech many times before, but this time the women who came proved unusually responsive. The next morning a group of Hillsboro women met for prayer and then marched through the town urging local merchants to stop selling liquor. Inspired by their success, the women kept up the pressure through the winter of 1873–1874. Neither jail nor a rain of curses, eggs, and sour beer could dampen their spirits.

The Crusade, as it came to be called, spread quickly into 31 states and territories. Druggists and hotel keepers promised to quit selling alcohol. Nearly 70 breweries closed. The women's fervor inspired crusaders to establish a permanent organization, the WCTU. In years to come, like-minded reformers set up "temperance saloons" that served ice cream or coffee. They opened YMCA chapters with reading rooms and employment agencies to co-opt services that bars had provided. Sunday schools recruited children to break from their parents' habits and to parade, chanting, "Tremble, King Alcohol! We shall grow up!"

But Americans' drinking habits hardly changed at all. Saloons throve. People went there not just to drink but to find companionship and release. Italians went there to read newspapers in their own language. Workers went there to find jobs listings, and foremen to do hiring. Bartenders knew everybody, which was one reason that saloons were tied closely to party machines. The fastest way to empty a Chicago council meeting, residents joked, was to shout, "Your saloon's on fire!"

In the end, lasting change took political action, first by creating local or statewide majorities for prohibiting alcohol, and then by forcing the minority to give way. So across the West, states and territories

served in the Civil War (and the one exception, Grover Cleveland, sent a substitute). But many Americans also came to feel deep concerns about a society becoming more diverse, urban, and industrial. Such issues would dominate public life by the close of the century.

Economic Issues Dominate National Politics

By the late nineteenth century, Americans were used to the idea that government should oversee the distribution of the nation's natural resources. After the Civil War, federal officials distributed public lands to homesteaders and railroads and granted rights to mining, ranching, and timber companies. During those same decades, the rise of big business led many Americans to believe that the government should regulate the outlawed the sale of alcohol, with the "dry" countryside imposing its will on the "wet" cities. Because women took leading roles in the cause, prohibitionists became the foremost advocates of woman suffrage.

For good reason, Frances Willard was the first woman honored with a statue in the US Capitol; for good reason, saloon keepers fought for a males-only suffrage to the last.

Protestors Outside an Ohio Saloon The WCTU's fight against alcohol could never have succeeded without the active support of many men. They felt as deep a concern at the moral and social consequences of too much tippling.

currency. Many others saw salvation in trade barriers to protect American commerce and workers from ruinous foreign competition. Because the two major parties commanded nearly even support at the national level, the outcome was that no issue could be finally settled. Shaped by clusters of special interests until they covered over 4,000 items, tariffs rose, fell, and rose again. Congresses tinkered with the currency, even while gold continued to hold a privileged place as backing for paper money. The bolder a policy initiative, the likelier it was to founder.

Greenbacks and Greenbackers

The money question demonstrated the inability of Gilded Age politicians to act decisively on major issues. To support the Union effort during the Civil War, the US government printed $450 million worth of "greenbacks," paper bills backed by the government's word but not by the traditional reserves of specie, meaning gold or silver. When the war ended, most Americans agreed that the greenbacks should be withdrawn from circulation until any paper dollar could be exchanged for a dollar in specie at the bank. But with the onset of the 1870s, wage cuts and tight money led to a debate. Resumptionists, those who wanted to return to the gold standard, found themselves battling debtors and industrialists who thought that a shrinking money supply would worsen the economy. Greenbackers went further. They called for issuing even more greenbacks, without any requirement that precious metals back the notes up. In the middle were many Republicans and Democrats who favored inflation, but by backing dollars in silver as well as gold. The currency had been backed in this way before Congress legislated silver out of its privileged place with the "Crime of 1873," as the Coinage Act of 1873 came to be called. Later reformers blamed a bankers' plot for the change: gold, in shorter supply, meant a smaller money supply, big enough for eastern needs and small enough to make every dollar more valuable. A dollar that could buy three times as much forced a farmer to work three times as hard to pay off debts contracted before the "Crime of '73." Holders of mortgages and bonds, agrarians shouted, had legislated themselves a bonanza.

To gold's defenders, any shift to silver or paper meant national dishonor. "Honest money," they cried, was morality itself. A flood of silver into Treasury vaults meant a flood of paper, with wild speculation, inflation out of control, and debts paid off in such depreciated currency that creditors would face ruinous losses. The Greenback-Labor Party peaked in 1878, when it garnered over a million votes and elected 14 congressmen. However, as economic skies brightened, its appeal dwindled. In 1879, resumption took place, with the $300 million in circulating greenbacks made convertible into gold. Support for silver did not die away, and every time the economy contracted, calls for limited silver coinage rose across the West and South. Farmers there found loans hardest to get, except at interest rates that (to their thinking) verged on extortion. Until times improved all over, neither side could win a final victory. They could take only half steps in one direction or the other.

Weak Presidents Oversee a Stronger Federal Government

Starting in the mid-1870s, the Democrats and Republicans had nearly equal electoral strength (see Table 17–1). From 1876 through 1896, no president took office with an overwhelming electoral mandate. The results of the 1880 election were typical of the era. Republican James A. Garfield won by a tiny margin. He received 48.5 percent of the votes, and Democrat Winfield Scott Hancock received 48.1 percent. Grover Cleveland won a plurality in 1888, but he lost the Electoral College. In both cases, the losers accused vote-buying Republicans of making the difference. But Republicans could reply that in the South, Republican votes never received a fair count. No president enjoyed a full term during which his own party controlled both houses of Congress. Reelected in 1872, Grant was the last president in the century to serve two consecutive terms.

In some cases, a president took office already discredited by the electoral process, as did Rutherford B. Hayes in 1877 (see Chapter 15). Furious that their presidential candidate, Samuel J. Tilden, had been "counted out" by three southern states juggling the returns to make Hayes the winner, Democrats threatened "His Fraudulency" with impeachment. Hayes's fellow Republicans protested his overtures to win over southern conservatives at the expense of protection for black voters, and guests resented his ban on liquor at state

Table 17-1 Razor-Thin Electoral Margins in the Gilded Age

Year	Popular Vote	% of Popular Vote	Electoral Vote
1876	4,036,572	48.0	185
	4,284,020	51.0	184
1880	4,453,295	48.5	214
	4,414,082	48.1	155
	308,578	3.4	–
1884	4,879,507	48.5	219
	4,850,293	48.2	182
1888	5,477,129	47.9	233
	5,537,857	48.6	168

dinners. The party bosses raged at his steps toward a professional civil service. Hayes forbade his party to exact tribute from Republican officeholders. He fought Roscoe Conkling, New York's ruthless Republican boss, for control of the New York Customs House—the most lucrative source of patronage in America. When the English writer Samuel Johnson defined patriotism as the last refuge of a scoundrel, Conkling snarled, he little anticipated the possibilities of the word "reform." With cabinet officers controlling civil service appointments, improvements were patchier than Hayes would have liked, and civil service reformers were crestfallen.

By sending federal troops to suppress the 1877 railroad strike (see Chapter 16), Hayes set an important precedent for federal intervention in industrial disputes. He vetoed the Chinese immigration exclusion legislation passed by Congress in 1879. Troubled as he was by widespread suffering, Hayes had no cure for the economic slump of the 1870s. To protect the public credit, he opposed any steps to end the deflation of currency that had forced wages and prices down so sharply and brought ruin to farmers and industrial workers. In 1878, he vetoed the Bland-Allison Act, hailed as a way to modestly inflate the currency by coining silver in amounts tied to the amount of gold being minted. (It passed anyway, with little effect on the money supply.) Though prosperity returned soon after, Republicans felt as much relief to see his term end as he did. They did not protest his decision not to stand for reelection.

Economic, rather than racial, issues dominated the 1880 campaign, although Democratic state governments were rolling back the gains blacks had made during Reconstruction. Both parties relied on the patronage system too much to press civil service reform. Democrats favored lower tariffs than the Republicans, though both parties had strong protectionist blocs (supporting high tariffs to protect American producers) as well as members who favored lower tariff rates. Neither party wanted free trade; the government needed the revenue from tariff duties. So Garfield's victory in 1880 did not foreshadow any major shifts in government policy. It took a national tragedy to bring that about.

On July 2, 1881, a neglected office seeker shot the president. Garfield died two months later, and Chester A. Arthur, the product of Conkling's patronage machine, became president. The assassination made it dangerous for the new president to resist the swell of popular support for civil service reform. The Republicans in control of Congress did resist, however, and Democrats swept into office on a tide of resentment against Republican corruption and patronage. The following year Congress passed, and President Arthur signed, the landmark Pendleton Civil Service Act. The Pendleton Act prohibited patronage officeholders from contributing to the party machine that gave them their jobs. More important, the law authorized the president to establish a Civil Service Commission to administer competitive examinations for federal jobs. Before the century ended, the majority of federal jobs were removed from the reach of the patronage machines. The Pendleton Act was a major turning point in the creation of a stable and professional civil service.

Dying of a kidney disease, Arthur could not win renomination. The corrupt Republican candidate, James G. Blaine, offended Liberals and gave Democrats a chance. They nominated Governor Grover Cleveland, who was elected after a mud-spattered campaign, complete with anti-Catholic slurs and a scandal about Cleveland's illegitimate child. His slogan, "Public office is a public trust," expressed the Liberals' ideal. However, Blaine would have won had he not alienated irate prohibitionists and had the black vote not been suppressed in the South.

Cleveland was upright, downright, and forthright. He carried out the Pendleton Act to the letter, though not much beyond it, and harried railroad interests that exploited public land, including some of his campaign contributors. Special veterans' pension bills met ringing vetoes. So did a bill to relieve drought victims on the plains. Union veterans shouted when he tried to return captured Confederate flags to the southern states, and for once Cleveland backed down. Believing in a cheap, limited national government, he offered no great programs, but neither did he thwart congressional moves to broaden government's scope. He signed legislation raising the Agriculture Department to cabinet status and the Dawes Severalty Act, parceling out a fraction of the Indians' land to them as private property (see Chapter 16). Equally important, he approved the Interstate Commerce Act, creating an Interstate Commerce Commission (ICC) with power to regulate the railroads. Ever since the 1860s, states had been creating similar commissions, some of them setting railroad rates and all of them able to investigate and publicize abuses. Although weak and sometimes captive to the interests they regulated, they represented a growing state role overseeing many activities. Like the state agencies, the ICC promised more in the way of controlling rates and unfair practices than it could deliver, especially with court decisions hobbling the regulators.

With few accomplishments beyond a White House wedding to Frances Folsom and ominous political rumblings at the midterm elections, Cleveland needed a stirring issue. He found it in the high protective tariff. The tariff had done its work too well. Government surpluses had been growing, tightening credit as Treasury vaults locked away more and more of the nation's money, and tempting politicians to spend the revenue for pensions and subsidies. Critics saw the tariff as taking money from consumers' pockets to fill those of the monopolists, who, safe from foreign competition, could keep their prices high. Cautious presidents like Arthur had left the tariff alone, but Cleveland devoted his annual message to Congress in December 1887 to tariff reform. Favoring free trade would be political suicide, but adjustments downward, especially for raw materials, might make American exports more competitive and drive prices down.

It might drive wages down, too; so Republicans warned. Shouting that rate reductions would shutter factories and flood America in cheaper British goods, they had the Senate votes to block any bill that the House passed. Even one less skewed to serve southern

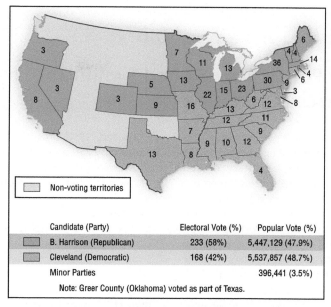

Candidate (Party)	Electoral Vote (%)	Popular Vote (%)
B. Harrison (Republican)	233 (58%)	5,447,129 (47.9%)
Cleveland (Democratic)	168 (42%)	5,537,857 (48.7%)
Minor Parties		396,441 (3.5%)

Note: Greer County (Oklahoma) voted as part of Texas.

Map 17-3   The Election of 1888 With the Solid South locked up, Democrats only needed two of the biggest northern states to win. They failed this year—just barely. But for Republicans, it was a wake-up call: either they must admit enough new states to pack the Electoral College their way or they must pass a law protecting a free, fair vote down South.

interests than the House-begotten Mills bill would have had no chance. Better in pointing the way than in working out the details of an actual measure, Cleveland did not push for the Mills bill or even for a strong endorsement of tariff reform in the 1888 Democratic platform. All the same, the issue dominated the campaign, with Republicans charging that free-trading England wanted a Cleveland victory. He won a majority of the popular vote but lost the Electoral College to Benjamin Harrison (see Map 17–3).

Having won House, Senate, and presidency on a protectionist platform, Republicans had two years to deliver. Under the forceful leadership of "Czar" Thomas Brackett Reed and with influence from President Harrison, the "Billion Dollar Congress" put through the new, higher McKinley Tariff, named for Congressman William McKinley of Ohio. At the same time, Congress gave the president the authority to lower tariffs with nations opening their markets to American goods, granting him important new power in the conduct of foreign affairs. Congress also passed a lavish Dependents' Pension Law, subsidies to encourage shipping, and a silver-purchase act that westerners hoped would inject more coinage into the money supply. The Sherman Anti-Trust Act of 1890 outlawed "combinations" in "restraint of trade," though what precisely that covered was uncertain. Five years later the Supreme Court even ruled out most manufacturing. Republicans also introduced—but failed to pass—both a federal enforcement bill that might have protected black southern voters and the Blair Education Bill, which might have provided federal money to guarantee black southerners an adequate education.

AMERICA AND THE WORLD

Foreign Policy: The Limited Significance of Commercial Expansion

Money was not everything—neither in domestic politics nor in foreign policy. In the 1860s, Secretary of State William Henry Seward shifted the emphasis of American foreign policy from the acquisition of territory to the expansion of American commerce. Working to open markets in the Americas and across the Pacific, Seward saw the nation's influence following its trade. He still dreamed of a nation extending beyond the water's edge. What he discovered was that, however adventurous American empire builders had been, the war had made them stingy in paying for new domains, either in money or in lives.

Expansionism in the Gilded Age, then, meant expanding markets, and even then not always through government action. Between 1860 and 1897, American exports tripled, surpassing $1 billion per year. In 1874, for the first time, Americans sold more than they bought. Nearly 85 percent of those exports were farm goods, but the share of industrial exports grew prodigiously as the century closed. Between

1889 and 1898, iron and steel exports jumped by 230 percent.

Mexico provided a different example of commercial expansion: investment abroad. Political instability had hindered investment, but Porfirio Díaz's seizure of power in 1876 brought decades of reassuring autocracy—at least for investors. They rushed south to build railroads, dig oil wells, sell life insurance, and invest in commercial farming. By 1910, Americans owned 43 percent of all the property in Mexico; Mexicans owned rather less.

Secretaries of state reaffirmed Seward's commitment to commercial expansion. Treaties with Japan and Korea opened new Asian markets. A treaty with King Kalakaua of Hawaii gave the islands' sugar favored treatment on the American market, prompting a huge influx into the United States (along with a backlash by sugar producers on the mainland). Worried that European nations would divert Latin American commerce from the United States, Secretary of State James G. Blaine became the champion of "reciprocity,"

Nothing offends like success. Derided as a "human iceberg," Harrison lacked the common touch. But he was not the problem. Democrats blamed higher prices on the tariff. White southerners rose in alarm at the threat of a full and fair black vote. Reformers considered the pensions a steal, and in the Midwest, Republicans ran into trouble when they tried to regulate parochial and German-language schools—the first step, immigrants cried, to foisting their own values on Catholic children. In 1890 voters put the Democrats back in control of the House of Representatives. Two years later, Cleveland won the presidency, this time with an outright majority.

breaking down American trade barriers in return for special access to foreign markets. In 1889, he convened the first Pan-American conference. Concern for access to foreign markets pushed successive administrations to assert America's exclusive right to build a canal across Central America. But that motive never stood alone—not in a world that every year Americans could see being devoured by European empires, and where Britain's and Germany's flags (and artillery) so often followed where their loans and exporters had ventured first.

Beyond that, America steered clear of foreign entanglements. In the 1880s, the United States, Germany, and England rattled sabers over disputed claims in Samoa; a riot in Valparaiso led to threats of naval force against Chile; and "jingoes," as friends of an aggressive foreign policy were called, complained about English mistreatment of Irish patriots and British claims in Latin America. If they had gotten their way, America would have gone to war to punish Spanish "insolence" in stopping American gunrunners to Cuba and to punish Canadian claims to sovereignty over the offshore fisheries and seal islands. They got no war.

Still, by the 1890s there were inklings of a new American assertiveness, mixing economic interest and a sense of America's

mission to spread democracy. That showed itself most clearly in Hawaii. By 1886, two-thirds of the islands' sugar was produced on American-owned plantations. American power in Hawaii grew so great that it provoked a backlash among native Hawaiians. Queen Liliuokalani's ascension to the throne in 1891 meant trouble for sugar growers. Two years later, they helped Hawaiians dethrone the queen and appealed for the United States to annex the islands. Undeceived by white planters pretending to speak for a Polynesian people, the Cleveland administration refused, but McKinley's carried annexation through. Nobody dreamed of statehood for so dark-skinned and foreign an electorate.

Only in the late 1880s did America's hemispheric interests begin to shape military policy. In 1890, Congress approved the construction of the first modern warships, and the Supreme Court extended the president's control over "our international relations." The growing links between commercial and diplomatic interests were reviving the powers of the American presidency. But as the story of domestic politics has made clear, those links were never the whole story—nor did the scramble for markets make America forge a steel navy in a world grown different and more dangerous.

Government Activism and Its Limits

Two themes dominate the traditional impression of late nineteenth-century political history: first, brazen corruption, and second, limited government that left the new industrial economy to develop as it pleased. The real heroes, according to this view, were those outside the party system, the Liberals and Populists, the moral crusaders and insurgents. While corruption was a problem, the foregoing view falls short as a true picture of the age.

Only by later standards was the national government limited. When peace came, Congress cut taxes, trimmed the army to a mere 25,000 men, and virtually abandoned any oceangoing navy. Yet it never returned to its proportions or role in 1861. Civilian federal employees rose from 53,000 in 1871 to 256,000 30 years later. Congress created a Department of Justice in 1870 and a Department of Agriculture in 1889. The postal service tripled in size over a quarter of a century, delivering 7 billion pieces of mail in 1900. More than a quarter of the national budget in 1900 went for veterans' pensions, awarded to over a million veterans and their dependents.

By the turn of the century, the rudiments of a modern federal government were in place. The Interstate Commerce Commission was able to compel safety machinery like automatic brakes and coupling devices on trains, but it lacked the power to enforce its own rulings, especially where unfair rates were concerned. It had to rely on courts friendly to government action protecting health, safety, and morals, but distrustful of any interference in the marketplace. Crippled by a damaging Supreme Court ruling in 1895, the weak Sherman Anti-Trust Act threatened few monopolies. In both cases, government action had not yet lived up to its potential. By comparison, state and municipal governments responded more aggressively to the problems of a transforming society.

States Discover Activism

Americans continued to clamor for state constitutions restricting government powers. They resented tax hikes and objected to bureaucrats. They had good reasons to distrust their officials. Lobbyists swarmed the capitols. Standard Oil did everything to the Pennsylvania legislators except refine them, a critic complained. Railroad tycoons, silvermine owners, and copper kings bought themselves Senate seats, and the insurance lobby in New York spent tens of thousands of dollars making friends in Albany every year.

But lawmakers kept doing more every year—and that, contradictory as it might seem, was what Americans also seem to have wanted. In spite of lobbyists, corporation taxes went up. So did spending. Public school systems expanded. School years lengthened. In 20 years, spending per pupil doubled, and in almost every state outside the South, attendance became compulsory. "Tramp laws" jailed jobless workers for bad reputations or "criminal idleness." Upset that customers might buy "butterine," made from animal or vegetable fats, dairy farmers got legislatures to require the new name "oleomargarine" and, in some places, unappetizing colors like pink. Unions put through laws establishing Labor Day and setting up fact-finding bureaus of labor statistics. Hundreds of laws went through to protect women workers or keep children out of the coal mines, to forbid employers from paying their workers in company-issued paper money, "scrip," and even to set up arbitration machinery, so that industrial disputes could be settled by negotiation rather than confrontation. The laws promised more than they performed: enforcement was sometimes spotty or nonexistent—much less stringent than for laws forbidding boycotting of shop owners and picketing by strikers. The courts weakened or killed many statutes, especially the ones that regulated workers' hours.

Cities: Boss Rule and New Responsibilities

States also intervened to help govern the swelling municipalities. One reason for that was the cities' reputation for boss rule and control by party machines such as New York City's Tammany Hall. With urban services expanding so fast, the city government had more than enough jobs to do, and every job bought the machine a friend. Trading services for votes, the ward and precinct captains working for the "boss" made government matter in the most personal way. But as reformers pointed out, the money to do that had to come from somewhere: shakedowns and graft, perhaps; protection money from gamblers and saloon keepers; and forced donations from storekeepers afraid to have an enemy in city hall. Government by two-bit politicians out to line their own pockets meant rotten government, and in many ways poorer neighborhoods suffered most. Boss rule meant garbage-choked streets, tenements that were firetraps, and police and fire chiefs turning their services into party armies.

Scandals and abuses gave legislatures the excuse to shift authority away from partisan elected officials to experts and specialists on unelected boards. Mayors, city council members, and aldermen lost much of their authority over budgets, schools, health, transportation, police, and parks to commissions generally staffed by middle-class professionals. The commissioners found help among city reformers, and in many cases, the bosses did not put up much of a fight. With competing private fire companies no longer rushing to a fire and beating each other up, and with patrolmen no longer paying a kickback for their appointment and expected to take it out of saloons, prostitutes, and shopkeepers, the quality of the fire and police departments could only improve.

Bosses were never the uncrowned emperors reformers made them out to be. Nowhere, not even in Tammany's New York, did they have total power. They had to accommodate interest groups, including labor and reform organizations. That was one reason why, in the late nineteenth century, city governments provided broader social services than anywhere else and produced some of the century's great urban achievements: New York's Central Park, San Francisco's Golden Gate Park, and the Brooklyn Bridge. Chicagoans literally reversed the flow of the Chicago River.

Challenging the New Industrial Order

In the late nineteenth century, disparate voices rose, arguing that something had gone wrong in a new, industrialized America where technology had made a few millionaires, living off the toil of unpropertied millions. Middle-class radicals argued that economic development had undermined individual liberty and equality. Yet although their attacks on capitalism were severe, their assumptions were traditional. They often worried that without substantial reforms, a discontented working class would threaten private property and social order. On the other hand, radicalized workers questioned one of the premises of producers' ideology—that American democracy was secured by a unique harmony between capital and labor. The Knights of Labor had called for a workers' party and carried their tickets in many local elections. In the mills and mines, labor agitation often became violent and was replied to with violence, as happened most notoriously in Haymarket Square in 1886. But even if the harmony of capital and labor had been destroyed, advocates of the producers' ideology continued to hold faith in political solutions to the labor problem.

Henry George and the Limits of Producers' Ideology

Henry George was born in Philadelphia in 1839 to middle-class parents. Although his formal education was limited, George traveled and read widely. Shocked that as the nation grew richer its number of poor people grew as well, he published his conclusions in 1879 in a best-selling book called *Progress and Poverty*.

George's explanation rested on what historians have called producers' ideology. He assumed that only human labor could create legitimate wealth and that anything of value, such as food, clothing, or steel rails, came from the world's producing classes. By contrast,

John F. Weir's 1877 Painting Forging the Shaft: A Welding Heat This painting graphically depicts the forms of industrial wage labor that Henry George feared. He advocated tax policies that would restore a Jeffersonian economy of small, independent producers.

stockbrokers, bankers, and speculators made money from money rather than from the goods they produced. Their wealth was therefore illegitimate. From these premises, George divided the world into two classes: producers and predators.

The harmony of capital and labor was a central theme of producers' ideology. Henry George dreamed of a world in which working people owned their own farms and shops, making them both capitalists and laborers, a vision that recalled Thomas Jefferson's ideal society of small farmers and independent shopkeepers. America used to be that way, George believed, but as society "progressed," the land was monopolized by a wealthy few. Producers were forced to work for wealthy landholders. Employers invested in technology that increased the productivity of their workers but kept the added wealth for themselves. George's solution was a so-called single tax on rents. Because all wealth derived from labor applied to land, he reasoned, rents were an unnatural transfer of wealth from the producers to the landlords. To discourage the landowning class from accumulating land, George suggested prohibitively high taxes on rents and improvements on land. All other taxes would be abolished, including the tariffs protecting big business.

George was no socialist. He presented his single tax as an alternative to the dangerous radical doctrines he thought were spreading among the working class. But his work challenged the Social Darwinists' idea that those who were poor owed it to their own inadequacies, and that the rich owed their place to their superiority. George depicted a world in which the system itself had made a cluster of winners and a host of losers, and in which government policy could right the balance.

Edward Bellamy and the Nationalist Clubs

In 1888, Edward Bellamy, a Massachusetts editor, published a best-selling critique of capitalism even more powerful than Henry George's. Bellamy's *Looking Backward* was a utopian novel set in the future, where technology had raised the standard of living for all. Industrial civilization's problems had been solved by overcoming the "excessive individualism" of Bellamy's day. Progress came, not through Social Darwinism's competition, but through its opposite: cooperation. Whereas *Progress and Poverty* proposed the restoration of the simple virtues of Jeffersonian society, *Looking Backward* imagined a high-tech future filled with consumer goods. In Bellamy's ideal world, production and consumption would no longer be subject to the whims of the market; instead, they would be harmonized by "nationalism," an obscure process of centralized planning. *Looking Backward* catered to a middle-class craving for order amid the chaos of industrial society. Decisions about what to produce were made collectively, and society as a whole owned the means of production. Whereas Henry George reasserted the values of hard work and self-restraint, Edward Bellamy embraced the modern cult of leisure and looked to the day when there would be little need for government. This vision inspired thousands of middle-class Americans to form "Bellamy Clubs" or "Nationalist Clubs," particularly in New England.

Agrarian Revolt

The late nineteenth century was a desperate time for American farmers in the grain and cotton belts of the West and South. To compete, they had to buy costly agricultural equipment, often from manufacturers who benefited from tariff protection. Then they had to ship their goods on railroads that charged higher rates to small farmers than to big industrialists. At the market, they faced steadily declining prices.

A global economy put southern cotton in competition with cotton from India and Egypt. Western wheat competed with Russian and eastern European wheat. To keep up, farmers increasingly went into debt, and in a deflationary spiral the money they borrowed to plant their crops was worth more when it came time to pay it back, whereas their crops were worth less. The proportion of owner-occupied farms declined, and the number of tenants rose. A few years of drought meant ruin on the plains. "In God we trusted, in Kansas we busted," one departing farmer wrote on his wagon.

Scattered over large sections of the country, farmers were committed to an ideology of economic independence and cool to government intervention. The industrial transformation of the late nineteenth century taught many of them that they could no longer stand alone. One of the first attempts to organize farmers was the Patrons of Husbandry, generally called the Grange. The Grange claimed 1.5 million members by 1874. Consistent with producers' ideology, the Grange organized cooperatives to eliminate the role of merchants and creditors. By storing grain collectively, farmers held their products back from the market in the hope of gaining control over commodity prices. But inexperience made the Grange cooperatives difficult to organize and sustain. After 1875, their membership dwindled.

The National Farmers' Alliance and Industrial Union, known simply as the Farmers' Alliance, was much more effective than the Grange. Founded in Texas in 1877, the Alliance spread rapidly across the South and West. Its goal was not to restore rural Jeffersonian simplicity but to bring American farmers into the modern world of industry and prosperity. The Alliance focused above all on education, broadly conceived. That meant public schools and the spread of scientific agriculture and sound business practices. The Alliance also built its own network of newspapers and lecturers to free farmers from their isolation. For rural men and women alike, the Farmers' Alliance offered the chance to share in the progress and prosperity of American life.

At its core the Alliance was a reform organization calling for a specific set of economic policies. Above all, the farmers wanted to inflate the currency, whether by the circulation of more silver currency or of more paper currency ("greenbacks") or a combination of the two. Inspired by the successes of highly organized corporations, especially railroads, the Alliance also supported a system of cooperative "subtreasuries" that would provide low-interest loans, backed by farmers' crops, held until the best prices were available.

By the late 1880s, the Farmers' Alliance had drawn millions of members, concentrated in the southern, western, and plains states. Created at a huge meeting at Ocala, Florida, in 1890, the Ocala Platform supported a host of new policies that joined economic progress to democratic reform. The platform called for the free coinage of silver, lower tariffs, government subtreasuries, and a constitutional amendment providing for direct election of senators. Finally, the Alliance called for strict government regulation, and if necessary direct government ownership, of the railroad and telegraph industries.

The Farmers' Alliance steered clear of politics and instead judged political candidates by their support of the Ocala Platform reforms. They elected shoals of congressmen and even a few senators by cooperating with Democrats in the West and, where neither party gave satisfaction, by running independent candidates. Out of these efforts came the most significant third party of the late nineteenth century, the People's Party, otherwise known as the Populists.

The Rise of the Populists

On February 22, 1892, a coalition of reform organizations met in St. Louis, including representatives of the Knights of Labor and the Farmers' Alliance. Together they founded the People's Party. At Omaha on July 4, they nominated General James B. Weaver of Iowa for president and drew up the Omaha Platform, demanding an inflationary currency policy and a subtreasury system. The Populists also called for a graduated income tax, direct government ownership of railroads and telegraph lines, and the confiscation of railroad land grants. But they also spoke for a government restored to the people by a

Time Line

▼**1867**
Patrons of Husbandry (the Grange) founded

▼**1869**
Noble and Holy Order of the Knights of Labor founded

▼**1870**
Department of Justice created

▼**1872**
Grant reelected

▼**1873**
"Crusade" against alcohol begins in Hillsboro, Ohio

▼**1874**
Women's Christian Temperance Union (WCTU) is formed

▼**1876**
Rutherford B. Hayes elected president
Porfirio Díaz seizes power in Mexico

▼**1877**
Farmers' Alliance founded

▼**1878**
Bland-Allison Act

▼**1879**
Frances Willard becomes president of the WCTU
Henry George publishes *Progress and Poverty*

▼**1880**
James Garfield elected president

▼**1881**
Garfield assassinated; Chester Arthur becomes president
WCTU endorses women's suffrage

▼**1883**
Pendleton Civil Service Act

Kansas Farm Families on the Road to a People's Party Gathering In a state usually locked up for the GOP, the farmer's revolt revived political competition and an evangelical passion about issues absent since the Civil War.

secret ballot, popularly elected senators, and the power of voters to make laws for themselves by initiative and referendum.

Populism took in more than wheat and cotton farmers. Small ranchers joined to fight the politically privileged cattle kings. Townspeople joined to oppose the railroads. Prohibitionists,

▼1884
Grover Cleveland elected
    president

▼1886
Nationwide strike for eight-hour
    day
Riot at Haymarket Square in
    Chicago

▼1887
Interstate Commerce Act
Four Haymarket anarchists
    executed
Dawes Severalty Act

▼1888
Benjamin Harrison elected
    president
Edward Bellamy publishes
    Looking Backward

▼1889
United States convenes first Pan-
    American Conference
Department of Agriculture
    created

▼1890
McKinley Tariff
Sherman Anti-Trust Act

Ocala Platform

▼1891
Queen Liliuokalani assumes the
    Hawaiian throne

▼1892
Omaha Platform of the People's
    Party
Grover Cleveland reelected

▼1893
Queen Liliuokalani overthrown

▼1898
Frances Willard dies

woman suffragists, and the dwindling membership of the Knights of Labor found friends aplenty in the People's Party. Rallies took on the spirit of a revival, with speakers promising a return to the lost promise of the Revolution. In the 1892 elections, Weaver won about 1 million votes, and the Populists elected several senators, representatives, governors, and state legislators. But wage earners in the industrial North and East still held back. The Populist platform, for all its talk of the unity of the toiling masses, offered industrial workers little. They depended on the protective tariff to shield them from cheap foreign labor. Higher prices for the farmer meant price hikes in the stores, when most workers had no hope of raising their wages to keep up. They knew how paper money worked: many were paid in company-issued "scrip," redeemable only at the company store at a steep discount. Conversely, farmers who hired workers had no zeal for an eight-hour day or laws restricting child labor. Wherever the Populists were strong, mainstream parties adopted their most popular causes.

Southern Populists faced a particularly difficult challenge. To win, they needed help from the largest class of impoverished farmers, black sharecroppers. Only by downplaying racial differences could they make such a coalition work. Not all whites could overcome their prejudices. The Farmers' Alliance had always been strictly segregated, with a separate Colored Farmers' Alliance. And in fact the economic interests of the two groups were not always compatible. Black leaders appreciated the limits of any alliance with white reformers, and most black southerners kept voting Republican. Coalitions between Republicans and Populists sometimes came about. But any multiracial alliance inspired the ugliest race-baiting that Democrats could devise, to break the partners apart and restore the color line. It gave them all the excuse they needed to stuff ballot boxes, count votes creatively, and remake the laws to cut as many Populists, white and black, out of the suffrage as possible—always in the name of reform.

Conclusion

Luna Kellie was not alone in seeing a nation on the edge of catastrophe by the early 1890s. Americans still went to the polls in record numbers, but the political system was showing serious strains. Strident voices rose, against Catholics, foreigners, Negroes, and Jews. Farmers cried out against the "money power." Bloody strikes convulsed the coalfields and Carnegie's mills. Culture wars disrupted politics in the Midwest, while southern Democrats fended off political challengers by invoking white supremacy in its rawest form. In big cities, reformers cried that boss rule had replaced government by the people. But Gilded Age politics offered more hope than it appeared. In its tumultuous variety, it showed a country bursting with reform impulses, and with the energy to regenerate a nation in crisis.

Who, What, Where

Comstock, Anthony 528
Farmers' Alliance 526
George, Henry 549
Greenbackers 542
Hawaii 546
Kellie, Luna 526

Mugwumps 539
Nationalist Clubs 551
Omaha Platform 552
Patronage 539
Pendleton Civil Service Act 544
Political machine 535

Review Questions

1. Discuss how constructions of gender defined what men and women could do and be.
2. How did urbanization and immigration challenge cultural norms in the late nineteenth century?
3. Describe the two major "styles" of politics in the late nineteenth century.
4. Describe the changes in the roles of national, state, and local government during this period.
5. What did Henry George, Edward Bellamy, and Frances Willard have in common? What did the Farmers' Alliance stand for?

Critical-Thinking Questions

1. Why did Victorian attitudes on gender and morality break down in this period?
2. What was the case that guardians of traditional culture made against a multicultural society?
3. Why did so many people participate in politics in the late nineteenth century? What did they expect to get out of it?
4. To what extent did the industrial revolution described in Chapter 16 affect politics and the issues politicians discussed in this period?
5. What were the major challenges to "politics as usual" in this age, and where did those challenges come from? Why did they arise, and how successful were they in remaking American society?

Suggested Readings

Burrows, Edwin G., and Mike Wallace. *Gotham: A History of New York to 1898.* New York: Oxford University Press, 1999.

Goodwyn, Lawrence. *The Populist Moment: A Short History of the Agrarian Revolt in America.* New York: Oxford University Press, 1978.

Morgan, H. Wayne. *From Hayes to McKinley: National Party Politics, 1877–1896.* Syracuse, NY: Syracuse University Press, 1969.

For further review materials and resource information, please visit www.oup.com/us/oakes-mcgerr

CHAPTER 17: THE CULTURE AND POLITICS OF INDUSTRIAL AMERICA, 1870–1892
Primary Sources

17.1 *NEW YORK WORLD*, "HOW TIM GOT THE VOTES" (1892)

New York City's Tammany Hall machine was nationally infamous, but no critic could deny that the Democratic organization knew how to bring every supporter to the polls. Local election-district leaders took pride in getting a full turnout, and those with political ambitions spared no effort on Election Day. One of the hardest working politicians was "Big Tim" Sullivan, a state assemblyman and rising star in downtown Manhattan. Helped by his cousins "Big Florry" and "Boston Tim" Sullivan, he demonstrated his skills during the 1892 Cleveland-Harrison presidential election, when he set the goal of carrying every man on the voter rolls.

"Now here comes a duck," whispered Tim, to his cousin Florry, "who's been gettin' drunk on Denny Shea. Watch me fix him."

"Say, young feller," demanded Tim with a frown, surrounded by eight fierce-looking Sullivans, "how are y' goin' to vote?"

"I'm fer Cleevelan' an' th' hull ticket," replied the fellow, with apparent enthusiasm.

"You're lyin' an' y' know it," said Tim, with painful frankness. "Do y' see this paster?"

He did.

"Well, jes' take it, an' slap it on a ballot. An' I want y' to slap it on so I can hear it, too. See?"

"All right," was the reply, "but you've gotto do dis fer me. You gotta promise to look out fer me if de cops take me in fer hittin' de bowl."

The agreement was made on the spot.

This was followed by sixty Tammany ballots which were above suspicion. Then the Republican district captain cast his vote.

"That's one fer Harrison," commented Tim, sadly.

Just then a woman came up to Tim and called him aside, confidentially.

"My husband's so drunk, begorra, he can't walk," she said. "Pfhat are yez goin' to do?"

"How many times have I told that duck," said Tim indignantly, "not to getta jag until after he voted. Here, Florry, get ten cents' worth o' ammonia and straighten 'im out."

Five minutes later the fellow came, supported by two Sullivans.

"You don't needa think I've been drinkin', Mr. Sullivan," he apologized. "I was workin' all night, an' I felt so tired I fell asleep. Hooray for Tim Sullivan an' Cleveland!"

Then there was a lull of five minutes. It was broken by the Republican Supervisor.

"That's two," said Tim, mournfully, "but I'll see that duck don't sling ink around here next year. The bloke who was here last year was a square feller."

There were twenty-eight votes still out by three o'clock, and among them were several who were under suspicion.

"Go hunt up Lake," he instructed his nephew, Tim, Jr: "He's another one o' Denny Shea's gang."

When Lake came he admitted frankly that he was going to vote for Harrison, but he promised to vote for the Tammany ticket.

"Do you wantta ruin my chances to get to th' Senate?" demanded Tim. "Are you goin' to be the only man in the district who's goin' back on me? What do you think Grover Cleveland'll say to me when he sees I let Gilroy have an extra vote? You'll be wantin' a favor, but when I got to Cleveland he'll fire me out."

Much as he loved Harrison, Jake would not have Tim put on the black list if he could help it. So he voted for Cleveland.

"But don't tell Denny," he enjoined Tim.

Next the Republican poll clerk voted. How aggravating it was to see him, with his cynical smile hand over a Republican ballot!

"That duck thinks he's smart," growled Tim, "but I know how to get even with 'im."

There were still half a dozen Baxter street clothiers who had not voted. Tim, Jr., reported they were busy selling clothing. Tim concluded to go around himself.

"Now here, Jake," he said to Jacob Harris, who keeps a store near Walker Street, "you gotta go out an' vote now."

"How can I, Mr. Sullivan," was protested. "I'm waitin' on a customer."

"Yes," responded Dry Dollar, "an' you've been waitin' on him fer two hours. How much are yer dickering over?"

"The gentleman wants it for two dollars less," was explained.

"Well, hully gee!" ejaculated Tim, "is that all? I'll pay the difference."

The Republican inspector had not yet voted. Tim looked in at him wistfully. Then he whistled to him and made a frantic endeavor to coax him out into the street, but the inspector was not in the market. A few minutes later he cast his ballot for Harrison and the agony was over.

"Now look here, Tim," consoled Florry, "wot's the use o' gettin' huffy over four votes? Those ducks couldn't get out of it. They had to vote for Harrison."

"I know," admitted Tim; "but it's pretty tough to come so near carryin' th' distric' unanimous, an' have four stubborn ducks hold out like that."

Judge Patrick Divver, when seen by a *World* reporter, said:

"Yes, Tim did first rate. He did all that could be expected of him. That boy's a good politician, and when he gets older he'll be a wonder."

Source: "How Tim Got the Votes," *New York World,* November 10, 1892.

17.2 *TAMMANY TIMES,* "AND REFORM MOVES ON" (1895)

In 1894, New York City reformers drove Tammany Hall from power and installed a Republican coalition. It only lasted a single term. When the new police commissioner, Theodore Roosevelt, began enforcing the state law forbidding the sale of alcohol on Sunday, his actions split working-class and immigrant voters from middle-class and native-born ones. The man with the "growler"—the bucket in which workers collected beer to consume on the job—narrowed all reform down to the narrow-mindedness of the prohibitionists. Tammany Hall had a winning issue and knew it, as these lyrics show, set to the tune of a popular favorite, "And the Band Played On."

New York on Sunday is awfully dry,
And Reform moves on,
Can't open the side-door, police standing by,
And Reform moves on.
The growler gets rusty, our throats are so dusty—
Oh dear, when will this end?—
When Roosevelt's dead or tucked snugly in bed,
As Reform moves on.
One Sunday our Roosevelt rode all over town,
When Reform moved on,

For side doors wide open he looked up and down,
As Reform moved on.
They say he was looking to have them closed up, but I'll give you a tip,
He simply was dry and he'd drink on the sly,
As Reform moves on.

Source: Tammany Times, November 18, 1895.

17.3 HENRY GEORGE, EXCERPTS FROM "THAT WE MIGHT ALL BE RICH" (1883)

As the author of *Progress and Poverty*, Henry George became a celebrated authority on class conflict and social injustice in industrializing America. Socialists agreed with his diagnosis of society, though not with his solutions, among which were a single tax falling on landed property and an end to protective tariffs. Nearly winning the New York City mayoral race in 1886 and at the forefront of efforts to create a workers' party, George campaigned on distrust of government and detestation of privilege. Many of his essays were gathered together in the book *Social Problems*, published in 1883.

The terms rich and poor are of course frequently used in a relative sense. Among Irish peasants, kept on the verge of starvation by the tribute wrung from them to maintain the luxury of absentee landlords in London or Paris, "the woman of three cows" will be looked on as rich, while in the society of millionaires a man with only $500,000 will be regarded as poor. Now, we cannot, of course, all be rich in the sense of having more than others; but when people say, as they so often do, that we cannot all be rich, or when they say that we must always have the poor with us, they do not use the words in this comparative sense. They mean by the rich those who have enough, or more than enough, wealth to gratify all reasonable wants, and by the poor those who have not.

Now, using the words in this sense, I join issue with those who say that we cannot all be rich; with those who declare that in human society the poor must always exist. I do not, of course, mean that we all might have an array of servants; that we all might outshine each other in dress, in equipage, in the lavishness of our balls or dinners, in the magnificence of our houses. That would be a contradiction in terms. What I mean is, that we all might have leisure, comfort and abundance, not merely of the necessaries, but even of what are now esteemed the elegancies and luxuries of life. I do not mean to say that absolute equality could be had, or would be desirable. I do not mean to say that we could all have, or would want, the same quantity of all the different forms of wealth. But I do mean to say that we might all have enough wealth to satisfy reasonable desires; that we might all have so much of the material things we now struggle for, that no one would want to rob or swindle his neighbor; that no one would worry all day, or lie awake at nights, fearing he might be brought to poverty, or thinking how he might acquire wealth.

Does this seem an utopian dream? What would people of fifty years ago have thought of one who would have told them that it was possible to sew by steam-power; to cross the Atlantic in six days, or the continent in three; to have a message sent from London at noon delivered in Boston three hours before noon; to hear in New York the voice of a man talking in Chicago?

Did you ever see a pail of swill given to a pen of hungry hogs? That is human society as it is.

Did you ever see a company of well-bred men and women sitting down to a good dinner, without scrambling, or jostling, or gluttony, each, knowing that his own appetite will be satisfied, deferring to and helping the others? That is human society as it might be.

"Devil catch the hindmost" is the motto of our so-called civilized society today. We learn early to "take care of No. 1," lest No.1 should suffer; we learn early to grasp from others that we may not want ourselves. The fear of poverty makes us admire great wealth; and so habits of greed are formed, and we behold the pitiable spectacle of men who have already more than they can by any possibility use, toiling, striving, grasping to add to their store up to the very verge of the grave—that grave which, whatever else it may mean, does certainly mean the parting with all earthly possessions however great they be.

In vain, in gorgeous churches, on the appointed Sunday, is the parable of Dives and Lazarus read. What can it mean in churches where Dives would be welcomed and Lazarus shown the door? In vain may the preacher preach of the vanity of riches, while poverty engulfs the hindmost. But the mad struggle would cease when the fear of poverty had vanished. Then, and not till then, will a truly Christian civilization become possible.

And may not this be?

. . .

The passenger who leaves New York on a trans-Atlantic steamer does not fear that the provisions will give out. The men who run these steamers do not send them to sea without provisions enough for all they carry. Did He who made this whirling planet for our sojourn lack the forethought of man? Not so. In soil and sunshine, in vegetable and animal life, in veins of minerals, and in pulsing forces which we are only beginning to use, are capabilities which we cannot exhaust—materials and powers from which human effort, guided by intelligence, may gratify every material want of every human creature. There is in nature no reason for poverty—not even for the poverty of the crippled or the decrepit. For man is by nature a social animal, and the family affections and the social sympathies would, where chronic poverty did not distort and embrute, amply provide for those who could not provide for themselves.

But if we will not use the intelligence with which we have been gifted to adapt social organization to natural laws—if we allow dogs in the manger to monopolize what they cannot use; if we allow strength and cunning to rob honest labor, we must have chronic poverty, and all the social evils it inevitably brings. Under such conditions there would be poverty in paradise.

"The poor ye have always with you." If ever a scripture has been wrested to the devil's service, this is that scripture. How often have these words been distorted from their obvious meaning to soothe conscience into acquiescence in human misery and degradation—to bolster that blasphemy, the very negation and denial of Christ's teachings, that the All-Wise and Most Merciful, the Infinite Father, has decreed that so many of his creatures must be poor in order that others of his creatures to whom he wills the good things of life should enjoy the pleasure and virtue of doling out alms! "The poor ye have always with you," said Christ; but all his teachings supply the limitation, "until the coming of the Kingdom." In that kingdom of God on earth, that kingdom of justice and love for which he taught his followers to strive and pray, there will be no poor. But though the faith and the hope and the striving for this kingdom are of the very essence of Christ's teaching, the staunchest disbelievers and revilers of its possibility are found among those who call themselves Christians. Queer ideas of the Divinity have some of these Christians who hold themselves orthodox and contribute to the conversion of the heathen. A very rich orthodox Christian said to a newspaper reporter, a while ago, on the completion of a large work out of which he is said to have made millions: "We have been peculiarly favored by Divine Providence; iron never was so cheap before, and labor has been a drug in the market."

. . .

The wealth-producing powers that would be evoked in a social state based on justice, where wealth went to the producers of wealth, and the banishment of poverty had banished the fear and greed and lusts that spring from it, we now can only faintly imagine. Wonderful as have been the discoveries and inventions of this century, it is evident that we have only begun to grasp that dominion which it is given to mind to obtain over matter. Discovery and invention are born of leisure, of material comfort, of freedom. These secured to all, and who shall say to what command over nature man may not attain?

It is not necessary that any one should be condemned to monotonous toil; it is not neces-sary that any one should lack the wealth and the leisure which permit the development of the faculties that raise man above the animal. Mind, not muscle, is the motor of progress, the force which compels nature and produces wealth. In turning men into machines we are wasting the highest powers. Already in our society there is a favored class who need take no thought for the morrow—what they shall eat, or what they shall drink, or wherewithal they shall be clothed. And may it not be that Christ was more than a dreamer when he told his disciples that in that kingdom of justice for which he taught them to work and pray this might be the condition of all?

Source: Henry George, "That We All Might Be Rich," from *Social Problems* (Chicago: 1883) quoted in William Benton, publ., *The Annals of America. Volume 10, 1866–1883: Reconstruction and Industrialization* (Chicago: Encyclopedia Britannica, Inc., 1968), pp. 601–606.

17.4 JACOB RIIS, EXCERPT FROM *HOW THE OTHER HALF LIVES* (1890) AND VISUAL DOCUMENT: JACOB RIIS, "BANDITS' ROOST" (1887)

In 1890, the Danish American police reporter Jacob Riis published a book about the slums of New York City entitled *How the Other Half Lives*. Its stark text, excerpted in the follow-ing, was accompanied by Riis's haunting photographs. In addition to being a pioneer in photojournalism, Riis contributed to the record that reformers used to advocate for public health programs, government policing of housing, and other public measures to relieve poverty and its accompanying ills.

The "Rock of Ages" is the name over the door of a low saloon that blocks the entrance to another alley, if possible more forlorn and dreary than the rest, as we pass out of the Alderman's court. It sounds like a jeer from the days, happily past, when the "wickedest man in New York" lived around the corner a little way and boasted of his title. One cannot take many steps in Cherry Street without encountering some relic of past or present prominence in the ways of crime, scarce one that does not turn up specimen bricks of the coming thief. The Cherry Street tough is all-pervading. Ask Superintendent Murray, who, as captain of the Oak Street squad, in seven months secured convictions for theft, robbery, and murder aggregating no less than five hundred and thirty years of penal servitude, and he will tell you his opinion that the Fourth Ward, even in the last twenty years, has turned out more criminals than all the rest of the city together.

But though the "Swamp Angels" have gone to their reward, their successors carry on business at the old stand as successfully, if not as boldly. There goes one who was once a shining light in thiefdom. He has reformed since, they say. The policeman on the corner, who is addicted to a pro-fessional unbelief in reform of any kind, will tell you that while on the Island once he sailed away on a shutter, paddling along until he was picked up in Hell Gate by a schooner's crew, whom he per-suaded that he was a fanatic performing some sort of religious penance by his singular expedition.

. . . .

We have crossed the boundary of the Seventh Ward. Penitentiary Row, suggestive name for a block of Cherry Street tenements, is behind us. Within recent days it has become peopled wholly with Hebrews, the overflow from Jewtown adjoining, pedlars and tailors, all of them. It is odd to read this legend from other days over the door: "No pedlars allowed in this house." These thrifty people are not only crowding into the tenements of this once exclusive district—they are buying them. The Jew runs to real estate as soon as he can save up enough for a deposit to clinch the bargain. As fast as the old houses are torn down, towering structures go up in their place, and

Jacob Riis's powerful exposures of the links between poverty, grime, crime, and exploitation were strengthened by the pictures he took in the slums of downtown New York. Danish-born, the reformer was one of the pioneers in what came to be called photojournalism. *Source:* Photograph by Jacob Riis.

Hebrews are found to be the builders. Here is a whole alley nicknamed after the intruder, Jews' Alley. But abuse and ridicule are not weapons to fight the Israelite with. He pockets them quietly with the rent and bides his time. He knows from experience, both sweet and bitter, that all things come to those who wait, including the houses and lands of their persecutors.

Here comes a pleasure party, as gay as any on the avenue, though the carry-all is an ash-cart. The father is the driver and he has taken his brown-legged boy for a ride. How proud and happy they both look up there on their perch! The queer old building they have halted in front of is "The Ship," famous for fifty years as a ramshackle tenement filled with the oddest crowd. No one knows why it is called "The Ship," though there is a tradition that once the river came clear up here to Hamilton Street, and boats were moored along-side it. More likely it is because it is as bewildering inside as a crazy old ship, with its ups and downs of ladders parading as stairs, and its unexpected pitfalls. But Hamilton Street, like Water Street, is not what it was. The missions drove from the latter the worst of its dives. A sailors' mission has lately made its appearance in Hamilton Street, but there are no dives there, nothing worse than the ubiquitous saloon and tough tenements.

Enough of them everywhere. Suppose we look into one? No. — Cherry Street. Be a little careful, please! The hall is dark and you might stumble over the children pitching pennies back there. Not that it would hurt them; kicks and cuffs are their daily diet. They have little else. Here where the hall turns and dives into utter darkness is a step, and another, another. A flight of stairs. You can feel your way, if you cannot see it. Close? Yes! What would you have? All the fresh air that ever enters these stairs comes from the hall-door that is forever slamming, and from the windows of dark bedrooms that in turn receive from the stairs their sole supply of the elements God meant to be free, but man deals out with such niggardly hand. That was a woman filling her pail by the hydrant you just bumped against. The sinks are in the hallway, that all the tenants may have access—and all be poisoned alike by their summer stenches. Hear the pump squeak! It is the lullaby of tenement-house babes. In summer, when a thousand thirsty throats pant for a cooling drink in this block, it is worked in vain. But the saloon, whose open door you passed in the hall, is always there. The smell of it has followed you up. Here is a door. Listen! That short hacking cough, that tiny, helpless wail—what do they mean? They mean that the soiled bow of white you saw on the door downstairs will have another story to tell—Oh! a sadly familiar story—before the day is at an end. The child is dying with measles. With half a chance it might have lived; but it had none. That dark bedroom killed it.

"It was took all of a suddint," says the mother, smoothing the throbbing little body with trembling hands. There is no unkindness in the rough voice of the man in the jumper, who sits by the window grimly smoking a clay pipe, with the little life ebbing out in his sight, bitter as his words sound: "Hush, Mary! If we cannot keep the baby, need we complain—such as we?"

Such as we! What if the words ring in your ears as we grope our way up the stairs and down from floor to floor, listening to the sounds behind the closed doors—some of quarrelling, some of coarse songs, more of profanity. They are true. When the summer heats come with their suffering they have meaning more terrible than words can tell. Come over here. Step carefully over this baby—it is a baby, spite of its rags and dirt—under these iron bridges called fire-escapes, but loaded down, despite the incessant watchfulness of the firemen, with broken household goods, with wash-tubs and barrels, over which no man could climb from a fire. This gap between dingy brick-walls is the yard. That strip of smoke-colored sky up there is the heaven of these people. Do you wonder the name does not attract them to the churches? That baby's parents live in the rear tenement here. She is at least as clean as the steps we are now climbing. There are plenty of houses with half a hundred such in. The tenement is much like the one in front we just left, only fouler, closer, darker—we will not say more cheerless. The word is a mockery. A hundred thousand people lived in rear tenements in New York last year. Here is a room neater than the rest. The woman, a stout matron with hard lines of care in her face, is at the wash-tub. "I try to keep the childer clean," she says, apologetically, but with a hopeless glance around. The spice of hot soap-suds is added to the air already tainted with the smell of boiling cabbage, of rags and uncleanliness all about. It makes an overpowering compound. It is Thursday, but patched linen is hung upon the pulley-line from the window. There is no Monday cleaning in the tenements. It is washday all the week round, for a change of clothing is scarce among the poor. They are poverty's honest badge, these perennial lines of rags hung out to dry, those that are not the washerwoman's professional shingle. The true line to be drawn between pauperism and honest poverty is the clothes-line. With it begins the effort to be clean that is the first and the best evidence of a desire to be honest.

What sort of an answer, think you, would come from these tenements to the question "Is life worth living?" were they heard at all in the discussion?

Source: Jacob A. Riis, *How the Other Half Lives: Studies Among the Tenements of New York* (New York: Charles Scribner's Sons, 1890), pp. 39–47.

17.5 VISUAL DOCUMENTS: "GIFT FOR THE GRANGERS" (1873) AND THE JORNS FAMILY OF DRY VALLEY, CUSTER COUNTY, NEBRASKA (1886)

The image of the self-sufficient "yeoman farmer" in close communion with nature always had been more fantasy than real; but on the bare prairies, where it took a family working full time just to keep body and soul together, the harsh reality made the old myths feel like bitter mockery. These contrasting documents depict two versions of farm life: the ideal and the real.

Source: "Gift for the Grangers," J. Hale Powers & Co. Fraternity & Fine Art Publishers, Cincinnati; Strobridge & Co. Lith.

Source: Photograph by Solomon D. Butcher, Library of Congress American Memory Historical Collections.

18

Industry and Empire

COMMON THREADS

How did industrial ideals of efficiency and organization change the practice of democracy in America during the early 1900s?

Did the choices Americans made about how to run their economy set the United States on a course for overseas conflict?

What did it mean to be modern? How did the pace of technological change affect Americans' outlook?

OUTLINE

< The Rough Riders

J. P. Morgan

It was a short distance from the Arlington Hotel to the White House, and although it was icy and dark, J. Pierpont Morgan chose to walk. He pulled his scarf up around a scowling face known to millions of newspaper readers. He had not wanted to come to Washington. There were "large interests" that depended on keeping the currency of the United States sound, he told a Treasury official, and those interests were now in jeopardy. The commander in chief of the nation's bankers was going to meet the president to keep the United States from going bankrupt.

The events leading up to this meeting stretched back five years to 1890, when business failures toppled London's Baring Brothers investment house and triggered a collapse in European stock prices. Depression spread through Britain, Germany, and France. Anxious European investors began selling off their large American holdings. In early 1893, the panic reached the United States. The Philadelphia and Reading Railroad folded in February. Fourteen thousand businesses soon followed, along with more than 600 banks.

Summer brought more bad news from abroad. The government of India stopped minting silver, causing US silver dollars to lose one-sixth of their value. Wall Street went into another tailspin. In New York, 55,000 men, women, and girls in the clothing industry were thrown out of work. Banks refused to cash checks, and coins vanished from circulation. Tens of thousands of homeless poor people filled the roads. Breadlines formed. "The world surely cannot remain as mad as it is," the historian Henry Adams observed.

For Grover Cleveland the madness was only starting. The anger of workers and farmers, simmering for decades, was boiling over. The president pledged to keep the dollar on the gold standard, but it was not enough. A wave of strikes swept the country. Unemployed workers battled police on the Capitol grounds. By January 1895 so many panicky investors were cashing government bonds that the Treasury's gold reserve was half gone, and it looked as if the remainder might last only two weeks. Reluctantly, Cleveland agreed to open negotiations with Morgan.

Admired and reviled, Morgan was known as the leading financial manipulator of the late nineteenth century. Born to wealth in Hartford, Connecticut, he had been a Wall Street fixture since before the Civil War. Like two of his contemporaries, steelmaker Andrew Carnegie and oil magnate John D. Rockefeller, Morgan's skill lay in organization. He restructured railroads, rooting out corruption, waste, and competition and driving down wages. Instead of taking risks, he eliminated them. He convinced leaders of warring firms to strike bargains and share the profits. Cleveland was about to place the Treasury in this man's hands.

The president opened the meeting by suggesting that things might not be so bad; a new bond issue might stabilize the dollar. No, Morgan replied flatly, the run on gold would continue until European investors regained confidence. If the president agreed, Morgan would arrange a private loan and personally guarantee the solvency of the US Treasury. After a stunned silence, the two men shook hands. News of the deal instantly calmed the bond markets. The crisis was over. The *New York Sun* reported that the deal "revived a confidence in the wealth and resources of this country," but Populist newspapers denounced it as a conspiracy and a "great bunco game."

Culminating two decades of turbulence, the Panic of 1893 permanently transformed the American political economy. Businessmen such as Morgan created even larger corporate combinations and placed them under professional managers. They used technology and "scientific management" to control the workplace and push laborers to work faster and harder. Workers resisted, and the 1890s saw brutal clashes between capital and labor. Looking for jobs and schools, country people moved to the city and found both promise and danger. Social mobility among African Americans aroused fears in whites, and southerners created a system of formal segregation, enforced by law and terror. Amid growing violence, industrial workers, Native Americans, and African Americans debated how best to deal with the overwhelming forces ranged against them.

The 1890s were also a turning point in American political history. After the 1896 election, many Americans walked away from the electoral process. Others were removed from the voter rolls through a process known as "disfranchisement." African American leaders and union organizers urged their followers to turn away from politics in favor of "bread-and-butter" economic issues. The masculine, public spectacle of nineteenth-century politics with its parades and flag raisings died out. Patriotism, once synonymous with partisanship, now stood for America's global military and economic ambitions. Civic events featured army bands and cannon salutes. Newspapers conjured up foreign threats. As Americans became more conscious of their military power, they watched the horizon for threats to their well-being.

Americans began to feel that their economy's links to the world—and the changes wrought by manufacturing and rapid communications—separated their times from all that had happened before. Morgan's rescue required transactions on two continents, instantaneously coordinated by telegraph. The speed of industry, trade, and information and the way carbon technologies spanned distance and time created a sense that the environment and the future could be controlled. Many felt that those who possessed this newfound control—citizens of modern countries—stood apart from those in other lands whose lives were not guided by science and information.

Between 1890 and 1900 Americans made their country recognizably modern. Those with the means to do so enlarged and refashioned many aspects of work and daily life. Financiers and giant corporations assumed control of the economy. Huge cities grew. The significance of voting declined, and a decade that opened with a global economic catastrophe ended with a dramatic display of the global reach of US power.

The Crisis of the 1890s

Financial convulsions, strikes, and the powerlessness of government against wealth rudely reminded Americans of how much their country had changed since the Civil War. When Illinois sent Abraham Lincoln to Congress, Chicago's population was less than 5,000; in 1890, it exceeded 1 million. Gone was the America of myth and memory, in which class tensions were slight and upward (or at least westward) and mobility seemed easy. Many Americans foresaw the collapse of civilization. Others, however, felt that the United States was passing into a new phase of history that would lead to still greater trials and achievements.

Hard Times and Demands for Help

Chicago in 1893 captured the hopes and fears of the new age. To celebrate the 400th anniversary of Columbus's discovery of America, the city staged the World's Columbian Exposition, transforming a lakefront bog into a gleaming vision of the past and the future. Just outside the exposition's gates was the city of the present. In December 1893, Chicago had 75,000 unemployed, and the head of a local relief committee declared that "famine is in our midst." In the nation's second-largest city, thousands lived in shacks or high-rise tenements with only a single bathroom on each densely packed floor. Jobs were scarce, and when men gathered at the exposition's gates to beg for work, the police drove them away.

As the depression deepened, the Cleveland administration ordered troops to guard Treasury branches in New York and Chicago. Jobless people banded together into "industrial armies," many with decidedly revolutionary aims. Hundreds heeded the call of Jacob Coxey, an Ohio landowner and Populist. In 1894, Coxey urged the unemployed to march on Washington and demand free silver and a public road-building program that would hire a half-million workers. When Coxey set out with 100 followers, reporters predicted the ragged band would disintegrate as soon as food ran out, but well-wishers turned out by the thousands to greet the Coxeyites with supplies for the trip.

Industrial armies set out from Boston, St. Louis, Chicago, Portland, Seattle, and Los Angeles. When Coxey arrived in Washington on May 1 with 500 marchers, Cleveland put the US Army on alert. The march ended ignominiously. In front of the Capitol, police arrested Coxey, and his disillusioned army dispersed. Still, no one could deny that something was seriously wrong and that, as Ray Stannard Baker, a reporter for the *Chicago Record*, noted, "the conditions in the country warranted some such explosion."

The Overseas Frontier

At noon on September 16, 1893, thousands of settlers massed along the borders of the Cherokee Strip, a 6-million-acre tract in northwestern Oklahoma. In the next six hours the last great land rush came to an end, and the line of settlement long marked on census maps ceased to exist.

Frederick Jackson Turner, a historian at the University of Wisconsin, described the implications of this event. Steady westward movement had placed Americans in "touch with the simplicity of primitive life," he explained, and helped renew the process of social development. The frontier furnished "the forces dominating the American character," and without its rejuvenating influence, democracy itself might be in danger. Turner's thesis resonated with Americans' fears that modernity had robbed their country of its unique strengths and that the end of free lands would put free institutions at risk. "There is no unexplored part of the world left suitable for men to inhabit," Populist writer William "Coin" Harvey claimed.

That assertion turned out to be premature. More homesteaders claimed more western lands after 1890 than before, and well into the next century new "resource frontiers"— oil fields, timber ranges, Alaskan ore strikes—were explored. Irrigation technology and markets for new crops created a boom for dry-land farmers. Nonetheless, the upheavals of the 1890s seemed to confirm Turner's contention that new frontiers lay overseas.

Whereas farmers had always needed to sell a large portion of their output abroad, until the 1890s the market for manufactured goods was almost exclusively domestic. As the volume of manufactured goods increased, the composition of exports changed. Oil, steel, textiles, typewriters, and sewing machines made up a larger portion of overseas trade. Americans still bought nine-tenths of domestic manufactures, but by 1898 the extra tenth was worth more than $1 billion (see Figure 18–1).

As American firms entered foreign markets, they discovered that other nations and empires also used restrictive tariffs to guard their markets and promote domestic manufacturing. Government and business leaders saw that the United States might have to use political or military leverage to open foreign markets to gain a larger share of world trade. Their social Darwinist view of the world—as a jungle in which only the fittest nations would survive—justified the global competition for trade and economic survival.

Recognizing that a strong navy could extend America's economic reach, Congress authorized the construction of three large battleships in 1890. Four years later, an official commission investigated the feasibility of a canal across Central America. A newly organized National Association of Manufacturers urged the government to open foreign markets. The administration created a Bureau of Foreign Commerce and urged US consuls to seize opportunities to extend sales of American industrial products abroad.

Congress also knew that tariff rates could influence the expansion of trade. Before 1890, taxes on imports had been set high to raise revenue and to help domestic manufacturers by making foreign goods unaffordable. The Harrison-McKinley Tariff of 1890 did something different. It allowed the president to use the tariff to punish countries that closed their markets to US goods or to reward them for lifting customs barriers. This "bargaining tariff" used the weight of the US economy to open markets around the world.

The United States began reorganizing to compete in a global marketplace. The struggle required the executive branch to enlarge the military and take on additional authority. It also meant that domestic industries had to produce higher quality goods at reduced cost to match those from Germany or Japan. Employers and workers had to gear up for the global contest for profits.

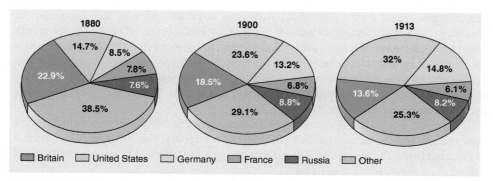

Figure 18-1   Relative Shares of World Manufacturing The United States was a significant industrial power by 1880, and by the turn of the century it moved into a position of dominance.

The Drive for Efficiency

In mines, factories, and mills, production relied on the knowledge of skilled workers. Laborers used their knowledge to set work routines, assure their own safety, and bargain with managers who wanted to change the nature of work. As profits stagnated and competition intensified, employers tried to prevent labor from sharing control over production. Employers relied on three allies: technology, scientific management, and federal power. Workers resisted, organizing themselves and enlisting the support of their communities.

Advances in management techniques enabled employers to dictate new methods. Frederick Winslow Taylor, the first "efficiency expert," reduced each occupation to a series of simple, precise movements that could be easily taught and endlessly repeated. To manage time and motion scientifically, Taylor explained, employers should convert traditional workplace skills and knowledge into "rules, laws, and formulae."

Taylor's stopwatch studies determined everything from how much pig iron a man should load into a boxcar in a day (75 tons) to how he should be paid (3.75 cents per ton). Even office work could be separated into simple, unvaried tasks. "Taylorism" created a new layer of college-educated "middle managers" who supervised production in offices and factories.

Although Taylorism accelerated production, it also increased absenteeism and worker dissatisfaction. Another new technique, "personnel management," promised to solve this problem with tests to select suitable employees, team sports to ward off boredom, and social workers to regulate the activities of workers at home.

As the nineteenth century ended, management was establishing a monopoly on expertise and using it to set the rhythms of work and play, but workers did not easily relinquish control. In the 1890s, the labor struggle entered a new phase. New unions confronted corporations in bloody struggles that forced the federal government to decide whether communities or property had more rights. Skilled workers rallied the labor movement to the cause of retaining control of the conditions of work.

The Struggle Between Management and Labor

To accelerate production, employers aimed to seize full control over the workplace. They had private detective agencies, the courts, and federal troops on their side and were ready to act. In Pennsylvania and Chicago, this antagonism led to bloody confrontations.

The most modern steelworks in the world, Andrew Carnegie's mill at Homestead, Pennsylvania, made armor plating for American warships and steel rails for shipment abroad. In June 1892, Carnegie's partner, Henry Clay Frick, broke off talks with the plant's American Federation of Labor–affiliated union and announced that the plant would close on July 2 and reopen a week later with a nonunion workforce. The union contended that Frick's actions were an assault on the community, and the town agreed. On the morning of July 6, townspeople equipped with a cannon confronted 300 armed company guards and forced them to surrender.

The victory was short-lived. A week later the governor of Pennsylvania sent in the state militia, and under martial law strikebreakers reignited the furnaces. The battle at Homestead broke the union and showed that corporations, backed by government, would defend their prerogatives at any cost.

The Pullman strike, centered in Chicago, paralyzed the railroads for two weeks in the summer of 1894. It pitted the American Railway Union (ARU) against 24 railroads and

HARPER'S WEEKLY
JOURNAL OF CIVILIZATION

NEW YORK, SATURDAY, JULY 16, 1892.

THE HOMESTEAD RIOT.—DRAWN BY W. P. SNYDER AFTER A PHOTOGRAPH BY DABBS, PITTSBURG.—[SEE PAGE 678.]
THE PINKERTON MEN LEAVING THE BARGES AFTER THE SURRENDER.

Homestead Strike When Carnegie Steel locked out all 3,800 employees of the Homestead Steel Works, local citizens and police battled with Carnegie guards for control of the plant. They believed that as producers they had a right to work and profit from their labor. Carnegie believed that he had a right to hire and fire whom he pleased.

the powerful Pullman Company over the company's decision to cut pay by 30 percent, an action taken in response to the economic crisis of 1893. Eugene V. Debs, the charismatic president of the ARU, urged strikers to obey the law, avoid violence, and respect strikebreakers. When Cleveland sent in the army over the governor's protests, enraged crowds blocked tracks and burned railroad cars. Police arrested hundreds of strikers. Debs went to jail for six months and came out a socialist. Pullman and Homestead showed that the law was now on the side of the proprietors.

Newspapers, magazines, and novels portrayed Pullman and Homestead as two more battles in an unending war against the savage opponents of progress, with the forces of government rescuing civilization from the unions.

The business elite's cultural influence allowed it to define the terms of this contest, to label its enemies as enemies of progress. Workers did not object to efficiency or modernization, but they wanted a share of its benefits and some control over the process of change. With state and corporate power stacked against them, their goals appeared beyond reach.

Just as the massacre at Wounded Knee in 1890 had ended the armed resistance of Native Americans, the violence at Homestead and Chicago marked a new phase in the struggle of industrial workers.

Corporate Consolidation

In a wave of mergers between 1897 and 1904, investment bankers consolidated leading industries under the control of a few corporate giants, and J. P. Morgan led the movement. His goal was to take industry away from the industrialists and give it to the bankers. Bankers, he felt, had better information about the true worth of an industry and so could make better decisions about its future. They could create the larger, leaner firms needed to take on foreign competitors.

Morgan's greatest triumph was the merger of eight huge steel companies, their ore ranges, rolling mills, railroads, and shipping lines into the colossal U.S. Steel. The 1901 merger created the world's largest corporation. Its capital amounted to 7 percent of the total wealth of the United States (by comparison, the largest US firm in 2008, Exxon Mobil, had assets valued at only six-tenths of 1 percent of gross domestic product). U.S. Steel's investors (Morgan especially) earned profits "greatly in excess of reasonable compensation," according to one government report.

Bankers outnumbered steelmakers on U.S. Steel's board, and they controlled the company. *McClure's* magazine reported that the new company was "planning the first really systematic effort ever made by Americans to capture the foreign steel trade."

A Modern Economy

Grover Cleveland's bargain with Morgan revived the industrial economy, but farm prices, wages, and the president's popularity remained flat. Cash-strapped farmers in the West and South disliked the president's hard-money policies and cozy relationships with plutocrats such as Morgan. Calling out troops to crush the Pullman strike cost Cleveland the support of northern workers. The escalating cycle of economic and political crises, farmer and labor insurgencies, middle-class radicalism, and upper-class conservatism fractured political parties. Democrats, Republicans, and Populists all called for stronger government action, but each party split over what action to take. In 1896, the "currency question" dominated a watershed election that transformed the two major parties and destroyed the third.

The year 1896 was the last time presidential candidates openly debated great economic questions in terms that had been familiar to voters since Thomas Jefferson ran for president in 1800; 1896 was also the first recognizably modern presidential election, the first time a successful candidate used the advertising and fund-raising techniques of twentieth-century campaigns.

Currency: Gold Versus Silver

The soundness of the dollar, which Morgan and Cleveland worked so hard to preserve, was a mixed blessing for Americans. Based on gold, the dollar helped sell American goods in foreign markets, especially in Europe, where currencies were also based on gold. The United States traded on a much smaller scale with countries—such as Mexico and China—that used silver. Gold, however, was valuable because it was scarce, and many Americans suffered from that scarcity. The low prices and high interest rates Populists complained of were a result of the gold standard.

Increasing the money supply would reduce interest rates and make credit more available. There were two ways to put more money in circulation: the government could print paper greenbacks, or it could coin silver. "Free silver" advocates generally favored coining a ratio of 16 ounces of silver for each ounce of gold. Both Populists and western mining interests pushed silver. The Republican and Democratic Parties officially endorsed the gold standard, but by 1896 each party had a renegade faction of silverites. In the 1890s, the crucial political issues—jobs, foreign trade, the survival of small farms, and the prosperity of big corporations—boiled down to one question: Would the dollar be backed by gold or silver? The election of 1896 was "the battle of the standards."

The Cross of Gold

A dark mood hung over Chicago as delegates arrived at the Democratic convention in July 1896. They had come to bury Cleveland and the party's commitment to the gold standard along with him. The draft platform denounced Cleveland for imposing "government by injunction" during the Pullman strike. When the platform came before the full convention, delegates had to decide whether the party would stand for silver or gold and who would replace Cleveland as the candidate for president.

Both questions were decided when a former congressman from Nebraska, William Jennings Bryan, mounted the stage. He was an electrifying speaker. "You come and tell us that the great cities are in favor of the gold standard," he said. "Destroy our farms, and the grass will grow in the streets of every city in the country!" Bryan spoke in the rhythmic cadence of a camp preacher. "We will answer their demand for a gold standard by saying to them"—he paused, stretching out his arms in an attitude of crucifixion— "You shall not press down upon the brow of labor this crown of thorns. You shall not crucify mankind upon a cross of gold!" The hall exploded with cheers. Bryan won the nomination handily.

Two weeks later the Populists, meeting in St. Louis, also nominated Bryan. The Ocala and Omaha platforms, which imagined comprehensive changes in the money system and American institutions, had been reduced to a single panacea: silver. Republicans overwhelmingly adopted a progold plank, drafted with the approval of J. P. Morgan, and nominated William McKinley, the governor of Ohio and a supporter of industry. The parties could hardly have offered two more different candidates or two more different visions of the future.

The Battle of the Standards

In one of the most exciting electoral contests since the Civil War, the candidates employed new techniques in radically different ways. McKinley ran like an incumbent: he never left his home. Instead, delegations came to him. Some 750,000 people from 30 states trampled McKinley's grass and listened to speeches affirming his commitment to high tariffs and sound money. The speeches were distributed as newspaper columns, fliers, and pamphlets across the country. The campaign used public relations techniques to educate the electorate on the virtues of the gold standard. Posters reduced the campaign's themes to pithy slogans like "Prosperity or Poverty" and "Vote for Free Silver and Be Prosperous Like Guatemala."

The genius behind the campaign was a Cleveland coal-and-oil millionaire named Marcus Hanna who bankrolled his publicity blitz with between $3 million and $7 million raised from industrialists. The combination of big money and advertising revolutionized presidential politics.

With only $300,000 to spend, Bryan ran like a challenger, even though his party occupied the White House. He logged 29,000 miles by rail and buggy and made more than 500 speeches in 29 states. Oratorical ability had won Bryan the nomination, but audiences were unaccustomed to hearing a candidate speak for himself, and many considered it undignified. "The Boy Orator has one speech," wrote an unsympathetic Republican, John Hay. "He simply reiterates the unquestioned truths that . . . gold is vile, that silver is lovely and holy."

Despite the scorn of eastern newspapers, industrialists feared the prospect of a Bryan presidency. Factory owners threatened to close shop if Bryan won. Just before Election Day, the global markets that McKinley praised returned the favor. Crop failures abroad doubled the price of wheat in the Midwest, raising farm incomes and alleviating the anxieties that drove farmers to Bryan. Bryan won the South and West decisively, but McKinley won the populous industrial Northeast and several farm states in the upper Midwest, capturing the Electoral College by 271 to 176 (see Map 18–1).

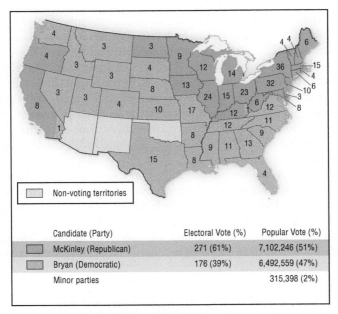

Candidate (Party)	Electoral Vote (%)	Popular Vote (%)
McKinley (Republican)	271 (61%)	7,102,246 (51%)
Bryan (Democratic)	176 (39%)	6,492,559 (47%)
Minor parties		315,398 (2%)

Map 18-1   The Election of 1896 William McKinley's "front-porch campaign" carried the northern industrial states, along with the key farm states of Iowa and Minnesota, securing a narrow victory over Bryan.

The election of 1896 changed the style of campaigns and shifted the political positions of both major parties. By pushing currency policies to improve the lives of workers and farmers, Bryan's Democrats abandoned their traditional Jacksonian commitment to minimal government. The Republicans recognized that voters would judge the president on his ability to bring them prosperity. Electoral democracy now had a distinctly economic cast. As president, McKinley asserted his leadership over economic policy, calling Congress into special session to pass the Dingley Tariff Act, which levied the highest taxes on imports in American history. He extended presidential power even more dramatically through an expansionist foreign and military policy.

In the election of 1896, basic economic questions—Who is the economy supposed to serve? What is the nature of money?—were at stake in a closely matched campaign. No wonder voter turnout hit an all-time high. Administrative agencies took over those issues after the turn of the century, but Americans long remembered that raucous campaign when the nation's economic future was up for grabs. As late as the 1960s, schoolchildren still recited the Cross of Gold speech.

The Retreat from Politics

The economy improved steadily after 1895, but this latest business panic left lasting marks on corporate and political culture. Industrial workers made a tactical retreat in the face of a new political and legal climate. In the South, depression, urbanization, and the modernizing influence of railroads accelerated the spread of legalized racial segregation and disfranchisement. What was happening in the South and the nation was part of a nationwide decline of participatory politics. With the slackening of both agrarian unrest and resistance to corporate capitalism, politics lost some of its value. Voter participation declined, and Americans felt less of a personal stake in elections. Disaffected groups—such as labor and African Americans—had to devise new ways to build community and express resistance.

The Lure of the Cities

In the South as in the North, people left the countryside and moved to towns and cities. By 1900, one out of six southerners lived in town. Except for Birmingham, Alabama, southern cities were not devoted to manufacturing but to commerce and services. Doctors' offices, clothing and dry goods stores, and groceries could be found near warehouses in which cotton was stored, ginned, and pressed and near the railway station, from which it was shipped to textile mills.

The growth of villages and towns in the South was the product of rural decay. Crop liens, which gave bankers ownership of a crop before it was planted, and debt drove people from farms. The young and the ambitious left first, while older and poorer residents stayed behind.

While white newcomers settled on the outskirts, African Americans moved into industrial districts along the railroad tracks. Still, towns offered things that were missing in the country, such as schools. A Little Rock, Arkansas, resident noted that newly arrived African American parents were "very anxious to send their children to school." Jobs were often available, too, although more frequently for women than for men. Men looked for seasonal labor at farms or lumber camps outside towns. This meant families faced a tough choice between poverty and separation.

Galveston, Texas, 1900

Looking back, many survivors would remember warning signs: an unusual stillness in the Gulf of Mexico, lightning flashes in a clear sky. But when the winds began to pick up early in the morning on September 8, 1900, the residents of Galveston believed their solid slate-roofed homes would protect them from what turned out to be the deadliest storm in American history.

Galveston was a Gilded Age boomtown, the "New York of the Gulf." Sited like Manhattan on an island at the mouth of a deep-water bay, it was Texas's principal port. Railroads brought cotton and cattle from San Antonio, Dallas, and Fort Worth to the wharves, where they met steamships from Hamburg, Cartagena, and Marseille. Galveston was a major arrival point for immigrants, who had their papers and throats checked at Pelican Island before setting foot in a land advertised as exuberantly fertile. Alongside hotels, offices, boutiques, and the Grand Opera House on the Strand were the consulates of 16 countries, including Russia and Japan.

Like many American cities, Galveston was ostensibly governed by a mayor and a council, comprised of aldermen elected by each of the 12 wards, but an elite of wealthy brokers and merchants maintained the city's dominance through private monopolies. The Galveston Wharf Company charged outrageous port fees and steered trade into the hands of favored clients. The Cotton Exchange set prices for the region's principal crop. Economics and politics were a kind of competition; for boosters it was not enough for Galveston to be prosperous; it also had to trounce its rival, Houston. Traders on the powerful (and unelected) Deepwater Port Commission used their connections to get federal money to dredge the shipping canals, removing protective sandbars and sealing Galveston's lead. Even the weather bureau joined in, playing up the tornado threat to inland cities while dismissing the danger from hurricanes as "an absurd delusion."

Galveston shared the confidence of the country at the dawn of a new century. Leaving the doldrums of the early 1890s, the national economy forged ahead. American armies were victorious in Cuba and Asia, and scientific advances—telecommunications, medicine, steam propulsion, and weather prediction—strengthened a sense that distance, disease, and nature itself could be tamed. Galveston was at the forefront of these changes, the first city in Texas with electric lights and telephones. Its streetcar line defied geography, traveling on elevated trestles over the Gulf itself. The city grew by 30 percent in the previous decade, the Galveston News reported on September 7, and "the prospects are bright even to surpass it."

The 1900 storm was not unprecedented. In 1886, the coastal town of Indianola was

Despite setbacks, newcomers gained a place for themselves in urban life. By 1890, every southern city had an African American business district with churches, insurance companies, lawyers, doctors, undertakers, and usually a weekly newspaper. Benevolent and reform organizations, sewing circles, and book clubs enriched community life.

wiped out by a hurricane. Still, when the red and black storm flags went up, Galvestonians and the thousands of tourists in town for a weekend at the beach sought shelter in the city rather than escaping to the mainland. It was a fatal choice. The storm surge pulverized the commercial district. The streetcar trestle, lifted by the flood, bulldozed through neighborhoods, smashing houses in its path. Thousands were swept out to sea, while thousands more drowned in the wreckage. The clouds cleared over a ruined city. From one end to the other along the high-water mark stretched a ridge of broken timbers, masonry, furniture, and human and animal corpses.

With hospitals, churches, and city hall destroyed, the victims organized their own relief. Middle- and upper-class women distributed thousands of pounds of supplies from the Red Cross. An ad hoc Women's Health Protective Committee rallied survivors to care for the injured, clear debris, and set up tent cities. Meanwhile, the Deep Water Commission struggled to clear wrecked ships and reopen the port. Together, WHPC and port officials petitioned the legislature to replace the city's elected government with a board of appointed commissioners who would head departments of finance, fire, police, water, sewage, and streets. Democratic institutions were not up to the challenge, they agreed; this emergency required experts.

The commissioner system unmasked the control that brokers and merchants had always had over Galveston's politics, but it also revealed the new power of educated women (who still lacked the vote) and reform groups. The commissioners launched an ambitious reconstruction scheme, beginning with data collection. They carefully mapped currents, wave patterns, and the debris wall, using it to mark the outer limits of new construction. Instead of relocating to the mainland, they laid plans for raising the city 17 feet and placing it behind a three-mile-long concrete seawall to hold back any future storm surge. The Women's Committee laid out lots for new houses separated by wide, well-drained streets and barriers of vegetation to disrupt flood currents.

Galveston lost the competition to become the state's largest city. The discovery of oil at Spindletop Dome a year later made Houston the next boomtown. But the commissioner system became a model of progressive reform imitated by over 500 cities, mostly in the Midwest. The "Galveston Plan" offered a cure for the corruption of urban machines. Commissioners agreed that "economy and business methods, not politics" should be the ruling principle. While efficient, it was also undemocratic. Only two members of the board were elected; the rest were appointed by the legislature. None were African American, despite black majorities in two of the wards. Residents were grateful for the speedy action, but uneasy about the new order. "Commission government is far from a perfect plan," wrote a journalist who survived the disaster; "it only marks a transition toward better things."

African American professionals such as lawyers, doctors, and nurses were limited to working within their community. Jobs on the bottom rung of the corporate ladder—clerk, salesman, telephone operator, stenographer, railroad conductor—were reserved for whites.

Inventing Jim Crow

In June 1892, Homer Plessy boarded the East Louisiana Railway in New Orleans for a trip to Covington, Louisiana. Having purchased a first-class ticket, he attempted to board the whites-only car and was arrested under a Louisiana law that required African Americans and whites to ride in "equal but separate accommodations." Before Judge John H. Ferguson could try the case, Plessy's lawyer appealed on the grounds that the separate-car law violated the Constitution's Fourteenth Amendment.

When *Plessy v. Ferguson* came before the Supreme Court in April 1896, the State of Louisiana argued that the law was necessary to avoid the "danger of friction from too intimate contact" between the races. In separate cars, all citizens enjoyed equal privileges. Plessy's lawyer, Albion Tourgée, replied that the question was not "the equality of the privileges enjoyed, but the right of the state to label one citizen as white and another as colored." In doing so, the government gave unearned advantages to some citizens and not to others. The issue for Tourgée was not racial conflict or even prejudice, but whether the government should be allowed to divide people arbitrarily. The court upheld the "separate but equal" doctrine, and the decision provided legal justification for the system of official inequality that expanded in the twentieth century. Informal segregation had existed since the Civil War, and unwritten local customs usually governed the public interaction of whites and African Americans—at work, in business, or when traveling. By the 1890s those informal customs were being codified in law. Railroads, as symbols of progress, were a chief point of contention.

The political and economic tensions created by the depression helped turn racist customs into a rigid caste division. Competition for jobs fed racial antagonisms, as did the migration into cities and towns of a new generation of African Americans, born since the war, who showed less deference to whites. New notions of "scientific" racism led intellectuals and churchmen to regard racial hostility as natural. Angry southern voters deposed the governing coalitions of landowners and New South industrialists and replaced them with Populist "demagogues."

Between 1887 and 1891, nine states in the South passed railroad segregation laws. Trains included separate cars for African Americans, called "Jim Crow" cars after the name of a character in a minstrel show. Soon Jim Crow laws were extended to waiting rooms, drinking fountains, and other places where African Americans and whites might meet.

Segregation was also enforced by terror. The threat of lynching poisoned relations

Lynchings Were Public Spectacles When 17-year-old Jesse Washington was killed in Waco, Texas, in 1916, a crowd of several thousand, including the mayor, police chief, and students from Waco High, attended the event on the lawn of city hall. Afterward, the murderers posed for a photograph and sold their victim's teeth for $5 apiece.

between the races, and African Americans learned that they could be tortured and killed for committing a crime, talking back, or simply looking the wrong way at a white woman. Between 1882 and 1903, nearly 2,000 African American southerners were killed by mobs. Victims were routinely tortured, flayed, castrated, gouged, and burned alive, and members of the mob often took home grisly souvenirs such as a piece of bone or a severed thumb.

Many African American southerners fought segregation with boycotts, lawsuits, and disobedience. Ida Wells-Barnett, a Nashville journalist, organized an international antilynching campaign (see Chapter 19). Segregation was constantly negotiated and challenged, but after 1896 it was backed by the US Supreme Court.

The Atlanta Compromise

When Atlanta invited African American educator Booker T. Washington to address the Cotton States Exposition in 1895, northern newspapers proclaimed a new era of racial progress. The speech made Washington the most recognized African American in the United States. Starting with 40 students and an abandoned shack, Washington had built Tuskegee Institute into the preeminent technical school for African Americans. Washington was a guest in the stately homes of Newport and at Andrew Carnegie's castle in Scotland. When Atlanta staged an exposition to showcase the region's industrial and social progress, the organizers asked Washington to speak.

Washington's address stressed racial accommodation. It had been a mistake, he argued, to try to attain equality by asserting civil and political rights, and he stated that progress "must be the result of severe and constant struggle rather than artificial forcing." He urged white businessmen to employ African American southerners "who have, without strikes and labor wars, tilled your fields, cleared your forests, built your railroads and cities." Stretching out his fingers and then closing them into a fist, he summarized his approach to race relations: "In all things that are purely social, we can be as separate as the fingers, yet one as the hand in all things essential to mutual progress." The largely white audience erupted into applause.

Washington's "Atlanta Compromise" stressed the mutual obligations of African Americans and whites. African Americans would give up the vote and stop insisting on social equality if white leaders would keep violence in check and allow African Americans to succeed in agriculture and business. White industrialists welcomed this arrangement, and African American leaders felt that for the moment it might be the best that could be achieved.

Disfranchisement and the Decline of Popular Politics

After the feverish campaign of 1896, elections began to lose some of their appeal. Attendance fell off at the polls, from 79 percent of voters in 1888 down to 65 percent in 1896. The public events surrounding campaigns also drew thinner crowds, and apathy seemed to have become a national epidemic.

In the South, the disappearance of voters was easy to explain. As Jim Crow laws multiplied, southern states disfranchised African Americans (and one out of four whites) by requiring voters to demonstrate literacy, property ownership, or knowledge of the Constitution in order to register. Louisiana added the notorious grandfather clause,

The Wilmington Race Riot

In 1894, the Populist-Republican "Fusion" ticket won both houses of the North Carolina General Assembly, the powerful state legislature. Fusion officials, anxious to overturn the machine style politics the Democratic Party had established since Reconstruction, set to restoring direct power to the people of North Carolina. Eliminating policies that benefited the white elite at the expense of the farming poor, unskilled labor, and black southerners, Fusionists terminated official appointments and made all positions subject to local election. They enacted new electoral laws and registration practices to encourage black voting. By 1896, the Fusionists, with their focus on class rather than racial solidarity, won every statewide race in North Carolina, and Daniel L. Russell, a Republican, was elected governor. A new brand of truly democratic politics seemed to be on the horizon.

Wilmington, the largest city in North Carolina, had a majority black population and had long been known for the political and economic opportunities it afforded African Americans. But in 1897, when city elections resulted in a Fusionist mayor and several Fusionist aldermen, the tide turned. Anxious at the results achieved by the Populist-Republican pairing, Democratic Party leaders were determined to redeem themselves politically. Embracing the language of "Negro rule" to frighten white voters and "white supremacy" to encourage racial solidarity, Democrats drew a sharp color line among voters, a strategy that coincided with the Jim Crow system of segregation that was rapidly spreading throughout the South.

A public exchange over the question of lynching and interracial relations galvanized the Democratic Party. In August 1897, Rebecca Felton, a Georgia feminist and white supremacist, declared the black rapist to be among the greatest threats faced by southern white farm women. She demanded that white men use vigilante justice to protect the virtue of their women. If necessary, men should be prepared to "lynch a thousand times a week." Alexander Manly, a black Wilmingtonian and editor of the only black-owned daily newspaper in the nation, the *Daily Record*, responded with an editorial in August 1898 in which he defended black men and attempted to dismantle the myth of the black sexual aggressor. He argued that rape claims against black men were exaggerated and that the majority of sexual relations between black men and white women were consensual.

This enraged white southerners. In the aftermath of the Manly editorial, a radical white supremacist faction of the Democratic Party, the Red Shirts, began a campaign of fear and coercion. In October which denied the vote to men whose grandfathers had been prohibited from voting (see Table 18–1).

Whites saw disfranchisement and segregation as modern, managed race relations. Demonizing African Americans enforced solidarity among white voters otherwise divided by local or class interests.

Wilmington White citizens stand before the destroyed *Daily Record* office, 1898.

1898, the Red Shirts terrorized interracial political alliances across eastern North Carolina by breaking up political meetings, destroying property, and committing violent acts. Their goal: keep Republican and Populist voters—especially black voters—from going to the polls. The night before the election, Wilmington Democratic Party leader Colonel Alfred Moor Waddell instructed a mass meeting of white citizens "Go to the polls tomorrow, and if you find the negro out voting, tell him to leave the polls, and if he refuses, kill him."

Democrats' tactics (including stuffed ballots and voter fraud) succeeded, and their candidates secured offices throughout the state. But many of those who had reclaimed Democratic seats in Wilmington were unwilling to accept Fusionists as their peers and colleagues. On November 9, the day after Election Day, a mass meeting of white Wilmingtonians adopted a Wilmington Declaration of Independence, which claimed white supremacy as a right, called for an end to black political participation and interracial politics, and demanded the expulsion of Manly from Wilmington (he had already left).

When black Wilmingtonians responded too slowly to the demands of the Declaration, the white citizenry was all too ready to strike. On November 10, armed, anxious white men filled the Wilmington armory; an early procession of about 500 men grew to 2,000. The first target was Manly's *Daily Record*. A mob ransacked the offices and torched the building. As the crowd marched into one of Wilmington's black neighborhoods, they used repeating rifles to outgun the black men who attempted to defend their property. Hundreds of black citizens escaped Wilmington, hoping to wait out the riot. The number of black deaths remains unknown; most estimates range from 7 to 20.

Those leading the insurrection demanded the resignation of Fusionist officials and then took power for themselves. Political opponents of the rioters were run out of the city. Over the course of the next month, 1,400 African Americans fled Wilmington. No one in Wilmington spoke out against the rioters and no outside forces came to the aid of black citizens. The tactics used in Wilmington spread a clear message throughout the Jim Crow South: those challenging a political system based on white supremacy and elite rule would suffer the consequences.

No new legal restrictions hampered voting in the North and West, but participation fell there, too. This withdrawal from politics reflected the declining importance of political pageantry and the disappearance of intense partisanship. A developing economy with new patterns of social and cultural life undermined partisanship, but so did the new style of campaigns. For American men, the cliffhanger contests of the late

Table 18-1 The Spread of Disfranchisement

Year	State	Strategies
1889	Florida	Poll tax
1889	Tennessee	Poll tax
1890	Mississippi	Poll tax, literacy test, understanding clause
1891	Arkansas	Poll tax
1893, 1901	Alabama	Poll tax, literacy test, grandfather clause
1894, 1895	South Carolina	Poll tax, literacy test, understanding clause
1894, 1902	Virginia	Poll tax, literacy test, understanding clause
1897, 1898	Louisiana	Poll tax, literacy test, grandfather clause
1899, 1900	North Carolina	Poll tax, literacy test, grandfather clause
1902	Texas	Poll tax
1908	Georgia	Poll tax, literacy test, understanding clause, grandfather clause

nineteenth century had provided a sense of identity that strengthened ethnic, religious, and neighborhood identities.

The new emphasis on advertising, education, and fund-raising reduced the personal stakes for voters. Educated middle- and upper-class voters liked the new style, feeling that raucous campaigns were no way to decide important issues. They sought to influence policy more directly, through interest groups rather than parties. Unintentionally, they discarded traditions that unified communities and connected voters to their country and its leaders.

Organized Labor Retreats from Politics

Workers followed organized labor as it turned away from political activity and redefined objectives in economic terms. As traditional crafts came under attack, skilled workers created new organizations that addressed immediate issues: wages, hours, and the conditions of work. The American Federation of Labor (AFL), founded in 1886, built a base around skilled trades and grew from 150,000 members to more than 2 million by 1904. The AFL focused on immediate goals to improve the working lives of its members. Its founder, Samuel Gompers, was born in London's East End and apprenticed as a cigar maker at the age of 10. After his family moved to New York, Gompers joined the Cigar Makers' International Union.

Although affiliated with the Knights of Labor, the cigar makers were more interested in shortening work hours and increasing wages than in remaking the economy. High dues and centralized control allowed the union to offer insurance and death benefits to members while maintaining a strike fund. Gompers applied the same practices to the AFL. His "pure and simple unionism" made modest demands, but it still encountered fierce resistance from corporations, which were backed by the courts.

In the 1895 case of *In re Debs*, the Supreme Court allowed the use of injunctions to criminalize strikes. The court then disarmed one of labor's last weapons, the boycott. In *Loewe v. Lawlor* (1908), known as the Danbury Hatters case, the court ruled that advertising a consumer boycott was illegal under the Sherman Anti-Trust Act.

Gompers believed that industrial unions, which drew members from all occupations within an industry, lacked the discipline and shared values needed to face down corporations and government, whereas unions organized around a single trade or craft would be stronger. However, because the AFL was organized by skill, it often ignored unskilled workers, such as women or recent immigrants. Because employers used unskilled newcomers to break strikes or to run machinery that replaced expert hands, Gompers excluded a large part of the labor force. Organizers recruited Irish and German workers while ignoring Italian, African American, Jewish, and Slavic workers. The union attacked female workers for "stealing" jobs that once belonged to men.

Other unions were built to represent the immediate interests of their members. Under Eugene V. Debs, railroad workers merged the old railroad brotherhoods into the ARU in 1893. The United Mine Workers (UMW), founded in 1890, unionized coal mines in Pennsylvania, Ohio, Indiana, and Michigan. The ARU and the UMW were industrial unions that tried to organize all of the workers in an industry. Able to disrupt the energy and transport systems on which the whole economy depended, these new unions had immense potential power. They faced determined opposition from business and its allies in government. "Our government cannot stand, nor its free institutions endure," the National Association of Manufacturers declared, "if the Gompers-Debs ideals of liberty and freedom of speech and press are allowed to dominate."

American Diplomacy Enters the Modern World

The Republican victory in 1896 gave heart to proponents of prosperity through foreign trade. Before the turn of the century, the new president announced, the United States would control the world's markets. "We will establish trading posts throughout the world as distributing points for American products," Senator Albert Beveridge forecast. "Great colonies, governing themselves, flying our flag and trading with us, will grow about our posts of trade." McKinley sought neither war nor colonies, but many in his party wanted both. These "jingoes" included Assistant Secretary of the Navy Theodore Roosevelt; John Hay, the ambassador to London; and Senators Beveridge and Henry Cabot Lodge. Britain, France, and Germany were seizing territory around the world, and jingoes believed the United States needed to do the same for strategic, religious, and economic reasons. Spain was the most likely target, clinging feebly to the remnants of its once-vast empire in Cuba, the Philippines, Guam, and Puerto Rico. Under Cleveland, the United States had moved away from confrontation with Spain, but McKinley pushed for the creation of an American empire that stretched to the far shores of the Pacific.

Sea Power and the Imperial Urge

Few men better exemplified the jingoes' combination of religiosity, martial spirit, and fascination with the laws of history than Alfred Thayer Mahan. A naval officer and strategist, he argued that since the Roman Empire, world leadership had belonged to the nation that controlled the sea. Published in 1890, his book *The Influence of Sea Power upon History, 1660–1783* became an instant classic.

Mahan connected naval expansion and empire to the problem of overproduction that the United States faced. A great industrial country needed trade; trade required a merchant fleet; and merchant shipping needed naval protection and overseas bases. Colonies could provide markets for goods and congregations for Christian missionaries, but, more important, they allowed naval forces to protect sea lanes and project power in Asia, Latin America, and Africa.

Mahan urged the United States to build a canal across Central America for better access to Asian markets. He urged the building of naval bases along routes to Latin America and the Far East. Congress and the Navy Department began implementing these recommendations even before McKinley took office (see Figure 18–2).

Mahan was not the only prophet who recalled the Roman Empire. Brooks Adams's *The Law of Civilization and Decay* (1895) detailed the effects of the closed frontier: greater concentration of wealth, social inequality, and eventual collapse. To repeal this "law," the United States needed a new frontier in Asia where it could regenerate itself through combat. Sharing the social Darwinist belief that nations and races were locked in a savage struggle for survival, Mahan and Adams expected the United States to win the approaching conflict.

If subduing continents with the cross, Constitution, and Gatling gun appealed to anyone, it was Theodore Roosevelt. Roosevelt paid keen attention to the forces that were magnifying the power of some nations and diminishing others. Imperialism seemed to him the essential characteristic of modernizing countries. A frontiersman, writer, soldier, and politician, Roosevelt was acutely conscious of how modern forces—globalized trade, instant communications, modern navies, and imperialism—had altered the rules of domestic and international politics. He sought to position the United States at the center of these modernizing currents, a place that would have to be earned, he felt, both on foreign battlefields and at home, where the gains of the nineteenth century had not yet been translated into the social and moral advancement that marked a true civilization.

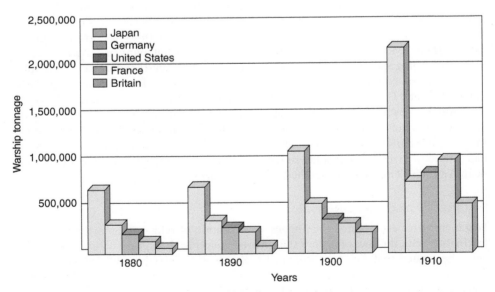

Figure 18-2 Warship Tonnage of the World's Navies Naval strength was the primary index of power before World War I. The United States held onto third place in the naval arms race, while Germany and Japan made significant gains.
Source: Paul Kennedy, *Rise and Fall of the Great Powers* (New York: Random House, 1987), p. 203.

Pears' Soap Advertisements emphasized the celebrated civilizing capacities of imperialism, as shown in this advertisement for Pears' Soap, 1899.

The first step towards lightening

The White Man's Burden

is through teaching the virtues of cleanliness.

Pears' Soap

is a potent factor in brightening the dark corners of the earth as civilization advances, while amongst the cultured of all nations it holds the highest place—it is the ideal toilet soap.

The Scramble for Empire

For jingoes, China was the ultimate prize in the global contest for trade and mastery. It had more people than any other country, hence more customers and more souls for Christ. The number of American missionaries in China doubled in the 1890s, many of them from the Student Volunteer movement, which had chapters on nearly every college campus. Even though no more than 1 or 2 percent of US exports had ever gone to China, manufacturers believed that China could absorb the output of America's overproductive factories. James B. Duke founded the British-American Tobacco Company based on "China's population of 450 million people, and assuming that in the future they might average a cigarette a day." In 1890, Standard Oil began selling kerosene in Shanghai. Fifteen years later, China was the largest overseas market for American oil. Mahan had predicted that China would be the arena for the coming struggle for industrial and military supremacy, and by 1897 he seemed to be right.

In 1894, Japan declared war on China and soon occupied Korea, Manchuria, and China's coastal cities. When the fighting was over, Western powers seized slices of Chinese territory. In 1897, German troops captured the port of Qingdao on the Shandong Peninsula. An industrial area, Shandong was the center of American missionary activity, investment, and trade. To Americans, the invasion of Shandong presaged an imperial grab for territory and influence. In the 1880s, European powers had carved up Africa. Now it appeared that the same thing was about to happen in China. The McKinley administration watched events in China carefully, but in the winter of 1897–1898 it had more pressing concerns closer to home.

War with Spain

While other European powers were expanding their empires, Spain was barely hanging on to the one it had. Since the 1860s, its two largest colonies, Cuba and the Philippines, had been torn by revolution. Between 1868 and 1878, Cuban nationalists fought for independence. Spain ended the war by promising autonomy but not independence. US officials wanted an end to Spanish rule, but the McKinley Tariff and the Panic of 1893 ruined Cuba's chief export industry, sugar. Under a crushing debt, Spain reneged on its promise, and in 1895 the rebellion resumed. The rebels practiced a scorched-earth policy, dynamiting trains and burning plantations in an attempt to force Spain out.

Spain retaliated with a brutal campaign of pacification, killing nearly 100,000 civilians, but it was no use. The Spanish army was disintegrating. Cuban rebels, in control of the countryside, prepared a final assault on the cities. US officials, many of whom wanted to annex the island, now worried that Cuba would gain full independence. McKinley explored the options of either purchasing it from Spain or intervening on the pretext of ending the strife. William Randolph Hearst's *New York Journal* and other newspapers favored the latter, inciting readers with lurid stories of Spanish atrocities and Cuban rioting. Cuba sold newspapers. McKinley moved quickly toward confrontation. When riots erupted in the Cuban capital, he ordered a warship to Havana. Theodore Roosevelt sent one of the newest battleships, the USS *Maine*. The arrival of the *Maine* reduced tensions for a while, but on February 15 an explosion ripped through the ship, killing 266 of a crew that had numbered 350. Navy investigators later concluded that boilers had exploded accidentally, but the newspapers blamed both Spanish and Cuban treachery. Hearst printed a full-page diagram of the ship being destroyed by a "sunken torpedo."

McKinley hesitated, mindful of the budget and events in China, but Roosevelt ordered Commodore George Dewey's Asiatic Squadron to ready an attack on the Philippines. Congress appropriated $50 million for arms. Spanish emissaries tried to gain support from other European countries, but they were rebuffed.

In March, the economic picture brightened, and McKinley sent Spain an ultimatum demanding independence for Cuba. On April 11, he asked Congress for authorization to use force, and Congress passed a declaration of war. Expansionists such as Roosevelt, Mahan, and Adams would not have succeeded if war had been less popular. Corporate interests favored it, immigrants and southerners saw it as a way to assert their patriotism, and newspapers found it made good copy. "We are all jingoes now," declared the *New York Sun*.

Neither side had many illusions about the outcome. Fighting Spain, novelist Sherwood Anderson wrote, was "like robbing an old gypsy woman in a vacant lot at night after the fair," but the war opened with a cliffhanger that even Hearst could not have invented. On May 1, news arrived that Dewey's forces were fighting the Spanish fleet in Manila Bay in the Philippines. The war had begun, not in Cuba, but instead half a world away. There the information stopped. The telegraph cable from Manila had been cut. Official Spanish reports alleged that the Americans had suffered a "considerable loss of life." Dewey's squadron contained only two modern cruisers, but in contrast to Spain's wooden vessels, all of its ships were steel hulled. For six anxious days Americans awaited word from the far edge of the Pacific.

It arrived early on May 7. The *New York Herald*'s Hong Kong correspondent had been at the battle. Dewey destroyed Spain's entire fleet of 12 warships without a single serious casualty. The country went wild with relief and triumph. New York staged a parade on Fifth Avenue. A Dewey-for-president movement began. In Washington, McKinley consulted a map to see where the Philippines were. Roosevelt quit his job and ordered up a uniform.

The war in Cuba unfolded more modestly. The navy bottled up Spain's ships in the Bay of Santiago de Cuba, and American warships cut the fleet to pieces as it attempted to escape. "Don't cheer, men," an officer ordered the gun crews. "Those poor devils are dying."

In the years before the war, Congress had poured money into the navy but not the army, and it took some time before soldiers could be trained and equipped. Recruits were

The Rough Riders Theodore Roosevelt's regiment, with its blend of educated men from the east and rough-and-tumble western frontiersmen, represented his idealized blend of American military manhood.

herded into camps in Florida without tents, proper clothing, or latrines. There were few medical supplies or doctors. In these unsanitary camps, soldiers died of dysentery and malaria. Of the 5,462 US soldiers who died in the war with Spain, 5,083 succumbed to disease, a scandal that forced the government to elevate the status of the surgeon general and to improve sanitation and disease prevention in the military.

The army landed on the Cuban coast and marched inland to engage Spanish defenders. Roosevelt came ashore with the First Volunteer Cavalry, known as the "Rough Riders." He recruited, trained, and publicized the regiment and wrote its history. An assortment of outlaws, cowboys, Ivy League athletes, New York City policemen, a novelist, and a Harvard Medical School graduate, its membership combined frontier heroism with eastern elite leadership. The regiment traveled with its own film crew and a correspondent from the *New York Herald*.

Spanish forces stubbornly resisted around the city of Santiago. At San Juan Hill, 500 defenders forced a regiment of the New York National Guard to retreat. The all–African American 9th and 10th Cavalry fought alongside the Rough Riders. "The negroes saved that fight," a white soldier reported. The capture of Santiago effectively ended Spanish resistance. When fighting ended in August, US troops occupied Cuba, Guam, Puerto Rico, and the city of Manila. The war had lasted only four months.

As American and Spanish diplomats met in Paris to conclude a peace treaty, McKinley had to decide which occupied territories to keep as colonies. Congress, not wanting to inherit the island's $400 million in debt, had already resolved not to annex Cuba. McKinley decided that Guam and Puerto Rico would make ideal naval bases (see Map 18–2).

The president also seized the opportunity to annex the island nation of Hawaii. In 1893, American sugar planters, led by Sanford Dole, overthrew the islands' last queen, Liliuokalani, and petitioned for annexation. They were motivated by the Harrison-McKinley Tariff, which would ruin the planters unless they could reconnect Hawaii's trade to the United States. Annexation was their best chance, and they had a powerful ally in the US Navy. Mahan had identified Pearl Harbor, on Oahu, as a vital base. McKinley decided to take up Dole's annexation offer.

The Philippines were more of a problem. The 7,000 islands were far from the United States and had a population of several million. The United States needed a naval base and supply station close to the China coast, but holding just one island would be impossible if another power controlled the others. Shortly after Dewey's victory, British and German warships anchored in Manila Bay, clearly intending to divide up the territory the United States did not claim. McKinley felt trapped.

Spain recognized Cuban independence and surrendered most of its empire to the United States for free, but it gave up the Philippines only after the United States agreed to

Map 18-2   The Spanish-American War: (a) Caribbean Theater; (b) Pacific Theater

pay $20 million, or, as an American satirist calculated, $1.25 for every Filipino. The treaty was signed December 10, 1898.

McKinley did not take into account the fact that the Philippines had already declared independence. With Dewey's encouragement, rebels under the command of Emilio Aguinaldo had liberated the countryside surrounding Manila and laid siege to the city. At Malolos, north of Manila, a national assembly, including lawyers, doctors, professors, and landowners, issued a constitution. By the time the US Army arrived in 1899, Filipinos had overthrown the Spanish and rallied to their new government.

The Anti-Imperialists

Many prominent Americans opposed both the annexation of new colonies and the approaching war with the Philippines. During the treaty fight in Congress in January 1899, they tried to mobilize opinion against the treaty. The movement included ex-presidents Grover Cleveland and Benjamin Harrison; William Jennings Bryan; labor unionists, including Samuel Gompers and Eugene Debs; writers such as Mark Twain and Ambrose Bierce; and industrialists, including Andrew Carnegie. The anti-imperialists advanced an array of moral, economic, and strategic arguments. Filipinos and Hawaiians, they said, had sought American help in good faith and were capable of governing themselves. The islands could not be defended, and US forces would be exposed to attack at Pearl Harbor or Manila. Carnegie argued that imperialism took tax dollars and attention away from domestic problems. White supremacists asked whether Filipinos would become citizens or be allowed to vote and emigrate to the mainland.

The most moving objections came from those who believed imperialism betrayed America's fundamental principles. To Mark Twain, imperialism was only the newest form of greed: "There is more money in it, more territory, more sovereignty, and other kinds of emolument, than there is in any other game that is played." Opponents of annexation organized an Anti-Imperialist League and lobbied for the rejection of the Paris Treaty.

Congress responded to anti-imperialist objections, banning Philippine immigration, placing the colonies outside the tariff walls, and promising eventual self-government. Jingoes had a military victory on their side. Anti-imperialists could not offer a vision comparable to naval supremacy, the evangelization of the world, or the China market. On February 6, 1899, the US Senate ratified the Paris Treaty and annexed the Philippines. A day earlier, on the other side of the world, the Philippine-American War began.

The Philippine-American War

McKinley believed he had annexed islands full of near savages "unfit for self-rule," but the Philippines by 1899 had an old civilization with a long tradition of resistance to colonialism. When Magellan discovered the islands in 1521, he found a literate population linked by trade ties to India, Japan, and China. The Spanish converted most Filipinos to Catholicism and established schools and a centralized government. Manila's oldest university was older than Harvard. By 1898, much of the upper class, the *illustrados*, had been educated in Europe.

Dewey gave Aguinaldo his word that America desired no colonies. Aguinaldo continued to trust the Americans despite the arrival of fresh US troops. On February 4, an argument between American and Filipino sentries ended in gunfire. Aguinaldo was despondent: "No one can deplore more than I this rupture. I have a clear conscience that I endeavored to avoid it at all costs."

Kansas volunteers drove the Filipino armies into the mountains. Aguinaldo adopted a guerilla strategy, which proved effective. Some 4,000 Americans were killed during the war and another 3,000 wounded out of a total force of 70,000. Frustrated by guerilla conflict, American soldiers customarily executed prisoners, looted villages, and raped Filipino women. An American general on the island of Samar ordered his soldiers to kill everyone over the age of 10. "No cruelty is too severe for these brainless monkeys," a soldier wrote home. "I am in my glory when I can sight some dark skin and pull the trigger."

The army's preferred mode of torture was "the water cure," in which a soldier forced water down a prisoner's throat until the abdomen swelled, and then kicked the prisoner's stomach to force the water out again. Military officials argued that Filipinos were "half-civilized" and that force was the best language for dealing with them.

Newspaper accounts of torture and massacres fueled American opposition to the war, just as US forces scored some victories. Recognizing that they were fighting a political war, US officers took pains to win over dissidents and ethnic minorities. In 1901, this strategy began to pay off. When American troops intercepted a messenger bound for Aguinaldo's secret headquarters, Brigadier General Frederick Funston devised a bold (and, under the rules of war, illegal) plan. He dressed a group of Filipinos loyal to the American side in the uniforms of captured Filipinos, and, posing as a prisoner, Funston entered Aguinaldo's camp and kidnapped the president.

After three weeks in a Manila prison, Aguinaldo issued a proclamation of surrender. When resistance continued in Batangas Province for another year, the US Army responded by herding people into concentration camps, a practice the United States had condemned in Cuba. It had the same tragic result. Perhaps a third of the province's population died of disease and starvation. On July 4, 1902, President Theodore Roosevelt declared the war over.

The American flag flew over the Philippines until 1942, but the colony never lived up to its imperial promise. Instead of defending American trade interests, US troops were pinned down in garrisons, guarding against uprisings and the threat of Japanese invasion. The costs of occupation far exceeded the profits generated by Philippine trade. The colony chiefly attracted American reformers and missionaries, who built schools, churches, and agricultural colleges. Some colonists sought statehood, but Americans liked their colonial experiment less and less. Labor unions feared a flood of immigration from the islands, and farmers resented competition from Philippine producers; in 1933, Congress voted to phase out American rule.

The Open Door

As Americans celebrated their victories, European powers continued to divide China into quasi-colonial "concessions." An alarmed imperial court in Beijing began a crash program of modernization, but reactionaries overthrew the emperor and installed the conservative "dowager empress" Cixi. In the countryside, Western missionaries and traders came under attack from local residents led by martial artists known as Boxers. Many Americans feared that the approaching disintegration of China would mean the exclusion of US trade.

Secretary of State John Hay watched events in China carefully. "The inherent weakness of our position is this," he wrote McKinley. "We do not want to rob China ourselves, and our public opinion will not allow us to interfere, with an army, to prevent others from robbing her. Besides, we have no army." Seeking some way to keep China's markets open, McKinley turned to William Rockhill, a legendary foreign service officer who had lived in China and had been the first westerner to visit Tibet. He, in turn, consulted his friend Alfred Hippisley, an Englishman returning from service with the British-run Chinese imperial customs.

Rockhill, Hippisley, and Hay drafted an official letter known as the Open Door Note. Sent to each of the imperial powers, it acknowledged the partitioning of China into spheres and observed that none of the powers had yet closed its areas to the trade of other countries. The note urged the powers to declare publicly their intention to continue this policy. The Open Door was mostly bluff. The United States had no authority to ask for such a pledge and no military power to enforce one. The foreign ministers of Germany, Japan, Russia, Britain, and France replied cautiously at first, but Hay adroitly played one power off another, starting with Britain and Japan. Once the two strongest powers in China had agreed, France and then Russia and Germany followed. The United States had secured access to China without war or partition, but the limits of Hay's success soon became apparent.

In early 1900, the antiforeign Boxer movement swept through Shandong Province. Armed Chinese attacked missions and foreign businesses, destroyed railroads, and massacred Chinese Christians. Empress Cixi recruited 30,000 Boxers into her army and declared war on all foreign countries. The Western powers rushed troops to China, but before they arrived, Chinese armies attacked Western embassies in Beijing. A British, Russian, Japanese, and French force gathered at Tianjin to march to the rescue. European powers appeared all too eager to capture the Chinese capital.

Without consulting Congress, McKinley ordered American troops into battle on the Asian mainland. Five thousand soldiers rushed from Manila to Tianjin. Hay issued a second Open Door Note, asking the allies to pledge to protect China's independence. Again, the imperial powers reluctantly agreed rather than admit their secret plans to carve up China. On August 15, 1900, US cavalry units reached Beijing, along with Russian Cossacks, French Zouaves, British-Indian sepoys, German hussars, and Japanese dragoons. After freeing the captive diplomats, the armies of the civilized world looted the city. The ,United States was unable to maintain the Open Door in China for long. Russia and Japan established separate military zones in northeast China, but the principle of the Open Door, of encouraging free trade and open markets, guided American foreign policy throughout the twentieth century. It rested on the assumption that, in an equal contest, American firms would prevail, spreading manufactured goods around the world and American influence with them. Under the Open Door, the United States was better off in a world without empires, a world in which consumers in independent nations could buy what they wanted. Just one year after the Spanish-American War, Hay rejected imperial expansion in favor of trade expansion. This new strategy promised greater gains, but it placed the United States on a collision course with the empires of the world (see Map 18–3).

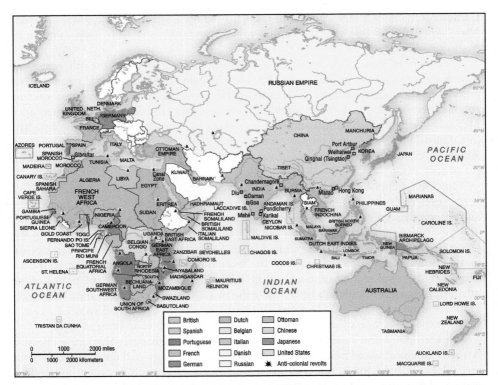

Map 18-3a   The Imperial World: Asia, Africa, and the Middle East Modern imperialism reached its apex between 1880 and 1945. Most of Africa, the Middle East, and Asia, a third of the world's population, was absorbed into global empires linked by telegraph and steamship to centers of government and commerce in London, Paris, Tokyo, and Washington, DC.

Time Line

▼**1890**

Global depression begins

United Mine Workers founded

Battle of Wounded Knee ends Indian wars

Harrison-McKinley Tariff passed

Alfred T. Mahan publishes *The Influence of Sea Power upon History, 1660–1783*

Standard Oil markets kerosene in China

▼**1892**

Homestead strike

▼**1893**

Financial crisis leads to business failures and mass unemployment

World's Columbian Exposition, Chicago

Cherokee Strip land rush

American sugar planters overthrow Queen Liliuokalani of Hawaii

▼**1894**

Coxey's Army marches on Washington

Pullman strike

US commission charts canal route across Nicaragua

▼**1895**

Morgan agrees to Treasury bailout

National Association of Manufacturers founded

Brooks Adams publishes *The Law of Civilization and Decay*

Booker T. Washington gives "Atlanta Compromise" address

Revolution begins in Cuba

Japan annexes Korea and Taiwan

▼**1896**

Plessy v. Ferguson declares "separate but equal" facilities constitutional

Map 18-3b   The Imperial World: the Pacific and the Americas

William McKinley elected
president

▼**1897**
Germany captures Qingdao, on
China's Shandong Peninsula
McKinley issues formal protest
to Spain

▼**1898**
USS *Maine* explodes in Havana's
harbor
United States declares war on
Spain
Dewey defeats Spanish fleet at
Manila Bay
In the Treaty of Paris, Spain
grants Cuba independence

and cedes Guam, Puerto Rico,
and the Philippines to the
United States
Aguinaldo proclaims Philippine
independence

▼**1899**
Senate votes to annex Puerto
Rico, Hawaii, and the
Philippines
Philippine-American War begins
Hay issues first Open Door Note

▼**1900**
Hay issues second Open Door
Note

US Army joins British, French,
Russian, German, and
Japanese forces in capture of
Beijing
Great Exposition of Paris
showcases American
technology
William McKinley reelected

▼**1901**
Aguinaldo captured
McKinley assassinated; Theodore
Roosevelt becomes president

▼**1902**
Roosevelt declares Philippine-
American War over

Conclusion

In the turbulent 1890s, the social and economic divisions among Americans widened. The hope that a solution to these divisions could be found outside the United States was short-lived. Imperialism promised new markets and an end to the cycle of depression and labor strife. The United States conquered an overseas empire and challenged other empires to open their ports to free trade, but the goal of prosperity and peace at home proved elusive.

In many ways social Darwinism became a self-fulfilling prophecy, as competition rather than compromise prevailed. Workers and businessmen, farmers and bankers, middle-class radicals and conservatives, whites and African Americans saw each other as enemies. Racial segregation showed that middle ground, on which whites and African Americans could meet on equal terms, had disappeared. Americans now had to decide what was politically possible and devise new bargaining strategies.

Economic recovery and military victory closed the decade on an optimistic note. Prosperity, power, and technology seemed to have rewritten the rules of human affairs to America's advantage. In the American exhibit at the Paris Exposition of 1900, Henry Adams contemplated a 40-foot dynamo—a "huge wheel, revolving within arm's length"—and felt as if he had crossed a "historical chasm." The machine's mysterious silent force, emanating from "a dirty engine house carefully kept out of sight," seemed a metaphor for the modern age.

Who, What, Where

Bryan, William Jennings 565

Crop liens 567

Cuba 568

Galveston 568

Gold standard 558

Gompers, Samuel 574

Hearst, William Randolph 578

Homestead Steel Works 563

Jim Crow laws 570

Open Door 582

The Philippines 575

Separate but equal 570

Taylorism 562

Washington, Booker T. 571

Wilmington 572

Review Questions

1. What new techniques and practices made US industries more efficient?
2. What motivated Americans to seek an empire?
3. Why did the weather bureau discount the hurricane threat to Galveston?
4. Which cities were the main centers of industry and culture in the 1890s?

Critical-Thinking Questions

1. How did the concept of individual rights evolve in reaction to new economic conditions? Name key figures who articulated a concept of democratic rights, and describe their ideas.

2. Contrast the arguments for empire with the rhetoric of the anti-imperialists. Which dangers to the nation and democracy did each side stress?

3. Why was the issue of currency so important to Americans in 1896? What was at stake?

Suggested Readings

Brewer, Susan A. *Why America Fights: Patriotism and War Propaganda from the Philippines to Iraq.* New York: Oxford University Press, 2009.

Edwards, Rebecca, and DeFeo, Sarah. The Presidential Campaign: Cartoons and Commentary. 2000. http://projects.vassar.edu/1896/1896home.html

Lears, Jackson. *Rebirth of a Nation: The Making of Modern America, 1877–1920.* New York: Harper Perennial, 2010.

Young, Jeremy C. *The Age of Charisma: Leaders, Followers, and Emotions in American Society, 1870–1940.* New York: Cambridge University Press, 2016.

For further review materials and resource information, please visit www.oup.com/us/oakes-mcgerr

CHAPTER 18: INDUSTRY AND EMPIRE, 1890–1900

Primary Sources

18.1 FREDERICK WINSLOW TAYLOR, EXCERPTS FROM *THE PRINCIPLES OF SCIENTIFIC MANAGEMENT* (1911)

Frederick Winslow Taylor aimed to identify the most basic movements of workplace skills to provide management with the means to train workers to complete tasks with the highest levels of efficiency. With managerial oversight and the cooperation of labor, industry could produce at higher levels, thereby benefiting owners, consumers, and through Taylor's imagined wage increases, workers.

Under the old type of management success depends almost entirely upon getting the "initiative" of the workmen, and it is indeed a rare case in which this initiative is really attained. Under scientific management the "initiative" of the workmen (that is, their hard work, their good-will, and their ingenuity) is obtained with absolute uniformity and to a greater extent than is possible under the old system; and in addition to this improvement on the part of the men, the managers assume new burdens, new duties, and responsibilities never dreamed of in the past. The managers assume, for instance, the burden of gathering together all of the traditional knowledge which in the past has been possessed by the workmen and then of classifying, tabulating, and reducing this knowledge to rules, laws, and formulæ which are immensely helpful to the workmen in doing their daily work. In addition to developing a science in this way, the management take on three other types of duties which involve new and heavy burdens for themselves.

These new duties are grouped under four heads:

First. They develop a science for each element of a man's work, which replaces the old rule-of-thumb method.

Second. They scientifically select and then train, teach, and develop the workman, whereas in the past he chose his own work and trained himself as best he could.

Third. They heartily cooperate with the men so as to insure all of the work being done in accordance with the principles of the science which has been developed.

Fourth. There is an almost equal division of the work and the responsibility between the management and the workmen. The management take over all work for which they are better fitted than the workmen, while in the past almost all of the work and the greater part of the responsibility were thrown upon the men.

It is this combination of the initiative of the workmen, coupled with the new types of work done by the management, that makes scientific management so much more efficient than the old plan. . . .

Perhaps the most prominent single element in modern scientific management is the task idea. The work of every workman is fully planned out by the management at least one day in advance, and each man receives in most cases complete written instructions, describing in detail the task which he is to accomplish, as well as the means to be used in doing the work. And the work planned in advance in this way constitutes a task which is to be solved, as explained above, not by the workman alone, but in almost all cases by the joint effort of the workman and the management. This task specifies not only what is to be done but how it is to be done and the exact time allowed for doing it. And whenever the workman succeeds in doing his task right, and within the time limit specified, he receives an addition of from 30 percent to 100 percent to his ordinary wages. These tasks are carefully planned, so that both good and careful work are called for in their performance, but it should be distinctly understood that in no case is the workman called upon to work at a pace which would be injurious to his health. The task is always so regulated that the man who is well suited to his job will thrive while working at this rate during a long term of years and grow happier and more prosperous, instead of being over-worked. Scientific management consists very largely in preparing for and carrying out these tasks. . . .

Doubtless some of those who are especially interested in working men will complain because under scientific management the workman, when he is shown how to do twice as much work as he formerly did, is not paid twice his former wages, while others who are more interested in the dividends than the workmen will complain that under this system the men receive much higher wages than they did before. . . .

It is not fair, however, to form any final judgment until all of the elements in the case have been considered. At the first glance we see only two parties to the transaction, the workmen and their employers. We overlook the third great party, the whole people—the consumers, who buy the product of the first two and who ultimately pay both the wages of the workmen and the profits of the employers.

[A] glance at industrial history shows that in the end the whole people receive the greater part of the benefit coming from industrial improvements. In the past hundred years, for example, the greatest factor tending toward increasing the output, and thereby the prosperity of the civilized world, has been the introduction of machinery to replace hand labor. And without doubt the greatest gain through this change has come to the whole people—the consumer. . . .

It is no single element, but rather this whole combination, that constitutes scientific management, which may be summarized as:

Science, not rule of thumb.

Harmony, not discord.

Cooperation, not individualism.

Maximum output, in place of restricted output.

The development of each man to his greatest efficiency and prosperity.

The writer wishes to again state that: "The time is fast going by for the great personal or individual achievement of any one man standing alone and without the help of those around him. And the time is coming when all great things will be done by that type of cooperation in which each man performs the function for which he is best suited, each man preserves his own individuality and is supreme in his particular function, and each man at the same time loses none of his originality and proper personal initiative, and yet is controlled by and must work harmoniously with many other men."

Source: Frederick Winslow Taylor, *The Principles of Scientific Management* (New York: Harper & Brothers, 1911), chapter 2.

18.2 BOOKER T. WASHINGTON, "THE ATLANTA COMPROMISE" (1895)

On September 18, 1895, noted black leader Booker T. Washington addressed a predominantly white audience at the Cotton States and International Exposition in Atlanta. The "Atlanta Compromise," as it came to be known, much like the curriculum of Washington's Tuskegee Institute, advocated hard work and morality as the path to upward mobility for the black population. As the South moved increasingly in the direction of Jim Crow segregation, white southerners celebrated the speech, pleased by Washington's emphasis on economic cooperation rather than social integration.

One-third of the population of the South is of the Negro race. No enterprise seeking the material, civil, or moral welfare of this section can disregard this element of our population and reach the highest success. I but convey to you, Mr. President and Directors, the sentiment of the masses of my race when I say that in no way have the value and manhood of the American Negro been more fittingly and generously recognized than by the managers of this magnificent Exposition at every stage of its progress. It is a recognition that will do more to cement the friendship of the two races than any occurrence since the dawn of our freedom.

Not only this, but the opportunity here afforded will awaken among us a new era of industrial progress. Ignorant and inexperienced, it is not strange that in the first years of our new life we began at the top instead of at the bottom; that a seat in Congress or the state legislature was more sought than real estate or industrial skill; that the political convention or stump speaking had more attractions than starting a dairy farm or truck garden.

A ship lost at sea for many days suddenly sighted a friendly vessel. From the mast of the unfortunate vessel was seen a signal, "Water, water; we die of thirst!" The answer from the friendly vessel at once came back, "Cast down your bucket where you are." A second time the signal, "Water, water; send us water!" ran up from the distressed vessel, and was answered, "Cast down your bucket where you are." And a third and fourth signal for water was answered, "Cast down your bucket where you are." The captain of the distressed vessel, at last heeding the injunction, cast down his bucket, and it came up full of fresh, sparkling water from the mouth of the Amazon River. To those of my race who depend on bettering their condition in a foreign land or who underestimate the importance of cultivating friendly relations with the Southern white man, who is their next-door neighbor, I would say: "Cast down your bucket where you are"—cast it down in making friends in every manly way of the people of all races by whom we are surrounded.

Cast it down in agriculture, mechanics, in commerce, in domestic service, and in the professions. And in this connection it is well to bear in mind that whatever other sins the South may be called to bear, when it comes to business, pure and simple, it is in the South that the Negro is given a man's chance in the commercial world, and in nothing is this Exposition more eloquent than in emphasizing this chance. Our greatest danger is that in the great leap from slavery to freedom we may overlook the fact that the masses of us are to live by the productions of our hands, and fail to keep in mind that we shall prosper in proportion as we learn to dignify and glorify common labour, and put brains and skill into the common occupations of life; shall prosper in proportion as we learn to draw the line between the superficial and the substantial, the ornamental gewgaws of life and the useful. No race can prosper till it learns that there is as much dignity in tilling a field as in writing a poem. It is at the bottom of life we must begin, and not at the top. Nor should we permit our grievances to overshadow our opportunities.

To those of the white race who look to the incoming of those of foreign birth and strange tongue and habits for the prosperity of the South, were I permitted I would repeat what I say to my own race, "Cast down your bucket where you are." Cast it down among the eight millions of Negroes whose habits you know, whose fidelity and love you have tested in days when to have proved treacherous meant the ruin of your firesides. Cast down your bucket among these people who have, without strikes and labour wars, tilled your fields, cleared your forests, builded your railroads and cities, and brought forth treasures from the bowels of the earth, and helped make possible this magnificent representation of the progress of the South. Casting down your bucket among my people, helping and encouraging them as you are doing on these grounds, and to education of head, hand, and heart, you will find that they will buy your surplus land, make blossom the waste places in your fields, and run your factories. While doing this, you can be sure in the future, as in the past, that you and your families will be surrounded by the most patient, faithful, law-abiding, and unresentful people that the world has seen. As we have proved our loyalty to you in the past, in nursing your children, watching by the sick-bed of your mothers and fathers, and often following them with tear-dimmed eyes to their graves, so in the future, in our humble way, we shall stand by you with a devotion that no foreigner can approach, ready to lay down our lives, if need be, in defense of yours, interlacing our industrial, commercial, civil, and religious life with yours in a way that shall make the interests of both races one. In all things that are purely social we can be as separate as the fingers, yet one as the hand in all things essential to mutual progress. . . .

Nearly sixteen millions of hands will aid you in pulling the load upward, or they will pull against you the load downward. We shall constitute one-third and more of the ignorance and crime of the South, or one-third [of] its intelligence and progress; we shall contribute one-third to the business and industrial prosperity of the South, or we shall prove a veritable body of death, stagnating, depressing, retarding every effort to advance the body politic.

Gentlemen of the Exposition, as we present to you our humble effort at an exhibition of our progress, you must not expect overmuch. Starting thirty years ago with ownership here and there in a few quilts and pumpkins and chickens (gathered from miscellaneous sources), remember the path that has led from these to the inventions and production of agricultural implements, buggies, steam-engines, newspapers, books, statuary, carving, paintings, the management of drug stores and banks, has not been trodden without contact with thorns and thistles. While we take pride in what we exhibit as a result of our independent efforts, we do not for a moment forget that our part in this exhibition would fall far short of your expectations but for the constant help that has come to our educational life, not only from the Southern states, but especially from Northern philanthropists, who have made their gifts a constant stream of blessing and encouragement.

The wisest among my race understand that the agitation of questions of social equality is the extremest folly, and that progress in the enjoyment of all the privileges that will come to us must be the result of severe and constant struggle rather than of artificial forcing. No race that has anything to contribute to the markets of the world is long in any degree ostracized. It is important and right that all privileges of the law be ours, but it is vastly more important that we be prepared for the exercise of these privileges. The opportunity to earn a dollar in a factory just now is worth infinitely more than the opportunity to spend a dollar in an opera-house.

In conclusion, may I repeat that nothing in thirty years has given us more hope and encouragement, and drawn us so near to you of the white race, as this opportunity offered by the Exposition; and here bending, as it were, over the altar that represents the results of the struggles of your race and mine, both starting practically empty-handed three decades ago, I pledge that in your effort to work out the great and intricate problem which God has laid at the doors of the South, you shall have at all times the patient, sympathetic help of my race; only let this be constantly in mind, that, while from representations in these buildings of the product of field, of forest, of mine, of factory, letters, and art, much good will come, yet far above and beyond material benefits will be that higher good, that, let us pray God, will come, in a blotting out of sectional differences and racial animosities and suspicions, in a determination to administer absolute justice, in a willing obedience among all classes to the mandates of law. This, coupled with our material prosperity, will bring into our beloved South a new heaven and a new earth.

Source: Louis R. Harlan, ed., *The Booker T. Washington Papers,* vol. 3 (Urbana: University of Illinois Press, 1974), pp. 583–587.

18.3 THEODORE ROOSEVELT, EXCERPTS FROM "THE STRENUOUS LIFE" (1899)

Drawing upon a national history that celebrated the rugged individual and the conquest of the frontier, Theodore Roosevelt saw an imperial future for the United States as the nineteenth century concluded. In Chicago in April 1899, he addressed an audience of wealthy businessmen at the Hamilton Club and called for bravery and decisive action from public leaders. Roosevelt believed those who wished to lead had a responsibility to uplift both white civilization and the American nation. Manliness was a fundamental part of national leadership, and Roosevelt believed manly, martial action was the only way for the United States to compete in the modern world.

We of this generation do not have to face a task such as that our fathers faced, but we have our tasks, and woe to us if we fail to perform them! We cannot, if we would, play the part of China, and be content to rot by inches in ignoble ease within our borders, taking no interest in what goes on beyond them, sunk in a scrambling commercialism; heedless of the higher life, the life of aspiration, of toil and risk, busying ourselves only with the wants of our bodies for the day, until suddenly we should find, beyond a shadow of question, what China has already found, that in this world the nation that has trained itself to a career of unwarlike and isolated ease is bound, in the end, to go down before other nations which have not lost the manly and adventurous qualities. If we are to be a really great people, we must strive in good faith to play a great part in the world. We cannot avoid meeting great issues. All that we can determine for ourselves is whether we shall meet them well or ill. Last year we could not help being brought face to face with the problem of war with Spain. All we could decide was whether we should shrink like cowards from the contest, or enter into it as beseemed a brave and high-spirited people; and, once in, whether failure or success should crown our banners. So it is now. We cannot avoid the responsibilities that confront us in Hawaii, Cuba, Porto Rico, and the Philippines. All we can decide is whether we shall meet them in a way that will redound to the national credit, or whether we shall make of our dealings with these new problems a dark and shameful page in our history. To refuse to deal with them at all merely amounts to dealing with them badly. We have a given problem to solve. If we undertake the solution, there is, of course, always danger that we may not solve it aright; but to refuse to undertake the solution simply renders it certain that we cannot possibly solve it aright.

The timid man, the lazy man, the man who distrusts his country, the over-civilized man, who has lost the great fighting, masterful virtues, the ignorant man, and the man of dull mind, whose soul is incapable of feeling the mighty lift that thrills "stern men with empires in their brains"—all these, of course, shrink from seeing the nation undertake its new duties; shrink from seeing us build a navy and an army adequate to our needs; shrink from seeing us do our share of the world's work, by bringing order out of chaos in the great, fair tropic islands from which the valor of our soldiers and sailors has driven the Spanish flag. These are the men who fear the strenuous life, who fear the only national life which is really worth leading. They believe in that cloistered life which saps the hardy virtues in a nation, as it saps them in the individual; or else they are wedded to that base spirit of gain and greed which recognizes in commercialism the be-all and end-all of national life, instead of realizing that, though an indispensable element, it is, after all, but one of the many elements that go to make up true national greatness. No country can long endure if its foundations are not laid deep in the material prosperity which comes from thrift, from business energy and enterprise, from hard, unsparing effort in the fields of industrial activity; but neither was any nation ever yet truly great if it relied upon material prosperity alone. All honor must be paid to the architects of our material prosperity, to the great captains of industry who have built our factories and our railroads, to the strong men who toil for wealth with brain or hand; for great is the debt of the nation to these and their kind. But our debt is yet greater to the men whose highest type is to be found in a statesman like Lincoln, a soldier like Grant. They showed by their lives that they recognized the law of work, the law of strife; they toiled to win a competence for themselves and those dependent upon them; but they recognized that there were yet other and even loftier duties—duties to the nation and duties to the race.

We cannot sit huddled within our own borders and avow ourselves merely an assemblage of well-to-do hucksters who care nothing for what happens beyond. Such a policy would defeat even its own end; for as the nations grow to have ever wider and wider interests, and are brought into closer and closer contact, if we are to hold our own in the struggle for naval and commercial supremacy, we must build up our power without our own borders. We must build the isthmian canal, and we must grasp the points of vantage which will enable us to have our say in deciding the destiny of the oceans of the East and the West.

So much for the commercial side. From the standpoint of international honor the argument is even stronger. The guns that thundered off Manila and Santiago, left us echoes of glory, but they also left us a legacy of duty. If we drove out a medieval tyranny only to make room for savage anarchy, we had better not have begun the task at all. It is worse than idle to say that we have no duty to perform, and can leave to their fates the islands we have conquered. Such a course would be the course of infamy. It would be followed at once by utter chaos in the wretched islands themselves. Some stronger, manlier power would have to step in and do the work, and we would have shown ourselves weaklings, unable to carry to successful completion the labors that great and high-spirited nations are eager to undertake.

The work must be done; we cannot escape our responsibility; and if we are worth our salt, we shall be glad of the chance to do the work—glad of the chance to show ourselves equal to one of the great tasks set modern civilization. But let us not deceive ourselves as to the importance of the task. Let us not be misled by vainglory into underestimating the strain it will put on our powers. Above all, let us, as we value our own self-respect, face the responsibilities with proper seriousness, courage, and high resolve. We must demand the highest order of integrity and ability in our public men who are to grapple with these new problems. We must hold to a rigid accountability those public servants who show unfaithfulness to the interests of the nation or inability to rise to the high level of the new demands upon our strength and our resources. . . .

Our army needs complete reorganization—not merely enlarging—and the reorganization can only come as the result of legislation. A proper general staff should be established, and the positions of ordnance, commissary, and quartermaster officers should be filled by detail from the line. Above all, the army must be given the chance to exercise in large bodies. Never again should we see, as we saw in the Spanish war, major-generals in command of divisions who had never before commanded three companies together in the field. Yet, incredible to relate, the recent Congress has shown a queer inability to learn some of the lessons of the war. There were large bodies, of men in both branches who opposed the declaration of war, who opposed the ratification of peace, who opposed the upbuilding of the army, and who even opposed the purchase of: armor at a reasonable price for the battle-ships and cruisers, thereby putting an absolute stop to the building of any new fighting-ships for the navy. If, during the years to come, any disaster should befall our arms, afloat or ashore, and thereby any shame come to the United States, remember that the blame will lie upon the men whose names appear upon the roll-calls of Congress on the wrong side of these great questions. On them will lie the burden of any loss of our soldiers and sailors, of any dishonor to the flag; and upon you and the people of this country will lie the blame if you do not repudiate, in no unmistakable way, what these men have done. The blame will not rest upon the untrained commander of untried troops, upon the civil officers of a department the organization of which has been left utterly inadequate, or upon the admiral with an insufficient number of ships; but upon the public men who have so lamentably failed in forethought as to refuse to remedy these evils long in advance, and upon the nation that stands behind those public men. . . .

When once we have put down armed resistance, when once our rule is acknowledged, then an even more difficult task will begin, for then we must see to it that the islands are administered with absolute honesty and with good judgment. If we let the public service of the islands be turned into the prey of the spoils politician, we shall have begun to tread the path which Spain trod to her own destruction. We must send out there only good and able men, chosen for their fitness, and not because of their partisan service, and these men must not only administer impartial justice to the natives and serve their own government with honesty and fidelity, but must show the utmost tact and firmness, remembering that, with such people as those with whom we are to deal, weakness is the greatest of crimes, and that next to weakness comes lack of consideration for their principles and prejudices.

I preach to you, then, my countrymen, that our country calls not for the life of ease but for the life of strenuous endeavor. The twentieth century looms before us big with the fate of many nations. If we stand idly by, if we seek merely swollen, slothful ease and ignoble peace, if we shrink from the hard contests where men must win at hazard of their lives and at the risk of all they hold dear, then the bolder and stronger peoples will pass us by, and will win for themselves the domination of the world. Let us therefore boldly face the life of strife, resolute to do our duty well and manfully; resolute to uphold righteousness by deed and by word; resolute to be both honest and brave, to serve high ideals, yet to use practical methods. Above all, let us shrink from no strife, moral or physical, within or without the nation, provided we are certain that the strife is justified, for it is only through strife, through hard and dangerous endeavor, that we shall ultimately win the goal of true national greatness.

Source: Theodore Roosevelt, "The Strenuous Life" (April 10, 1899).

18.4 VISUAL DOCUMENT: LOUIS DALRYMPLE, "SCHOOL BEGINS" (1899)

Toward the end of the nineteenth century, some Americans expressed concern about the motivation behind American imperial action and empire building. The original caption to Louis Dalyrmple's 1899 cartoon, "School Begins," published in *Puck* magazine read: "School Begins. Uncle Sam (to his new class in Civilization): Now, children, you've got to learn these lessons whether you want to or not! But just take a look at the class ahead of you, and remember that, in a little while, you will feel as glad to be here as they are!" The blackboard in the background reads: "The consent of the governed is a good thing in theory, but very rare in fact. . . . England has governed her colonies whether they consented or not. By not waiting for their consent she has greatly advanced the world's civilization. . . . The U.S. must govern its new territories with or without the consent of the governed until they can govern themselves."

Source: *Puck* 44, no. 1142 (January 25, 1899). Copyright 1899 by Keppler & Schwarzmann. Library of Congress Prints and Photographs Division Washington, DC.

19

A United Body of Action

1900–1916

< The Hull House Choir in Recital, 1910

589

Helen Keller

Like many women of her generation, Helen Keller, born in 1880 to a wealthy family in Tuscumbia, Alabama, attended college. Of her first day, she later wrote, "It was a day full of interest for me. I had looked forward to it for years." In 1904, she graduated cum laude from Radcliffe College, the all-women sister institution to Harvard College. Diploma in hand, Keller joined many turn-of-the-century middle-class Americans as they assessed an America in need of change and dedicated themselves to improving it.

Keller, though, was unlike her peers. Blind and deaf since she had been stricken by "brain fever" when she was 19 months old, Keller had completed her university education with the assistance of her long-time friend and teacher, Anne Sullivan, who signed for Helen all the lectures and readings that were not available in Braille. As the first deaf and blind person to earn a college degree, Helen was an object of public fascination, something of a celebrity. The public celebrated her as an example of the triumph of the individual against the most difficult of circumstances. With hard work and dedication, she had overcome unimaginable hurdles.

But Keller, like so many activists at the turn of the century, rejected this model of individualism. An ongoing commitment to the rights of the disabled, coupled with continued reading on society and philosophy by radical authors such as Karl Marx, H. G. Wells, and Eugene Debs, led Keller, in 1908, to join the American Socialist Party, which assessed modern problems as economic in nature and advocated on behalf of (ideally, non-violent) revolution.

The leading causes of disability in the United States, Keller determined, were related to accidents occurring and diseases acquired in the industrial workplace. These accidents and health issues arose as a result of employer greed and negligence, a refusal to make worker safety a priority. Once disabled, people were dismissed, Keller argued, and constituted a class that, as a rule, were poor. They joined the ranks of the impoverished as they were cut off from educational and employment opportunities, condemned to live in overcrowded slums, and received often limited and insufficient medical care.

While Keller claimed the necessity of a full-scale revolution, she echoed the views of those who believed in the need to reform the existing social structure. In her conception of disability rights, the issue was not that disabled people did not fit into society as it was. The issue was that society was constructed in such a way that it failed to fit all of its existing members. She extended this view to a class analysis, believing that capitalism inevitably subjugated the working class and resulted in tremendous inequality. In a 1913 lecture, she made clear the limits of individualism and the need to change society: "[N]o one of us can do anything alone . . . we are bound together. I do not like this world as it is. I am trying to make it a little more as I would like to have it."

Many of Keller's contemporaries likewise believed in the necessity of cooperation and similarly wished to make the world more as they would like to have it. The majority of

American reformers—known as progressives—did not, however, share her political radicalism. The possibility of a violent conflict between rich and poor seemed a very real threat. As a whole, progressive reformers—social workers, journalists, lawyers—optimistically believed in people's ability to improve society and each other (a radicalism of its own kind). They believed in the need for the establishment of and adherence to a moral, distinctly middle-class model, cultivated and spread by new institutions and enforced by new laws. Progressives employed science and religion to justify their beliefs and, upon that basis, advocated for the supervision of human affairs by qualified experts. Critical of the rich and the poor, progressives believed in the necessity of an activist government to oversee the actions and behaviors of both. The radicalism espoused by socialists like Keller pushed conservatives who had long supported a laissez-faire style of government to respond to progressive calls for reform rather than face the possibility of a full-scale political uprising.

Toward a New Politics

Progressivism displaced the intensely partisan politics of the late nineteenth century. The political and economic crises of the 1890s left Americans disillusioned with traditional parties. A growing socialist movement threatened more radical action if moderate reform failed. Protestant churches spoke out against capitalism's abuses, and new interpretations of Christian ethics lent a moral urgency to reform. The dangers of urban life gave educated, affluent Americans a sense that civic problems needed to be dealt with immediately. Women took leading roles, using pressure groups to extend their influence while also seeking the vote.

Egged on by the press, progressives organized to solve the problems of the new industrial world. Although they sometimes idealized smaller towns and bygone eras, progressives recognized that large-scale industrial capitalism was here to stay. They worked as troubleshooters to make an erratic and brutal system more predictable, efficient, and humane. In pushing for reform, they were willing to enlarge the power of the state and to use it to tell people what was good for them. As reform gained momentum, mayors, governors, and presidential candidates identified themselves and their agendas as progressive.

The Insecurity of Modern Life

Most people who lived in cities at the turn of the century had grown up in the country (see Figure 19–1). They remembered living in communities where people knew each other, where much of what they ate and wore was made locally. In the modern city, water, fuel, and transportation were all supplied by large, anonymous corporations. Unknown executives made decisions that affected the livelihoods, savings, and safety of thousands of people. City dwellers felt more sophisticated than their parents but also less secure.

City living carried risks. Inspecting a Chicago market, journalist Upton Sinclair found milk laced with formaldehyde, peas colored green with copper salts, and sausage doctored with toxic chemicals. Dozens of patent medicines—including aspirin, cocaine, and heroin—were sold as remedies for everything from hay fever to cancer.

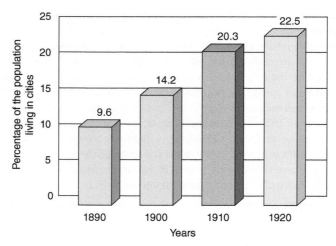

Figure 19-1 Percentage of the Population Living in Cities, 1890-1920 Cities and towns underwent dramatic growth around the turn of the century. Offices, department stores, and new forms of mass entertainment—from vaudeville to professional sports—drew people to the city center. Railroads and trolleys allowed cities to spread outward, segregating residents by class.
Source: Paul Kennedy, *Rise and Fall of the Great Powers* (New York: Random House, 1987), p. 200.

Tenement blocks housing hundreds of people often had no fire escapes or plumbing. Tragedy reminded New Yorkers of these dangers on March 25, 1911, when fire engulfed the Triangle Shirtwaist Company on the top three floors of a 10-story building. Five hundred Jewish and Italian seamstresses were trapped; many jumped from ledges in groups, holding hands. In all, 146 died. Such episodes demonstrated that an unregulated economy could be both productive and deadly.

Government added to the problem. Regulation often created kickbacks and bribery. In 1904 and 1905, journalist Lincoln Steffens uncovered corruption in state after state. In New York, insurance companies paid off elected officials in return for favorable legislation. In San Francisco, boss Abraham Ruef ruled the city with a slush fund from public utilities. The Minneapolis police, along with the mayor's office, protected brothels and gambling dens in return for bribes. Elections made the system less accountable, not more. By creating a demand for campaign funds and jobs, elections became invitations to graft.

The rising middle class found public and corporate irresponsibility infuriating. In stately Victorian "streetcar suburbs," business managers, accountants, engineers, lawyers, and doctors became aware of themselves as a class, but one trapped between two groups, the rich and the masses of wage laborers. Because of education and experience, members of the middle class had their own ideas on how organizations, such as utility companies, cities, and states, should run. Modern corporations needed clear lines of authority, an emphasis on efficiency, and reliable sources of information. Yet these virtues were frustratingly absent from civic life.

Triangle Shirtwaist Fire Disasters often galvanized support for new laws. After the March 25, 1911, fire at the Triangle Shirtwaist Company in Greenwich Village killed 146 young workers, many of whom jumped from the seventh, eighth, and ninth stories of the building to escape flames, New York finally enacted legislation on factory safety.

The Decline of Partisan Politics

Participation in elections declined by choice and coercion. Nationally, 79 percent of the electorate voted in 1896, but four years later only 73 percent voted, and by 1904 the total fell to 65 percent (see Figure 19–2). Literacy tests accounted for much of the decline in the South, but in all regions the old spectacular style of electioneering, with parades and rallies, gave way to campaigns that were more educational and less participatory. Worse for the parties, the voters split their tickets. The ethnic and sectional loyalties that led to straight party ballots in the late nineteenth century seemed to be weakening.

Increasingly, Americans participated in politics through associations. Voluntary and professional societies took over functions that once belonged to the parties: educating voters and even making policy. These "interest groups" worked outside the system to gather support for a cause or proposal. Many were patterned after corporations, with a board of directors and state and local chapters. Built on the idea that reform was a continuous process, they strove for permanence. Some, such as the National Association for the Advancement of Colored People (NAACP), the Salvation Army, and the Sierra Club, are still prominent.

Social Housekeeping

The mounting clamor for change aroused political strength in unexpected places. Women's social clubs had been nonpolitical before the turn of the century. Dedicated to developing public talents such as art, speaking, reading, and conversation, they were highly organized, with local, state, and national chapters. A General Federation of Women's Clubs was formed in 1890. Within 10 years, the urgency of social problems led many clubs to campaign for free kindergartens, civil service reform, and public health.

A growing cohort of professional women energized reform. The first generation of graduates from the new women's colleges had reached adulthood, and some, like Helen Keller, had attained advanced degrees at a time when few men went to college. These "new women," as historians have called them, had ambitions and values different from those of their mothers' generation. About half did not marry. With career paths closed to them, educated women found careers by finding problems that needed solving. Florence Kelley, trained as a lawyer, became Illinois's first state factory inspector and later directed the National Consumers League. Margaret Sanger, a New York public health nurse, distributed

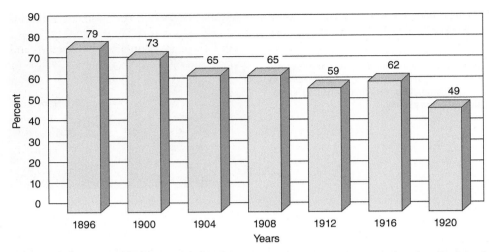

Figure 19-2 Voter Participation, 1896–1920 After the intense partisanship and high-stakes elections of the 1890s, campaigns became more "educational" and voters lost interest.

literature on birth control and sex education when it was illegal to do so. Sophonisba Breckinridge, with a doctorate from the University of Chicago, led the struggle against child labor. Female activists discovered problems, publicized them, lobbied for new laws, and then staffed the bureaus and agencies administering the solutions.

Women's professional associations, unions, business clubs, ethnic and patriotic societies, and foundations changed the practice of democracy. What was once considered charity or volunteer work became political. Some groups, such as the Young Women's Christian Association (YWCA, 1894) and the International Council of Nurses (1899), had a global reach. The experiences of women's groups taught activists the importance of cooperation, organization, and expertise. When women's clubs built a playground and donated it to the city, they increased their stake in the political system. Likewise, advocating on behalf of women's political role was the National Association of Colored Women's Clubs (NACWC, 1896), which launched campaigns against lynching and Jim Crow laws. All of these organizations gave women new reasons to demand full citizenship.

The women's suffrage movement grew quietly in the early years of the century. Women had gained the vote in four states—Colorado, Wyoming, Utah, and Idaho—but between 1896 and 1910 no other states adopted a women's suffrage amendment. The movement was stubbornly opposed by the Catholic Church, machine politicians, and business interests.

Competing suffrage organizations joined forces under the National American Woman Suffrage Association (NAWSA). Led by Carrie Chapman Catt and Anna Howard Shaw, NAWSA developed a strategy based on professional lobbying and publicity. Suffragists appealed to clubwomen and middle-class reformers by cultivating an image of Victorian respectability and linking suffrage to moderate social causes, such as temperance and education. At first, NAWSA's strategy paid off. After 1910, five states adopted suffrage amendments, but the opposition rallied and defeated referenda in three states.

Frustrated with the glacial pace of progress, Alice Paul's National Woman's Party adopted more radical tactics, picketing the White House and staging hunger strikes. Despite setbacks, women led the transformation of politics through voluntary organizations and interest groups and were on the threshold of even greater gains.

Evolution or Revolution?

Founded in 1901, the Socialist Party's swelling membership seemed to confirm its claims that the future would be revolutionary rather than progressive. In 1912, Eugene V. Debs, the party's candidate for president, won almost a million votes, or 6 percent of the total. "Gas and water" Socialists, who demanded public ownership of utilities, captured offices in many smaller cities. In the plains states, socialism drew strength from primitive Baptist and Holiness churches and held revival-style tent meetings. In Oklahoma, almost one-quarter of the electorate voted Socialist in 1914.

Although tinged with religion, Socialists' analysis of modern problems was economic. They maintained that the profit motive distorted human behavior, forcing people to compete for survival as individuals instead of joining to promote the common good. Driven by profits, corporations could not be trusted with the welfare of consumers or workers. Socialists demanded the collective ownership of industries, starting with ones that most directly affected people's lives: railroads and city utilities. Socialists had faith that America could make the transition without violence and that socialism was surely "coming like a prairie fire," a Socialist newspaperman told his readers. "Social Gospel" clergymen preached this coming millennium. Washington Gladden, a Congregationalist pastor from Ohio; Walter Rauschenbusch, a Baptist minister from New York; William Dwight Porter Bliss, who founded the Society for Christian Socialists; and George Herron, an Iowa Congregationalist, were among the prominent ministers who interpreted the Bible as a call to social action. Their visions of the Christian commonwealth ranged from reform to revolution, but they all believed that corporate capitalism was organized sin and that the church had an obligation to stand against it.

When the Industrial Workers of the World (IWW) talked about revolution, they meant class war, not elections. Founded in 1905, the IWW (known as the "Wobblies") unionized some of the most rugged individuals in the West: miners, loggers, and even rodeo cowboys (under the Bronco Busters and Range Riders Union). Gathering unskilled workers into "one big union," the Wobblies challenged the AFL's elite unionism and the Socialists' gradualism. With fewer than 100,000 members, the union and its leader, William "Big Bill" Haywood, had a reputation for radicalism. In Lawrence, Massachusetts, and Paterson, New Jersey, IWW strikers clashed with police and paraded under red flags with thousands of marchers. To an anxious middle class, these activities looked like signs of an approaching conflict between rich and poor.

Conservatives and reformers alike felt the hot breath of revolution on their necks, and socialism's greatest influence may have been the push it gave conservatives to support moderate reform. Theodore Roosevelt warned that without reform the United States would divide into two parties, one representing workers, the other capital.

The failure of the two parties to deal with urgent problems created a chance to redefine democracy. As the new century began, Americans were testing their political ideals, scrapping old rules, and getting ready to fashion new institutions and laws to deal with the challenges of modern society.

The Progressives

Historians have found it difficult to define the progressives. They addressed a wide variety of social problems with many different tactics but appealed to a broad audience. A rally to end child labor, for instance, might draw out young lawyers, teachers, labor unionists, woman suffragists, professors, and politicians. A series of overlapping movements, campaigns, and crusades defined the era from 1890 to 1920.

Progressivism was a political style, a way of approaching problems. Progressives had no illusions that wage labor or industrialism could be eliminated or that it was possible to re-create a rural commonwealth. Big cities and big corporations, they believed, were permanent features of modern life, but progressives were convinced that modern institutions could be made humane, responsive, and moral.

In choosing solutions, progressives relied on scientific expertise as a way to avoid the clash of interests. Those raised during the Civil War knew democracy was no guarantee against mass violence. Rival points of view could be reconciled more easily by impartial authority. Like the salaried managers many of them were, progressives valued efficiency and organization. No problem could be solved in a single stroke, but only by persistent action.

Sure that science and God were on their side, progressives did not balk at imposing their views on other people, even if democracy got in the way. Such measures as naming "born criminals" to be put on probation before committing a crime were called "progressive." To southern progressives, "scientific" principles justified racial segregation. Progressives demanded more democracy when it led to "good government," but if the majority was wrong, in their view, progressives handed power to unelected managers. The basic structure of American society, they felt, should not be open to political debate.

Above all, progressives shared an urgency. "There are two kinds of people," reformer and occupational health expert Alice Hamilton learned from her mother, "the ones who say, 'Someone ought to do something about it but why should it be I?' and the ones who say, 'Somebody must do something about it, then why not I?'" Hamilton and other progressives never doubted which kind they were.

Social Workers and Muckrakers

Among the first to hear the call to service were the young women and men who volunteered to live among the urban poor in "settlement houses." Stanton Coit established the first on New York's Lower East Side in 1886, but the most famous was Hull House, which opened in Chicago three years later. Its founders, Jane Addams and Ellen Starr, bought a rundown mansion at the center of an inner-city ward thick with sweatshops, factories, and overcrowded tenements. The women of Hull House opened a kindergarten and a clinic, took sweatshop bosses to court, investigated corrupt landlords, criticized the ward's powerful alderman, and built the city's first public playground.

Addams drew together at Hull House a remarkable group of women with similar backgrounds. Florence Kelley organized a movement for occupational safety laws. Julia Lathrop headed the state's Children's Bureau. All three women were raised in affluent Quaker homes during or shortly after the Civil War, and their parents were all abolitionists. Like Helen Keller, all three attended college and traveled or studied in Europe.

As the fame of Hull House spread, women (and some men) organized settlement houses in cities across the country. By the turn of the century there were more than 100, and by 1910 more than 400. Reformers often began by using social science techniques to

The Hull House Choir in Recital, 1910 Chicago, according to Lincoln Steffens, was "loud, lawless, unlovely, ill-smelling, new; an overgrown gawk of a village." Addams and other settlement workers sought to tame this urban wilderness through culture and activism.

survey the surrounding neighborhoods, gathering information on the national origins, income, housing conditions, and occupations of residents. Addams released *Hull-House Maps and Papers*, a survey of the 19th Ward, in 1895. One of the most ambitious research projects was the Pittsburgh Survey, a massive investigation of city living and working conditions published between 1909 and 1914. Its data confirmed that the causes of poverty were social, not personal, contradicting a common belief that the poor had only themselves to blame. Settlements did "social work" rather than charity.

Surveys also used maps, photographs, and even three-dimensional models. In 1900, housing reformers exhibited a scale cutaway model of a New York tenement block, showing how airless, overcrowded rooms contributed to disease and crime. Shelby Harrison, director of surveys for the Russell Sage Foundation, explained that the survey itself was reform, stimulating popular action with "the correcting power of facts."

This statistical outlook motivated settlement workers to attack urban problems across a broad front. Social workers labored to ensure food safety, repair housing, and sponsor festivals and pageants. Working conditions, especially for women and children, drew special attention, but employers, landlords, and city bosses were not the only targets: those involved in working-class vices—in gambling establishments, saloons, and brothels—were also attacked. The loudest voice of progressivism came from a new type of journalism introduced in 1902. In successive issues, *McClure's* magazine published Lincoln Steffens's investigation of graft in St. Louis and Ida Tarbell's "History of the Standard Oil Company," sensational exposés of the crimes of the nation's political and economic elite. As periodicals competed for readers, the old partisan style of journalism gave way to crusades,

STRUGGLES FOR DEMOCRACY

Public Response to *The Jungle*

Like other reform-minded journalists of the Progressive Era, Upton Sinclair believed in the power of the pen to bring attention to various social troubles and inspire demands for social, economic, and political reform. In 1904, Sinclair began an investigation of Chicago's Packingtown during which he learned firsthand of workers' challenges as they attempted to make a living doing the foul work available in Chicago's stockyards. The result of his investigation was the 1906 novel *The Jungle*. The title reflected Sinclair's critique of the United States' capitalist economy—a cutthroat system, he believed, that robbed people of their humanity as they struggled to survive. Chronicling the travails of the working poor and revealing the horrors of the American meatpacking enterprise through the struggles of Lithuanian immigrant Jurgis Rudkus and his family, the book revealed the limits to the rugged individualism so celebrated by Gilded Age leaders and those who touted the virtues of social Darwinism. Sinclair hoped readers would empathize with workers who toiled under atrocious work conditions, lived in squalor,

and suffered from political corruption, all while struggling to achieve the upward mobility they had imagined American life would provide. Socialism, the book concludes, with its focus on equity and cooperation, could lead the American people to a more humane existence.

The novel was an immediate sensation. In the first month and a half after publication, the book sold 25,000 copies. Audiences read Sinclair's fictional account as though it were fact and were outraged by what they read. But the outrage—and calls for reform—differed from what Sinclair had intended. Rather than creating cross-class consciousness or fostering a sense of solidarity with the working-class immigrants described in the text, the novel succeeded in outraging middle-class citizens in their identification as consumers, horrified by descriptions of diseased meat and chemical preservatives in products they might have purchased.

President Theodore Roosevelt, no fan of muckrakers, was persuaded by Sinclair's indictment of the meatpacking industry. A self-identified progressive, Roosevelt was inclined to regulate food and drugs

celebrities, and "sob sister" features. The new 10-cent magazines, such as *Everybody's*, *Cosmopolitan*, and *McClure's*, had audiences and budgets big enough to pay for in-depth investigations. The result was a type of reporting Theodore Roosevelt disdainfully called "muckraking." Readers loved it, and an article exposing some new corporate or public villainy could easily sell half a million copies.

Muckrakers named names. Upton Sinclair described the grisly business of canning beef. Ray Stannard Baker investigated railroads and segregation. Samuel Hopkins Adams catalogued the damage done by narcotics in popular medicines. Tarbell exposed Standard Oil's camouflaged companies, espionage, sweetheart deals, and predatory pricing.

Meat Inspectors Hogs receive a final inspection at Swift & Co., Chicago, 1906.

to prevent misbranding and adulteration. Direct response from readers pushed him to act. When angry letters from those who had read *The Jungle* began to arrive at the White House, Roosevelt authorized the Department of Agriculture to investigate meatpacking in Chicago. Their claim that conditions were fine came as no surprise to Sinclair, who told the president that sending those officials was tantamount to sending a criminal to investigate a crime. When the two men met in the aftermath of this first investigation, Roosevelt resolved to send the US labor commissioner Charles P. Neill and Assistant Treasury Secretary James Bronson Reynolds, assisted by Socialist activist and political organizer Ella Reeve Bloor, to conduct an independent investigation. Their June 1906 report matched descriptions from Sinclair's text. They described "a humid atmosphere heavy with the odors of rotten wood, decayed meats, stinking offal, and entrails" and "dirty, blood-soaked, rotting wood floors, fruitful culture beds for the disease germs of men and animals."

In the aftermath of the report—and as a result of the efforts of other muckrakers like Samuel Hopkins Adams, who called attention to the patent medicine industry's false claims and peddling of often dangerous products—President Roosevelt endorsed the Pure Food and Drug Act of 1906 as well as the Federal Meat Inspection Act of the same year. The laws created sanitary standards for the meatpacking industry and federal inspections of animals to be slaughtered, and made criminal the misbranding of food and drugs. Demonstrating the progressive commitment to research, problem solving, and government oversight, the legislation also represented the power of the public voice in effecting real change.

Her series shattered the notion that industrial giants competed in a free market and pushed the Justice Department to sue Standard Oil in 1906 for conspiracy to restrain trade.

The 10-cent magazines projected local problems onto a national canvas. Newspapers had covered municipal corruption before, but Steffens's series in *McClure's* revealed that bribery, influence peddling, and protection rackets operated in nearly every major city. Magazines also reported on progressive victories, allowing solutions adopted in Toledo or Milwaukee to spread quickly. Muckraking declined after 1912, the victim of corporate advertising boycotts and declining readership, but while it lasted, "public opinion" became a force that could shake the powerful.

Dictatorship of the Experts

For doctors, lawyers, and engineers, reform offered a chance to apply their skills to urgent problems, and the Progressive Era coincided with the rise in influence of the social sciences and the professions. Experts could mediate potentially violent conflicts and eliminate the uncertainties of democracy. Scientific advances seemed to justify this faith. In just a generation, antiseptic techniques, X-rays, and new drugs created a new understanding of disease. Electric light, recorded sound, motion pictures, radio, and flight confirmed science's ability to shape the future.

Social workers copied doctors, diagnosing each case with clinical impartiality. Newly professionalized police forces applied the techniques of fingerprinting, handwriting analysis, and psychology to law enforcement. Dietitians installed bland but nutritionally balanced meals in school cafeterias. Reformers tried (but failed) to simplify spelling and bring "efficiency" to the English language.

Trust in science sometimes led to extreme measures. One was the practice of eugenics, an attempt to rid society of alcoholism, poverty, and crime through selective breeding. "If the knowledge [of eugenics] were applied, the defective classes would disappear within a generation," the president of the University of Wisconsin predicted. Persuaded that genetics could save the state money, the Indiana legislature passed a law in 1907 authorizing the forced sterilization of "criminals, idiots, rapists, and imbeciles." Patients with epilepsy, psychiatric disorders, or mental handicaps who sought help at state hospitals were surgically sterilized. Criminals received the same treatment. Seven other states also adopted the "Indiana Plan."

The emphasis on expertise hid a thinly veiled distrust of democracy. Professional educators, for example, took control of the schools away from local boards and gave it to expert administrators and superintendents. They certified teachers and classified students based on "scientific" intelligence tests. To reformers, education was too important to be left to amateurs, such as teachers, parents, or voters.

Progressivism created new social sciences and made universities centers of advocacy. Sociology was a product of the progressive impulse. The study of government became political science, and "scientific" historians searched the past for answers to modern problems. John R. Commons, Richard Ely, and Thorstein Veblen used economics to study how modern institutions developed and functioned. Legal scholars such as Louis Brandeis and Roscoe Pound called for revising the law to reflect social realities.

This stress on expertise made Progressive Era reforms different from those of earlier periods. Instead of trying to succeed at a single stroke—by passing a law or trouncing a corrupt politician—progressives believed in process and established organizations and procedures that would keep the pressure on and make progress a habit.

Progressives on the Color Line

In her international crusade against lynching, Ida B. Wells-Barnett pioneered some of the progressive tactics of research, exposure, and organization. A schoolteacher in Memphis, Wells-Barnett documented mob violence against African Americans and mobilized opinion in the United States and Britain. Cities that condoned extralegal executions soon faced a barrage of condemnation from church groups and women's clubs. As her Afro-American Council grew, Wells-Barnett joined forces with white suffragists, social workers, and journalists, but her cause was not fully embraced. Many reform groups sympathized with white southerners or wanted to avoid dividing their membership over race.

Ida B. Wells-Barnett with Her Children Ida Wells-Barnett, journalist and activist, made lynching an international issue through her writing and speaking tours.

Reformers debated how much progress non-Anglo-Saxons were capable of, but they were inclined to be pessimistic. Eugenics gave white supremacy the endorsement of science. A new technology, the motion picture, showed its power to rewrite history from a racial viewpoint in D. W. Griffith's classic *Birth of a Nation* (1915), which romanticized the Klan's campaign of terror during Reconstruction. Policy was often based on racial assumptions. Trade schools, not universities, were deemed appropriate for educating Filipinos and Hawaiians. Progressives took Native American children from their families and placed them in boarding schools. Electoral reform in Texas meant disfranchising Spanish-speaking voters.

Wells-Barnett was not alone in finding doors through this wall of racial ideology. William Edward Burghardt DuBois documented the costs of racism in *The Philadelphia Negro* (1898). The survey spoke the progressives' language, insisting that discrimination was not just morally wrong but inefficient, because it took away work and encouraged alcoholism and crime. DuBois transformed the politics of race as profoundly as Addams transformed the politics of cities.

Raised in Massachusetts, DuBois learned Latin and Greek in public schools. At 17, he went to Fisk University in Tennessee, where he "came in contact for the first time with a sort of violence that [he] had never realized in New England." He also had his first encounter with African American religion and gospel music, which was "full of the voices of the past." DuBois later studied at Harvard and Berlin.

DuBois and Booker T. Washington espoused opposing visions of African Americans' place in the United States. Both emphasized the importance of thrift and hard work. DuBois, however, rejected Washington's willingness to accept legal inequality. DuBois came to believe that the Atlanta Compromise (see Chapter 18) led only to disfranchisement and segregation. He disliked the way Washington's influence with white philanthropists silenced other voices. Five years after the Atlanta speech he opened a sustained attack on Washington's "Tuskegee Machine."

In *The Souls of Black Folk* (1903), DuBois argued that the strategy of accommodation contained a "triple paradox": Washington had urged African Americans to seek industrial training, build self-respect, and become successful in business, while asking them to stop striving for higher education, civil rights, or political power. How could a people train themselves without higher education or gain self-respect without having any of the rights other Americans enjoyed—or succeed in business without the power to protect themselves or their property? Economic, political, and educational progress had to move together. Like other progressives, DuBois insisted on the importance of process and organization. African Americans could not stop demanding the vote, equality, or education.

In July 1905, DuBois and 28 African American leaders met on the Canadian side of Niagara Falls (no hotel on the US side would admit them) to organize a campaign against racial violence, segregation, and disfranchisement. The Niagara Movement was one of several such organizations. In 1909, Wells-Barnett, Addams, and other reformers created the National Association for the Advancement of Colored People to carry on the fight in the courts. In 1915, the NAACP won a Supreme Court decision outlawing the grandfather clause, which denied the vote to descendants of slaves; but another 40 years passed before it succeeded in overturning *Plessy v. Ferguson.*

Progressives in State and Local Politics

Progressives were of two minds about the public. Walter Lippmann, a journalist and reformer, could write fondly of "the voiceless multitudes" and contemptuously of the "great dull mass of people who just don't care." Progressives' tactics betrayed this split vision. Their reforms made city government less democratic and more "businesslike." Reforms at the state level, however, expanded voters' power to initiate legislation and remove officeholders. In both cases, the changes enlarged the influence of small-town and urban-middle-class reformers while reducing that of immigrants and the working class.

Redesigning the City

The machine politicians who ran American cities adapted well to change. To immigrants and factory workers, the local boss was one of the few people looking out for the average person. He rushed to fire scenes to aid homeless victims. He distributed turkeys in poor neighborhoods at Christmas. He could be counted on to post bail or find someone a job. Jane Addams acknowledged that she could not compete with Johnny Powers, the popular local ward boss, this "big manifestation of human friendliness, this stalking survival of village kindness."

Powers and other aldermen sheltered the brothels, saloons, and gambling dens that, in Addams's view, exploited honest workers. Hull House organized to beat Powers in 1895, and in defeat the reformers revealed their frustrations with democracy. The reformers nominated an Irish bricklayer, William Gleeson, whom they thought would appeal to the 19th Ward's working-class voters. But voters said they wanted someone grander to represent them, such as Powers, with his big house and diamond buttons. Gleeson was trounced. Addams was "puzzled, then astounded and indignant" at the outcome.

With officials like Powers in charge, corporations could do what they liked if they padded the right wallets. "If you want to get anything out of the council," the head of the Chicago Chamber of Commerce advised, "the quickest way is to pay for it—not to the city, but to the aldermen." City machines lost their appeal by providing not too few services but too many. As tax burdens grew, wealthier voters clamored for reform. Progressives set out to replace paternalism with efficient, scientific administration.

After the depression of 1893, many groups sprang up to criticize municipal government, which often resembled the federal system in miniature. A mayor, elected by the whole city, presided over a council of representatives from each neighborhood, or ward. This system diluted the influence of the "better classes" and allowed a few powerful wards to rule the city. In 1899, Louisville's Conference for Good City Government proposed a new model, later known as the "strong mayor" system. It gave more power to the mayor and required each council member to represent the whole city. Two years later, after the hurricane and tidal wave destroyed Galveston, Texas, the devastated city tried an even bolder plan (see Chapter 18). The recovery would be run by a commission of five unelected officials, each managing a city department. Des Moines, Iowa, improved on Galveston's design, and by 1911 some 160 cities had commission governments.

The commission resembled a corporate board of directors. Professionalism and accountability, the keys to business success, could make a city run, too. This philosophy led Detroit voters to elect Ford Motor Company's chief efficiency expert, James Couzens, as mayor. Other cities, led by Dayton, Ohio, tried to improve on the city-commission plan by placing local government in the hands of an unelected "city manager."

Middle- and upper-class professionals led this revolution in city government, and they gained the most from it. The new officials could explain where tax money was spent, but there were no turkeys at Christmas. Getting a job from the city meant filling out the proper forms. Reform administrations targeted urban "vice," which included most working-class recreations. Voters also learned that efficiency did not lower taxes. Budgets grew along with the public's demand for services.

Reform Mayors and City Services

While commissioners rewrote the rules, a new breed of reform mayors cleaned up their cities. Samuel "Golden Rule" Jones, a Welsh immigrant who earned a fortune in the oil fields, won election three times as independent mayor of Toledo. He enacted the eight-hour day for city employees, pushed for public ownership of city utilities, and staged free concerts in the parks. Like Tom Johnson in Cleveland and Hazen Pingree in Detroit, Jones worried less about saloons and more about utilities. Milwaukee, Schenectady, and other cities bought or regulated the private monopolies that supplied lighting, garbage removal, water, and streetcars.

The reform mayors' efforts to humanize the city were supported by architects and engineers who looked to improve urban life through the arrangement of public space. The City Beautiful movement sought to soften the urban landscape with vistas, open spaces, and greenery. The District of Columbia, with its commission government, broad avenues, and parks, furnished a model of city planning, and Congress sought to make it a model of municipal reform as well by introducing a model child-labor law, slum-clearance plan, and school system. The new urban spaces performed social and educational functions as well, especially to Americanize and uplift immigrant city dwellers. New York enacted zoning laws in 1916, and "city planners" joined the ranks of specialists by organizing themselves as a profession.

Progressives and the States

State reform varied by region. The East mimicked the agenda of urban reform. New York's progressive governor, Charles Evans Hughes, passed laws that prohibited gambling and created a state commission to regulate utilities. In southern states, progressivism often meant refining the techniques of segregation and disfranchisement. Lynching and mob

Daniel Burnham's City Plan for Chicago, 1909 Through comprehensive planning, Burnham sought to save cities from "the chaos incident to rapid growth." He drafted designs for Washington, Cleveland, San Francisco, and Manila.

assaults on African Americans were weekly occurrences in the Progressive Era. White leaders justified segregation and violence in terms used to justify urban reform in the North: the "better classes" had an obligation to rein in the excesses of democracy.

States in the West and Midwest produced the boldest experiments. Oregon introduced the secret ballot, voter registration, and three measures originally proposed by the Populists: the initiative, recall, and referendum. The initiative allowed voters to place legislation on the ballot by petition; the referendum let the legislature put proposals on the ballot; and the recall gave voters the chance to remove officials from office before the end of their terms. Other states soon adopted all or part of the "Oregon system."

The best known of the progressive governors was Robert M. "Fighting Bob" La Follette, whose model of state government came to be known as the "Wisconsin Idea." Elected in 1900, La Follette pushed through a comprehensive program of social legislation. Railways and public utilities were placed under public control. One commission designed a "scientific" distribution of the tax burden, including an income tax, whereas others regulated hours and working conditions and protected the environment. Wisconsin also implemented the direct primary, which allowed party nominees to be chosen directly by voters rather than by party caucuses.

Few machine politicians had as much personal power as the reform governors did. Wisconsin papers would call La Follette a "demagogue," but the reform governors brought policy making out of the "smoke-filled rooms." By shaking up city halls and statehouses, progressives made the public less cynical and government more responsive to reform. They knew, however, that social problems did not respect political boundaries: national corporations and nationwide problems had to be attacked at the federal level, and that meant capturing the White House.

A Push for "Genuine Democracy" and a "Moral Awakening"

If Theodore Roosevelt stood at the center of the two great movements of his age, imperialism and progressivism, it was because he prepared himself for the part. The Roosevelt family was wealthy and one of the oldest in New York, but Theodore embarked instead on pursuits that were unusual for a man of his class. After graduating from Harvard in 1880, he married, started law school, wrote a history of the War of 1812, bought a cattle ranch in the Dakota Territory, and, most surprisingly, ran for the state legislature.

For Roosevelt's family and friends, government was no place for gentlemen. Roosevelt himself described his colleagues as "a stupid, sodden, vicious lot, most of them being equally deficient in brains and virtue." Avoiding the "rough and tumble," he argued, only conceded high offices to those less fit to lead. Roosevelt's flair for publicity got him noticed, and in 1886 the Republican Party nominated him for mayor of New York. He finished third, behind the Tammany nominee and the Socialist candidate.

A turn as head of New York's board of police commissioners from 1895 to 1897 deepened Roosevelt's commitment to reform. The commission supervised an army of 38,000 policemen. Roosevelt's crackdown on saloons and corruption in the police department earned him a reputation as a man who would not be intimidated, even by his own party's bosses, and when McKinley won the presidency, he named Roosevelt assistant secretary of the navy. The Spanish-American War catapulted him to national fame, and in quick succession he became governor of New York, vice president, and then president of the United States.

Roosevelt believed that to restore democracy—"genuine democracy"—America needed a mission, "a genuine and permanent moral awakening." In the White House, he sought great tasks—duties to be carried out, principles to be upheld, isthmuses to be cut, and lands to be conserved—to inspire a common purpose and test the national will. In the process, he rewrote the president's job description, seizing new powers for the executive branch and turning the presidency into "the administration."

The Executive Branch Against the Trusts

Roosevelt approached politics the way Jane Addams approached poverty: studying it, living in its midst, and carefully choosing his battles. His fear of radicalism was borne out in September 1901. President William McKinley was shaking hands at the Pan American Exposition in Buffalo, New York, when a man thrust a pistol into his chest and fired twice. The assassin, Leon Czolgosz, came from the Cleveland slums and claimed to seek vengeance for the poor.

At age 42, Roosevelt was the youngest man to attain the presidency. He was the first president to call himself a progressive, and the first, according to Lippmann, "who realized clearly that national stability and social justice had to be sought deliberately and had consciously to be maintained." Unsatisfied merely to lead his party, he set out to remake the executive as the preeminent branch of government, initiating legislation, shaping public opinion, and protecting the national interest at home and abroad. "I believe in power," he explained. Instead of asking Congress for legislation, he drafted bills and lobbied for them personally. He believed government should intervene in the economy to protect citizens or to save business from itself. McKinley had already planned against the trusts, but his plans were not as bold as his successor's.

Challenging the corporations would not be easy. Roosevelt took office less than a decade after J. P. Morgan rescued the federal Treasury. In 1895, the Supreme Court gutted the Sherman Act, one of the few laws allowing federal action against monopolies. The underfunded Interstate Commerce Commission possessed few powers. Roosevelt told Congress "publicity is the only sure remedy which we can now invoke." He used it to the limit, putting Wall Street on notice in his first inaugural when he asserted that trusts "are creatures of the State, and the State not only has the right to control them, but it is duty bound to control them." In 1903, Roosevelt established a Department of Commerce and Labor that required annual reports, making corporate activities transparent.

The Justice Department revitalized the Sherman Act with vigorous prosecutions, and Roosevelt selected cases for maximum publicity value. Attorney General Philander Knox filed suit against J. P. Morgan's holding company, Northern Securities. Morgan expected the matter to be settled in the usual way, and his attorney asked how they might "fix it up." "We don't want to fix it up," Knox replied. "We want to stop it." When the Court handed Roosevelt a victory in 1904, Americans cheered.

With this case, Roosevelt gained an undeserved reputation as a "trust buster." He did oppose serious abuses, but he distinguished between good and bad trusts and believed that government should encourage responsible corporations to grow. He agreed with such progressive writers as Herbert Croly, editor of the *New Republic*, who imagined a central government staffed by nonpartisan experts who would monitor big corporations to assure efficiency and head off destructive actions.

Not all progressives agreed. Louis Brandeis and Woodrow Wilson envisioned a political economy of small, highly competitive firms kept in line by regular use of the Sherman Act. To Roosevelt, there was no future in a small-business economy. Only large combinations could compete on a world scale, and government's obligation was not to break them up but to regulate them. He secured passage of the Hepburn Act (1906), which allowed the commission to set freight rates and banned "sweetheart" deals (of the kind Standard Oil enjoyed) with favored clients. The Elkins Act (1910) regulated telephone, telegraph, and cable communications. The Pure Food and Drug Act (1906) responded to Upton Sinclair's exposé of the meatpacking industry by making it a crime to ship or sell contaminated or fraudulently labeled food and drugs. Under Roosevelt, the federal government gained the tools to counterbalance the power of business. It grew to match its responsibilities. The number of federal employees almost doubled between 1900 and 1916.

The Square Deal

Roosevelt's exasperation with big business reached a peak during the coal strike of 1902. The United Mine Workers represented 150,000 miners in the coalfields of eastern Pennsylvania. The miners, mostly Polish, Hungarian, and Italian immigrants, earned less than $6 a week, and more than 400 died yearly to supply the coal to run railroads and heat homes. Seventy percent of the mines were owned by six railroads, which in turn were controlled by the usual financiers, including Morgan and Rockefeller. The owners refused to deal with the union, declaring it a band of outlaws. When the miners struck in May, they had the public's sympathy. Editorials, even in Republican newspapers, urged the president to take the mines away from the owners.

The "gross blindness of the operators" infuriated Roosevelt. Coal was the only fuel for heating, and a strike might cause hundreds to freeze. After failing to get the sides to negotiate, he invited union officials and the operators to Washington so that he could personally arbitrate. John Mitchell, head of the mine workers, eagerly accepted the offer, but the owners refused.

For Roosevelt this was the final straw. He prepared the army to move into the coal-fields and put the mines under government control. The owners capitulated, agreeing to submit the dispute to a federal commission. The result was a compromise: miners received a 10 percent increase in pay and a nine-hour workday, but owners did not have to recognize the union.

Roosevelt's direct action made the federal government a third force in labor disputes. For the first time a strike was settled by federal arbitration, and for the first time a union had struck a strategic industry without being denounced as a radical conspiracy. The government would no longer automatically side with the corporations. "We demand that big business give the people a square deal," Roosevelt explained. "In return, we must insist that when anyone engaged in big business honestly endeavors to do right, he shall be given a square deal."

Conserving Water, Land, and Forests

When Roosevelt felt important issues were at stake, he pushed the limits of his office. He enraged Congress by stretching the definitions of presidential power, especially in the area of conservation (see Map 19–1). When Congress sent him a bill to halt the creation of new national forests in the West, Roosevelt first created or enlarged 32 national forests and then signed the bill. To stop private companies from damming rivers, he reserved 2,500 of the best hydropower sites by declaring them "ranger stations." Behind his program was Gifford Pinchot, the chief forester of the United States, who saw conservation as a new frontier. Unsettled, undeveloped lands were growing scarce, and Pinchot convinced the president of the value in managing resources more efficiently. Forests, deserts, and ore ranges were to be used wisely, scientifically, and in the national interest.

One of Roosevelt's first victories was the Newlands Reclamation Act (1902), which gave the Agriculture Department authority to build reservoirs and irrigation systems in the West. In the next four years, 3 million acres were "reclaimed" from the desert and turned into farms. To prevent waste, Roosevelt put tighter controls on prospecting, grazing, and logging. Big lumber and mining companies accepted rationalized resource administration, but small-scale prospectors and ranchers were shut out of federal lands. Naturalists like John Muir also resisted, pointing out that nature was to be appreciated, not used.

By 1909, conservation had become a national issue and created a new constituency of hikers, sightseers, and tourism entrepreneurs. By quadrupling the acreage in federal reserves, professionalizing the Forest Service, and using his "bully pulpit" to build support for conservation, Roosevelt helped create the modern environmental movement.

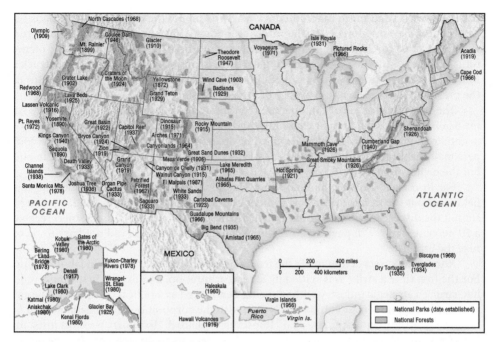

Map 19-1 Growth of Public Lands Responding to a national conservation movement, Roosevelt set aside public lands for use as parks and managed-yield forests. The National Park Service was founded in 1916.

TR and Big Stick Diplomacy

Imperial and commercial expansion put new strains on foreign and military policy after the turn of the century. US investors wanted Washington to protect their overseas factories and railroads against civil wars and hostile governments. Diplomatic and military budgets grew to meet these demands. Diplomats were no longer political cronies but trained professionals, and diplomacy was no longer a matter of weathering "incidents" but of making policy.

Roosevelt's view of world affairs flowed from his understanding of the past and the future. Global trade and communications, he believed, united "civilized" nations. His foreign policy aimed to keep the United States in the mainstream of commerce, imperialism, and military (particularly naval) modernization. He felt a duty to interfere with "barbarian" governments in Asia, Latin America, or Africa that blocked progress. The United States was obliged, he felt, to overthrow governments and even to seize territory when it was acting in the interests of the world as a whole.

Building an interoceanic canal topped Roosevelt's list of foreign policy priorities. A canal would be a hub of world trade and naval power in the Atlantic and Pacific, and Roosevelt aimed to prevent France or Britain from building it. He negotiated a deal to buy out a failed French venture in the Colombian province of Panama.

A civil war in Colombia complicated his plans. In 1902, American diplomats brokered a peace between modernizers led by José Marroquín and traditionalists who fiercely opposed the canal. Marroquín favored it but knew war would erupt again unless the Americans gave Bogotá full control over the canal. For Roosevelt, control was not negotiable.

In the spring of 1903, Panamanian senators, upset by the rejection of the US offer, began planning to secede. Panama had had revolutions before, but the United States had always stepped in to preserve Colombia's sovereignty. Together with Philippe Bunau-Varilla, who represented the French company, the Panamanians lobbied US officials to support their plot. Bunau-Varilla predicted a revolution for November 3, thereby ensuring that the rebels, the Colombian army (which had been bribed into surrendering), and US warships would all be on hand.

The revolution went off without a hitch, and Roosevelt presented the new Panamanian government with a treaty that gave less and took more than the one offered to Colombia. Congress launched an investigation. "I took the canal and let Congress debate," Roosevelt said, "and while the debate goes on the canal does also." The canal, a 50-mile cut built under the direction of George W. Goethals at a cost of $352 million and more than 5,600 lives, opened in 1914.

With construction under way, Roosevelt acted to protect the canal from other powers. Poverty in the region created opportunities for imperial governments to establish bases on Panama's doorstep. In 1902, Germany almost invaded Venezuela over an unpaid loan, but Roosevelt stepped in to mediate. When the Dominican Republic later reneged on its loans, four European nations laid plans for a debt-collecting expedition.

Roosevelt went before Congress in December 1904 and announced a policy later known as the Roosevelt Corollary. It stipulated that when chronic "wrongdoing or impotence" in a Latin American country required "intervention by some civilized nation," the United States would do the intervening. In Roosevelt's view, white "civilized" nations acted; nonwhite "impotent" nations were acted on. The next month, the United States took over the Dominican Republic's customs offices and began repaying creditors. The economic intervention turned military in 1916, when the United States landed marines to protect the customs from Dominican rebels. US troops stayed in the Dominican Republic until the early 1920s.

By enforcing order and efficiency in the Caribbean, Roosevelt extended progressivism beyond the borders of the United States. The movement spread to the Far East, too. In 1906, a US federal court was created in Shanghai, China, to control prostitution in the American community there.

Taft and Dollar Diplomacy

Enormously popular at the end of his second term, Roosevelt chose his friend William H. Taft to succeed him. Taft gained national attention as a circuit judge whose decisions enlarged federal power to regulate trusts. As governor general of the Philippines, he brought reform to Manila. Taft easily defeated William Jennings Bryan in the 1908 election, and as president he began consolidating Roosevelt's gains. He sent to the states constitutional amendments for the direct election of senators and for the income tax. He increased antitrust enforcement and levied the first tax on corporations. Satisfied that his legacy would continue, Roosevelt left for a tour of Africa.

In the Caribbean, Taft put the Roosevelt Corollary into action (see Map 19–2). The United States bought up the debts of Honduras and Nicaragua. Taft persuaded New York banks to refinance Haiti's debt to prevent German intervention there. Taft intended "dollar diplomacy" to replace force as an instrument of policy, but in most cases, dollars

The Hetch Hetchy Valley

When landscape painter Albert Bierstadt visited in 1875, he saw a panorama of waterfalls. The canyon walls towered 2,500 feet above a wide, forested meadow populated by herds of elk. Twenty-five years later, San Francisco's mayor James Phelan beheld the cliffs and the pure glacier water pouring into the Tuolumne River and saw his city's answer to the problems of "monopoly and microbes."

The Hetch Hetchy Valley hypnotized naturalists and engineers equally because of its magnificence and its location. It was only 152 miles from San Francisco, close enough both to lure visitors and to channel its waters to the city. A village of less than a thousand in 1848, the City by the Bay was, by 1900, the nation's ninth largest, with 340,000 people. Only water kept it from growing larger.

Hemmed in by ocean on three sides, San Francisco faced a chronic scarcity of fresh water. As the Gold Rush swelled the population, entrepreneurs bought up all available water supplies and formed the Spring Valley Water Company, which monopolized the city's water for 60 years. Water tycoons supported the political machine, led by "Boss" Abe Ruef. The company's water

was neither cheap nor safe, causing occasional outbreaks of cholera and typhus.

When voters elected Phelan and a reform ticket in 1897, they expected something to be done about water. The Republican mayor proposed to dam the Hetch Hetchy and build an aqueduct across the Central Valley, breaking the monopoly and making water an abundant, safe public utility.

Many obstacles stood in the way. The city's board of superintendents, controlled by Ruef, sided with Spring Valley and blocked plans for a city reservoir. But it was even harder to get permission from the federal government. Hetch Hetchy was located in Yosemite National Park, one of the first nature preserves, created in 1890 to save its peaks and waterfalls. The parks system was new, and the philosophy of conservation—how to preserve natural resources, and for what purposes—was evolving rapidly. Phelan found an ally in Gifford Pinchot, who filled the newly created office of chief forester.

Pinchot's father had made millions in the lumber trade. Gifford argued that the job of forestry was "to grow trees as a crop." He and Phelan agreed that the two main threats to any resource were inefficient

preceded bullets. For Caribbean nations, American protection meant high import taxes. A revolt usually followed. Marines went into Honduras and Nicaragua in 1912 and stayed until 1933.

Dollar diplomacy also aimed to harness economic power for diplomatic purposes. Taft mobilized a consortium to finance China's Chinchow-Aigun railway. Railroads were instruments of power in North China, and Taft felt he could drive a wedge between the imperial powers—Britain, Russia, and Japan—and compel them to resume open-door trade. Instead, they joined forces against the United States and the Open Door.

use and monopoly control. The few hikers who might enjoy Hetch Hetchy's magnificence were less important than the need "to supply pure water to a great center of population."

Natural and political disasters worked to Phelan's advantage. After the 1906 San Francisco earthquake and fire vividly demonstrated the need for a water supply, Congress allowed the city to apply to use part of Yosemite's land. The following year, a lurid scandal led to a bribery conviction for Ruef and disgrace for his followers. But just as the way seemed clear, a public outcry urged the secretary of the interior to save the Hetch Hetchy.

Behind the campaign were the 1,000-member Sierra Club and its ascetic founder, John Muir. A wilderness explorer and naturalist, Muir was popular for his writings on the transcendent, spiritual aspects of the natural world. "Dam Hetch Hetchy!" he remonstrated. "As well dam for water tanks the people's cathedrals and churches." Historians have characterized the debate between Muir and Pinchot as a contest between rival concepts of environmentalism—conservation for use versus preservation for nature's sake—but the two men also represented opposing interpretations of democracy and the dangers it faced.

"Conservation is the most democratic movement this country has known for generations," Pinchot believed. The Hetch Hetchy project would replace unbridled corporate power with management of natural resources for the public good.

Democratic values were scientific values: efficiency, expertise, and "the greatest good, for the greatest number, for the longest time." For Muir, nature was a refuge where democratic values could survive amid the culture of self-interest and scientific progress. The valley had to be preserved, not just to save the trees but also to "save humans for the wilderness." Only there could people share the nonmaterial values in which democracy took root.

The Sierra Club did not advocate leaving the area pristine. They imagined making Hetch Hetchy a retreat for harried city dwellers, managed by the park service. The public outcry surprised dam advocates, but they managed to cast the "nature lovers" as unwitting tools of the water and power monopolies.

The Roosevelt administration wavered, but in 1913, Phelan got his dam. Muir died a year later. Today the Hetch Hetchy aqueduct delivers 300 million gallons of water a day to San Francisco. But the battle for the valley gave birth to a modern environmental movement. When municipal and mining interests encroached on the Yosemite and Yellowstone preserves in the following decades, they were opposed by a national constituency that saw both activism and wilderness as part of America's heritage.

Despite the setback, Taft still believed that economic power, not military force, was what mattered.

Taft disappointed both conservatives and progressives in his party. He first urged Congress to reduce the tariff, but then he signed the Payne-Aldrich Tariff in 1909, which raised rates on key imports. Taft's secretary of the interior, Richard Ballinger, sided with ranchers and miners who opposed Roosevelt's resource-management policies. When Pinchot, the chief forester, fought back, Taft fired him. When the Ballinger-Pinchot affair revealed the party's divisions, Roosevelt felt his country needed him back.

Map 19-2   United States in the Caribbean US troops intervened repeatedly in the Caribbean and Central America to protect investments and guard against perceived threats to order. Panama, Nicaragua, Haiti, and the Dominican Republic were under nearly constant US occupation until the mid-1920s.
Source: Thomas Paterson et al., *American Foreign Relations* (Lexington, MA: D.C. Heath, 1995), vol. 2, pp. 55, 40.

Rival Visions of the Industrial Future

After Roosevelt returned from Africa in 1910, Pinchot, La Follette, Croly, and others trooped to his home at Sagamore Hill to complain about Taft. The former president denied any interest in the Republican nomination, but he could not keep his pledge. Roosevelt reentered politics because his views had evolved and because politics was what he knew best. Just 54 years old, his energy undiminished, he took more radical positions on corporations, public welfare, and labor than he had while president. The election of 1912 would define the future of industrial America.

The New Nationalism

At a sun-baked junction in Osawatomie, Kansas, in August 1910, Roosevelt declared that "the essence of any struggle for liberty . . . is to destroy privilege and give the life of every individual the highest possible value." He laid out a program he called the New Nationalism.

It included the elimination of corporate campaign contributions, the regulation of industrial combinations, an expert commission to set tariffs, a graduated income tax, banking reorganization, and a national workers' compensation program. "This New Nationalism regards the executive power as the steward of the public welfare." The message drew cheers.

Roosevelt had the newspapers, whereas Taft had the delegates. The nomination fight tested the new system of direct primaries. Taft's control of the party machinery helped him in states that chose delegates by convention, but in key states Roosevelt could take his campaign to the voters. At the convention in Chicago in June 1912, Taft's slim but decisive majority allowed him to control the platform and win over undecided delegates. Grumbling that he had been robbed, Roosevelt walked out.

Roosevelt returned to Chicago in August to accept the nomination of the newly formed Progressive Party. The delegates were a mixed group. They included Hiram Johnson, the reform governor of California; muckraking publisher Frank Munsey; imperialist senator Albert Beveridge; and J. P. Morgan's business partner George W. Perkins. The party platform endorsed the New Nationalism, along with popular election of senators, popular review of judicial decisions, and women's suffrage. Women were delegates, and Jane Addams seconded Roosevelt's nomination. The gathering had an evangelical spirit. "Our cause is based on the eternal principles of righteousness," Roosevelt said. "We stand at Armageddon and we battle for the Lord."

The 1912 Election

In Baltimore the Democrats nominated a former college professor and governor of New Jersey. Like Roosevelt, the young Woodrow Wilson defied his family's expectations by pursuing a political career. He took an unusual route. While studying for a doctorate in government at Johns Hopkins University in 1886, he published his first book, *Congressional Government*, at the age of 28. It advocated enlarging the power of the executive branch. As a professor and later president of Princeton University, he became a well-known lecturer and commentator for new national political magazines such as *Harper's* and the *Atlantic Monthly*. In 1910, he was elected governor of New Jersey and enacted sweeping progressive reforms. For Democrats, smarting from losses under Bryan's leadership, Wilson offered a new image and the ability to unite the South and the East under a progressive program.

With Roosevelt in the race, Wilson had to stake his own claim to the progressive constituency. With the help of Louis Brandeis, Wilson devised a program called the New Freedom. It challenged Roosevelt on his approaches to the economy and politics. Simply regulating the trusts, Wilson argued, would not help consumers, workers, or small entrepreneurs. Instead, it would create a paternalistic bureaucracy. Wilson wanted a lean, strong government and antitrust laws to encourage a return to competition and economic mobility. Both agreed on the importance of a strong executive, but they had different economic formulas. Roosevelt appealed to a collective, national interest, whereas Wilson stressed the needs of individual consumers and investors. The New Nationalism was evangelical, aiming to inspire people to work for the common good. Wilson appealed to reason and self-interest.

On Election Day, the split in the Republican Party gave Wilson a plurality. He won 42 percent of the popular vote, compared with 27 for Roosevelt, 23 for Taft, and 6 for Debs (see Map 19–3). Although his margin was thin, Wilson could interpret Taft's loss and the large combined vote for the progressive candidates as a mandate for change. "What the Democratic Party proposes," he told his followers, is "to do the things the Republican Party has been talking about doing for sixteen years."

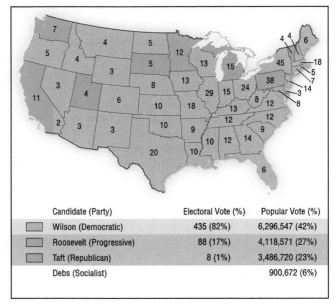

Candidate (Party)	Electoral Vote (%)	Popular Vote (%)
Wilson (Democratic)	435 (82%)	6,296,547 (42%)
Roosevelt (Progressive)	88 (17%)	4,118,571 (27%)
Taft (Republican)	8 (1%)	3,486,720 (23%)
Debs (Socialist)		900,672 (6%)

Map 19-3 The Election of 1912 The election pitted rival visions of progressivism against each other. The decentralized regulation of Wilson's "New Freedom" had more appeal than Roosevelt's far-reaching "New Nationalism."

Time Line

▼**1889**
Hull House founded

▼**1890**
General Federation of Women's Clubs founded

▼**1893**
Illinois passes eight-hour day for women

▼**1900**
Robert La Follette elected governor of Wisconsin

▼**1901**
Socialist Party of America founded
Galveston introduces commission government

McKinley assassinated; Theodore Roosevelt inaugurated president

▼**1902**
Newlands Reclamation Act funds construction of dams and irrigation systems
McClure's publishes first episodes of Ida Tarbell's "History of the Standard Oil Company" and Lincoln Steffens's "The Shame of the Cities"
Roosevelt settles anthracite strike

▼**1903**
Roosevelt establishes Department of Commerce and Labor
Panama declares independence from Colombia

W. E. B. DuBois publishes *The Souls of Black Folk*

▼**1904**
Justice Department sues Standard Oil under the Sherman Anti-Trust Act
US Supreme Court orders Northern Securities Company dissolved as an illegal combination
Roosevelt elected president
The Roosevelt Corollary announced

▼**1905**
United States takes over Dominican customs
Industrial Workers of the World founded

The New Freedom

Within a year and a half of his inauguration, Wilson produced one of the most coherent and far-reaching legislative programs ever devised by a president. Drawing on his long study of congressional politics, he seized the advantage of his party's majority and exercised an unprecedented degree of personal control through the majority leaders in both houses. The New Freedom advocated lower tariffs, increased competition, and vigorous antitrust enforcement. Three monumental bills passed through Congress in rapid succession.

The first bill was the Underwood-Simmons Tariff (1913), which made the first deep cuts in tariff rates since before the Civil War. The bill overturned a cornerstone of Republican economic policy, the protectionist tariff. It helped farmers and consumers by lowering prices and increasing competition, but Wilson argued that its real beneficiaries would be manufacturers. Lower tariffs would help persuade other countries to reduce taxes on imports from the United States, opening new markets for American-made goods. Wilson created an expert Tariff Commission in 1916 to improve tariff bargaining. The most-favored-nation policies it implemented (and which remain in place) induced European powers to open their empires to American goods. The Singer, Ford, and Camel brand names began appearing in markets from Caracas to Mandalay.

Wilson next targeted the banking system. When Steffens and Lippmann investigated banking for *Everybody's* magazine in 1908, they found that its structure was "strikingly like that of Tammany Hall," with a similar concentration of power, lack of accountability, and extralegal maneuvering. The Federal Reserve Act of 1913 set up a national board to supervise the system and created 12 regional reserve banks throughout the country.

▼1906
Hepburn Act passed, allowing the Interstate Commerce Commission to set freight rates
Pure Food and Drug Act requires accurate labeling

▼1907
Indiana passes forcible sterilization law

▼1908
William H. Taft elected president
Helen Keller joins the American Socialist Party

▼1909
Payne-Aldrich Tariff goes into effect
NAACP founded

▼1910
Taft fires chief forester Gifford Pinchot
Elkins Act authorizes Interstate Commerce Commission to regulate electronic communications
Roosevelt announces the New Nationalism

▼1911
Triangle Shirtwaist Company fire

▼1912
US troops occupy Nicaragua
Woodrow Wilson elected president

▼1913
Federal Reserve Act reorganizes banking system
Underwood-Simmons Tariff

▼1914
Panama Canal completed
Clayton Antitrust Act strengthens antitrust enforcement

▼1916
New York City enacts zoning laws
Federal workers' compensation, child-labor, and eight-hour-day laws passed

Banks were now watched to ensure that their reserves matched their deposits. The system's real advantage was the flexibility it gave the currency. The board could put more dollars into circulation when demand was high and retire them when it subsided. Regional banks could adjust the money supply to meet local needs. The system broke Wall Street's stranglehold on credit and opened new opportunities for entrepreneurship and competition.

Finally, Wilson attacked the trusts. He established the Federal Trade Commission (FTC), an independent regulatory commission assigned to enforce free and fair competition. It absorbed the functions of Roosevelt's Bureau of Corporations, but with more authority, including the right to subpoena corporate records and issue cease-and-desist orders. The Clayton Antitrust Act (1914) prohibited price fixing, outlawed interlocking directorates, and made it illegal for a company to own the stock of competitors. To enforce these provisions, citizens were entitled to sue for triple the amount of the actual damages they suffered. In 1916, Wilson produced more reform legislation, including the first national workers' compensation and child-labor laws, the eight-hour day for railroad workers, and the Warehouse Act, which extended credit to cash-strapped farmers.

These programs furthered Wilson's goal of "releasing the energies" of consumers and entrepreneurs, but they also helped business. Businessmen headed many of the regulatory boards, and the FTC and Federal Reserve Board helped stabilize unruly markets. The New Freedom brought reform without the elaborate state machinery of the New Nationalism or European industrial nations. The New Freedom linked liberal reform to individual initiative and free markets.

Conclusion

By 1900, America's political economy had outgrown the social relationships and laws that served the rural republic for most of the nineteenth century. Squeezed between corporate elites and the large, transient immigrant communities that controlled urban politics, middle-class reformers created a new style of political participation. They experimented with new forms of political decision making and vested the state with responsibility for the quality of life of its citizens. Progressives challenged but never upset the system. Science and the pressure of informed opinion, they believed, could produce managed, orderly change without open conflict.

The progressive presidents took this movement to the national stage. Roosevelt and Wilson touted their programs as attacks on privilege, but both presidents helped position the federal government as a broker among business, consumer, and labor interests. In less than two decades, the federal government overcame its reputation for corruption and impotence and moved to the center of economic and social life. The concept of a "national interest" greater than individual and property rights was now firmly ingrained; so, too, was the need to protect it. The president's leadership now extended beyond the administration to Congress and public opinion. These achievements created a modern central government just as military, diplomatic, and economic victories made the United States a global power. War and its aftermath would curtail the progressive movement, as support for a strong central government would be tested by events unfolding in Europe.

Who, What, Where

Review Questions

1. Why did reformers feel that privately owned utilities caused corruption?

2. What were the Oregon system and the Wisconsin Idea?

3. Choose one level of government—local, state, or federal—and describe three key progressive reforms.

Critical-Thinking Questions

1. Were the progressives' goals conservative or radical? What about their strategies? Explain your answers.

2. Theodore Roosevelt has been called the first modern president. In what ways did he change the presidency?

3. Did the progressives' emphasis on research and documentation indicate their respect for public opinion or not? Explain your answer.

Suggested Readings

Bederman, Gail. *Manliness and Civilization: A Cultural History of Gender and Race in the United States, 1880–1917.* Chicago: University of Chicago Press, 1997.

Library of Congress. Progressive Era to New Era. http://www.loc.gov/teachers/classroommaterials/presentationsandactivities/presentations/timeline/progress/

Marten, James, ed. *Children and Youth During the Gilded Age and Progressive Era.* New York: New York University Press, 2014.

McGerr, Michael. *A Fierce Discontent: The Rise and Fall of the Progressive Movement in America, 1870–1920.* New York: Free Press, 2003.

Painter, Nell Irvin. *Standing at Armageddon: The United States, 1877–1919.* New York: W. W. Norton, 1987.

For further review materials and resource information, please visit www.oup.com/us/oakes-mcgerr

CHAPTER 19: A UNITED BODY OF ACTION, 1900–1916
Primary Sources

19.1 JANE ADDAMS, EXCERPTS FROM *TWENTY-YEARS AT HULL HOUSE WITH AUTOBIOGRAPHICAL NOTES* (1910)

Jane Addams, inspired by Oxford University graduates who worked in London's poorest neighborhoods, led the settlement house movement in the United States. Addams co-founded Hull House in Chicago, which offered the city's poor a variety of social services and educational opportunities, and advocated on behalf of their rights against corrupt landlords and politicians. Addams celebrated the desire expressed by educated young people of financial means to follow the path of progressive reform and worked to improve life for Americans across social class and status.

This paper is an attempt to analyze the motives which underlie a movement based, not only upon conviction, but upon genuine emotion, wherever educated young people are seeking an outlet for that sentiment of universal brotherhood, which the best spirit of our times is forcing from an emotion into a motive. These young people accomplish little toward the solution of this social problem, and bear the brunt of being cultivated into unnourished, oversensitive lives. They

Jane Addams in 1914, 25 years after she founded Chicago's Hull House.

Source: Library of Congress Prints and Photographs Division, Washington, DC.

have been shut off from the common labor by which they live which is a great source of moral and physical health. They feel a fatal want of harmony between their theory and their lives, a lack of coordination between thought and action. I think it is hard for us to realize how seriously many of them are taking to the notion of human brotherhood, how eagerly they long to give tangible expression to the democratic ideal. These young men and women, longing to socialize their democracy, are animated by certain hopes which may be thus loosely formulated; that if in a democratic country nothing can be permanently achieved save through the masses of the people, it will be impossible to establish a higher political life than the people themselves crave; that it is difficult to see how the notion of a higher civic life can be fostered save through common intercourse; that the blessings which we associate with a life of refinement and cultivation can be made universal and must be made universal if they are to be permanent; that the good we secure for ourselves is precarious and uncertain, is floating in mid-air, until it is secured for all of us and incorporated into our common life. It is easier to state these hopes than to formulate the line of motives, which I believe to constitute the trend of the subjective pressure toward the Settlement.

There is something primordial about these motives, but I am perhaps overbold in designating them as a great desire to share the race life. We all bear traces of the starvation struggle which for so long made up the life of the race. Our very organism holds memories and glimpses of that long life of our ancestors which still goes on among so many of our contemporaries. Nothing so deadens the sympathies and shrivels the power of enjoyment, as the persistent keeping away from the great opportunities for helpfulness and a continual ignoring of the starvation struggle which makes up the life of at least half the race. To shut one's self away from that half of the race life is to shut one's self away from the most vital part of it; it is to live out but half the humanity to which we have been born heir and to use but half our faculties. We have all had longings for a fuller life which should include the use of these faculties. . . .

"It is true that there is nothing after disease, indigence and a sense of guilt, so fatal to health and to life itself as the want of a proper outlet for active faculties." I have seen young girls suffer and grow sensibly lowered in vitality in the first years after they leave school. In our attempt then to give a girl pleasure and freedom from care we succeed, for the most part, in making her pitifully miserable. She finds "life" so different from what she expected it to be. She is besotted with innocent little ambitions, and does not understand this apparent waste of herself, this elaborate preparation, if no work is provided for her. There is a heritage of noble obligation which young people accept and long to perpetuate. The desire for action, the wish to right wrong and alleviate suffering haunts them daily. Society smiles at it indulgently instead of making it of value to itself.

We have in America a fast-growing number of cultivated young people who have no recognized outlet for their active faculties. They hear constantly of the great social maladjustment, but no way is provided for them to change it, and their uselessness hangs about them heavily. . . . These young people have had advantages of college, of European travel, and of economic study, but they are sustaining this shock of inaction. They have pet phrases, and they tell you that the things that make us all alike are stronger than the things that make us different. They say that all men are united by needs and sympathies far more permanent and radical than anything that temporarily divides them and sets them in opposition to each other. If they affect art, they say that the decay in artistic expression is due to the decay in ethics, that art when shut away from the human interests and from the great mass of humanity is self-destructive. They tell their elders with all the bitterness of youth that if they expect success from them in business or politics or in whatever lines their ambition for them has run, they must let them consult all of humanity; that they must let them find out what the people want and how they want it. It is only the stronger young people, however, who formulate this. Many of them dissipate their energies in so-called enjoyment. Others not content with that, go on studying and go back to college for their second degrees; not that they are especially fond of study, but because they want something definite to do, and their powers have been trained in the direction of mental accumulation. Many are buried beneath this mental accumulation with lowered vitality and discontent. . . .

Other motives which I believe make toward the Settlement are the result of a certain renaissance going forward in Christianity. The impulse to share the lives of the poor, the desire to make social service, irrespective of propaganda, express the spirit of Christ, is as old as Christianity itself. . . .

I believe that there is a distinct turning among many young men and women toward this simple acceptance of Christ's message. They resent the assumption that Christianity is a set of ideas which belong to the religious consciousness, whatever that may be. They insist that it cannot be proclaimed and instituted apart from the social life of the community and that it must seek a simple and natural expression in the social organism itself. The Settlement movement is only one manifestation of that wider humanitarian movement which throughout Christendom, but preeminently in England, is endeavoring to embody itself, not in a sect, but in society itself.

The Settlement, then, is an experimental effort to aid in the solution of the social and indus-trial problems which are engendered by the modern conditions of life in a great city. It insists that these problems are not confined to any one portion of a city. It is an attempt to relieve, at the same time, the overaccumulation at one end of society and the destitution at the other; but it assumes that this overaccumulation and destitution is most sorely felt in the things that pertain to social and educational advantages. From its very nature it can stand for no political or social propa-ganda. It must, in a sense, give the warm welcome of an inn to all such propaganda, if perchance one of them be found an angel. The one thing to be dreaded in the Settlement is that it lose its flexibility, its power of quick adaptation, its readiness to change its methods as its environment may demand. It must be open to conviction and must have a deep and abiding sense of tolerance. It must be hospitable and ready for experiment. It should demand from its residents a scientific patience in the accumulation of facts and the steady holding of their sympathies as one of the best instruments for that accumulation. It must be grounded in a philosophy whose foundation is on the solidarity of the human race, a philosophy which will not waver when the race hap-pens to be represented by a drunken woman or an idiot boy. Its residents must be emptied of all conceit of opinion and all self-assertion, and ready to arouse and interpret the public opinion of their neighborhood. They must be content to live quietly side by side with their neighbors, until they grow into a sense of relationship and mutual interests. Their neighbors are held apart by differences of race and language which the residents can more easily overcome. They are bound to see the needs of their neighborhood as a whole, to furnish data for legislation, and to use their influence to secure it. In short, residents are pledged to devote themselves to the duties of good citizenship and to the arousing of the social energies which too largely lie dormant in every neighborhood given over to industrialism. They are bound to regard the entire life of their city as organic, to make an effort to unify it, and to protest against its overdifferentiation.

It is always easy to make all philosophy point to one particular moral and all history adorn one particular tale; but I may be forgiven the reminder that the best speculative philosophy sets forth the solidarity of the human race; that the highest moralists have taught that without the ad-vance and improvement of the whole, no man can hope for any lasting improvement in his own moral or material individual condition; and that the subjective necessity for Social Settlements is therefore identical with that necessity, which urges us on toward social and individual salvation.

Source: Jane Addams, *Twenty-Years at Hull House with Autobiographical Notes* (New York: The Macmillan Company, 1910; twenty-fifth printing, 1968), pp. 200–204.

19.2 UPTON SINCLAIR, EXCERPTS FROM *THE JUNGLE* (1906)

Muckraking journalist Upton Sinclair used the power of his pen to expose the corrupt conditions of Packingtown, Chicago's meatpacking district in the early 1900s. In 1906, after spending weeks interviewing and living among workers, Sinclair wrote *The Jungle*, the story of Jurgis Rudkus and his family, which chronicles working-class poverty and the immigrant experience. In the novel, Sinclair detailed the ways packing houses "doctored" the meat sold to the American public. Outrage at the conditions exposed by Sinclair led to nationwide reform.

The people of Chicago saw the government inspectors in Packingtown, and they all took that to mean that they were protected from diseased meat; they did not understand that these hundred and sixty-three inspectors had been appointed at the request of the packers, and that they were paid by the United States government to certify that all the diseased meat was kept in the state.

They had no authority beyond that; for the inspection of meat to be sold in the city and state the whole force in Packingtown consisted of three henchmen of the local political machine!

And shortly afterward one of these, a physician, made the discovery that the carcasses of steers which had been condemned as tubercular by the government inspectors, and which therefore contained ptomaines, which are deadly poisons, were left upon an open platform and carted away to be sold in the city; and so he insisted that these carcasses be treated with an injection of kerosene—and was ordered to resign the same week! So indignant were the packers that they went farther, and compelled the mayor to abolish the whole bureau of inspection; so that since then there has not been even a pretense of any interference with the graft. There was said to be two thousand dollars a week hush money from the tubercular steers alone; and as much again from the hogs which had died of cholera on the trains, and which you might see any day being loaded into boxcars and hauled away to a place called Globe, in Indiana, where they made a fancy grade of lard.

Jurgis heard of these things little by little, in the gossip of those who were obliged to perpetrate them. It seemed as if every time you met a person from a new department, you heard of new swindles and new crimes. There was, for instance, a Lithuanian who was a cattle butcher for the plant where Marija had worked, which killed meat for canning only; and to hear this man describe the animals which came to his place would have been worthwhile for a Dante or a Zola. It seemed that they must have agencies all over the country, to hunt out old and crippled and diseased cattle to be canned. There were cattle which had been fed on "whisky-malt," the refuse of the breweries, and had become what the men called "steerly"—which means covered with boils. It was a nasty job killing these, for when you plunged your knife into them they would burst and splash foul-smelling stuff into your face; and when a man's sleeves were smeared with blood, and his hands steeped in it, how was he ever to wipe his face, or to clear his eyes so that he could see? It was stuff such as this that made the "embalmed beef" that had killed several times as many United States soldiers as all the bullets of the Spaniards; only the army beef, besides, was not fresh canned, it was old stuff that had been lying for years in the cellars.

Then one Sunday evening, Jurgis sat puffing his pipe by the kitchen stove, and talking with an old fellow whom Jonas had introduced, and who worked in the canning rooms at Durham's; and so Jurgis learned a few things about the great and only Durham canned goods, which had become a national institution. They were regular alchemists at Durham's; they advertised a mushroom-catsup, and the men who made it did not know what a mushroom looked like. They advertised "potted chicken,"—and it was like the boardinghouse soup of the comic papers, through which a chicken had walked with rubbers on. Perhaps they had a secret process for making chickens chemically—who knows? said Jurgis' friend; the things that went into the mixture were tripe, and the fat of pork, and beef suet, and hearts of beef, and finally the waste ends of veal, when they had any. They put these up in several grades, and sold them at several prices; but the contents of the cans all came out of the same hopper. And then there was "potted game" and "potted grouse," "potted ham," and "deviled ham"—de-vyled, as the men called it. "De-vyled" ham was made out of the waste ends of smoked beef that were too small to be sliced by the machines; and also tripe, dyed with chemicals so that it would not show white; and trimmings of hams and corned beef; and potatoes, skins and all; and finally the hard cartilaginous gullets of beef, after the tongues had been cut out. All this ingenious mixture was ground up and flavored with spices to make it taste like something. Anybody who could invent a new imitation had been sure of a fortune from old Durham, said Jurgis' informant; but it was hard to think of anything new in a place where so many sharp wits had been at work for so long; where men welcomed tuberculosis in the cattle they were feeding, because it made them fatten more quickly; and where they bought up all the old rancid butter left over in the grocery stores of a continent, and "oxidized" it by a forced-air process, to take away the odor, rechurned it with skim milk, and sold it in bricks in the cities! Up to a year or two ago it had been the custom to kill horses in the yards—ostensibly for fertilizer; but after long agitation the newspapers had been able to make

Upton Sinclair wrote about the hazardous working conditions immigrant and American workers endured as they took up employment in Chicago's meatpacking industry. But while Sinclair hoped to outrage readers about the plight of workers, such as those pictured here, readers generally focused more on the potential health risks they faced as consumers of the meat processed in Chicago's stockyards.

Source: Copyright 1909, by Kelley & Chadwick. Library of Congress Prints and Photographs Division Washington, D.C.

the public realize that the horses were being canned. Now it was against the law to kill horses in Packingtown, and the law was really complied with—for the present, at any rate. Any day, however, one might see sharp-horned and shaggy-haired creatures running with the sheep and yet what a job you would have to get the public to believe that a good part of what it buys for lamb and mutton is really goat's flesh!

There was another interesting set of statistics that a person might have gathered in Packingtown—those of the various afflictions of the workers. When Jurgis had first inspected the packing plants with Szedvilas, he had marveled while he listened to the tale of all the things that were made out of the carcasses of animals, and of all the lesser industries that were maintained there; now he found that each one of these lesser industries was a separate little inferno, in its way as horrible as the killing beds, the source and fountain of them all. The workers in each of them had their own peculiar diseases. And the wandering visitor might be skeptical about all the swindles, but he could not be skeptical about these, for the worker bore the evidence of them about on his own person—generally he had only to hold out his hand.

There were the men in the pickle rooms, for instance, where old Antanas had gotten his death; scarce a one of these that had not some spot of horror on his person. Let a man so much as scrape his finger pushing a truck in the pickle rooms, and he might have a sore that would put him out of the world; all the joints in his fingers might be eaten by the acid, one by one. Of the butchers and floorsmen, the beef-boners and trimmers, and all those who used knives, you could scarcely find a person who had the use of his thumb; time and time again the base of it had been slashed, till it was a mere lump of flesh against which the man pressed the knife to hold it. The hands of these men would be criss-crossed with cuts, until you could no longer pretend to count them or to trace them. They would have no nails,—they had worn them off pulling hides; their knuckles were swollen so that their fingers spread out like a fan. There were men who worked in the cooking rooms, in the midst of steam and sickening odors, by artificial light; in these rooms the germs of tuberculosis might live for two years, but the supply was renewed every hour. There were the beef-luggers, who carried two-hundred-pound quarters into the refrigerator-cars; a fearful kind of work, that began at four o'clock in the morning, and that wore out the most pow-erful men in a few years. There were those who worked in the chilling rooms, and whose special disease was rheumatism; the time limit that a man could work in the chilling rooms was said to be five years. There were the wool-pluckers, whose hands went to pieces even sooner than the hands of the pickle men; for the pelts of the sheep had to be painted with acid to loosen the wool, and then the pluckers had to pull out this wool with their bare hands, till the acid had eaten their fingers off. There were those who made the tins for the canned meat; and their hands, too, were a maze of cuts, and each cut represented a chance for blood poisoning. Some worked at the stamp-ing machines, and it was very seldom that one could work long there at the pace that was set, and not give out and forget himself and have a part of his hand chopped off. There were the "hoisters," as they were called, whose task it was to press the lever which lifted the dead cattle off the floor. They ran along upon a rafter, peering down through the damp and the steam; and as old Dur-ham's architects had not built the killing room for the convenience of the hoisters, at every few feet they would have to stoop under a beam, say four feet above the one they ran on; which got them into the habit of stooping, so that in a few years they would be walking like chimpanzees. Worst of any, however, were the fertilizer men, and those who served in the cooking rooms. These people could not be shown to the visitor,—for the odor of a fertilizer man would scare any ordinary visitor at a hundred yards, and as for the other men, who worked in tank rooms full of steam, and in some of which there were open vats near the level of the floor, their peculiar trouble was that they fell into the vats; and when they were fished out, there was never enough of them left to be worth exhibiting,—sometimes they would be overlooked for days, till all but the bones of them had gone out to the world as Durham's Pure Leaf Lard!

Source: Upton Sinclair, *The Jungle* (1906; Project Gutenberg EBook, 2006), accessed at http://www.gutenberg.org/files/140/140-h/140-h.htm#link2HCH0009.

19.3 VISUAL DOCUMENTS: LEWIS WICKES HINE, NATIONAL CHILD LABOR COMMITTEE PHOTOGRAPHS (EARLY 1900s)

Lewis Hine worked as an investigative photographer for the National Child Labor Com-mittee, an organization dedicated to child labor reform, between 1908 and 1924. Through his photography, Hine chronicled labor conditions in sites such as coal mines, textile mills, and family farms. Hine's images brought public attention to the conditions under which children labored and effectively underscored the difference between the idealized vision of American childhood and the reality in which many children lived.

Three adults and six children from seven years to twelve years hard at work on a sugar beet farm near Greeley, Colorado. July 1915.

A 14-year-old spinner in a Brazos Valley Cotton Mill in West, Texas. November 1913.

Young drivers and trapper boy, Brown Mine, Brown, West Virginia. September 1908.

Source: Lewis Wickes Hine, 1874–1940, photographer. National Child Labor Committee Collection. Library of Congress Prints and Photographs Division, Washington, DC.

19.4 HELEN KELLER, EXCERPTS FROM "BLIND LEADERS" (1913)

When she expressed politically and economically radical views, Helen Keller often faced charges that her disabilities made her unfit for social commentary, that her ailments impeded her ability to think rationally. Keller continued to advocate a Socialist position and charged that those who saw the horrors of unfettered industrial capitalism and the inequalities it created, yet allowed the system to continue, were the truly and willfully blind members of American society.

I do not doubt that many persons who read what I am going to write will say to themselves: "She is indeed blind. She is so blind she imagines everybody else to be blind." As a matter of fact, I have been thinking for a long time that most of us are afflicted with spiritual blindness. Certainly, very few people open fresh, fearless eyes upon the world they live in. They do not look at anything straight. They have not learned to use their eyes, except in the most rudimentary ways. They will usually see a lamp-post—if it is a large one—and sometimes they are able to read the danger signal on a railway crossing, but not always. Most of the time they expect some one else to see for them. They often pay fabulous sums to lawyers, doctors, ministers, and other "experts" to do their seeing for them; but, unfortunately, it frequently happens that those hired guides and leaders are also blind. Of course they deny that their sight is imperfect. They claim to have extraordinary powers of vision and many people believe them. Consequently, they are permitted to lead their fellows. But how often do they steer them to their destruction!

When we look about us with seeing eyes, what do we behold? Men and women at our very doors wrung with hard labor, want or the dread of want, needing help and receiving none, toiling for less than a living wage! If we had had penetrating vision, I know that we could not, we would not, have endured what we saw—cruelty, ignorance, poverty, disease—almost all preventable, unnecessary. Our blind leaders whom we have sent away told us that the poverty and misery of mankind were divinely ordained. They taught us that the words, "Ye have the poor always with you," mean that Christ sanctioned poverty as necessary and irremediable. Now we read the Gospel with our own eyes, and we see that Christ meant no such thing.

Much poverty is abominable, unnecessary, a disgrace to our civilization, or rather a denial that we are civilized. Let us try to understand poverty. What is the cause of it? Simply this: that the land, the machinery, the means of life, belong to the few, while the many are born and live with nothing that they can call their own except their hands and their brains. They live by selling their hands and their brains to the few; and all the work they do makes the rich more rich, and gains for the workers a mere livelihood, or less than a livelihood. The ownership of the world by a small class is the main cause of poverty. Strange that we could not see it before, and that when we did see it we accepted it in blind contentment! Our blind guides consoled us by saying that there was much charity, and that the rich were generous and gave to the poor. We now see that what the rich give is only a small part of the money which is made for them by the labor of the poor! They never stop to think that if the workers received an equitable share of their product, there would be no rich, there would be little need of philanthropy. Charity covers a multitude of sins. It does something worse than that. It covers the fact so that they cannot be seen. It covers the fact that the property of the few is made by the labor of the many. The rich are willing to do everything for the poor but to get off their backs. . . .

When we inquire why things are as they are, the answer is: The foundation of society is laid upon a basis of individualism, conquest, and exploitation, with a total disregard of the good of the whole. The structure of society built upon such wrong basic principles is bound to retard the development of all men, even the most successful ones, because it tends to divert man's energies into useless channels and to degrade his character. The result is a false standard of values. Trade and material prosperity are held to the be the main objects of pursuit, and consequently the lowest instincts in human natures—love of gain, cunning, and selfishness—are fostered. The output of a cotton mill or a coal mine is considered of greater importance than the production of healthy, happy-hearted, free human beings.

This unmoral state of society will continue as long as we live under a system of universal competition for the means of existence. The workers cannot lift up their heads so long as a small favored class in each generation is allowed to inherit the accumulated labor of all preceding generations, and many who produce the wealth inherit nothing. (We often forget what wealth is. It is the stored-up labor of men, women, and little children. Money does not create anything. Money is about as productive as a wheel revolving in a void. It has value only in proportion to the toil and sweat of human hands that went into the getting of it.)

During the past century man has gained greater mastery over the forces of nature than he ever had before. Consequently the wealth produced in the world has increased a hundredfold. With the help of the machines he has invented, man can produce enough to provide necessaries, comforts, and even some luxuries for every human being. But in spite of this enormously greater productive power the condition of the workers has not essentially improved. Because the industrial system under which we live denies them the fruits of their labor, they have not received their fair share in the products of civilization.

As a matter of fact, machinery has widened the gulf between those who own and those who toil. It has become a means of perpetuating man's slavery, because it may be run by unskilled laborers who receive low wages, which of course increase the profits of employers and stock holders. So the worker become part of the machine they manipulate; but the machine is expensive, while human life is cheap. When the workers can no longer live, they go on strike, and what happens? The masters evict them from the hovels that they call home; the police and militia break up their protest-meetings, imprison their leaders, and when they can, drive them out of town. This appalling condition of things exists in many different parts of our country at this moment. For even the Constitution does not safeguard the liberties of the workers when their interests are opposed to those of the capitalist. Our administration of justice, which blind leaders used to tell us was a splendid inheritance from our fathers, is grossly unequal and unjust. It is based on a system of money fees. It is so encumbered at every step with technicalities that it is necessary to employ experts at great cost to explain and interpret the law. Then, too, all the petty offenses are punishable by fine or imprisonment. This means the poor will always be punished, while the rich are usually allowed to go free.

We cannot longer shut our eyes to these glaring evils. They divide the world into economic classes antagonistic to each other it is because of all these undeniable evils that I am the determined foe of the capitalist system, which denies the workers the rights of human beings. I consider it fundamentally wrong, radically unjust and cruel. It inflicts purposeless misery upon millions of my fellow men and women. It robs little children of the joy of life, embitters motherhood, breaks the bodies of men and degrades their manhood. It must, therefore, be changed, it must be destroyed, and a better, saner, kinder social order established. Competition must give place to co-operation, and class antagonism to brotherhood. "Each for all" is a far more stimulating and effective doctrine than "each for himself." Private ownership of land and the means of production and distribution of the necessaries of life must be replaced by public ownership and democratic management.

Oh, no, it is not human nature that we have to change. Our task is not so difficult as that. All that is necessary to make this world a comfortable abode for man is to abolish the capitalist system. In the words of Sir Oliver Lodge, "we have entered upon the period of conscious evolution, and have begun the adaptation of environment to organism." In other words, we have learned to curb and utilize the forces of nature. The time of blind struggle is drawing to a close. The forces governing the law of the survival of the fittest will continue to operate; but they will be under the conscious, intelligent control of man.

Source: Helen Keller, "Blind Leaders," *Outlook* 105 (September 27, 1913), 231–236.

20

A Global Power

1914–1919

< French Children in a Red Cross Hospital

619

AMERICAN PORTRAIT

Walter Lippmann

Walter Lippmann had just landed in Brussels in July 1914 when the trains stopped running. At the station, "crowds of angry, jostling people" were struggling to leave the city. This looked, he confided to his diary, like the beginning of a war. Four weeks earlier, Austria-Hungary's crown prince, Archduke Ferdinand, had been shot in the Serbian city of Sarajevo. Austria threatened to attack unless Serbia punished the terrorists. Russia mobilized to come to Serbia's defense. As stock markets tumbled and banks collapsed, Lippmann found himself caught in a conflict between the world's most powerful states: Austria and Germany on one side, Russia, France, and Britain on the other. As land borders closed, he escaped across the channel to England.

In the twilight of August 4, he stood with an anxious crowd outside the House of Commons, as Parliament passed a war resolution. In Berlin, the Reichstag declared war on France. "We sit and stare at each other and make idiotically cheerful remarks," Lippmann wrote, "and in the meantime, so far as anyone can see, nothing can stop the awful disintegration now."

Twenty-four years old, Lippmann had come of age in the Progressive Era. As a student at Harvard, he came to believe that reason and science would allow his generation to "treat life not as something given but as something to be shaped." After graduation, he set out to become a journalist, studying under the legendary investigator Lincoln Steffens and helping to start a magazine called the *New Republic*. "It was a happy time, those last few years before the First World War," he later remembered; "the air was soft, and it was easy for a young man to believe in the inevitability of progress, in the perfectibility of man and of society, and in the sublimation of evil."

The European war crushed those hopes. Just days after Lippmann left Belgium, German armies slashed through the neutral nation in a great maneuver designed to encircle the French army, but before the ring could be closed, reserve troops from Paris, many of them rushed to the front in taxicabs, stopped the German advance at the Marne River. By November, the western front had stabilized into the bloody stalemate that would last the next four years, taking between 5,000 and 50,000 lives a day. Two inventions first used in the American West, barbed wire and the machine gun, defeated all attempts to break through the enemy's trench lines. Colossal artillery, poison gas, submarine warfare, aerial bombardment, and suicide charges would each be used in desperate bids to break the deadlock, and all would fail.

The carnage horrified Americans. German soldiers terrorized Belgian civilians in retaliation for guerilla attacks, killing over 5,000 hostages and burning the medieval city of Louvain. The gruesome tragedy of modern war made Americans feel both fortunate and guilty to be so uninvolved. "We Americans have been witnessing supreme drama, clenching our fists, talking, yet unable to fasten any reaction to realities," Lippmann told his readers. For three years, Americans watched a civilization they had admired sink into barbarism. They recoiled from the war's violence and the motives behind it, and they debated what, if anything, they could do to stop it.

When the United States entered the fight in 1917, it mobilized its economy and society to send an army of a million to Europe. The war disrupted and culminated the progressive movement. In the name of efficiency, the state stepped in to manage the economy as never before, placing corporations under federal supervision but allowing them profits and some autonomy. The war transformed controversial items on the progressive agenda—women's suffrage, prohibition of alcohol, restrictions on prostitution—into matters of national urgency. The federal government punished political dissenters. On the battlefield, American forces brought swift triumph, but not the permanent peace Wilson sought. Defeated powers collapsed into revolution and anarchy. New ideologies threatened American ideals. The experience of war brought home the dangers of a modern, interdependent world, but it also revealed the United States' power to shape the global future.

The Challenge of Revolution

Like other progressives, Wilson saw threats to democracy arising from rapid change in industrial society. Revolution, militarism, and imperial rivalries threatened global stability just as surely as labor wars, reckless corporations, and corrupt officials endangered the republic. Wilson opposed radicalism at home and abroad, and he tried to foster orderly change. Stability, like reform, was a process, not a goal, but Wilson believed it had to be forced on those who resisted.

Imposing order, the president believed, was both a duty and an opportunity. An expanding commercial power such as the United States had talent, technology, and capital to share. "Prosperity in one part of the world ministers to prosperity everywhere," he declared, but only in safe markets. Imperialism and revolution endangered the trade necessary for peace in the world and growth at home. It was the government's duty to safeguard goods and investments in order to secure American prosperity and its benefits for the world.

This combination of idealism and self-interest, humanitarianism and force, produced a seemingly contradictory policy. Wilson renounced "dollar diplomacy" only to use Taft's tactics himself in China. He atoned for US imperialism but intervened repeatedly in Central America. Secretary of State William Jennings Bryan negotiated a series of "cooling-off" treaties that required arbitration before resorting to war, but Wilson seldom submitted his own policies to arbitration. He believed the United States had a mission to promote democracy, yet he considered many peoples—including Filipinos—unready to govern themselves.

These contradictions arose from Wilson's view of history. As he saw it, modern commerce and communications were creating a global society with new rules of international conduct. Meanwhile, relics of the past—militarism and revolution—threatened to "throw the world back three or four centuries." Resolving the struggle between the past and the future would require "a new international psychology," new norms and institutions to regulate conflict. Wilson's sympathies lay with Britain and France, but with Europe aflame, the United States, the sole voice of reason, had to remain aloof. "Somebody must keep the great economic processes of the world of business alive," he protested. He was also preoccupied with matters closer at hand. In April 1914, American troops invaded Mexico in an attempt to overthrow its revolutionary government.

The Mexican Revolution

In May 1911, rebels took control of Mexico City, ending over three decades of enforced order and rapid industrialization under the dictatorship of Porfirio Díaz. Díaz and a clique of intellectuals and planners known as the *científicos* had made Mexico one of the world's leading oil exporters. They confiscated communal lands, forcing Indians to farm as tenants on commercial haciendas. Foreign investment poured in, and by 1911 Americans owned 40 percent of the property in the country. Mexicans grew to resent foreign business and the regime's taxes. When Francisco Madero's revolt broke out, the army folded, Díaz fled to Spain, and power changed hands in a nearly bloodless coup.

The fall of Díaz hardly troubled the United States: Madero held an election to confirm his presidency. But in February 1913, two weeks before Wilson's inauguration, General Victoriano Huerta seized power and had Madero shot. Mexican states raised armies and revolted against Huerta's regime, beginning one of the twentieth century's longest and bloodiest civil wars. In the mountains south of Mexico City, Emiliano Zapata led a guerilla resistance. Meanwhile, along Mexico's northern border, Venustiano Carranza organized a constitutionalist army.

Wilson denounced Huerta, gave arms to Carranza's soldiers, and sent 7,000 marines to occupy Mexico's largest port, Veracruz, in April 1914. The invasion radicalized the revolution, unifying all sides against the United States. When Carranza deposed Huerta a few months later, he promised to nationalize US oil fields. Wilson pressured Carranza to resign while providing arms to his enemy, Francisco "Pancho" Villa. Villa briefly seized the capital at the end of 1914, but Carranza drove Villa's army north toward the border. Reluctantly, Wilson recognized the Carranza government and cut ties to Villa. Stung by Wilson's betrayal, Villa crossed the border and attacked the 13th Cavalry outpost at Columbus, New Mexico, killing 17 Americans and stealing horses and guns.

Furious, Wilson sent 10,000 troops under General John J. Pershing into Mexico (see Map 20–1). Pershing never found Villa, but the invasion again unified Mexicans against the United States. Rather than declare war, Wilson ordered Pershing home. After three years of trying to bring democracy and stability to Mexico, Wilson had nothing to show for his efforts. He failed to tame nationalism and revolution in Mexico. The civil war still raged, and American property was more in danger than ever.

Bringing Order to the Caribbean

In principle, Wilson opposed imperialism, but his desire to bring order to neighboring countries led him to use force again and again. He sent the marines into more countries in Latin America than any other president. Marines quashed a revolution in Haiti in 1915 and then occupied the country. They landed in the Dominican Republic the following year to supervise an election and stayed to fight a guerilla war until 1924. Wilson kept marines in Honduras, Panama, and Nicaragua and briefly sent troops into Cuba.

Progressive senators wondered why Wilson busted trusts and reorganized banks at home but put the marines at their service abroad. Senators Robert La Follette and George

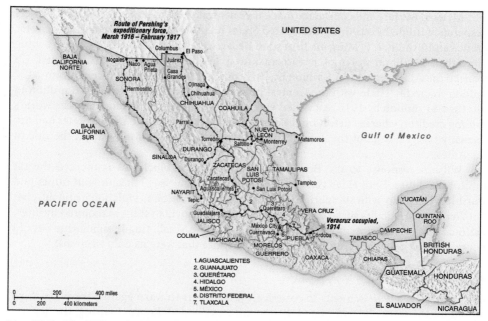

Map 20-1   The US Invasions of Mexico, 1914, 1917 General John Pershing led 10,000 troops together with observation aircraft and a convoy of trucks 419 miles into Mexico on a fruitless hunt for Francisco Villa's band. Federal forces loyal to Carranza confronted Pershing near Parral, bringing the US advance to a halt.

Norris argued that revolutions might be necessary in some countries to protect the many against the few. On August 29, 1914, some 1,500 women, dressed in black, marched down Fifth Avenue in New York City to oppose wars in the Caribbean and Europe. Peace advocates, such as Jane Addams, saw signs of a country being drawn toward war.

A One-Sided Neutrality

As German armies crossed Belgium in August 1914, Wilson declared a policy of strict neutrality. The war took him by surprise, and like Addams he found it "incredible" that civilized nations could display such savagery. His first worry was that America's immigrant communities would take sides. Shortly after the crisis began, 450 steelworkers from Gary, Indiana, enlisted in the Serbian army. Irish Americans, who wanted independence for their homeland, sided with Germany against England. The Allies (Britain, France, Italy, and Russia) and the Central powers (Germany, Austria-Hungary, and Turkey) each used propaganda to manipulate US opinion.

Wilson sent his closest aide, Colonel Edward House, to Europe with offers to broker a peace agreement. Privately the president believed that a German victory would be a catastrophe. Protected by Britain's control of the seas, the United States had expanded its influence during the previous century. In an Allied defeat, he said, "the United States, itself, will have to become a military nation, for Germany will push her conquests into South America." With Europe and possibly Asia controlled by a single power, the United States would be vulnerable and alone.

Modern warfare and commerce made true neutrality difficult. The belligerent powers desperately needed everything the United States had to export. As purchasing agent for France and Britain, J. P. Morgan's firm soon became the world's largest customer, buying more than $3 billion worth of armaments, food, textiles, steel, chemicals, and fuel. US loans to the Allies grew to $2.5 billion by 1917, but the Central powers received only $127 million in credit. Trade with the Central powers meanwhile sank from $170 million to less than $1 million by 1916. An Allied victory would make the United States the world's leading creditor, whereas defeat might mean financial collapse. The United States had not formally taken sides, but the American economy was already in the war on the side of the Allies.

Wilson's response to the British and German naval blockades reinforced the tilt toward the Allies. Both sides violated the "freedom of the seas," Britain with mines and warships, Germany with submarines. Wilson considered Britain's violation justifiable, but not Germany's. Britain's surface fleet was able to capture civilian ships as required by international law, but a German *Unterseeboot*, or U-boat—a small, fragile submarine—could not do that without giving up the stealth and surprise that were its only weapons.

The *Lusitania*'s Last Voyage

Germany used advertisements in American newspapers to warn against travel on ships bound for the war zone. The State Department was divided. Robert Lansing, the department's counselor, condemned submarine attacks as an offense against law and morality, but Bryan wanted to bar Americans from traveling on belligerent ships. Wilson sided with Lansing and declared that Germany would be held to "strict accountability" for American lives or property.

On the afternoon of May 7, 1915, submarine U-20 sighted the luxury liner *Lusitania* off the coast of Ireland and fired a torpedo that detonated against the starboard side. In 18 minutes, the *Lusitania* broke apart and sank. Of almost 2,000 passengers aboard, 1,198 drowned, including 94 children and 124 Americans. The newspapers reacted with rage and horror, but Wilson's advisers again disagreed on how to respond. Bryan wanted to balance a protest with a denunciation of Britain's violation of neutral rights. Wilson ignored him and demanded that submarine warfare stop altogether. He hinted that unless his demands were met, the United States would break relations.

Public opinion was equally divided. Lippmann told a friend in England that "the feeling against war in this country is a great deal deeper than you would imagine by reading editorials." When Germany promised not to attack passenger liners without warning, Wilson accepted this pledge as a diplomatic triumph. It momentarily restored calm, but official and public opinion had turned against Germany. The *Lusitania* crisis, Lippmann predicted, "united Englishmen and Americans in a common grief and a common indignation" and might "unite them in a common war."

The Drift to War

The *Lusitania* disaster divided progressives on the issue of the war. Peace advocates such as Addams, Bryan, and La Follette urged a stricter neutrality. Others believed war, or preparations for war, were justified. Theodore Roosevelt clamored for it. He endorsed the preparedness campaign mounted by organizations such as the National

Security League and the American Defense Society. Thousands marched down New York's Fifth Avenue under an electric sign declaring "Absolute and Unqualified Loyalty to Our Country."

Preparedness leagues, headed by businessmen and conservative political figures, called attention to the state of the armed forces, equipped only for tropical wars and lacking trucks, planes, and modern arms. The preparedness campaign appropriated patriotic rituals once reserved for elections. Wilson himself led the parade in Washington in 1916, wearing a red tie, white trousers, and a blue blazer. Hundreds of young Americans, positive that a German victory would mean the defeat of civilization, went to Paris to enlist. The French army soon had an American Volunteer Corps and a squadron of American fliers, the Lafayette Escadrille, whose exploits filled American newspapers. Magazines featured the poems of Alan Seeger, a Harvard graduate who joined the foreign legion. While Americans slept "pillowed in silk and scented down," Seeger wrote, "I've a rendezvous with death/At midnight in some flaming town." Wilson felt that to shape the world after the war, Americans would have to meet that rendezvous.

The Election of 1916

Although Wilson believed the United States would need to enter the fight, he campaigned for reelection under the slogan "He kept us out of war." The preparedness issue reunited Theodore Roosevelt and the Republicans behind Supreme Court Justice Charles Evans Hughes, who attacked Wilson for failing to defend American honor in Mexico and Europe. Woman suffragists campaigned against Wilson and picketed the White House with signs asking, "Mr. President? How long must women wait for liberty?" Although the Republicans remained dominant, Hughes was an inept campaigner. He won New York, Pennsylvania, and Illinois but lost in the South and West. Wilson won narrowly, whereas Republicans controlled the House and the Senate. Still, reelection freed Wilson to pursue a more vigorous foreign policy. As Lippmann realized, "What we're electing is a war president—not the man who kept us out of war."

The Last Attempts at Peace

After the election, Wilson launched a new peace initiative. Looking for an opening after years of stalemate, he asked each of the belligerent powers to state its war aims. Each insisted on punishing the other and enlarging its own territories. Before Congress in January 1917, the president called for a "peace without victory," based on the self-determination of all nations and the creation of an international organization to enforce peace.

Germany toyed with accepting Wilson's proposals but decided to wait. With the defeat of Russia in 1917, it could shift armies from the eastern front to France. U-boats again torpedoed British passenger liners and American merchant ships. In late February, British intelligence officers showed the US ambassador in London a telegram from the German foreign minister, Arthur Zimmermann, plotting an alliance with Mexico. With the Zimmermann Telegram revealed, if Wilson did not declare war now, Roosevelt declared, he would "skin him alive."

Americans disagreed then, as historians do today, on why the United States went to war. Critics pointed to the corporate interests that stood to gain. Publicly and in private, Wilson stressed two considerations: the attacks on American ships and the peace settlement. The treaty conference would settle scores of issues affecting American interests. Unless it went to war, Wilson told Jane Addams, the United States would have to shout "through a crack in the door."

War Aims

Rain was falling on the evening of April 2, 1917, as Wilson went to ask Congress for war. Some on Pennsylvania Avenue cheered and waved flags, whereas others stared silently at the president's limousine. The war, Wilson told the assembly, was in its last stages. American armies could bring it to a merciful end. The United States had tried to stand apart, but it had failed. Neutrality had provided no safety for travelers or trade. The only hope for avoiding even more dangerous future wars was for the United States to dictate the peace, to establish a "concert of free peoples." This would be a war to end all wars, to make the world safe for democracy.

In urging the vote for war, the president explicitly rejected the aims of the Allies. "We have no quarrel with the German people," he said, but with the kaiser and all other emperors and autocrats who blocked his road to a new world order. Wilson realized, however, that imperial France and Britain did not stand for democracy or self-determination, either. The United States would fight with Britain and France as an "associated power."

Edward House assembled a secret committee, known as the Inquiry, to draft a peace proposal both generous enough to show "sympathy and friendship" to the German people and harsh enough to punish their leaders. Made up of economists, historians, geographers, and legal experts, with Lippmann as its secretary, the Inquiry produced a set of 14 recommendations that redrew the boundaries of Europe, created a league of nations, and based peace on the principles of freedom of the seas, open-door trade, and ethnic self-determination.

The Fight in Congress

During the ovation after Wilson's speech to Congress, one senator stood silently, his arms folded. La Follette told his colleagues that if this was a war for democracy, it should be declared democratically. The country had voted for the peace candidate for president, and there were strong reasons to suspect a declaration would fail a national vote. Representatives found that voters opposed American entry, often by two to one. Midwestern farmers, William Allen White reported from Iowa, "don't seem to get the war."

Prowar representatives blocked La Follette's move for a referendum and brought the declaration to a vote on April 6, when it passed 82 to 6 in the Senate and 373 to 50 in the House. Divisions resurfaced over questions of how to pay for the war and who would fight in it. Wilson wanted universal conscription, the first draft since the Civil War. The 1917 draft law deputized 4,000 local boards to induct men between 18 and 45. Both supporters and opponents believed the draft would mold citizens. It would "break down distinctions of race and class," said one representative, turning immigrants into "new Americans." La Follette countered that the new Americans would be like the new Germans, indoctrinated by the army.

Newspapers and politicians denounced the antiwar progressives as traitors. They had too few votes to stop conscription, but they did create an exemption for conscientious objectors and reduced some taxes used to pay for the war. Opposition voices were soon silenced by patriotic calls for unity. "I pray God," Wilson avowed, "that some day historians will remember these momentous years as the years which made a single people of the great body of those who call themselves Americans."

Mobilizing the Nation and the Economy

News of the war declaration, carried in banner headlines on Easter Sunday, 1917, set the nation abuzz with activity. Wilson recognized that he was asking for an unprecedented effort. Raising an army of over 3 million, supplying it with modern equipment, and transporting it across submarine-infested waters were herculean feats. By midsummer, there were more men at work building barracks than had been in both armies at Gettysburg. Americans would send to Europe 1.8 million tons of meat, 8.8 million tons of grain, and 1.5 million tons of sugar. Factories that produced sewing machines and automobiles would retool to make howitzers and tanks.

The strain war placed on the American people and economy was severe. Wilson and others feared that it could widen political divisions and destroy 15 years of progressive achievements. Others felt that sharing the sacrifices of war would consolidate the gains. "We shall exchange our material thinking for something quite different," the General Federation of Women's Clubs predicted. "We shall all be enfranchised, prohibition will prevail, many wrongs will be righted." Lippmann hoped war would bring a new American revolution.

Enforcing Patriotism

Authorities dealt severely with dissent. Suspicions about the loyalties of ethnic communities and rumors of German saboteurs fed the hysteria. On July 30, 1916, across the river from New York City, the largest arms storage facility in the country blew up. The explosion destroyed thousands of pounds of shells and guns bound for Russia and tore away parts of the Statue of Liberty. Federal agents responded by rounding up aliens. However, domestic opinion posed a greater danger to the war effort than enemy agents. While initial enthusiasm ran high, the skepticism La Follette expressed was just beneath the surface.

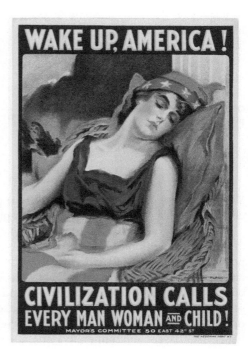

Wake Up, America! After a prolonged effort at neutrality, the United States faced the challenge of preparedness upon entering World War I. Propaganda posters encouraged Americans to support the war effort.

STRUGGLES FOR DEMOCRACY

Eugene V. Debs Speaks Out Against the War

When the United States declared war on Germany in April 1917, the Socialist Party convened to draft a response to the war. The party committed to an ongoing, active opposition to the war, the draft, and all funding of the war effort. This public stance, combined with steadily increasing membership due to antiwar sentiments from both farm and urban working-class communities, made the Socialist Party a target for those dedicated to promoting "Americanism," unquestioning loyalty, and total support for the war effort. Those who failed to demonstrate their patriotism sufficiently were subject to harassment, violence, or worse. Legislation such as the Sedition Act and Espionage Act made dissent not only unpopular, but illegal.

Eugene V. Debs, a long-time Socialist leader, watched much of this occur from his home in Indiana. After a lifetime of advocating on behalf of the American worker and attempting to spread the party's message, the 63-year-old Debs suffered from poor health and was confined to his bed. But as he saw his friends and associates beaten and jailed, and as he read Socialist views misrepresented in the press, he felt compelled to defend the party to which he had dedicated so much of his life.

Debs traveled to Canton, Ohio, where three local party leaders had been imprisoned under the Espionage Act for publicly opposing the war. After visiting with these men, Debs addressed a crowd of more than 1,000 people in nearby Nimisilla Park. He angrily asserted that his comrades had been persecuted merely for exercising their "constitutional right of free speech." Debs critiqued the American government for failing to live up to its promise as a free republic. He lamented the power of the business elite, who claimed to set the standard for American patriotism even as they made handsome profits from the war effort. These men, Debs proclaimed, "shout their claim from the housetops that they are the only patriots, and who have their magnifying glasses in hand, scanning the country for evidence of disloyalty, eager to apply the brand of treason to the men who dare to even whisper their opposition."

Victories might not come quickly, and if the public should start to turn against the war, consent would have to be manufactured by propaganda or the police.

Congress gave the president sweeping powers to suppress dissent. The Espionage Act (1917) and the Sedition Act (1918) effectively outlawed opposition to the war and used the postal service to catch offenders. Although there was no link between the labor movement and sabotage, unions were the prime target. The Justice Department raided the Chicago offices of the Industrial Workers of the World and sent 96 leaders to prison on charges of sedition. William D. "Big Bill" Haywood was sentenced to 20 years. Eugene V. Debs, leader of the Socialist Party, received 10 years for telling Ohioans they were "fit for something better than slavery and cannon fodder."

The wealthy, he asserted, fervently promoted the war as they happily allowed other men to fight it. To that end, Debs told the crowd, "You are fit for something better than slavery and cannon fodder. You need to know that you were not created to work and produce and impoverish yourself to enrich an idle exploiter. You need to know that you have a mind to improve, a soul to develop, and a manhood to sustain."

In his speech, Debs said nothing he had not said before, but his supporters were not the only ones in the crowd. Also present were stenographers hired by the US Attorney for Northern Ohio, E. S. Wertz. Although the Justice Department in Washington, DC, was not enthusiastic about the possibility of prosecution, Wertz obtained an indictment, charging Debs with 10 violations of the Espionage Act.

When Debs went to trial, he instructed his lawyers not to contest the charges, which had been reduced to two violations. He had given the speech and would stand by it. In his estimation, he had been well within his rights of free speech. As Debs addressed the jury, he invoked great American patriots like George Washington and Thomas Paine, men who had spoken out against injustice, just as he had. Those men were heroes, but contemporaries who followed their examples were subject to persecution. His defense mattered not. The jury found Debs guilty and he was sentenced to 10 years in jail.

Debs's speech and sentencing initially electrified American Socialists, but optimism on the left was short-lived. Debs appealed the decision, but in March 1919, the US Supreme Court upheld his conviction. Ohio Senator Atlee Pomerene feared leniency for Debs would suggest national weakness against the perceived growing threat from radicals and revolutionaries inspired by the Bolshevik Revolution in Russia. Attorney General A. Mitchell Palmer, who would go on to lead raids against political radicals as part of the post–World War I Red Scare, rejected the possibility of clemency altogether.

Debs ultimately served less than three years of his sentence. While in prison, he ran as the Socialist candidate for president of the United States and received nearly a million votes. When he emerged from prison in December 1921, however, he was hobbled by poor health and his party was hampered by an increasingly conservative political climate that would limit radical activism for much of the decade ahead. The rights and freedoms advocated by Debs would be restricted for the foreseeable future.

States also passed laws criminalizing "unpatriotic" activity. Indiana's Council for Defense licensed citizens to raid German homes, prevent church services in German, and make sure German Americans bought war bonds. Towns, schools, and clubs with German-sounding names changed them. East Germantown, Indiana, became Pershing. Hamburgers became "liberty sandwiches." Schools in the Midwest stopped teaching German altogether. Americans who had once proudly displayed their ethnicity now took pains to disguise it.

Pacifist faiths had their own ordeals. Some sects had come to America to avoid conscription in Germany or Russia. Many could not comply with the conscientious objector statute, which required submission to military control. Fifteen hundred Mennonites fled to Canada to avoid being placed in camps. Thirty-four Russian Pentecostals were arrested in Arizona, turned over to the army, court-martialed, and sent to Leavenworth.

The government's propaganda effort was managed by the Committee on Public Information (CPI) under former muckraker George Creel. It made films, staged pageants, and churned out ads, billboards, and press releases. The CPI sold the war by telling Americans they were fighting to save their own homes. One poster showed German bombers over a shattered, headless Statue of Liberty. Like Wilson, propaganda distinguished between Germany and the German people. CPI leaflets in German offered "Friendly Words to the Foreign Born." It cast immigrants as potential patriots and women as symbols of progress and sacrifice. Creel drafted Charles Dana Gibson, whose "Gibson Girl" ads personified glamour, to depict women as mothers, nurses, and patriotic consumers. As advertising mobilized American thought for the war effort, it also advanced progressive agendas.

Regimenting the Economy

The first prolonged conflict between industrial nations, World War I introduced the term "total war." By 1917, all of the resources, manpower, and productive capacities of the combatants had been mobilized. It soon became clear that the economy of the United States would have to be organized in new ways.

The navy planned a vast shipyard on Hog Island, near Philadelphia, with 250 buildings, 80 miles of railroad track, and 34,000 workers. It would be larger than Britain's seven largest shipyards combined, but in April 1917, Hog Island was 847 acres of swamp. Steelmaker Charles M. Schwab, in charge of the project, signed contracts for machinery, cement, steel, and timber. Materials were loaded on trains headed east. The result was the Great Pile Up, the biggest traffic jam in railroad history. Without enough workers to unload, cars began to back up on sidings in Philadelphia and then all the way back to Pittsburgh and Buffalo, their loads dumped on the outskirts of cities. Schwab begged the railroads to cooperate, to no avail. The voluntary system had failed, and on January 1, 1918, Wilson nationalized the railroads.

The Hog Island fiasco demonstrated the need for supervision of the economy. Wilson created a War Industries Board (WIB) to regulate prices, manufacturing, and transport. The job was enormous, and Wilson found the overseer he needed in Bernard Baruch, a Wall Street financier, who believed in regulation by "socially responsible" businessmen. Baruch recruited corporate executives for top positions and paid them a dollar a year. The president of the Aluminum Company of America became chairman of the WIB's aluminum committee, and a former top executive of John Deere headed the agricultural implements section.

The dollar-a-year men regimented the economy and put business to work for government, but they also guaranteed profits and looked after their own interests. One of their innovations, the "cost-plus" contract, assured contractors the recovery of costs plus a percentage for profit. Under these arrangements, the Black and Decker Company made gun sights, Akron Tire made army cots, and the Evinrude Company stopped making outboard motors and turned out grenades. Each company built up revenues to launch new product lines after the war. Standardization also helped industry. The WIB set standard designs and sizes for everything from shirts to lug nuts. One steel executive observed, "We are all making more money out of this war than the average human being ought to."

Hog Island Shipyard Building the massive shipyard at Hog Island was a major feat. The railroad network broke down under the strain, leading Wilson to nationalize the railroads.

Not all businesses submitted willingly to "war socialism." The Ford Motor Company had just set up a national dealer network, and it refused to stop delivering cars. When other automakers followed suit, the board threatened to cut off the industry's supply of coal and steel. After long negotiations, the automakers agreed to cut production by three-fourths. The delay hurt. When American troops went into battle, they had a grand total of two tanks.

The war economy was a culmination of two movements: Wall Street's drive for corporate consolidation and the progressives' push for federal regulation. Businessmen saw that the WIB could rationalize the economy. These "New Capitalists" wanted to end cutthroat competition and make business predictable. They encouraged workers to identify with the company through stock sharing and bonus plans. The WIB's example of government-industry cooperation would serve as a model in national crises to come.

The Great Migration

The war economy gave Americans new choices and opportunities. As factories geared up, they faced a shortage of labor. The draft took eligible employees from the cities, and the usual source of new workers—Europe—was sealed off by a screen of U-boats. Employers found eager workers in the South. In small towns and rural junctions, labor recruiters arrived offering free rides to the North and well-paid employment on arrival. Manufacturers came to rely on the labor of former sharecroppers. Westinghouse employed 25 African Americans in 1916; by 1918, it employed 1,500. The Pennsylvania Railroad recruited 10,000 workers from Florida and Georgia. Veterans saw no reason to go back to sharecropping after the war. In some northern cities, a thousand migrants were arriving each week. This massive movement from the rural South to the urban North and West came to be called the Great Migration.

Lynchings, intimidation, and a declining southern economy encouraged migration. Almost half a million people came north during the war years—so many that some counties emptied out, creating panic among whites left behind. Mississippi alone lost 75,000 workers. "We must have the Negro in the South," the Macon, Georgia, *Telegraph* pined. "It is the only labor we have. . . . If we lose it, we go bankrupt." Southern states banned recruiters. In some places violence provoked migration. "Every time a lynching takes place in a community down south," one observer noted, "you can depend on it that colored people will arrive in Chicago within two weeks."

African American workers moved into jobs at the bottom of the pay scale: janitors, domestics, and factory hands. Rent, groceries, and other necessities were substantially more expensive in the cities. Still, African American workers could earn wages 70 percent higher than what they were used to at home. Almost no one went back, and the new arrivals adapted to the rhythms of city life. "South State Street was in its glory then, a teeming Negro street with crowded theaters, restaurants, and cabarets," Langston Hughes wrote of Chicago in 1918. Housing was scarce, and African American renters were limited to overcrowded districts wedged between industrial zones and hostile white neighborhoods. W. E. B. DuBois noted that African Americans had lived in many neighborhoods of Philadelphia before the war, but by the end of the war they were concentrated in just one ward. Ghetto neighborhoods were both expensive and decrepit. On Chicago's South Side, rents were 15 to 20 percent higher than in white neighborhoods, and the death rate was comparable to that of Bombay, India. White property owners and real estate agents worked to create the ghettos, enforce their boundaries, and "Make Hyde Park White." A real estate agent said that African American homeowners "hurt our values." When discrimination failed, there was dynamite. From 1917 to 1919, whites bombed 26 African American residences in Chicago. On July 2, 1917, in East St. Louis, an arms manufacturing center in southern Illinois, competition for housing and political offices led a mob of white workers to attack "Black Valley," an African American neighborhood along the Southern Railroad track. Forty-seven people were killed and six thousand left homeless.

After East St. Louis, white mobs found black neighborhoods less easy to attack. When a mob invaded a Washington, DC, ghetto three years later, residents fought back with guns. The novelist Alden Bland wrote that the mood in Chicago's Black Belt, under attack in the hot summer of 1919, was "get them before they get you." An African American newspaper explained drily that "New Negroes are determined to make their dying a costly investment for all concerned." The New Negro, urban, defiant, often a war veteran who demanded rather than asked for rights, became the subject of admiring and apprehensive reports. Police kept files on suspected militants, but the mobility and anonymity of northern cities translated into freedom.

Reforms Become "War Measures"

On August 3, 1917, thousands of protestors marched in New York under signs demanding "Why not make America safe for democracy?" In the wake of the East St. Louis outrage, the NAACP urged Congress to outlaw lynching as a "war measure." African Americans were not alone in using the president's language to justify reform. Carrie Chapman Catt told Wilson that he could enact women's suffrage as a "war measure." Advocates of progressive change demanded that the United States practice at home the ideals it fought for abroad.

Suffragists hitched their cause to the national struggle. Catt's National American Woman Suffrage Association (NAWSA) abandoned its state-by-state lobbying to identify women with the national cause. Members sold liberty bonds and knitted socks for the Red Cross, making it clear they expected a constitutional amendment in return. Alice Paul's National Woman's Party (NWP) picketed the White House with signs quoting Wilson's demand for all peoples to "have a voice in their own governments." When Wilson announced his support in 1918, he cited women's war service as the reason. The Nineteenth Amendment was finally ratified in 1920, "so soon after the war," according to Jane Addams, "that it must be accounted as the direct result of war psychology."

As it had for African Americans, the labor shortage increased opportunities for women. Although most women workers were already in the labor force, many took jobs previously considered "inappropriate" for their sex. Women replaced men as bank tellers, streetcar operators, mail carriers, and steelworkers. Many of these opportunities vanished when the war ended, but in expanding sectors such as finance, communications, and office work, women made permanent gains. By 1920, more than 25 percent worked in offices or as telephone operators, and 13 percent were in professions such as teaching, nursing, and social work. The new opportunities gave women a source of prestige and enjoyment. Alice Hamilton remarked on the "strange spirit of exaltation among the men and women who thronged to Washington, engaged in all sorts of 'war work' and loving it." Army General Order 13 set standards for women's work, including an eight-hour day, prohibitions on working at night or in dangerous conditions, and provisions for rest periods, lunchrooms, and bathrooms. The government also empowered women consumers, encouraging them to report on shopkeepers who charged above the official price.

Wilson authorized a National War Labor Board to intervene in essential industries. The board set an unofficial minimum wage. For the first time, the federal government recognized workers' rights to organize, bargain collectively, and join unions. Unskilled workers earned higher real wages than ever before. When the Smith and Wesson Company refused to acknowledge its workers' right to bargain collectively, the army seized the factory and recognized the union. There were limits, however, for the administration. When skilled machinists at the Remington Arms plant made demands the board considered excessive, Baruch threatened to have them drafted and sent to France.

Prohibition did not please workers, either, but beer, wine, and spirits were early casualties of war. The Anti-Saloon League and the Woman's Christian Temperance Union had built a powerful antiliquor coalition by 1916. Congress would have passed

Prohibition without war, but temperance became a patriotic crusade. Military regulations prohibited liquor near army camps. Finally, in 1919 the states ratified the Eighteenth Amendment, banning the "manufacture, sale, or transportation of intoxicating liquors." The Anti-Saloon League celebrated the dawn of "an era of clear thinking and clean living." America was "so dry it couldn't spit," according to Billy Sunday. He overstated the case. By some estimates, after the ban illegal speakeasies in New York outnumbered the saloons they replaced. Bootleggers and smugglers slaked American thirsts, but liquor prices rose and consumption declined. Americans never again drank anything like the average two and a half gallons of pure alcohol per person annually imbibed before Prohibition.

The war also lent patriotic zeal to antivice crusaders. During the Progressive Era, muckrakers exposed the police-protection rackets that allowed gambling dens and brothels to thrive. Within days of the declaration of war, reformers identified prostitutes as enemies of the health of American troops. Gonorrhea afflicted a quarter of the Allied forces in France, and middle-class Americans were appalled. Before 1917, reformers targeted commercial vice as a source of political and social corruption, but afterward they directed their efforts at women as carriers of disease.

The army acted against liquor and prostitution to protect the welfare of soldiers, but it did not challenge racial injustice, even when lives were at stake. At camps in the South, it was often unclear who had more authority, uniformed African American soldiers or white local officials. Clashes could easily turn violent. A riot in Houston in August 1917 began when soldiers from nearby Camp Logan rushed to the aid of an African American woman being beaten by police. Twenty policemen and soldiers were killed, and 54 soldiers received life sentences in the largest court-martial in US history.

After the Houston riot, African American units were dispersed across the country, and the army remained segregated. Worse, many southern communities used military discipline to strengthen their own Jim Crow laws. Encouraged by the army's "work or fight" order, which required draft-age men to either enlist or get a job, states and localities passed compulsory work laws that applied to women and older men. The laws were intended to keep laborers in the fields and servants in the kitchens at prewar wages.

In this "war welfare state," the government mediated among labor, industry, and other organized interests. Social activism became a matter of lobbying federal agencies that could either dictate sweeping changes or use wartime powers to maintain the status quo. Success required organization and an ability to tie one's goals to the government's ambitions.

Over There

When the Senate took up the enormous war budget Wilson submitted in April 1917, the finance committee questioned Major Palmer E. Pierce about what would be done with the money. "Clothing, cots, camps, food, pay," he replied, "and we may have to have an army in France." "Good Lord!" exclaimed Senator Thomas Martin of Virginia. "You're not going to send soldiers over there, are you?" After the horrors of the Somme and Verdun, where men were fed to machine guns by the tens of thousands, it hardly seemed reasonable to send Americans to such a place. "One would think that, after almost four years of war, after the most detailed and realistic accounts of murderous fighting, . . . it would have been all but impossible to get anyone to serve," one veteran later recalled. "But it was not so; we and many thousands of others volunteered."

Americans went to France optimistically believing they could change the war and the peace. Trench warfare was not for them. They planned to fight a war of movement, sweeping in formations across open fields, like those at Antietam and Gettysburg. To a remarkable degree, they got the war they wanted. Europeans watched their civilization destroy itself in the Great War, but Americans saw theirs rising. Soldiers, "doughboys," said so in their letters, echoing the words of their leaders, their newspapers, and the volumes of poetry they carried with them into battle.

Citizens into Soldiers

Enlisting, training, and transporting soldiers began in a rush. Camps housing 400,000 recruits went up in the first 30 days. Conscription went smoothly, and soon 32 camps were housing 1.3 million men. Commander John J. Pershing arrived in France in June with 40,000 men and the first of some 16,000 women who would serve in the American Expeditionary Force (AEF).

Neither the Wilson administration nor the Allies initially anticipated that soldiers would be the United States' main contribution to the war effort. Britain urgently needed financial support, and Wilson advanced $200 million immediately, the first of an eventual $10 billion in loans to the Allies. Funds, food, and ammunition were needed more urgently than men, but that changed in October 1917, when German and Austrian forces smashed through the Italian lines at Caporetto, capturing 275,000 men and finishing the war on that front. When the Bolshevik Revolution curtailed Russian resistance in the East in November, Britain and France saw that by the next spring Germany would be able to mass its armies on the line from Belgium to Switzerland and break through to Paris. The war became a race to the western front between the United States and Germany.

Getting troops to the war required ships, but the American merchant fleet was smaller in 1917 than it was during the Civil War. For a time the United States had to cut back draft calls because it lacked ships to transport soldiers. The navy, meanwhile, cured the U-boat problem. The American destroyer fleet drove submarines from the sea lanes with depth charges, allowing the Allies to convoy effectively for the first time. By July 18, some 10,000 troops a day boarded the "Atlantic Ferry" for the ride to France.

The Fourteen Points

In December 1917, the Inquiry sent the president a memorandum titled "The War Aims and the Peace Terms It Suggests." Wilson redrafted it and presented it to Congress on January 8, 1918. The Fourteen Points outlined US objectives, but more fundamentally they offered an entirely new basis for peace. Unlike nineteenth-century wars waged for limited territorial or political objectives, the Great War was a total war, fought for unlimited aims. The principal belligerents—Britain, France, Russia, Germany, and Austria-Hungary—were global empires. Germany hoped both to defeat Britain and to take its empire. France wanted to destroy Germany's future as a great power, economically and militarily. Wilson replaced these imperial visions of total victory with a peace based on limited gains for nations, not empires.

The Fourteen Points addressed four themes: national self-determination; freedom of the seas; enforcement of peace by a league of nations; and open diplomacy. The Inquiry's memorandum included maps marked with new European boundaries based on national, ethnic identities. The new state of Poland, for instance, should govern only territories with "indisputably Polish populations." Point three restated the Open Door, urging international free trade, reflecting Wilson's hope of eliminating what he saw as the two leading causes of war, imperial ambition and commercial rivalry. By calling for an end to secret diplomacy, he appealed directly to the people of Europe. The expectation was that the hope of a just peace would weaken the enemy nations' will and inspire the Allies to fight harder. Creel printed 60 million copies and had them distributed around the world. Planes dropped copies over Germany and Austria.

Wilson hoped the Fourteen Points would dispel both the old dream of empire and the new one of socialist revolution. On November 7, two months before Wilson presented the points to Congress, Russian workers overthrew the Provisional Government of Alexander Kerensky. The one-party regime of the Bolsheviks, led by Vladimir Lenin, summoned workers everywhere to rise against their governments and to make peace without indemnities or annexations. "The crimes of the ruling, exploiting classes in this war have been countless. These crimes cry out for revolutionary revenge." In December, Lenin revealed the contents of the secret treaties, unmasking the imperial ambitions of the Allies. He sued for peace based on the principle of self-determination. The Council of People's Commissars allocated 2 million rubles to encourage revolutions around the world and called "upon the working classes of all countries to revolt."

Two world leaders—Lenin and Wilson—now offered radically different visions of the new world order, and Lenin was putting his into effect. The Bolsheviks' contempt for democracy angered Wilson, but he hoped that Russia would stay in the war. Those hopes ended with the Treaty of Brest-Litovsk, signed by Russia and Germany in March 1918. The treaty showed the fearful price of defeat in modern war. Russia lost the Ukraine, Poland, and Finland, most of its iron, steel, and best farmland, and one-quarter of its population. Those assets went into the German war machine, which began transferring 10 divisions a month to the West, its eastern front now secure.

Wilson was the first, but not the last, American president to be haunted by the specter of a German-Russian alliance, uniting the immense war-making resources of Europe and Asia. In Wilson's strategic vision, the great land powers of Eurasia, not Alfred Thayer Mahan's sea powers, most threatened US security. He refused to recognize the Bolshevik government and sent 7,000 American troops to Russia to support anti-Bolshevik forces on the eastern front. US and Japanese forces invaded Siberia from the east. The Bolshevik government now counted the United States among its enemies. Meanwhile, the battle for the control of Europe was about to begin.

The Final Offensive

The German high command knew the spring offensive would be the last. Their exhausted economy no longer could supply food or ammunition for a sustained effort. Breadlines, strikes, and industrial breakdowns foreshadowed the chaos that would follow defeat. Risking everything, the German commander Erich Ludendorff launched his offensive on March 21, 1918 (see Map 20–2). Shock troops hurled the British Fifth Army back to Amiens. In May they penetrated French lines as far as Soissons, 37 miles from Paris. As gaps split the lines, French general Ferdinand Foch and General Douglas Haig of Britain appealed urgently to Pershing to put American troops under British and French command. Pershing opposed the idea. He wanted the American army to play its own part in the war.

Map 20-2   Western Front, 1918 On the western front, the opposing armies fought from trenches forti-fied with earthworks and barbed wire. The parallel trench lines stretched thousands of miles from the North Sea to Switzerland.

Pershing criticized European commanders for remaining on the defensive instead of "driving the enemy out into the open and engaging him in a war of movement." Trained at West Point in Civil War tactics, he imagined himself a General Grant replacing European McClellans and saw trenches as symbols of inertia. Pershing favored massed assaults in which the sheer numbers of American troops would overwhelm the Germans, rifles against machine guns. In seeing Europe's war as a replay of the US Civil War, Pershing revealed a habit of mind that would typify American geopolitical thinking for the next century: the belief that Americans could understand the world through the prism of their own experience. He was not alone in wanting a decisive alternative to trench warfare. Billy Mitchell, head of the army's aviation section, noted that "we could cross the lines of these contending armies in a few minutes in our aeroplanes."

On May 27, German divisions pierced French lines at Château-Thierry and began ad-vancing on Paris at a rate of 10 miles a day. The French government considered whether to abandon the capital or surrender. Bowing to urgent requests, Pershing threw the AEF into the breach. Column upon column of fresh American troops filled the roads from Paris to the front. "We are real soldiers now and not afread [*sic*] of Germans," John F. Dixon, an African American infantryman from New York, wrote home. "Our boys went on the battlefield last night singing." Ahead lay five German divisions, poison gas, minefields, rolling artillery barrages, and machine guns in interlocking fields of fire. The Germans were stopped, but at a fearful cost. The marine brigade that took Belleau Wood suffered 4,600 casualties, half the force. Without artillery or tanks, they assaulted machine gun nests head-on, with rifles.

By mid-July, the initiative passed to the Allies. On September 12, Foch allowed Pershing to try his tactics against the St. Mihiel salient, a bulge in the French lines which, unknown to the Allies, the Germans had already begun to evacuate. The doughboys raced behind the retreating enemy past their planned objectives. Pershing was delighted. St. Mihiel had vindicated his strategy, and he yearned for another chance. It came two weeks later, at the battle of the Meuse-Argonne.

Ten miles northwest of Verdun, the Argonne Forest contained some of the most formidable natural and man-made defenses on the western front. Atop parallel ridges lay three fortified trench lines, *Stellungen*—barriers of concrete pillboxes, barbed wire, artillery, and observation posts. Half a million German troops had defended these fortifications for four years. Against this force, Pershing arrayed the American First Army, 1,031,000 men. The average doughboy at the Meuse-Argonne had a total of four months of training, and some had as little as 10 days. Pershing's battle plan called for overwhelming the German defenses with speed and numbers, reaching the second trench line, 10 miles inside the German front, the first day.

The Western Front From 1914 to 1918 the western front was the largest metropolis on earth, in Robert Cowley's phrase, an "unreal city" whose inhabitants—8,000 of whom died each day—worked in an industry of destruction. Here, Australian soldiers tread through the wasteland near Ypres, Belgium, in October 1917.

"Moving slowly forward, never heeding the bursting shells, nor gas, we followed a road forking to the left . . . into no man's land. It was soon noticed that we were in the bracket of a German barrage," a soldier wrote from the battlefield. They broke through the first line of German trenches after a day and a half; then the battle turned into a deadly crawl. In two weeks of fighting, 26,277 Americans died. French soldiers reported seeing the American dead lying in rows, cut down by machine guns as they marched in formation. Finally, on November 10, American troops reached their objective and dynamited the rail line connecting the cities of Metz and Sedan. Meanwhile, Germany announced that it would accept the Fourteen Points as the basis for an armistice and negotiations. At 11:00 a.m. on November 11, 1918, the guns fell silent.

American intervention had been decisive. The American economy, two and a half times the size of Germany's, lent its industrial and agricultural strength to the Allies at a crucial moment. American military power also tipped the balance. Pershing failed to transform strategy—it remained a mechanized war of attrition until the end—but by striking the final blow, Americans had the illusion that their way of war had been triumphant. American losses, 116,516 dead, were smaller than those of the British (908,371), the French (1.4 million), or the Germans (1.8 million), but they still show the colossal destructiveness of industrial war. In just six months, the United States suffered twice as many combat deaths as it would in the Vietnam War and almost a third as many as in World War II.

Americans and Europeans fought two vastly different wars on the same battlefields. The Americans' war was swift and victorious, but the Europeans experienced a catastrophe that consumed an entire generation. For Europeans, their faith in modernity and in the ability of science and democracy to create a better future vanished forever. Confidence in the inevitability of progress became a distinctive feature of US culture in the postwar era. In much of the world, "American" became almost synonymous with "modern," but not everywhere. In the East, another political and economic system shouted its claim to the future.

Revolutionary Anxieties

Americans celebrated the armistice with bonfires, church bells, automobile horns, and uplifted voices. Wilson told Congress that "everything for which America fought has been accomplished," but he observed that the situation in Russia cast doubt on the durability of peace. Even before the armistice, German revolutionaries took power in Bavaria. Over the next months, revolutions broke out throughout eastern Europe. From the trenches of Flanders to the Sea of Japan, not a single government remained intact, and in Moscow the new Soviet state towered above the ruins of the old regimes.

Wilson in Paris

For Wilson, the moment he had planned for in 1917 had arrived—the United States could help set the terms of peace—but war had exhausted the president. Confident that the public would view the nation's victory as his victory, he committed mistakes. Had he remained in Washington, some historians argue, he could have taken credit for the peace while keeping a close eye on his critics. Instead, he went to Paris, staking the treaty's success on his own popularity. He passed up a chance to include in the delegation a prominent Republican, such as Henry Cabot Lodge, who could guide the treaty through Congress.

Wilson in Paris Woodrow Wilson received a hero's welcome on the Rue Royale when he arrived in France to join the other Allied Powers in crafting the postwar world. His triumph was short-lived, however, as many of his Fourteen Points fell to the wayside during treaty talks at the Palace of Versailles.

In December 1918, Walter Lippmann, now an army captain, watched Wilson's triumphal entry into Paris. Crowds lined the streets, and as the procession crossed the Pont du Concorde, a great cheer echoed off the walls of the Chamber of Deputies. "Never has a king, never has an emperor received such a welcome," *L'Europe Nouvelle* declared. For the next month, Wilson toured France, Italy, and Britain to cries of "Viva Veelson." "They say he thinks of us, the poor people," a workingman remarked, "that he wants us all to have a fair chance; that he is going to do something when he gets here that will make it impossible for our government to send us to war again. If he had only come sooner!"

By the time Wilson arrived for treaty talks at the Palace of Versailles, two of the Fourteen Points had already been compromised. Britain refused to accept the point on freedom of the seas, which would thwart the use of the Royal Navy in a future conflict. Wilson also undercut his own position on point six, respect for Russia's sovereignty, as American troops were occupying Russian Siberia. Wilson was unable to prevent Britain, France, and Japan from dividing Germany's colonies among themselves and imposing harsh peace terms. Germany had to sign a humiliating "war guilt" clause and pay $33 billion in reparations, enough to cripple its economy for decades. Wilson concentrated on the League of Nations, which might make up for the treaty's other weaknesses and provide some safety against the rising tide of revolution. He took the lead in drafting the League Covenant, which committed each member to submit disputes to arbitration and pledged them to take action against "any war or threat of war."

The Senate Rejects the League

To many observers in the United States the Treaty of Versailles betrayed the goals Americans had fought to attain. "This Is Not Peace," declared the *New Republic*. Congress saw the League of Nations less as a way to prevent wars than as a guarantee that the United States would be involved. Americans were "far more afraid of Lenin than they ever were of the Kaiser," Lippmann wrote. To Republican leaders such as Henry Cabot Lodge, the United States' best bet was to look to its own security, keep its options open, and work out its international relations independently rather than as part of an alliance or league.

In March 1919, before the treaty was concluded, Lodge and 38 other senators—more than enough to defeat the treaty—signed a petition opposing the League of Nations. James A. Reed of Missouri said the covenant would turn American foreign policy over to foreigners. Editorials feared that American troops would be summoned to settle blood feuds in the Balkans. Wilson expected to fight, but he believed that the Senate would not reject the treaty.

In September, Wilson went "over the heads" of Congress and stumped for the treaty on a nationwide tour. He assured listeners in Sioux Falls that "the peace of the world cannot be established without America." He promised the citizens of Salt Lake City that China's independence would be respected. Traveling more than 8,000 miles and speaking before large audiences without loudspeakers took a toll on his health. After a speech in Pueblo, Colorado, he became so ill that he was rushed back to Washington, where he suffered a stroke that left him partially paralyzed and unable to concentrate for more than a few minutes a day. Mrs. Wilson and the president's physician kept his condition a secret and refused to allow anyone to see him.

With Wilson secluded in the White House, the Senate voted against ratification. To the end, Wilson refused to allow Senate Democrats to accept any modifications. Even Lippmann's *New Republic*, a mouthpiece for Wilson throughout the war, called the treaty's demise "desirable and wholesome." Lodge and the Republicans were not ready for isolation, but they preferred diplomatic strategies based on economic strength rather than a relatively weak military. They also saw Latin America as more critical than Europe to US security. Meanwhile, European governments organized the League of Nations without delegations from the United States or the Soviet Union.

Over the next decade, US influence abroad grew enormously. American automobiles, radios, and movies could be seen in far corners of the globe. The United States still practiced cautious diplomacy in Europe and Asia, to avoid being drawn into what the *New York Tribune* called the "vast seething mass of anarchy extending from the Rhine to the Siberian wastes."

Red Scare

On May 1, 1919, a dozen or more mail bombs were sent to prominent Americans: J. P. Morgan, John D. Rockefeller, senators, cabinet officials, and Supreme Court Justice Oliver Wendell Holmes. None of the packages reached its intended target, but one injured a maid in the home of Senator Thomas Hardwick and another exploded at the residence of Attorney General A. Mitchell Palmer in Washington, nearly injuring Franklin and Eleanor Roosevelt, who lived next door. Investigations later showed that the bombings were the work of lone lunatics, but many people quickly concluded that the United States was under attack. Since the Russian Revolution, newspapers, evangelists, and government officials had fed fears of Bolshevism. Revolution, Palmer alleged, was "licking at the altars of the churches, leaping into the belfry of the school bell, crawling into the sacred corners of American homes."

Revolutions in Europe terrified conservatives in the United States and led them to look for Soviet terrorists, particularly among immigrants and unionized workers. They drew no distinctions among Socialists, anarchists, Communists, and labor unionists; they were all "red." Seattle's mayor called in the army to break a dockworkers' strike. When steelworkers in Gary, Indiana, struck for higher wages and shorter hours in September 1919, Judge Elbert Gary, president of U.S. Steel, denounced them as followers of Russian "anarchy and Bolshevism." During the war they had worked 12 hours a day, 7 days a week, for an average wage of $28 a week. With the help of local loyalty leagues, Gary broke the strike.

AMERICA AND THE WORLD

The American Red Cross and Wartime Civilian Aid

Beyond the financial and material assistance provided by the American government and the military reinforcement provided by the American Expeditionary Force (AEF), Europeans received vital support from the American Red Cross (ARC). Founded in 1881, the ARC was part of the International Red Cross, dedicated to providing neutral wartime aid to soldiers and assisting during natural disasters, famine, and other times of unrest, internationally or at home. During World War I, the ARC moved away from its origins as a neutral organization and engaged in expansive and wide-ranging assistance to soldiers and civilians of Allied nations, supporting the United States' diplomatic efforts to foster global goodwill through the spread of American ideals.

While the ARC had been active in providing assistance to wartime nations since the beginning of World War I, American entry into the conflict marked a turning point for the organization. One-third of the US population became members of the ARC, and donations exceeded $400 million. The vast resources generated by the ARC's popularity allowed the organization to send volunteers to and lead civilian relief efforts in 24 countries, many to which American troops had never been deployed. Influenced by the writings of famed ARC ambulance drivers Earnest

Hemingway and John Dos Passos, popular memory of the ARC often tends toward the organization's military assistance when, in fact, much of its aid targeted the needs of civilian populations.

The model for ARC aid was its operation in France. Homer Folks, a former social worker from New York, became head of the Department of Civil Affairs and worked collaboratively with existing French and American aid efforts. Folks led ARC efforts to establish a vast infrastructure that provided both immediate aid (food, housing, and gainful employment) and set into motion plans for long-term health and welfare programs (an anti-tuberculosis campaign, educational training about public health and nursing for local women, and extensive infant and child health and wellness programs). The ARC justified its focus on education and preventative public health work as war relief, noting that such programs were fundamental to France's long-term stability. In many ways, the strategy and organizational methods of the ARC mirrored the tactics employed by American Progressives of the prewar period, informed as they were by a social scientific method and a commitment to planning, efficiency, and oversight.

The perspectives of the ARC's programs were communicated across numerous forms of media: propaganda

French Children in a Red Cross Hospital The ARC assisted civilian populations affected by the tumult of World War I.

posters, films, popular magazines, and its own publication, *Red Cross Magazine*. For progressives and those committed to an effort to establish global health, welfare, and social reform, the ARC's programs provided a model of organization and efficiency, evidence that international reform views were the views of the future, as were international fellowship and global cooperation. Indeed, many ARC volunteers headed overseas were thrilled by the prospect of practicing their ideals, wishing to communicate a global sense of American benevolence and commitment to democracy, contributing to international well-being, and finding professional satisfaction and possible career advancement. Even more, the ARC's efforts to appease civilian suffering provided an answer to those who critiqued the United States' delayed entry into World War I as evidence of its failure to fulfill its responsibility as an ally. Officially, the ARC leadership claimed to assist Allied nations "not in the American way," but in a way "satisfying" to the native populations they assisted. Still, these ways were based on American middle-class values and a faith in expertise, and it was the United States that held the upper hand by providing rather than receiving assistance.

As the war came to a close, the ARC ceded authority to the American Relief Administration and focused on famine relief. The ARC remained committed to a global view of the United States and continued to provide aid to war-torn European nations, but its mission was complicated by the fact that some Europeans objected to a continued American presence and what appeared to be ARC workers' sense of superiority, while volunteers grew frustrated with the limited change they were able to achieve. Many Americans began to yearn for a "return to normalcy" and a decline in international engagement. Yet the ARC remained internationally engaged, assisting when disaster struck across the globe and providing health and hygiene reform in US territories. Even as the US government moved toward a policy of isolation in the 1920s and 1930s, the ARC served an important symbolic function of American international humanitarianism and aid that continues to be among its hallmarks to the present day.

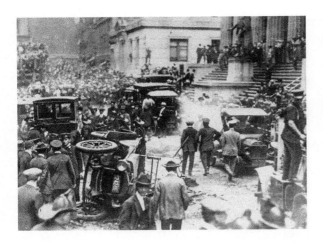

Wall Street Bombing On September 16, 1920, Mario Buda detonated a horse-drawn wagon filled with dynamite and scrap metal in front of the J. P. Morgan offices on Wall Street. It was the first use of a new technology of terror, the car bomb. Sending shock waves through an America already anxious about revolutionaries, the blast intensified the hunt for radicals and "reds."

Using the patriotic rhetoric of the war, industry leaders labeled strikers as dangerous aliens. They persuaded allies in the courts to take action, and a series of Supreme Court decisions made union activity virtually illegal. In 1919, the Court allowed antitrust suits to be filed against unions and later outlawed boycotts and picketing. Then, in January 1920, a series of crackdowns known as the Palmer raids rounded up and deported 250 members of the Union of Russian Workers. In one night, 4,000 suspected Communists were arrested in raids across the country.

The most notorious case associated with the "Red Scare" began in May 1920 when Nicola Sacco and Bartolomeo Vanzetti, a shoemaker and a fish peddler, were arrested for robbing a shoe company in South Braintree, Massachusetts. Two men died of gunshot wounds during the robbery, and ballistics experts claimed the bullets came from Sacco's gun.

Time Line

▼**1911**
Mexican Revolution begins

▼**1914**
US troops occupy Veracruz, Mexico
World War I begins

▼**1915**
US troops occupy Haiti (until 1934)
Lusitania sunk

▼**1916**
US forces invade Mexico in search of Pancho Villa
US forces enter the Dominican Republic
Woodrow Wilson reelected

▼**1917**
Russian czar abdicates; parliamentary regime takes power

United States declares war on Germany
East St. Louis riot
Houston riot
October Revolution overthrows Russian government; Lenin takes power

▼**1918**
Wilson announces US war aims: the Fourteen Points
Wilson nationalizes railroads

The trial, however, focused less on the evidence than on the fact that the defendants were Italian and anarchists. The state doctored evidence and witnesses changed testimony, but the judge favored the prosecution. The appeals lasted six years, as protests for their release mounted. With the execution approaching, labor parties organized worldwide boycotts of American products. Riots in Paris took 20 lives. Uruguayan workers called a general strike. Governments called on the president to intervene, but on August 23, 1927, Sacco and Vanzetti died in the electric chair.

Americans who had talked in 1917 about making the world safe for democracy now seemed ready to restrict their own freedoms out of fear. Lippmann found it "incredible that an administration announcing the most spacious ideals in our history should have done more to endanger fundamental American liberties than any group of men for a hundred years." By the end of 1920, the terror subsided, but labor unions and social radicals would have to fight the charge of communism for decades to come.

Conclusion

Wilson tried to lead America toward what he called a new world order, in which nations and international law would count more than empires and in which the United States could light the way toward progress, stability, and peace. He failed to recognize that for many Americans this future was filled with terrors, as well as promise. The strains of war had introduced new divisions into American society. Progressivism, which had given coherence and direction to social change, was a spent force. The growth of federal administration, the new powers of big business, internal migrations, and new social movements and values added up to what Lippmann called a "revolutionary world." Many of the changes that began during the war had not fully played out, nor were their consequences apparent, but Americans entered the 1920s with a sense of uneasiness. They knew that their nation was now the world's strongest, but they were unsure about what that might mean for their lives.

Sedition Act outlaws criticism of the US government
US troops stop German advance
Wilson sends troops to Siberia
Armistice ends fighting on the western front
Influenza pandemic peaks in September

▼1919
Eighteenth Amendment outlaws manufacture, sale, and transport of alcoholic beverages
Versailles Treaty signed in Paris
Mail bombs target prominent government and business figures
Gary, Indiana, steel strike
US Senate rejects Versailles Treaty

▼1920
Nineteenth Amendment secures the vote for women
Palmer raids arrest thousands of suspected Communists
Sacco and Vanzetti arrested on charges of robbery and murder

Who, What, Where

Review Questions

1. Wilson encouraged Americans to fight a war for democracy, but what other goals did US intervention serve?

2. How did mobilization for war advance the progressive agenda? In what ways did it set progressives back?

3. Where were the main battles in which US troops fought?

Critical-Thinking Questions

1. Allied commanders wanted to use American troops as a reserve, but Pershing wanted his soldiers to enter the battle as an army. Why was that so important to him?

2. Why did Senate Republicans reject the League of Nations? Did they want the United States to withdraw from the world, or did they want to deal with the world in a different way?

3. Managing the pace of change posed a tricky problem for leaders in the early twentieth century. How did Wilson try to control the dynamic of social and political change? What methods of change was he unwilling to accept?

4. Why were American leaders so much more concerned about sedition and dissent during World War I than they were during the Civil War or World War II?

Suggested Readings

Capozzola, Christopher. *Uncle Sam Wants You: World War I and the Making of the Modern American Citizen*. New York: Oxford University Press, 2008.

Irwin, Julia F. *Making the World Safe: The American Red Cross and a Nation's Humanitarian Awakening*. New York: Oxford University Press, 2013.

National Archives. World War I Centennial. https://www.archives.gov/topics/wwi#event-/timeline/item/archduke-assassination

Neiberg, Michael S. *The Path to War: How the First World War Created Modern America.* New York: Oxford University Press, 2016.

For further review materials and resource information, please visit www.oup.com/us/oakes-mcgerr

CHAPTER 20: A GLOBAL POWER, 1914–1919
Primary Sources

20.1 WORLD WAR I–ERA MUSIC: "I DIDN'T RAISE MY BOY TO BE A SOLDIER" (1915) AND "OVER THERE" (1917)

Americans viewed their nation's potential involvement in World War I with a healthy dose of skepticism. Many saw no need for the United States to become involved in what they regarded as a European conflict. After the United States joined the war, the Wilson administration recognized right away the need for propaganda efforts to boost support for American war efforts. Music played a fundamental role in reflecting the evolving mood of the population.

Alfred Bryan and Al Piantadosi, "I Didn't Raise My Boy to Be a Soldier," 1915

Ten million soldiers to the war have gone,
Who may never return again.
Ten million mothers' hearts must break,
For the ones who died in vain.
Head bowed down in sorrow in her lonely years,
I heard a mother murmur thro' her tears:

Chorus:
I didn't raise my boy to be a soldier,
I brought him up to be my pride and joy,
Who dares to put a musket on his shoulder,
To shoot some other mother's darling boy?
Let nations arbitrate their future troubles,
It's time to lay the sword and gun away,
There'd be no war today,
If mothers all would say,
I didn't raise my boy to be a soldier.

What victory can cheer a mother's heart,
When she looks at her blighted home?
What victory can bring her back,
All she cared to call her own?
Let each mother answer in the year to be,
Remember that my boy belongs to me!
(Chorus)

George M. Cohan, "Over There," 1917

Johnnie, get your gun
Get your gun, get your gun
Take it on the run
On the run, on the run

Hear them calling, you and me
Every son of liberty
Hurry right away
No delay, go today
Make your daddy glad
To have had such a lad
Tell your sweetheart not to pine
To be proud her boy's in line

Chorus:
Over there, over there
Send the word, send the word over there
That the Yanks are coming
The Yanks are coming
The drums rum-tumming
Everywhere
So prepare, say a prayer
Send the word, send the word to beware
We'll be over, we're coming over
And we won't come back till it's over
Over there

Johnnie, get your gun
Get your gun, get your gun
Johnnie show the Hun
Who's a son of a gun
Hoist the flag and let her fly
Yankee Doodle do or die
Pack your little kit
Show your grit, do your bit
Yankee to the ranks
From the towns and the tanks
Make your mother proud of you
And the old Red, White and Blue
(Chorus)

Sources: Al Piantadosi and Alfred Bryan, "I Didn't Raise My Boy to Be a Soldier," http://historymatters.gmu.edu/d/4942.
George M. Cohan, "Over There," http://www.loc.gov/teachers/classroommaterials/presentationsandactivities/
activities/songs/song2.php.

20.2 EUGENE V. DEBS, EXCERPTS FROM CANTON, OHIO, SPEECH (1918)

Eugene V. Debs, a leader of the Socialist Party of America, vehemently opposed American involvement in World War I. In June 1918, after visiting several local Socialist leaders who had been jailed for their opposition to the war, Debs spoke in Canton, Ohio. During his speech, he criticized the war as a capitalist undertaking and charged that those who led the patriotic charge did so for purely financial purposes. He called for the working classes to join the Socialist Party and fight for a socialist republic in America. In the aftermath of his speech, Debs was convicted for sedition under the Espionage Act of 1917 and sentenced to 10 years in prison. President Warren Harding commuted his sentence in 1921.

I hate, I loathe, I despise junkers and junkerdom. I have no earthly use for the junkers of Germany, and not one particle more use for the junkers in the United States. They tell us that we live in a great free republic; that our institutions are democratic; that we are a free and self-governing people. This is too much, even for a joke. But it is not a subject for levity; it is an exceedingly serious matter.

To whom do the Wall Street junkers in our country marry their daughters? After they have wrung their countless millions from your sweat, your agony and your life's blood, in a time of war as in a time of peace, they invest these untold millions in the purchase of titles of broken-down aristocrats, such as princes, dukes, counts and other parasites and no-accounts. Would they be satisfied to wed their daughters to honest workingmen? To real democrats? Oh, no!

They scour the markets of Europe for vampires who are titled and nothing else. And they swap their millions for the titles, so that matrimony with them becomes literally a matter of money. These are the gentry who are today wrapped up in the American flag, who shout their claim from the housetops that they are the only patriots, and who have their magnifying glasses in hand, scanning the country for evidence of disloyalty, eager to apply the brand of treason to the men who dare to even whisper their opposition to junker rule in the United States. No wonder Sam Johnson declared that "patriotism is the last refuge of the scoundrel." He must have had this Wall Street gentry in mind, or at least their prototypes, for in every age it has been the tyrant, the oppressor and the exploiter who has wrapped himself in the cloak of patriotism, or religion, or both to deceive and overawe the people.

They would have you believe that the Socialist Party consists in the main of disloyalists and traitors. It is true in a sense not at all to their discredit. We frankly admit that we *are* disloyalists and traitors to the real traitors of this nation. . . .

Every solitary one of these aristocratic conspirators and would-be murderers claims to be an arch-patriot; every one of them insists that the war is being waged to make the world safe for democracy. What humbug! What rot! What false pretense! These autocrats, these tyrants, these red-handed robbers and murderers, the "patriots," while the men who have the courage to stand face to face with them, speak the truth, and fight for their exploited victims—they are the disloyalists and traitors. If this be true, I want to take my place side by side with the traitors in this fight. . . .

Socialism is a growing idea; an expanding philosophy. It is spreading over the entire face of the earth: It is as vain to resist it as it would be to arrest the sunrise on the morrow. It is coming, coming, coming all along the line. Can you not see it? . . . It is the mightiest movement in the history of mankind. What a privilege to serve it! . . .

Our hearts are with the Bolsheviki of Russia. Those heroic men and women, those unconquerable comrades have by their incomparable valor and sacrifice added fresh luster to the fame of the international movement. Those Russian comrades of ours have made greater sacrifices, have suffered more, and have shed more heroic blood than any like number of men and women anywhere on earth; they have laid the foundation of the first real democracy that ever drew the breath of life in this world. And the very first act of the triumphant Russian revolution was to proclaim a state of peace with all mankind, coupled with a fervent moral appeal, not to kings, not to emperors, rulers or diplomats but to *the people* of all nations. Here we have the very breath of democracy, the quintessence of the dawning freedom. The Russian revolution proclaimed its glorious triumph in its ringing and inspiring appeal to *the peoples* of all the earth. In a humane and fraternal spirit new Russia, emancipated at last from the curse of the centuries, called upon all nations engaged in the frightful war, the Central Powers as well as the Allies, to send representatives to a conference to lay down terms of peace that should be just and lasting. Here was the supreme opportunity to strike the blow to make the world safe for democracy. Was there any response to that noble appeal that in some day to come will be written in letters of gold in the history of the world? Was there any response whatever to that appeal for universal peace? [*From the crowd, "No!"*] No, not the slightest attention was paid to it by the Christian nations engaged in the terrible slaughter. . . .

Wars throughout history have been waged for conquest and plunder. In the Middle Ages when the feudal lords who inhabited the castles whose towers may still be seen along the Rhine concluded to enlarge their domains, to increase their power, their prestige and their wealth they declared war upon one another. But they themselves did not go to war any more than the modern feudal lords, the barons of Wall Street go to war. The feudal barons of the Middle Ages, the economic predecessors of the capitalists of our day, declared all wars. And their miserable serfs fought all the battles. The poor, ignorant serfs had been taught to revere their masters; to believe that when their masters declared war upon one another, it was their patriotic duty to fall upon one another and to cut one another's throats for the profit and glory of the lords and barons who held them in contempt. And that is war in a nutshell. The master class has always declared the wars; the subject class has always fought the battles. The master class has had all to gain and nothing to lose, while the subject class has had nothing to gain and all to lose—especially their lives.

They have always taught and trained you to believe it to be your patriotic duty to go to war and to have yourselves slaughtered at their command. But in all the history of the world you, the people, have never had a voice in declaring war, and strange as it certainly appears, no war by any nation in any age has ever been declared by the people.

And here let me emphasize the fact—and it cannot be repeated too often—that the working class who fight all the battles, the working class who make the supreme sacrifices, the working class who freely shed their blood and furnish the corpses, have never yet had a voice in either declaring war or making peace. It is the ruling class that invariably does both. They alone declare war and they alone make peace.

What a compliment it is to the Socialist movement to be thus persecuted for the sake of the truth! The truth alone will make the people free. And for this reason the truth must not be permitted to reach the people. The truth has always been dangerous to the rule of the rogue, the exploiter, the robber. So the truth must be ruthlessly suppressed. That is why they are trying to destroy the Socialist movement; and every time they strike a blow they add a thousand new voices to the hosts proclaiming that socialism is the hope of humanity and has come to emancipate the people from their final form of servitude. . . .

[Socialists] are pressing forward, here, there and everywhere, in all the zones that girdle the globe. Everywhere these awakening workers, these class-conscious proletarians, these hardy sons and daughters of honest toil are proclaiming the glad tidings of the coming emancipation; everywhere their hearts are attuned to the most sacred cause that ever challenged men and women to action in all the history of the world. Everywhere they are moving toward democracy and the dawn; marching toward the sunrise, their faces all aglow with the light of the coming day. These are the Socialists, the most zealous and enthusiastic crusaders the world has ever known. They are making history that will light up the horizon of coming generations, for their mission is the emancipation of the human race. They have been reviled; they have been ridiculed, persecuted, imprisoned and have suffered death, but they have been sufficient to themselves and their cause, and their final triumph is but a question of time.

Do you wish to hasten the day of victory? Join the Socialist Party! Don't wait for the morrow. Join now! Enroll your name without fear and take your place where you belong. You cannot do your duty by proxy. You have got to do it yourself and do it squarely and then as you look yourself in the face you will have no occasion to blush. You will know what it is to be a real *man* or *woman*. You will lose nothing; you will gain everything. . . .

Source: Jean Y. Tussey, ed., *Eugene V. Debs Speaks* (New York: Pathfinder Press, 1970), pp. 243–279.

20.3 GEORGE CREEL, EXCERPTS FROM *HOW WE ADVERTISED AMERICA* (1920)

In April 1917, after the United States entered World War I, President Woodrow Wilson created the Committee on Public Information (CPI) headed by George Creel (1876–1953), a former muckraking journalist, newspaper editor, and politician. The CPI managed the nation's propaganda effort, creating films, staging pageants, and turning out advertisements, billboards, and press releases intended to educate the American public and build support for war efforts such as bond drives and rationing. In this memoir of his years at the CPI, published in 1920, Creel defended the work of the CPI against those who saw the agency as engaging in promotion of the war effort in any way other than an "open" and "positive" manner.

As Secretary Baker points out, the war was not fought in France alone. Back of the firing-line, back of armies and navies, back of the great supply-depots, another struggle waged with the same intensity and with almost equal significance attaching to its victories and defeats. It was the fight for the *minds* of men, for the "conquest of their convictions," and the battle-line ran through every home in every country.

It was in this recognition of Public Opinion as a major force that the Great War differed most essentially from all previous conflicts. The trial of strength was not only between massed bodies of armed men, but between opposed ideals, and moral verdicts took on all the value of military decisions. Other wars went no deeper than the physical aspects, but German *Kultur* raised issues that had to be fought out in the hearts and minds of people as well as on the actual firing-line. The approval of the world meant the steady flow of inspiration into the trenches; it meant the strengthened resolve and the renewed determination of the civilian population that is a nation's second line. The condemnation of the world meant the destruction of morale and the surrender of that conviction of justice which is the very heart of courage. The Committee on Public Information was called into existence to make this fight for the "verdict of mankind," the voice created to plead the justice of America's cause before the jury of Public Opinion. . . .

In no degree was the Committee an agency of censorship, a machinery of concealment or repression. Its emphasis throughout was on the open and the positive. At no point did it seek or exercise authorities under those war laws that limited the freedom of speech and press.

In all things, from first to last, without halt or change, it was a plain publicity proposition, a vast enterprise in salesmanship, the world's greatest adventure in advertising.

Under the pressure of tremendous necessities an organization grew that not only reached deep into every American community, but that carried to every corner of the civilized globe the full message of America's idealism, unselfishness, and indomitable purpose. We fought prejudice, indifference, and disaffection at home and we fought ignorance and falsehood abroad. We strove for the maintenance of our own morale and the Allied morale by every process of stimulation; every possible expedient was employed to break through the barrage of lies that kept the people of the Central Powers in darkness and delusion; we sought the friendship and support of the neutral nations by continuous presentation of facts. We did not call it propaganda, for that word, in German hands, had come to be associated with deceit and corruption. Our effort was educational and informative throughout, for we had such confidence in our case as to feel that no other argument was needed than the simple, straightforward presentation of facts.

There was no part of the great war machinery that we did not touch, no medium of appeal that we did not employ. The printed word, the spoken word, the motion picture, the telegraph, the cable, the wireless, the poster, the sign-board—all these were used in our campaign to make our own people and all other peoples understand the causes that compelled America to take arms. All that was fine and ardent in the civilian population came at our call until more than one hundred and fifty thousand men and women were devoting highly specialized abilities to the work of the Committee, as faithful and devoted in their service as though they wore the khaki. While America's summons was answered without question by the citizenship as a whole, it is to be remembered that during the three and a half years of our neutrality the land had been torn by a thousand divisive prejudices, stunned by the voices of anger and confusion, and muddled by the pull and haul of opposed interests. These were conditions that could not be permitted to endure. What we had to have was no mere surface unity, but a passionate belief in the justice of America's cause that should weld the people of the United States into one white-hot mass instinct with fraternity, devotion, courage, and deathless determination. The *war-will*, the will-to-win, of a democracy depends upon the degree to which each one of all the people of that democracy can concentrate and consecrate body and soul and spirit in the supreme effort of service and sacrifice. What had to be driven home was that all business was the nation's business, and every task a common task for a single purpose. . . .

As swiftly as might be, there were put into pamphlet form America's reasons for entering the war, the meaning of America, the nature of our free institutions, our war aims, likewise analyses of the Prussian system, the purposes of the imperial German government, and full exposure of the enemy's misrepresentations, aggressions, and barbarities. Written by the country's foremost publicists, scholars, and historians, and distinguished for their conciseness, accuracy, and simplicity, these pamphlets blew as a great wind against the clouds of confusion and misrepresentation. Money could not have purchased the volunteer aid that was given freely, the various universities lending their best men and the National Board of Historical Service placing its three thousand members at the complete disposal of the Committee. Some thirty-odd booklets, covering every phase of America's ideals, purposes, and aims, were printed in many languages other than English. Seventy-five million reached the people of America, and other millions went to every corner of the world, carrying our defense and our attack.

The importance of the spoken word was not underestimated. A speaking division toured great groups like the Blue Devils, Pershing's Veterans, and the Belgians, arranged mass-meetings in the communities, conducted forty-five war conferences from coast to coast, coordinated the entire speaking activities of the nation, and assured consideration to the crossroads hamlet as well as to the city.

The Four Minute Men, an organization that will live in history by reason of its originality and effectiveness, commanded the volunteer services of 75,000 speakers, operating in 5,200 communities, and making a total of 755,190 speeches, every one having the carry of shrapnel.

With the aid of a volunteer staff of several hundred translators, the Committee kept in direct touch with the foreign-language press, supplying selected articles designed to combat ignorance and disaffection. It organized and directed twenty-three societies and leagues designed to appeal to certain classes and particular foreign-language groups, each body carrying a specific message of unity and enthusiasm to its section of America's adopted peoples.

It planned war exhibits for the state fairs of the United States, also a great series of interallied war expositions that brought home to our millions the exact nature of the struggle that was being waged in France. In Chicago alone two million people attended in two weeks, and in nineteen cities the receipts aggregated $1,432,261.36. The Committee mobilized the advertising forces of the country—press, periodical, car, and outdoor—for the patriotic campaign that gave millions of dollars' worth of free space to the national service.

It assembled the artists of America on a volunteer basis for the production of posters, window cards, and similar material of pictorial publicity for the use of various government departments and patriotic societies. A total of 1,438 drawings was used. . . .

It organized a bureau of information for all persons who sought direction in volunteer war-work, in acquiring knowledge of any administrative activities, or in approaching business dealings with the government. In the ten months of its existence it gave answers to eighty-six thousand requests for specific information.

It gathered together the leading novelists, essayists, and publicists of the land, and these men and women, without payment, worked faithfully in the production of brilliant, comprehensive articles that went to the press as syndicate features. One division paid particular attention to the rural press and the plate-matter service. Others looked after the specialized needs of the labor press, the religious press, and the periodical press. The Division of Women's War Work prepared and issued the information of peculiar interest to the women of the United States, also aiding in the task of organizing and directing. Through the medium of the motion picture, America's war progress, as well as the meanings and purposes of democracy, were carried to every community in the United States and to every corner of the world. "Pershing's Crusaders," "America's Answer," and "Under Four Flags" were types of feature films by which we drove home America's resources and determinations, while other pictures, showing our social and industrial life, made our free institutions vivid to foreign peoples.

Turning away from the United States to the world beyond our borders, a triple task confronted us. First, there were the peoples of the Allied nations that had to be fired by the magnitude of the American effort and the certainty of speedy and effective aid, in order to relieve the war weariness of the civilian population and also to fan the enthusiasm of the firing-line to new flame. Second, we had to carry the truth to the neutral nations, poisoned by German lies; and third, we had to get the ideals of America, the determination of America, and the invincibility of America into the Central Powers. . . .

Source: George Creel, *How We Advertised America* (New York: Harper and Brothers, 1920), pp. 3–8.

20.4 WOODROW WILSON, "FOURTEEN POINTS" SPEECH (1918)

As Woodrow Wilson addressed Congress on January 8, 1918, he attempted to link American involvement in World War I to a moral cause, much as he had when he asked for a declaration of war in order to "make the world safe for democracy." As he outlined his goals for peace, he attempted to address many of the issues that had led to the outbreak of the war. By eliminating the main causes of the war—imperial desire and commercial competition—and establishing a just peace, he hoped to avoid such conflicts in the future.

It will be our wish and purpose that the processes of peace, when they are begun, shall be absolutely open and that they shall involve and permit henceforth no secret understandings of any kind. The day of conquest and aggrandizement is gone by; so is also the day of secret covenants entered into in the interest of particular governments and likely at some unlooked-for moment to upset the peace of the world. It is this happy fact, now clear to the view of every public man whose thoughts do not still linger in an age that is dead and gone, which makes it possible for every nation whose purposes are consistent with justice and the peace of the world to avow now or at any other time the objects it has in view.

We entered this war because violations of right had occurred which touched us to the quick and made the life of our own people impossible unless they were corrected and the world secured once and for all against their recurrence. What we demand in this war, therefore, is nothing peculiar to ourselves. It is that the world be made fit and safe to live in; and particularly that it be made safe for every peace-loving nation which, like our own, wishes to live its own life, determine its own institutions, be assured of justice and fair dealing by the other peoples of the world as against force and selfish aggression. All the peoples of the world are in effect partners in this interest, and for our own part we see very clearly that unless justice be done to others it will not be done to us. The programme of the world's peace, therefore, is our programme; and that programme, the only possible programme, as we see it, is this:

I. Open covenants of peace, openly arrived at, after which there shall be no private international understandings of any kind but diplomacy shall proceed always frankly and in the public view.

II. Absolute freedom of navigation upon the seas, outside territorial waters, alike in peace and in war, except as the seas may be closed in whole or in part by international action for the enforcement of international covenants.

III. The removal, so far as possible, of all economic barriers and the establishment of an equality of trade conditions among all the nations consenting to the peace and associating themselves for its maintenance.

IV. Adequate guarantees given and taken that national armaments will be reduced to the lowest point consistent with domestic safety.

V. A free, open-minded, and absolutely impartial adjustment of all colonial claims, based upon a strict observance of the principle that in determining all such questions of sovereignty the interests of the populations concerned must have equal weight with the equitable claims of the government whose title is to be determined.

VI. The evacuation of all Russian territory and such a settlement of all questions affecting Russia as will secure the best and freest cooperation of the other nations of the world in obtaining for her an unhampered and unembarrassed opportunity for the independent determination of her own political development and national policy and assure her of a sincere welcome into the society of free nations under institutions of her own choosing; and, more than a welcome, assistance also of every kind that she may need and may herself desire. The treatment accorded Russia by her sister nations in the months to come will be the acid test of their good will, of their comprehension of her needs as distinguished from their own interests, and of their intelligent and unselfish sympathy.

VII. Belgium, the whole world will agree, must be evacuated and restored, without any attempt to limit the sovereignty which she enjoys in common with all other free nations. No other single act will serve as this will serve to restore confidence among the nations in the laws which they have themselves set and determined for the government of their relations with one another. Without this healing act the whole structure and validity of international law is forever impaired.

VIII. All French territory should be freed and the invaded portions restored, and the wrong done to France by Prussia in 1871 in the matter of Alsace-Lorraine, which has unsettled the peace of the world for nearly fifty years, should be righted, in order that peace may once more be made secure in the interest of all.

IX. A readjustment of the frontiers of Italy should be effected along clearly recognizable lines of nationality.

X. The peoples of Austria-Hungary, whose place among the nations we wish to see safeguarded and assured, should be accorded the freest opportunity of autonomous development.

XI. Rumania, Serbia, and Montenegro should be evacuated; occupied territories restored; Serbia accorded free and secure access to the sea; and the relations of the several Balkan states to one another determined by friendly counsel along historically established lines of allegiance and nationality; and international guarantees of the political and economic independence and territorial integrity of the several Balkan states should be entered into.

XII. The Turkish portions of the present Ottoman Empire should be assured a secure sovereignty, but the other nationalities which are now under Turkish rule should be assured an undoubted security of life and an absolutely unmolested opportunity of autonomous development, and the Dardanelles should be permanently opened as a free passage to the ships and commerce of all nations under international guarantees.

XIII. An independent Polish state should be erected which should include the territories inhabited by indisputably Polish populations, which should be assured a free and secure access to the sea, and whose political and economic independence and territorial integrity should be guaranteed by international covenant.

XIV. A general association of nations must be formed under specific covenants for the purpose of affording mutual guarantees of political independence and territorial integrity to great and small states alike.

In regard to these essential rectifications of wrong and assertions of right we feel ourselves to be intimate partners of all the governments and peoples associated together against the Imperialists. We cannot be separated in interest or divided in purpose. We stand together until the end.

For such arrangements and covenants we are willing to fight and to continue to fight until they are achieved; but only because we wish the right to prevail and desire a just and stable peace such as can be secured only by removing the chief provocations to war, which this programme does remove. We have no jealousy of German greatness, and there is nothing in this programme that impairs it. We grudge her no achievement or distinction of learning or of pacific enterprise such as have made her record very bright and very enviable. We do not wish to injure her or to block in any way her legitimate influence or power. We do not wish to fight her either with arms or with hostile arrangements of trade if she is willing to associate herself with us and the other peace-loving nations of the world in covenants of justice and law and fair dealing. We wish her only to accept a place of equality among the peoples of the world,—the new world in which we now live,—instead of a place of mastery.

Neither do we presume to suggest to her any alteration or modification of her institutions. But it is necessary, we must frankly say, and necessary as a preliminary to any intelligent dealings with her on our part, that we should know whom her spokesmen speak for when they speak to us, whether for the Reichstag majority or for the military party and the men whose creed is imperial domination.

We have spoken now, surely, in terms too concrete to admit of any further doubt or question. An evident principle runs through the whole programme I have outlined. It is the principle of justice to all peoples and nationalities, and their right to live on equal terms of liberty and safety with one another, whether they be strong or weak. Unless this principle be made its foundation no part of the structure of international justice can stand. The people of the United States could act upon no other principle; and to the vindication of this principle they are ready to devote their lives, their honor, and everything that they possess. The moral climax of this the culminating and final war for human liberty has come, and they are ready to put their own strength, their own highest purpose, their own integrity and devotion to the test.

Source: Woodrow Wilson, Address on the Fourteen Points for Peace, January 8, 1918.

21

THE NEW NEGRO
HAS NO FEAR

Edwin's
CIGAR
STORE

The Modern Nation

1919–1928

UNIA Parade

649

AMERICAN PORTRAIT

"America's Sweetheart"

By the end of World War I, 26-year-old Mary Pickford had become "America's sweetheart." After a decade in Hollywood, the diminutive, long-haired actress was one of the first and greatest stars of the movies. Fans flocked to her films, eagerly read news about her, and mobbed her in public. The actress, earning hundreds of thousands of dollars a year, was one of the richest women in the United States.

Mary Pickford's phenomenal success was certainly a product of her talent and good luck. But her career was also a product of increasingly important trends after World War I. A dynamic industrial economy, drawing on such rapidly developing technologies as motion pictures, seemed effortlessly to produce plenty of prosperity, leisure, and consumer goods. More than ever before, Americans had both the money and time to enjoy themselves, to consume a host of pleasures.

Pickford exemplified the new national culture that emerged from the needs of the booming consumer economy. Breaking with the past, this modern culture celebrated innovation, modernity, and the future. "One should always go forward," Pickford declared. "It isn't good to go back to anything, not even to the old home farm, or one's old loves." The new culture welcomed leisure, including moviegoing, spectator sports, and other diversions. Pickford worked hard but she entertained lavishly and took highly publicized vacations, too. The new culture also glorified conspicuous consumption. Living well, Pickford bought such indulgences as a miniature, glass-enclosed, two-seater Rolls-Royce automobile, one of only three in the world.

The movie star embodied still other aspects of the new culture—its fascination with youth and its infatuation with independent, nontraditional women. Well into her 20s, "Little Mary" still portrayed plucky, playful young girls. Although married, Pickford focused on her career and increasingly took control of the production of her films. Like the new culture, Pickford broke free from old restraints. Americans, as she wrote, had seen divorce as a "dreadful disease," but even so, in March 1920, she divorced her first husband and married the star Douglas Fairbanks Sr. Her popularity did not decrease.

Going her own way so often, Pickford also exemplified a resurgent individualism that shaped the Republican-dominated politics of the 1920s. In the movies and real life, she seemed to prove that individuals, even immigrants and the poor, could still find opportunity and achieve great things in an increasingly corporatized and bureaucratized society. Born to poverty in Canada, Pickford had found success in America. Remaking her identity, she changed her name from Gladys Smith. In 1919, she escaped the control of the big movie studios by joining with Douglas Fairbanks Sr., comic actor Charlie Chaplin, and director D. W. Griffith to create their own distribution company, United Artists.

The new culture helped redefine the United States in the eyes of the world. Pickford's films were popular around the globe. When she and Fairbanks traveled to Europe in the 1920s, they met huge crowds and near riots. Even citizens of the communist Union of Soviet Socialist Republics lionized the visiting "Little Mary."

Amid all the trappings of Mary Pickford's popularity, it was easy to conclude that Americans loved the emerging cultural and political order as much as they loved "America's sweetheart." In fact, many people were troubled by the changes of the 1920s. The modern order did not reflect the values of millions of Americans. For all the celebration of the individual, many Americans felt they did not have enough power over their lives. American democracy seemed too limited. As a result, the new cultural and political order faced a powerful backlash as the decade went on.

A Dynamic Economy

By and large, the 1920s were a prosperous time for America. After a recession during 1920 to 1921, the economy continued to grow. Consumer prices remained steady throughout the decade, and jobs were plentiful; the unemployment rate dropped as low as 1.8 percent in 1926. Wages jumped: the nation's net income—the value of its earnings from labor and property—leapt from $64 billion in 1921 to $86.8 billion in 1929. This prosperity was driven by a dynamically evolving industrial economy featuring new technologies, increased efficiency, a maturing automobile industry, and new businesses.

Despite general prosperity, the transformation of the economy involved defeats for organized labor and decline for many farmers. The relative weakness of agriculture and the strength of industry helped to turn the United States into a predominantly urban nation. In the prosperous 1920s, as always, industrial capitalism was a transforming force.

The Development of Industry

Several long-term factors shaped the development of American industry in the 1920s. Searching for more efficient production, businessmen used a flood of new technologies, other innovations, and new technical expertise. More patents were issued for new inventions—421,000 of them—than in any preceding decade. During the 1920s, the number of engineers in the country nearly doubled.

The switch from coal to electricity, under way since the 1910s, was a critical innovation. By the end of the 1920s, electricity powered more than two-thirds of American manufacturing plants. Henry Ford's car company pioneered another crucial innovation, the system that became known as Fordism, or mass production. By the 1910s, Ford, like other American manufacturers, used interchangeable parts, simple and accurate machine tools, and electric power to speed output at its Highland Park plant in Detroit. But traditional manufacturing practice slowed production. Frames, transmissions, and other key subassemblies waited on stands while teams of workers moved from one stand to another. Eager to meet the rising demand for the popular Model T car, Ford's managers reversed the process by "moving the work to the men." Beginning in 1913, conveyor belts and chains sent subassemblies past groups of stationary workers. Instead of making an entire engine, a worker might tighten a few bolts or install a single part. The results were astonishing: in 1914, Ford produced 300,000 Model Ts; in 1923, more than 2 million. Other manufacturers raced to copy Ford's techniques.

Ford Assembly Line Mass production at work: the assembly line at the Ford Motor Company plant in Dearborn, Michigan, 1928.

Mass production, electrification, and other innovations spurred an extraordinary increase in productivity for American industry. Output per worker skyrocketed 72 percent from 1919 to 1929.

Along with increased productivity, the rise of several industries drove the economy. Auto production now dominated as textiles, railroads, iron, and steel had earlier. In 1921, there were 9.3 million cars on American roads; by 1929, there were 23 million. The manufacture of all those cars stimulated demand for plate glass, oil, gasoline, and rubber.

Other sectors of the economy also grew rapidly. The demand for processed foods, household appliances, office machinery, and chemicals increased dramatically. Emerging industries such as aircraft demonstrated their potential importance.

Arguably the first powered, fixed-wing flight had occurred in December 1903, when Wilbur and Orville Wright's "Flyer" flew 120 feet in 12 seconds over the beach at Kitty Hawk, North Carolina. But the civilian airplane industry did not take off until the 1920s. Aircraft production rose from fewer than 300 in 1922 to more than 6,000 in 1929. By then, fledgling airlines were flying passengers on scheduled flights.

The Trend Toward Large-Scale Organization

The development of industry reinforced the trend toward large-scale organization that was basic to US capitalism. Only giant corporations, with thousands of employees and hundreds of millions of dollars in capitalization, had the financial resources to pay for mass production. A wave of mergers meant that these big businesses controlled more factories and assets than ever. By 1929, corporations produced 92 percent of the nation's manufactured goods.

The largest firms also benefited from more efficient organization. When the recession of 1920 to 1921 left them with too many unsold goods, companies reorganized. Top managers, aided by financial, legal, and other experts, now oversaw semiautonomous divisions that supplied different markets. At General Motors, the Chevrolet division produced huge numbers of relatively inexpensive cars, while the Cadillac division turned out a smaller number of expensive cars. The new system made corporations more flexible, efficient, and responsive to consumer demand.

Corporate growth was not confined to industry. Chains such as A. & P. grocers and F. W. Woolworth variety stores increased their share of retail sales from 4 percent to 20 percent. One percent of the nation's banks managed nearly half of the country's financial assets. By 1929, just 200 corporations held about one-fifth of national wealth.

Giant firms and their leaders had often been targets of hostility and reform during the Progressive Era, but the decade's prosperity led many Americans to soften their attitude toward business. There were fewer calls to break up or regulate giant corporations. Big businessmen had seemed to be selfless patriots during World War I. Now their companies were apparently creating a new period of economic well-being. To ensure a better image, businessmen paid for public relations campaigns that stressed their commitment to ethical behavior and social service. Basking in the glow of public approval, big business was confident about its role in the nation's destiny.

The Transformation of Work and the Workforce

The quest for productivity had dramatic consequences for American workers. Industrial efficiency was not just a matter of electricity and machines. To speed up production, the managers at Ford and other factories had to change the nature of work.

Accordingly, the spirit of scientific management continued to sweep across the factory floor. Under ever-tighter supervision, workers were pushed to work faster and harder. In textile mills, the "stretch-out" required workers to tend more looms than before. Ford's system of mass production shared Frederick Winslow Taylor's determination to simplify and regiment labor. The result was less-satisfying work. Instead of making a whole engine, a Ford assembly-line worker might spend his day turning a few nuts on one engine after another. In 1913, Ford's labor turnover rate soared to 380 percent as unhappy workers quit their jobs.

As production grew more efficient, about a million workers lost manufacturing, mining, and railroading jobs. The growth of other kinds of employment more than compensated for this decrease, however. The ranks of white-collar workers increased 80 percent from 1910 to 1930, or nearly one worker in three. The nation had already begun to evolve from an industrial economy based on manual labor to a postindustrial economy based on sales and service.

Economic development also encouraged the gradual movement of women into the paid workforce. By the end of the 1920s, women, most of them unmarried, made up a majority of clerical workers. In 1900, 22 percent of women had worked for pay; by the 1940s, the percentage would reach 27.

Despite these changes, women still faced discrimination. Mary Pickford was exceptional. Overwhelmingly concentrated in low-wage occupations such as domestic service, factory work, and agriculture, they were paid less than men who did comparable work. Female sales workers earned between 42 and 63 percent of the wages paid to their male counterparts. Few women held high-level managerial jobs. Moreover, most people continued to believe that a woman's place was in the home, especially if she had children, and many men feared that paid labor would make women too independent. Only economic necessities reconciled American society to women's employment in the 1920s.

The Defeat of Organized Labor

The American labor movement did not respond effectively to the transformation of work and the workforce. In an age of increasing economic organization, workers became less organized. In 1920 nearly 1 nonagricultural worker in 5 belonged to a union. By 1929, little more than 1 in 10 did. The labor movement was especially weak in such developing mass-production industries as automobiles and steel and barely addressed the growing ranks of clerks and other white-collar workers.

Prosperity also weakened organized labor. Earning relatively good wages, many workers were less interested in joining unions. To show that unions were unnecessary, corporations promoted welfare capitalism, highly publicized programs ranging from lunch-hour movies to sports teams to profit-sharing plans. Many firms created company unions, but when it became clear that they did not give employees a real voice in management, their membership dwindled.

Although some firms tried to win over their workers with baseball teams and company unions, many others used tougher tactics to battle the labor movement. Management crusaded for the "open shop"—a workplace free of labor organization—and found an ally in the judicial system. Rulings by the US Supreme Court, such as *Duplex Printing Press Co. v. Deering* (1921) and *Bedford Cut Stone Co. v. Journeymen Stone Cutters' Assn.* (1927), made it easier for state and federal courts to grant injunctions to stop unions from striking and exercising their rights. Businesses could sue unions for damages. They also demanded that workers sign "yellow-dog contracts" promising not to join a union.

The labor movement also hurt its own cause. The leadership of the major national organization, the American Federation of Labor, was increasingly conservative and timid. The heads of the AFL, mostly white males of western European extraction who represented skilled crafts, had little interest in organizing women workers and wanted nothing to do with Socialists, radical unionists, or African American workers. The AFL was slow to acknowledge the Brotherhood of Sleeping Car Porters, the assertive union of African American workers organized in 1925 under Socialist A. Philip Randolph. Despite pleas from Randolph and others, the AFL failed to organize unskilled workers, many of whom were African Americans or white immigrants from eastern and southern Europe.

Weakened by internal divisions, welfare capitalism, the open-shop crusade, and the courts, the labor movement did not effectively challenge the transformation of industrial labor. Nationwide, the number of strikes and lockouts dropped from 3,411 in 1920 to 604 in 1928. These labor actions often ended in defeat for workers.

The Decline of Agriculture

Despite national prosperity, American agriculture continued its long decline. Prices for basic crops such as cotton and wheat fell, and the number of farms dropped.

The larger story of decline obscured important signs of growth and health. Some agricultural sectors were as dynamic as industry and for the same reasons—increased efficiency promoted by new technologies and large-scale organization. Mechanization, including the introduction of powerful tractors, made farm labor more efficient. So did the development of irrigation systems. By the 1920s, the irrigated farms of the Southwest were producing bumper crops of cotton, fruits, and vegetables. The Southwest also witnessed the rise of huge mechanized farms with hundreds and even thousands of irrigated acres. These "factories in the fields" depended not only on size and technology but also on the old-fashioned exploitation of farm labor. In California's Imperial Valley and elsewhere, migrant workers labored in harsh conditions for low pay on modern farms.

Ironically, the dynamic agricultural economy created a problem for many farmers. Midsize farms, too big to be run by their owners alone and too small for mechanization, could not compete with the vast "factories in the fields." Increased efficiency, meanwhile, led to bumper crops that did not always find a good market price. Farmers were hurt by a changing American diet, with declining consumption of bread and potatoes, and by the rise of competitors overseas. Productive American farmers could no longer export enough of their surplus. The resulting glut reduced the price of farm products. As their incomes lagged behind those of urban workers, farmers yearned for the return of high pre–World War I agricultural prices to restore parity between city and country. As a Georgia farmer observed, "The hand that is feeding the world is being spit upon."

The Urban Nation

The woes of agriculture contributed to a long-term shift in the American population. For the first time, according to the census of 1920, a majority of Americans—54 million out of 105 million—lived in urban territory. The census defined "urban territory" as places with as few as 2,500 people, many of them small towns close to country life. Still, the population of the United States was no longer predominantly rural.

The decline of farming spurred this shift. As agricultural prices fell, millions of Americans fled the nation's farms. The total US population increased by 17 million during the 1920s, but the farm population declined by more than 1.5 million.

At the same time, the growth of the industrial economy swelled the population of towns and cities. In the 1920s, factory production was still centered in urban areas and gave many cities their identity. Detroit was becoming the "Motor City." Akron was the home of rubber production. Pittsburgh and Birmingham symbolized the steel industry. Most of the new white-collar jobs were located in cities. Corporations also put their headquarters in cities, especially the two largest, Chicago and New York.

The rise of the automobile further contributed to the emergence of the urban nation. The car made it practical for Americans to live in suburbs and drive into the city to work and shop. In the 1920s, the suburban lifestyle was still reserved mostly for the well-to-do. Elite suburbs, such as Grosse Pointe and Ferndale outside Detroit and Beverly Hills and Glendale outside Los Angeles, grew explosively. The transformation of farms into suburbs symbolized the new urban nation.

A Modern Culture

The 1920s saw the full emergence of a modern culture that had been taking shape for decades and that now surrounded Americans with something fundamentally new. Symbolized by Mary Pickford, the new culture extolled the virtues of modernity and pleasure. Rooted in the nation's economic development, the new culture reflected both the needs of businessmen with goods to sell and the desires of Americans with more money and free time than ever. Supported by advertising and installment buying, the culture of leisure and consumption offered movies, spectator sports, popular music, radio, and sex. It also offered new views of gender, family life, and youth and renewed old values of individualism in an increasingly organized society.

The Spread of Consumerism

Encouraged by big business, many Americans now defined life as the pursuit of pleasure and found happiness in leisure and consumption rather than in work. This philosophy of consumerism saturated society by the end of the decade.

Increased efficiency and profitability enabled American employers to allow their workers higher wages and more leisure hours. Some employers, notably Ford, also raised wages in order to hold on to workers alienated by the drudgery of mass production. And Ford himself increased workers' pay to enable them to buy the products of modern factories. The incomes of workers and other employees reached a new high in the 1920s. Factory workers' real wages rose 19 percent from 1914 to 1923.

Many workers had more time to enjoy their wages. For salaried, middle-class workers, the annual vacation had become a tradition by the 1910s. Although blue-collar workers seldom enjoyed a vacation, they spent less time on the job. Some employers, including Henry Ford, instituted a five-day workweek during the 1920s. More businesses shortened their workdays, and the average workweek fell from 47.4 hours in 1920 to 44.2 in 1929. "The shorter work day brought me my first idea of there being such a thing as pleasure," said one young female worker. "Before this time it was just sleep and eat and hurry off to work."

A change in attitude accompanied these changes in wages and workdays. The work ethic seemed less necessary in a prospering economy. Thanks to Fordism and Taylorism, work was also less satisfying, and people justified pleasure as an essential antidote to labor.

The advertising industry encouraged the new attitude toward pleasure. Although advertising agencies had first appeared in the 1850s and 1860s, the business did not mature until the 1920s. Now, ads appeared everywhere—in newspapers and magazines, on billboards and big electric signs. Major advertising agencies such as J. Walter Thompson and Batten, Barton, Durstine, and Osborn concentrated in New York City, home to so many corporations. Impressed by successful ad campaigns for Listerine mouthwash and Fleischmann's yeast, big business hired ad agencies to sell goods and services. Expenditures for advertising leapt from $682 million in 1914 to nearly $3 billion by 1929.

Advertising, like the new culture, optimistically embraced change and trumpeted the new. In advertisements, purchasing the right products solved problems, made up for the drudgery of work, and brought fulfillment. To enthusiastic ad men, advertising was as important as the products it sold. In his best-selling book *The Man Nobody Knows* (1925), ad pioneer Bruce Barton portrayed Jesus Christ as a great advertiser, whose disciples "conquered the world" by selling a new product, Christianity. Along with advertising, business used installment loans to encourage Americans to buy goods and services "on time." Credit buying spread so rapidly that total consumer debt more than doubled from 1922 to 1929. The sales of such consumer goods as pianos, washing machines, and automobiles boomed. Americans bought 181,000 automobiles in 1910; they bought 4,455,000 in 1929. Thanks to the availability of another kind of loan, the mortgage, more Americans were able to invest in a home of their own. Spending on new private housing jumped from $2 billion in 1920 to $5 billion by 1924. Loan-driven spending helped power the economic prosperity of the 1920s.

New Pleasures for a Mass Audience

The culture of the 1920s offered many escapes, especially sports, movies, popular music, and radio. Although people still played games themselves, they also watched other people's games more than ever before. Tennis, boxing, and auto racing flourished as spectator sports during the decade. The American Professional Football Association, which became the National Football League, played its first season in 1920. Although crowds packed college football stadiums, baseball remained the most popular American sport. Minor-league baseball covered the nation. Meanwhile, the popularity of major-league baseball surged, thanks in part to the exploits of home run–hitting Babe Ruth and his New York Yankees.

Spectator sports enthralled millions, but another passive enjoyment, the movies, was the most popular consumer attraction of the 1920s (see Table 21–1). A novelty in the mid-1890s, silent films had become a big business. In city neighborhoods in the 1900s, crowds packed into stuffy "nickelodeons"—storefront theaters showing short, silent one-reel films for the price of a nickel. The movies became longer and more sophisticated, and theaters became larger and more lavish. Nationwide, weekly attendance doubled from 40 million in 1922 to 80 million in 1929.

Booming attendance fueled the growth of a handful of corporate movie studios, including Warner Brothers and RKO, that dominated the film industry. By the 1920s, the center of movie production had shifted from New York to Hollywood, California. Now called "Hollywood," the film industry grew still bigger toward the end of the decade, when studios learned to synchronize sound and moving images in such films as *The Jazz Singer* of 1927.

It was fitting that one of the first "talking pictures" was about jazz. Popular music in general and jazz in particular played an important role in the new consumer culture. Created by African Americans in the 1910s, jazz was a rhythmically and harmonically innovative music that featured improvised solos and a hot beat. The new music emerged around the country, but its first great center was the streets, brothels, and dives of New Orleans. The Louisiana city was home to the first major jazz composer, Jelly Roll Morton, and to the first jazz superstar, trumpeter and singer Louis Armstrong. As jazz became nationally popular, Morton, Armstrong, and the focus of jazz moved on, as did so many African Americans, to Chicago and New York City (see Chapter 20).

Table 21–1 Spending for Recreational Services, 1909–1929

Year	Total (millions of dollars)	Motion Picture Theaters (millions of dollars)	Spectator Sports (millions of dollars)
1909	377	###	###
1914	434	###	###
1919	806	###	###
1921	911	301	30
1923	1,082	336	46
1927	1,405	526	48
1929	1,670	720	66

Source: Historical Statistics of the United States, Millennial Online Edition (Cambridge: Cambridge University Press, 2008), Table Dh309–318.

Note: ### = no data.

The Premiere of *The Jazz Singer* The dazzling allure of a new pleasure—the "talking picture"—draws a big opening-night crowd to Warners' Theatre, New York City, October 6, 1927.

The new music quickly attracted white Americans, especially the young, who yearned for something more daring than the relatively sedate popular music of the day. Even its name—a reference perhaps to speed or sexual intercourse—conjured up pleasure and liberation. Soon white musicians were contributing to the music. For many whites, jazz summed up a period marked by the pursuit of liberating pleasures. The 1920s became known as the "Jazz Age," after the title of a 1922 book of short stories by F. Scott Fitzgerald.

The great popularity of jazz and other musical genres was made possible by the phonograph, originated by Thomas Edison in the 1870s and modified by other inventors. In the 1920s, the electrical recording microphone dramatically improved sound quality and made the new music accessible to millions of Americans.

A newer technological innovation, the radio, also allowed Americans to hear popular music. In 1895, Italian inventor Guglielmo Marconi transmitted the first radio waves; by 1920, commercial radio broadcasting began in the United States. The federal government started licensing radio stations the next year.

Like the movies, radio quickly became corporatized big business. By 1923, there were more than 500 stations, and by 1926, the first permanent radio network, the National Broadcasting Company (NBC). Americans tuned in to broadcasts of live music, news, sports, and soap operas. By 1925, manufacturers turned out more than 2 million radios a year. Radio, like the movies, disseminated the values of consumerism, as corporations rushed to advertise their products by sponsoring radio programs.

A Sexual Revolution

Along with such new pleasures as radio and movies, the modern culture offered a new attitude toward an old pleasure, sex. By the 1920s, Americans' sexual attitudes and behavior were changing. People openly discussed sex and placed a new emphasis on the importance of sexual satisfaction, primarily in marriage. And there were signs of greater sexual exploration among unmarried young people.

In the nineteenth century, Americans, especially middle-class Victorians, had largely kept a discreet silence about sex. That silence gave way in the twentieth century. Progressive-Era reformers had forced public discussion of issues such as prostitution and venereal disease. The reformers, anxious to control extramarital sexual behavior, hardly wanted to glorify sexual pleasure. But they helped pave the way for an approving depiction of sexuality.

Popular amusements of the 1910s and 1920s were filled with sexual images. The movies explored sexual topics in such films as *The Anatomy of a Kiss* and *A Bedroom Blunder*. Popular music featured suggestive songs about sex, such as "It's Tight Like That" and "I Need a Little Sugar in My Bowl." Popular dances such as the grizzly bear and the turkey trot promoted close physical contact or sexually suggestive steps. As early as 1913, a magazine concluded that "Sex O'Clock" had struck in the United States.

The increased openness about sex reflected the growing belief that sexual pleasure was necessary and desirable, particularly within marriage. Married couples increasingly considered intercourse an opportunity for pleasure, as well as procreation. Experts insisted that healthy marriages required sexual satisfaction for both partners.

The new view of marital sexuality helped change attitudes toward contraception. By the 1910s, a grassroots movement, led by Socialists and other radicals, promoted sex education and contraceptives, which were largely illegal. The crusade's best-known figure was the fiery former nurse and Socialist organizer Margaret Sanger, who coined the term "birth control." Although Sanger once had to flee the country to avoid prosecution, birth control became respectable—and widely practiced—in the 1920s.

At the same time, most adult Americans still condemned premarital sex. Nevertheless, premarital intercourse apparently became more common. Many couples believed that intercourse was acceptable if they were "in love" and intended to marry. There was also an apparent increase in "petting"—sexual contact short of intercourse.

While changing some of their attitudes about sexual behavior, most heterosexual Americans still condemned homosexuality. Nevertheless, a sexual revolution was under way.

Changing Gender Ideals

Shifting sexual attitudes were tied to new gender ideals. By the 1920s, Americans' sense of what it meant to be female was changing. Since the late nineteenth century, Americans had been talking about the independent, assertive "New Woman" who claimed the right to attend school, vote, and have a career. The "New Woman" of the 1920s, exemplified by Mary Pickford, was now a sexual being, too, a fun-loving individual with desires of her own.

The sexual nature of women was central to a new movement, known as feminism, that had emerged in the 1910s. The feminists, like earlier female reformers, were generally white, well-educated, Protestant, urban women. Concentrated in New York's Greenwich Village, feminists broke with older reformers by insisting on sharing the sexual

STRUGGLES FOR DEMOCRACY

Flappers and Feminists

Chronicling the excitement of 1920s New York City nightlife, the *New Yorker* column "Table for Two" allowed readers to live vicariously through the exploits of the author known as "Lipstick." Lois Long, the woman behind "Lipstick," spent her nights traveling from one nightclub to the next, often ending her evenings at one of the famed mixed-race clubs of Harlem. With her smoking, drinking, and dancing, she embraced all that the Roaring Twenties had to offer.

Long embodied the flapper figure that captured American imaginations during the 1920s with her devil-may-care attitude, bobbed hair, rouged cheeks, and fashionable dress. Reveling in the freedom enjoyed by the New Woman of the decade, Long described her life with verve and wit and apologized for nothing, delighting in the adventure modern life afforded. Typical of her column was her description of a raid on a New York City bar. She wrote, a "big Irish cop regarded me with a sad eye and remarked, 'Kid, you're too good for this dump,' and politely opened a window leading to the fire escape. I made a graceful exit." After such a night, it was not uncommon for Long to stroll into the *New Yorker* offices, sometimes at 3 or 4 a.m., and type up a column in time to meet a deadline.

While many readers idolized Lipstick and women across the country embraced the flapper style, others were scandalized by this kind of behavior. Those unnerved by the power of the urban center to shape American values, Victorians unwilling to cede their visions of men and women's appropriate roles, and Christian moralists abhorred the flapper's influence. But some of the harshest critics of women like Long were the suffragettes who had advocated on behalf of women's right to vote in the years leading up to the 1920 passage of the Nineteenth Amendment. Lillian Symes, a veteran of the suffrage cause and feminist journalist, lamented how little her generation had in common with "the post-war, spike-heeled, over-rouged flapper," a figure she saw as completely devoid of political engagement. Educated women like Long, a Vassar College graduate, should be doing

opportunities that men had presumably long enjoyed. Unlike the older generation of activist women, feminists were unwilling to give up marriage and children for careers outside the home. Feminism insisted on women's right to pleasure and satisfaction in all phases of life, from the most public to the most intimate.

Small in number, the feminists commanded a great deal of attention. Several of their ideas and practices were too radical for many American men and women, such as some feminists' decision to retain their maiden names in married life or to explore sexual relationships outside of marriage. Most fundamentally, many Americans were unwilling to accept the feminist insistence on full equality with men.

American culture proved rather open to a more liberated view of female sexuality. The most popular image of the American woman of the 1920s was the vivacious "flapper," more with her life than hopping from one mindless entertainment to the next.

Imagining a new political landscape in which women wielded greater power and influence, veteran feminists were disappointed by the world of the 1920s. But the younger generation's embrace of the flapper image, with a focus on leisure rather than political action, was only part of the problem for a movement that had begun to splinter. Having achieved their objective—the right to vote—the conflicting identities and allegiances of women across race, class, ethnicity, region, age, and ideology prevented the creation of a powerful women's political bloc. Feminists were divided in their beliefs about the relationship between men and women—were they fundamentally different or did the pursuit of sexual equality rest on the premise that men and women were the same? How would this debate shape goals of the future? Furthermore, the political tide had shifted. In the aftermath of the activism and reform of the Progressive Era, the 1920s bore witness to a far more conservative political culture, one characterized by a focus on individualism and a largely disinterested electorate. The flapper, then, was only part of the problem, but her visibility, her direct rejection of causes greater than herself,

and her mishandling of the freedom feminists had fought so hard to achieve made her a direct target for criticism.

Dorothy Dunbar Bromley, a prominent writer on women's issues, defended the New Women of the 1920s with the celebrated language of individualism. She imagined these women as a new kind of feminist: she "knows that it is her American, her twentieth-century birthright to emerge from a creature of instinct into a full-fledged *individual* who is capable of molding her own life. And in this respect she holds that she is becoming man's equal." Flappers embraced the gains made by feminists who had come before them, but they embraced those gains in unexpected ways and with little recognition of feminists' efforts. In a culture increasingly shaped by the influences of the consumer marketplace and mass media, for some women, equality had little to do with the traditional style of politics and much more to do with the opportunity to inhabit public space and enjoy entertainments previously off limits. This was not the style of politics imagined by suffragettes or their Progressive-Era contemporaries, but as Americans living in this new modern age were coming to learn, times had changed.

with her short skirt, bound breasts, and bobbed hair. The flapper was likely to wear cosmetics and to smoke cigarettes—practices once associated only with prostitutes.

Notions of masculinity were also changing. With the growing emphasis on female needs and desires, men were urged to be attentive and responsive and to focus on the home. As the world of work became less satisfying, experts told men to look for fulfillment in family life. The family man of the 1920s was no longer to be a distant, stern patriarch but a companion to his wife and a doting friend to his children.

In practice, many men still defined themselves in terms of their work rather than their domestic life, and society still regarded women as the primary caretakers of children. Despite the change in domestic values, many men were still relative outsiders in the home.

"Flaming Youth" on Campus

During the 1920s, college and university campuses were laboratories for "flaming youth," as male and female college students created a distinctive youth culture. Campus life reflected central features of the larger society: the desire for individual freedom and the need to cope with organization. The world of the "advance guard of the younger generation" also reflected the uneven development of American democracy in the Jazz Age.

Traditionally for the elite, higher education was anything but democratic. In 1899, only 238,000 students—some 2 percent of Americans ages 18 to 24—enrolled in colleges and universities. Only 85,000 of those students were women. But as the dynamic economy demanded educated white-collar workers, more middle-class families found the means to send their sons and daughters to college. By 1929, 1.1 million students—7.2 percent of 18- to 24-year-olds—were enrolled. Thanks to changing attitudes toward women, 480,000 of those students were female. The development of public-supported colleges and universities

made this growth possible. From 1919 to 1922, enrollments doubled from 3,000 to 6,000 at the University of Illinois and from 4,000 to 8,000 at Ohio State University. The public schools were at the forefront of a more democratic student culture.

That culture celebrated independence. "To me the Jazz Age signifies an age of freedom in thought and action," explained a female student at the University of Denver. Liberated from the traditional constraints of home and workplace, college students could pursue their desires. "We were big-eyed with wanting," said the songwriter Hoagy Carmichael, then a student at Indiana University, "with making fun."

Students held "petting parties." They forced college officials to tolerate racy new dances such as the toddle, the shimmy, the Charleston, and the black bottom. By the end of the decade, about two out of three students defied Prohibition (see Chapter 20) by drinking on and off campus. Public drunkenness was no longer a scandal. Women students engaged in the "unladylike," sexually suggestive practice of smoking. "College,"

The Family and Youth

Changing gender ideals were directly related to a reconsideration of family life and youth. Although whole families still labored together in fields and mills, most Americans no longer regarded the family as a group of productive workers. Child-labor laws increasingly made sure that boys and girls went to school rather than to work. The family became primarily a unit of leisure and consumption. The home was where men, women, and children, gathered around the radio, found pleasure and fulfillment.

Reflecting modern cultural values, parents became more likely to indulge their children, who enjoyed more toys, possessions, and spending money than had earlier generations. The automobile gave young people more mobility, too. With their new freedom,

Northwestern Co-eds   Women students at Northwestern University show their school spirit by hoisting a banner and megaphones before a campus building, 1929.

sniffed a dean at Princeton, "has unfortunately become a kind of glorified playground . . . a paradise of the young."

Students' quest for pleasure shaped their politics. Although Carmichael and his friends cared little about most public issues, they believed strongly in individual rights. Students regarded sex and other satisfactions as a private matter. College newspapers criticized Prohibitionists and other reformers who wanted to regulate individual behavior.

Even as they reflected the individualist values of modern culture, college students adapted to the growing power of organization. As enrollments rose, collegiate life became more crowded and more bureaucratic. Students turned to organizations: in the 1920s, the number of fraternities and sororities shot up. By 1930, about one student in three belonged to one; Hoagy Carmichael joined Kappa Sigma. Greek

houses often included most student leaders and set the tone of campus fashion for the "barbs": the "barbarians" who made up the rest of the student body.

While fraternities and sororities offered spaces for freedom and expression, they also forced members to come to terms with organization. As the campus newspaper at Cornell University explained, the fraternity "crushes individuality." Initiation rites and hazing taught new members they were expected to conform to the norms of the group. The distinctive culture of "flaming youth," like the new national culture, embraced organization and freedom, conformity and individualism.

they began to create their own separate culture. One sign was the dramatic spread of petting among high school youth, newly free from parental control.

Most adults accepted this situation partly because they admired and envied youthfulness. The modern culture, unsatisfied with work and anxious for fun, glorified sexually adventurous, fast-living young people. The title of the 1923 novel *Flaming Youth* became a catchphrase for the youth culture of the 1920s.

The Celebration of the Individual

The emphasis on the individual, so evident in changing views of sex, gender, family, and youth, was fundamental to the modern culture. In addition to Babe Ruth, Americans admired a host of sports heroes and heroines, and the movie industry increasingly showcased the distinctive personalities of such stars as Mary Pickford and Douglas Fairbanks Sr. Individualism was basic to the "New Woman," too.

The resurgence of individualism was not surprising. The belief in the importance of the individual was deeply ingrained in American culture. Paradoxically, the development of industrial capitalism intensified the importance of both individuals and organizations. As corporations grew larger and produced more, they needed to stimulate consumerism, the gratification of individual needs and desires.

There were serious obstacles to true individualism in the 1920s. Powerful organizations, including corporations, controlled individual life. Even the most famous individual exploit of the decade depended on organization. On May 20–21, 1927, Charles A. Lindbergh flew the *Spirit of St. Louis* from New York City to Paris. This first nonstop solo crossing of the Atlantic made Lindbergh an international symbol of individual achievement, but his feat relied on businessmen who put up the money and a corporation that built the plane. So, too, Mary Pickford's individual success culminated in the creation of a corporation, United Artists. Organization and individualism, the new and the old, were interdependent in the 1920s.

The Limits of the Modern Culture

The modern culture had clear limits in the 1920s. For millions of Americans, much of the consumer lifestyle was out of reach. Many Americans, including artists and intellectuals, chose not to define themselves by the pursuit of pleasure, leisure, and consumption. For them, modern society—with its emphasis on the new, including the "New Negro," the "New Woman," and the "New Era"—represented an unwelcome abandonment of old values. In different ways, fundamentalist Christians, immigration restrictionists, and the Ku Klux Klan demanded a return to an earlier United States. Mexican Americans, African Americans, and others found that the new culture, like the old, treated them like second-class citizens.

The Limits of Prosperity

Despite the aura of prosperity, low incomes and poverty persisted in the 1920s. As late as 1928, 6 out of 10 families made less than the $2,000 a year required for the "basic needs of life." Despite the housing boom, most American household heads did not own their own homes.

The towns and cities of the increasingly urban nation were still divided by social class. In *Middletown* (1929), their pioneering study of a small midwestern city in the 1920s, Helen and Staughton Lynd discovered that the "division into the working class and business class . . . constitutes the outstanding cleavage." The working class of "Middletown"— Muncie, Indiana—had less money and leisure to enjoy the new culture. About a third of the city still did not own automobiles.

The "Lost Generation" of Intellectuals

Many artists and intellectuals felt alienated from the United States in the 1920s. For white, mostly male writers and artists who came of age during World War I, the conflict represented a failure of civilization, a pointless exercise in destruction. Its aftermath left them angry, alienated, and rootless. In a nation supposedly devoted to individualism, they did not feel free. They were, as the writer Gertrude Stein described them, a "Lost Generation." Some of them, such as Stein and her fellow writer Ernest Hemingway, left the United States for Paris and other places in Europe.

However prosperous and peaceful, the postwar years did not reassure the Lost Generation that American life had changed much. In such works as *Winesburg, Ohio* (1919), novelist Sherwood Anderson portrayed a still-repressive society that denied people real freedom and individuality. The acid-tongued H. L. Mencken, editor of the *American Mercury*, condemned a provincial culture still dominated by the "booboisie" and its rural values.

Still other American artists and intellectuals feared their country had changed too much. Although excited by the potential of the machine, they criticized the routinized work and superficial pleasures of modern life. In his 1922 novel *Babbitt*, Sinclair Lewis satirized a midwestern Republican businessman whose consumerism made him a conformist, not an individualist. F. Scott Fitzgerald, in such fiction as *This Side of Paradise* (1920) and *The Great Gatsby* (1925), conveyed the sense of loss and emptiness in the lives of fashionable "flaming youth" in the "Jazz Age."

From a different angle, 12 southern intellectuals, including Allen Tate, Robert Penn Warren, Donald Davidson, and John Crowe Ransom, attacked the modern culture in *I'll Take My Stand: The South and the Agrarian Tradition* (1930). Their essays offered a defense of rural culture and a critique of a consumer society that demeaned work and exalted individualism.

Artists and intellectuals did not set off a mass rebellion against modern culture, but they did express a widespread ambivalence and uneasiness. In different and contradictory ways, they laid out an agenda for Americans as they came to terms with modern, consumer society.

Fundamentalist Christians and "Old-Time Religion"

For many Americans of faith, the modern culture promoted a sense of deep, unsettling change. "The world has been convulsed," declared *Presbyterian Magazine*. "The most settled principles and laws of society have been attacked." The new culture was troubling because it was so secular and seemed to define life in terms of material satisfaction rather than spiritual commitment. Many Protestants, feeling betrayed by their own churches, resented the influence of liberal Protestants who had tried to accommodate religion to science and scholarship.

Fundamentalists, the opponents of liberalism, took their name from *The Fundamentals*, a series of essays by conservative Protestant theologians that began to appear in 1909. Emerging across the continent, fundamentalists were strongest in the countryside and in the South and West. By the end of World War I, they dominated the Southern Baptist Convention and were fighting liberals for control of northern churches.

Fundamentalists rejected liberalism above all for its willingness to question the historical truth of the Bible. The fundamentalist movement urged a return to biblical, patriarchal, and denominational authority, to what came to be called "old-time religion."

The high point in the fundamentalist-liberal battle came in a Tennessee courtroom in 1925. That year, a high school biology teacher, John Scopes, defied a new state law banning the teaching of "any theory that denies the story of the divine creation of man as taught in the Bible, and that teaches instead that man has descended from a lower order of animals." Scopes's trial became a national media event. The chief lawyer for the prosecution was William Jennings Bryan, the former Democratic presidential candidate and now a leading crusader for fundamentalism. While Bryan was a champion of rural America, Scopes's attorneys—Clarence Darrow and Dudley Field Malone—represented the city and modern culture. In a dramatic confrontation, Darrow called Bryan to the stand and forced him to concede that the Bible might not be literally accurate. Although Scopes was convicted and fined, the fundamentalists lost some credibility. Other southern and western states later passed antievolution laws, but similar measures failed in the more urbanized Northeast.

The Scopes trial did not end the war between fundamentalism and liberalism. Fundamentalists were numerous. Their hostility to liberal Protestantism and modern culture would affect American life for decades to come.

Nativists and Immigration Restriction

While fundamentalist Christianity sought a return to old-time religion, a resurgent nativist movement wanted to go back to a supposedly more homogeneous America. As mass migration from Europe resumed after World War I, nativist feeling revived among Americans from western European backgrounds. Thanks to the Russian Revolution and the domestic Red Scare, they associated immigrants with anarchism and radicalism and derided Asians and southern and eastern Europeans as inferior races that would weaken the nation.

In response, Congress overwhelmingly passed the Immigration Act of 1921, which limited annual immigration from any European country to 3 percent of the number of its immigrants living in the United States in 1910. This quota sharply reduced the number of new immigrants from southern and eastern Europe, but nativists wanted tougher action. Congress responded with the Immigration Act of 1924, which reduced the annual intake from a European country to 2 percent of the number of its immigrants living in the United States in 1890, when there were far fewer southern and eastern Europeans in America. The act also effectively excluded Asian immigrants altogether. The legislation worked: immigration fell from 805,000 arrivals in 1921 to 280,000 in 1929 (see Table 21–2).

The Rebirth of the Ku Klux Klan

Nativism and fundamentalism helped spur another challenge to the new order of the 1920s. In 1915, the Ku Klux Klan, the vigilante group that had terrorized African Americans in the South during Reconstruction, was reborn in a ceremony on Stone Mountain, Georgia. It enjoyed explosive growth after World War I, inspired, in part, by

Table 21–2 The Impact of Nativism: Immigration, 1921–1929

Origin	Arrivals (in thousands)		
	1921	1925	1929
Eastern Europe and Poland	138	10	14
Southern Europe	299	8	22
Asia	25	4	4
Mexico	31	33	40
Total	805	294	280

Source: Historical Statistics of the United States (Cambridge: Cambridge University Press), vol. I, p. 401.

Note: Itemized groups do not add up to totals.

D. W. Griffith's film *The Birth of a Nation* (1915), which depicted African Americans as sexual aggressors and the Klan of the 1860s as a heroic and necessary force. The "Invisible Empire" borrowed the rituals of the nineteenth-century Klan, including its white robes and hoods. The twentieth-century KKK adopted cross burnings based upon popular remembrances of its predecessor. The new Klan was still driven by a racist hatred of African Americans, but it took on new targets, including Jews, Roman Catholics, immigrants, religious liberalism, and change in general.

The Invisible Empire condemned big business and modern culture for valuing "money above manhood." The Klan condemned pleasure, "the god of the young people of America," and was hostile to the new gender ideals, birth control, freer sexuality, and the independence of youth. Klansmen and Klanswomen yearned for an earlier America in which white Protestant males controlled women, youth, and other groups and had nothing to fear from big business.

The Klan's tactics blended old and new. Seeing themselves as a secret army of vigilantes, some Klan members supported the age-old tactics of moral regulation—intimidation, flogging, and sometimes lynching—to scare people into good behavior. At the same time, much of the Invisible Empire repudiated violence and used the latest advertising techniques and modern technology to boost its membership.

For several years, the Klan proved extraordinarily successful. Despite its extremist views, the Invisible Empire had a mainstream membership in every region, in cities and the countryside. At its peak, there were perhaps 3 to 5 million secret members. Because so many politicians and newspaper editors feared or sympathized with it, the Klan had considerable political influence. It helped to elect governors, senators, and other officials from both major parties.

The Klan collapsed, however, when its leaders were revealed to be caught up in financial scandal, alcohol, pornography, adultery, kidnapping, and murder. Most people realized they had nothing to fear from such Klan targets as Communists, unions, and Jews. Millions of Americans, however uneasy about the new culture, had no desire to support prejudice, lawbreaking, and violence in a futile attempt to go back to the past. The Klan's membership dropped precipitously in the late 1920s.

Mexican Americans

Despite the efforts of immigration restrictionists and the Klan, the United States became more diverse than ever. Up to a million and a half Mexicans entered the United States legally or surreptitiously between 1890 and 1929. Many left to avoid the upheaval of the Mexican Revolution of 1910 (see Chapter 20) and to escape the agricultural changes driving the rural poor from the land. The dynamic US economy created opportunities for impoverished Mexican immigrants, as did, ironically, the restrictionist immigration legislation of the 1920s. Unable to get enough European or Asian workers, employers turned eagerly to Mexico as a source of cheap seasonal labor. The Southwest's rapidly developing economy particularly needed Mexican workers for mines, railroads, construction gangs, and, above all, farms.

Like many immigrants from Europe, many Mexican migrants did not plan to stay in the United States. They traveled back and forth to their homeland or returned permanently. Gradually, many chose to stay as they developed economic and family ties in the United States, The National Origins Act, which made it costly, time-consuming, and often humiliating for Mexicans to cross the border, also encouraged migrants to remain in the

United States. As a result, the official Mexican population of the United States rose from 103,000 in 1900 to 478,000 by 1920. At the turn of the century, the majority of immigrants lived in Texas and Arizona, but California, with its booming agriculture, rapidly became the center of the Mexican population. Los Angeles, growing phenomenally in the early twentieth century, attracted perhaps 190,000 Mexicans by 1930.

Mexican immigrants, like so many other ethnic groups in the United States, wrestled with questions about their national identity. Were they still Mexicans, or had they become Americans or some unique combination of the two nationalities? In varying degrees, the migrants clung to old identities and adapted to their new home. Mexican Americans, eager to hold on to the advantages they had won by birth and residence in the United States, feared that newcomers would compete for jobs and cause native-born whites to denigrate all Mexicans alike. The immigrants, in turn, often derided Mexican Americans as *pochos*—bleached or faded people—who had lost their true Mexican identity.

Nevertheless, ethnic Mexicans created a distinctive culture in the United States. For all their differences, they shared a sense of common origins and common challenges. In a white-dominated society, they saw themselves as *La Raza*—The Race—set apart by heritage and skin color.

Poverty and discrimination also contributed to a sense of common identity. In many towns and cities, ethnic Mexicans were effectively segregated in certain neighborhoods—*barrios*—in poor conditions. Largely ignored by national corporations, Mexican Americans supported their own businesses and listened to their own Spanish-language radio programs. Anglo-American prejudice also drove Mexicans together. Many whites stereotyped them as a lazy and shiftless race that would take jobs from native-born workers but could not be assimilated into American life. Still other white Americans, drawing on the reform agenda of the Progressive Era, wanted to "Americanize" ethnic Mexicans by teaching them English and middle-class values.

Their sense of shared identity encouraged Mexican Americans to struggle for economic progress and equal rights. In 1928, farm workers in California created La Unión de Trabajadores del Valle Imperial (Imperial Valley Workers Union) in a successful fight for higher wages. A year later, Mexican American businessmen and professionals formed the League of United Latin American Citizens (LULAC) in Texas.

African Americans and the "New Negro"

Like Mexican Americans, African Americans found the new cultural terrain of the United States appealing but unsatisfying. They enjoyed and helped to create the new culture, but it did little to affect racial discrimination. South and North, African Americans still lived with economic and political inequality.

Although discrimination had not changed, many African Americans insisted that they had. It was the decade of both the "New Woman" and the "New Negro." In 1900, Booker T. Washington titled one of his books *A New Negro for a New Century*. By the 1920s, the increased use of "New Negro" reflected a fresh sense of freedom as African Americans left the rural South for cities. It was also the product of frustration as African Americans encountered inequality along with opportunity. The "New Negro" was assertive in the face of mistreatment. "The time for cringing is over," said an African American newspaper.

The "New Negro" was also defined by a deep sense of racial difference and pride. Applauding their distinctive life and culture, African Americans spurred the Harlem Renaissance. Harlem, the section of upper Manhattan in New York where many African

Americans had moved, became a center of artistic and intellectual creativity. Novelists such as Zora Neale Hurston, Jessie Fauset, Claude McKay, Jean Toomer, and Dorothy West; poets such as Langston Hughes, Sterling Brown, and Countee Cullen; and artists such as Aaron Douglas and Augusta Savage produced a new birth of African American creativity. In different ways, these women and men explored and honored the nature of American blackness in 1920s America and its origins in Africa. The consideration of these African origins reflected a more international celebration of blackness occurring during the 1920s.

The militancy of the "New Negro" was reflected in the development of the NAACP, which turned increasingly to African American leadership. Its key figure, W. E. B. DuBois, became more critical of whites and more determined that white colonizers return Africa to Africans. The NAACP also pushed the cause of African American civil rights more aggressively and attacked the white primary system that denied African Americans any say in the southern Democratic Party. The NAACP continued a longtime antilynching campaign, which bore fruit in the 1920s, as southern whites were increasingly embarrassed by vigilante justice.

For a time, the NAACP's efforts were overshadowed by the crusades of Marcus Garvey. A Jamaican immigrant to New York City, Garvey founded the Universal Negro Improvement Association (UNIA), which became the largest African American activist organization of the 1920s. Less interested in political rights and integration, Garvey focused on African American pride and self-help and on Africa. He exalted "a new Negro who stands erect, conscious of his manhood rights and fully determined to preserve them at all times." Garvey urged African Americans to develop their own businesses and become economically self-sufficient. Like DuBois, he insisted that the imperial powers give up their control of Africa. Sure that blacks could never find equality in a white-dominated nation, Garvey believed African Americans should return to Africa.

Unlike the mostly middle-class NAACP, Garvey's UNIA developed a vast following among the African American working class. In 1919, he launched an economic self-help

UNIA Parade A parade organized by the United Negro Improvement Association in Harlem, 1920.

project, the Black Star Line, which, he promised, would buy ships and transport passengers and cargo from the United States to the West Indies, Central America, and Africa. Many of his followers invested in the venture, but it collapsed due to mismanagement. Garvey was indicted for mail fraud in connection with the project. In 1927, he was deported to Jamaica, and the UNIA lost its mass following.

As the fate of the UNIA suggested, militancy could be costly for African Americans. The NAACP also saw its membership drop dramatically during the decade. Nevertheless, African Americans' struggles laid the groundwork for more successful struggles in the future.

A "New Era" in Politics and Government

The economic and cultural transformations of the 1920s shaped American democracy in important but contradictory ways. Modern culture helped empower ordinary people and transform the style of politics. But organized groups—big business above all—affected public life more decisively while a succession of conservative Republican presidents monopolized the White House during the decade. In a society fascinated by all things "new," the Republicans claimed to represent a "New Era" in politics and government. But the Republican ascendancy of the 1920s mostly meant the return of an older vision of minimalist government, individualism, and a less internationalist foreign policy. The mix of old ideology and new political styles failed to galvanize the democratic system: the prosperous 1920s became an age of apathy and low voter turnout.

The Modern Political System

In some ways, the cultural changes of the 1920s stimulated equality and reinforced the idea that the individual could make a difference in politics, too. The emphasis on female freedom and empowerment encouraged women to exercise their newly won right to vote.

The modern culture also hastened the emergence of a political style taking shape since the late nineteenth century. Copying big business, politicians used advertising to appeal to the electorate. In the Gilded Age, voters had been active participants in political campaigns. Now, citizens were political consumers choosing candidates just as they chose mouthwash or automobiles.

The shift to advertising was necessary, too, because the major parties' control over the media had dramatically decreased. Once partisan, many newspapers now took a more independent stand. The new radio stations and movie theaters had no political affiliations at all. With the decline of partisanship, political ad campaigns focused more on individual candidates than on their parties.

Economic and cultural change also benefited big business and other organized groups. Congress was besieged by lobbyists from corporations, business groups, professional organizations, and single-issue pressure groups such as the Anti-Saloon League. Organizations employed a political style that used supposedly objective facts to educate legislators and voters. Unorganized Americans had less chance of influencing the political process.

The new, less partisan politics did a poor job of mobilizing voters. Nationwide, voter turnout fell from 79 percent in the presidential election of 1896 to just 49 percent in 1920 and 1924 (Figure 21–1). A number of factors accounted for this drop-off: African Americans in the South had been effectively disfranchised, and newly enfranchised women were less likely to vote than men; but white male turnout dropped dramatically, too.

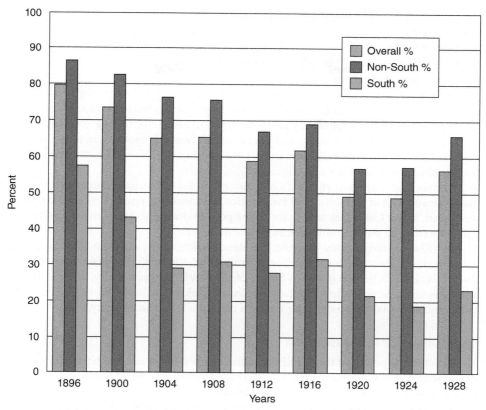

Figure 21-1   Declining Voter Turnout, 1896–1928 Why was turnout so much lower in the South?

The Republican Ascendancy

The chief beneficiaries of the new politics were the Republicans. Determined to regain the White House in 1920, the Republican Party chose an uncontroversial, conservative ticket. Presidential nominee Warren G. Harding of Ohio, handsome and charismatic, had accomplished little during a term in the Senate. His running mate, Governor Calvin Coolidge of Massachusetts, was best known for his firm stance against a strike by the Boston police.

The Republican ticket was not imposing, but neither was the opposition. The Democratic presidential nominee, Governor James M. Cox of Ohio, was saddled with the unpopularity of the Wilson administration. His running mate, Franklin Roosevelt of New York, was a little-known cousin of former president Theodore Roosevelt who had served as assistant secretary of the navy. While the Democrats ran an ineffective campaign, the Republicans made excellent use of advertising. Harding cleverly appealed to the reaction against Wilson's activist government, offering a return to "normalcy" after years of unsettling progressive innovations. Harding won a huge victory with 60.3 percent of the popular vote, a new record; he won 37 states for a total of 404 electoral votes. The Republican Party substantially increased its majorities in Congress.

The Harding administration was plagued by revelations of fraud and corruption, some involving the so-called Ohio Gang of cronies from Harding's home state. The director of the Veterans' Bureau, caught making fraudulent deals with federal property, went to prison. One of the Ohio Gang, fearing exposure of the group's influence-peddling schemes, committed suicide.

A shaken Harding died suddenly of a misdiagnosed heart attack in August 1923, but the troubles continued. Congressional hearings revealed that former secretary of the interior Albert B. Fall had apparently accepted bribes in return for leasing US Navy oil reserves at Teapot Dome, Wyoming, and Elk Hills, California. Teapot Dome, as the scandal came to be called, earned Fall a fine and a jail term. In 1924, Harding's attorney general resigned because of his role in the Ohio Gang.

The scandals damaged Harding's reputation but did not seriously harm his party or his successor, Calvin Coolidge. The former vice president—so reserved in public that he was called "Silent Cal"—was well suited to the political moment. The picture of rectitude, Coolidge restored public confidence in the presidency.

In 1924, Coolidge easily won the presidency against the Democrat John W. Davis, a colorless, conservative corporate lawyer from West Virginia, and Wisconsin's senator Robert M. La Follette, the standard-bearer of the new Progressive Party. The choice, insisted Republicans, was either "Coolidge or Chaos." Holding on to the White House and to their majorities in Congress, the Republicans continued their ascendancy.

The Politics of Individualism

The Republicans practiced the politics of individualism. Eager to serve big business, they denounced the activist, progressive state and called for less government and more individual freedom. Coolidge declared, "The chief business of the American people is business."

Despite such slogans, Republicans sometimes used government power to spur economic development. The Federal Highway Act of 1921 provided federal matching grants to improve roads, and the Fordney-McCumber Tariff of 1922 restored high protective taxes on imports.

These measures were exceptions, however. Above all, the Harding and Coolidge administrations called for "economy"—reduced government spending and lower taxes. The Republicans also condemned budget deficits and pledged to reduce the national debt; they succeeded on all counts. Federal expenditures dropped from $6.4 billion in 1920 to $3.1 billion in 1924. Congress repeatedly cut income and other taxes, but the federal government still produced annual budget surpluses and reduced its debt.

Republicans' commitment to minimal government was obvious in their lax enforcement of Progressive-Era legislation. Under Harding and Coolidge, the federal government made only weak attempts to carry out Prohibition. The Republicans also allowed regulatory commissions to atrophy. The Interstate Commerce Commission (ICC) and the Federal Trade Commission (FTC) were effectively controlled by the businesses they were supposed to regulate.

Herbert Hoover, the secretary of commerce for both Harding and Coolidge, had a more activist view of the government's role in the economy. Sensitive to business interests, Hoover used the Commerce Department to promote "associationalism"—organized cooperation among business trade groups. However, businessmen did not trust one another enough to make voluntary cooperation effective, and Hoover did not advocate federal action to force cooperation. Afraid of too much government, Hoover believed above all in what he called "American individualism."

Republican Foreign Policy

After America's intense involvement in international affairs during World War I, the 1920s were a period of relative withdrawal. But even without a foreign policy crisis, the United States, the world's greatest economic power, played an active role around the globe.

In the aftermath of World War I, Americans were eager to reduce the size of the military and to avoid new conflict. Horrified by the "Great War," women's groups and religious organizations joined a surging international peace movement. Activists' calls for disarmament helped push the Harding administration to organize the Washington Naval Conference of 1921–1922. In the first international arms-reduction accord, the United States, Great Britain, and Japan agreed to scrap some of their largest warships and, along with France and Italy, promised to limit the tonnage of their existing large ships, abandon gas warfare, and restrict submarine warfare.

The peace movement was less successful in its second goal, outlawing war. In 1928, the United States and 14 other countries signed the Kellogg-Briand Pact forswearing war as an instrument of national policy. Enthusiastically received, the measure lacked an effective mechanism to stop a nation from going to war. US membership in a world court, the third major goal of the peace movement, was not achieved in the 1920s. Too many Americans believed that the court, like the League of Nations, would undermine US sovereignty.

Meanwhile, the United States became an increasingly active member of the world economy. During the 1920s, Americans made investments and loans around the world. American corporations, including movie studios and automobile companies, exported their products. More US corporations became multinational firms by building plants overseas.

The growth of American economic activity abroad complicated the priorities of the Harding and Coolidge administrations. In the 1920s, the United States had more interests than ever to protect overseas, but Americans were wary of policies that might lead to war. Many were also uneasy about imperialism, the nation's military role in its own possessions and in supposedly sovereign nations.

The Harding and Coolidge administrations tried to pull back from some of the imperial commitments made by presidents Taft and Wilson in the 1910s. US Marines withdrew from the Dominican Republic in 1924. They also withdrew from Nicaragua in 1925 but returned the next year when the country became politically unstable.

The Harding and Coolidge administrations also attempted to promote a stable world for American business. During the 1920s, the United States helped negotiate an increase in Chinese sovereignty to reduce the chances of conflict in Asia. The United States also tried to stabilize Europe after World War I. With the quiet approval of Republican presidents, American businessmen intervened to help resolve the controversial issue of how much Germany should pay in reparation to the Allies.

Extending the "New Era"

With their cautious foreign and domestic policies so popular, Republicans faced no serious challenge as the decade came to a close. The Democrats were also hurt by the backlash against modern culture. The Democratic Party depended on support not only from nativists, fundamentalists, and Klansmen but also from their frequent targets— urban Catholics and Jews. The antagonism among these constituencies helped doom the Democrats' chances in the 1924 and 1928 elections.

In 1928, the Democrats nominated Al Smith, the governor of New York, for president. The first Irish Catholic presidential nominee of a major party, Smith displeased fundamentalists

AMERICA AND THE WORLD

J. Walter Thompson and International Markets

Even without an activist foreign policy, the United States played an important global role throughout the 1920s. As American manufacturers mastered the science of mass production, their goods saturated the American domestic market. In the United States, many businesses began relying on the services of expanding advertising agencies to enhance the consumer appeal of their products at home and overseas.

At the forefront of American advertising's overseas expansion was the top firm of J. Walter Thompson (JWT). The agency had opened a London branch in 1899, closed it during World War I, and, with its reopening, saw substantial growth during the first half of the 1920s. In 1927, JWT acquired the international business of automobile manufacturer General Motors (GM), and agreed to open a branch office wherever GM had a manufacturing plant.

By the early 1930s, JWT had thirty-four branch offices across Europe, the Middle East, Australia, South America, South Africa, and India. While the branches aimed to solicit local accounts, they also enhanced the reach of American products to a global consumer population.

In addition to making GM a recognizable global name, JWT also established modern and professional American advertising practices throughout the world. With its unprecedented number of branches and its international agents' dedication to research and reports (in the first year and a half abroad, the agency produced 222 research reports, based on 44,086 interviews), JWT outpaced its competitors on the international market and positioned itself to be the leading international agency for decades to come. Its methods became *the* methods of modern advertising, at home and abroad.

Time Line

▼**1913**
Introduction of the assembly line at Ford Motor Company

▼**1919**
Black Star Line founded by Marcus Garvey
Original Dixieland Jazz Band and Will Marion Cook's Southern Syncopated Orchestra bring jazz to England

▼**1920**
Commercial radio broadcasting
Warren G. Harding elected president

▼**1922**
Fordney-McCumber Tariff
Sinclair Lewis, *Babbitt*

▼**1923**
Teapot Dome scandal
Calvin Coolidge succeeds Harding as president

▼**1924**
National Origins Act

Yet even as the various JWT branches compiled data that spoke to the cultural specificity of their individual locations, the advertisements produced for GM differed little from country to country. At the New York office, the international department generated "pattern" copy and illustrations, largely standardizing GM advertising worldwide. Part of the reason for this was practical: stock images and text cut down on creative work. International branches could devote themselves instead to signing new clients. Additionally, a standard image of GM lines, recognized globally, was believed to enhance the power of the brand.

Advertisements generally featured art more prominently than text. Depictions of people suggested where they stood in the larger social structure, a practice that situated consumers within the anticipated class structure of the various GM lines, from the affordable Chevrolet to the highest end vehicle, the Cadillac. JWT primarily emphasized relationships between men, women, and automobile selection and the differences in the appeal of automobiles across class lines. While automobile advertisements in the United States were far more likely to foreground the significance of the nuclear family, there was some commonality in international consumer appeals. Many of JWT's international advertisements continued to echo familiar American themes, especially those intended to appeal to an upper-class clientele: luxury, style, and leisure.

With the onset of the Great Depression and a decline in sales, GM severed its relationship with JWT. While the agency closed many of its international branches, its global business sustained and potentially strengthened JWT during the 1930s, as domestic billings declined 25 percent and international business increased 43 percent. The worldwide presence of JWT had far-reaching cultural and economic consequences in promoting American goods, ideals, and business practices. The agency's expansion in the aftermath of the Great Depression and World War II would lead *Fortune* magazine in 1947 to liken the firm to the British Empire at its height, noting "the sun never sets on J. Walter Thompson."

▼1925
Founding of the Brotherhood of Sleeping Car Porters
Bruce Barton, *The Man Nobody Knows*
Scopes trial

▼1927
Charles Lindbergh's solo transatlantic flight

▼1928
Kellogg-Briand Pact
Herbert Hoover elected president

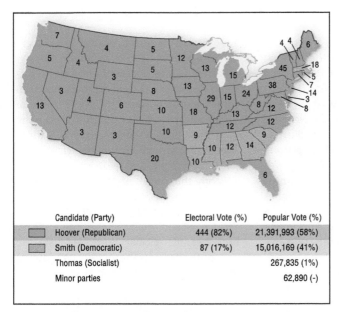

Candidate (Party)	Electoral Vote (%)	Popular Vote (%)
Hoover (Republican)	444 (82%)	21,391,993 (58%)
Smith (Democratic)	87 (17%)	15,016,169 (41%)
Thomas (Socialist)		267,835 (1%)
Minor parties		62,890 (-)

Map 21-1   The Election of 1928 Herbert Hoover's landslide victory extends the Republican "New Era."

and nativists. Moreover, his brassy, urban style—his campaign theme song was "The Sidewalks of New York"—alienated many rural Americans. Smith represented a new generation of urban, ethnic Democrats ready to use activist government to deal with social and economic problems. Their brand of urban liberalism would be influential in later years, but Smith could not galvanize a majority of voters in 1928.

Meanwhile, Herbert Hoover, the Republican nominee, polled 58.2 percent of the popular vote and carried 40 states for a total of 444 electoral votes—the Republicans' largest electoral triumph of the decade (see Map 21–1). Republicans also increased their majorities in the House and Senate. The New Era would continue.

Conclusion

The Republicans' victory in 1928 underscored the triumph of modern culture. The "New Era" had swept past the challenges of nativists, fundamentalists, and Klansmen. As Hoover prepared to take office, the appeal of the modern culture, rooted in the industrial economy, appeared undeniable. It offered a renewed sense of individual worth and possibility. It promised new freedom to women and youth. It held out an alluring vision of material pleasures—a life devoted to leisure and consumption—to all Americans. Mary Pickford still embodied the promise of the new culture and the "New Era." In 1929, moving with the times, she made her first "talking picture," *Coquette*. Her performance won her an Oscar, an award for the best performance by a female actor, from the American Academy of Motion Picture Arts and Sciences, which she had helped found.

Nevertheless, Pickford, the modern culture, and its Republican defenders were vulnerable. The political "New Era" of the 1920s was especially dependent on the state of the economy. Perhaps more than ever before in their history, Americans equated happiness with the capacity to pay for pleasures. What would happen if Americans lost their jobs and their purchasing power? What would happen when they began to wonder whether their country was really so democratic after all? The new culture and the "New Era" had survived the dissent of alienated and excluded Americans in the 1920s. It would not survive the sudden end of prosperity.

Who, What, Where

Review Questions

1. What factors created the dynamic industrial economy of the 1920s?
2. What were the main values of the modern culture that emerged after World War I?
3. What groups opposed or resisted the modern culture?

Critical-Thinking Questions

1. Why was individualism such a powerful force in America despite the growing power of corporations? Did individuals really influence American life?
2. Why did the Republican Party dominate the emerging political system of the 1920s?
3. Did the United States become more or less democratic in the 1920s?
4. How would the emergence of consumer culture shape the United States beyond the 1920s?

Suggested Readings

Baldwin, Davarian L. *Chicago's New Negroes: Modernity, the Great Migration, and Black Urban Life.* Chapel Hill: University of North Carolina Press, 2007.

Duke University. Ad Access. https://repository.duke.edu/dc/adaccess

Dumenil, Lynn. *The Modern Temper: American Culture and Society in the 1920s.* New York: Hill and Wang, 1995.

McGirr, Lisa. *The War on Alcohol: Prohibition and the Rise of the American State.* New York: W. W. Norton & Co., 2016.

Murphy, Paul V. *The New Era: American Thought and Culture in the 1920s.* Lanham, MD: Rowman and Littlefield, 2012.

For further review materials and resource information, please visit www.oup.com/us/oakes-mcgerr

21.1 HIRAM WESLEY EVANS, EXCERPTS FROM "THE KLAN: DEFENDER OF AMERICANISM" (1925)

While many Americans eagerly embraced the modernity and excitement of the "Roaring Twenties," others rejected the cultural changes under way. Hiram Wesley Evans, the Imperial Wizard of the Ku Klux Klan from 1922 to 1939, made clear the organization's rejection of diversity and inclusivity in the body politic. Members of the Ku Klux Klan regarded differences in race, ethnicity, and religion as threats to what they imagined to be the "true" American character, possessed by the white, the Protestant, and the native born.

We believe that the pioneers who built America bequeathed to their own children a priority right to it, the control of it and of its future, and that no one on earth can claim any part of this inheritance except through our generosity. We believe, too, that the mission of America under Almighty God is to perpetuate and develop just the kind of nation and just the kind of civilization which our forefathers created. This is said without offense to other civilizations, but we do believe that ours, through all possible growth and expansion, should remain *the same kind* that was "brought forth upon this continent." Also, we believe that races of men are as distinct as breeds of animals; that any mixture between races of any great divergence is evil; that the American stock, which was bred under highly selective surroundings, has proved its value and should not be mongrelized; that it has automatically and instinctively developed the kind of civilization which is best suited to its own healthy life and growth; and that this cannot safely be changed except by ourselves and along the lines of our own character. Finally, we believe that all foreigners were admitted with the idea, and on the basis of at least an implied understanding, that they would become a part of us, adopt our ideas and ideals, and help in fulfilling our destiny along those lines, but never that they should be permitted to force us to change into anything else.

That is the basic idea of the Klan. There is, perhaps, much to be said for the liberal idea of making America a mongrel nation, but that involves the two points which, as I have pointed out, the Klan will not debate. We hold firmly that America belongs to Americans, and should be kept American. All who believe this have much in common with us, and . . . belong with us in spirit if not in actual membership. The whole purpose of the Klan is to bring this belief to fulfilment. We make many mistakes, but we are doing this one thing, and no one else is even trying to do it. Within a few years the America of our fathers will either be saved or lost, and unless some other way is found, all who wish to see it saved must work with us. If they think our methods wrong, or the details of our ideas, we will be glad of correction.

There can be no doubt about the traditional American spirit, the Americanism of the pioneers, which we are trying to save. It is to be seen in the character and spirit of those pioneers, far more than in formal political documents. Americanism is not wholly lovely, perhaps. It is certainly neither soft nor lax, neither easily ductile nor imitative, neither silken nor oily. It is a thing of rugged steel, tempered and forged in the terrific stress of the task of wresting a continent from savages and from the wilderness. It is welded of convictions, independence, self-reliance, freedom, justice, achievement, courage, acceptance of responsibility, and the guidance of his own conscience by each man personally. If inheritance counts for anything, it is to be found in the children of the pioneers far more than in any other group on earth, for only those who had this spirit survived. . . .

We are drifting away from national unity: in fact, we are being carefully and deliberately driven away from it by alien ideas and excessive liberalism toward them. The Klan, knowing this, believes the whole tendency must be stopped, and that control of the nation should return to, and remain in, the hands of men of the character and spirit of the pioneers who made the nation, a spirit most often found in the descendants of those pioneers.

We believe, also, that all who foment this disruption through alienism threaten the very foundations of all the things that have made America great. It is because of this that the Klan is intolerant—prejudiced. It is intolerant of this attack; intolerant of the people who are trying to destroy our traditional Americanism. We do not admit that we are more intolerant than our opponents; it seems to us as intolerant to condemn the Klan's attempts to save Americanism as it is for us to condemn the attempts to subvert it. But, if that is intolerance, we are proud of it.

And in our intolerance, as in other things, we are true to the American tradition; for this is our intolerance: We will not endure attempts to tear down the fundamentals on which the whole structure of our nation and our civilization is based. So long as these are not threatened, tolerance should be unlimited; we of the Klan do not wish or try to limit it. But the ideas upon which the nation rests, and which set us apart from other nations, are in a way like a corral fence. While the fence is undamaged there is no need to worry, no matter how much the animals inside may kick up and mill around. But when the fence is weakened or threatened, then it is time for action. So, in the nation, toleration becomes a vice when fundamentals are in danger. That time has come, and we who are the heirs of the American tradition are called upon to act. . . .

To sum up: The Klan speaks for the plain people of America, who believe in an American nation, built on that unity of mind and spirit which is possible only to an homogeneous people, and growing out of the purposes, spirit, and instincts of our pioneer ancestors. We know that the melting pot has failed; the reasons are unimportant now. We believe that definite steps must now be taken to prevent ours from becoming a mongrel nation, or a milling and distraught mass of opposed groups, in which the mental and spiritual qualities that made America great will be lost forever. Therefore, we oppose all alienism in any form and the excessive liberalism that supports it. We grant to all the right to their own ideas, but we claim the same right for ourselves, and a prior right to control America.

Source: Hiram Wesley Evans, "The Klan: Defender of Americanism," *The Forum* (December 1925), 801–814.

21.2 BRUCE BARTON, EXCERPTS FROM *THE MAN NOBODY KNOWS: A DISCOVERY OF THE REAL JESUS* (1925)

Bruce Barton, one of the best known advertising men of the twentieth century, was also famous for publishing guides to personal success. His most famous book, *The Man Nobody Knows*, reconsidered the success of Jesus Christ through the lens of the 1920s business-man. Celebrating Jesus's leadership and ability to manage a team and spread his message as core virtues of the business world, the book became a bestseller, selling more than 750,000 copies in two years.

For some, formal theology has diminished the thrill to be found in His life by assuming that He knew everything from the beginning—that His three years of public work were a kind of dress rehearsal, with no real problems or crises. What interest would there be in such a life? What in-spiration? You who read these pages have your own creed concerning Him; I have mine. Let us forget all creed for the time being, and take the story just as the simple narratives give it—a poor boy, growing up in a peasant family, working in a carpenter shop; gradually feeling His powers expanding, beginning to have an influence over His neighbors, recruiting a few followers, suffering disappointments, reverses and finally death. Yet building so solidly and well that death was only the beginning of His influence! Stripped of all dogma, this is the grandest achievement story of all! In the pages of this book let us treat it as such. If, in so doing, we are criticized for overemphasizing the human side of His character, we shall have the satisfaction of knowing that our overemphasis rends a little to offset the very great overemphasis which has been exerted on the other side. Books and books and books have been written about Him as the Son of God; surely we have a reverent right to remember that His favorite title for Himself was the Son of Man.

Nazareth, where He grew up, was a little town in an outlying province. In the fashionable circles of Jerusalem it was quite the thing to make fun of Nazareth—its crudities of custom and speech, its simplicity of manner. "Can any good thing come out of Nazareth?" they asked derisively when the report spread that a new prophet had arisen in that country town. The question was regarded as a complete rebuttal of His pretensions. . . .

In New York one day a luncheon was tendered by a gathering of distinguished gentlemen. There were perhaps two hundred at the tables. The food was good and the speeches were impressive. But what stirred one's imagination was a study of the men at the speakers' table. There they were—some of the most influential citizens of the present-day world; and who were they? At one end an international financier—the son of a poor country parson. Beside him a great newspaper proprietor—he came from a tiny town in Maine and landed in New York with less than a hundred dollars. A little farther along the president of a world-wide press association—a copy boy in a country newspaper office. And, in the center, a boy who grew up in the poverty of an obscure village and became a commanding statesman.

When and how and where did the eternal miracle occur in the lives of those men? At what hour, in the morning, in the afternoon, in the long quiet evenings, did the audacious thought enter the mind of each of them that he was larger than the limits of a country town, that his life might be bigger than his father's? When did the thought come to Jesus? Was it one morning when He stood at the carpenter's bench, the sun streaming in across the hills? Was it late in the night, after the family had retired, and He had slipped out to walk and wonder under the stars? Nobody knows. All we can be sure of is this—that the consciousness of His divinity must have come to Him in a time of solitude, of awe in the presence of Nature. The Western Hemisphere has been fertile in material progress, but the great religions have all come out of the East. The deserts are a symbol of the infinite; the vast spaces that divide men from the stars fill the human soul with wonder. Somewhere, at some unforgettable hour, the daring filled His heart. He knew that He was bigger than Nazareth. . . .

The mastery of ideas, the achievement of ideals—what we call success is always exciting; we never grow tired of asking what and how. What, then, were the principal elements in His power over men? How was it that the boy from a country village became the greatest leader?

First of all, He must have had the voice and manner of the leader—the personal magnetism which begets loyalty and commands respect. The beginnings of it were present in Him even as a boy. John felt them. On the day when John looked up from the river where he was baptizing converts and saw Jesus standing on the bank, he drew back in protest. "I have need to be baptized of thee," he exclaimed, "and comest thou to me?" The lesser man recognized the greater instinctively. We speak of personal magnetism as though there were something mysterious about it—a magic quality bestowed on one in a thousand and denied to all the rest. This is not true. The essential element in personal magnetism is a consuming sincerity—an overwhelming faith in the importance of the work one has to do. . . .

Most of us go through the world mentally divided against ourselves. We wonder whether we are in the right jobs, whether we are making the right investments, whether, after all, anything is as important as it seems to be. Our enemies are those of our own being and creation. Instinctively we wait for a commanding voice, for one who shall say authoritatively, "I have the truth. This way lies happiness and salvation." There was in Jesus supremely that quality of conviction.

. . . This blazing conviction was the first and greatest element in the success of Jesus. The second was His powerful gift of picking men and recognizing hidden capacities in them. It must have amazed Nicodemus[1] when he learned the names of the twelve whom the young teacher had chosen to be His associates. What a list! Not a single well-known person on it. Nobody who had ever accomplished anything, A haphazard collection of fishermen and small-town businessmen, and one tax collector—a member of the most hated element in the community. What a crowd!

Nowhere is there such a startling example of success in leadership as the way in which that organization was brought together. Take the tax collector, Matthew, as the most striking instance. His occupation carried a heavy weight of social ostracism, but it was profitable. He was probably well-to-do according to the simple standards of the neighborhood; certainly he was a busy man and not subject to impulsive action. His addition to the group of disciples is told in a single sentence:

"And as Jesus passed by, he called Matthew."

Amazing. No argument; no pleading. A small leader would have been compelled to set up the advantages of the opportunity. "Of course you are doing well where you are and making money," He might have said. "I can't offer you as much as you are getting; in fact you may have some difficulty in making ends meet. But I think we are going to have an interesting time and shall probably accomplish a big work." Such a conversation would have been met with Matthew's reply that he would "have to think it over," and the world would never have heard his name.

There was no such trifling with Jesus. As He passed by He called Matthew. No leader in the world can read that sentence without acknowledging that here indeed is the Master.

He had the born leader's gift for seeing powers in men of which they themselves were often almost unconscious. One day as He was coming into a certain town a tremendous crowd pressed around Him. There was a rich man named Zacchaeus in the town, small in stature, but with such keen business ability that he had got himself generally disliked. Being curious to see the distinguished visitor, he had climbed up into a tree. Imagine his surprise when Jesus stopped under the tree and commanded him to come down, saying, "Today I intend to eat at your house." The crowd was stunned. Some of the bolder spirits took it on themselves to tell Jesus of His social blunder. He couldn't afford to make the mistake of visiting Zacchaeus, they said. Their protests were without avail. They saw in Zacchaeus merely a dishonest and greedy little man; He saw in him a person of unusual generosity and a fine sense of justice, who needed only to have those qualities revealed by someone who understood. So with Matthew—the crowd saw only a despised tax gatherer. Jesus saw the potential writer of a book which will live forever. . . . Having gathered together His organization, there remained for Jesus the tremendous task of training it. And herein lay the third great element of His success—His vast unending patience. The Church has attached to each of the disciples the title of Saint, and it may be that thinking of them exclusively as Saints robs us of an essential reality. They were very far from sainthood when He picked them up. For three years He had them with Him day and night, His whole energy and resources poured out in an effort to create an understanding in them. Yet through it all they never fully understood. We have seen, at the beginning of this chapter, an example of their petulance. The narratives are full of similar discouragements.

In spite of all He could do or say, they were persuaded that He planned to overthrow the Roman power and set Himself up as ruler in Jerusalem. Hence they never tired of wrangling as to how the offices should be divided. Two of them, James and John, got their mother to come to Him and ask that her sons might sit, one on His right hand and one on His left. When the other ten heard of it they were angry with James and John; but Jesus never lost His patience. He believed that the way to get faith out of men is to show that you have faith in them.

Of all the disciples Simon was most noisy and aggressive. It was he who was always volunteering advice, forever proclaiming the stanchness of his own courage and faith. One day Jesus

---

[1] Nicodemus was a wealthy and popular holy man in Jerusalem.

said to him, "Before the cock crows tomorrow you will deny me thrice." Simon was indignant. Though they killed him, he cried, he would never deny! Jesus merely smiled—and that night it happened. . . . A lesser leader would have dropped Simon. "You have had your chance," he would have said, "I am sorry, but I must have men around me on whom I can depend." Jesus had the rare understanding that the same man will usually not make the same mistake twice. To this frail, very human, very likable former fisherman He spoke no words of rebuke. Instead He kept His faith that Peter would carry on bravely. It was daring, but He knew His man. The shame of the denial had tempered the iron of that nature like fire; from that time on there was no faltering in Peter even at the death.

Source: Bruce Barton, *The Man Nobody Knows: A Discovery of the Real Jesus* (New York: Grosset & Dunlap, 1925).

21.3 VISUAL DOCUMENT: COLGATE & CO. ADVERTISEMENT (1925)

As American culture underwent a transformation whereby workers found satisfaction not in their work but in their leisure time, the advertising industry encouraged the pursuit of pleasure. As new products flooded the market, advertisements—in magazines, on billboards, in trolley cars—educated American consumers about products they had once lived without but would now absolutely need in order to compete in the modern world.

Source: Literary Digest/Courtesy Duke University Libraries.

21.4 ROBERT LYND AND HELEN LYND, EXCERPT FROM "REMAKING LEISURE IN MIDDLETOWN" (1929)

Just as Henry Ford's moving assembly line and system of mass production changed business forever, so too did the product coming off his factory lines: the automobile. Robert and Helen Lynd's pioneering 1929 study of social and economic life in Muncie, Indiana, revealed the influence of new goods and entertainments and the resulting changes to patterns of modern American life. The car, in particular, took people away from the traditional influences of home and church and revealed the new power of media and peer culture.

Although lectures, reading, music, and art are strongly intrenched in Middletown's traditions, it is none of these that would first attract the attention of a newcomer watching Middletown at play.

"Why on earth do you need to study what's changing this country?" said a lifelong resident and shrewd observer of the Middle West. "I can tell you what's happening in just four letters: A-U-T-O!"

The first real automobile appeared in Middletown in 1900. About 1906 it was estimated that "there are probably 200 in the city and county." At the close of 1923 there were 6,221 passenger cars in the city, one for every 6.1 persons, or roughly two for every three families. Of these 6,221 cars, 41 per cent were Fords; 54 per cent of the total were cars of models of 1920 or later, and 17 per cent models earlier than 1917. These cars average a bit over 5,000 miles a year. For some of the workers and some of the business class, use of the automobile is a seasonal matter, but the increase in surfaced roads and in closed cars is rapidly making the car a year-round tool for leisure-time as well as getting-a-living activities. As, at the turn of the century, business class people began to feel apologetic if they did not have a telephone, so ownership of an automobile has now reached the point of being an accepted essential of normal living.

Into the equilibrium of habits which constitutes for each individual some integration in living has come this new habit, upsetting old adjustments, and blasting its way through such accustomed and unquestioned dicta as "Rain or shine, I never miss a Sunday morning at church"; "A high school boy does not need much spending money"; "I don't need exercise, walking to the office keeps me fit"; "I wouldn't think of moving out of town and being so far from my friends"; "Parents ought always to know where their children are." The newcomer is most quickly and amicably incorporated into those regions of behavior in which men are engaged in doing impersonal, matter-of-fact things; much more contested is its advent where emotionally charged sanctions and taboos are concerned. No one questions the use of the auto for transporting groceries, getting to one's place of work or to the golf course, or in place of the porch for "cooling off after supper" on a hot summer evening; however much the activities concerned with getting a living may be altered by the fact that a factory can draw from workmen within a radius of forty-five miles, or however much old labor union men resent the intrusion of this new alternate way of spending an evening, these things are hardly major issues. But when auto riding tends to replace the traditional call in the family parlor as a way of approach between the unmarried, "the home is endangered," and all-day Sunday motor trips are a "threat against the church"; it is in the activities concerned with the home and religion that the automobile occasions the greatest emotional conflicts.

Group-sanctioned values are disturbed by the inroads of the automobile upon the family budget. A case in point is the not uncommon practice of mortgaging a home to buy an automobile. Data on automobile ownership were secured from 123 working class families. Of these, sixty have cars. Forty-one of the sixty own their homes. Twenty-six of these forty-one families have mortgages on their homes. Forty of the sixty-three families who do not own a car own their homes. Twenty-nine of these have mortgages on their homes. Obviously other factors are involved in many of Middletown's mortgages. That the automobile does represent a real choice in the minds of some at least is suggested by the acid retort of one citizen to the question about car ownership: "No, sir, we've *not* got a car. *That's* why we've got a home." According to an officer of a Middletown automobile financing company, 75 to 90 per cent of the cars purchased locally are bought on time payment, and a working man earning $35.00 a week frequently plans to use one week's pay each month as payment for his car.

The automobile has apparently unsettled the habit of careful saving for some families. "Part of the money we spend on the car would go to the bank, I suppose," said more than one working class wife. A business man explained his recent inviting of social oblivion by selling his car by saying: "My car, counting depreciation and everything, was costing mighty nearly $100.00 a month, and my wife and I sat down together the other night and just figured that we're getting along, and if we're to have anything later on, we've just got to begin to save." The "moral" aspect of the competition between the automobile and certain accepted expenditures appears in the remark of another business man, "An automobile is a luxury, and no one has a right to one if he can't afford it. I haven't the slightest sympathy for any one who is out of work if he owns a car."

. . . Many families feel that an automobile is justified as an agency holding the family group together. "I never feel as close to my family as when we are all together in the car," said one business class mother, and one or two spoke of giving up Country Club membership or other recreations to get a car for this reason. "We don't spend anything on recreation except for the car. We save every place we can and put the money into the car. It keeps the family together," was an opinion voiced more than once. Sixty-one per cent of 337 boys and 60 per cent of 423 girls in the three upper years of the high school say that they motor more often with their parents than without them.

But this centralizing tendency of the automobile may be only a passing phase; sets in the other direction are almost equally prominent. "Our daughters [eighteen and fifteen] don't use our car much because they are always with somebody else in their car when we go out motoring," lamented one business class mother. And another said, "The two older children [eighteen and sixteen] never go out when the family motors. They always have something else on." "In the nineties we were all much more together," said another wife. "People brought chairs and cushions out of the house and sat on the lawn evenings. We rolled out a strip of carpet and put cushions on the porch step to take care of the unlimited overflow of neighbors that dropped by. We'd sit out so all evening. The younger couples perhaps would wander off for half an hour to get a soda but come back to join in the informal singing or listen while somebody strummed a mandolin or guitar." "What on earth *do* you want me to do? Just sit around home all evening!" retorted a popular high school girl of today when her father discouraged her going out motoring for the evening with a young blade in a rakish car waiting at the curb. The fact that 348 boys and 382 girls in the three upper years of the high school placed "use of the automobile" fifth and fourth respectively in a list of twelve possible sources of disagreement between them and their parents suggests that this may be an increasing decentralizing agent.

An earnest teacher in a Sunday School class of working class boys and girls in their late teens was winding up the lesson on the temptations of Jesus: "These three temptations summarize all the temptations we encounter today: physical comfort, fame, and wealth. Can you think of any temptation we have today that Jesus didn't have?" "Speed!" rejoined one boy. The unwanted interruption was quickly passed over. But the boy had mentioned a tendency underlying one of the four chief infringements of group laws in Middletown today, and the manifestations of Speed are not confined to "speeding." "Auto Polo next Sunday!!" shouts the display advertisement of an amusement park near the city. "It's motor insanity—too fast for the movies!" The boys who have cars "step on the gas," and those who haven't cars sometimes steal them: "The desire of youth to step on the gas when it has no machine of its own," said the local press, "is considered responsible for the theft of the greater part of the [154] automobiles stolen from [Middletown] during the past year."

The threat which the automobile presents to some anxious parents is suggested by the fact that of thirty girls brought before the juvenile court in the twelve months preceding September 1, 1924, charged with "sex crimes," for whom the place where the offense occurred was given in the records, nineteen were listed as having committed the offense in an automobile. Here again the automobile appears to some as an "enemy" of the home and society.

Sharp, also, is the resentment aroused by this elbowing new device when it interferes with old established religious habits. The minister trying to change people's behavior in desired directions through the spoken word must compete against the strong pull of the open road strengthened by endless printed "copy" inciting to travel. Preaching to 200 people on a hot, sunny Sunday in midsummer on "The Supreme Need of Today," a leading Middletown minister denounced "automobilitis—the thing those people have who go off motoring on Sunday instead of going to church. If you want to use your car on Sunday, take it out Sunday morning and bring some shut-ins to church and Sunday School; then in the afternoon, if you choose, go out and worship God in the beauty of nature—but don't neglect to worship Him indoors too." This same month there appeared in the *Saturday Evening Post,* reaching approximately one family in six in Middletown, a two-page spread on the automobile as an "enricher of life," quoting "a bank president in a Mid-Western city" as saying, "A man who works six days a week and spends the seventh on his own doorstep certainly will not pick up the extra dimes in the great thoroughfares of life." "Some sunny Sunday very soon," said another two page spread in the *Post,* "just drive an Overland up to your door—tell the family to hurry the packing and get aboard—and be off with smiles down the nearest road—free, loose, and happy—bound for green wonderlands." Another such advertisement urged Middletown to "Increase Your Week-End Touring Radius."

. . . "We had a fine day yesterday," exclaimed an elderly pillar of a prominent church, by way of Monday morning greeting. . . . "dinner. It's a fine thing for people to get out that way on Sundays. No question about it. They see different things and get a larger outlook."

"Did you miss church?" he was asked.

"Yes, I did, but you can't do both. I never missed church or Sunday School for thirteen years and I kind of feel as if I'd done my share. The ministers ought not to rail against people's driving on Sunday. They ought just to realize that they won't be there every Sunday during the summer, and make church interesting enough so they'll want to come."

Source: Robert Lynd and Helen Lynd, *Middletown: A Study in Contemporary American Culture,* foreword by Clark Wissler (New York: Harcourt, Brace & World, Inc., 1956), pp. 251–261.

A Great Depression and a New Deal

1929–1940

< FDR Giving a Fireside Chat, 1936

AMERICAN PORTRAIT

Dorothea Lange

The city she loved had changed and Dorothea Lange resolved to capture that change on film. In the spring of 1932, Lange descended from her fashionable second-story portrait studio and began to document the effects of the Great Depression on the streets of San Francisco. Noting the throng of men standing outside the White Angel soup kitchen, Lange recalled that she took three shots and "then I got out of there." Those three shots marked the beginning of a tremendous change in the life and career of Dorothea Lange and would forever influence the way Americans, present and future, would visualize the Great Depression.

One of San Francisco's most celebrated portrait photographers, Lange had long catered to an upscale clientele who loved the intimacy and emotion she evoked from her subjects. But as the nation fell deeper into the Depression, Lange felt a desire to move beyond photographing the city's elite. The desperation of the Depression propelled Lange in a more political, more public direction.

Lange's early 1930s images focused on urban scenes of the Depression: a woman waiting on a food distribution line; an unemployed man leaning against a wall; a 1934 strike by the city's longshoremen. When Paul Taylor, an economics professor at the University of California at Berkeley, contacted Lange about using some of her images to accompany his article on the strike, Lange became even more politicized. Through a professional and personal partnership with Taylor, Lange left San Francisco and became one of the preeminent photographers of the rural Depression experience.

Lange accompanied Taylor on travels throughout California, where she photographed the work and living conditions of migrant laborers and "Okies" who had fled the Dust Bowl hoping to find employment and opportunity in California. Pushing the Farm Security Administration (FSA), a New Deal agency intended to aid agricultural laborers and combat rural poverty, for government-built camps to house migratory workers, Taylor provided economic and sociological evidence while Lange documented the desperate living conditions of these workers and the grueling labor that men, women, and children completed in order to survive. With her images and accompanying captions, which often outlined the background and experiences of her subjects, Lange successfully depicted farmworkers as hardworking and capable—people who did not deserve their poverty, but had come to it through a range of circumstances, many of them rooted in the inequity of the American economy.

Hoping to hold off conservative critics by demonstrating the value of its efforts, the FSA adopted a photography project that ultimately became its most influential activity. By documenting the Depression and sharing the images with journalists and popular media, the FSA drew national attention to the plight of the rural poor. Lange, with her skilled portrait style, was essential in depicting this population with dignity and grace. Her images communicated a New Deal view of American citizens during the Depression. Like Progressives, New Dealers refused to believe that immoral character led to poverty. It was the structure of the American economy, not the character of the American people, that needed correction.

With great intent, Lange used her photographs to communicate that the people she photographed were better than their current circumstances. She depicted efforts to keep an orderly pantry in a lean-to shelter as a means of maintaining some measure of domesticity. She showed families gathered by their cars, loaded down with possessions, taking to the road to look for work. She captured the back-breaking nature of farm labor migrant workers were willing to endure. And most famously, in "Migrant Mother," she showed the resolve of a maternal figure, worrying over her children, determined to continue on. These people deserved more, Lange believed, and in the spirit of the New Deal, Americans were coming to believe that the government had a responsibility to see that they got it.

The Great Depression

In the fall of 1929, declining confidence in the stock market shook the economy. By Thursday, October 24, panic had set in as brokers rushed to unload their stocks. Prices rallied briefly, but on October 29, "Black Tuesday," stock values lost over $14 billion, and within the month the market stood at only half its precrash worth. Hundreds of corporations and thousands of individuals were wiped out. On Wall Street, the symbol of prosperity in the 1920s, mounted police had to keep angry mobs away from the stock exchange. Although the crash did not cause the Depression, it did expose underlying weaknesses and shatter the confidence President Herbert Hoover relied on for recovery. His optimistic speeches would ring false over the years of unemployment, hunger, and homelessness.

Causes

No single factor explains the Great Depression. Politicians, bureaucrats, and business leaders had no clear idea why things had gone so wrong. Economists and historians still debate the issue today. Yet, even without a definitive account, it is clear that structural flaws in the national and international economies and ill-conceived government policies were at fault.

In the 1920s, the base of the economy had begun to shift. No longer was it driven by steel, coal, textiles, railroads, and other heavy industries. New industries that sold complex consumer goods such as automobiles became the driving force. In addition to cars, sales of radios, clothing, processed foods, and a whole range of consumer products grew dramatically. This shift toward a new consumer-oriented economy was fueled by favorable business conditions, job growth, and plentiful consumer credit. The limits of this market had, however, been reached even before the great crash. When the stock market fell, the collapse of purchasing power caused by mass unemployment and the loss of savings slowed the transition to the new economy.

A rickety credit and financial system added to the problems of the late 1920s. Even in good times, banks failed by the hundreds. For rural banks these failures could be traced to low farm prices, but financial institutions everywhere suffered from inept and even criminal management. Banks were virtually unregulated, and in the booming 1920s many bet depositors' money on stocks or large, risky loans. Bank failures magnified the impact of the crash; many thousands lost money they thought was safe.

Like banks, corporate finance was free from regulation and given to misrepresentation, manipulation, and corrupt insider deals. Few could be sure whether investments were going into sound companies or worthless paper.

Government missteps and poor policies also had a role. The Republican administrations of the 1920s reduced government interference in the economy, lowered taxes on the wealthy, and reduced spending. They failed to address the banking mess, the problems of farmers, or the growing reliance on credit. The Federal Reserve could have dampened speculation in stocks or, after the Depression began, expanded the currency to promote growth. Concerned more about a strong dollar than about stable employment, the Harding and Coolidge administrations cut spending and the money supply, worsening the eventual collapse.

The Depression was magnified by an international economy still reeling from the effects of World War I. Under the peace terms, Germany owed $33 billion in reparations to Britain and France, who in turn owed billions in debts to the United States. Only US bank loans to Germany made these huge payments possible, so throughout the 1920s, funds that could have created jobs and industries went instead into this financial merry-go-round. The cycle was broken by the depression in the United States. European nations tried to protect themselves by devaluing their currencies and raising trade barriers. The result was a steady economic decline that made payments on reparations or loans impossible. The cycle reached a breaking point in 1931, and the international financial system came crashing down, bringing with it many more American banks and further deepening the crisis.

Descending into Depression

The statistics describing the Great Depression were alarming. Between 1929 and 1933, every index of economic activity steadily worsened. The gross national product shrank from $104.4 billion in 1929 to $74.2 billion in 1933. The combined incomes of American workers fell by more than 40 percent. Bank failures increased, from 640 in 1928 to 2,294 in 1931. A *New York Times* index of business activity dropped from 114.8 in June of 1929 to 63.7 in March of 1933. Both exports and imports fell by more than two-thirds.

As business activity collapsed, joblessness skyrocketed. Periods of unemployment had always been a feature of capitalist economies, even in good times. What distinguished the Great Depression was the extent and duration of unemployment. At the lowest point of the slump, in the early 1930s, between 20 and 30 percent of wage earners were out of work (see Table 22–1). In some cities the jobless rate was much higher, with Chicago and Detroit near 50 percent, Akron 60 percent, and Toledo a crushing 80 percent. In 1933, the Bureau of Labor Statistics estimated that as many as one in three workers, more than 12,600,000 Americans, were unemployed.

Behind the grim statistics lay terrible human costs. In the spring of 1930, as the first Depression winter came to an end, breadlines appeared in major cities. The unemployed could be seen in the thousands, Sherwood Anderson wrote, "creeping through the streets of American cities, eating from garbage cans." Unemployed men and women stood outside factory gates desperately seeking work, at soup kitchens hoping for a meal, and at homeless shelters that were already overflowing.

Table 22-1 Labor Force and Unemployment, 1929–1941 (numbers in millions)

Year	Labor Force	Number	% of Labor Force
1929	49.2	1.6	3.2
1930	49.8	4.3	8.7
1931	50.4	8.0	15.9
1932	51.0	12.1	23.6
1933	51.6	12.8	24.9
1934	52.2	11.3	21.7
1935	52.9	10.6	20.1
1936	53.4	9.0	16.9
1937	54.0	7.7	14.3
1938	54.6	10.4	19.0
1939	55.2	9.5	17.2
1940	55.6	8.1	14.6
1941	55.9	5.6	9.9

Source: United States Department of Commerce, *Historical Statistics of the United States* (1960), p. 70.

Food, clothing, and shelter were suddenly hard to get. Schoolteachers reported that growing numbers of students were listless from hunger. Hospitals began receiving patients suffering from nutritional disorders, including children with rickets, a disease caused by a lack of vitamin D. *Fortune* magazine ran an article on Americans who had starved to death. Embarrassed mothers sent children to school in rags. Men wrapped newspapers beneath their shirts as protection from the cold. Desperate families, unable to pay the rent, "doubled up" with relatives. More and more tenants were evicted; more and more banks foreclosed on mortgages. Apartments stood vacant and homes went unsold, yet by 1932 more than a million homeless men, women, and children occupied shantytowns or slept in doorways and alleys. Hoboes were everywhere, searching for something to eat, somewhere to live, someplace to work.

Farmers faced both economic and environmental disaster. Farmers in the plains states and the West aggressively increased production in the 1920s and then saw the markets for corn, wheat, beef, and pork collapse. Between 1929 and 1932, farmers' income dropped by two-thirds. Then drought struck. Between 1930 and 1936, rains all but stopped in much of the South, the Southwest, and the Great Plains (see Map 22–1). Exposed by decades of wasteful farming practices and a more recent propensity to plow fields immediately following the previous harvest, the earth dried up and blew away. Spectacular dust storms carried topsoil hundreds of miles through the air, giving a new name—the Dust Bowl—to much of the southern plains. Dust and depression ripped thousands of farm families from the land in Texas, Kansas, Oklahoma, and Arkansas, sending these "Okies," "Arkies," and "Texies" off to California in search of work.

The Great Depression affected nearly everyone in America, but it was most severe for those already disadvantaged. Although the shock of the Dust Bowl affected many poor white farmers, the larger agricultural depression was even more devastating for

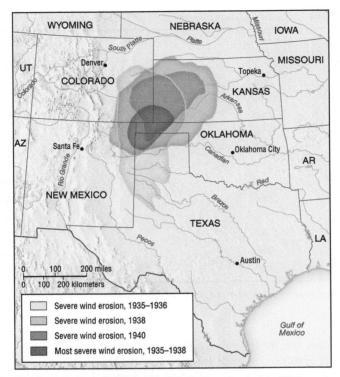

Map 22-1   Extent of the Dust Bowl   The Dust Bowl of the 1930s eventually spread across thousands of square miles of the southern plains.

sharecroppers on the southern cotton lands, workers in the wheat fields of the Midwest, and the vast migrant labor pools that traveled the East and West Coasts picking fruits and vegetables. In cities, African Americans, who held the least-secure jobs, found themselves pushed from menial service tasks and unskilled work by desperate white workers.

By 1932, private charities, the major social safety net, failed to meet the needs of desperate citizens. Ethnic organizations such as the Bohemian Charitable Association or Jewish Charities in Chicago found themselves overwhelmed. Arthur T. Burns, the president of the Association of Community Chests and Councils, flatly declared, "The funds we have are altogether inadequate to meet the situation."

Public monies were also scarce. Only eight states provided any form of unemployment insurance; most of it was meager. The few state welfare agencies were poorly funded and now stretched beyond their limits. Cities faced insolvency as their tax bases dwindled. Many states were forbidden by their constitutions to borrow for social welfare expenditures. Frustrated Americans looked to the federal government for a solution, but there was little help beyond pensions for veterans. There was no social security for the elderly and disabled, no federal unemployment insurance for those who lost their jobs, and no food stamp program to relieve hunger.

Dust Storm Drought and modern agriculture churned the Great Plains into silica powder that was carried by windstorms. Over half the patients in Kansas hospitals in 1935 suffered from dust pneumonia.

The federal government was under unprecedented pressure to do something, anything, to relieve the Depression. Even bankers and businessmen abandoned their resistance to a strong central government. The president of Columbia University suggested that a dictatorship might provide more effective leadership. Others warned of social revolution. Most of the pleas for action were aimed at the administration, and Herbert Hoover himself came to symbolize the failures of government. The newspapers that jobless men wrapped themselves in were called "Hoover shirts"; shantytowns were "Hoovervilles." In the popular imagination, Hoover and the Great Depression became inseparable.

Hoover Responds

In many ways, Hoover was ideally qualified to handle this emergency. He had experience with natural and human catastrophes. Orphaned at a young age, Hoover worked hard to educate himself. Trained as an engineer at Stanford University, he roamed the world building and managing mining operations and was a millionaire by his mid-20s. Like other young progressives, Hoover sought to use business skills to solve social problems. He won fame as an administrator of emergency relief, saving Belgium from starvation during World War I and overseeing rescue efforts during the Great Mississippi Flood of 1927.

He brought to the presidency a well-developed theory of the role of government in a modern economy. Hoover believed that complex societies required accurate economic information, careful planning, and large-scale coordination. His political philosophy, associationalism, envisioned a federal government that gathered information and encouraged voluntary cooperation among businesses but did not intervene further. He feared that an overbearing government would crush the creativity essential to a capitalist economy. This voluntarist dream fit well with America's dominant ideology, and Hoover easily won the presidency in 1928.

Hoover acted quickly. One of his first achievements was the Agricultural Marketing Act of 1929, designed to raise farm incomes and rationalize production. Since the turn of the century, farmers had been plagued by a "paradox of plenty." They produced more food and fiber than Americans could consume, so the more farmers grew, the less they earned. The bill established a Federal Farm Board to create cooperatives for purchasing and distributing surplus crops. It issued $500 million in loans to stabilize prices but did not limit production or dictate prices.

A Hooverville in Seattle, Washington As the Depression deepened, the homeless settled in "Hoover-villes" on the edge of city centers.

When the market crashed, Hoover's initial response reflected his overall vision. His goal was to get business to promise to cooperate to maintain wages and investment. In 1931, as 25 banks a week were failing, he encouraged formation of the National Credit Corporation, in which banks were urged to pool resources to stave off collapse. Rather than distribute unemployment insurance or poor relief, he tried to persuade companies not to lay off workers and to contribute to charities for the homeless and unemployed. But the breadth and depth of the Depression overwhelmed Hoover's schemes. Crop prices fell so low that farmers blockaded cities and demanded compensation for their crops.

Hoover had never failed before, and he worked tirelessly to fight the Depression. By 1932, he reluctantly agreed to more aggressive government action, even at the risk of deficit spending. He proposed a Reconstruction Finance Corporation (RFC) authorized to loan $2 billion to revive large corporations. Plans to increase government revenues and distribute farm surpluses to the needy were also enacted. But it was too little, too late. The Depression was three years old and showed no signs of lifting.

Hoover's policies increased the Depression's severity. Unable to control his own party, Hoover watched Congress pass the Hawley-Smoot Tariff in 1930. The tariff raised import duties to record levels, stifling hopes that international trade might help the economy and damaging the weak nations of Europe. Despite misgivings, he signed the bill into law. At the same time, Hoover opposed other measures that might have relieved poverty or stimulated recovery. He vetoed massive public works bills sponsored by congressional Democrats. Finally, Hoover's commitment to the gold standard and a balanced budget also prevented a potential turnaround.

Hoover, whose popularity had plummeted as the Depression deepened, reinforced his reputation as a protector of the privileged by his response to the Bonus Marchers in 1932. In 1924, Congress had issued the veterans of World War I a "bonus" to be paid in 1945. But as the Depression threw millions out of work, veterans asked to have their bonuses paid early. In the summer of 1932, veterans formed a "Bonus Expeditionary Force" to march on Washington. Arriving on freight cars and buses, over 20,000 Bonus Marchers and their families encamped on Capitol grounds. Hoover ordered the army to remove the marchers. Against orders, General Douglas MacArthur attacked with tanks and mounted cavalry. Major George S. Patton, saber drawn, galloped through the encampment, setting fire to its miserable tents and shacks. Among those he attacked was Joseph T. Angelino, who won the Distinguished Service Cross in 1918 for saving Patton's life. Photographs of government brutality shocked Americans. Hoover's silence solidified his reputation for callousness.

As Congress struggled to relieve unemployment and suffering, Hoover dismissed the "futile attempt to cure poverty by the enactment of law." He questioned the motives of everyone who disagreed with his policies. By the end of his term the "Great Humanitarian" had become sullen and withdrawn. It was a dispirited Republican Convention that met in Chicago to nominate Hoover for reelection in 1932.

The First New Deal

When the Democratic Convention chose a presidential candidate in 1932, Franklin Delano Roosevelt flew from Albany, New York, to Chicago to accept the nomination in person, a dramatic gesture in an age new to air travel and personal politics. "I pledge myself," he told the enthusiastic crowd, "to a new deal for the American people." The phrase stuck, and the reforms enacted between 1933 and 1938 have come to be known as the New Deal. The programs came in two great waves, the "first" and "second" New Deals. The first New Deal began with the Hundred Days, a burst of executive and legislative activity following FDR's inauguration, and continued through 1934.

The Election of 1932

The Depression reached its lowest depths as the 1932 election approached, and the Republicans seemed headed for disaster. Their inability to develop a legislative program to attack the Depression had already cost them control of the House. But to take advantage of the situation, Democrats had to overcome internal divisions.

Throughout the 1920s the Democratic Party had been split between the ethnically diverse, wet (anti-Prohibition), urban wing concentrated in the North and the East and the Anglo-Saxon Protestant, rural southern and western wings. Ideological divisions on many issues separated northeastern business Democrats from western populists and urban progressives from southern conservatives.

The leading candidate for the Democratic nomination, New York's governor Franklin D. Roosevelt, had the background to overcome many of these divisions. He came from an upstate rural district, and his interest in conservation endeared him to many westerners. He had built ties to southern Democrats while serving as Wilson's assistant secretary of the navy and as a sometime resident of Warm Springs, Georgia. As governor of New York, his strong record of support for progressive social reforms appealed to urban liberals.

Roosevelt turned out to be the ideal candidate. As a distant cousin of Theodore Roosevelt, he had a recognizable name. FDR also had immense personal charm. Despite having been crippled by polio since 1921, he was a tireless campaigner and would become one of the most visible of modern presidents. Raised in wealth and educated at Groton and Harvard, he spoke in clear, direct language that ordinary Americans found reassuring.

During the campaign, Roosevelt simultaneously embraced old orthodoxies and enticed reformers with hints of radical changes. He promised to cut government spending and provide relief for the poor. FDR did not say how he would do both, but it hardly mattered. In November 1932, the Republicans were swept out of office in a tide of popular repudiation (see Map 22–2). FDR and the Democrats took control of the government with the promise of "a new deal" for the American people.

Roosevelt worked hard to develop a program to fight the Depression. While governor of New York, FDR had recruited intellectuals who provided him with an influential

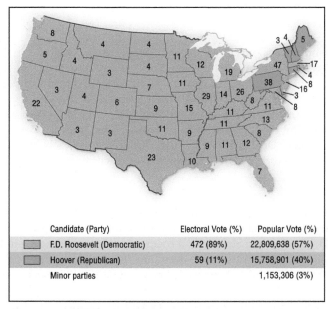

Candidate (Party)	Electoral Vote (%)	Popular Vote (%)
F.D. Roosevelt (Democratic)	472 (89%)	22,809,638 (57%)
Hoover (Republican)	59 (11%)	15,758,901 (40%)
Minor parties		1,153,306 (3%)

Map 22-2   The Presidential Election of 1932 By November 1932, most American voters blamed the Depression on Hoover and the Republicans. The Democrats, led by FDR, swept into office by huge electoral margins.

diagnosis of the Great Depression. Known as the "Brains Trust," they attempted to convince Roosevelt that the Depression was caused by the economy's fundamental defects. The core issue was the maldistribution of wealth. Because the rich held on to too large a share of the profits of American industry, the economy was producing much more than Americans could consume.

Roosevelt never fully bought the ideas of the Brains Trust nor allowed any one group to dominate his thinking. FDR's comfort with experimentation and chaos would hold his administration together and enable it to confront the complexities of the Depression. Where Hoover had retreated into dogmatism, FDR endorsed "bold, persistent experimentation." Above all, he ordered his officials, "try something." And rather than trying to unite his followers behind a single idea or policy, Roosevelt seemed to enjoy watching his advisers feud while he orchestrated their final compromises. The president, an adviser said, was "the boss, the dynamo, the works."

FDR Takes Command

In the weeks before the inauguration, the ailing American banking system took a sharp turn for the worse. In mid-February, the governor of Michigan declared an eight-day bank holiday. In one of the most important manufacturing states, nearly a million depositors could not get their money. Stock prices dropped when the news came, and the rich began shipping their gold to safer countries. Panic struck, and funds flew out of bank tellers' windows. On the morning of the inauguration, New York and Illinois joined most of the other states in calling a bank holiday. The New York Stock Exchange and Illinois Board of Trade also closed. To many, it seemed like the end of the American economy.

With commerce at a standstill, the nation turned to the new president, and Roosevelt did not disappoint. "First of all," he declared, "let me assert my firm belief that the only thing we have to fear is fear itself—nameless, unreasoning, unjustified terror." In the midst of a frightening financial collapse, these words revitalized the nation almost overnight.

Roosevelt knew words alone would not end the crisis. On his first day in office, he declared a national bank holiday to last through the end of the week. He instructed his new secretary of the Treasury to draft emergency legislation and called Congress into special session. When Congress convened on March 9, the drafting team had barely finished the bill, but Congress

FDR During One of His Fireside Chats Hoover broadcast his speeches on radio, but Roosevelt's "fireside chats" took advantage of the intimacy of the new medium.

was ready to act. Breaking all precedent, the House unanimously shouted its approval of the bill after less than a half hour of debate; the Senate voted to do the same with only seven dissents, and the president signed it into law that night. The Emergency Banking Act was a modest reform. It gave the Treasury secretary the power to determine which banks could safely reopen and which had to be reorganized. It also enabled the RFC to strengthen sound banks by buying their stocks.

On Sunday night, a week after taking office, FDR went on national radio to deliver the first of his many "fireside chats." Sixty million people tuned in to hear Roosevelt explain, in his resonant, fatherly voice, his response to the banking crisis. He assured Americans that their money would be "safer in a reopened bank than under the mattress." The government was not fully sure how solid most banks were, but the gamble worked. The next day, 12,756 banks reopened, the run stopped, and deposits started flowing into the system. The immediate crisis was over.

Once the banking crisis had been resolved in March 1933, Roosevelt wanted to ensure that the financial system would remain sound for the long run. He moved to restrict banks' speculations while guaranteeing their profitability. The Glass-Steagall Banking Act of 1933 imposed conservative banking practices nationwide. Chancy loans, stock investments, and shady business practices were outlawed, and close federal oversight guaranteed bank stability until Glass-Steagall was repealed in 1999. In addition, the new Federal Deposit Insurance Corporation protected deposits. The Banking Act of 1935 reorganized the Federal Reserve under more centralized and democratic control. Together, these laws established the credibility of the US banking system. One reason the banking system had become so vulnerable was its ties to the unregulated securities markets. So in 1933 the administration sponsored a Truth in Securities Act that required all companies issuing stock to disclose accurate information to all prospective buyers. In 1934, Congress passed the Securities and Exchange Act. Whereas the 1933 law regulated companies, the 1934 legislation regulated the markets, prohibiting insider trading and other forms of manipulation. It gave the Federal Reserve Board the power to control the supply of credit and established the Securities and Exchange Commission, which quickly became one of the largest and most effective regulatory agencies in the country.

Federal Relief

Roosevelt's unemployment programs departed sharply from Hoover's relief strategies. In May, Congress passed a bill providing a half-billion dollars for relief and creating the Federal Emergency Relief Administration (FERA) to oversee it. Local and state agencies dispensed the funds. Headed by Harry Hopkins, a shrewd social worker and Roosevelt confidant, FERA distributed money at a rapid rate. As winter came on, Hopkins convinced Roosevelt that only a massive new federal program could avert disaster. At FDR's request, Congress created the Civil Works Administration (CWA), which employed 4 million men and women. During the winter, the CWA built or renovated over half a million miles of road and tens of thousands of schools and other public buildings. The CWA was eliminated in the spring—Roosevelt did not want the nation to get used to a federal welfare program—but FERA continued to run programs on a smaller scale.

Of all the relief programs, Roosevelt was most enthusiastic about one, the Civilian Conservation Corps (CCC). FDR believed that life in the countryside and service to the nation would have a positive moral impact on the young men of the cities and on those Depression "wild boys" roaming the nation. For the CCC, these young men built roads and trails in the national parks. By the time the program ended in 1942, it had transformed America's public lands and employed over 3 million teenagers and young adults.

The Farm Crisis

"I don't want on the relief if I can help it," a Louisiana farm woman wrote to the first lady, Eleanor Roosevelt, in the fall of 1935. "I want to work for my livin'." But she was desperate. She asked Mrs. Roosevelt to send money to save the family cow "for my little children to have milk." The doctor was no longer able to give her sick child medicine "unless we pay him some for he is in debt for it." The landlord was threatening to evict them. She had turned to the first lady because of Mrs. Roosevelt's reputation for caring about the poor, but political realities would limit what the first lady, or her husband, could do to help.

By the spring of 1933, farmers were desperate. Prices of commodities such as corn, cotton, wheat, and tobacco had fallen so low that it was not even worth the cost of harvesting. The banking crisis left farmers without access to necessary credit, and millions faced foreclosure, homelessness, or dust storms.

FDR saw a stark "imbalance" between city and country as a root cause of the Depression. While the land remained the only real source of wealth, modern cities absorbed all of the countryside's water, produce, talent, and people. The Dust Bowl was a result of this ecological distortion. His aim was to restore a more even pattern of development, with small manufacturing towns, suburbs, and farms linked to centers of culture and commerce. The New Deal program that came closest to fulfilling these goals was the Tennessee Valley Authority (TVA). In his campaign, Roosevelt had endorsed a proposal to develop the Muscle Shoals property along the Tennessee River. Congress created the TVA within the first Hundred Days. The TVA was a "corporation clothed with the power of government but possessed of the flexibility and initiative of a private enterprise." According to its administrator, it aimed to change the environment, the economy, the way of life, and the "habits, social, economic, and personal" of a region that spanned nine states.

One of the most ambitious projects of the entire New Deal, the TVA was also astonishingly successful. The dams built by the TVA controlled flooding, created reservoirs for irrigation, and provided cheap hydroelectric power (see Map 22–3). Electricity improved life for millions of farm families and made it possible for industry to move into new areas, bringing jobs to some of the poorest parts of the country. The TVA took responsibility for soil conservation, reforestation, improved navigation, and the manufacture of fertilizer and aluminum. During the Roosevelt administration, the poor Tennessee–North Carolina border region went from growing cotton to manufacturing aircraft and components for nuclear weapons. Average incomes in the area increased tenfold. As a comprehensive, centrally planned development scheme, the TVA came closest to the Brains Trusters' vision of how a modern "democracy on the march" should work.

STRUGGLES FOR DEMOCRACY

The Civilian Conservation Corps and a New Brand of Environmentalism

As Franklin Roosevelt delivered his inaugural address on March 4, 1933, he proclaimed "Our greatest primary task is to put people to work." Upon his arrival in the White House, FDR immediately proposed legislation that would do just that. On March 31, Congress passed the bill establishing the Civilian Conservation Corps (CCC), a program designed to employ young men in the conservation of national forests, the prevention of soil erosion, and the creation and maintenance of state parks. Beyond putting people to work, the program changed the shape of the American landscape and the way citizens viewed both their natural environment and the federal government. Directly rejecting the small government views of the recent past, programs like the CCC highlighted the benefits of extensive government programs and an active government role in citizens' lives.

The CCC demonstrated the government's commitment not only to creating employment opportunities but also to the broader goal of responsible land use and conservation, expanding views about the nature of federal power. From 1933 to 1942, the CCC employed 3 million men who planted 2 billion trees; worked to slow soil erosion on 40 million acres of farm land; and developed 800 new state parks nationwide. The nation's terrain was forever changed by the physical labor of CCC volunteers, as was the nature of American environmentalism. From a fairly small group of progressive conservationists at the turn of the twentieth century, the movement grew in size and scope during the Great Depression, thanks to the work and education received by CCC volunteers, the benefits enjoyed by those in the communities surrounding the more than 5,000 CCC camps, and the regular media coverage—much of it positive—the general public received about this popular New Deal program. The CCC began the process by which environmental politics shifted from a purview of the elite to a concern shared by a broader segment of the American population. Those politicized by the program advocated on behalf of environmental protection and conservation long after the CCC ceased to exist.

Headed by Henry Wallace, founder of the Pioneer Hi-Bred Corn Company, the Agriculture Department was an idea factory in the first Hundred Days. An emergency farm bill gave Wallace powers to control production, buy up surpluses, regulate marketing, and levy taxes. Conservation and reclamation projects drained swamps, irrigated deserts, and sheltered the Great Plains from windstorms. The Agricultural Adjustment Act (AAA) turned agriculture into a regulated industry. After 1933, farmers, once fiercely independent, essentially worked for the federal government. The New Deal farm system

Building on conservationist views developed during the early part of the twentieth century, CCC labor created outdoor spaces intended for leisure, recreation, and renewal. Travelers could visit state parks to escape the hustle and bustle of urban life and restore themselves both mentally and physically. During the lean years of the Depression, a camping trip to a state park provided an affordable alternative to an expensive vacation at an elite hotel or resort. According to the South Carolina Forestry Commission (SCFC), parks would provide "areas where families can find rest and relaxation . . . where they can absorb the principles of forest conservation." Parks were prized for the leisure they afforded as well as for the appreciation of the natural landscape they instilled in visitors.

South Carolina was one state tremendously influenced by the CCC. Demonstrating the possibility of cooperation between national and local programs, the CCC joined forces with the SCFC to create and maintain a state park system. When the Depression began, the state had no parks. By 1942, laborers had constructed 16 state parks and 6 wayside parks along state roadways. Unlike other state parks, particularly those in the West, South Carolina parks were not created based on an area's scenic value or natural beauty. Rather, the state used land that had been overworked and stripped of agricultural

value. Through the work of the CCC, land was repurposed and value was restored toward an alternative use: recreation. CCC volunteers cleared overgrowth, planted seedling trees, and built structures or facilities, from roads and bridges to lodges and campsites, to dams and lakes. In an effort to preserve and enhance the existing landscape and history of a region, volunteers often used natural materials and local architectural styles to create continuity with the surrounding area.

Like so many New Deal programs, the CCC fundamentally changed national views. The federal government made clear its dedication to preserving the natural environment and providing public access to nature. In return, Americans became more accepting and even expectant of an active government and the possibility that they, as citizens, might play a more active role. Many of those who had volunteered in the CCC continued their conservation efforts well beyond the Depression era, taking jobs in the federal government and with conservation agencies, joining environmental groups, and advocating on behalf of similar conservation programs in the postwar years. Through New Deal programs, people came to believe not only that they had the right to respond to and benefit from public policy but also that they had the right to a voice in its creation.

permanently altered the American diet by making processed grains, grain-fed meat, sugar, and dairy products cheap and plentiful relative to unsubsidized fresh vegetables, fruits, and fish.

In many respects, however, the New Deal did little for the rural poor. Price supports and production controls helped farmers who owned their own land, whereas soil conservation, irrigation, and rural electrification tended to benefit independent commercial farmers. Subsistence farmers and the landless poor—Mexican migrant workers in the

Map 22-3   TVA Projects The Tennessee Valley Authority (TVA) was one of the most ambitious of all New Deal projects. A network of dams provided electricity, irrigation, and flood control to many of the poorest regions of the South.

Far West and tenants and sharecroppers, black and white, in the cotton South—gained little. An unintended consequence of New Deal production limits was to take work away from the poorest Americans, pushing them to migrate from the country to industrial cities.

Native Americans suffered an especially severe form of rural poverty. Shunted onto reservations in the late nineteenth century, most American Indians by 1930 were landless, miserably poor, and subjected to the corrupt paternalism of the Bureau of Indian Affairs. Alcoholism, crime, and infant mortality plagued reservations. John Collier, FDR's commissioner of Indian affairs, was determined to correct the situation, and the Indian Reorganization Act of 1934 gave him the power to try. Collier reversed decades of federal attempts to assimilate Native Americans into the mainstream. Under the New Deal, forced land sales ended, and reservations were enlarged. Tribal democracy replaced bureaucratic authority. But congressional opponents, even western liberals, resented attempts to preserve traditional culture. Indians themselves were divided over policies and goals, and what suited Pueblo communities might not work for the Navajo. As a result, although the New Deal relieved some poverty among Native Americans, it did not develop a satisfactory long-term solution.

The Blue Eagle

FDR had no fixed plan for industrial recovery and preferred to wait for business interests to agree on one before acting. Congress, however, moved independently to pass a bill aimed at spreading employment by limiting the workweek to 30 hours. Heading off what he thought an ill-conceived plan, Roosevelt offered his last proposal to become law in the first Hundred Days: the National Industrial Recovery Act. It mandated that business, labor, and government officials negotiate a "code" restructuring each industry into a national cartel. The code would set trade practices, wages, hours, and production quotas. The hope was to raise prices by limiting production while protecting the purchasing power of workers. The NIRA reversed decades of antitrust law. The act protected organized labor by guaranteeing unions the right of collective bargaining. Finally, $3.3 billion was earmarked for jobs creation through a Public Works Administration.

The NIRA was a bold idea, but it suffered from many of the same problems as Hoover's earlier schemes. It brought together hundreds of industries to draw up their codes, but the process tended to be dominated by business. Few strong unions existed, and smaller businesses were shut out, leaving the largest corporations to write the codes in their interest. For a time in 1933 and 1934, the Blue Eagle banner, the symbol of compliance with the codes, flew proudly in the windows of shops and factories. Dissatisfaction with the program soon dampened enthusiasm, and by 1935 the eagle had come to roost atop a shaky and unpopular agency.

The Second New Deal

The first Hundred Days had been extraordinary by any standard. Congress had given the president unprecedented power to regulate the economy. The financial system had been saved from collapse. Federal relief reached the unemployed. The agricultural economy was given direct federal support. The TVA had created a yardstick for public utilities. A bold experiment in industrial planning had been attempted. Almost everyone was dazzled, but not everyone was pleased. Critics noted that much of this legislation was poorly drafted, overly conservative, or just self-contradictory. If Hoover had been too rigid, FDR struck even his admirers as hopelessly flexible. By 1935, the New Deal was besieged by critics from all directions. But Roosevelt responded to political criticism and judicial setbacks by keeping Congress in session throughout the hot summer of 1935. The result was another dramatic wave of reforms known as the second New Deal.

Critics Attack from All Sides

In May 1935, one of William Randolph Hearst's emissaries traveled to Washington to warn Roosevelt that the New Deal was becoming too radical. Hearst was one of the most powerful newspaper publishers in America and, like many businessmen, had "no confidence" in Roosevelt's advisers. But by 1935 Roosevelt was losing patience with the business community. Saving capitalism was always one of Roosevelt's goals, but shortsighted capitalists never appreciated his efforts. They had their own reasons for detesting the New Deal, and they proved more potent critics than all of Roosevelt's radical opponents combined.

The fate of the Communist Party illustrates the difficulties radicals faced during the New Deal. On the one hand, the 1930s were the "heyday of American Communism," as perhaps a quarter of a million disillusioned Americans joined the Communist Party (CPUSA). The Communists organized labor unions and took the lead in defending the Scottsboro Boys, nine young African American men falsely accused of raping two white women in Alabama. On the other hand, the party's appeal was greatest after 1935, when, on orders from the Soviet Union, it adopted a "popular front" strategy in support of the New Deal. The Communists were most popular when they surrendered their revolutionary aims. Most of those who joined had left the party by the end of the decade.

Populist radicals gave Roosevelt more trouble. Father Charles Coughlin was a Catholic priest in Detroit who attracted listeners to his weekly radio show by blaming the Depression on international bankers and Wall Street. His solution was to nationalize the banking system and inflate the currency. At first the radio priest defended Roosevelt and blamed the New Deal on Communist and Jewish influence. But by 1935 Coughlin turned on the president. He formed his own organization, the National Union for Social Justice, to pressure Congress for further reforms.

A California physician, Dr. Francis Townsend, offered an agenda appealing to older Americans devastated by the Depression. Through a transaction tax of 2 percent, the government would fund retirement pensions of $200 per month. By requiring elderly retirees to spend all of their pensions each month, the program was supposed to pump money into the economy and stimulate a recovery. Huey Long's "Share Our Wealth" program was more comprehensive than Townsend's and more popular than Coughlin's. As governor of Louisiana, Long slapped steep taxes on the oil industry that he used for roads, schools, hospitals, and Louisiana State University. In the process, he amassed nearly dictatorial powers, controlling the legislature and the state police. At first, Long was a loyal but critical supporter of FDR, but by 1934 he was proposing his own alternative to the New Deal.

Long believed the Depression was caused by the maldistribution of income. His program for recovery called for the radical redistribution of wealth through confiscatory taxes on the rich and a guaranteed minimum income of $2,500 per year. Townsend's, Coughlin's, and Long's plans all contained truths about the American economy. The currency did need to be inflated. Elderly Americans were indeed desperate, and wealth was unequally distributed. Roosevelt eventually defused these movements by adopting parts of their programs.

The business community's rising hostility concerned FDR as he prepared for his 1936 campaign. It would be years before bankers admitted that the New Deal had saved the financial system. Wall Street never admitted it. And most industrialists became vocal critics of the NIRA. As criticism grew, a conservative US Supreme Court moved to strike down many of the key laws of the first Hundred Days. On May 27, 1935, in *Schechter Poultry Corporation v. United States*, the Court invalidated the NIRA. The case had been brought by a small poultry company but was financed by larger companies out to kill the Blue Eagle. The justices ruled the NIRA unconstitutional in a way that made it difficult for Congress to regulate the national economy to any significant degree. Roosevelt feared the setback would undo most of his achievements, and his fears were borne out in January 1936, when the Court overturned the Agricultural Adjustment Act.

The Second Hundred Days

FDR loved a good fight. No longer concerned about attracting support from business, he welcomed criticism and shot right back. After 1935 the rhetoric became noticeably more radical. When the Supreme Court invalidated the NIRA, Roosevelt kept Congress in session through a sweltering summer and forced through a raft of legislation in a "second Hundred Days," which began the second New Deal.

A few of the new proposals were meant to salvage pieces of the NIRA and AAA or to silence radical critics. Hoping to undermine the "crackpot ideas" of Huey Long, Roosevelt proposed a Revenue Act to encourage a "wider distribution of the wealth." It raised estate and corporate taxes and pushed personal income taxes in the top bracket up to 79 percent. Despite the political motives behind the bill, it made economic sense. Before the 1935 Revenue Act, most New Deal programs had been financed by regressive sales and excise taxes. Thereafter, programs were funded with progressive income taxes that fell most heavily on those best able to pay.

The first New Deal had been preoccupied with the emergency of 1933. The second New Deal left a more enduring legacy. The administration finished its program to ensure the long-term security of the financial system and extend the relief programs that had helped so many to survive. It created a social security system that anchored the American welfare state for the rest of the century. With organized labor it created a new and powerful Democratic Party coalition. By the time Congress adjourned in late August 1935, the most important achievements of the New Deal were in place.

Social Security for Some

Bolstered by big Democratic gains in the 1934 elections, FDR pursued a massive effort to fund work relief by sponsoring the Emergency Relief Appropriations Bill. Providing nearly $5 billion, more than the entire 1932 federal budget, the bill rejuvenated the relief programs of the first New Deal and created a new Works Progress Administration (WPA), headed by Harry Hopkins. The WPA lasted for eight years, employing as many as 3.3 million Americans. WPA workers built bridges, schools, libraries, sewer systems, the Blue Ridge Parkway, and more than 800 airports. The WPA commissioned artists to decorate post offices and historians to collect the stories of mill workers and former slaves. At Indiana University, the WPA paid undergraduates to build a student union. WPA lexicographers wrote a Hebrew-English dictionary. The program was hugely popular.

Critics of the WPA complained with some justice about meaningless "make-work" jobs and unqualified workers. Political corruption was a more serious problem. WPA officials, especially at the local level, often used the agency as a patronage machine, favoring loyal party regulars with contracts and jobs. In many states, particularly in the South, officials openly discriminated against African Americans. The WPA was never able to employ all those who needed work, but for millions of Americans it provided immediate relief from the very real prospect of hunger and misery.

WPA Mural Japanese artist Eitaro Ishigaki painted this mural showing American Revolutionary War figures at the Harlem Courthouse in New York City in 1938.

The New Deal also created a permanent system of long-term economic security. In 1932, there were no national programs of unemployment insurance, workers' compensation, old-age pensions, or aid to needy children, and the states were only slightly more able to care for citizens. Most Americans had little or no protection from economic calamity.

The Social Security Act of 1935 took a critical first step toward providing such protection. It established matching grants to states that set up their own systems of workers' compensation, unemployment insurance, and aid to families with dependent children. More important, the federal government itself created a huge social security system that guaranteed pensions to millions of elderly Americans. FDR insisted that it be funded as an insurance plan, with payroll taxes paid by employees and employers. He hoped that this would protect the system from the political attacks that welfare programs typically encountered.

Most New Dealers hoped to go much further. Secretary of Labor Frances Perkins wanted to include agricultural laborers and domestic servants, mostly women and African Americans, in the new social security system. But that would have provoked enough opposition from southern conservatives to kill the entire program. The administration also preferred federal- rather than state-run programs. There was, however, no federal bureaucracy in place to run such programs, and there was fierce opposition to the idea of taking such programs away from the states.

Local and factional opposition limited the New Deal's plans for nationalized social welfare and economic security. Welfare and insurance programs were weaker in the South than in the North and weaker for women and African Americans than for white men. Despite such strong opposition, the New Deal accomplished many of its goals. By 1939 every state had a program of unemployment insurance and assistance to the elderly. Almost overnight the social security system became the federal government's first huge social welfare bureaucracy. More Americans than ever before were now protected from the ravages of unemployment, disability, poverty, and old age.

Labor and the New Deal

During the 1930s, unions took a new role in America's political and economic life. The number of Americans organized in unions leaped by the millions, and by 1940 nearly one in four non–farm workers was unionized. Labor organizations were able to enroll workers in core industries, including steel, rubber, electronics, and automobiles. Unions also became key players in the Democratic Party. None of the leading New Dealers, Roosevelt included, had anticipated this in 1932, but in critical ways the New Deal fostered the growth of organized labor and its inclusion in the Democratic electoral coalition.

Unlike past administrations, Roosevelt's had never demonstrated outright hostility toward unions. Rather, through the 1930s FDR moved from grudging acceptance to open support for organized labor. Across the country, workers responded to the change. Unions were now allowed to run organizing drives, and labor began to flex its muscle with a spontaneous wave of strikes. Mill workers in the South launched brave, but doomed, strikes against textile manufacturers. Dockworkers in San Francisco organized a successful general strike throughout the city. At the same time, the NIRA inspired a talented group of national leaders, in particular John L. Lewis of the United Mine Workers, Sidney Hillman of the Amalgamated Clothing Workers, and David Dubinsky of the International Ladies' Garment Workers.

Employers fought back against this new militancy. They used all the methods to intimidate workers—espionage, blacklisting, and armed assault—that had once worked so well. But when it became clear that the federal government would now protect workers seeking to organize and bargain collectively, employers formed company unions to thwart workers' independent action. By 1935, the employers seemed to be winning, particularly when the Supreme Court declared the NIRA, and its protection of union rights, unconstitutional. In 1935, worker militancy declined, and the unionization drive seemed stalled. But the hopes of organized labor were kept alive by an influential and imaginative liberal senator from New York named Robert Wagner.

Wagner took the lead in expanding the NIRA's limited labor protections into the National Labor Relations Act, also known as the Wagner Act. Although he had few ties to organized labor, Wagner believed workers had a basic right to join unions. He also hoped that effective unions would stimulate the economy by raising wages, thereby building consumer purchasing power. Like the NIRA provisions, the Wagner Act guaranteed workers the right to bargain collectively with their employers, but it also outlawed company unions, prohibited employers from firing workers after a strike, and restricted many other antiunion tactics. Most important, the Wagner Act created the National Labor Relations Board (NLRB) to enforce these provisions. In the summer of 1935, FDR declared the Wagner Act "must" legislation, and the bill became law.

While Wagner and his colleagues moved in Congress, John L. Lewis and Sidney Hillman took another course. In 1935, they pressed the conservative leadership of the American Federation of Labor to accept the principle of industrial unions, which would organize workers in an entire sector of the economy, such as steel. AFL traditionalists rejected the idea and held fast to the notion that workers should be organized by their crafts, not by whole industries. Thwarted by AFL leadership, Lewis, Hillman, and their allies formed a rival organization that eventually became the Congress of Industrial Organizations (CIO).

The CIO began organizing some of the most powerful and prosperous industries in the country. The government's new attitude toward organized labor played an important role in the CIO's initial success. For example, when the United Automobile Workers initiated a series of sit-down strikes against General Motors, neither Roosevelt nor the Democratic governor of Michigan sent in troops to remove workers from the factories they were occupying. This clear message to the leaders of industry helped to win the strike against America's most powerful corporation. The NLRB also protected the new unions from an employer counterattack during the recession of 1937.

By the late 1930s, a crucial political alliance had formed. A newly vigorous labor movement had become linked to a reinvigorated national Democratic Party. Thanks to this alliance, American industrial workers entered a new era. Having won the ability to organize with the help of the government, industrial workers used their power to increase wages, enhance job security, improve working conditions, and secure their retirements. Organized labor now had a stake in preserving the system from collapse. As much as the banking and financial reforms of the first New Deal, the successful unionization of industrial workers helped stabilize American capitalism.

The New Deal Coalition

Roosevelt believed that to overcome his varied opposition and win reelection he needed to create a coalition far broader than that of 1932. By 1936, the Democratic Party was transformed in fundamental ways. For the first time since the Civil War, a majority of voters identified themselves as Democrats, and the Democrats remained the majority party for decades to come. FDR achieved this feat by forging a powerful coalition between the competing wings of the party. In the end, however, the same coalition that made the New Deal possible also limited its progressivism.

The rural South had been overwhelmingly Democratic for a century, but urban voters in the North became the party's new base. This shift was well under way during the 1920s, when Al Smith's two presidential bids attracted ethnic blue-collar voters. FDR offered prominent ethnic Americans an unprecedented number of federal appointments. Jews and Catholics (Italian, as well as Irish) served Roosevelt as advisers, judges, and cabinet officers. More important, thousands of working-class city dwellers found jobs with the CWA, the WPA, or the CCC. Those New Deal programs generated a flood of patronage appointments that endeared Roosevelt to local Democratic machines. Finally, the unions reciprocated FDR's support for labor. The CIO alone poured $600,000 into Roosevelt's campaign, replacing the money no longer forthcoming from wealthy donors, and its members formed an army of campaign volunteers. By 1940, the Democratic Party became the party of the urban working class.

The New Deal's programs also explain a dramatic shift of allegiance among African American voters. Since Reconstruction, southern blacks had supported the party of Lincoln, but as they migrated to the urban North they gained voting strength and abandoned the Republican Party. By 1936, northern blacks voted overwhelmingly for FDR, even though the Democrats were weak on the issue of civil rights. The New Deal included no legislation against discrimination, and FDR silently allowed Congress to reject anti-lynching laws. New Deal agencies did offer more assistance to poor, unemployed African Americans than previous federal programs, and some leading New Dealers supported equal rights. Mary McLeod Bethune, a prominent African American educator and close friend of Eleanor Roosevelt, served the New Deal as director of the National Youth Administration's Office of Negro Affairs, which gave jobs and training to some 300,000 young African Americans. Besides controlling her own Special Negro Fund, Bethune convinced other New Deal administrators to open their programs to blacks. With perhaps a million African American families depending on the WPA by 1939, black voters had solid reasons for joining the New Deal coalition.

A similar logic explains why women reformers threw their support to the Democrats in the 1930s. Once again, FDR had no feminist agenda, and New Deal programs discriminated against women by offering lower pay and restricting jobs by sex. But women also benefited in unprecedented numbers from New Deal welfare and jobs programs. For the first time in American history, a woman, Frances Perkins, was appointed to the cabinet.

The most prominent female reformer associated with the New Deal was Eleanor Roosevelt. She was in many ways the last great representative of a woman's reform tradition that flourished in the Progressive Era. She had worked in a settlement house and campaigned for suffrage and progressive causes. Eleanor and Franklin made a remarkable political couple. Millions of Americans read Eleanor's opinions in her weekly newspaper column, "My Day." She became for many the conscience of the New Deal, the person closest to the president who spoke most forcefully for the downtrodden. Her well-deserved reputation for compassion also protected her husband. Liberals who might have been more critical of the New Deal instead relied on Eleanor Roosevelt to push the president toward more progressive reform. At the same time, conservatives who were charmed by FDR's personality blamed the faults of the New Deal on his wife. "It was very simple," one southern journalist explained. "Credit Franklin, better known as He, for all the things you like, and blame Eleanor, better known as She, or 'that woman,' for all the things you don't like."

Although four years of the New Deal had not lifted the Depression, the economy was making headway. Jobs programs had put millions of Americans to work; the banking crisis was over; the rural economy had been stabilized. Based on this record and the backing of his powerful coalition of southern whites, northern urban voters, the labor movement, and many other Americans, FDR won reelection by a landslide in 1936. He captured over 60 percent of the popular vote and, in the Electoral College, defeated his Republican opponent Alf Landon in every state but Maine and Vermont. Landon, the governor of Kansas, even lost his home state. The new Democratic coalition also won sweeping command of the Congress, and Roosevelt now stood at the peak of his power.

Crisis of the New Deal

In 1937, it seemed as if Roosevelt was unbeatable, but within a year the New Deal was all but paralyzed. A politically costly fight to "pack" the Supreme Court at last gave FDR's conservative opponents a winning issue. A sharp recession encouraged the New Deal's enemies and provoked an intellectual crisis within the administration. In 1938, when the Republicans regained much of their congressional strength, the reform energies of the New Deal were largely spent. Within a year the nation turned its attention to rising threats from overseas.

Conservatives Counterattack

With conservative opponents vanquished, it seemed as if New Dealers could finish the job begun in 1933. Administration progressives such as Frances Perkins hoped that existing legislation could now be strengthened.

FDR seemed poised to launch the next great wave of New Deal reforms, but one apparently immovable barrier stood in the way: the US Supreme Court. The Court had already struck down the NIRA and the AAA, and recent rulings made it seem that neither Social Security nor the Wagner Act was safe from the Court's nine "old men." Roosevelt wanted to change the Court. He had not yet had the opportunity to appoint any new justices, and pundits joked that the elderly judges refused to die. Sure that a constitutional amendment supporting his program would take too long or fail, FDR launched a reckless and unpopular effort to "reform" the Court. He proposed legislation that would allow the president to appoint a new justice for every sitting member of the Court over 70 years of age. This "court packing" plan, as opponents labeled it, would have given the president as many as six new appointments.

Conservatives had long complained of FDR's "dictatorial" powers, and the court plan seemed to confirm their warnings. They skillfully cultivated congressional allies, giving Democrats the lead in opposing the court reform. Even his allies refused to campaign for the president's bill, and it took all of FDR's political power and prestige to keep it before a hostile Congress. By the end of the summer of 1937, the bill was defeated.

Ironically, Roosevelt won his point. Several justices soon retired, giving FDR the critical appointments he needed, and the Supreme Court backed away from its narrow

AMERICA AND THE WORLD

The 1936 Olympics

Whereas Franklin Roosevelt offered the American people a New Deal to reform capitalism and preserve democracy, other governments responded differently to the global economic crisis. In 1933, Germany came under control of the National Socialist or Nazi Party. Led by Adolf Hitler, the Nazi government suspended civil liberties, eliminated political opposition, and embraced a nationalist edict based on the celebrated racial superiority of the Aryan race. A fascist dictatorship replaced the nation's fledgling democracy.

In 1931, before the Nazi seizure of power, in an effort to bring Germany back into the global fold and support its democratic government, the International Olympic Committee (IOC) chose Berlin, Germany, as the host city for the 1936 Summer Olympics. After Hitler's rise to power, the international community questioned the morality of participating in the games, given his government's anti-Semitism and the repressive policies targeting Germany's Jewish population. In response to international concerns, in June 1933, the German Olympic Committee declared that German Jews would not be excluded from the German Olympic teams. In December 1933, Germany pledged a policy of nondiscrimination, reprinted in the New York Times, which, while inconsistent with Nazi practices that had essentially banned German Jews from athletic events and sports clubs, was accepted by the IOC, reflecting the organization's priority of ensuring the successful growth of the Olympic Games.

As they considered whether or not to boycott the Games, many nations looked to the United States, given its cadre of formidable athletes. American opinion, reflected by debate within the Amateur Athletic Union (AAU), was divided. Jeremiah Titus Mahoney, a former Olympian and New York Supreme Court justice, believed participation in the Games would hurt the Olympic movement and violated the American Olympic Committee's (AOC) rules against discrimination based on race or creed. On the other side, Avery Brundage, a self-made Chicago millionaire, also of the AAU, opposed the idea of a boycott and believed politics and sports should be regarded separately. In 1934, as president of the AOC, Brundage traveled to Germany and received further assurances of nondiscrimination, reaffirming his support for US participation in the Berlin games. In December 1935, the AAU narrowly voted in support of sending a US team to the Games.

The American government remained committed to nonintervention on the issue, claiming no legal or moral obligation to oppose the Games. Some of Roosevelt's

conception of the role of the federal government. Nevertheless, FDR's court plan proved a costly mistake, and its defeat emboldened his opponents. In November 1937, the administration's critics issued a Conservative Manifesto calling for balanced budgets, states' rights, lower taxes, and the defense of private property and the capitalist system,

1936 Olympics Nazi flags draped Olympic Stadium in Berlin as the Olympic torch arrived on August 1, 1936.

advisers feared diplomatic pressure would worsen the condition of German Jews while others focused on the need to maintain civil relations with Germany in order to ensure the collection of German war debt. Rather than act decisively on behalf of Germany's Jewish population, Roosevelt walked a political tightrope to appease interests at home and maintain international calm.

Joseph Goebbels, minister of propaganda, had convinced Hitler of the positive publicity the Games might afford his regime. A successful hosting of the Olympic Games would enhance Germany's global reputation, highlight its technological and military might, and demonstrate the rightfulness of Hitler's views regarding the supremacy of the Aryan race. The Berlin Games could legitimize modern Germany.

The Nazis masterfully orchestrated the Games, presenting a sanitized Germany to the international community. The nation took a temporary reprieve from the persecution of its Jewish citizens, intended to distract international visitors, especially the international press, from the harsh anti-Semitic realities of the Third Reich. The Games began with a spectacular opening ceremony (the first of its kind) in a newly constructed stadium seating 100,000 spectators, where flags of the Olympic Rings and the Nazi swastika flew side by side. The Olympic torch arrived in Berlin after a journey that began in Greece (the first use of the torch in the modern Olympics). The Reich greeted members of the international press as VIPs and provided them carte blanche to any of the advanced technological communication tools Germany had to offer. The expectation, of course, was communication of Germany's might and modernity. Given their limited access to critical sources and Germany's allowance of a token Jewish competitor (fencer Helene Meyer), members of the press took away a positive impression of their host nation whose leadership understood very clearly the powerful pairing of politics and sport.

themes that would rally conservatives for the remainder of the century. Behind the manifesto lay some hard political realities that drove the conservatives into opposition.

Southern congressmen, for example, desired to preserve white privilege. The new federal programs disturbed entrenched systems of political and economic dominance.

Southern conservatives blamed the New Deal. "You ask any nigger in the street who's the greatest president in the world. Nine out of ten will tell you Franklin Roosevelt," one white southerner declared. "That's why I think he's so dangerous."

In the rural South and West, there were fears that the New Deal was growing too close to the urban working class in the Northeast. Against this trend, conservatives appealed to the deeply rooted American suspicion of central government. Still, conservatives were not strong enough to block all New Deal legislation. Farm-state representatives needed Roosevelt's support. In late 1937, the administration succeeded in passing housing and farm tenancy reforms. In 1938, Congress passed the Fair Labor Standards Act, requiring the payment of overtime after 40 hours of work in a week, establishing a minimum wage, and eliminating child labor. Even with flagging support, FDR could enact proposals blocked during the Progressive Era.

The 1938 congressional elections gave conservatives the strength they needed to bring New Deal reform to an end. The president campaigned against leading conservatives, but he failed. Republicans gained 75 seats in the House and were now strong enough in the Senate to organize an effective anti–New Deal coalition with southern Democrats. By then, a jolting recession had created a crisis of confidence within the New Deal itself.

The Liberal Crisis of Confidence

During the 1936 campaign, Roosevelt was stung by conservative criticism of his failure to balance the budget. He had leveled the same charge against Hoover four years earlier, but the demands of the Depression made it difficult and dangerous to reduce government spending. Deficit spending seemed to help resuscitate the economy.

Hoping to silence conservative critics, Roosevelt ordered a sharp cutback in relief expenditures in 1937. On top of an ill-timed contraction of the money supply and the removal of $2 billion from the economy by the new Social Security taxes, the measure had a disastrous effect. Once again, the stock market crashed and industrial production plummeted. Even the relatively healthy automobile, rubber, and electrical industries were seriously hurt. Opponents carped about the "Roosevelt Recession" and accused the administration of destroying business confidence.

Time Line

▼**1929**
Stock market crash

▼**1930**
Hawley-Smoot Tariff enacted

▼**1931**
National Credit Corporation
  authorized

▼**1932**
Franklin D. Roosevelt elected
  president

▼**1933**
FDR declares a bank holiday
First Hundred Days
Emergency Banking Act passed

Civilian Conservation Corps
  (CCC)
United States goes off the gold
  standard
Agricultural Adjustment Act
  (AAA)
Tennessee Valley Authority (TVA)
Truth in Securities Act
National Industrial Recovery Act
  (NIRA)

Among the president's advisers, the competition between the budget balancers and the deficit spenders intensified. This was an important turning point in the New Deal and in twentieth-century American politics. Until 1938, the orthodoxy that associated economic health with balanced budgets was entrenched in government and the business community. The recession of 1937–1938 converted young New Dealers to the newer economic theories associated with John Maynard Keynes, the great English economist. During periods of economic stagnation, Keynes argued, the government needs to stimulate recovery through deficit spending. The goal of fiscal policy was no longer to encourage production, but rather to increase the purchasing power of ordinary consumers. Roosevelt never fully embraced these theories, but more and more members of his administration did. Moreover, the breathtaking economic revival created by massive government expenditures in World War II seemed to validate Keynesian economics. Until the 1980s, presidents of both parties subscribed to Keynesian theory, although they differed on what kind of government programs federal spending should buy.

Conclusion

The New Deal did not bring an end to the Depression, and this was undoubtedly its greatest failure. Nevertheless, FDR achieved other important goals. "I want to save our system," he said in 1935, "the capitalistic system." By this standard, the New Deal was a smashing success. By allowing Americans to survive the worst collapse in the history of capitalism while preserving core freedoms, the New Deal reaffirmed democracy at a time when most of the industrialized world chose dictatorship. Through the expansion of the federal government, the New Deal also created a system of security for the vast majority of Americans. National systems of unemployment compensation, old-age pensions, and welfare programs were born during the 1930s, and the nature of Americans' relationship to the government changed fundamentally. With the creation of the federal system of security, the government accepted at least some responsibility for citizens' economic security. Farm owners received new protections, as did the very soil of the nation. Workers were granted the right to organize, hours of labor were limited, child

Glass-Steagall Banking Act
Farm Credit Act

▼**1935**
Second Hundred Days
NIRA declared unconstitutional
National Labor Relations
(Wagner) Act
Social Security Act

▼**1936**
Agricultural Adjustment Act
(AAA) overturned
FDR reelected

▼**1937**
FDR announces "court packing"
plan
Economy goes into recession

▼**1938**
Second Agricultural Adjustment
Act
Fair Labor Standards Act
New Deal opponents win big in
Congress

▼**1939**
Administrative Reorganization
Act

labor ended, and wages were held above the bare minimum. The financial system was stabilized and strengthened. America was a safer place at the end of the 1930s, but the world had become more dangerous. After 1938 the Roosevelt administration was increasingly preoccupied with the threatening behavior of nations that had responded poorly to the challenge of the Great Depression.

Who, What, Where

Berlin 702

Civilian Conservation Corps (CCC) 691

Dust Bowl 680

Hoover, Herbert 685

Hoovervilles 685

Long, Huey 696

New Deal 680

Roosevelt, Eleanor 691

Roosevelt, Franklin D. 687

Social Security 697

Tennessee Valley Authority (TVA) 691

Wagner Act 699

Review Questions

1. Did the stock market crash cause the Great Depression?

2. How did Roosevelt's philosophy of government differ from Hoover's?

3. What setbacks caused FDR to launch a second New Deal?

Critical-Thinking Questions

1. Compare the American response to the Depression with that of Britain, Germany, and Japan. Why did other industrial countries choose different paths?

2. What were Roosevelt's attributes as a leader? What aspects of his style inspired confidence or animosity?

3. Histories of the Depression focus on national statistics and large-scale programs. How could you retell the story of the 1930s from a local, personal perspective?

Suggested Readings

Brinkley, Alan. *The End of Reform: New Deal Liberalism in Depression and War.* New York: Knopf, 1995.

Cohen, Lizabeth. *Making a New Deal: Industrial Workers in Chicago, 1919–1939.* New York: Cambridge University Press, 1990.

Dickstein, Morris. *Dancing in the Dark: A Cultural History of the Great Depression.* New York: W. W. Norton, 2009.

George Washington University. The Eleanor Roosevelt Papers. https://erpapers.columbian.gwu. edu/

Wall, Wendy. *Inventing the "American Way": The Politics of Consensus from the New Deal to the Civil Rights Movement.* New York: Oxford University Press, 2008.

For further review materials and resource information, please visit www.oup.com/us/oakes-mcgerr

CHAPTER 22: A GREAT DEPRESSION AND A NEW DEAL, 1929–1940
Primary Sources

22.1 FRANKLIN D. ROOSEVELT, FIRST INAUGURAL ADDRESS (1933)

As he faced the nation on March 4, 1933, the newly elected President Franklin Delano Roosevelt spoke candidly, but optimistically, to the American people. While admitting the terrible realities of the Depression, he also reassured the American public that they had not failed, that the nation could—and would—be restored. He called upon citizens to trust in his leadership and articulated a plan for government action as a means of solving the economic crisis.

I am certain that my fellow Americans expect that on my induction into the Presidency I will address them with a candor and a decision which the present situation of our Nation impels. This is preeminently the time to speak the truth, the whole truth, frankly and boldly. Nor need we shrink from honestly facing conditions in our country today. This great Nation will endure as it has endured, will revive and will prosper. So, first of all, let me assert my firm belief that the only thing we have to fear is fear itself—nameless, unreasoning, unjustified terror which paralyzes needed efforts to convert retreat into advance. In every dark hour of our national life a leadership of frankness and vigor has met with that understanding and support of the people themselves which is essential to victory. I am convinced that you will again give that support to leadership in these critical days.

In such a spirit on my part and on yours we face our common difficulties. They concern, thank God, only material things. Values have shrunken to fantastic levels; taxes have risen; our ability to pay has fallen; government of all kinds is faced by serious curtailment of income; the means of exchange are frozen in the currents of trade; the withered leaves of industrial enterprise lie on every side; farmers find no markets for their produce; the savings of many years in thousands of families are gone. More important, a host of unemployed citizens face the grim problem of existence, and an equally great number toil with little return. Only a foolish optimist can deny the dark realities of the moment.

Yet our distress comes from no failure of substance. We are stricken by no plague of locusts. Compared with the perils which our forefathers conquered because they believed and were not afraid, we have still much to be thankful for. Nature still offers her bounty and human efforts have multiplied it. Plenty is at our doorstep, but a generous use of it languishes in the very sight of the supply. Primarily this is because rulers of the exchange of mankind's goods have failed through their own stubbornness and their own incompetence, have admitted their failure, and have abdicated. Practices of the unscrupulous money changers stand indicted in the court of public opinion, rejected by the hearts and minds of men.

True they have tried, but their efforts have been cast in the pattern of an outworn tradition. Faced by failure of credit they have proposed only the lending of more money. Stripped of the lure of profit by which to induce our people to follow their false leadership, they have resorted to exhortations, pleading tearfully for restored confidence. They know only the rules of a generation of self-seekers. They have no vision, and when there is no vision the people perish.

The money changers have fled from their high seats in the temple of our civilization. We may now restore that temple to the ancient truths. The measure of the restoration lies in the extent to which we apply social values more noble than mere monetary profit. Happiness lies not in the mere possession of money; it lies in the joy of achievement, in the thrill of creative effort. The joy and moral stimulation of work no longer must be forgotten in the mad chase of evanescent profits. These dark days will be worth all they cost us if they teach us that our true destiny is not to be ministered unto but to minister to ourselves and to our fellow men.

Recognition of the falsity of material wealth as the standard of success goes hand in hand with the abandonment of the false belief that public office and high political position are to be valued only by the standards of pride of place and personal profit; and there must be an end to a conduct in banking and in business which too often has given to a sacred trust the likeness of callous and selfish wrongdoing. Small wonder that confidence languishes, for it thrives only on honesty, on honor, on the sacredness of obligations, on faithful protection, on unselfish performance; without them it cannot live.

Restoration calls, however, not for changes in ethics alone. This Nation asks for action, and action now.

Our greatest primary task is to put people to work. This is no unsolvable problem if we face it wisely and courageously. It can be accomplished in part by direct recruiting by the Government itself, treating the task as we would treat the emergency of a war, but at the same time, through this employment, accomplishing greatly needed projects to stimulate and reorganize the use of our natural resources.

Hand in hand with this we must frankly recognize the overbalance of population in our industrial centers and, by engaging on a national scale in a redistribution, endeavor to provide a better use of the land for those best fitted for the land. The task can be helped by definite efforts to raise the values of agricultural products and with this the power to purchase the output of our cities. It can be helped by preventing realistically the tragedy of the growing loss through foreclosure of our small homes and our farms. It can be helped by insistence that the Federal, State, and local governments act forthwith on the demand that their cost be drastically reduced. It can be helped by the unifying of relief activities which today are often scattered, uneconomical, and unequal. It can be helped by national planning for and supervision of all forms of transportation and of communications and other utilities which have a definitely public character. There are many ways in which it can be helped, but it can never be helped merely by talking about it. We must act and act quickly.

Finally, in our progress toward a resumption of work we require two safeguards against a return of the evils of the old order: there must be a strict supervision of all banking and credits and investments, so that there will be an end to speculation with other people's money; and there must be provision for an adequate but sound currency.

These are the lines of attack. I shall presently urge upon a new Congress, in special session, detailed measures for their fulfillment, and I shall seek the immediate assistance of the several States.

Through this program of action we address ourselves to putting our own national house in order and making income balance outgo. Our international trade relations, though vastly important, are in point of time and necessity secondary to the establishment of a sound national economy. I favor as a practical policy the putting of first things first. I shall spare no effort to restore world trade by international economic readjustment, but the emergency at home cannot wait on that accomplishment.

The basic thought that guides these specific means of national recovery is not narrowly nationalistic. It is the insistence, as a first consideration, upon the interdependence of the various elements in and parts of the United States—a recognition of the old and permanently important manifestation of the American spirit of the pioneer. It is the way to recovery. It is the immediate way. It is the strongest assurance that the recovery will endure. In the field of world policy I would dedicate this Nation to the policy of the good neighbor—the neighbor who resolutely respects himself and, because he does so, respects the rights of others—the neighbor who respects his obligations and respects the sanctity of his agreements in and with a world of neighbors.

If I read the temper of our people correctly, we now realize as we have never realized before our interdependence on each other; that we cannot merely take but we must give as well; that if we are to go forward, we must move as a trained and loyal army willing to sacrifice for the good of a common discipline, because without such discipline no progress is made, no leadership becomes effective. We are, I know, ready and willing to submit our lives and property to such discipline, because it makes possible a leadership which aims at a larger good. This I propose to offer, pledging that the larger purposes will bind upon us all as a First Inaugural Address sacred obligation with a unity of duty hitherto evoked only in time of armed strife.

With this pledge taken, I assume unhesitatingly the leadership of this great army of our people dedicated to a disciplined attack upon our common problems. Action in this image and to this end is feasible under the form of government which we have inherited from our ancestors. Our Constitution is so simple and practical that it is possible always to meet extraordinary needs by changes in emphasis and arrangement without loss of essential form. That is why our constitutional system has proved itself the most superbly enduring political mechanism the modern world has produced. It has met every stress of vast expansion of territory, of foreign wars, of bitter internal strife, of world relations. It is to be hoped that the normal balance of Executive and legislative authority may be wholly adequate to meet the unprecedented task before us. But it may be that an unprecedented demand and need for undelayed action may call for temporary departure from that normal balance of public procedure.

I am prepared under my constitutional duty to recommend the measures that a stricken Nation in the midst of a stricken world may require. These measures, or such other measures as the Congress may build out of its experience and wisdom, I shall seek, within my constitutional authority, to bring to speedy adoption.

But in the event that the Congress shall fail to take one of these two courses, and in the event that the national emergency is still critical, I shall not evade the clear course of duty that will then confront me. I shall ask the Congress for the one remaining instrument to meet the crisis—broad Executive power to wage a war against the emergency, as great as the power that would be given to me if we were in fact invaded by a foreign foe. For the trust reposed in me I will return the courage and the devotion that befit the time. I can do no less.

We face the arduous days that lie before us in the warm courage of national unity; with the clear consciousness of seeking old and precious moral values; with the clean satisfaction that comes from the stern performance of duty by old and young alike. We aim at the assurance of a rounded and permanent national life. We do not distrust the future of essential democracy. The people of the United States have not failed. In their need they have registered a mandate that they want direct, vigorous action. They have asked for discipline and direction under leadership. They have made me the present instrument of their wishes. In the spirit of the gift I take it.

In this dedication of a Nation we humbly ask the blessing of God. May He protect each and every one of us. May He guide me in the days to come.

Source: The Public Papers and Addresses of Franklin D. Roosevelt with a Special Introduction and Explanatory Notes by President Roosevelt, Volume 2: The Year of Crisis, 1933 (New York: Random House, 1938), pp. 11–16.

22.2 VISUAL DOCUMENTS: DOROTHEA LANGE, FARM SECURITY ADMINISTRATION PHOTOGRAPHS (1930s)

Dorothea Lange photographed men and women as part of the Farm Security Administration's photography project. Through her work she portrayed the challenges people faced as they attempted to make a living during the harsh economic circumstances of the Great Depression. Images of families traveling in cars tightly packed with possessions as they searched for employment, living in makeshift tents as they moved from one work site to the next, and attempting to maintain some element of normalcy in the midst of financial struggle revealed the toll the Depression took on the American people.

Drought refugees from Oklahoma looking for work in the pea fields of California, near San Jose Mission. March 1935.

Florence Owens Thompson, age 32, mother of seven children. Nipomo, California. February or March 1936.

Wife and child of migrant worker encamped near Winters, California. November 1936.

Source: Dorothea Lange, photographer. US Farm Security Administration, Office of War Information Photograph Collection. Library of Congress Prints and Photographs Division, Washington, DC.

22.3 LETTERS TO ELEANOR ROOSEVELT (1936)

As American citizens suffered through the lean years of the Great Depression, they often found themselves having to do without the most basic necessities. New Deal programs helped many to regain their footing, but families still struggled to get by. The relationship President Franklin D. Roosevelt and First Lady Eleanor Roosevelt cultivated through their media outreach and demonstration of compassion for the poor led some citizens to contact the Roosevelts directly as they searched for assistance through hard times.

Anderson County Schools
Clinton, Tennessee
January 26, 1936

Mrs. Franklin D. Roosevelt
Washington, D.C.

My dear Mrs. Roosevelt,
You may think I am a very insignificant person to be writing to a person of your standing and ability but by reading your article and hearing your talks I know you are real and have an interest in people even my dear little needy boys and girls of the mountain schools.

I am Rural Supervisor of schools in my county. I have forty schools to supervise. Due to insufficient clothing and food many are unable to attend schools.

I wish it were possible for you to see some of the conditions. It is not uncommon for a child to have but one dress or one shirt. They have to stay at home the day the mother laundries them.

I am just wishing that in some of your groups that it would be possible to interest them in our needs. The Save the Children Fund, with headquarters in New York, has helped me some. Many children of my schools would be unable to attend school had it not been for this organization.

I hope you will not consider me rude for writing. I have my heart in the work. I realize a hungry or a cold child cannot learn too much.

Yours very truly,
C. B. S.

Star Route One
Albertville, Ala.
January 1, 1936

Dear Mrs. Roosevelt,
For some time I have wished to be aqainted with you. Or merly to receive a letter from you. I haved wish much to see you, but as I am a poor girl and have never been out of our state that will be impossible I guess.

Mrs. Roosevelt since I have been in high school I have been studying modern things and conveniences. I took your family for my study. I have found the study to be the most interesting subjects I could have found. In the study I, at all times know where you are, by reading all papers I find at school and elsewhere. I find what you are doing. You may never had given this a thought, but to think over our daily lives there is a good story to it.

My life has been a story to me and most of the time a miserable one. When I was 7 years old my father left for a law school and never returned. This leaving my mother and 4 children. He left us a small farm, but it could not keep us up. . . . I am now 15 years old and in the 10th grade. I have always been smart but I never had a chance as all of us is so poor. I hope to complete my education, but I will have to quit school I guess if there is no clothes can be bought. (Don't think that we are on the relief.) Mother has been a faithful servent for us to keep us to gather. I don't see how she has made it.

Mrs. Roosevelt, don't think I am just begging, but that is all you can call it I guess. There is no harm in asking I guess eather. Do you have any old clothes you have throwed back. You don't realize how honored I would feel to be wearing your clothes. I don't have a coat at all to wear. The clothes may be too large but I can cut them down so I can wear them. Not only clothes but old shoes, hats, hose, and under wear would be appreciated so much. I have three brothers that would appreciate any old clothes of your boys or husband. I wish you could see the part of North Alabama now. The trees, groves, and every thing is covered with ice and snow. It is a very pretty scene. But Oh, how cold it is here. People can hardly stay comfortable.

I will close now as it is about mail time. I hope to hear from you soon. (ans real soon)

Your friend,
M. I.

Source: Anonymous letter, 1936, in *Dear Mrs. Roosevelt: The Letters*, New Deal Network, http://newdeal.feri.org/eleanor/bs0136.htm, accessed July 25, 2012.

Anonymous letter, 1936, in *Dear Mrs. Roosevelt: Letters from Children of the Great Depression*, ed. Robert Cohen (Chapel Hill: University of North Carolina Press, 2002), p. 105.

22.4 REMEMBERING THE GREAT DEPRESSION, EXCERPTS FROM STUDS TERKEL'S *HARD TIMES* (1970)

Americans experienced the Great Depression in different ways, and those experiences evolved as the economic crisis continued. One constant, however, seemed to be a sense that the nation had changed and was continuing to change in fundamental ways. During the 1960s, famed radio host and oral historian Studs Terkel interviewed Americans to gain a sense of how they had endured the crisis and how they remembered the Great Depression and FDR's New Deal.

James Ward: James lost his job at a publishing house in 1935; he was out of work for six months until he began work as part of the Illinois Writers' Project.

I was out of work six months. I was losing my contacts as well as my energy. I kept going from one publishing house to another. I never got past the telephone operator. It was just wasted time. One of the worst things was occupying your time, sensibly. You'd go to the library.

You took a magazine to the room and sat and read. I didn't have a radio. I tried to do some writing and found I couldn't concentrate. The day was long. There was nothing to do evenings. I was going around in circles, it was terrifying. So I just vegetated.

With some people I knew, there was a coldness, shunning: I'd rather not see you just now. Maybe *I'll* lose my job next week. On the other hand, I made some very close friends, who were merely acquaintances before. If I needed $5 for room rent or something, it was available. . . .

I went to apply for unemployment insurance, which had just been put into effect. I went three weeks in succession. It still hadn't come through. Then I discovered the catch. At that time, anybody who earned more than $3,000 a year was not paid unemployment insurance unless his employer had O.K.'d it. It could be withheld. My employer exercised his option of not O.K.'ing it. He exercised his vindictive privilege. I don't think that's the law anymore.

I finally went on relief. It's an experience I don't want anybody to go through. It comes as close to crucifixion as. . . . You sit in an auditorium and are given a number. The interview was utterly ridiculous and mortifying. In the middle of mine, a more dramatic guy than I dived from the second floor stairway, head first, to demonstrate he was gonna get on relief even if he had to go to the hospital to do it.

There were questions like: Who are your friends? Where have you been living? Where's your family? I had sent my wife and child to her folks in Ohio, where they could live more simply. Why should anybody give you money? Why should anybody give you a place to sleep? What sort of friends? That went on for half an hour. I got angry and said, "Do you happen to know what a friend is?" He changed his attitude very shortly. I did get certified some time later. I think they paid $9 a month.

I came away feeling I didn't have any business living any more. I was imposing on somebody, a great society or something like that.

Joe Marcus: an economist who graduated from college in 1935 and went to work as part of the New Deal in 1936.

The New Deal was a young man's world. Young people, if they showed any ability, got an opportunity. I was a kid, twenty-two or twenty-three. In a few months, I was made head of the department. We had a meeting with hot shots: What's to be done? I pointed out some problems: let's define what we're looking for. They immediately had me take over. I had to set up the organization and hire seventy-five people. Given a chance as a youngster to try out ideas, I learned a fantastic amount. The challenge itself was great.

It was the idea of being asked big questions. The technical problems were small. These you had to solve by yourself. But the context was broad: Where was society going? Your statistical questions became questions of full employment. You were not prepared for it in school. If you wanted new answers, you needed a new kind of people. This is what was exciting.

Ordinarily, I might have had a job at the university, marking papers or helping a professor. All of a sudden, I'm doing original research and asking basic questions about how our society works. What makes a Depression? What makes for pulling out of it? Once you start thinking in these terms, you're in a different ball game.

The climate was exciting. You were part of a society that was on the move. You were involved in something that could make a difference. Laws could be changed. So could the conditions of people.

The idea of being involved close to the center of political life was unthinkable, just two or three years before all this happened. Unthinkable for someone like me, of lower middle-class, close to ghetto, Jewish life. Suddenly you were a significant member of society. It was not the kind of closed society you lived in before. . . .

You were really part of something, changes could be made. Bringing *immediate* results to people who were starving. You could do something about it: that was the most important thing. This you felt.

A feeling that if you had something to say, it would get to the top. As I look back now, memoranda I had written reached the White House, one way or another. The biggest thrill of my life was hearing a speech of Roosevelt's, using a selection from a memorandum I had written.

Everybody was searching for ideas. . . . there was a search, a sense of values . . . that would make a difference in the lives of people.

We weren't thinking of remaking society. That wasn't it. I didn't buy this dream stuff. What was happening was a complete change in social attitudes at the central government level. The questions was: How can you do it within this system? People working in all the New Deal agencies were dominated by this spirit. . . .

At one stage Harry Hopkins met with his staff, a lot of people, in a huge auditorium. He explained they'd have to work day and night to get this particular job done. He asked for volunteers, who would start off tonight and work straight through. Practically everybody in the auditorium raised their hands. Youth and fervor.

Normally, administrative people were much older. But even the young of the old bureaucracy were stodgy. They came to work, left their jobs when the day was over, went out for their lunches. . . . Frankly, they didn't work very hard and knocked off whenever they could. What right-wingers say about Government employees was very true in many cases.

The New Dealers were different. I'm not only talking about policy people. I'm talking about the clerks, who felt what they were doing was important. You didn't take time out for lunch because of a job that had to be done. You had a sandwich on the desk. Their jobs made sense. . . .

Source: Studs Terkel, *Hard Times: An Oral History of the Great Depression* (New York: Pantheon Books, 1970), 421–422, 265–267.

The Second World War

1941–1945

< Pearl Harbor, December 7, 1941

709

AMERICAN PORTRAIT

A. Philip Randolph

"**W**ho is this guy Randolph," Joseph Rauh wondered, and "what the hell has he got on the President of the U.S.?" It was June 1941, and Rauh, a government attorney, had just been instructed to draft a presidential order prohibiting discrimination on grounds of "race, color, creed, or national origin" in defense industries. It was a radical departure from decades of official support for legalized racism. It would use the economic muscle of the federal government to overturn job segregation and, in the process, make enemies for President Franklin Roosevelt. Rauh was enthusiastic, but he couldn't understand why FDR, with his reliance on southern votes, would even consider it. The president was bending to pressure, Rauh learned, from African Americans led by a charismatic organizer named A. Philip Randolph.

Raised in Florida and educated at New York's City College, Randolph had founded the largest African American labor union, the Brotherhood of Sleeping Car Porters, in 1925. Porters traveled the railroads as baggage handlers and valets, and during the Depression Randolph's influence extended into every station and depot reached by the Brotherhood's magazine, the *Messenger*.

In 1941, it looked to Randolph like only a matter of months before the United States entered the war raging in Europe and Asia. He believed, according to FBI informants, "that Negroes make most fundamental gains in periods of great social upheaval." War would create a chance to achieve equality, but only if African Americans demanded it. "The Negro sat by idly during the First World War thinking conditions would get better," he told an audience in Oklahoma City. "That won't be the procedure during the duration of this conflict."

In January 1941, Randolph called for African Americans to march to Washington to demand an end to job discrimination. Only 3 percent of workers in war industries were people of color. "The administration leaders in Washington will never give the Negro justice," he declared, "until they see masses, ten, twenty, fifty thousand Negroes on the White House lawn." The March on Washington movement was largely bluff, but Roosevelt and the FBI believed it enough to try to head it off.

A protest march would embarrass the government, and Roosevelt had the power to accept Randolph's demands. Leveraging federal defense contracts, the president could desegregate a large portion of the economy without even asking Congress. He opened negotiations with Randolph through Eleanor Roosevelt. The organizers agreed to cancel the march in return for a presidential directive—Executive Order 8802—establishing a Fair Employment Practices Committee to assure fairness in hiring.

It was a victory for civil rights and for Randolph personally. If the Emancipation Proclamation had ended physical slavery, the New York *Amsterdam News* declared, E.O. 8802 ended "economic slavery." Within a year, thousands of African Americans would be working at high-tech jobs in aircraft factories and arms plants. Randolph had recognized that war created an opening for changing the economic and political rules of the game. War touched all Americans. Millions were sent to serve and fight everywhere from the Arctic to the tropics.

Millions of others left home to work in plants producing war materiel. Government stepped in to run the economy and created new relationships with corporations, labor, the states, and universities. The war stimulated revolutionary advances in science, industry, and agriculture. The United States itself became the foremost military and economic power in a world destroyed by war.

These changes enlarged the discretionary powers of the presidency and the federal government. Americans willingly accepted personal sacrifices and greater federal authority as part of the price of victory. As the March on Washington movement proved, the president's enhanced powers could enlarge freedom and opportunity—but they could also restrict individual liberties. Many Japanese Americans spent the war imprisoned in "relocation centers," and the FBI placed Randolph's name on a list of persons to be placed in "custodial detention" in the event of a national emergency. The war unsettled the economy and society, enlisting all Americans in a global crusade and arousing both idealism and fear.

Island in a Totalitarian Sea

Randolph's movement capitalized on a world crisis that reached back to the treaty that ended World War I. The Depression heightened international tensions, turning regional conflicts in Africa, Europe, and Asia into tests of ideology and power. In 1937, Japan attacked China. Two years later, when Germany invaded Poland, France and Britain declared war, beginning World War II in Europe. As with the previous war, Americans had time to reflect on the world crisis. Most blamed it on the failures of the Versailles Treaty and the desperation caused by the global Depression. Nations and empires were solving economic problems with military force.

Americans were divided, however, on how their country ought to respond, on its role in the world and its responsibilities at home. Isolationists wanted to stay out of war and secure the Western Hemisphere against attack. But Roosevelt and other internationalists believed the United States had to support the nations fighting Germany and Japan. Internationalists saw a free-trading, open-door world economy as a solution to international conflict. Isolationists worried about growing federal power and the ambitions of Britain and the Soviet Union. The threat of fascism forced Americans to ask whether their economy and government could compete in the world.

Both camps knew war would change American society. The future of world politics and the world economy would be shaped by America's choice of allies and aims. In 1940, most Americans feared involvement and opposed aid to the enemies of fascism. When France's defeat left Britain to fight alone, more Americans saw aid to Britain as an alternative to US involvement. Japan's attack on Pearl Harbor ended a debate that divided the nation.

A World of Hostile Blocs

The Depression destroyed the liberal international order based on free trade. For a century, governments had favored policies that increased the movement of goods, people, and investment across borders. The steamship and telegraph accelerated that trend.

Movement toward an open-door world slowed during World War I and the 1920s, and then stopped completely with the Depression. World trade shrank from almost $3 billion a year in 1929 to less than $1 billion in 1933. Empires and nations began to restrict the movement of goods, capital, and people and to regiment their societies for self-sufficiency. Everywhere, it seemed, governments became more ruthless and less free.

Dictators offered visions of imperial conquest and racial supremacy. Mussolini promised a new Roman Empire in Africa and the Mediterranean. Japanese schoolchildren learned they belonged to a "Yamato race," purer and more virtuous than the inferior peoples they would one day rule. Hitler urged Germans to defend themselves against the *Untermenschen*, subhumans, in their midst—Jews, Gypsies, homosexuals. He built a state based on racism, total control, and brutality, where secret police, the Gestapo, hunted down enemies of the regime, and a Nazi army, the SS, enforced party rule.

Jews were the main target of Nazi terror. In 1935, the Nuremberg Laws stripped Jews of citizenship and outlawed intermarriage with members of the "Aryan race." On the night of November 9, 1938, Nazi stormtroopers and ordinary citizens rampaged throughout Germany, burning synagogues and destroying Jewish shops, homes, and hospitals, killing 100 Jews and arresting 30,000 more. Until *Kristallnacht*, this "night of the broken glass," FDR thought international opinion would restrain Hitler. Now he was no longer sure.

Roosevelt grew apprehensive as Germany, Italy, and Japan, the Axis powers, sought to solve their economic problems through military conquest. Italy invaded Ethiopia in 1935. In July 1937, Japan attacked China. In 1938, Hitler's troops marched into Austria. Roosevelt worried that the Axis would soon control most of Europe and Asia, but American leaders had an even darker fear, one they scarcely breathed: that totalitarianism would outcompete democracy. America's free markets and free labor might be no match for the ruthless efficiency of the fascist states. The United States would have to regiment its own citizens just to keep up, and to enlist industry, labor, and agriculture into a "state system," *Fortune* magazine predicted, "which, in its own defense, would have to take on the character of Hitler's system."

The Good Neighbor

Some believed the United States ought to retreat into its own sphere. The Hawley-Smoot Tariff of 1930 blocked most imports, but within a year, FDR reversed course and began pushing trade as the answer to America's economic problems. He reacted mainly to the vision of his single-minded secretary of state, Cordell Hull. A conservative former senator from Tennessee, Hull believed that equal access for all to the world's markets was the cure for dictatorship and depression and the best way to ensure peace. In a world of empires and blocs, Hull turned an old foreign policy tradition, the Open Door, into a bold plan for peace and prosperity.

Roosevelt and Hull slowly began to reopen markets in Latin America. FDR expanded Hoover's "Good Neighbor" policy, encouraging trade and renouncing the use of force. A new Export-Import Bank financed transactions, and tariffs were lowered. Hull surprised the 1933 Pan-American Conference by approving a declaration that no nation had the right to intervene in the affairs of another. Good Neighbor policies undermined German and Japanese economic ventures, and Latin American governments invited the FBI to track down Axis agents on their soil.

In 1938, after absorbing Austria, Hitler demanded part of Czechoslovakia's territory. Fearing that a small war over the territory would escalate into a larger war, Czechoslovakia's allies, Britain and France, agreed to negotiations. In a meeting at Munich in September, they yielded to Hitler's demands. FDR cabled Hitler a last-minute appeal for restraint but accepted the final decision. After World War II, the term "Munich" came to symbolize the failed attempts to appease aggressors, but in 1938 Americans were unsure how best to guard their freedoms in a hostile world.

America First?

As the Axis threat grew, Roosevelt pushed for a buildup of US forces, but Congress and the public disagreed. Disillusioned by the last war, the public wanted to stay out of the conflicts in Europe and Asia. Polls indicated that more than 70 percent believed the United States had been tricked into World War I. Half a million students pledged their refusal to serve in another war. Senator Gerald P. Nye charged that the munitions industry was lobbying for war. Pacifists, economic nationalists, and veterans groups, backed by the *Chicago Tribune* and the Hearst newspapers, composed a powerful isolationist constituency.

From 1935 to 1937, Congress passed annual Neutrality Acts prohibiting loans and credits to nations engaged in war. The action took place against the backdrop of the Spanish Civil War, in which Fascist forces, aided by Germany and Italy, fought against democratic Loyalist forces aided by the Soviet Union. Some 3,000 Americans volunteered to fight with the Loyalists. For that reason, Congress decided to stay out of the conflict; the Neutrality Acts also restricted the president's ability to aid the enemies of fascism.

In late 1939, Roosevelt's worst nightmare came true, as the United States became an island in a world dominated by force. The Soviet Union signed a nonaggression treaty with Germany. The full terms of the Nazi-Soviet pact were secret, leading diplomats to fear the worst, a totalitarian alliance stretching from the Rhine to the Pacific. In September, German armies struck Poland, using tanks and dive-bombers in a *Blitzkrieg*, or "lightning war." Hitler and Soviet leader Josef Stalin split Poland between them. Britain and France declared war on Germany.

The following April, Nazi armies invaded Denmark and Norway. On May 10, 1940, Hitler launched an all-out offensive in the West. Tank columns pierced French lines in the Ardennes Forest and headed toward the English Channel. France, Belgium, and the Netherlands were defeated; Britain faced the German onslaught alone. Roosevelt now had to consider the possibility of a British surrender, placing the Royal Navy, control of the Atlantic, and possibly even Canada in Hitler's hands. The German air force, the *Luftwaffe*, was already dueling for control of the skies over England.

Determined to shore up this last line of defense, Roosevelt used his powers as commander in chief to bypass the Neutrality Acts. In June 1940, he submitted a bill to create the first peacetime draft in American history. He declared army weapons and supplies "surplus" so they could be donated to Britain. In September 1940, he traded Britain 50 destroyers for leases to naval bases in Canada, Bermuda, and the Caribbean.

The isolationists were now isolated. Sympathy for Britain grew as radio audiences heard the sounds of air attacks on London. Two-thirds of the public favored the draft, but isolationists were not finished. In September 1940, the America First Committee launched a new campaign that urged Americans to turn from Europe and prepare for their own defense. Charles A. Lindbergh and Senator Burton Wheeler headlined America

First rallies. The only reason for United States involvement, Lindbergh argued, "is because there are powerful elements in America who desire us to take part. They represent a small minority . . . but they control much of the machinery of influence and propaganda."

Roosevelt worried that the 1940 election would become a referendum on intervention. Isolationist senator Robert Taft was a leading contender for the nomination, but the Republicans chose Wendell L. Willkie, an anti–New Deal internationalist who endorsed the draft and expressed sympathy for Britain. With defense and foreign policy off the table, FDR won an unprecedented third term by a 5-million-vote margin.

Means Short of War

British Prime Minister Winston Churchill could now broach the delicate but urgent issue of war finances. Britain had been buying arms on a "cash and carry" basis but was now out of funds. The Neutrality Act prohibited new loans, but without arms Britain would have to surrender. FDR gave his cabinet a weekend to devise a plan, and the following Monday he produced the answer himself. Instead of loaning money, the United States would lend arms and equipment. Roosevelt compared the idea to lending a garden hose to a neighbor whose house was on fire. "There would be a gentleman's obligation to repay," but because there would be no loans, it would not violate the Neutrality Act. Lend-Lease, as the program was called, put the US "arsenal of democracy" on Britain's side and granted FDR unprecedented powers to arm allies. The Lend-Lease bill, H.R. 1776, passed the Senate by a two-to-one margin in 1941.

Repayment took the form of economic concessions. Hull saw Lend-Lease as a chance to crack one of the largest autarkic blocs, the British Empire. He insisted that in return for aid, Britain had to discard the Ottawa Accords and open its empire's door to American trade. Churchill's economic adviser, John Maynard Keynes, reluctantly agreed. Later that year, Churchill and Roosevelt met aboard the cruiser *Augusta* to issue a declaration of war aims, the Atlantic Charter. It ensured all nations, "victor and vanquished," equal access to the trade and raw materials of the world.

In June 1941, Hitler stunned the world again with a lightning invasion of the Soviet Union. Three million men and 3,000 tanks slashed through Soviet defenses toward Moscow and Leningrad. Secretary of War Henry Stimson predicted that in three months the Axis would control Europe and Asia, but George C. Marshall, the army's chief of staff, saw that this might be a turning point. If the Soviet army could hold the area between Moscow and the Black Sea, the Germans would have a long winter. Roosevelt shared his optimism. The eastern front took pressure off Britain and gave the Allies a real chance to defeat Hitler. Roosevelt extended Lend-Lease aid to Moscow. The German columns advanced steadily, but they were no longer moving through Poland or France. "Even when encircled, the Russians stood their ground and fought," a Nazi general reported.

German U-boats worked to cut Britain's lifelines, sinking half a million tons of shipping a month. To help the British, Roosevelt fought an undeclared naval war against Germany in the western Atlantic. The US Navy convoyed merchant ships as far as Iceland, where British destroyers took over. FDR said he was offering "all aid short of war," but it was not far short. In September a U-boat fired torpedoes at the USS *Greer*, and the destroyer threw back depth charges. When Roosevelt ordered patrols to expel German and Italian vessels from the western Atlantic, he had crossed the line from neutrality to belligerency and seemed to be seeking an incident that would make it official.

Japan, meanwhile, moved into Southeast Asia. In 1939, the Japanese adopted a "go south" strategy to capture oil fields in the Dutch East Indies and encircle China. Because the Philippines, a US territory, blocked the invasion route, the question for the Japanese was not whether to declare war on the United States, but when. In July 1941, Japan established bases in French Indochina. Roosevelt saw this as a threat, but, preoccupied with Europe, he wanted to forestall war in the Pacific. US diplomats opened talks with Japan while Marshall dispatched a fleet of B-17s in an attempt to deter an attack. When Japanese troop convoys moved into the South China Sea, Hull ended negotiations and placed an embargo on oil exports to Japan, denying the nation its primary source of fuel. On November 27, Marshall warned commanders in Hawaii and the Philippines to expect "an aggressive move by Japan" in the next few days. The Philippines, Thailand, and Malaya were the likely targets.

On Sunday afternoon, December 7, Americans listening to the radio heard that aircraft "believed to be from Japan" had attacked US bases at Pearl Harbor in Hawaii. At 7:40 a.m. Hawaii time, 181 planes had bombed and strafed airfields on Oahu, destroying or damaging more than 200 planes on the ground. Bombers then attacked the 96 ships of the US Pacific Fleet anchored next to each other. Three torpedoes struck the battleship *Oklahoma*, capsizing it with 400 crew members aboard. Alongside her the *Maryland* went

Pearl Harbor Japan's attack on the US Navy's principal Pacific base at Pearl Harbor brought the United States into World War II. For Japan, it was the opening phase of a campaign to capture European and American colonies in Asia.

down. A bomb exploded in the *Arizona*'s forward magazine, breaking the ship in half and killing over a thousand men. In the Philippines, Japanese bombers also caught American planes on the ground. The following day, President Roosevelt appeared before Congress to ask for a declaration of war against Japan. Only one representative, Montana's Jeannette Rankin, voted no. On December 11, Germany honored its alliance with Japan and declared war on the United States.

Some historians have argued that Roosevelt knew of the approaching attack but withheld warnings in order to draw the United States into war. In fact, naval authorities at Pearl Harbor anticipated an attack but doubted that Japan could project air and sea power across the Pacific in secrecy. When Japanese planes destroyed American aircraft on the ground in the Philippines nine hours after the Pearl Harbor attack, Douglas MacArthur said Germans must have flown the bombers. Such preconceptions blinded commanders to the warning signs.

Turning the Tide

For the Allies there was only bad news in the first half of 1942. Japanese invaders walked over the larger British and Dutch armies in Southeast Asia and captured the American islands of Guam and Wake. In February, the "impregnable" fortress of Singapore surrendered with most of the Australian and Indian armies still inside. Japan's Combined Fleet ruled the seas between Hawaii and India, striking at will. MacArthur abandoned Manila and staged an Alamo-style defense of the Bataan Peninsula and the fortress island of Corregidor.

But the tide was beginning to turn. The Soviets stopped the German advance outside Moscow. On April 18, Colonel James Doolittle's B-25 bombers raided Tokyo. Roosevelt wanted to hold the line in the Pacific while coming to the aid of Britain and the Soviet Union as soon as possible. This meant stopping Japan, creating an American army, and sending it to the other side of the Atlantic. None of those jobs would be easy.

Midway and Coral Sea

"We can run wild for six months or a year," Admiral Isoroku Yamamoto prophesied before the victorious attack on Pearl Harbor, "but after that I have utterly no confidence." Panic-stricken Americans imagined enemy landings in California, but Japan was never so ambitious. It called for fortifying a defensive screen of islands in the western Pacific (see Map 23–1) and holding the Allies at bay until they sued for peace. "The fact that the Japanese did not return to Pearl Harbor and complete the job was the greatest help for us," Chester W. Nimitz, the US Pacific commander, later remembered.

After the Doolittle raid, the Japanese realized their error and laid plans to lure the US Pacific Fleet into battle. The increase in radio traffic helped Commander Joseph Rochefort, who had already partly broken the Japanese codes. In late April, he was able to tell Nimitz that Japan was planning an attack on Port Moresby on the island of New Guinea. Nimitz dispatched two carriers, *Lexington* and *Yorktown*, to intercept the Japanese carrier force. The Battle of Coral Sea was the first between carrier task forces, an entirely new type of sea battle. Sailors never saw the enemy's ships, only their aircraft, which struck with devastating speed. Planes from *Yorktown* turned back the Japanese transports while Lexington's torpedo- and dive-bombers sunk the carrier *Shoho*. The Japanese

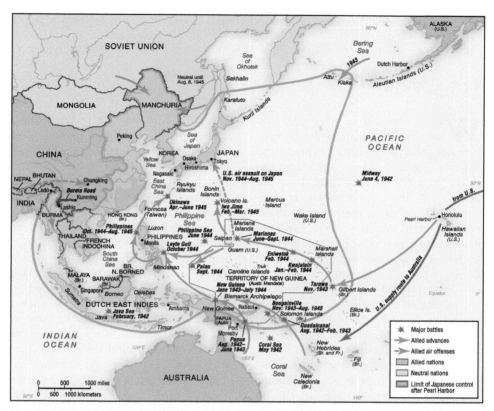

Map 23-1   World War II in the Pacific, 1942-1945 Japan established a barrier of fortified islands across the western Pacific. US forces penetrated it westward from Hawaii and from Australia northward through the Solomon Islands to the Philippines.

fatally crippled *Lexington* and tore a hole in *Yorktown*'s deck. The two sides pulled back after fighting to a draw.

Yamamoto next chose to attack the US fleet directly. Sending a diversionary force toward the Aleutians, he aimed his attack at Midway, the westernmost island of the Hawaiian chain. Yamamoto gambled that Nimitz would divide his forces, allowing the Combined Fleet to crush the remnant guarding Hawaii. But trusting Rochefort's code breakers, Nimitz knew the real target was Midway. He also learned from Coral Sea that aircraft, not battleships, were the winning weapons. He hastily assembled task forces around the carriers *Hornet* and *Enterprise* and reinforced airfields on Midway and Oahu. Crews worked night and day to repair *Yorktown*. The American fleet was still outnumbered, but surprise was now on its side.

When Japanese aircraft met stiff resistance from Midway's guns on the morning of June 4, they returned to their carriers and prepared for an unplanned second attack. With bombers, bombs, and fuel littering their decks, Japan's four carriers were vulnerable, their defending Zeros busy intercepting US torpedo bombers. At that moment dive-bombers

AMERICA AND THE WORLD

The Carrier

William Meredith, a navy pilot and later a poet laureate, wrote a sonnet in honor of his carrier, a craft as proud and majestic as an old queen: "The planes rise heavy from her whining deck. Then the bomb's luck, the gun's poise and chattering, the far-off dying are her near affair." Prior to World War II, admirals saw little grace in the new species of vessel they described as "a barn door laid atop a bathtub." Compared to the battleship, or even the destroyer, it lacked elegance and purpose.

The aircraft carrier joined the US Navy almost by accident. To head off a naval arms race after World War I, the Harding administration wanted to scrap the largest battleships, the dreadnought-class warships then being built in Virginia, Britain, and Japan. The problem was what to do with dreadnoughts already partially built. As a compromise, the Washington Naval Treaty of 1922 allowed each navy to place a flat deck atop the unfinished hulls to serve as a landing place for observation planes. In 1928, the Norfolk shipyard launched two ungainly "flattops," *Saratoga* and *Lexington*. "They are the weirdest ships in the Navy," noted the *Washington Post*, pointing out that their chief defense was speed—33 knots—which would enable them to escape enemy shells by running away.

Even after battleships' vulnerability to aerial bombing became apparent, naval strategists had difficulty envisioning a role for the carrier. Future battles, it was thought, would be slugfests between heavily armored gunships throwing shells at each other from a distance of up to 23 miles. Until the attack on Pearl Harbor, the carrier's worth was unproven.

Meanwhile, the Japanese navy made the carrier the principal element of its battle plan. After destroying the ships at Hawaii, Japan's six-carrier Combined Fleet roved the Pacific and Indian Oceans from New Zealand to India virtually unchallenged. Pacific Commander Chester W. Nimitz, himself a former submariner, rebuilt US forces around the carriers *Enterprise*, *Hornet*, *Lexington*, and *Yorktown*.

The result was a new kind of warfare in which carrier battle groups struck each other across wide tracts of ocean using torpedo planes and bombers. The first such encounter came at the Coral Sea, where both sides displayed their inexperience. Signals intelligence revealed the target but not the location of the Japanese fleet, while Japanese submarines sent to scout for the American carriers missed them entirely. Groping toward each other, the two commanders struck blindly. Planes from the *Lexington* spotted one of the enemy carriers, the *Shoho*, and sank it. Meanwhile Japanese squadrons mistook a destroyer and an oiler for the US carriers and, after sinking the

from *Yorktown* and *Enterprise* burst out of the clouds. They destroyed three carriers in a matter of minutes. The mighty Combined Fleet was almost entirely destroyed. Midway put Japan on the defensive and allowed the United States to concentrate on building an army and winning the war in Europe.

wrong ships, found the *Yorktown*, took it for one of their own carriers, and tried to land. The following day Vice Admiral Takeo Takagi had better luck, and each side lost one carrier before breaking off.

Success in this new type of battle required information, timing, and luck, but unlike the bloody land battles in New Guinea and the Solomons, the result was quick and decisive. Since the beginning of the twentieth century, modern weapons and industrial mobilization had reduced the significance of battle; victory went not to the swift but to the side that could overwhelm its enemies with organization and materiel. Carrier war was different; an empire's fortunes could turn in a single day. Nowhere was this clearer than at the Battle of Midway. Outnumbered four carriers to three (including the badly damaged *Yorktown*), Nimitz was able to inflict a crushing defeat on the Combined Fleet. Navy code breakers had given him advance warning, but victory might not have been possible had Admiral Raymond Spruance not launched planes from *Hornet* and *Enterprise* at the right time and in the right direction, and had they not arrived above Admiral Nagumo Chuichi's fleet just when Japanese planes were refueling on deck.

A carrier was a small city, with its own telephone network, hospital, commissaries, crime, and residential districts. The crew of 3,000 men had one job, launching and landing planes, but between flights were long spells of idleness. "Most of them sleep, curled up on the naked deck; others sharpen their knives, write letters or read," Joseph Bryan, an officer on the *Yorktown*, wrote in his diary. "There is a man in the compartment at the foot of the Exec's ladder who is as expert and delicate an embroiderer as I've ever seen." Living quarters were strictly segregated by rank and race. Despite regulations, navy custom kept African Americans off carriers except as stewards. In 1945, veterans groups picketed the carrier *Croatan* after its commander refused to allow African American quarter-masters to board.

The golden age of carrier warfare lasted just three years. After the last Japanese flattop sank in the Battle of the Philippine Sea in 1944, American carriers provided air cover over invasion beaches as the navy closed the ring around Japan's home islands. Spruance's battle group at Okinawa contained 40 carriers and a "fleet train" of fuel and supply ships that enabled it to remain continually at sea.

Immense nuclear-propelled carriers later proved ideal for the containment and symbolic missions of the cold war. In 1968, Moshe Dayan, an Israeli general and hero of the Yom Kippur War, visited the *Constellation* off the coast of Vietnam. Its five-acre deck gave him a "breathtaking impression" of American power. The carrier, he said, was "not fighting against guerrillas, or against North Vietnamese leader Ho Chi Minh, but against the entire world. Their real aim was to show everybody—including Britain, France, and the USSR—their power and determination so as to pass this message: wherever Americans go, they are irresistible."

Gone with the Draft

The German army that overran France in May 1940 consisted of 136 mechanized divisions of 17,000 men each. The United States had only five divisions and was still using horse cavalry. "Against Europe's total war," *Time* observed, "the U.S. Army looked like a few nice boys with BB guns." Military officials drew up plans for a 10-million-man force. As in World War I, the United States had to find ways to house, equip, and transport the army, but this time it would be five times larger. By December 1941, 2 million men and 80,000 women had enlisted. A year later the total exceeded 5 million.

Buses rolled into the new boot camps and unloaded recruits, called selectees, in front of drill instructors. Basic training aimed to erase the civilian personality and replace it with an instinct for obedience and action. Eugene Sledge left college to join the marines and found himself at a camp in San Diego. "Your soul may belong to Jesus," his drill instructor bellowed, "but your ass belongs to the Marines." After 13 weeks of calisthenics, close-order drill, marches, and rifle practice, Sledge was assigned to the infantry.

Recruits hungered for a weekend pass, but in the South and West, where many bases were located, there was little to do. The War Department joined several charities in creating the United Services Organization (USO) to provide a "home away from home" with meals, dances, and wholesome entertainment. Still, wherever they were on leave, soldiers often fought with each other and with the locals. Distinctions of apparel and race could stimulate violence. Southerners lynched African American soldiers for wearing their uniforms. In 1943, riots erupted in Harlem after police arrested an African American soldier in uniform. The same year, sailors in Los Angeles attacked Mexican American shipyard workers who wore distinctive "zoot suits." In both cases the clothes signified a disruption of the established social order, a process accelerated by the war.

Army leadership struggled to preserve racial traditions amid wartime changes. Like the multiethnic armies of Britain and France, the US Army consisted of segregated units, some with special functions. The Japanese American 442nd Regimental Combat Team and the marines' Navajo "code talkers" became well known. African Americans served in the army in segregated units and, until 1942, were excluded from the Marine Corps altogether. Roosevelt ordered the services to admit African Americans and appointed an African American brigadier general, Benjamin O. Davis, but injustices remained. Even blood plasma was segregated in military hospitals.

Two issues aroused the most anger among African Americans: exclusion from combat and the treatment of soldiers at southern bases. Many GIs in uniform experienced the indignity of being refused service at restaurants where German prisoners of war were allowed to eat. Mutinies and race riots erupted at bases in Florida, Alabama, and Louisiana, where African American soldiers were housed separately and denied furlough privileges. The army responded by sending African American GIs to the war theaters.

Though desperately short of infantrymen, the army kept African Americans out of front-line units and assigned them to menial chores. Combat symbolized full citizenship, and the NAACP pressed Roosevelt to create African American fighting units. An African American infantry division, the 92nd, fought in Italy; three air units—among them the 99th Pursuit Squadron, known as the Tuskegee Airmen—flew against the Luftwaffe; and one mechanized battalion, the 761st Tanks, received a commendation for action in the Ardennes. Most African Americans went into the line individually as replacements, and racially mixed units aroused few complaints in the field. Resistance to desegregation came mainly from Washington.

With manpower in short supply, the armed forces reluctantly enlisted women. The Women's Army Corps (the WACs) was created in 1942, while the navy signaled its reluctance in the title of its auxiliary, the Women Accepted for Volunteer Emergency Service

The 99th Pursuit Squadron, Known as the Black Eagles The Black Eagles trained at the Tuskegee Institute and engaged the Luftwaffe in the skies over North Africa.

(WAVES). Eventually more than 100,000 women served as mechanics, typists, pilots, cooks, and nurses, an unusually low rate of mobilization. Nearly every other warring country enlisted women for industry and combat, leaving the state to perform traditionally female jobs: caring for children, the sick, and the elderly. This government role came to be accepted in Europe, Canada, and Australia, but in the United States "welfare" continued to be associated with poor relief.

The Winning Weapons

During World War II, weapons technology advanced with blinding speed. Entering the war late, the United States gained a technological edge. American factories produced models using the latest innovations, but many of these would not see combat until 1943 or later.

Until then, troops had to make do with inferior weapons. Marines landed on Guadalcanal wearing World War I–era helmets and carrying the 1903 Springfield rifle. Japan's Zero was faster and lighter than any American fighter. After 1943, the advantage began to pass to the Americans. The M1 rifle was the finest infantry weapon in the war. Artillery was precise and lethal, and American crews were skilled in the devastating "time-on-target" technique, which delivered shells from several directions simultaneously.

The elegant P-51 Mustang, a high-speed ultra-long-range fighter, could escort bombers from Britain to Berlin. It dominated the skies after D-Day. American four-engine bombers—the B-17 Flying Fortress and the B-24 Liberator—were superior to German or Japanese counterparts. In 1944, the B-29 Superfortress, with its 10-ton bomb load and unrivalled range, took to the skies over the Pacific and incinerated one Japanese city after another. American tanks, however, remained inferior to their German counterparts throughout the war, owing to the flawed logistical decisions of American forces.

Quantity often trumped quality, however, and the results were impressive. When Allied troops landed in France in 1944, they enjoyed a superiority of 20 to 1 in tanks and 25 to 1 in aircraft. When Roosevelt set a production target of 50,000 aircraft in 1940, the Germans considered it a bluff, but American factories turned out almost 300,000 planes during the war (see Figure 23–1). Sometimes sheer American numbers defeated Axis skill. An American soldier in Salerno asked a captured German lieutenant why he had surrendered. "The Americans kept sending tanks down the road," the German replied. "Every time they sent a tank, we knocked it out. Finally, we ran out of ammunition, and the Americans didn't run out of tanks."

Americans also developed secret weapons. The War Department funded defense laboratories at Johns Hopkins, MIT, Harvard, and other universities, forging a permanent link between government, science, and the military. American and British scientists invented one of the first "smart" bombs, the proximity fuse. American and British scientific collaboration also produced improvements in sonar and radar, penicillin, and the atomic bomb.

The Manhattan Project that produced the atomic bomb was the war's largest military-scientific-industrial enterprise. In 1939, Albert Einstein warned Roosevelt that the Germans might invent a nuclear weapon. The National Academy of Sciences concluded that a weapon of "superlatively destructive power" could be built, and General Leslie R. Groves was put in charge of the project, which eventually employed 600,000 people and cost $2 billion. World War II's marriage of technology and war changed

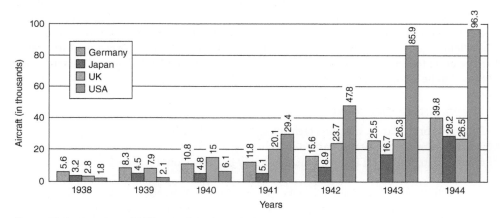

Figure 23-1 Number of Military Aircraft Produced US production of military equipment lagged at first, but once in high gear it dwarfed that of the rest of the world.
Source: I. C. B. Dear and M. R. D. Foot, eds., *The Oxford Companion to World War II* (New York: Oxford University Press, 1995), p. 22.

warfare, and it also changed science. Researchers and inventors had once worked alone on their own problems. Now they worked in teams at government-funded laboratories on problems assigned by Washington.

The Second Front

To reassure Britain and the Soviet Union, FDR adopted a "Europe First" strategy, holding the line against Japan while directing the main effort at Nazi Germany. The Allies had little in common except that Hitler had chosen them as enemies. Britain was struggling to preserve its empire. The Soviet Union had once been allied with Germany and had a nonaggression pact with Japan. Roosevelt needed to keep this shaky coalition together long enough to defeat Hitler. His greatest fear was that one or both of the Allies would make a separate peace or be knocked out of the war. Stalin and Churchill each had their own opinions about how to use American power, and their conflicting aims produced bitter disputes over strategy.

As the Nazis closed in on the Soviet oil fields during 1942, Stalin pleaded with Britain and the United States to launch an invasion of France. Roosevelt and Marshall also wanted a second front against Germany in northern Europe. But to the British, the idea of a western front evoked the horrors of the trench warfare of World War I and the losses it could no longer sustain. Instead, Churchill wanted to encircle the Nazis and attack the "soft underbelly" of the Axis from the Mediterranean.

Concerned about U-boats and the inexperience of American troops, FDR reluctantly accepted Churchill's plan (see Map 23–2). A month after Pearl Harbor he had promised Stalin a second front "this year." In late 1942, he postponed it to the spring of 1943. Finally, in June 1943, he told Stalin it would not take place until 1944. The delays reinforced Stalin's suspicions that the capitalist powers were waiting for the USSR's defeat.

Instead of invading Europe, the Americans chose a softer target, North Africa, where troops under Lieutenant General Dwight Eisenhower landed in Algeria and Morocco on November 8, 1942. As they moved east to link up with British forces attacking into Tunisia, German tank divisions under General Erwin Rommel burst through the Kasserine Pass and trapped American columns in high, rocky terrain. Panicky troops fled, blowing up their ammunition stores. Once through the pass, Rommel had a chance to encircle and defeat the Allied forces, but his Italian commanders ordered him to advance in another direction. The Americans and British regrouped for a counterattack.

Ernie Pyle, the popular war correspondent, reassured readers that despite the rout, "there was never at any time any question about the American bravery." Eisenhower was not so sure. He sacked the commander responsible for Kasserine and replaced him with Major General George S. Patton. The army increased basic training from 13 to 17 weeks and reviewed its doctrine and weapons. For Patton, Kasserine showed that firepower delivered by air, tanks, and artillery was more reliable than infantry. His preference for technology over bravery became ingrained in American strategy.

On May 7, Allied forces captured Tunis and Bizerte and took 238,000 German and Italian prisoners. Rommel escaped to fight again in France a year later. There he would encounter a different American army, larger, more experienced, and equipped with the newest weapons. As it mobilized, the United States was changing, too.

Map 23-2   World War II in Europe, 1942–1945 While the Soviets reduced the main German force along the eastern front, the British and American Allies advanced through Italy and France.

Organizing for Production

To defeat totalitarian regimes, Americans had to gear their economy for war. Big government and corporations made possible the "miracle of production" that was winning the war and raising living standards. During the height of the Depression, FDR did not use deficit spending to stir the economy (a technique economists call a "Keynesian stimulus"), but during the war, half the money the federal government spent was borrowed, and nobody complained. The economy boomed. War contracts created 17 million new jobs. Industrial production doubled. The employment dial reached "full" in 1942 and stayed there until Japan surrendered.

War industries worked by a new set of rules. Contractors depended on the government for financing, materials, and labor. New war plants, built at taxpayer expense, went up in towns with little industry. As industry moved, workers moved with it into the new boomtowns, organizing themselves into a powerful political and economic force.

A Mixed Economy

The Roosevelt administration added new war agencies to control prices, assign labor, and gear up industry. It dusted off methods from World War I—dollar-a-year men and "cost-plus" contracts—and added new incentives, such as tax breaks, federal loans, and subsidies. "You have to let business make money out of the process," Secretary of War Henry Stimson explained, "or business won't work." Sometimes it didn't, and the government seized at various times the steel industry, the railroads, the coal mines, and a department store chain.

Output soared. A Ford plant at Willow Run, Michigan, turned out a fleet of B-24s larger than the whole Luftwaffe. Cargo ships, which took more than a year to build in 1941, were coming out of the Kaiser Shipyards in an average of 56 days. Entirely new industries such as synthetic rubber and Lucite (a clear, hard plastic used for aircraft windshields) appeared overnight. Industrial techniques applied to agriculture—mechanization and chemical herbicides and pesticides—raised output with fewer farmers. Corporations patriotically increased their market share. Coca-Cola's mobile bottling plants followed the front lines, creating a global thirst for their product. Wrigley added a stick of gum to each K ration and made chewing gum a national habit.

Business leaders regained the prestige lost during the Depression. Major corporations such as General Electric, Allis-Chalmers, and Westinghouse ran parts of the super-secret Manhattan Project. Edwin Witte, a member of the National War Labor Board, called this partnership "a mixed economy, which is not accurately described as either capitalism or socialism." Most business was still small; 97 percent of manufacturing came from firms with just a few hundred employees. During the war, Congress and the administration drew a line between large high-tech firms, its partners in defense, and "small business" that needed tax breaks and loans. Small business acquired its own federal agency and lobbying groups, while major corporations such as Boeing and General Electric negotiated long-term contracts with the federal government. World War II permanently divided the economy into separate "government" and "market" sectors, each with its own rules and ways of dealing with Washington.

Industry Moves South and West

Although Detroit got its share, the bulk of war contracts went to states in the South and Southwest and on the Pacific coast, shifting industry's center of gravity. Airplanes flown in World War I came from Dayton and Buffalo, but the B-29 Superfortress was made in Seattle, Washington; Omaha, Nebraska; Wichita, Kansas; and Marietta, Georgia. The Manhattan Project's largest facilities at Oak Ridge, Tennessee; Hanford, Washington; and Los Alamos, New Mexico, also broke the historic concentration of industry in the Northeast and Midwest (see Map 23–3).

There were several reasons for this shift. Like other industries moving to the huge hydroelectric grids created by the New Deal, aluminum plants went up along the Tennessee and Columbia Rivers to tap abundant power from federal dams. The government also encouraged construction in the middle of the country to lessen the danger of enemy attacks. Corporations moved south and west to find low-wage nonunion workers. Powerful

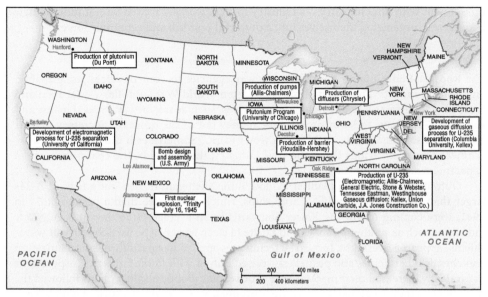

Map 23-3   The Manhattan Project The Manhattan Project created a new kind of collaboration between industry, government, and science. In a pattern of federal spending that would continue after the
war, much of the new infrastructure was located in the South and West.

southern and western senators, who controlled military appropriations, steered new development into their states.

The results were visible. The population of the West increased by 40 percent. San
Diego doubled in size in 1942. Los Angeles, Houston, Denver, Portland, and Seattle
became boomtowns. Whereas "old" industries such as automobiles and steel remained
strong above the Mason-Dixon Line, the Sunbelt states became home to the gleaming
industries of the future: plastics, aluminum, aircraft, and nuclear power.

Few objected to government direction of the economy when it meant new jobs and
industry in poor regions. A 1942 Gallup poll showed that two-thirds of Americans wanted
the government to register all adults and assign them to war work as needed. The Office
of Price Administration enlisted women consumers to enforce price ceilings by informing
on their local grocers. Citizens started scrap drives, bond drives, blood drives, and victory gardens. The war effort was so popular that the administration did not worry much
about propaganda. Roosevelt and other leaders—many of them former progressives—had
learned a lesson from World War I: in gaining public support, inducements worked better
than coercion.

New Jobs in New Places

As it had during World War I, the need for workers pushed up wages, added new
employees to the workforce, and set people on the move. It also swelled the ranks of
organized labor from 10 million to almost 15 million between 1941 and 1945. Enlisted as a partner in the war effort, unions grew because of a federally mandated

"maintenance of membership" policy, by which new employees automatically joined the union. Through the National Defense Mediation Board (NDMB), the administration encouraged cooperation, a process begun by the New Deal. When wildcat locals of the United Auto Workers struck North American Aviation plants in Los Angeles in 1941, Stimson sent the army to break the strike, but the NDMB then forced management to accept the union's wage demands. Using carrots and sticks, federal administrators encouraged a more collaborative, managerial style of union leadership. Unions did not have to struggle for membership or recognition; in return, they curbed militant locals and accepted federal oversight. Decision making moved from one-story brick "locals" in factory towns to the marble headquarters of national unions in Washington, DC.

People moved to jobs, rather than the other way around, and some 4 million workers, and with them another 5 million family members, migrated to the new sites of war production. Some 200,000 Mexican *braceros* crossed the border to harvest crops. San Francisco's African American population doubled in a year. In Los Angeles, African Americans were arriving at a rate of 300 to 400 a day. By leaving Mississippi to take a factory job in California, a sharecropper could increase his salary six- or sevenfold.

Workers were generally happy with higher wages, but many lacked a decent place to live. New York, with plenty of housing, suffered from unemployment while new factories were located in places with no housing. There were no rooms to rent within miles of Willow Run. In many towns, workers "hot bedded"—slept in shifts in boardinghouses—or lived in cars. Frustrations over the housing shortage sometimes boiled over into racial conflict. In 1943, two days of mob violence erupted in Detroit over who would take possession of 1,000 new units of federal housing. Housing remained a chronic problem during the war and for several years afterward.

Women in Industry

"Rosie the Riveter," the image of the glamorous machinist laboring to bring her man home sooner, was largely a creation of the Office of War Information. Some 36 percent of the wartime labor force was female, but that was only slightly higher than the peacetime figure (see Figure 23–2). Few women left housework to take a job in a factory solely for patriotic reasons. Instead, the war economy shifted women workers into new roles, some from service jobs into industry and others from factory jobs to better-paid positions.

The number of manufacturing jobs for women grew from 12 million to 16.5 million, with many women moving into heavy industry as metalworkers, shipwrights, and assemblers of tanks and aircraft, jobs that had been off-limits before. Women worked coke ovens, blast furnaces, and rolling mills. For many women, the war and its demands offered the first real chance for mobility.

Even so, employers did not offer equal pay or help to women trying to juggle job and family. Unions either refused women membership or expelled them when the war ended. The Lanham Act provided the first federal support for day care, but the 2,800 government centers were not nearly enough. "Latchkey children," left home alone while their mothers worked, were said to be a major problem. Experts saw female labor as necessary during the war but dangerous in the long run. "Many of them are rejecting their feminine roles," a social worker complained. After the war, women were expected to yield their jobs to

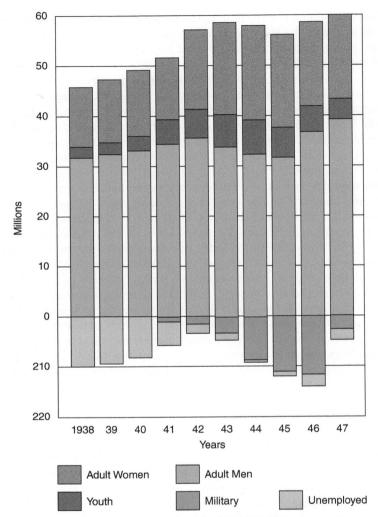

Figure 23-2 Makeup of US Labor Force, 1938–1947 Flush riveting of aluminum wing panels required a steady hand. War industries employed thousands of women.
Source: I. C. B. Dear and M. R. D. Foot, eds., *Oxford Companion to World War II* (Oxford: Oxford University Press, 2001), p. 1182.

returning servicemen. They were also blamed for neglecting their domestic duties and encouraging juvenile delinquency.

Between Idealism and Fear

In the movies, Americans marched to war (and war plants) singing patriotic tunes by George M. Cohan, but in real life this war was noticeably free of high-minded idealism. Americans had already fought once to end all wars and to keep the world safe for democracy. They were not ready to buy that bill of goods again. Journalist John Hersey asked marines on Guadalcanal what they were fighting for. "Scotch whiskey. Dames. A piece of blueberry pie. Music," they replied. Things were no clearer at home, where to writer Dwight Macdonald the war seemed to represent "the maximum of physical devastation accompanied by the minimum of human meaning."

If Americans weren't sure what they were fighting for, they knew what they were fighting against: totalitarianism, gestapos, and master races. Throughout the war and after, totalitarianism was a powerful symbol of what America and Americans ought to oppose. The president of the US Chamber of Commerce denounced the New Deal as "fascist" and "totalitarian." Labor unions and civil rights groups used the same words against their enemies, but wartime rhetoric also held Americans to a higher standard of tolerance. "All races and religions; that's America to me," sang Frank Sinatra in *The House I Live In* (1945).

Wartime leaders struggled to fill the inspirational vacuum with some of the century's most stirring restatements of the democratic creed. Winston Churchill spoke of protecting the liberty and culture of the "English-speaking peoples." In his State of the Union address in January 1941, Franklin Roosevelt aspired to a world based on the "Four Freedoms": freedom of speech, freedom of worship, freedom from want, and freedom from fear. A month later, *Life* magazine published an essay by its founder, Henry Luce, entitled "The American Century." It was a powerfully optimistic vision of globalized democracy and abundance, "a sharing with all people of our Bill of Rights, our Declaration of Independence, our Constitution, our magnificent industrial products, our technical skills." In response, Vice President Henry Wallace proclaimed that in the "Century of the Common Man," nations would "measure freedom by standards of nutrition, education and self-government." He equated democracy—as American leaders would do after the war—with schools, jobs, food, and a New Deal for the world.

African Americans sought their four freedoms in an atmosphere of increasing racial hostility. Detroit was just one city in which rapid growth touched off racial conflict. In Maryland, Michigan, New York, and Ohio, white workers engaged in "hate strikes" to prevent the hiring of African American workers. Over 3,000 white employees of a naval shipyard burned African American neighborhoods in Beaumont, Texas, in June 1943. Curfews, rumors of riots, and white citizens' committees kept many other cities on edge.

African Americans responded by linking their struggle for rights at home to the global war against fascism. Thurgood Marshall, chief counsel for the NAACP, compared the Detroit rioters to "the Nazi Gestapo." In 1942, the *Pittsburgh Courier* launched the "Double V" campaign to connect the fight against racism to the one against fascism. "Defeat Hitler, Mussolini, and Hirohito," it urged, "by Enforcing the Constitution and Abolishing Jim Crow." NAACP membership grew tenfold during the war. In Chicago, students and activists inspired by the nonviolent tactics of Mohandas Gandhi organized the Congress of Racial Equality (CORE), which desegregated restaurants and public facilities in the North. The NAACP won a legal victory in the Supreme Court case of *Smith v. Allwright* (1944), which invalidated all-white primary elections.

The experience of war may have been the greatest catalyst to change. Many African Americans returned from combat determined not to accept discrimination any longer. Amzie Moore came home to Cleveland, Mississippi, after serving in the army and was elected head of the local NAACP chapter. "Here I am being shipped overseas," he said of

Dorothea Lange Photograph Memorial Day at Manzanar Even after wartime relocation, many of the interned Japanese Americans maintained their American patriotism. In 1942, Boy Scouts, members of the American Legion, and other internees participated in a Memorial Day service at Manzanar.

his service in the Pacific, "and I been segregated from this man who I might have to save or he save my life. I didn't fail to tell it." The war prepared Moore and his generation for the struggle ahead.

Japanese Internment

Idealism was no match for fear, and in the days after Pearl Harbor, panicky journalists, politicians, and military authorities perpetrated an injustice on American citizens of Japanese descent. Ominous signs reading "Civilian Exclusion Order" went up in California and the Pacific Northwest in February 1942. They instructed "Japanese aliens and non-aliens" to report to relocation centers for removal from the Pacific coast "war zone." The Western Defense Command of Lieutenant General John L. DeWitt and the *Los Angeles Times*, believing the Japanese planned to invade the West Coast, aroused the public against the Japanese "menace." FBI investigators found no suspicious plots and told the president so, but the press continued to print rumors. Responding to the press, DeWitt, and the California congressional delegation, Roosevelt ordered the relocation.

Internees and lawyers challenged the legality of confining American citizens without charge or trial. Fred Korematsu, a welder from San Leandro, California, took a new name and had his face surgically altered in a futile attempt to stay out of the camps. When he was arrested, the American Civil Liberties Union used his case to challenge the evacuation order. Supreme Court Justice Hugo Black upheld the policy as justified by "military necessity." In January 1947, the Western Defense Command praised the evacuation program and suggested that it could be used as a model for the treatment of suspect populations during the next national emergency.

No Shelter from the Holocaust

The United States might have saved more of the victims of Hitler's "final solution" had it chosen to do so. A combination of fear, anti-Semitism, and a desire to avoid unwanted burdens led American leaders to dismiss the Holocaust as someone else's problem. The State Department, worried that spies and saboteurs would sneak in with the refugees, erected a paper wall of bureaucratic restrictions. Refugees found it easier to get a visa from China than from the United States. In 1939, the *St. Louis* steamed from Hamburg with 930 Jewish refugees aboard. American immigration officials refused to let the refugees ashore because they lacked proper papers—papers that only their Nazi persecutors could have furnished. The ship and its passengers returned to Germany.

Nazi Germany's systematic extermination of the Jews made news in the United States. Stories in the *New York Times* as early as 1942 described the deportations and concluded that "the greatest mass slaughter in history" was under way. At Auschwitz, Poland, in the most efficient death camp, 2,000 people an hour could be killed with Zyklon-B gas. Jewish leaders begged the War Department to bomb the camp or the rail lines leading to it. The city of Auschwitz was bombed twice in 1944, but John J. McCloy, the assistant secretary of war, refused to target the camp, dismissing it as a humanitarian matter of no concern to the army. Roosevelt knew of the Holocaust, but his inaction, according to historian David Wyman, was "the worst failure of his presidency."

When American soldiers entered Germany in 1945, they saw clearly why they were fighting. On April 15, Patton's Third Army liberated the Buchenwald death camp. Correspondent Edward R. Murrow described the scene to radio listeners in the United States: the skeletonlike survivors, the piles of the dead, the ovens. "I pray you to believe what I have said about Buchenwald," he said. "I have reported what I saw." Eisenhower had photographs and films taken, and he brought German civilians from nearby communities to witness the mass burial, by bulldozer, of the corpses. Many GIs doubted anyone would believe what they had witnessed. "We got to talk about it, see?" one soldier told reporter Martha Gellhorn. "We got to talk about it if anyone believes us or not."

Americans entered the World War I flushed with idealism and became disillusioned in victory's aftermath. World War II reversed this trajectory. Americans slowly came to see the power of their shopworn ideals against the hatred and bigotry that afflicted all nations, including their own. Rose McClain wrote her husband in the Pacific to promise "that our children will learn kindness, patience, and the depth of love . . . that they shall never know hate, selfishness and death from such [a war] as this has been."

The Zoot Suit Riots

On May 31, 1943, a group of servicemen stationed in Los Angeles engaged in a violent confrontation with a group of young Mexican American men, all members of a vibrant pachuco street culture identified by the oversized coats and wide-legged pants of the men's zoot suits and their distinct long, greased-back, "ducktail" hairstyle. Ostensibly a fight over the servicemen's approaching a group of pachucas, the female counterpart to the pachuco, the violent interaction reflected broader hostilities against Mexican Americans that long had simmered throughout Los Angeles's white community.

Concern about pachuco "gangs" and their "hoodlumism" was rampant in Los Angeles throughout the 1940s. Authorities interpreted the young men's defiance, expressed both by their behavior and their flamboyant dress, as an assault on American sensibilities, especially during wartime. In 1942, the War Production Board outlawed the production of zoot suits, claiming the need to ration fabric for soldiers' uniforms. Pachucos, typically American born and often straining against a traditional Mexican upbringing, resented the fact that they were expected to show loyalty, submit to the draft, and fight for a country that treated them as second-class citizens. Authorities' attempts to curtail their signature style gave rise to a bootleg market of zoot suits, which more than ever, reflected Mexican American youths' resistance and rebellion.

Apprehension about Mexican American youth escalated following the August 1942 murder of a young man named José Diaz at a reservoir in Southeast Los Angeles known as Sleepy Lagoon. Local media depicted Diaz's death as the result of a Mexican American gang war. In the aftermath of what became known as the "Sleepy Lagoon Murder," the Los Angeles Police Department raided Mexican American neighborhoods and brought in more than 600 men and women for questioning. Twenty-two men were tried en masse in *The People v. Zammora*. They were made to sit separately from their lawyers and given no opportunity to seek counsel until the day's proceedings had concluded. They were not allowed to change out of their zoot suits or cut their long hair. "Scientific" evidence submitted by the sheriff's department claimed they were like wild cats, with a predisposition to violence. In January 1943, an all-white jury found three defendants guilty of first-degree murder, and they were sentenced to life in prison; nine were convicted of second-degree murder and received sentences of five years to life.

Closing with the Enemy

"The Americans are so helpless," Joseph Goebbels, Hitler's propaganda minister, said in 1942, "that they must fall back again and again upon boasting about their matériel." After the North Africa campaign, the United States made good on its boasts. The

Zoot Suit Riots American service-men walked the streets of Los Angeles in search of zoot-suited Mexican American pachucos they wished to defrock.

From the conclusion of the Sleepy Lagoon case until May of 1943, more than 50 confrontations between servicemen and zoot-suited pachucos took place. Servicemen took particular affront to the zoot suit: their uniforms, they believed, represented American service and patriotism, and the zoot suit revealed the pachucos' disregard for both the nation and soldiers' and sailors' service. When Seaman Second Class Joseph Coleman sustained a serious head injury and a broken jaw during a clash, servicemen stationed in Los Angeles undertook a full-scale attack on Mexican American youth, their targets easily identified by the pachucos' hallmark zoot suit. The ensuing "Zoot Suit Riots" raged for the better part of a week as sailors and soldiers hunted down pachucos. The servicemen feared neither interruption nor consequence from the Los Angeles Police Department.

Whites raided bars, dancehalls, movie theaters, and other public amusements. When they found someone wearing a zoot suit, they beat the individual, stripped him of his clothes, lit the zoot suit on fire, and cut his long hair. In some instances, they followed up on their assault by depositing the individual in a garbage can. In the aftermath of an attack, the Los Angeles Police Department often would place the beaten and humiliated Mexican American (although sometimes Filipino or African American) under arrest. The attackers, depicted in local Los Angeles newspapers as white knights, restoring the city to law and order, went free.

Manuel Reyes, serving his sentence in the aftermath of the Sleepy Lagoon trial, observed the Zoot Suit Riots from behind the walls of San Quentin Prison. As he listened to the radio, read articles, and saw images of the assaults, he wrote, "It sure is terrible what's going on in L.A. I never dream[ed] that things like that would happen in the U.S.A., a land of freedom. I thought it only happens in Germany and Japan."

American army was small—only 5 million compared with Germany's 9 million—but it was amply supplied and agile, emphasizing speed and firepower. In 1944 and 1945, the United States carried the war to Japan and into the heart of Europe with a singular destructiveness. As the war drew to a close, Americans began to anticipate the difficulties of reconstructing the postwar world and to create institutions to structure a global economy at peace.

Taking the War to Europe

Using North Africa as a base, the Anglo-American Allies next attacked northward into Italy, knocking one of the Axis powers out of the war. In Sicily, where the Allies landed in July 1943, Patton applied the mobile, aggressive tactics he had advocated since 1940. Slicing the island in half and trapping a large part of the Italian army, he arrived at Messina too late to block the Germans' escape. The defeat shook Italy. Parliament deposed Mussolini and ordered his arrest. German troops took control and fiercely resisted the Allied landings at Salerno in September, and winter rains stopped the Anglo-American offensive south of Rome. American troops finally broke through to Rome on June 5, 1944.

The next day, D-Day, finally began the second front the Soviets had asked for. Early on the morning of June 6, 1944, the massive Allied invasion armada assembled off England's Channel coast and launched the assault on France's Normandy coast on beaches

Invasion of Normandy The failure to seize an intact port nearly foiled the Normandy invasion plans, but low-ranking boat pilots saved the Allies from disaster. They invented the technique of driving large landing ships onto shore at high tide and unloading directly onto the beach. When the tide came in, the now-empty ships would float off and return to England for more cargo.

designated Juno, Gold, Sword, Utah, and Omaha. Hitler had fortified the beaches with an "Atlantic Wall" of mines, obstacles, heavy guns, and cement forts. Americans waded ashore on the lightly held Utah Beach without much difficulty, but on Omaha the small boats headed straight into concentrated fire. The boats unloaded too soon, and men with full packs plunged into deep water. Floating tanks overturned and sank with crews inside. Commanders briefly considered calling off the attack, but soldiers in small groups began moving inland to outflank German batteries. By the end of the day, they held the beach.

Eisenhower's greatest fear was another Italy. The hedgerow country behind the beaches contained the most defensible terrain between the Channel and Germany. Each field and pasture was protected by earthen mounds topped with shrubs, natural walls that isolated troops. When GIs crossed a hedgerow, "the Germans could knock off the first one or two, cause the others to duck down behind the bank and then call for his own mortar support," according to one infantryman. "The German mortars were very, very efficient." However, just as had happened on Omaha Beach, the defects of the generals' strategy were compensated for by the initiative of ordinary soldiers. On their own, tankers hand-built devices to help their tanks cut through the thick hedgerows. By the end of the month, the US advance broke through German defenses and captured the critical port city of Cherbourg.

Once in open country, highly mobile American infantry chased the retreating enemy across France to the fortified German border. There, in the Ardennes Forest, Hitler's armies rallied for a final desperate counterattack. Thirty divisions, supported by 1,000 aircraft, hit a lightly held sector of the American lines, broke through, and opened a "bulge" 40 miles wide and 60 miles deep in the Allied front. Two regiments were forced to surrender, but the 101st Airborne, encircled and besieged at Bastogne, held on to a critical road junction, slowing the German advance until Allies brought in reinforcements. The Battle of the Bulge lasted a month and cost more than 10,000 American dead and 47,000 wounded, but the German army had lost the ability to resist.

Island Hopping in the Pacific

To get close enough for a knockout blow at Japan, the United States had to pierce the barrier of fortified islands stretching across the western Pacific. The army and the navy each had a strategy and bickered over supplies and the shortest route to Tokyo. MacArthur favored a thrust from Australia through the Solomon Islands and New Guinea to retake the Philippines. Nimitz, in keeping with the US Navy's prewar plans, preferred a thrust across the central Pacific to seize islands as staging areas for an air and land assault on Japan.

By November 1943, MacArthur's American and Australian forces had advanced to Bougainville, the largest of the Solomon Islands and the nearest to the Japanese air and naval complex at Rabaul. Jungle fighting on these islands was especially vicious. Each side treated the other without mercy, killing prisoners, mutilating the dead, and fighting with "a brutish, primitive hatred," according to Eugene Sledge, whose marine comrades kept gold teeth and skulls as trophies. Air attacks pulverized Rabaul in early 1944, opening the way for an advance into the southern Philippines.

Meanwhile, Nimitz launched a naval attack on Japan's island bases. With 11 new aircraft carriers, the Fifth Fleet attacked Tarawa, a tiny atoll with 4,500 Japanese troops protected by bunkers and hidden guns. Coral reefs snagged landing craft, forcing troops to wade ashore under heavy fire. Americans were shocked by the losses, more than 3,000 dead and wounded, for such a small piece of territory, but it was only one of many island battles. "Island hopping" from Tarawa to the Marshall Islands and the Marianas, American forces bypassed strongly held islands and moved the battle closer to Japan.

The Allied capture of Saipan, Tinian, and Guam in July 1944 brought Japan within range of B-29 bombers. General Curtis LeMay landed his 21st Bomber Command on Saipan in January 1945 and began a new kind of air offensive, known as "city busting," against Japanese cities. LeMay experimented with low-level attacks using high explosives (to shatter houses) and incendiaries (to set fire to the debris). The proper mix could create a "firestorm," a flaming tornado hundreds of feet high. On the night of March 9, 1945, 334 bombers lit a fire in Tokyo that destroyed 267,000 buildings. The heat was so intense that the canals boiled and 83,000 people died from flames and suffocation. LeMay went on to burn more than 60 percent of Japan's cities. Americans felt the attacks justified, but, as historian Ronald Spector has written, bomber crews "realized that this was something new, something more terrible than even the normal awfulness of war."

Building a New World

As the war progressed across Europe and the Pacific, Allied leaders met to discuss their visions of the world after victory. In Casablanca in 1943, Roosevelt and Churchill agreed to demand the unconditional surrender of the Axis powers to give the Allies a free hand to set the terms of peace. No country planned for peace as thoroughly as the United States. The State, War, and Navy Departments undertook a comprehensive survey of the world, examining each country and territory to determine its importance to the United States. Planners had only sketchy ideas about future threats, but based on experience they believed that American security would depend on having a functioning international organization, a global system of free trade, and a worldwide network of American military bases.

The weak League of Nations stood little chance of maintaining the peace in the 1930s. Roosevelt envisioned a stronger organization led by regional powers acting as "policemen" within designated spheres of influence. The new organization would disband empires, placing "trusteeships" over colonial territories preparing for self-government. The world after victory would be a world of nations, not empires or blocs. In September 1944, delegates from 39 nations met at the Dumbarton Oaks estate in Washington, DC, and sketched out a plan for a United Nations (UN) organization comprising a general assembly, in which all nations would be represented, and an executive council made up of the United States, China, the Soviet Union, Britain, and France.

To American leaders, the lesson of the 1930s had been that without prosperity there could be no peace. They wanted to remove the economic conditions that caused desperate people to follow dictators into war. A true victory, they imagined, would create an open-door world, in which goods and money could move freely, eliminating the need or justification for conquest. In 1943, before the UN existed as an organization, the United States created the United Nations Relief and Rehabilitation Administration (UNRRA) to provide food and medicine to areas retaken by the Allies. The next year, the Bretton Woods Conference set conditions for a postwar expansion of trade with new institutions, the International Monetary Fund and the World Bank, to manage the flow of money in a global economy. The army established schools at universities, where officers studied languages and discussed strategies for instilling a democratic culture in enemy nations. The invasion of Italy provided a first test of these techniques, and the United States drew on its resources as an immigrant nation to staff units with Italian-speaking officers.

Military planners were not ready to stake America's future security entirely on trade or international organizations. Pearl Harbor had shown that oceans offered no protection against aggression. Military leaders could imagine aircraft and rockets striking deep into the American heartland without warning. Beginning in 1943, they laid plans for a global system of military bases from the Azores to Calcutta to Manila, encircling the vast Eurasian land mass. Planners could not say who the next enemy would be, but with such an extensive base network, the United States could act against any challenger before it could strike. Britain and the Soviet Union looked upon this plan warily, suspecting that they might be its targets, but American leaders were willing to take diplomatic risks to attain the security they felt they required.

The Fruits of Victory

Despite rumors of his failing health, Americans elected Franklin Roosevelt to a fourth term in 1944 by a margin of 53.5 percent to 46 percent for the challenger Thomas E. Dewey. On April 12, 1945, less than three months after his inauguration, Roosevelt died suddenly of a cerebral hemorrhage at Warm Springs, Georgia. "Mr. Roosevelt's body was brought back to Washington today for the last time," reporter I. F. Stone wrote on April 21, 1945. "The marching men, the solemn bands, the armored cars, the regiment of Negro soldiers, the uniformed women's detachments. . . . In that one quick look thousands of us said goodbye to a great and good man, and to an era." In Paris, French men and women offered condolences to American GIs. Flags flew at half-staff on Guadalcanal, Kwajalein, and Tarawa. Roosevelt died just days before Allied troops in Europe achieved the great victory for which he had struggled. On April 25, American and Soviet troops shook hands at Torgau in eastern Germany. On April 30, with Soviet soldiers just a few hundred yards away, Hitler committed suicide in his Berlin bunker. On May 8, all German forces surrendered unconditionally.

Harry S. Truman, the new vice president and former senator from Missouri, was now commander in chief. Shortly after he took office, aides informed him that the Manhattan Project would soon test a weapon that might end the war in Asia. The first atomic explosion took place in the desert near Alamogordo, New Mexico, on July 16, 1945. Truman, meeting with Churchill and Stalin at Potsdam, Germany, was elated by the news. He informed Stalin while Churchill looked on, watching the expression of the Soviet leader. The bomb had been developed to be used against the Axis enemy, but by the time Truman learned about it, American leaders already saw it as a powerful instrument of postwar diplomacy.

Hiroshima The Museum of Science and Technology following the blast of the nuclear bomb.

Time Line

▼**1933**
Hitler becomes chancellor of
  Germany

▼**1935**
Congress passes first Neutrality
  Act

▼**1937**
War begins in Asia

▼**1938**
Munich agreement gives Hitler
  Sudetenland

▼**1939**
War begins in Europe

▼**1940**
Germany defeats France, the
  Netherlands, and Belgium
Destroyers-for-bases deal
  between the United States
  and Britain

▼**1941**
Lend-Lease passed
Executive Order 8802 ends
  discrimination in defense
  industries
Roosevelt and Churchill sign
  Atlantic Charter
Germany invades the Soviet
  Union
Japan attacks the United States
  at Pearl Harbor
United States declares war on
  Axis powers

As American forces neared the Japanese home islands, defenders fought with suicidal ferocity. On Okinawa, soldiers and civilians retreated into caves and battled to the death. GIs feared the invasion of Japan's home islands, where resistance could only be worse. Then, on August 6, a B-29 dropped an atomic bomb on Hiroshima. Two days later, the Soviet Union declared war on Japan, and Soviet armies attacked deep into Manchuria. On August 9, the United States dropped a second atomic bomb, this time on Nagasaki. It detonated 1,900 feet above Shima Hospital. In a fraction of a second, the hospital and nearly a square mile of the city ignited. Bricks and granite melted in the nuclear fire. People were vaporized, some leaving shadows on the pavement. In the ruins of Hiroshima, a French Red Cross worker saw "not a bird or an animal. . . . On what remained of the station facade the hands of the clock had been stopped by the fire at 8:15. It was perhaps the first time in the history of humanity that the birth of a new era was recorded on the face of a clock."

Conclusion

Emperor Hirohito announced Japan's unconditional surrender on August 14. In New York, crowds celebrated, but everywhere there was silence and reflection. Thirty million people had been killed; great cities lay in ruins. At the end of the war, the United States' economic, scientific, and military mastery reached a pinnacle never attained by any of the great empires of history. Two-thirds of the world's gold was in American treasuries; half of the world's manufactured goods were made in the United States. At its height, imperial Britain controlled 25 percent of the world's wealth. In 1945, the United States controlled 40 percent. America's air force, almost 80,000 planes, dominated the skies; its fleet had more ships than the navies of all its enemies and allies combined. Then there was the atomic bomb. The rest of the world looked to see how the United States would use its formidable wealth and power.

▼1942
Philippines fall to Japan
Internment of Japanese Americans begins
Battles of Coral Sea and Midway turn the tide in the Pacific
Allies land in North Africa

▼1943
Allies land in Sicily
Churchill and Roosevelt meet at Casablanca

US troops advance to Bougainville
Marines capture Tarawa

▼1944
US troops capture Rome
Allied landings in Normandy
US troops capture Saipan
Bretton Woods Conference
Roosevelt reelected for fourth term

▼1945
Roosevelt dies
Harry S. Truman becomes president
Germany surrenders
Truman meets Churchill and Stalin at Potsdam
Atomic bombs dropped on Hiroshima and Nagasaki
Japan surrenders

The war's sudden end meant Americans had to reconvert to a peacetime economy, preferably one more stable and prosperous than the depression economy of the 1930s. A. Philip Randolph predicted government would have to take a larger role in raising wages and stimulating key industries, such as housing, if returning soldiers were to find jobs and goods to buy. The postwar future looked tenuous. America could either succumb to "a native variety of fascism" or open an era of expanding rights, democracy, and material abundance.

Who, What, Where

Atomic bomb 722

Auschwitz 731

Braceros 727

City busting 736

Davis, Benjamin O. 720

Hiroshima 739

Internment 730

Lindbergh, Charles A. 713

Midway 716

Nimitz, Chester W. 716

Patton, George S. 723

Pearl Harbor 711

Rosie the Riveter 727

Review Questions

1. Which was more important to victory at Midway, planning or luck?

2. Why did the population of the West grow so rapidly during the war?

3. According to American leaders, what caused World War II? How did their answers to that question affect their plans for the postwar world?

4. Thurgood Marshall worried about the emergence of "gestapos" in America. What did he mean?

Critical-Thinking Questions

1. Contrast isolationist and internationalist viewpoints. How did they imagine different futures for the United States?

2. The government used propaganda and repressive laws to control domestic opinion during World War I. Why was there no repeat of those policies in World War II?

3. Some historians blame Roosevelt for luring the United States into war. How might that historical view be rooted in the isolationist/internationalist debate?

Suggested Readings

Blum, John Morton. *V Was for Victory: Politics and American Culture During World War II.* New York: Harcourt Brace Jovanovich, 1976.

Borgwardt, Elizabeth. *A New Deal for the World: America's Vision for Human Rights* Cambridge, MA: Belknap, 2005.

Kersten, Andrew E. *Labor's Home Front: The American Federation of Labor During World War II.* New York: New York University Press, 2009.

Kruse, Kevin, and Stephen Tuck, eds. *Fog of War: The Second World War and the Civil Rights Movement.* New York: Oxford University Press, 2012.

The National World War II Museum. https://www.archives.gov/topics/wwi#event-/timeline/item/archduke-assassination

For further review materials and resource information, please visit www.oup.com/us/oakes-mcgerr

23.1 FRANKLIN D. ROOSEVELT, "FOUR FREEDOMS" SPEECH (1941)

Before American entry into World War II, in his annual State of the Union address, Franklin D. Roosevelt spoke candidly about the likelihood that the nation would face war. Even as he outlined the steps the nation and its citizens should take toward preparedness, he continued to highlight the goals of his New Deal programs. Additionally, Roosevelt outlined the "Four Freedoms," values upon which he hoped the postwar world could be based. Importantly, Roosevelt envisioned these freedoms not only for Americans but also for people all around the world.

As your President, performing my constitutional duty to "give to the Congress information of the state of the Union," I find it, unhappily, necessary to report that the future and the safety of our country and of our democracy are overwhelmingly involved in events far beyond our borders.

Armed defense of democratic existence is now being gallantly waged in four continents. If that defense fails, all the population and all the resources of Europe, Asia, Africa and Australasia will be dominated by the conquerors. Let us remember that the total of those populations and their resources in those four continents greatly exceeds the sum total of the population and the resources of the whole of the Western Hemisphere—many times over.

In times like these it is immature—and incidentally, untrue—for anybody to brag that an un-prepared America, single-handed, and with one hand tied behind its back, can hold off the whole world.

No realistic American can expect from a dictator's peace international generosity, or return of true independence, or world disarmament, or freedom of expression, or freedom of religion—or even good business.

Such a peace would bring no security for us or for our neighbors. "Those, who would give up essential liberty to purchase a little temporary safety, deserve neither liberty nor safety."

As a nation, we may take pride in the fact that we are soft-hearted; but we cannot afford to be soft-headed.

We must always be wary of those who with sounding brass and a tinkling cymbal preach the "ism" of appeasement.

We must especially beware of that small group of selfish men who would clip the wings of the American eagle in order to feather their own nests.

I have recently pointed out how quickly the tempo of modern warfare could bring into our very midst the physical attack which we must eventually expect if the dictator nations win this war.

There is much loose talk of our immunity from immediate and direct invasion from across the seas. Obviously, as long as the British Navy retains its power, no such danger exists. Even if there were no British Navy, it is not probable that any enemy would be stupid enough to attack us by landing troops in the United States from across thousands of miles of ocean, until it had acquired strategic bases from which to operate.

But we learn much from the lessons of the past years in Europe—particularly the lesson of Norway, whose essential seaports were captured by treachery and surprise built up over a series of years.

The first phase of the invasion of this Hemisphere would not be the landing of regular troops. The necessary strategic points would be occupied by secret agents and their dupes—and great numbers of them are already here, and in Latin America.

As long as the aggressor nations maintain the offensive, they—not we—will choose the time and the place and the method of their attack.

That is why the future of all the American Republics is today in serious danger.

That is why this Annual Message to the Congress is unique in our history.

That is why every member of the Executive Branch of the Government and every member of the Congress faces great responsibility and great accountability.

The need of the moment is that our actions and our policy should be devoted primarily—almost exclusively—to meeting this foreign peril. For all our domestic problems are now a part of the great emergency.

Just as our national policy in internal affairs has been based upon a decent respect for the rights and the dignity of all our fellow men within our gates, so our national policy in foreign affairs has been based on a decent respect for the rights and dignity of all nations, large and small. And the justice of morality must and will win in the end.

Our national policy is this:

First, by an impressive expression of the public will and without regard to partisanship, we are committed to all-inclusive national defense.

Second, by an impressive expression of the public will and without regard to partisanship, we are committed to full support of all those resolute peoples, everywhere, who are resisting aggression and are thereby keeping war away from our Hemisphere. By this support, we express our determination that the democratic cause shall prevail; and we strengthen the defense and the security of our own nation.

Third, by an impressive expression of the public will and without regard to partisanship, we are committed to the proposition that principles of morality and considerations for our own security will never permit us to acquiesce in a peace dictated by aggressors and sponsored by appeasers. We know that enduring peace cannot be bought at the cost of other people's freedom.

In the recent national election there was no substantial difference between the two great parties in respect to that national policy. No issue was fought out on this line before the American electorate. Today it is abundantly evident that American citizens everywhere are demanding and supporting speedy and complete action in recognition of obvious danger.

Therefore, the immediate need is a swift and driving increase in our armament production.

Leaders of industry and labor have responded to our summons. Goals of speed have been set. In some cases these goals are being reached ahead of time; in some cases we are on schedule; in other cases there are slight but not serious delays; and in some cases—and I am sorry to say very important cases—we are all concerned by the slowness of the accomplishment of our plans.

The Army and Navy, however, have made substantial progress during the past year. Actual experience is improving and speeding up our methods of production with every passing day. And today's best is not good enough for tomorrow.

I am not satisfied with the progress thus far made. The men in charge of the program represent the best in training, in ability, and in patriotism. They are not satisfied with the progress thus far made. None of us will be satisfied until the job is done.

No matter whether the original goal was set too high or too low, our objective is quicker and better results. To give you two illustrations:

We are behind schedule in turning out finished airplanes; we are working day and night to solve the innumerable problems and to catch up.

We are ahead of schedule in building warships but we are working to get even further ahead of that schedule.

To change a whole nation from a basis of peacetime production of implements of peace to a basis of wartime production of implements of war is no small task. And the greatest difficulty comes at the beginning of the program, when new tools, new plant facilities, new assembly lines, and new ship ways must first be constructed before the actual materiel begins to flow steadily and speedily from them.

The Congress, of course, must rightly keep itself informed at all times of the progress of the program. However, there is certain information, as the Congress itself will readily recognize, which, in the interests of our own security and those of the nations that we are supporting, must of needs be kept in confidence.

New circumstances are constantly begetting new needs for our safety. I shall ask this Congress for greatly increased new appropriations and authorizations to carry on what we have begun.

I also ask this Congress for authority and for funds sufficient to manufacture additional munitions and war supplies of many kinds, to be turned over to those nations which are now in actual war with aggressor nations.

Our most useful and immediate role is to act as an arsenal for them as well as for ourselves. They do not need man power, but they do need billions of dollars worth of the weapons of defense.

The time is near when they will not be able to pay for them all in ready cash. We cannot, and we will not, tell them that they must surrender, merely because of present inability to pay for the weapons which we know they must have.

I do not recommend that we make them a loan of dollars with which to pay for these weapons—a loan to be repaid in dollars.

I recommend that we make it possible for those nations to continue to obtain war materials in the United States, fitting their orders into our own program. Nearly all their materiel would, if the time ever came, be useful for our own defense.

Taking counsel of expert military and naval authorities, considering what is best for our own security, we are free to decide how much should be kept here and how much should be sent abroad to our friends who by their determined and heroic resistance are giving us time in which to make ready our own defense.

For what we send abroad, we shall be repaid within a reasonable time following the close of hostilities, in similar materials, or, at our option, in other goods of many kinds, which they can produce and which we need.

Let us say to the democracies: "We Americans are vitally concerned in your defense of freedom. We are putting forth our energies, our resources and our organizing powers to give you the strength to regain and maintain a free world. We shall send you, in ever-increasing numbers, ships, planes, tanks, guns. This is our purpose and our pledge."

In fulfillment of this purpose we will not be intimidated by the threats of dictators that they will regard as a breach of international law or as an act of war our aid to the democracies which dare to resist their aggression. Such aid is not an act of war, even if a dictator should unilaterally proclaim it so to be.

When the dictators, if the dictators, are ready to make war upon us, they will not wait for an act of war on our part. They did not wait for Norway or Belgium or the Netherlands to commit an act of war.

Their only interest is in a new one-way international law, which lacks mutuality in its observance, and, therefore, becomes an instrument of oppression.

The happiness of future generations of Americans may well depend upon how effective and how immediate we can make our aid felt. No one can tell the exact character of the emergency situations that we may be called upon to meet. The Nation's hands must not be tied when the Nation's life is in danger.

We must all prepare to make the sacrifices that the emergency—almost as serious as war itself—demands. Whatever stands in the way of speed and efficiency in defense preparations must give way to the national need.

A free nation has the right to expect full cooperation from all groups. A free nation has the right to look to the leaders of business, of labor, and of agriculture to take the lead in stimulating effort, not among other groups but within their own groups.

The best way of dealing with the few slackers or trouble makers in our midst is, first, to shame them by patriotic example, and, if that fails, to use the sovereignty of Government to save Government.

As men do not live by bread alone, they do not fight by armaments alone. Those who man our defenses, and those behind them who build our defenses, must have the stamina and the courage which come from unshakable belief in the manner of life which they are defending. The mighty action that we are calling for cannot be based on a disregard of all things worth fighting for.

The Nation takes great satisfaction and much strength from the things which have been done to make its people conscious of their individual stake in the preservation of democratic life in America. Those things have toughened the fibre of our people, have renewed their faith and strengthened their devotion to the institutions we make ready to protect.

Certainly this is no time for any of us to stop thinking about the social and economic problems which are the root cause of the social revolution which is today a supreme factor in the world.

For there is nothing mysterious about the foundations of a healthy and strong democracy.

The basic things expected by our people of their political and economic systems are simple. They are:

Equality of opportunity for youth and for others.
Jobs for those who can work.
Security for those who need it.
The ending of special privilege for the few.
The preservation of civil liberties for all.
The enjoyment of the fruits of scientific progress in a wider and constantly rising standard of living.

These are the simple, basic things that must never be lost sight of in the turmoil and unbelievable complexity of our modern world. The inner and abiding strength of our economic and political systems is dependent upon the degree to which they fulfill these expectations.

Many subjects connected with our social economy call for immediate improvement.
As examples:

We should bring more citizens under the coverage of old-age pensions and unemployment insurance.
We should widen the opportunities for adequate medical care.
We should plan a better system by which persons deserving or needing gainful employment may obtain it.

I have called for personal sacrifice. I am assured of the willingness of almost all Americans to respond to that call.

A part of the sacrifice means the payment of more money in taxes. In my Budget Message I shall recommend that a greater portion of this great defense program be paid for from taxation than we are paying today. No person should try, or be allowed, to get rich out of this program; and the principle of tax payments in accordance with ability to pay should be constantly before our eyes to guide our legislation.

If the Congress maintains these principles, the voters, putting patriotism ahead of pocket-books, will give you their applause.

In the future days, which we seek to make secure, we look forward to a world founded upon four essential human freedoms.

The first is freedom of speech and expression—everywhere in the world.

The second is freedom of every person to worship God in his own way—everywhere in the world.

The third is freedom from want—which, translated into world terms, means economic understandings which will secure to every nation a healthy peacetime life for its inhabitants—everywhere in the world.

The fourth is freedom from fear—which, translated into world terms, means a world-wide reduction of armaments to such a point and in such a thorough fashion that no nation will be in a position to commit an act of physical aggression against any neighbor—anywhere in the world.

That is no vision of a distant millennium. It is a definite basis for a kind of world attainable in our own time and generation. That kind of world is the very antithesis of the so-called new order of tyranny which the dictators seek to create with the crash of a bomb.

To that new order we oppose the greater conception—the moral order. A good society is able to face schemes of world domination and foreign revolutions alike without fear.

Since the beginning of our American history, we have been engaged in change—in a perpetual peaceful revolution—a revolution which goes on steadily, quietly adjusting itself to changing conditions—without the concentration camp or the quick-lime in the ditch. The world order which we seek is the cooperation of free countries, working together in a friendly, civilized society.

This nation has placed its destiny in the hands and heads and hearts of its millions of free men and women; and its faith in freedom under the guidance of God. Freedom means the supremacy of human rights everywhere. Our support goes to those who struggle to gain those rights or keep them. Our strength is our unity of purpose. To that high concept there can be no end save victory.

Source: Franklin D. Roosevelt, "Four Freedoms," Annual Message to Congress on the State of the Union, January 6, 1941.

23.2 CHARLES LINDBERGH, AMERICA FIRST COMMITTEE ADDRESS (1941)

Anxious at the prospect of American involvement in another world war, many Americans expressed a desire that the United States remain outside the conflict taking place overseas. Those who joined the organization America First were especially vocal about the need for the United States to maintain its independence from the conflict while developing its military capabilities for its own defense rather than the defense of its allies.

In time of war, truth is always replaced by propaganda. I do not believe we should be too quick to criticize the actions of a belligerent nation. There is always the question whether we, ourselves, would do better under similar circumstances. But we in this country have a right to think of the welfare of America first, just as the people in England thought first of their own country when they encouraged the smaller nations of Europe to fight against hopeless odds. When England asks us to enter this war, she is considering her own future, and that of her Empire. In making our reply, I believe we should consider the future of the United States and that of the Western Hemisphere. . . .

There are many . . . interventionists in America, but there are more people among us of a different type. That is why you and I are assembled here tonight. There is a policy open to this nation that will lead to success—a policy that leaves us free to follow our own way of life, and to develop our own civilization. It is not a new and untried idea. It was advocated by Washington. It was incorporated in the Monroe Doctrine. Under its guidance, the United States became the greatest nation in the world. It is based upon the belief that the security of a nation lies in the strength and character of its own people. It recommends the maintenance of armed forces sufficient to defend this hemisphere from attack by any combination of foreign powers. It demands faith in an independent American destiny. This is the policy of the America First Committee today. It is a policy not of isolation, but of independence; not of defeat, but of courage. It is a policy that led this nation to success during the most trying years of our history, and it is a policy that will lead us to success again. . . .

War is not inevitable for this country. Such a claim is defeatism in the true sense. No one can make us fight abroad unless we ourselves are willing to do so. No one will attempt to fight us here if we arm ourselves as a great nation should be armed. Over a hundred million people in this nation are opposed to entering the war. If the principles of Democracy mean anything at all, that is reason enough for us to stay out. If we are forced into a war against the wishes of an overwhelming majority of our people, we will have proved Democracy such a failure at home that there will be little use fighting for it abroad.

The time has come when those of us who believe in an independent American destiny must band together, and organize for strength. We have been led toward war by a minority of our people. This minority has power. It has influence. It has a loud voice. But it does not represent the American people. During the last several years, I have travelled over this country, from one end to the other. I have talked to many hundreds of men and women, and I have had letters from tens of thousands more, who feel the same way as you and I. Most of these people have no influence or power. Most of them have no means of expressing their convictions, except by their vote which has always been against this war. They are the citizens who have had to work too hard at their daily jobs to organize political meetings. Hitherto, they have relied upon their vote to express their feelings; but now they find that it is hardly remembered except in the oratory of a political campaign. These people—the majority of hard-working American citizens are with us. They are the true strength of our country. And they are beginning to realize, as you and I, that there are times when we must sacrifice our normal interests in life in order to insure the safety and the welfare of our nation.

Such a time has come. Such a crisis is here. That is why the America First Committee has been formed—to give voice to the people who have no newspaper, or news reel, or radio station at their command; to the people who must do the paying, and the fighting, and the dying, if this country enters the war.

Whether or not we do enter the war, rests upon the shoulders of you in this audience, upon us here on this platform, upon meetings of this kind that are being held by Americans in every section of the United States today. It depends upon the action we take, and the courage we show at this time. If you believe in an independent destiny for America, if you believe that this country should not enter the war in Europe, we ask you to join the America First Committee in its stand. We ask you to share our faith in the ability of this nation to defend itself, to develop its own civilization, and to contribute to the progress of mankind in a more constructive and intelligent way than has yet been found by the warring nations of Europe. We need your support, and we need it now. The time to act is here.

Source: Charles Lindbergh, Speech delivered at America First Committee Meeting, April 23, 1941, http://www.charleslindbergh.com/americanfirst/speech2.asp.

23.3 LETTER FROM JAMES G. THOMPSON TO THE EDITOR OF THE *PITTSBURGH COURIER* (1942)

Black Americans served in every theater of World War II. By 1945, over 1.2 million black soldiers were in uniform at home in the United States, in Europe, and in the Pacific. Despite their bravery and commitment to American war aims, black servicemen and women continued to face discrimination, both at home and abroad. Hoping that the United States would honor its claims to ensure the Four Freedoms for everyone "everywhere in the world," African Americans embraced a "Double Victory" campaign, intended to conquer fascism overseas and Jim Crow at home.

Letter to the Editor, *Pittsburgh Courier*, January 31, 1942

Dear Editor:

Like all true Americans, my greatest desire at this time, this crucial point of our history, is a desire for a complete victory over the forces of evil, which threaten our existence today. Behind that desire is also a desire to serve, this, my country, in the most advantageous way. Most of our leaders are suggesting that we sacrifice every other ambition to the paramount one, victory. With this I agree; but I also wonder if another victory could not be achieved at the same time.

After all, the things that beset the world now are basically the same things which upset the equilibrium of nations internally, states, counties, cities, homes and even the individual.

Being an American of dark complexion and some 26 years, these questions flash through my mind: "Should I sacrifice my life to live half American?" "Will things be better for the next generation in the peace to follow?" "Would it be demanding too much to demand full citizenship rights in exchange for the sacrificing of my life?" "Is the kind of America I know worth defending?" "Will America be a true and pure democracy after this war?" "Will colored Americans suffer still the indignities that have been heaped upon them in the past?"

These and other questions need answering; I want to know, and I believe every colored American, who is thinking, wants to know.

This may be the wrong time to broach such subjects, but haven't all good things obtained by men been secured through sacrifice during just such times of strife?

I suggest that while we keep defense and victory in the forefront that we don't lose sight of our fight for true democracy at home.

The "V for Victory" sign is being displayed prominently in all so-called democratic countries which are fighting for victory over aggression, slavery and tyranny. If this V sign means that to those now engaged in this great conflict then let colored Americans adopt the double VV for a double victory. The first V for victory over our enemies from without, the second V for victory over our enemies within. For surely those who perpetrate these ugly prejudices here are seeing to destroy our democratic form of government just as surely as the Axis forces.

This should not and would not lessen our efforts to bring this conflict to a successful conclusion; but should and would make us stronger to resist these evil forces which threaten us. America could become united as never before and become truly the home of democracy.

In way of an answer to the foregoing questions in a preceding paragraph, I might say that there is no doubt that this country is worth defending; things will be different for the next generation; colored Americans will come into their own, and America will eventually become the true democracy it was designed to be. These things will become a reality in time; but not through any relaxation of the efforts to secure them.

In conclusion let me say that though these questions often permeate my mind, I love America and am willing to die for the America I know will someday become a reality.
James G. Thompson

Source: James G. Thompson, letter to the editor, *Pittsburgh Courier*, originally printed January 31, 1942; reprinted April 11, 1942, p. 5.

23.4 LETTERS FROM POLLY CROW TO HER HUSBAND DURING WORLD WAR II (1944)

Polly Crow's husband, William, was drafted in the fall of 1943. When he was shipped to Europe in the summer of 1944, Polly and their son William moved to Louisville, Kentucky, to be near her mother. During her time in Louisville, Polly took a number of war-related jobs, and her workplace experiences made up much of her correspondence to her husband. Her letters reveal the challenges of balancing motherhood and labor, her pride in taking on new responsibilities and earning a living, and her suspicion about the nature of American business during war time.

Louisville, June 12, 1944

Darlin'

You are now the husband of a career woman—just call me your little Ship Yard Babe! Yeh! I made up my mind that I wanted to work from 4:00 p.m. 'till midnight so's I could have my cake and eat it too. I wanted to work but didn't want to leave Bill all day—in the first place it would be too much for Mother altho' she was perfectly willing and then Bill needs me. This way Mother will just have to feed him once and tuck him in which is no trouble at all any more as I just put him in bed and let him play quietly until he's ready to go to sleep and he drops right off. . . . I finally ended up with just what I wanted. Comptometer [calculator] job—4:00 'till midnite—70 cents an hour to start which amounts to $36.40 a week, $145.60 per month, increase in two months if I'm any good and I know I will be. Oh yeh! At Jeffersonville Boat and Machine Co. I'll have to go over to Jeffersonville, Ind. which will take about 45 minutes each way. Hope I can get a ride home each nite as that's the only feature I dislike but I'm not gonna be a sissy. If I can't get a ride, I'll get tags for our buggy and probably use it. . . . If I don't need it for work I may not get them but will just have to see how things work out. Want to take Bill out swimming a lot this summer so I may need it for that. . . .

Opened my little checking account too and it's a grand and a glorious feeling to write a check all your own and not have to ask for one. Any hoo, I don't want it said I charged things to 'em and didn't pay it so we don't owe anybody anything and I'm gonna start sockin' it in the savings and checking too so's we'll have something when our sweet little Daddy comes home.
Good nite, Darlin'
I love you,
Polly

Louisville, June 13, 1944

Darlin':

Just got home from work at 12:30 a.m. Got a ride both ways with one of the girls in the office who lives about ten blocks from here—certainly am glad 'cause I didn't go for the idea of coming home alone. Like my job fine and it was great fun to get going on a comptometer again. I'm figuring the pay checks as everyone with Jefferson Boat is paid by the hour so that makes plenty of work. I haven't sat in one position and an erect one at that for so long that it was rather hard to do so I made several trips to the water fountain mainly for the exercise. We have 30 minutes for lunch at 7:15 and go across the park to a little cafe which slings out pretty good hash. At about 9:30 we all give the boss, Mr. Toby, a nickel and he goes and gets all a good old ice cold coke which is most refreshing. Haven't counted the office force but there must be about 20 of us in the nite shift. They seemed very generous with my work last nite and couldn't get over the most legible figures I made. They must be used to sloppy jobs or something. I turned over as much work as the other girls and didn't make one single error which they couldn't get over. . . . Will write you before I go to work each day so's I can tuck me in just as soon as I get home so I get plenty of good old shut eye.

I dreamed this morning that you'd come home on furlough but had to return shortly 'n you were in civilian clothes and had received 4 of ten boxes we'd sent you. I was so glad to see you I almost popped, then I woke up.
Shucks.
Good nite, Darlin'
I love you terribly,
Polly

Louisville, Nov. 6, 1944

Darlin':
. . . Have an appointment to take the car in Thursday morning to get it simonized. Have to have it in by 10:00 a.m. and it will be ready about 5:00 p.m. so I'll have to pick it up as I don't want to leave it there overnite. The strip of rubber padding came off the right door so I want to get that fixed also. Will cost about $7.00 but I figured I'd better get it done to protect the finish as it hasn't been done since you left. About time, wouldn't you say? Had 6 qts. of anti-freeze put in it yesterday and it's a good thing I did as it was 26 degrees at 7:00 a.m. and everyone will probably make a mad rush for it now. Have used all my gas coupons now up to Dec. 21st and cain't figure how I did it as I've never run short before. I guess the leak must have lost a lot before I discovered it. . . . That's where my money goes! But I want to take good care of the buggie. . . . After the simonize job, I shouldn't have to spend any more on it for a while any hoo. 'Tiz worth every penny to have it ready whenever we want to go.
"Tiz time to go."
Good nite, Darlin'.
I love you,
Polly

Louisville, March 17, 1945

Darlin':
. . . The more I see of war plants the more I believe that they're dragging this damn war out as long as possible on purpose, and no one will even make me believe that politics hasn't everything to do with the finishing or rather the prolonging of it. Jefferson Boat was bad enough I thought when it came to wasting materials and man hours as they had so many men in the yards they'd practically fall all over one another doing nothing as there was such a great surplus of help but out here it seems as tho' they have so much money they don't know what to do with it and are just throwing it away. They'll spend two weeks putting in water fountains, cooling systems or such and when they're completed they'll decide that isn't what they want and spend another two weeks taking them out, then start all over again. They build a building then decide it isn't what

they want and knock out a wall here, one there or even tear it completely down. Hell, if they'd make up their feeble minds in the first place and know what they need and want before they start it blindly they'd save millions of dollars and man hours and get this thing over with—if this is supposed to be the hottest job now the way they are going at it certainly won't help you all much—better stop as I'm feeling so hot I might burn up the paper if I continue.

I love you terribly, Darlin',

Polly

Louisville, April 3, 1945

Darlin':

. . . The boss called us all together yesterday afternoon and said when the news of victory came the plant would shut for the rest of the day but if the news came at nite we were to report the next morning as usual. He went on to explain that this plant is making a product which is . . . used or to be used in the Pacific and will continue in full force after the European victory. Everyone is expecting the exciting news any minute but I'm beginning to believe it is already over and they just aren't releasing the news yet for fear everyone will go wild with celebrating. I'm not gettin' enthused tho' until I know for true that the word is official.

Gotta go to work.

I love you terribly, Darlin',

Polly

Source: Judy Barrett Litoff and David C. Smith, eds., *Since You Went Away: World War II Letters from American Women on the Home Front* (Lawrence: University of Kansas Press, 1995), pp. 146–151.

The Cold War

1945–1954

< **George Tooker,** *Government Bureau* **(1956)**

AMERICAN PORTRAIT

John Turchinetz

In January 1946, John Turchinetz finally headed home to Boston, Massachusetts, from World War II. Just out of high school, this son of a Romanian-born father and Ukrainian-born mother had joined the Navy three years earlier at the age of 18. Serving as a seaman aboard the cruiser named for his home city, John had manned an antiaircraft gun, suffered a disabling injury, and won medals in the Pacific. After the Japanese surrender, he and some of his shipmates from the *Boston* toured the city of Hiroshima, devastated by the first atomic bomb. "It was unbelievable," the seaman recalled. Like other Americans, John and his shipmates had had enough of war. "We were glad that it was over," he said. "We wanted peace."

At first, they found it. Back in Boston, John had a joyful reunion with his family. The mayor threw a big party for the crew of the *Boston*. Living with his parents again, John went to work at the federal Navy Yard in the harbor. The government needed the veteran, but not his beloved ship, in the new era of peace: the *Boston* was taken out of service—"mothballed," they called it. Although John, like many veterans, "felt a little different," his neighborhood and his country seemed the same. After the experience of war, people were friendly and united. "We were trying to help each other," John remembered. "We were trying to be normal."

The sense of normality—the feeling of friendliness, unity, and peace—did not last long at all. Before the end of 1946, the cold war, a tense confrontation with the Soviet Union, began to disrupt American life. Soviet influence quickly spread in Eastern Europe. The USSR absorbed Ukraine, the homeland of John Turchinetz's father, and took territory from Romania, his mother's homeland, which then became a Soviet ally. Convinced the Soviets would keep trying to expand their power and spread communism across Europe, US leaders challenged their former allies. While the cold war developed, Americans also faced the task of maintaining prosperity in peacetime. Laborers, women, and African Americans struggled to preserve and extend their rights and opportunities. President Harry Truman and the Democratic Party struggled as well to preserve their power and implement a liberal agenda.

The cold war quickly became the dominant fact of national life in the late 1940s. To contain Soviet and communist expansion, the US government took unprecedented peacetime actions. But massive foreign aid, new alliances, and a military buildup did not prevent the cold war from widening and intensifying. By 1950, the nation was fighting a hot war on the other side of the world in Korea. By then, too, Americans knew that the Soviet Union had nuclear weapons that could conceivably devastate the United States. In turn, the Truman administration stepped up military spending and developed more powerful nuclear weapons. As the cold war seemed to spiral out of control, fear gripped American society. Emigres from Eastern Europe—people like John Turchinetz's parents—could be suspect. A frenzied search for communist subversives at home threatened civil liberties. In one way or another, the cold war unsettled the lives of all Americans for years to come.

John Turchinetz was not completely surprised by what happened. "I was hoping that . . . there would be no more war," he said, "but people being what they are . . . it didn't happen." Mostly he blamed the Soviet Union, dominated by communist Russians. "Even at that time, I knew about Russia," John declared many years later. "I still don't trust them."

Origins of the Cold War

In a span of two years, the United States and the Soviet Union went from a wartime alliance to the protracted rivalry known as the cold war. The sweeping, long-term consequences of the cold war made it particularly important for Americans to understand the origins of the conflict. From the outset, the United States and the Soviet Union tried to pin the blame for the cold war on each other. For a long time, Americans, like John Turchinetz, wanted to believe that the Soviet Union, authoritarian and expansionist, was solely responsible. However, historians have gradually offered a more critical perspective, and they generally agree that actions by both countries caused the cold war.

Ideological Competition

There is less agreement about the precise sources of the conflict. Ideological, political, military, and economic factors all clearly played a role. Ever since the founding of the Soviet Union toward the end of World War I, Soviets and Americans were ideological adversaries with different political systems. The Soviet Union was committed to communism and socialism, and the United States was committed to democracy and capitalism. Despite their differences, the two countries fought as allies in World War II. Wartime decisions, especially about the postwar world, laid the groundwork for animosity after 1945. In peacetime, the Soviet Union and the United States were the only countries strong enough to threaten each other, and World War II showed that with modern arms both sides could strike with devastating suddenness. Moreover, they had different political, military, and economic ambitions. By 1947, those different goals produced open antagonism. With the United States' vow to combat the spread of communism, the cold war was under way.

The Union of Soviet Socialist Republics (USSR) emerged from the Russian Revolution of 1917 and the civil war that followed. Vladimir Lenin's Bolshevik Party introduced a socialist economy in which the state—the government—owned factories and farms. At home, the Soviet Union practiced forms of economic and social regimentation Americans recognized from Nazi Germany and imperial Japan, limiting individual rights, including freedom of speech and religion, and achieving a self-contained autarkic economy. Abroad, the new nation endorsed the revolutionary overthrow of capitalism.

The Soviets' Marxist ideology obviously set them at odds with American ideals. The vast majority of Americans favored a capitalist economy, in which private citizens owned property. They celebrated individualism, freedom of speech, freedom of religion, and democratic government based on free elections. Communists believed all modern societies would eventually eliminate religion and private property and set the collective good over the rights of the individual.

Nevertheless, open conflict was not inevitable. Although American leaders hated communism, the USSR was weak and hemmed in by powerful neighbors, Germany in the West and Japan in the East. It posed no military threat to the United States in the 1920s and 1930s and could even be helpful to American interests. President Franklin Roosevelt, eager to promote trade and restrain Japanese expansion, officially recognized the Soviet Union in 1933.

Uneasy Allies

World War II demonstrated that, despite their differences, the United States and the Soviet Union could become allies. After the German invasion of the USSR and the Japanese attack on Pearl Harbor, the United States and the Soviets were thrown together in the war against fascism. They were uneasy allies at best. For many Americans, the lesson of the war was that the United States could not tolerate aggression. No new dictator should ever be able to take over other European countries unopposed, as Hitler did, nor should any single power be allowed to dominate Eurasia. By 1945, some Americans already equated the Soviets with the Nazis by denouncing "Red Fascism."

Different experiences drove each country to protect itself from future disasters. American leaders believed autarkic trade blocs had caused both the Great Depression and the war that followed, and they resolved to rebuild the world economy as a single system, with reduced trade barriers and uniform rules. Soviet leaders feared a repeat of the last two wars, when Poland and Eastern Europe had been staging areas for invasions that claimed millions of Russian lives. But the lessons they drew from war led to opposite solutions: American leaders favored an interdependent system, with open borders allowing goods, information, and people to move freely; Soviet leaders felt only a closed system and tight controls would give it real protection.

Wartime decisions also aggravated tensions. In 1943, the American government created ill feeling by excluding the Soviets from the surrender of Italy. The delay of the Allied invasion of France until 1944 embittered the Soviets, who were desperately resisting the Germans at the cost of millions of lives. The American government further strained relations by sharing news of its secret atomic bomb project with the British but not with the Soviets.

Decisions about the postwar world led to trouble as well. At a conference in Yalta in the Soviet Union in February 1945, Franklin Roosevelt, Josef Stalin, and British Prime Minister Winston Churchill proposed a self-contradictory vision of the postwar world. The "Big Three" supported national self-determination, the idea that countries should decide their own futures. They agreed that countries should act collectively to deal with world problems and laid plans for the United Nations, which would encourage states to cooperate for security. But they also believed powerful nations should dominate other nations within a "sphere of influence." In these areas—Latin America and the Pacific for the United States; Africa and the Middle East for Britain; and Eastern Europe for the Soviet Union—each power could act independently and limit the self-determination of smaller states. Clearly, spheres of influence and unilateral action conflicted with democracy, self-determination, and collective action.

The conflict was made apparent when the three leaders dealt with the future of Poland, the Soviets' neighbor to the west. Despite talk of self-determination and democracy, Stalin wanted to install a loyal Polish government that would not become a gateway for another invasion. Churchill and Roosevelt favored a self-governing Poland under its prewar leaders. Stalin agreed to elections but believed that Roosevelt had given him a free hand in Poland. This lack of clarity set the stage for future misunderstandings.

From Allies to Enemies

The United States' ambitions for global security appeared threatening to the Soviet Union. To prevent a future Pearl Harbor, the Pentagon erected a circle of air and naval bases around Europe and Asia. Thanks to the Bretton Woods agreement, the United States led a global economy that worked to the disadvantage of controlled, socialist economies. To Roosevelt these steps were not antagonistic, but to Stalin their effect was to block his ambitions with bombers and dollars.

Disagreements over Germany sharpened these suspicions. The United States wanted defeated Germany to rejoin the world economy. The Soviets wanted the country that attacked them twice in 50 years divided and weakened forever. In the end, the Big Three agreed to split it into four zones of occupation. The United States, the USSR, Great Britain, and France would each administer a zone. Although Berlin lay within the Soviet zone, the four powers would each control a section of the capital. The Big Three also agreed that eventually Germany would be reunified but did not indicate when or how.

The uncertainties and contradictions of Yalta led to disagreements even before the war ended. When Vice President Harry Truman succeeded Roosevelt in April 1945, he objected to the Soviets' attempt to take tight control of Poland. Promising to "stand up to the Russians," the new president met in Washington with the Soviet foreign minister, V. M. Molotov. Truman "gave it to him straight 'one-two to the jaw.'" "I have never been talked to like that in my life," Molotov answered. "Carry out your agreements," snapped Truman, "and you won't get talked to like that."

When Truman met with Stalin and the British prime minister in Potsdam in July, relations were more cordial. Because Soviet troops occupied most of Eastern Europe and much of Germany, Truman could do little about Stalin's actions there. There was no progress on planning the future reunification of Germany. But Truman learned during the meeting of the successful test of the atomic bomb in New Mexico. The new weapon would increase US influence everywhere in the world.

National Security

After the war, relations between the United States and the Soviet Union deteriorated. Although Stalin was still committed to overthrowing capitalism, his immediate concerns were in Eastern Europe and along the southern border with Turkey and Iran. The Soviet leader also wanted to keep Germany and Japan from menacing his country again. As an added measure of security, the USSR built a completely self-reliant economy. The United States, by contrast, did not have to worry about securing its borders or supplies. Armed with nuclear weapons, it was stronger than any rival. But American leaders feared that impoverished and vulnerable states would voluntarily align themselves with Soviet power. Every election in Europe, coup in the Middle East, or uprising in Asia had the potential to build a Communist war machine. Recalling the collapse of empires and alliances in the late 1930s, they could imagine the United States suddenly alone and vulnerable.

The Truman Doctrine

To avoid this scenario, American leaders favored the quick reconstruction of nations, including Germany and Japan, within a world economy based on free trade. They also needed military bases to keep future aggressors far from American shores. The opposing interests of the Soviet and US systems soon translated into combative rhetoric. In February 1946, Stalin declared capitalism and communism incompatible. A month later, Winston Churchill, the former British prime minister, spoke at Fulton, Missouri. Introduced by Truman, Churchill ominously declared that "an Iron Curtain has descended across the Continent" of Europe. Central and Eastern Europe, he warned, "lie in the Soviet sphere." Churchill called for an alliance against this menace.

In February 1946, George Kennan, an American consul in Moscow, sent the State Department a long telegram. The Soviet leadership, he wrote, believed "there can be no permanent peaceful coexistence" between capitalism and socialism. Stalin's regime was sure that capitalist nations, beset by internal problems, would attack socialist nations. Acting on this fear, the USSR would, Kennan insisted, try to destabilize other nations and align them with the Communist bloc. The Communist system had to expand to survive.

Iron Curtain In Winston Churchill's image, an "iron curtain" divided Europe, but soon similar barriers would mark the frontiers of containment in Asia and the Middle East.

More concerned than ever, Truman took aggressive steps to counter apparent Soviet expansion in the Mediterranean. The USSR had been pressing Turkey for control of the Dardanelles, a key waterway. Meanwhile, in Greece, a civil war pitted Communist guerillas against a monarchist government backed by Britain. By 1947, the British could no longer afford the war and wanted to pass the burden to the Americans. Truman told Congress on March 12, 1947, that the world faced a choice between freedom and totalitarianism. He announced what became known as the "Truman Doctrine." The United States must "support free peoples who are resisting attempted subjugation by armed minorities or by outside pressures." The speech, said *Life* magazine, was "a bolt of lightning." Congress voted overwhelmingly to send aid to Greece and Turkey.

The crisis marked a turning point. In 1947, Walter Lippmann coined the term "cold war" to describe the American-Soviet confrontation. There was no formal declaration of war, but with the Truman Doctrine, confrontation had certainly begun. Dividing the world into good and evil, the United States would support "free peoples" and oppose Communism. Former allies were now bitter antagonists.

Was the confrontation inevitable? There is no way for historians to prove it was, but the United States and the Soviet Union realistically could not have avoided friction. They had a history of hostility, and both possessed great military power. It is also not clear that the form the confrontation took—the cold war—was inevitable. It was the product of choices, such as Truman's decision to aid Greece, and perceptions, such as Kennan's judgment about Soviet expansion. Those choices and judgments were not the only ones that could have been made, and Americans, with good reason, would wonder for decades whether the cold war could have been different.

Containment

As the United States implemented diplomatic, economic, and military strategies for containing Soviet expansion, the scope of the confrontation widened to include the entire world. In 1949 China's civil war ended in a Communist victory. In 1950, five years after the end of World War II, the United States went to war again, this time to save a non-Communist regime in South Korea. The cold war spread and became more dangerous. When the Soviets exploded their atomic bomb, the United States also increased military spending and built a hydrogen bomb. As the arms race spiraled, the cold war seemed out of control.

Committed to opposing Soviet and Communist expansion, the Truman administration had to learn just how to fight the cold war. It would be, in George Kennan's words, "a long-term, patient but firm and vigilant containment of Russian expansive tendencies."

The term *containment* aptly described American policy for the cold war. The United States worked to hold back the Soviets for the next 40 years, but "containment," as Kennan described it in 1947, was still a vague concept. Truman and his successors had to decide where and when to contain the Soviet Union and what combination of diplomatic, economic, and military programs to use.

Containment would not, however, rely primarily on the United Nations. Like the United States, the Soviet Union had a veto over actions by the United Nations Security Council and used it to frustrate American efforts. The United Nations would become another arena for rivalry, not an instrument of American policy.

Truman and his advisers revolutionized American policies on foreign aid, overseas alliances, and national defense. Fearing that a ruined and impoverished Europe would embrace Communism, they were determined to help Europe rebuild. In June 1947, Truman's new secretary of state, General George C. Marshall, proposed a "European Recovery Plan" to combat "hunger, poverty, desperation and chaos" and to promote "political and social conditions in which free institutions can exist." The Soviets declined to join and refused to allow Eastern European countries to participate, but 16 nations eagerly supported what became known as the "Marshall Plan."

"The Marshall Plan saved Europe," Truman boasted. From 1948 to 1952, $13 billion went to boost agricultural and industrial output, increase exports, and promote economic cooperation. Whole cities were rebuilt. By 1950, participating countries had already exceeded prewar production. Prosperity helped stabilize Western European governments, bind them to the United States, and weaken Communist parties. Containment required more than aid. It also demanded the kind of military alliances that the United States had historically avoided as dangerous entanglements. But, challenged by the cold war, leaders now saw alliances as a way of preventing, rather than provoking, armed conflict. In 1949, the United States joined 10 Western European nations and Canada to form the North Atlantic Treaty Organization (NATO) (see Map 24–1). Under NATO, an attack on any member nation would be treated as an attack on all. To strengthen the American commitment to Western Europe, Congress appropriated $1.3 billion in military aid for NATO countries, and Truman ordered American troops to the Continent. General Dwight D. Eisenhower, the commander of the Allied invasion of France in World War II, became the supreme commander of NATO forces.

Containment also required vigilance. In 1947, Congress passed the National Security Act, creating a Central Intelligence Agency (CIA) to gather and assess information for the president and a National Security Council (NSC) to advise him on military and political threats. The act placed the army, navy, and air force under a single command, the Joint Chiefs of Staff, and a single cabinet secretary, the secretary of defense. The term "national security" provided a blanket justification for responses to all kinds of threats—for actions such as election rigging, proxy wars, and other "covert operations." Congress passed a new Selective Service Act creating a draft for men between 19 and 25 years old.

Taking Risks

Containment entailed risks. There was always the chance that simmering conflict could boil over into world war. One particularly dangerous hot spot was Berlin. In 1948, the Americans, British, and French began to unify their zones of occupation in Germany into a single unit under a new currency, the deutschmark. Faced with an anti-Communist western Germany, Stalin sealed off his own German zone of occupation. On June 24, the Soviets cut road and rail transport into Berlin, the jointly occupied German capital. "We stay in Berlin, period," Truman snapped, calling what he felt was Stalin's bluff. But 2.5 million Berliners were at risk of running out of food and coal. Sending an armed supply convoy through the Soviet blockade could provoke a shooting war.

Instead, Berlin was supplied by air. American transport planes carried 2,500 tons of food and fuel a day. Along with this massive airlift, the Truman administration sent to Britain two squadrons of B-29 bombers, the kind that dropped the atomic bombs on Japan. In May 1949, the Soviets ended the blockade. Tested, the strategy of containment had worked: Soviet expansion had seemingly been deterred. But the risks were clear.

Map 24-1   Cold War in Europe, 1950 Five years after World War II, the cold war had divided Europe into hostile camps, with NATO members allied with the United States and Warsaw Pact signers tied to the Soviet Union.

Those risks became even clearer later that year. In early September, American planes found radioactivity in the air over the Pacific, evidence that the Soviet Union had exploded an atomic bomb. The US nuclear weapon monopoly was over. Suddenly, confrontation with the Soviets had potentially lethal consequences. It was now, a Republican senator somberly observed, "a different world."

Global Revolutions

The cold war soon spread from Europe to shape the politics of the world. Civil and post-colonial strife in Asia, Africa, the Middle East, and Latin America came to be seen as part of the conflict between the nuclear superpowers.

The Nevada Test Site

Near the southern tip of Nevada, between the Great Basin and Mojave deserts, the land was tough and unpromising. With temperatures as high as 120 degrees Fahrenheit and very little rain, places such as Frenchman Flat, Yucca Flat, and Skull Mountain remained hot and dry. Springs sustained sagebrush and creosote bushes, along with coyotes, deer, rabbits, and rattlesnakes, but over time few people settled there. Sparsely populated, the land seemed perfect when the federal government needed vast space for the Army Air Forces to practice bombing just before World War II. And it seemed perfect again in 1950 when the government needed space for the Atomic Energy Commission (AEC) to test nuclear weapons in the midst of the cold war.

At 5:44 a.m. on January 27, 1951, an Air Force B-50D bomber dropped a small atomic bomb that exploded in the light of dawn above the new Nevada Test Site. It was the first of 928 controlled nuclear explosions that would occur over the next four decades. In addition to testing the weapons themselves, the AEC measured their effects on land, structures, animals, and people.

The government did not intentionally use human beings as test subjects in obviously lethal situations. In March 1953, for instance, Operation Annie assessed the impact of an atomic blast on "Doom Town," a collection of houses, bomb shelters, automobiles, a school bus, and department-store mannequins dressed as people. But in order to understand the effect of atomic warfare on soldiers, the AEC did have US troops observe the tests from hundreds and thousands of yards away and then had them move quickly into the blast zone.

By 1955, the Nevada Test Site grew to 1,350 square miles. Yet even this vast expanse could not contain either the spectacle of nuclear explosions or the radioactive fallout they produced. Approximately 70 miles to the south, people in the gambling resort of Las Vegas got a clear view of the flash and clouds from the tests. Thanks to wind patterns, Las Vegas did not experience much fallout. But the winds did send radioactive clouds east over Utah and on to the East Coast.

Federal officials, concerned about the public reaction to atomic testing on US soil, downplayed the dangers of nuclear fallout. "Your best action," a government pamphlet told Americans, "is not to be worried about fallout." In 1958, a leading physicist even publicly suggested that fallout "might be slightly beneficial or have no effect at all." When it became clear that fallout did have ill effects, the government tried to cover them up. After fallout from the tests killed thousands of sheep in Utah in 1953, AEC officials lied and claimed that there was no evidence of radiation found in the sheep.

Reassured by the government, most Americans accepted atomic testing at the

In China, the nationalist government of Jiang Jieshi had waged a civil war against Mao Zedong's Communist rebels since the 1920s. Both sides joined forces to fight the Japanese in World War II, but whereas combat strengthened the Communists, it weakened Jiang's corrupt and unpopular regime. When Japan surrendered, US forces helped

Nevada Nuclear Tests Unprotected members of a secret federal unit film an atomic bomb explosion at the test site in Nevada, 1957. A number of the group's filmmakers would die of cancer.

Nevada Test Site as a necessary part of fighting the cold war. Atomic-inspired consumer goods such as Starburst-pattern dinnerware and Santas with eyes like the nucleus of an atom became popular.

In Nevada, politicians saw the site as a welcome boost to the state's economy. "We had long ago written off that terrain as wasteland," Governor Charles Russell insisted, "and today it's blooming with atoms." Las Vegas, home to workers from the site and host to tourists eager to see the explosions, eagerly celebrated testing. "Heck," ran a local newspaper headline, "We're Not Scared!" A casino show girl, "radiating loveliness instead of deadly atomic particles," was crowned Miss Atomic Blast.

Despite such reassurances, people in Utah were concerned about the radioactive fallout that descended on their state. "Utahns may be accumulating small doses of atomic radiation, which would some day mean the difference between life and death," a newspaper suggested. This raised the question as to whether or not people should trust the government and its scientists. "There are still many things which even our top scientists do not yet know—specifically the long-range effects of radiation," a paper in Salt Lake City worried.

There was reason to worry. Soldiers who participated in the tests lost their teeth, developed cancers, and suffered declining health. Communities in Utah, especially the town of St. George, had abnormal rates of leukemia and other cancers. Nevertheless, the government continued to avoid the issue and people did not protest against the testing. "Our state was so stupid, they wouldn't even admit the damage it was doing," lamented Jackie Maxwell, a hospital worker, who suffered miscarriages. "We were hyper-trusting because we are taught to trust authority figures."

Complying with international treaties, the US government stopped aboveground nuclear testing in the 1960s and underground testing in the 1990s. In the twenty-first century, the Nevada Test Site, pockmarked with craters from underground tests, remains a lonely expanse, hot and dry, home to sagebrush, animals, and stored nuclear waste.

Jiang regain control of Chinese cities. Truman urged a permanent settlement, but the civil war resumed. Congressional Republicans saw China as a key cold war battleground, but Truman doubted the United States could influence the outcome. He sent the nationalists $2 billion in aid but refused to send troops. In December 1949, the defeated nationalists fled the Chinese mainland for the island of Taiwan, and Republicans angrily blamed the administration for the "loss" of China.

With most of Asia now in Communist hands, American strategists began to rethink containment. Before 1949, the danger zones were in the world's industrial heartlands, Europe and Japan. Now it seemed brushfire wars could spread nearly anywhere. Peasants had manned Mao's armies, and the rural "third world" seemed especially vulnerable. To contain Latin America, Truman organized the Rio Pact, through which the United States would provide training, weapons, and advisers for Latin American militaries. The Organization of American States (OAS), created in 1948, promoted stability and economic development from its headquarters in Washington.

Territories formerly of little strategic interest, such as Southeast Asia and Africa, became vital to security. Although the Truman administration favored self-determination, it tolerated Latin American dictatorships, European colonial dominion, and South Africa's white supremacist rule because these undemocratic regimes opposed Communism.

Korea

Working to hold off Communism at so many points, it was probably not surprising that the United States was eventually drawn into war. Nevertheless, the news that US troops were fighting in Korea startled Americans in 1950, because the conflict was so far from areas considered strategically important. But the Korean War was firmly rooted in the logic of the cold war.

Korea, a peninsula bordering China and the Soviet Union, had been liberated from the Japanese in 1945. American and Soviet troops jointly occupied the territory, splitting it into two zones at the 38th parallel. The United States opposed the popular nationalist Kim Il Sung, a Communist, and acted unilaterally to install a regime in the South under Syngman Rhee, an anti-Communist. By 1948, Korea had two governments, each claiming jurisdiction over the whole. In June 1950, after incidents along the 38th parallel, Kim's army, led by Soviet-made tanks, invaded the South (see Map 24–2).

Truman responded boldly. By itself, South Korea was not important, but the administration believed the Soviet Union was behind the North Korean attack. After the "loss" of China, Truman could not afford another Communist victory in Asia. He secured United Nations approval for international action. Troops from 15 countries eventually fought in the UN force, but nine-tenths came from the United States. Was America at war, then? Claiming the conflict was only a "police action," Truman never asked Congress for a declaration of war. For the first time, but not the last, a president sent troops to battle in the cold war without regard for the Constitution.

At first, the fighting did not go well. Ill-prepared US troops fell back toward the coast. But in the summer, General Douglas MacArthur used the US Navy's control of the seas to put troops ashore at Inchon, deep behind enemy lines. North Korea's main armies were cut off and destroyed. Within weeks, the South had been reclaimed.

Then Truman and his advisers made a fateful decision. Rather than just contain Communism, they wanted to roll it back. Truman gave the order to invade North Korea and reunify the peninsula. MacArthur, who privately wanted war with the Chinese Communists, pushed ever closer to China. Fearing an invasion, the Chinese issued warnings, sent their forces into North Korea, and, on November 25, unleashed a massive attack on UN troops. MacArthur's shattered army pulled back to defend South Korea.

Map 24-2 The Korean War, 1950–1953 The shifting lines of advance mark the back-and-forth struggle that would end with stalemate and the division of Korea.

The Korean "police action" became a stalemate. A frustrated MacArthur wanted to fight aggressively, but the chastened Truman administration gave up reunification and accepted the 38th-parallel division. That was too much for MacArthur, who broke the military's unwritten rule against public criticism of civilian leaders. "There is no substitute for victory," MacArthur lectured in 1951. Fed up, Truman fired his popular general in April as the war dragged on.

The Korean stalemate underscored hard truths of the cold war. Containment could mean sacrificing American lives in minor, nondecisive wars. As nuclear war was not an option, US troops had to be prepared, as the saying went, to "die for a tie"—to fight for something less than victory. In this kind of conflict, leaders had to convince allies, undecided nations, and citizens at home that, despite setbacks, the West would eventually win. Psychology was more important than territory.

NSC-68

Before Korea, the Truman administration tried to balance its international and domestic agendas. But by the 1950s, containment became the first priority. The administration escalated efforts against revolutionary movements even in peripheral areas, such as Southeast Asia. Colonial struggles, such as the Vietnamese rebellion against their French overlords, were seen as critical challenges.

In April 1950, the National Security Council approved a secret guideline known as NSC-68. Citing a growing list of threats and the "possibility of annihilation," it called for the United States to triple defense spending, impose order in postcolonial areas, and seek more powerful weapons. Truman worried about the cost, but the Korean War convinced him. By 1952, defense expenditures had nearly quadrupled, to $44 billion. Meanwhile, the armed forces grew—to 3.6 million by 1952—along with the list of combat theaters, now including Vietnam. Truman ordered the building of "the so-called hydrogen or superbomb." Successfully tested in November 1952, the thermonuclear bomb was far more powerful than the atomic bomb, but it did not stop the arms race. Less than a year later, the USSR had its own "H-bomb."

Although it remained top secret until the 1970s, NSC-68 profoundly changed the US economy and political system. The military buildup was paid for with deficit financing, and federal borrowing generated jobs and growth, particularly in the South and West. To fight the cold war, Americans accepted things they had long feared: secrecy, debt, alliances, a massive standing army, and centralized direction of the economy. Each of these magnified the role of the federal government.

The Reconversion of American Society

While the cold war intensified, domestic policy focused on restoring the economy and society to a peacetime footing. "Reconversion" was welcomed by a nation tired of war, but it was also a cause for worry. Americans feared a return to the desperate conditions of the 1930s. Labor, women, and African Americans, especially, wanted to hold on to and extend wartime gains.

The Postwar Economy

As World War II ended, the economy threatened to slide back into depression. Millions of unemployed servicemen came home at a time when government was cutting spending. The disaster never happened. Unemployment did rise in 1946 but never approached the double-digit rates of the 1930s. Despite brief downturns, the economy was vibrant. Its resilience reflected several factors, including veterans' choices, the federal role, the transformation of industry, and US economic dominance. Returning veterans did not strain the economy, partly because half of them went to school rather than work. Under the GI Bill of 1944, the federal government paid for up to three years of college tuition for veterans.

The GI Bill in Action William Oskay, Jr. lived in a trailer with his wife and daughter while attending Pennsylvania State College (now University) under the GI Bill in 1946.

Federal spending also helped prevent a return to the economic troubles of the 1930s. With World War II over, federal expenditures decreased dramatically, but spending was still far greater than it was during the 1930s. The GI Bill showed how spending stimulated the economy. Pumping nearly $14.5 billion into education, the bill encouraged colleges and universities to expand. As veterans swelled enrollments, institutions hired new faculty, and entire new systems, such as the State University of New York, were created.

Reconversion accelerated the economic change started by World War II. In the late 1940s, industrial production was still concentrated in the Northeast and Midwest, but new military spending was helping to shift factories and population south and west. In the 1940s, the population of the western states grew by 50 percent, compared with 10 percent in the East. The nature of the economy was changing, too. Oil and natural gas replaced coal as the chief source of power. New industries, such as plastics, electronics, and aviation, were growing rapidly.

Finally, the dominance of the United States in the world economy helped reconversion. At the end of World War II, the US economy was roughly the size of the European and Soviet economies combined. As late as 1950, America, with only 6 percent of the world's population, accounted for 40 percent of the value of all the goods and services produced in the world. Demand for American exports created jobs but also stoked inflation. Production caught up, and in the late 1940s, the economy began a prolonged peacetime boom.

The Challenge of Organized Labor

Organized labor had never been more powerful than at the end of World War II. One-third of nonagricultural civilian workers belonged to unions. The Democratic Party paid attention to influential unions, such as the Congress of Industrial Organizations (CIO), and after pledging not to strike during World War II, organized labor was eager to test its clout. Workers wanted wage increases to cope with inflation and as a reward for their contribution to wartime profits. In Europe and Japan, unions were gaining control over the way corporations did business, and some American unions also wanted a role in management. Not surprisingly, corporations were reluctant to give up any of their power or profits. Along with conservatives in Congress, they branded the unions as agents of Communism.

The result was a huge wave of strikes as soon as the war ended in August 1945. In 1946, 2 million machinists, longshoremen, and other workers around the country called a record 4,985 strikes. "[L]abor has gone crazy," an anxious Truman told his mother.

Significant work stoppages hit automobile factories, coal mines, and railroad yards. Late in 1945, the United Auto Workers (UAW) struck General Motors (GM) for a 30 percent raise in hourly wages, access to the company's books, and more say in company decisions. GM rejected union interference in management decisions. When the strike finally ended after 113 days, the UAW won only some of its wage demands. It marked a turning point for labor. Unions never again demanded to participate in management, but instead focused on pay and benefits.

The coal and railroad strikes were even more contentious. Members of the United Mine Workers (UMW) and the railway unions refused to accept federal arbitration. As the coal supply dwindled, power systems suffered "brownouts," and railroad passengers were stranded. The situation tested the strong relationship, forged in the New Deal, between the Democratic Party and organized labor. Truman ordered federal takeovers of the mines and the railroads. "Let Truman dig coal with his bayonets," snarled John L. Lewis, leader of the UMW. But the strikes ended in May. Many Americans applauded the president's action and believed that Lewis and other union leaders had become too powerful and demanding.

Counting on this unhappiness with unions, probusiness Republicans in Congress soon moved to limit the power of organized labor. In 1947, a coalition of Republicans and conservative, mostly southern Democrats passed the Taft-Hartley Act, a sweeping modification of federal labor law. The bill made it easier for employers to hire nonunion workers and to oppose the formation of unions. It also limited unions' right to organize and engage in political activity. Most humiliating, it compelled union leaders to swear that they did not belong to the Communist Party.

Despite these setbacks, workers and unions prospered. Landmark contract negotiations between the UAW and GM offered a model of labor relations. In 1948, the UAW won guaranteed cost-of-living adjustments, known as COLAs, and an annual wage increase tied to rises in worker productivity. In the so-called Treaty of Detroit, signed in 1950, the UAW won other increases and a pension plan in a long five-year contract. In return for pensions and protection against inflation, autoworkers gave management stable, predictable labor relations over the long term.

The Treaty of Detroit ended a difficult period for organized labor. Thanks to lucrative contracts, many workers were more secure than ever before, but reconversion also limited the power of organized labor and the support of the Democratic Party. Aggressive strikes produced mixed results, public hostility, and government interference. With the end of the strike wave, unions effectively abandoned their demand to participate in management.

Opportunities for Women

Reconversion also posed special challenges to the status of American women. During World War II, the shortage of male labor had expanded women's opportunities for employment. Working women prized the income and the sense of satisfaction they gained from performing jobs traditionally monopolized by men. But employers and government officials encouraged the belief that women should surrender jobs to returning veterans. The number of women in the labor force dropped 13 percent from 1945 to 1946, but reconversion did not send female workers home for good. Three-quarters of the women who wanted to stay at work after the war managed to find jobs.

Most women, of course, needed to earn a living for themselves or their families. By 1953, the number of women in the workforce matched the level of 1945. The number in nontraditional jobs increased, too. More women than ever before were skilled craftspersons, forepersons, physicians, and surgeons.

The number of married women in the postwar labor force was especially notable, as economic necessity overcame cultural prejudice against working mothers and married women. By 1947, there were more married women than single women in the wage labor force.

The armed forces, like civilian employers, initially cut back the number of women in the ranks when the war ended, but Congress granted women permanent status in the armed forces and merged the separate women's military organizations, such as the Women's Army Corps, into the regular armed services.

Despite these gains, women still faced discrimination. The majority had to settle for traditionally female, low-paying jobs in offices, stores, and factories. Women's hourly pay rose only half as much as men's pay in the first years after the war. In the military, women were largely confined to noncombatant roles such as nursing. There were no women generals.

In the larger society there was little interest in women's rights. After a meeting with female activists, Truman dismissed a constitutional amendment guaranteeing equal rights for women as a "lot of hooey."

Despite the lack of support for women's rights, women's opportunities were gradually expanding in the postwar years; the combination of women's desires and the economy's needs was slowly promoting the feminization of the labor force.

Civil Rights for African Americans

Like women, African Americans had made significant gains during World War II. They filled new roles in the military and higher-paying jobs in the civilian economy and pushed their demand for civil rights. Like women, African Americans sought to preserve and extend these rights and opportunities in the face of substantial resistance.

Several factors, including economic change, legal rulings, and wartime experiences, stimulated the postwar drive for equal rights and opportunities. By the end of the war, the transformation of the southern economy was undermining the system that segregated African Americans and denied them the right to vote. As mechanization reduced the need for field hands, African Americans left for the region's growing cities and for the North and West. One of the basic rationales for segregation—the need for an inexpensive, submissive labor force in the fields—was disappearing. The developing southern economy also attracted whites from other regions who were less committed to segregation and disfranchisement. Meanwhile, by migrating to northern and western cities, African Americans increased their votes and political influence.

In fighting the Nazis during the war and the Communists afterward, the United States dedicated itself to universal freedoms. The United Nations Declaration on Human Rights committed member states to guarantee rights to education, free movement, assembly, and personal safety. African Americans appealed to the UN, the courts, and the press to have the United States recognize these commitments.

During the 1940s, a series of US Supreme Court decisions struck at racial discrimination and encouraged African Americans to challenge inequality. In *Smith v. Allwright* in 1944, the Court had banned whites-only primary elections. In *Morgan v. Virginia* in 1946, the Court ruled that interstate bus companies could not segregate passengers. In *Shelley v. Kraemer* in 1948, the court banned restrictive covenants, the private agreements between property owners not to sell houses to African Americans and other minorities. These and other court decisions weakened discriminatory practices and suggested that African Americans might have a judicial ally in the struggle for justice.

African Americans' war experiences also encouraged them to demand more and to expect justice from the country they fought for. "Our people are not coming back with the idea of just taking up where they left off," an African American private wrote. "We are going to have the things that are rightfully due us or else."

That kind of determination spurred civil rights activism after the war. In the South, African Americans increasingly demanded the right to vote after *Smith v. Allwright*. The National Association for the Advancement of Colored People (NAACP) set up citizenship schools in the South to show African American voters how to register. The campaign was driven, too, by individual actions. In July 1946, Medgar Evers, a combat veteran who had just reached his 21st birthday, decided to try to vote in the Democratic Party's primary election in Decatur, Mississippi.

Such activism was resisted by whites deeply committed to disfranchisement and segregation. A white mob kept Evers from voting in 1946. In Georgia, whites killed an African American voter. More often, they manipulated registration laws to disqualify voters. A voter seeking to register might have to answer such questions as "How many bubbles are there in a bar of soap?" Still, African American voter registration in the South, only 2 percent in 1940, rose to 12 percent by 1947. The result was the election of a few African American officials and improved service from local government.

Alongside the campaign for voting rights, civil rights activists fought segregation across the country. The interracial Congress of Racial Equality (CORE) took the lead in protesting public discrimination. To test the Supreme Court's decision in *Morgan*, CORE sent an integrated team on a bus trip through the upper South, where they met with violence and arrests. Activists hardly dented segregation in the South in the 1940s but had more success promoting antidiscrimination laws in the North. By 1953, fair employment laws had been adopted in 30 cities and 12 states.

Activists also pressured Truman to support civil rights. In the spring and summer of 1946, picketers marched outside the White House with signs that read, "SPEAK, SPEAK, MR. PRESIDENT." Racial discrimination was an embarrassment for a nation claiming to represent freedom and democracy in the world, but support for civil rights was a risk for a politician dependent on white support. Nevertheless, Truman took significant steps.

In the fall of 1946, Truman supported a presidential committee report, *To Secure These Rights*, that called for strong federal action against lynching, vote suppression, job discrimination, and civil rights violations, including segregation in the armed forces. Furious white southern politicians and newspapers said Truman was "stabbing the South in the back."

African Americans, meanwhile, kept the heat on Truman. To protest discrimination in the military, A. Philip Randolph, the head of the Brotherhood of Sleeping Car Porters, proposed a boycott of the draft. In July 1948, Truman responded with Executive Order 9981, creating a committee to phase out discrimination in the military. He also established the Fair Employment Board, which moved more slowly against discrimination in federal hiring.

Jackie Robinson Steals Home for the Brooklyn Dodgers His daring, speed, and power helped force the integration of Major League Baseball.

During the Truman years, the most publicized blow to racial inequality came not from the White House but the baseball diamond. When the Brooklyn Dodgers called up infielder Jackie Robinson from the minor leagues in 1947, he became the first African American to play in the major leagues since the late nineteenth century. A strong, self-disciplined former soldier, Robinson took taunts and beanballs on the field and death threats in the mail. Fast, powerful, and exciting, he finished the season as the National League's Rookie of the Year. Robinson's success paved the way for increasing numbers of African American players in the majors over the next several years.

Robinson's success also spelled the end of the Negro Leagues, created when African Americans were banned from the major leagues. Integration would sometimes undermine distinctly African American institutions. Nonetheless, the achievements of Robinson, Larry Doby, and other pioneering African American players sent a powerful message for civil rights and underscored the limits of reconversion. On the whole, African Americans preserved and sometimes expanded their wartime gains while still encountering injustice and inequality. In one respect, African Americans, women, and organized labor shared a common experience in the first years after World War II. For each of these groups, struggling for rights and opportunities, reconversion turned out to be better than feared and worse than hoped. They all confronted the limits of their power to change the society around them.

The Frustrations of Liberalism

During the Great Depression, New Deal liberalism had reshaped American democracy, thrusting the federal government more deeply than ever into economic and social life. But the liberal Democratic agenda of federal activism, which stalled during World War II, met more frustration afterward. Liberals and the Democratic Party strained to provide answers for a nation no longer facing an economic or military emergency. Harry Truman struggled to prove that he was a worthy successor to Franklin Roosevelt.

The Democrats' Troubles

Many Americans were skeptical about their accidental president. Liberals who wondered whether Truman shared their ideals were incensed when he fired FDR's trusted aide Henry Wallace after Wallace criticized Truman's policy toward the USSR. Conservatives and moderates also had their doubts. During the Depression, Americans had been willing to endorse government interventions in the economy, but they felt less need for government and more need for individual freedom in a prosperous peacetime.

The president was more liberal than the liberals expected. Shortly after he took office in 1945, he presented a legislative program that included proposals on education, employment, insurance, social security, and civil rights. Yet a full-employment bill, giving the federal government responsibility for securing jobs and prosperity, met overwhelming conservative and moderate opposition. Watered down by Congress, the resulting Employment Act of 1946 created a presidential Council of Economic Advisors but did nothing to increase the economic role of the federal government.

Truman and the liberals suffered an even sharper defeat over the president's sweeping proposal for a national health insurance system that would guarantee medical care to all Americans. Under the plan, the federal government would manage the insurance system and set doctors' and hospitals' fees. Conservatives and the medical profession promptly condemned the proposal as socialism. The bill failed, and so did most of Truman's domestic proposals.

Nevertheless, the federal role in national life continued to grow. Medical care offered a notable example. The Veterans Administration established a vast network of federal hospitals to care for returning soldiers. In 1946, the Hill-Burton Act appropriated federal money for new hospitals. That same year, Congress created a research lab in Atlanta, later called the Centers for Disease Control, to monitor infectious diseases. Congress also established the National Institute of Mental Health in 1949.

As Truman struggled with domestic and foreign policy, he became increasingly unpopular. "To err is Truman," went the joke. "Had enough?" asked Republicans. Many had. In the 1946 congressional elections, the voters gave the Republicans a majority in the House of Representatives and the Senate for the first time in 16 years.

Truman's Comeback

The 1946 elections seemed to presage a defeat for Truman in two years, but the president managed a stunning comeback. It began with the Republican majority that took control in Congress in 1947. Led by Senator Robert Taft of Ohio, Republicans hoped to replace New Deal liberalism with a different understanding of American democracy. Refuting "the corrupting idea" that prosperity, equality, or opportunity can be legislated, Taft wanted "free Americans freely working out their destiny." The Taft-Hartley Act was a blow to liberals and the administration, but Republicans found themselves trapped by Americans' ambivalence about liberalism. Only a minority was enthusiastic about such innovations as national health insurance, but there was little sentiment to roll back the New Deal and its benefits. Besides Taft-Hartley, the Eightieth Congress did not accomplish much, and soon Truman was campaigning against a "do-nothing Congress."

Still, things looked bad for Truman. By March 1948 his approval rating was 35 percent. His party was also splitting apart. On the left, his former secretary of commerce Henry Wallace was running for president as a "Progressive." On the right, Democratic governor Strom Thurmond of South Carolina was running as a "Dixiecrat," appealing to white supporters of segregation. Truman seemed certain to lose in November. Or so his Republican opponent, Governor Thomas E. Dewey of New York, thought. Dewey believed an uncontroversial campaign would do the trick, but Truman pulled the New Deal majority back together. The president reached out to African Americans, labor, farmers, senior

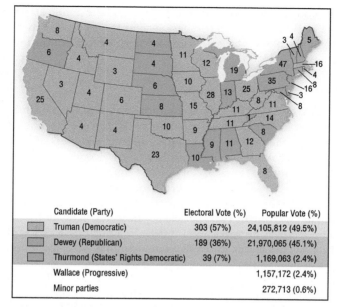

Candidate (Party)	Electoral Vote (%)	Popular Vote (%)
Truman (Democratic)	303 (57%)	24,105,812 (49.5%)
Dewey (Republican)	189 (36%)	21,970,065 (45.1%)
Thurmond (States' Rights Democratic)	39 (7%)	1,169,063 (2.4%)
Wallace (Progressive)		1,157,172 (2.4%)
Minor parties		272,713 (0.6%)

Map 24-3   The 1948 Presidential Election Segregationist and progressive candidacies were expected to undermine the Democratic majority, but the Roosevelt coalition returned Truman to the White House for a second term.

citizens, and other beneficiaries of New Deal liberalism. "Give 'em hell, Harry," the crowds shouted, and he did, driving home his vision. "The Democratic Party puts human rights and human welfare first," he declared. "These Republican gluttons of privilege . . . want a return of the Wall Street economic dictatorship."

On Election Day, Wallace and Thurmond received only a million votes each. Dewey attracted fewer votes than he had four years before. Leading Roosevelt's coalition, Truman won the presidency with only 49.5 percent of the vote (see Map 24–3). The Democrats recaptured the House and the Senate, but the triumph did not last long. Like Taft two years before, Truman soon discovered that a victory did not mean a mandate. In his State of the Union address in January 1949, Truman declared that "every individual has a right to expect from our Government a fair deal." But his "Fair Deal" legislation stalled in Congress. Despite Truman's comeback, the liberal vision could not dominate the politics of cold war America.

Fighting the Cold War at Home

Beyond the battles over domestic policy, the cold war increasingly intruded into every aspect of life. Billions of dollars in defense expenditures stimulated economic growth and kept John Turchinetz employed at the Boston Navy Yard, but fear, doubt, and insecurity pervaded the late 1940s. Americans added a new fear of nuclear weapons to their old fear of immigrants, and society succumbed to a largely irrational dread of hidden traitors in Hollywood, Washington, the universities, and the public library. To fight the cold war at home, anti-Communist crusaders such as Joseph McCarthy hunted for disloyal Americans. By the 1950s, McCarthyism was capable of destroying the lives of thousands of Americans.

Doubts and Fears in the Atomic Age

Despite triumph in World War II, American culture was dark and pessimistic in the late 1940s. The rise of fascism, the Holocaust, and the bombings of Hiroshima and Nagasaki raised questions about the direction of progress and the goodness of humankind. The cold war did nothing to calm those concerns. Even the welcome prosperity of the reconversion period did not soothe this sense of doubt. People felt small and powerless in an age of big corporations, big unions, big government, and superbombs.

Americans revealed their unease in a variety of ways. Not long after the announcement of the Truman Doctrine in 1947, people began seeing lights in the sky, and "flying saucers" were reported over 35 states and Canada. In a nuclear-armed world, columnist Joseph Alsop observed, the saucer scare was a reminder that "man-made horrors are quite real, quite imminent possibilities."

Meanwhile, Hollywood films explored popular fears. In 1946, *The Best Years of Our Lives* traced the difficult, sometimes humiliating readjustment of three returning veterans. The same year, *It's a Wonderful Life* told the story of a small-town banker forced to accept the disappointment of his unfulfilled dreams. Both films expressed reservations about the morality of capitalism and the chances of achieving happiness in the modern world. A new genre, film noir, offered an even darker view. Such films as *Fear in the Night* (1947) and *Kiss Me Deadly* (1955) told the harrowing stories of individuals trapped in a confusing, immoral world.

As the greatest source of fear, nuclear weapons dominated the popular imagination. Many Americans dealt with their anxiety about the Atomic Age in a variety of ways, including dark attempts at humor. Americans drank "atomic cocktails" and danced the "atomic polka." American women wore the new "bikini," the explosively scanty bathing suit named for the Pacific atoll where the United States tested the H-bomb. The Soviets' development of the atomic bomb and the hydrogen bomb was impossible to laugh away.

Americans' fear was also reflected in the hardening of attitudes toward foreigners. In 1945, the nation welcomed the foreign wives of American servicemen by passing the War Brides Act, but as the cold war intensified, other potential migrants met a hostile reception. The Immigration and Nationality Act of 1952 tightly restricted immigration, particularly from Asia. It kept out Communists and gays and allowed the deportation of American citizens suspected of disloyalty.

The Anti-Communist Crusade

Americans may have feared disloyalty most of all. Many believed the real Communist threat came from within. Historians debate the origins of this second "Red Scare." Some trace the anti-Communist crusade to a conservative reaction against the rise of labor, African Americans, women, and other disempowered groups. Others blame the Truman administration for using fear to justify unprecedented military activity and spending. Although anti-Communism had deep roots in American culture, politicians in both parties gave domestic anti-Communism its particularly dangerous form.

The crusaders had to search hard for local Communists. The Communist Party of the United States of America (CPUSA), a legal political party, was tiny and losing followers. Infiltrated by FBI and police informants, it never received more than 0.3 percent of the popular vote. Just to be sure, the Truman administration charged 12 party leaders with violating the Smith Act, which criminalized membership in "a group advocating . . . the overthrow of the government by force." In 1949, 11 were convicted and sent to jail.

Open Communists seemed to pose less of a threat than secret ones. In the late 1940s, self-professed former Communists and spies eagerly turned informant to reveal America's presumed hidden network of traitors. The hunt for these "subversives" was led by the House of Representatives' Un-American Activities Committee (HUAC). In 1947, HUAC held hearings on supposed Communist plots in Hollywood. The film industry cooperated, but eight screenwriters, a producer, and a director cited their First Amendment rights and declined to testify. The "Hollywood Ten" were convicted of contempt of Congress and sent to jail for up to a year. Film studios got the message and "blacklisted"—refused to hire—writers, directors, and actors even remotely suspected of Communist ties. Avoiding controversial subjects, studios put out overwrought anti-Communist movies such as *The Red Menace* and *I Was a Communist for the FBI*.

Afraid of looking "soft" on Communism, the Truman administration declared there was a real problem with domestic Communism. "Communists," said Truman's attorney general, Tom Clark, "are everywhere . . . and each carries with him the germs of death for society." In 1947, the president created an "employee loyalty" program. Any civil servant

George Tooker, *Government Bureau* (1956) Modernist painter George Tooker captured the claustro-phobic anxiety of the McCarthy era in paintings like *Government Bureau* and *The Subway* (1950). In popular fiction and noir films, social conformity thinly concealed a mounting hysteria.

STRUGGLES FOR DEMOCRACY

The Hollywood Ten

With the passage of time, the enormity of the anti-Communist crusade becomes harder to understand. In the midst of a violent century that saw two world wars, the search for Communist subversives seems fairly tame. Little blood was shed. Relatively few people went to jail. Yet the anti-Communist crusade damaged American democracy. As the case of the Hollywood Ten illustrates, the Red Scare harmed the careers and lives of Americans who were not traitors. In turn, the fate of these victims intimidated the American public, as well as the leaders of powerful institutions, into silence and acquiescence. Democracy, dependent on the right to free speech and dissent, suffered.

The crusade against Communism rested on the authority of the US government. The case of the Hollywood Ten began in 1947 when the House Committee on Un-American Activities (HUAC), as part of its longtime search for disloyalty, investigated "alleged Communist influence and infiltration in the motion-picture industry." Using its subpoena power, the committee compelled director Edward Dmytryk, writers Dalton Trumbo and Ring Lardner, Jr., and

seven other suspected Communists to testify as so-called unfriendly witnesses at hearings in Washington, DC. The chair of the committee, J. Parnell Thomas of New Jersey, allowed only one of the Ten to read a prepared statement; the rest were not given this customary right. Badgering the witnesses, Thomas did not let them respond to accusations against them and he had three of them forcibly removed from the hearing room. Thomas also insisted that each of the Ten answer what he called the "$64 question": "Are you now, or have you ever been a member of the Communist Party of the United States?" When the witnesses declined to answer directly, HUAC had all of them cited for contempt of Congress.

In conjunction with the legal power of government, the anti-Communist crusade depended on the willing cooperation of individual Americans. Film stars such as Gary Cooper and Robert Montgomery appeared at the HUAC hearings as "friendly witnesses" to reveal the names of alleged Communists.

The Red Scare also depended on the help of powerful institutions. The Screen Actors Guild, a union led by actor and

could lose his or her job by belonging to any of the "totalitarian, Fascist, Communist or subversive" groups listed by the attorney general. The program had little regard for due process. People accused of disloyalty could not challenge evidence or confront their accusers and were presumed guilty until they proved their innocence. Although only about 300 employees were discharged, the loyalty program helped create the impression of a serious problem in Washington.

future president of the United States, Ronald Reagan, gave the names of suspected Communist sympathizers. Faced with damaging publicity about Communism in Hollywood, the major movie studios ostentatiously joined the anti-Communist crusade. In November 1947, studio heads issued a statement vowing not to rehire "any of the ten until such time as he is acquitted or has purged himself of contempt and declares under oath that he is not a Communist." The studios proceeded to discriminate against suspected Communists and to make safe films that could not possibly be considered pro-Communist. In this way, HUAC managed to reshape a powerful national institution without passing a law.

The anti-Communist crusade flourished because many Americans did not speak out against it for fear of persecution. The Hollywood Ten had some famous defenders in the film industry, including actors Lauren Bacall and Humphrey Bogart. But few people were willing to risk accusations of Communism and disloyalty by supporting the "unfriendly witnesses."

Help from the judicial system was also essential to fueling the Red Scare. The courts were willing to endorse or at least ignore the often unconstitutional treatment of suspected Communists. In the spring of 1948, the US District Court in Washington, DC, speedily convicted two of the Hollywood Ten, screenwriters John Howard Lawson and Dalton Trumbo, for contempt of Congress. When the US Supreme Court refused to review their cases, the rest of the Ten were convicted in 1950. As author E. B. White observed, "Ten men have been convicted, not of wrong-doing but of wrong thinking; that is . . . bad news."

The combination of government power, "friendly witnesses," discriminatory studios, intimidated supporters, and complaisant courts defeated the Hollywood Ten. In addition to their fines and jail sentences, they faced being blacklisted. Only one of them, director Edward Dmytryk, immediately denounced communism and went back to work in Hollywood. Some of the rest wrote screenplays under pseudonyms. But they could not work openly in Hollywood again until the 1960s, when the hysteria of the Red Scare had died down. In the meantime, HUAC had successfully used the Hollywood Ten to intimidate the film industry and send a powerful message to the rest of American society not to interfere in the search for supposed Communists. Basic rights and freedoms disappeared amid the persecution of a minority and the silence of the majority.

The Hunt for Spies

There was, in fact, spying going on inside the government. The Soviet Union, like the United States, carried out espionage abroad. The Canadian government found evidence of a spy ring that had passed American atomic secrets to the Soviets during World War II. Through interceptions of Soviet communications, the CIA knew about the spy ring but chose not to share this information with Congress, prosecutors, or even the president.

Thanks to the Canadian evidence, the FBI began to suspect that Alger Hiss, an aide to the secretary of state, was a Soviet agent. Hiss was quietly eased out of his job. Then, in 1948, HUAC took testimony from Whittaker Chambers, a *Time* magazine editor who claimed to have been a Soviet agent in the 1930s. Chambers accused Hiss of passing secret documents. The patrician Hiss denied the charges and said he had never even met Chambers. He seemed more credible than the rumpled Chambers, an admitted perjurer, but Congressman Richard Nixon of California, a Republican member of HUAC, forced him to admit that he had known Chambers under an alias. With help from the FBI, Chambers charged that Hiss had given him secret information in the 1930s. When Chambers produced microfilmed photographs of the secret documents, Hiss could not explain them. Under the statute of limitations, it was too late to try Hiss for spying, but not too late to indict him for lying to Congress. Hiss's perjury trial ended in a hung jury in 1949, but a second jury convicted him in 1950, and he served almost four years in federal prison. The case was a triumph for Republicans and conservatives and a blow to Democrats and liberals.

As the Hiss case ended, another scandal stoked Americans' fears. In early 1950, British authorities arrested Klaus Fuchs, a physicist who had worked at the US nuclear research facility in Los Alamos, New Mexico. The investigation led to David Greenglass, who worked on the atomic bomb project, and his brother-in-law, Julius Rosenberg. Julius, a former member of the CPUSA, and his wife, Ethel, were convicted of conspiring to steal atomic information in a trial controversial for its anti-Semitic overtones and because the act protecting atomic secrets became law after the spying allegedly took place. Though they had two young sons, both Rosenbergs were sentenced to death. Ignoring appeals for clemency, the federal government electrocuted the Rosenbergs in 1953.

There now seems little doubt that the USSR obtained American nuclear secrets, but the impact was probably not as great as conservatives feared or as small as liberals insisted. Most likely, espionage sped up work on an atomic bomb the Soviets would have eventually produced anyway.

Time Line

▼**1945**
Yalta conference
Harry S. Truman inaugurated
Potsdam Conference
Industrial strikes break out

▼**1946**
Winston Churchill's "Iron Curtain" speech
George Kennan's "long telegram" on Soviet expansionism
Employment Act of 1946

Morgan v. Virginia
Election of Republican majorities in House and Senate

▼**1947**
Announcement of Truman Doctrine
Beginning of Federal Employee Loyalty Program
Integration of Major League Baseball by Jackie Robinson
HUAC Hollywood hearings
Rio Pact

Taft-Hartley Act
National Security Act
Presidential commission reports on civil rights

▼**1948**
Shelley v. Kraemer
Congressional approval of Marshall Plan
Truman's Executive Order 9981
Beginning of Berlin crisis
Selective Service Act
Truman elected president

The Rise of McCarthyism

Two weeks after Hiss's conviction, one week after Truman's announcement of the decision to build the hydrogen bomb, and days after the arrest of Klaus Fuchs, Senator Joseph McCarthy of Wisconsin spectacularly took command of the anti-Communist crusade. Speaking to the Republican Women's Club of Wheeling, West Virginia, the previously obscure senator claimed to have names of 205 Communists working in the State Department. In fact, McCarthy had no new information, only a handful of old accusations.

Nevertheless, McCarthy was instantly popular and powerful. Frightened by new dangers, many people wanted to believe in a senator bold enough to fight back. Some shared McCarthy's resentment of privileged elites—New Dealers, diplomats, scientists—whom he derided as "egg-sucking phony liberals" and "bright young men . . . born with silver spoons in their mouths." For some Americans—immigrants, Midwesterners, Catholics, and fundamentalists—support for McCarthy was a way to prove their patriotism. Even Democratic legislators voted for the Internal Security Act of 1950, which forced the registration of Communist and Communist-front groups, provided for the deportation of allegedly subversive aliens, barred Communists from defense jobs, made picketing a federal court house to affect a case a felony, and granted the president emergency powers to detain individuals who might engage in espionage. Refusing to "put the Government of the United States in the thought control business," Truman vetoed the bill, but Congress overrode his veto.

Eventually, McCarthy went too far. Angry that one of his aides, David Schine, had not received a draft deferment, he launched an investigation of the army. The secretary of the army, Robert T. Stevens, refused to cooperate and claimed McCarthy had tried to get preferential treatment for Schine. In April 1954, before a television audience of 20 million people, McCarthy failed to come up with evidence of treason in the army. When he tried to smear a young army lawyer as a Communist, the senator was exposed. "Have you no sense of decency, sir, at long last?" asked the army's chief counsel, Joseph Welch. It was an electric moment. The Senate hearings came to no judgment, but Americans

▼1949
Formation of North Atlantic Treaty Organization
Communist takeover of mainland China

▼1950
NSC-68
Alger Hiss's conviction for perjury
Joseph McCarthy's speech in Wheeling, West Virginia

Treaty of Detroit
Beginning of Korean War
Internal Security Act of 1950

▼1951
Truman fires General Douglas MacArthur

▼1952
Immigration and Nationality Act
Test of hydrogen bomb

▼1953
Execution of Ethel and Julius Rosenberg

▼1954
Army-McCarthy hearings

did. McCarthy's popularity plummeted. By year's end, the Senate condemned him for "unbecoming conduct."

The fall of McCarthy did not end McCarthyism. Schools forced teachers to sign loyalty oaths. Faculty members at several universities lost their jobs, and deans gave the names of suspect students to the FBI. Communism had become a useful charge to hurl at anything that anybody might oppose—labor unions, civil rights, even modern art. To protect themselves, groups policed their own membership. Labor unions drove out Communist leaders and unions. The Cincinnati Reds renamed their team the "Redlegs."

Americans became more careful about what they said out loud. Many had come to believe, along with McCarthy, that the civility of democracy, the attention to rights and fairness, exposed America to a ruthless adversary not bound by similar codes of conduct. Even as the Senate was censuring McCarthy, James Doolittle, the heroic World War II aviator, handed the CIA a report on counterespionage and countersubversion. It explained that the goal of America's enemy is "world domination by whatever means and at whatever cost." "If the United States is to survive," it concluded, "long-standing American concepts of 'fair play' must be reconsidered."

Conclusion

To contain Communism, the United States had transformed its economy. American society dealt with the unfinished business of reconversion, including the role of government and the rights and opportunities of labor, women, and African Americans. Despite these changes, the cold war had widened and intensified. Just seven years after dropping the first atomic bomb on Japan, Americans were again at war in the Far East and were forced to live with the threat of nuclear annihilation. They lived, too, with the frenzied search for subversives. America seemed to be out of control.

As McCarthyism flourished, most Americans longed for peace. They wanted the fighting in Korea to end. Anxious to avoid a nuclear holocaust, they wanted the confrontation with the Soviets to stabilize. Meanwhile, American society, adjusting to the postwar economy, sorted out the roles that government, labor, race, and gender would play in the cold war order. In the midst of upheaval, Americans went on with their lives. John Turchinetz, still working at the Boston Navy Yard, went to night school and got married. A disabled veteran, he wasn't needed on the frontlines of the cold war. But in 1952, the US government took his old ship, the *Boston*, out of mothballs and began to equip it with state-of-the-art missiles for duty around the cold war world.

Who, What, Where

Review Questions

1. How did the National Security Act change the executive branch?

2. Why did Truman see Korea as important enough to defend?

3. Why were struggles in the workplace more intense in the late 1940s than during the Depression or World War II?

Critical-Thinking Questions

1. McCarthyism attacked government, science, education, theater, and Hollywood. What does this pattern reveal about the nature of American anxiety in the 1950s?

2. Two-thirds of the world's peoples gained their independence between 1945 and 1961. How did the cold war affect this movement toward nationhood?

3. In the 1950s and 1960s, historians debated the question of who started the cold war. In the 1990s, it became more interesting to ask when it started. Why the change, and what questions might today's historians ask?

Suggested Readings

Harry S. Truman Presidential Library and Museum. Online Documents. https://www.trumanlibrary.org/online-collections.htm

Storrs, Landon R. Y. *The Second New Deal and the Unmaking of the American Left.* Princeton, NJ: Princeton University Press, 2012.

Westad, Odd Arne. *The Cold War: A World History.* New York: Basic Books, 2017.

For further review materials and resource information, please visit www.oup.com/us/oakes-mcgerr

CHAPTER 24: THE COLD WAR, 1945–1954
Primary Sources

24.1 X (GEORGE F. KENNAN), EXCERPTS FROM "THE SOURCES OF SOVIET CONDUCT" (1947)

Convinced that the Soviet Union and communism posed a fundamental threat to the United States, American policy makers needed a clear overarching strategy based on an understanding of the Soviets. Diplomat George Kennan gave them just that in an article formally titled "The Sources of Soviet Conduct" published in 1947. Writing under the pseudonym "X," Kennan argued for "a long-term, patient but firm and vigilant containment of Russian expansive tendencies." While optimistic about the outcome of the cold war, he made clear that containment could take a long time to work. Kennan did not invent the strategy of containment by himself; rather, his article neatly summed up emerging American ideas and gave them new focus.

. . . We have seen that the Kremlin is under no ideological compulsion to accomplish its purposes in a hurry. Like the Church, it is dealing in ideological concepts which are of long-term validity, and it can afford to be patient. It has no right to risk the existing achievements of the revolution for the sake of vain baubles of the future. . . . Here caution, circumspection, flexibility and deception are the valuable qualities; and their value finds natural appreciation in the Russian or the oriental mind. Thus the Kremlin has no compunction about retreating in the face of superior force. And being under the compulsion of no timetable, it does not get panicky under the necessity for such retreat. Its political action is a fluid stream which moves constantly, wherever it is permitted to move, toward a given goal. Its main concern is to make sure that it has filled every nook and cranny available to it in the basin of world power. But if it finds unassailable barriers in its path, it accepts these philosophically and accommodates itself to them. The main thing is that there should always be pressure, unceasing constant pressure, toward the desired goal. There is no trace of any feeling in Soviet psychology that that goal must be reached at any given time. . . .

In these circumstances it is clear that the main element of any United States policy toward the Soviet Union must be that of a long-term, patient but firm and vigilant containment of Russian expansive tendencies. It is important to note, however, that such a policy has nothing to do with outward histrionics: with threats or blustering or superfluous gestures of outward "toughness." While the Kremlin is basically flexible in its reaction to political realities, it is by no means unamenable to considerations of prestige. Like almost any other government, it can be placed by tactless and threatening gestures in a position where it cannot afford to yield even though this might be dictated by its sense of realism. The Russian leaders are keen judges of human psychology, and as such they are highly conscious that loss of temper and of self-control is never a source of strength in political affairs. They are quick to exploit such evidences of weakness. For these reasons, it is a sine qua non of successful dealing with Russia that the foreign government in question should remain at all times cool and collected and that its demands on Russian policy should be put forward in such a manner as to leave the way open for a compliance not too detrimental to Russian prestige.

In the light of the above, it will be clearly seen that the Soviet pressure against the free institutions of the western world is something that can be contained by the adroit and vigilant application of counter-force at a series of constantly shifting geographical and political points, corresponding to the shifts and manoeuvres of Soviet policy, but which cannot be charmed or talked out of existence. The Russians look forward to a duel of infinite duration, and they see that already they have scored great successes. . . .

[T]he future of Soviet power may not be by any means as secure as Russian capacity for self-delusion would make it appear to the men in the Kremlin. . . .

It is clear that the United States cannot expect in the foreseeable future to enjoy political intimacy with the Soviet régime. It must continue to regard the Soviet Union as a rival, not a partner, in the political arena. It must continue to expect that Soviet policies will reflect no abstract love of peace and stability, no real faith in the possibility of a permanent happy coexistence of the Socialist and capitalist worlds, but rather a cautious, persistent pressure toward the disruption and weakening of all rival influence and rival power.

Balanced against this are the facts that Russia, as opposed to the western world in general, is still by far the weaker party, that Soviet policy is highly flexible, and that Soviet society may well contain deficiencies which will eventually weaken its own total potential. . . .

[I]n actuality the possibilities for American policy are by no means limited to holding the line and hoping for the best. It is entirely possible for the United States to influence by its actions the internal developments, both within Russia and throughout the international Communist movement, by which Russian policy is largely determined. . . . It is . . . a question of the degree to which the United States can create among the peoples of the world generally the impression of a country which knows what it wants, which is coping successfully with the problems of its internal life and with the responsibilities of a World Power, and which has a spiritual vitality capable of holding its own among the major ideological currents of the time. To the extent that such an impression can be created and maintained, the aims of Russian Communism must appear sterile and quixotic, the hopes and enthusiasm of Moscow's supporters must wane, and added strain must be imposed on the Kremlin's foreign policies. For the palsied decrepitude of the capitalist world is the keystone of Communist philosophy. . . .

It would be an exaggeration to say that American behavior unassisted and alone could exercise a power of life and death over the Communist movement and bring about the early fall of Soviet power in Russia. But the United States has it in its power to increase enormously the strains under which Soviet policy must operate, to force upon the Kremlin a far greater degree of moderation and circumspection than it has had to observe in recent years, and in this way to promote tendencies which must eventually find their outlet in either the break-up or the gradual mellowing of Soviet power. . . .

Thus the decision will really fall in large measure on this country itself. The issue of Soviet-American relations is in essence a test of the over-all worth of the United States as a nation among nations. To avoid destruction the United States need only measure up to its own best traditions and prove itself worthy of preservation as a great nation.

Source: George F. Kennan, "The Sources of Soviet Conduct," *Foreign Affairs* 25 (July 1947): 566–578, 580–582.

24.2 HIGH SCHOOL AND COLLEGE GRADUATES IN THE COLD WAR (1948–1950)

In the first years of the cold war, graduates from high school and college entered an uncertain, fearful adult world. Here, two newspaper editors and a columnist offer advice to young people graduating from 1948 to 1950 amid the intensifying international nuclear arms race and the domestic Red Scare. Are these pieces optimistic or pessimistic? What challenges do these graduates face? Is the advice sincere and realistic?

Editorial, *Binghamton Press and Sun Bulletin*, June 14, 1948: June graduates of high school and college are hearing the same old commencement orations. They are being told that they should concentrate on improving the world. The world, of course, could stand improvement. . . . Some day a starry-eyed youngster is going to ask a commencement speaker how it happened that his generation got the world into such shape. . . .

No one really should feel too much concern about the future of today's boys and girls. They're a little weak in the three R's, in spelling and grammar. But they look out on horizons that are wider than those of their parents. Today's youngsters in the main know what it is all about. Yes, they're smart. They have to be, considering the burdens the older generation so unfairly has thrust upon their shoulders. They'll probably do better than the older generation. They couldn't do much worse.

Editorial, *Iowa City Press-Citizen*, June 10, 1949: Graduates are being told these are troublesome times, that the threat of war hangs over us, that freedom is in peril from communism, that population is outrunning world resources, that our health, security and education need new safeguards, that a hundred other dire circumstances prevail. Most of this may well be true. Certainly there have been more restful moments in history. . . .

For long years every graduating class has been told to stick out its chin and face down the world. . . .We voice the fervent wish, however, that this time the speakers cut through the welter of the world's dilemmas and talk in simple, human terms that may serve as real guide approach we have found that we would like to repeat:

"You students are leaving the college world, where truth is the great, single, unifying goal. You are entering the outside world, where truth competes openly and violently with falsehood, half-truth, and propaganda. You will bump into baffling mixtures of these elements. If you are ever to play any useful part in bettering the world, learn quickly to recognize these cheap alloys that corrupt truth. Resist their intrusion into your own thinking. . . . Distortions of truth are a prized weapon in the battle of ideas raging today. But truth is stronger and will blunt that weapon, however lethal it sometimes is. You will need courage to combat the users of falsehood and propaganda. They will too seldom be your avowed enemies. They may be in positions of power. They may even be, on occasion, your friends.

But if you flinch from fighting, you will go down in the struggle to bring peace and order and justice to this complex world.

Hal Boyle, 1950: An open letter to Joe College, class of 1950:

Dear Joe:

Welcome to the brave new world, kid. . . . There is one word of advice I'd like to give you. It's this: "Relax."

These are jittery times, perhaps the most jittery ever known. A census might even show there are more ulcers alive in the world today than there are people. There's a growing habit to be afraid of shadows, which are usually larger than the things that cast them.

So, relax, Joe. Show the older people the example they need: That courage doesn't die in rompers, but also wears long pants.

What really is there to be afraid of? War today is only the threat of a needless possibility. There is more mass security in the United States today than there was when young Thomas Jefferson wrote the Declaration of Independence, and he lived to be an old, old man. More people live a wider, freer life than at previous periods of our national story. The good old days are a legend. The good present time is here to be enjoyed.

There's a job waiting for you to find, Joe. There's a girl for you to marry, and you'll want to bring up some kids. And the prospect for bringing them up in a happy world was never really better. But you don't find happiness by being tense. Relax, Joe. . . . Good luck.

Hal Boyle

Sources: "Same Old Graduation Speeches," *Binghamton Press and Sun Bulletin*, June 14, 1948, p. 6; "Advice to Graduates," *Iowa City Press-Citizen*, June 10, 1949, p. 4; Hal Boyle, "Word of Advice to Graduates Entering Jittery World— Relax," *Marshfield News Herald*, June 2, 1950.

24.3 STATEMENTS BY THE UNITED AUTO WORKERS AND GENERAL MOTORS (1945)

The United Auto Workers' (UAW) strike against General Motors in 1945–1946 laid bare basic differences over the past and future of labor relations in the United States. As President Truman appointed a fact-finding board to make recommendations on a settlement, the union and the corporation disagreed over the proper roles of the federal government, unions, and corporations. As this statement by UAW official Walter Reuther makes clear, the union wanted the government to help force corporations into supporting the buying power of all Americans. In response, General Motors flatly rejected giving up any of its power. The UAW and General Motors also had different understandings of just how good things had been before World War II.

Reuther: The President's fact-finding board will shortly report its findings and recommendations in the UAW-CIO-General Motors wage dispute to President Truman. If those findings and recommendations are based upon the arithmetic of the case, and if the President and the American people will insist that the Wall Street managers of General Motors Corporation honestly negotiate an agreement based on the economic facts of the case, General Motors workers and the American people will be spared a winter of industrial war that may spread to all of American industry. . . . [T]he General Motors workers, who have already sacrificed so much in this strike, will not accept less than the 30 per cent increase in wage rates needed to maintain take-home pay, except and to the extent that the economic facts may show that General Motors cannot pay that increase without increasing prices to the consumers.

. . . The Wall Street lawyers who have been substituted for the operating management raise the motheaten battle flags that the forces of special privilege have carried for the past hundred and fifty years. Theirs are the voices and the slogans of the past. America is going forward to a better future, of full employment, full production and full consumption.

We believe that the American people will not be frightened by hysterical screams of "revolution." We are through with blind acceptance of the bad old days of boom and bust, of chronic mass unemployment. . . .

The workers' demands to maintain take-home pay, keep prices down and thereby maintain and increase purchasing power are geared to the welfare of the whole community, the needs of the whole nation. We refuse to operate as an economic pressure group attempting to make progress at the expense of the community. We want to make progress with the community. . . .

Free enterprise is killing itself when it refuses to recognize that the maintenance and increase of purchasing power to keep pace with technological progress is its own life blood.

Free enterprise, to survive, must learn that it has more and greater responsibilities than merely producing a cash return for its investors. It must make its contribution to the welfare of the community as a whole; it must meet and help solve the problem of unemployment and recurrent depressions. . . .

The GM strikers walking the picket lines in Detroit and Flint and Janesville, Wis., and all the other cities where GM plants are on strike, are fighting the fight of the majority of Americans in city and farm alike. . . . They are fighting to give economic substance to ideals for which the war was fought. . . . This fight is for keeps. Upon its outcome hangs the future of America. If we win, we and those from whom we buy our food and clothes and fuel and other necessities and comforts of life will win ground on which to build an America of new economic and political freedom. Should we lose, it would be 1919 and the Twenties all over again. We are right and we will win.

General Motors: America is at the crossroads. It must preserve the freedom of each unit of American business to determine its own destinies. Or it must transfer to some governmental bureaucracy or agency, or to a union, the responsibility of management that has been the very keystone of American business. Shall this responsibility be surrendered? That is the decision the American people face. America must choose!

General Motors has made its choice. It refuses to subscribe to what it believes will ultimately become, through the process of evolution, the death of the American system of competitive enterprise. It will not participate voluntarily in what stands out crystal clear as the end of the road—a regimented economy. If this is what the American people want, they must make that choice through their accredited representatives in Congress. General Motors declines for itself to take such a great responsibility.

It may be said that this is an exaggeration. It is not. All business questions are interrelated. Costs, prices, wages, profits, schedules, investments must be the responsibility of management. Political determination of such relationships means regimentation.

The idea of ability to pay, whatever its validity may be, is not applicable to an individual business within an industry as a basis for raising its wages beyond the going rate.

Consider the implications of such a principle. Who would risk money to develop or expand a business under such circumstances?

. . . The President of the United States has appointed a fact-finding board to inquire into the circumstances involved in the demands of the UAW-CIO upon General Motors and to make recommendations related thereto. . . . [T]he board has ruled that General Motors' ability to pay will be considered as a factor in determining an increase in wages. . . . Thus the board would assume the most vital functions of management. . . .

Source: "Statements by GM and UAW on Issues," *New York Times*, December 30, 1945, p. 2.

24.4 HARRY S. TRUMAN, EXCERPTS FROM SPECIAL MESSAGE TO THE CONGRESS RECOMMENDING A COMPREHENSIVE HEALTH PROGRAM (1945)

The campaign for federally supported national health insurance summed up the frustrations of liberals who hoped to expand the New Deal after World War II. In this message to Congress in November 1945, President Truman proposed a system of compulsory medical insurance that would stand with the Social Security pension plan enacted in the 1930s. With the help of new taxes, a federally supervised system would ensure that all Americans had access to both health care and benefits if illness kept them from working. Truman knew that increased taxes and federal power would provoke opposition: note his careful effort to insist that his plan did not add up to "socialized medicine."

. . . Millions of our citizens do not now have a full measure of opportunity to achieve and enjoy good health. Millions do not now have protection or security against the economic effects of sickness. The time has arrived for action to help them attain that opportunity and that protection. . . .

In the past, the benefits of modern medical science have not been enjoyed by our citizens with any degree of equality. Nor are they today. Nor will they be in the future—unless government is bold enough to do something about it.

People with low or moderate incomes do not get the same medical attention as those with high incomes. The poor have more sickness, but they get less medical care. People who live in rural areas do not get the same amount or quality of medical attention as those who live in our cities. . . .

We should resolve now that the health of this Nation is a national concern; that financial barriers in the way of attaining health shall be removed; that the health of all its citizens deserves the help of all the Nation. . . .

The principal reason why people do not receive the care they need is that they cannot afford to pay for it on an individual basis at the time they need it. This is true not only for needy persons. It is also true for a large proportion of normally self-supporting persons.

In the aggregate, all health services—from public health agencies, physicians, hospitals, dentists, nurses and laboratories—absorb only about 4 percent of the national income. We can afford to spend more for health.

But 4 percent is only an average. It is cold comfort in individual cases. Individual families pay their individual costs, and not average costs. They may be hit by sickness that calls for many times the average cost—in extreme cases for more than their annual income. When this happens they may come face to face with economic disaster. Many families, fearful of expense, delay calling the doctor long beyond the time when medical care would do the most good. . . .

I recommend solving the basic problem by distributing the costs through expansion of our existing compulsory social insurance system. This is not socialized medicine.

Everyone who carries fire insurance knows how the law of averages is made to work so as to spread the risk, and to benefit the insured who actually suffers the loss. If instead of the costs of sickness being paid only by those who get sick, all the people—sick and well—were required to pay premiums into an insurance fund, the pool of funds thus created would enable all who do fall sick to be adequately served without overburdening anyone. That is the principle upon which all forms of insurance are based. . . .

Socialized medicine means that all doctors work as employees of government. The American people want no such system. No such system is here proposed.

Under the plan I suggest, our people would continue to get medical and hospital services just as they do now—on the basis of their own voluntary decisions and choices. Our doctors and hospitals would continue to deal with disease with the same professional freedom as now. There would, however, be this all-important difference: whether or not patients get the services they need would not depend on how much they can afford to pay at the time.

I am in favor of the broadest possible coverage for this insurance system. I believe that all persons who work for a living and their dependents should be covered under such an insurance plan. . . . In addition, needy persons and other groups should be covered through appropriate premiums paid for them by public agencies. Increased Federal funds should also be made available by the Congress under the public assistance programs to reimburse the States for part of such premiums, as well as for direct expenditures made by the States in paying for medical services provided by doctors, hospitals and other agencies to needy persons. . . .

But no matter what we do, sickness will of course come to many. Sickness brings with it loss of wages.

Therefore . . . the workers of the Nation and their families should be protected against loss of earnings because of illness. A comprehensive health program must include the payment of benefits to replace at least part of the earnings that are lost during the period of sickness and long-term disability. This protection can be readily and conveniently provided through expansion of our present social insurance system, with appropriate adjustment of premiums. . . .

Source: Harry S. Truman, Special Message to the Congress Recommending a Comprehensive Health Program, November 19, 1945.

24.5 JOSEPH MCCARTHY, EXCERPTS FROM WHEELING, WEST VIRGINIA SPEECH (1950)

At Wheeling, West Virginia, in February 1950, Republican Senator Joseph McCarthy of Wisconsin gave a speech that summed up the fervent anti-Communist worldview that had gripped the United States. Rather than trace the cold war to differences over economic or national security interests, he blamed the conflict on religion. Rather than trace the Soviets' success to their own efforts, he blamed the disloyalty of privileged men in the US government. In particular, he accused Dean Acheson, then secretary of state, of condoning the treason of Alger Hiss, an aide to the secretary accused of being a Soviet agent. McCarthy also claimed to have the names of 57 Communists or Communist sympathizers in the State Department—a claim that was never substantiated. To some observers, such claims epitomized McCarthyism.

Five years after a world war has been won, men's hearts should anticipate a long peace, and men's minds should be free from the heavy weight that comes with war. But this is not such a period—for this is not a period of peace. This is a time of the "cold war." This is a time when all the world is split into two vast, increasingly hostile armed camps—a time of a great armaments race. . . .

We are now engaged in a show-down fight—not the usual war between nations for land areas or other material gains, but a war between two diametrically opposed ideologies.

The great difference between our western Christian world and the atheistic Communist world is not political, ladies and gentlemen, it is moral. . . .

The real, basic difference . . . lies in the religion of immoralism—invented by Marx, preached feverishly by Lenin, and carried to unimaginable extremes by Stalin. This religion of immoralism, if the Red half of the world wins—and well it may—this religion of immoralism will more deeply wound and damage mankind than any conceivable economic or political system. . . .

As one of our outstanding historical figures once said, "When a great democracy is destroyed, it will not be because of enemies from without, but rather because of enemies from within."

The truth of this statement is becoming terrifyingly clear as we see this country each day losing on every front. . . .

The reason why we find ourselves in a position of impotency is not because our only powerful potential enemy has sent men to invade our shores, but rather because of the traitorous actions of those who have been treated so well by this Nation. It has not been the less fortunate or members of minority groups who have been selling this Nation out, but rather those who have had all the benefits that the wealthiest nation on earth has had to offer—the finest homes, the finest college education, and the finest jobs in Government we can give.

This is glaringly true in the State Department. There the bright young men who are born with silver spoons in their mouths are the ones who have been worst. . . .

In my opinion the State Department, which is one of the most important government departments, is thoroughly infested with Communists.

I have in my hand 57 cases of individuals who would appear to be either card carrying members or certainly loyal to the Communist Party, but who nevertheless are still helping to shape our foreign policy.

One thing to remember in discussing the Communists in our Government is that we are not dealing with spies who get 30 pieces of silver to steal the blueprints of a new weapon. We are dealing with a far more sinister type of activity because it permits the enemy to guide and shape our policy. . . .

This brings us down to the case of one Alger Hiss who is more important not as an individual any more, but rather because he is so representative of a group in the State Department. . . .

As you hear this story of high treason, I know that you are saying to yourself, "Well, why doesn't the Congress do something about it?" Actually, ladies and gentlemen, one of the important reasons for the graft, the corruption, the dishonesty, the disloyalty, the treason in high Government positions—one of the most important reasons why this continues is a lack of moral uprising on the part of the 140,000,000 American people. In the light of history, however, this is not hard to explain.

It is the result of an emotional hang-over and a temporary moral lapse which follows every war. It is the apathy to evil which people who have been subjected to the tremendous evils of war feel. As the people of the world see mass murder, the destruction of defenseless and innocent people, and all of the crime and lack of morals which go with war, they become numb and apathetic. . . .

However, the morals of our people have not been destroyed. They still exist. This cloak of numbness and apathy has only needed a spark to rekindle them. Happily, this spark has finally been supplied.

As you know, very recently the Secretary of State proclaimed his loyalty to a man guilty of what has always been considered as the most abominable of all crimes—of being a traitor to the people who gave him a position of great trust. The Secretary of State in attempting to justify his continued devotion to the man who sold out the Christian world to the atheistic world, referred to Christ's Sermon on the Mount as a justification and reason therefor. . . .

When this pompous diplomat in striped pants, with a phony British accent, proclaimed to the American people that Christ on the Mount endorsed communism, high treason, and betrayal of a sacred trust, the blasphemy was so great that it awakened the dormant indignation of the American people.

He has lighted the spark which is resulting in a moral uprising and will end only when the whole sorry mess of twisted, warped thinkers are swept from the national scene so that we may have a new birth of national honesty and decency in Government.

Source: *Major Speeches and Debates of Senator Joe McCarthy Delivered in the United States Senate, 1950–1951* (Washington, DC: United States Government Printing Office, 1953), pp. 7–14.

The Consumer Society

1945–1961

< A Crowd at First Baptist Church in Montgomery, Alabama, 1956

The Ricardos

On the evening of October 15, 1951, millions of Americans turned the channel knob and adjusted the antenna on their television sets to watch the first episode of a new comedy about bandleader and club owner Ricky Ricardo and his madcap wife, Lucy. Broadcast in black and white, *I Love Lucy* quickly became one of television's biggest hits. The show aired until 1957 and over the course of 181 half-hour long episodes, viewers laughed as homemaker Lucy schemed endlessly to get a job or buy a fur coat, while Cuban-born Ricky responded to Lucy's antics with comic exasperation. During the show's run, the couple had a baby and moved from the city to the suburbs.

Part of the fun for the audience was the relationship between the fictional *I Love Lucy* and the characters' real lives. The show's stars, Lucille Ball and Desi Arnaz, were married. *I Love Lucy* attracted an especially large audience for the groundbreaking episode about the birth of the Ricardos' son, "Little Ricky," which aired on the same day as the birth of the Arnazes' own son, Desi, Jr.

I Love Lucy's reflection of real American life was another reason for the show's success. Leaving behind the economic limits and constraints of the Depression and World War II, the 1950s marked the full emergence of the consumer society foreshadowed in the 1920s. *I Love Lucy* reassured Americans that television, suburban houses, and other consumer pleasures were acceptable. The show also let people laugh away the tensions generated by a renewed emphasis on women as stay-at-home mothers in the midst of a huge baby boom. As a full-time actress and businesswoman, Lucille Ball had to reassure her audience that she was a devoted mother—"a typical woman" and "a homebody."

I Love Lucy, like other pleasures of consumerism, helped Americans forget about the cold war. The Red Scare search for American communists was never a topic addressed by the fictional Ricardos, but it was an issue for the real-life Arnazes. In 1953, Americans learned that Lucille Ball had signed a pledge to vote for Communist Party candidates in the 1930s. With her career and her show in jeopardy, Ball testified that she had only signed the pledge as a young woman to please her dictatorial grandfather. Lucille's red hair, Desi laughed, was "the only thing red about her." Despite conservative attacks, most Americans accepted her explanation—a sign that there were limits to the Red Scare.

In later years, American culture would look back nostalgically at the 1950s as a prosperous golden age. But the consumer society did not benefit every group, end racial inequality, or win the cold war. Underneath the prosperity and good times of the decade, there were developing tensions over race, gender, generation, the confrontation with communism, and consumerism itself. Despite their image as "America's best-loved couple," Lucille and Desi were beset by his alcoholism and adultery. The fictional Ricardos stayed married; the real-life Arnazes would divorce in 1960. By then, Americans worried about the limits of the consumer society, even as they enjoyed its benefits.

Living the Good Life

Much of the consumer lifestyle was in place by the 1920s (see Chapter 21), but only in the 1950s did consumer values and habits finally dominate the American economy and culture. Never before had so many Americans had the chance to live the good life.

They tended to define that "good life" in economic terms. A dynamic, evolving economy offered more leisure and income. Sure of prosperity, Americans confidently spent more of their time and money in the pursuit of pleasure. Millions lived the dream of a home in new suburbs, bought flashy automobiles, purchased their first televisions, and enjoyed a new openness about sex.

Economic Prosperity

Consumerism could not have flourished without prosperity. Despite short recessions, the 1950s was a period of economic boom. The gross national product—the value of all the country's output of goods and services—grew solidly at an average of 3.2 percent a year.

Several major factors spurred this economic growth. Because of the cold war, federal spending for defense and foreign aid stimulated demand for American goods and services. The shortage of consumer goods during and just after World War II left Americans with money to spend. Robust capital spending by businesses helped ensure economic growth. The industrial economy was also evolving. Traditional heavy manufacturing—steel and automobiles—was still crucial to prosperity, but newer industries, such as electronics, chemicals, plastics, aviation, and computers, became increasingly important.

The emergence of computing was especially significant for the long run. In 1946, two engineers at the University of Pennsylvania, J. Presper Eckert Jr. and John William Mauchly, completed the first fully electronic digital computer. The Electronic Numerical Integrator and Computer (ENIAC) weighed over 30 tons and filled a large room. Then Eckert and Mauchly produced the more advanced UNIVAC 1 (Universal Automatic Computer), which counted census data in 1951 and presidential election returns in 1952.

As tiny solid-state transistors replaced bulky vacuum tubes, computers became smaller, more powerful, and more common. By 1958, American companies were producing $1 billion worth of computers annually. Still large and expensive, computers were used mostly by universities, corporations, and the federal government. With about 10,000 computers in use by 1961, the nation was on the brink of the digital age.

As industry evolved, the nation's distribution and service sectors played a larger role than ever. While the number of manufacturing jobs barely changed, employment in stores increased 19 percent. Jobs in the service sector, such as restaurants, hotels, repair shops, hospitals, and universities, jumped 32 percent. The nation had begun to develop a postindustrial economy, less dependent on production and more dependent on service and consumption.

Economic prosperity greatly benefited big business. New corporations emerged and grew. Thanks to a wave of mergers, established corporations became still larger. By 1960, corporations earned 18 times as much income as the rest of the nation's businesses combined.

Prosperity boosted corporations' confidence and popularity. Even liberals, once critical of corporate power, now celebrated the benefits of large-scale enterprise. "What is good for the country is good for General Motors, and vice versa," Charles Wilson, the head of GM, supposedly declared.

Eisenhower's Interstate Highway System

Along with the construction of new suburbs, the creation of a true interstate highway system promised to remake the American landscape in the 1950s. Since the 1910s, the need for a national system of high-speed roads had been clear. The US Army, in particular, had pushed for a network of transcontinental highways that would make it easier to defend the nation. Although the federal government had begun providing funds for the creation and maintenance of national highways during World War I, the roads remained woefully inadequate in the 1950s.

Dwight D. Eisenhower's election as president changed the situation dramatically. As a young officer in 1919, Eisenhower participated in the Army's first transcontinental convoy, a slow, accident-ridden journey across the primitive Lincoln Highway. That trip helped make the president a fervent supporter of national highways. In a message to Congress in February 1955, Eisenhower declared that the nation's highways were dangerous, costly, and unable to support the growing volume of traffic. A new, comprehensive system, the president maintained, would strengthen the economy, promote defense, especially in the event of evacuations in a nuclear war, and make the country a genuinely "United States." Rather than turn to private ownership, Eisenhower called this "a public enterprise" that should be shared by the federal and state governments.

In June 1956, Congress overwhelmingly passed the Federal-Aid Highway Act, then

American workers enjoyed high employment, low inflation, and rising incomes. Less than 5 percent of the workforce was unemployed at any one time. Factory workers' average hourly pay more than doubled between 1945 and 1960, while consumer prices rose less than 2 percent per year. The percentage of Americans living in poverty fell from as much as 30 in the late 1940s to 18 in 1959.

Americans also had more leisure time. By the 1950s, the 40-hour workweek was commonplace. Many workers now looked forward to two- or three-week paid vacations. As life expectancy increased and the economy boomed, more Americans expected to retire at age 65 and live off pensions and Social Security.

Workers' well-being produced labor peace, which in turn stimulated prosperity. After the contentious 1940s, workers and employers were more likely to resolve differences without strikes and lockouts. When the relatively aggressive Congress of Industrial Organizations (CIO) merged with the American Federation of Labor (AFL) to become the gigantic AFL-CIO in 1955, the union movement became more bureaucratic and complacent. "American labor never had it so good," crowed a union leader.

The Suburban Dream

For growing numbers of people, the good life meant a house in the suburbs. Most Americans had never owned their own homes. Suburbs had been mainly for the well-to-do.

the largest peacetime government project in history. A tax on gasoline helped the federal government ultimately pay $114 billion, or 90 percent of the cost of constructing more than 46,000 miles of new highways. The vast project would not be essentially complete until the 1990s; even now a small part of the system remains incomplete.

Nevertheless, the interstate highway system's impact on the landscape and the nation quickly became clear. "More than any single action by the government since the end of the war, this one would change the face of America with straightaways, cloverleaf turns, bridges, and elongated parkways," Eisenhower wrote in 1963. "Its impact on the American economy—the jobs it would produce in manufacturing and construction, the rural areas it would open up—was beyond calculation."

Such interstates as the 3,020-mile I-90 from Boston, Massachusetts, to Seattle, Washington, and the 1,920-mile I-95 from Miami, Florida, to Houlton, Maine, doubly affected the environment. Cutting across farmland and running through towns and cities, the roads remade the land. In Boston and other cities, the interstates obliterated workers' homes, isolated neighborhoods, and created new traffic jams. Rather than bring Americans back to live in the cities, as many interstate proponents had hoped, the new highways enabled more Americans to move to the suburbs and commute to urban jobs. "When Interstate comes," a reporter wrote, "can anything once familiar ever be the same?"

Although the creation and improvement of federal highways made it easier to drive automobiles, highways also contributed to increased air pollution. Despite the benefits of Eisenhower's interstates, the nation would also have to deal with their negative impact on the land and the environment, too.

But entrepreneurship, new construction methods, cheap land, and federal aid made possible affordable housing outside the nation's cities. Much of America moved to the suburbs in the 1950s.

William J. Levitt's pioneering development, Levittown, illustrated the suburban housing boom. Back from World War II, Levitt optimistically believed he could make houses affordable for middle- and working-class people. Drawing on his military experience and Henry Ford's assembly-line techniques, Levitt intended to build houses so efficiently that they could sell at remarkably low prices. He put up simple houses, with prefabricated parts, no basements, and low price tags, on 1,000 acres of cheap farmland on New York's Long Island. Levitt's original Cape Cod–style house cost $7,990, ideal for young couples financing their first home.

Levittown quickly became a huge success. Buyers contracted for 1,400 houses on one day in 1949. The development grew to 17,500 dwellings housing 82,000 people. Levitt soon built more Levittowns, as did imitators all around the country.

The federal government made those suburbs more affordable by allowing buyers to deduct mortgage interest payments from their federal income taxes and by guaranteeing loans to military veterans. To make commuting practical, the Federal-Aid Highway Act of 1956 encouraged the construction of interstate freeways connecting cities and suburbs.

Under such favorable conditions, the United States quickly became a nation of suburban homeowners. As home ownership increased 20 percent between 1945 and 1960, nearly one-third of Americans lived in places like Levittown. The suburban dream had become an everyday reality.

The Pursuit of Pleasure

The consumer society depended on Americans' eagerness to pursue pleasure. Businesses made sure that nothing prevented people from buying. If their wages and salaries were not enough, consumers could borrow. In 1950, the Diners Club introduced the credit card for New Yorkers. By 1960, Sears Roebuck credit cards allowed more than 10 million Americans to spend borrowed money. In 1945, Americans owed only $5.7 billion for consumer goods other than houses. By 1960, they owed $56.1 billion.

In the 1950s, discount stores such as E.J. Korvettes made shopping simpler and more attractive. So did another new creation, the shopping mall. In 1956, Southdale, the first enclosed suburban mall, opened outside Minneapolis. Consumers ate more easily, too. The first McDonald's fast-food restaurant opened in San Bernardino, California, in 1948. Taken over by Ray Kroc, McDonald's began to grow into a national chain in the mid-1950s.

To get to McDonald's, Southdale, or Levittown, Americans needed cars. In the 1950s, automobiles reflected a new sense of affluence and self-indulgence. Big, high-compression engines burning high-octane gasoline powered ever-bigger cars stuffed with new accessories—power steering, power brakes, power windows, and air conditioning. Unlike

Icons of the Consumer Society The first enclosed mall in the United States—Southdale, outside Minneapolis, Minnesota.

the drab sedans of the Depression, the new models featured "Passion Pink" and "Horizon Blue" interiors and two- and even three-tone exteriors studded with shiny chrome.

Automakers used that chrome to solve one of the problems of a consumer society—getting people who already had plenty to buy even more. How could Detroit persuade Americans to trade in cars that were running just fine for new ones? The answer was what General Motors' chief designer called "dynamic obsolescence," the feeling that last year's model was somehow inadequate. So automakers changed chrome, colors, and tailfins from year to year (see Table 25–1).

The cars of the 1950s reflected a driver's identity and affluence. General Motors' line rose up the socioeconomic ladder, from the ordinary Chevrolet to the more prosperous Pontiac, Oldsmobile, and Buick, and up to the sumptuous success symbol Cadillac.

Automobiles also spoke to gender identities. To appeal to women, car interiors seemed like living rooms. The exterior offered men power and sexuality. While the back of a 1950s car could look like a jet's afterburner, the front might evoke the female body. A car, as a Buick ad promised, "makes you feel like the man you are."

In the 1950s, television became central to the consumer society. As TV sets became less expensive and sales boomed, broadcasters seized opportunity. By 1950, the Federal Communications Commission (FCC) had licensed 104 TV stations, mostly in cities. As television undermined the popularity of radio and movie theaters, the three major broadcasting companies quickly created TV networks and dominated the new industry.

Table 25-1 Automobiles and Highways, 1945–1960

Year	Factory Sales (in 1,000s)	Registrations (in 1,000s)	Miles of Highway Completed (in 1,000s)
1945	69.5	25,796.9	3,035
1946	2,148.6	28,217.0	5,057
1947	3,558.1	30,849.3	15,473
1948	3,909.2	33,355.2	21,725
1949	5,119.4	36,457.9	19,876
1950	6,665.8	40,339.0	19,876
1951	5,338.4	42,688.3	17,060
1952	4,320.7	43,823.0	22,147
1953	6,116.9	46,429.2	21,136
1954	5,558.8	48,468.4	20,548
1955	7,920.1	52,144.7	22,571
1956	5,816.1	54,210.9	23,609
1957	6,113.3	55,917.8	22,424
1958	4,257.8	56,890.5	28,137
1959*	5,591.2	59,453.9	32,633
1960	6,674.7	61,682.3	20,969

Source: Historical Statistics of the United States, Millennial Online Edition (Cambridge: Cambridge University Press, 2008), Table Df347–352 and Table Df213-217.

*Denotes first year for which figures include Alaska and Hawaii.

Table 25-2 Television, 1941–1960

Year	Television Stations	Households with Television Sets (in 1,000s)
1941	2	–
1945	9	–
1950	104	3,875
1955	458	30,700
1960	579	45,750

Source: George Thomas Kurian, *Datapedia* (Lanham, MD: Bernan Press, 1994), pp. 299–300.

By 1960, 90 percent of the nation's households had a television (see Table 25–2). In 15 years, TV had become part of everyday life.

From its early days, television reinforced the consumer society's values. Advertisements for consumer products paid for programming. There were operas, documentaries, and live dramas in what critics consider television's golden age, but variety shows, sports, westerns, and situation comedies, such as *I Love Lucy*, filled most of the broadcast day. Nightly national news broadcasts lasted only 15 minutes.

Sexual openness also defined consumer society. Dr. Alfred C. Kinsey commanded enormous public attention with two pioneering academic studies—*Sexual Behavior in the Human Male* (1948) and *Sexual Behavior in the Human Female* (1953). Kinsey surprised Americans by reporting more sexual activity outside of marriage than had been thought. The Supreme Court contributed to sexual openness by overturning a ban on a film version of D. H. Lawrence's often erotic novel, *Lady Chatterley's Lover*, in 1959. *Playboy* magazine, first published by Hugh Hefner in December 1953, epitomized the new sexual candor. Featuring bare-breasted women, *Playboy* blended sex into a hedonistic lifestyle of flashy cars, expensive stereos, and fine liquor.

A Homogeneous Society?

The spread of consumerism reinforced a sense of sameness in America. The United States seemed a homogeneous society whose people bought the same products, watched the same TV shows, worked for the same corporations, and dreamed the same dreams. Critics worried that Americans had sacrificed individuality for conformity. Declining class differences and renewed emphasis on religion and family strengthened the feeling that people were becoming more alike.

Nevertheless, the United States remained a heterogeneous society. Although class and ethnic differences among whites decreased, race remained a powerful divider. Despite fears of conformity, the nation still encouraged difference and individuality.

The Discovery of Conformity

After World War II, sociologists and other writers discovered an increasing uniformity in American society for a variety of reasons. During the frenzied search for domestic Communists, people did not want to risk accusations by appearing different or unusual. As corporations merged and small businesses disappeared, more Americans worked for the same giant companies. Levittown and the other new suburbs intensified the sense of sameness. In 1957, one writer described suburbanites as "people whose age, income, number of children, problems, habits, conversations, dress, possessions, perhaps even blood types are almost precisely like yours."

The Decline of Class and Ethnicity

The apparent decline of social class differences reinforced the sense of homogeneity. By the 1950s, the old upper class—the families of the Gilded Age—no longer ran American industry and finance. Thanks to taxes and the Depression, the largest American fortunes were smaller than at the beginning of the twentieth century. The corporate leaders of the 1950s did not have the swagger, the palaces, or the dynastic ambitions of the Gilded Age robber barons.

Meanwhile, the ranks of American farmers continued to shrink. As agriculture became more efficient and corporatized, the number of farms fell from over 6 million in 1944 to 3.7 million in 1959. Although manual and service workers remained the largest occupational group, they seemed a less distinctive social class. In an era of labor peace, well-paid blue-collar workers appeared content with American society. Labor leaders endorsed consumerism and anti-Communism. Some observers argued that American workers had become middle class in their habits and values. The middle class itself was burgeoning. By 1960, the white-collar sector made up 40 percent of the workforce.

Even ethnic differences no longer seemed significant. Whites from different national and religious backgrounds mixed together in the new suburbs. The rate of intermarriage between ethnic groups increased. Anxious to prove their loyalty during the cold war, newer Americans avoided emphasizing their origins. Ethnicity apparently disappeared in the consumer society's melting pot.

Many Americans, especially powerful ones, had long wanted to believe theirs was a unified society devoted to middle-class values. In the 1950s, there was more basis for this belief than ever before.

The Resurgence of Religion and Family

A renewed emphasis on religion and family contributed to social homogeneity. Political leaders, fighting the cold war, encouraged religiosity. Freedom of religion, they insisted, set the United States apart from allegedly godless Communist nations. To underscore this commitment to religion, the federal government put the words "In God We Trust" on all currency. Meanwhile, religion adapted to the consumer society. Charismatic preachers such as Roman Catholic bishop Fulton J. Sheen and Protestant evangelist Billy Graham now brought religion to Americans by television.

People participated more in organized religion. In 1945, 45 percent of Americans belonged to a religious denomination; by 1960, that figure had reached 61 percent. Weekly church attendance increased to a peak of 49 percent in 1958. By 1960, there were 64 million Protestants, 42 million Roman Catholics, and fewer than 6 million Jews (see Table 25–3).

American culture also celebrated what *McCall's* magazine christened family "togetherness." Manufacturers promoted TV viewing as a way of holding families together. Detroit called its big automobiles "family" cars.

"Togetherness" meant the nuclear family, with a mother, a father, and plenty of children. After decades of decline, the birthrate rose in the 1940s. Beginning in 1954,

Table 25-3 Religious Revival and Baby Boom, 1945-1960

Year	Membership of Religious Bodies (in 1,000s)	Live Births (in 1,000s)
1945	71,700	2,858
1946	73,673	3,411
1947	77,386	3,817
1948	79,436	3,637
1949	81,862	3,649
1950	86,830	3,632
1951	88,673	3,823
1952	92,277	3,913
1953	94,843	3,965
1954	97,483	4,078
1955	100,163	4,104
1956	103,225	4,218
1957	104,190	4,308
1958*	109,558	4,255
1959**	112,227	4,245
1960	114,449	4,258

Source: George Thomas Kurian, *Datapedia* (Lanham, MD: Bernan Press, 1994), pp. 37, 146.

*Includes Alaska.

**Denotes first year for which figures include Alaska and Hawaii.

Americans had more than 4 million babies a year. Thanks to new drugs, nearly all these infants survived. Antibiotics reduced the risk of diphtheria, typhoid fever, and other infections. The Salk and Sabin vaccines virtually wiped out polio. As a result, the average number of children per family went from 2.4 in 1945 up to 3.2 in 1957, and the population grew by a record 29 million people to 179 million.

Like the religious revival, the "baby boom" is somewhat difficult to explain. For over a century, Americans had reduced the size of their families to ease financial and personal burdens. Prosperity may have persuaded couples that they could afford more children. But affluence alone did not explain why American culture became more child centered in the 1950s. In his *Common Sense Book of Baby and Child Care* (1946), pediatrician Benjamin Spock urged parents to raise their children with less severity and more attention, warmth, tenderness, and fun. It outsold every other book in the 1950s except the Bible.

Maintaining Gender Roles

As many social differences decreased, American culture nevertheless reemphasized the distinctions between the sexes. During the baby boom, women were expected to be helpful wives and devoted mothers. Men were encouraged to define themselves primarily as family providers.

The 1950s underscored the differences between genders in a variety of ways. Blue became the color for boys and pink the color for girls. Standards of beauty highlighted physiological differences between women and men. Voluptuous actresses such as Jayne Mansfield and Marilyn Monroe defined femininity.

Nevertheless, gender roles grew more similar during the 1950s. Society stressed a man's domestic role more than before. Husbands were urged to do housework and spend more time nurturing their children, although few men lived up to the new ideal.

Female roles evolved more dramatically. To help pay for the consumer lifestyle, many wives had to find jobs. In 1940, 15.6 percent of married women participated in the paid workforce. By 1960, that percentage had nearly doubled to 31.0, and women made up more than one-third of the labor force, mostly in clerical and sales positions. In the cold war competition with the Soviets, Americans celebrated the supposedly greater freedom and opportunity for women in the United States. Nevertheless, women had little help coping with their jobs and bigger families. Congress voted an income tax deduction for child-care costs in 1954, but little first-class child care was available. At work, women were expected to watch men get ahead of them. Women's income was only 60 percent of men's in 1960.

American culture strongly condemned women and men who strayed outside conventional gender norms. *Modern Woman: The Lost Sex*, a 1947 bestseller by Marynia Farnham and Ferdinand Lundberg, censured feminism as the "deep illness" of "neurotically disturbed women" with "penis envy." Psychologists and other experts demonized lesbians and gay men. As police cracked down on gay bars, unmarried men risked accusations of homosexuality. In 1950, a small group of gay men formed the Mattachine Society to work for homosexual rights. Five years later, a group of lesbians formed a counterpart organization, the Daughters of Bilitis. But there were no large protests against the treatment of gays and lesbians. The dominant culture expected males to be heterosexual husbands and fathers and women to be heterosexual wives and mothers.

Persisting Racial Differences

Despite pressures toward conformity, American society remained heterogeneous. As whites left for the suburbs, African Americans took their place in cities. By 1960, more than half of the black population lived in cities, where they were typically barred from white neighborhoods. Although suburbanization broke down ethnic differences among whites, it intensified the racial divide. The suburbs were 95 percent white in 1950. That was no accident: the first Levittowns, for instance, refused to sell houses to African Americans.

Living on reservations, Native Americans were also set apart. In 1953, Congress tried to "Americanize" the Indians by terminating their special legal status as sovereign groups and, with it, the traditional rights and reservations of more than 11,000 Native Americans. Termination was intended to turn them into members of the consumer society.

It did not turn out that way. As reservations became counties in the 1950s and early 1960s, Indians had to sell valuable mineral rights and lands to pay taxes. Tribes still faced poverty, unemployment, and social problems. Encouraged by the federal government's new Voluntary Relocation Program, about one in five Native Americans moved to the city. Some tribes, including the Catawba, the Coquille, and the Klamath, began legal fights to reclaim tribal status. But whether they lived on reservations or on crowded city blocks, a quarter of a million Indians remained largely separate and ignored.

The increasing migration of Puerto Ricans reinforced the nation's multiracial character. Beginning in the 1940s, a large number of Puerto Ricans, who were US citizens, left their island for more economic opportunity. By 1960, 887,000 Puerto Ricans lived on the mainland, two-thirds of them in the East Harlem section of New York City. They found opportunities but also separation and discrimination in their new homes.

Mexican immigration also added to racial diversity. After 1945, increasing numbers of Mexicans left their impoverished country for the United States, particularly the booming Southwest. Congress, bowing to southwestern employers, continued the Bracero Program, the supposedly temporary agreement that had brought hundreds of thousands of laborers, or *braceros*, to the wartime United States. Meanwhile, illegal Mexican migration increased dramatically.

Like other Mexican migrants before them, the newly arrived met a mixed reception. As in the years before World War II, Mexicans already living in the United States worried that the new migrants would compete for jobs, drive down wages, and feed American prejudice. Many white Americans indeed derided them as *mojados*, or "wetbacks," because so many had supposedly swum the Rio Grande River to enter the country illegally. Mexican Americans feared that the federal government would use the Internal Security Act of 1950 and the Immigration and Nationality Act of 1952 to deport Mexicans and break up families. The government's intention became clear in 1954 with Operation Wetback, which sent more than 1 million immigrants back to Mexico in that year alone.

The Plight of Mexican "Wetbacks" Illegal immigrants taken off freight trains in Los Angeles, after two days without food or water, in 1953. They were probably sent back to Mexico.

About 3.5 million Mexican Americans were living in the United States by 1960. The great majority worked for low wages in the cities and on the farms of the Southwest. Many lived in *barrios* apart from whites. Because of Operation Wetback and other instances of prejudice, some Mexican Americans became more vocal about their rights. The League of United Latin American Citizens denounced the impact of the Immigration and Nationality Act. More outspoken was the American GI Forum, an organization of Mexican American veterans formed when a Texas funeral parlor would not bury a deceased comrade. Such assertiveness made it harder to ignore the presence of Mexican Americans in the consumer society.

The experiences of Hispanics, Mexican Americans, Native Americans, and African Americans underscored the continuing importance of race in the United States. Mostly living apart, whites and nonwhites faced different conditions and different futures. Prosperity and consumerism did not change that reality. As long as race was so potent a factor, the United States would never be a homogeneous society.

The Survival of Diversity

Along with race, other forces ensured the survival of diversity, especially regional differences. As in the past, internal migration and the expansion of national boundaries promoted change. During the 1950s, more than 1.6 million people, many of them retired,

"160 Acres of Happiness" This ad for the opening of Disneyland in 1955 embodies the promise of pleasure for Americans in the consumer society.

moved to Florida. As a result, the state increasingly played a distinctive national role as a center for leisure and entertainment.

Other Americans headed westward. During the 1950s, over 3 million people moved to California, which earned a reputation as the pioneer state of the consumer society, home of the first Disney amusement park and the first McDonald's.

The admission of two new states highlighted the nation's continuing diversity. In 1959, Alaska and Hawaii became, respectively, the 49th and 50th states in the Union. Racially and culturally diverse, climatically and topographically distinctive, they demonstrated that America was not simply a land of corporations and Levittowns.

Popular music also exemplified this continuing diversity. Big swing bands gave way to such popular singers as Frank Sinatra and Patti Page. Jazz split into different camps—traditional, mainstream, and modern. Country music featured cowboy songs, western swing, honky-tonk, bluegrass, and the suburbanized "Nashville sound." A range of African American musical forms, including blues, jazz, and vocal groups, became known as "rhythm and blues" (R & B). Gospel music thrilled white and black audiences. Mexican Americans made Tejano music in Texas, and Polish Americans danced to polka bands in Illinois.

R & B collided with country music to create rock and roll. By 1952, white disc jockey Alan Freed was playing R & B on his Cleveland radio show, "Moondog's Rock 'n' Roll Party." In 1954, a white country group, Bill Haley and the Comets, recorded the first rock-and-roll hit, "Rock Around the Clock." Early rock and roll produced both African American and white heroes—Chuck Berry, Fats Domino, Jerry Lee Lewis, and Buddy Holly, among others.

The biggest rock-and-roll sensation was a young white singer and guitar player, Elvis Presley. Born in Mississippi and raised in near poverty in Memphis, Presley drew on a variety of genres to create a distinctive personal style. "Who do you sound like?" he was asked. "I don't sound like nobody," he said.

Because of Presley and other musicians, the sound of America was anything but homogeneous. Because of Florida, California, Alaska, Hawaii, and other states, the United States hardly looked monolithic. In these ways, American society avoided uniformity after World War II.

The Eisenhower Era at Home and Abroad

Prosperity subtly changed Americans' understanding of democracy. On one hand, they expected more from politics and government. Along with guarantees of national security and civil rights, people wanted government to assure their opportunity to consume. The good life became the test of democracy. On the other hand, people expected less from politics and government in the 1950s. Since the country was so prosperous and middle class, democracy must be working. As long as the federal government maintained the economy and national security, Americans did not demand dramatic, new liberal programs. The politics of the decade were dominated by President Dwight D. Eisenhower, whose middle-of-the-road domestic program, "Modern Republicanism," appealed to a prosperous electorate wary of government innovation. But Eisenhower's anti-Communist foreign policy did little to diminish popular anxieties about the cold war and laid the groundwork for future trouble in the Middle East and Southeast Asia.

"Ike" and 1950s America

Eisenhower, a charismatic military hero with a bright, infectious grin, would have been an ideal public figure in almost any era of American history, but the man known as "Ike" was especially suited to the 1950s. The last president born in the nineteenth century, he had successfully accommodated the changes of the twentieth. Raised on the individualism of the rural Midwest, Eisenhower adopted the bureaucratic style of modern organizations. He succeeded in the military not because he was a great fighter but because he was a great manager, a classic "organization man." As a commander in World War II, Eisenhower worked to keep fractious allies together. After the war, he deepened his organizational experience as president of Columbia University and as the first commander of NATO armed forces. Just as he adapted to big organizations, Eisenhower accommodated America's expanding commitment abroad. Raised among people who often feared American involvement in the world's problems, Ike had made his career in the world.

Eisenhower easily fit the dominant culture of the 1950s. He was an involved, loving husband and father. In a society pursuing pleasures, he was famous for his hours on the golf course. His wife, Mamie, wore the "New Look" fashions inspired by designer Christian Dior and avidly watched television soap operas.

Nominated for president by the Republicans in 1952, Eisenhower ran against Adlai Stevenson, the liberal Democratic governor of Illinois. Running a moderate campaign, Eisenhower avoided attacks on the New Deal and promised to work for an end to the Korean War. Meanwhile, his tough-talking running mate, Senator Richard Nixon of California, accused Stevenson of being soft on Communism. Eisenhower handily won 55 percent of the popular vote and 442 electoral votes. The Republicans took control of the White House and both houses of Congress for the first time in 20 years.

Modern Republicanism

Eisenhower's Modern Republicanism steered a middle course between traditional Republican conservatism and Democratic liberalism. With a conservative's faith in individual freedom, the president favored limited government and balanced budgets, but Eisenhower the organization man believed that Washington had an important role in protecting individuals. He also knew that most Americans wanted to keep such liberal programs as Social Security and farm subsidies.

Accordingly, his administration limited government by decreasing regulation of business and cutting taxes for the wealthy. The Submerged Lands Act of 1953 turned over offshore oil resources to the states for private exploitation. The Atomic Energy Act of 1954 allowed private firms to sell power produced by nuclear reactors.

Nevertheless, the administration left the legacy of the New Deal and the Fair Deal intact. Eisenhower accepted increases in Social Security benefits and farm subsidies. In some cases, the president wanted the government to take a more active role. The expansion of the interstate system was largely his initiative, which he justified as a matter of national defense. Despite his belief in balanced budgets, Eisenhower's administration produced several budget deficits. Federal spending helped fuel the consumer economy.

Modern Republicanism frustrated liberals, as well as conservative "Old Guard" Republicans, but "the public loves Ike," a journalist observed. "The less he does the more they love him."

"The Fantastic, Real-Life, Dream-Come-True Adventure of the Barstow Family of Wethersfield, Connecticut"

In the 1950s, American democracy rested on the faith in growing economic equality. A generation after the rigors of the Great Depression, more Americans were able to enjoy a middle-class life. With the rise of the consumer society, the middle-class standard of living became more comfortable and pleasurable than before. Additionally, unions offered workers protection, and the wealthy and big corporations no longer seemed to pose a threat to the power and prosperity of ordinary Americans.

For the Barstow family of Wethersfield, Connecticut, the sense of change was real. Robbins Barstow Jr. and his wife, Margaret, came from middle-class backgrounds; unusual for the time, both had graduated from college. Yet they did not take a comfortable life for granted. They were overjoyed in 1951, when, like so many young couples after World War II, they managed to buy their first home. A two-story house in the popular Cape Cod style, 190 Stillwold Drive was a modest 1,737 square feet on a

quarter acre of land—a tight fit for 32-year-old Robbins, 30-year-old Margaret, and their three small children. But the Barstows happily christened their home "Fairacre," where, as Barstow recalled, "the American dream came to fulfillment."

The Barstows had seen democratic values reach a kind of fulfillment, too. A passionate amateur filmmaker, Robbins had made a short film about President Franklin D. Roosevelt's Four Freedoms in the 1940s. Freedom of speech, freedom of worship, freedom from want, and freedom from fear had seemed to triumph in World War II. Labor unions, another value of Roosevelt's New Deal, had triumphed as well. In the 1950s, Robbins, a former teacher, made a living as a union official for the Connecticut Education Association, in the nearby city of Hartford. Like many suburban husbands, Robbins made the daily drive to work, while Margaret stayed home to take care of the house and the children. With only one income, the Barstows had to economize. Robbins

Eisenhower's popularity was confirmed at the polls in 1956. Repeating 1952, Eisenhower and Nixon again defeated Stevenson, this time with a bigger victory—58 percent of the popular vote and 457 electoral votes.

An Aggressive Cold War Strategy

Like Truman, Eisenhower opposed Communism at home and around the world. The president helped the crusade against alleged Communist subversives and tolerated its gave his sons haircuts and Margaret made matching "Davy Crockett" jackets for the family's trips. Like many Americans, the Barstows took vacations but could not afford their dream trip to the newly opened Disneyland in California.

In 1956, the Barstows entered a contest, sponsored by the 3M Corporation, for the best advertising tribute to Scotch tape: the reward was a family trip to Disneyland. Four-year-old Danny Barstow won with his slogan, "I like 'Scotch' brand cellophane tape because when some things tear then I can just use it." The Barstows shared in the excitement of flying across the country on an airplane and spending a week touring Disneyland and other sites.

The trip was a lesson in democracy. Thanks to 3M, the Barstows stayed in a fine hotel that had once been the playground of the very rich who had been defeated by the Depression and federal taxes. Swimming in the pool, the Barstows enjoyed what Robbins called "the by-gone days of . . . upper-class style and elegance."

Disneyland was a lesson in democratic progress, too. The Barstows' trip through the park traced an optimistic history of the United States, from the inaccurate depiction of a bloodless white settlement of the West in "Frontierland" to the quaint nostalgia of turn-of-the-twentieth-century "Main Street U.S.A." to the safe cars circling the roads of "Autopia" and the futuristic space travel of "Tomorrowland." Enjoying the excitement, the Barstows did not pay attention to the stereotypical depiction of African tribesmen in "Adventureland" or the few black faces among the tourists.

What struck the Barstows was the "magic" of it all. Even the bathrooms drove home the message that Disneyland was a special place. Looking fruitlessly for men's and women's rooms in "Fantasyland," the family realized they were marked "Prince" and "Princess." "And we remembered," Robbins noted, "that everybody in Fantasyland is a prince or princess." The new Disneyland was indeed a special, fantastical place, but it was also part of an emerging, middle-class America that more and more people could enjoy. It did not worry the Barstows that the park was the product of a corporation. And the family was, as Robbins put it, "forever grateful" that 3M, another corporation, had made their "marvelous Disneyland dream actually come true."

Robbins used the product of a third corporation—a 16-millimeter movie camera, made by Kodak—to record his family's adventure. "The Fantastic, Real-Life, Dream-Come-True Adventure of the Barstow Family of Wethersfield, Connecticut" so perfectly evoked the wonder and possibility of a middle-class America that the film became one of the first amateur productions added to the National Film Registry of the Library of Congress.

excesses. He refused to criticize publicly Senator Joseph R. McCarthy and declined to stop the execution of the convicted spies, Julius and Ethel Rosenberg, in 1953. Eisenhower denied the security clearance that J. Robert Oppenheimer, the former director of the Manhattan Project, needed to work on federal nuclear projects. Thousands of others allegedly deemed security risks also lost their federal jobs during the Eisenhower era.

Whereas Truman had pledged only to contain Communist expansion, Eisenhower and his advisers talked of rolling back Soviet power in Europe and freeing "captive

The "New Look" of Defense in the Eisenhower Era A ceremony honors the production of the 1,000th B-47 Stratojet, the long-range bomber capable of delivering nuclear weapons in an attack on the Soviet Union.

peoples" from Communism. Secretary of State John Foster Dulles threatened "instant, massive retaliation" with nuclear weapons in response to any Soviet aggression. To support this threat, the US military adopted the "New Look" strategy, named after Mamie Eisenhower's favorite fashions, that de-emphasized conventional armies and increased the nuclear arsenal with long-range bombers, missiles, and nuclear-powered submarines.

The president also used the CIA to counter Communism by stealthier means. At his direction, the CIA carried out secret activities once considered unacceptable. At home, the agency explored possible uses of lysergic acid diethylamide—the dangerous hallucinogenic drug known as LSD—by testing it on hundreds of unwitting Americans. Abroad, the agency secretly aided pro-American regimes and ran programs against uncooperative governments.

In August 1953, a covert CIA operation, code-named Ajax, orchestrated a coup that removed Mohammad Mossadeq, the nationalist prime minister of oil-rich Iran. Eisenhower and Dulles feared that this "madman," who had nationalized Iran's oil fields, would shut out US business in favor of Communism and the Soviet Union. Mossadeq's successor, the young monarch, Shah Mohammad Reza Pahlavi, accepted $45 million in US aid, turned his back on the Soviets, and made low-priced oil available to American companies.

In 1954, PBSUCCESS, a secret CIA operation modeled on Ajax, overthrew another foreign leader. Eisenhower and Dulles worried that a "Communist infection" in the Central

American nation of Guatemala could spread to the United States–controlled Panama Canal and to Mexico. In fact, the Soviet Union had made no effort to help Guatemala's new president, Jacobo Arbenz Guzmán, who supported redistribution of land and threatened the interests of a powerful American corporation, United Fruit. In June, PBSUCCESS used misleading "disinformation," a force of Guatemalan exiles, and CIA-piloted bombing raids to persuade Arbenz Guzmán to resign.

More openly, Eisenhower intensified efforts to shape perceptions of American culture and values abroad. In 1953, the administration created the United States Information Agency (USIA), overseen by the State Department. Active in 76 countries by 1960, the agency published pamphlets, promoted the exchange of visitors with other nations, broadcast Voice of America radio around the world, and worked with the CIA on propaganda and psychological warfare.

Avoiding War with the Communist Powers

Despite its tough talk, the Eisenhower administration avoided direct confrontation with the two major Communist powers, the People's Republic of China and the Soviet Union. Eisenhower knew he had to end the Korean conflict. As he promised in his 1952 campaign, Eisenhower traveled to Korea to end the military stalemate that ultimately killed 33,629 Americans. A cease-fire agreement in July 1953 left North and South Korea divided and the United States without a victory. It was, Eisenhower declared, "an acceptable solution." In October 1956, Hungarians, spurred on by American broadcasts, rose up against their pro-Soviet government. The Soviet Union sent troops to break the rebellion, but Eisenhower did not intervene with "massive retaliation," after all.

Fundamentally, Eisenhower maintained Truman's policy of containment. Cautious about military confrontation with the Soviets and the Chinese, Eisenhower declined to unleash nuclear weapons that would "destroy civilization." Although he sent CIA agents to conduct covert operations, the president was more reluctant than Truman to send American soldiers into open battle.

At the same time, Eisenhower, like Truman, knew the cold war was an economic, political, and cultural war, waged by foreign aid and propaganda. The Eisenhower administration took modest steps to improve relations with the Soviets. Responding to the Soviets' interest in "peaceful coexistence," Eisenhower told the United Nations that he wanted disarmament and the peaceful use of atomic power. He proposed the "Atoms for Peace" plan in which an international agency would explore nonmilitary uses for nuclear materials. The Soviets dragged their feet.

In 1955, Eisenhower took another step when he joined Khrushchev in Geneva for the first meeting between an American president and a Soviet leader since World War II. Eisenhower's proposal for "Open Skies"—a plan to allow each side to fly over the other's territory—sparked optimism about better relations. In 1958, the United States and the Soviets also agreed to a program of cultural exchanges. But in May 1960, optimism plummeted when the Soviets downed an American U-2 spy plane over the USSR. After the United States denied the affair, Khrushchev triumphantly produced the captured pilot, Francis Gary Powers, along with pieces of the plane. The rivalry would continue.

Crises in the Third World

Although Eisenhower worried most about Western Europe, his administration increasingly focused on the threat of Communist expansion in Africa, Asia, Latin America, and the Middle East. These relatively rural, unindustrialized regions, which made up the "third world," were enmeshed in the confrontation between the "first world" of industrialized non-Communist nations and the "second world" of industrialized Communist countries. Plagued by poverty, violence, and civil war, many third-world societies struggled against imperial domination.

Under Khrushchev, the Soviet Union tried to exploit third-world discontent and conflict. Anxious to preserve America's influence and access to natural resources, the Eisenhower administration countered Soviet moves with the tools of containment—aid, trade, and alliances. Eisenhower offered increased foreign aid and trade opportunities to third-world countries. He pursued closer military ties, including defense pacts with the Philippines, South Korea, and Taiwan.

This approach was sorely tested in Southeast Asia. When Eisenhower took office in 1953, the United States supported France's war to hold on to Vietnam and its other Southeast Asian colonies. Despite vast American aid, the French could not defeat the nationalist forces of the Viet Minh, led by the Communist Ho Chi Minh and helped by the mainland Chinese. By 1954, the Viet Minh had surrounded French troops at Dien Bien Phu. Unwilling to fight another land war in Asia, Eisenhower refused to send American troops and rejected the use of atomic bombs. France surrendered in May.

In 1954, peace talks at Geneva produced an agreement to cut Vietnam, like Korea, in half. Ho Chi Minh's forces would stay north of the 17th parallel; his pro-French Vietnamese enemies would stay to the south. The agreement called for a popular election to unite Vietnam in 1956. Certain that Ho Chi Minh and the Communists would win the election, the United States refused to sign the agreement. The president feared that a Communist Vietnam would deprive the West of raw materials and encourage Communism elsewhere. Comparing the nations of Asia and the Pacific to "a row of dominoes," Eisenhower explained that the fall of the first domino—Vietnam—would lead to the fall of the rest, including Japan and Australia.

Instead, the Eisenhower administration worked to create an anti-Communist nation south of the 17th parallel. To protect South Vietnam, the United States joined with seven nations to create the Southeast Asia Treaty Organization (SEATO) in 1954 (see Map 25–1). To ensure South Vietnam's loyalty, the Eisenhower administration backed Ngo Dinh Diem, an anti-Communist who established a corrupt, repressive government, with military advisers and hundreds of millions of dollars.

By thwarting the Geneva Accords and installing an unpopular regime in the South, Eisenhower ensured that Vietnam would be torn by civil war. In the short run, however, he had avoided war and seemingly stopped the Asian dominoes from falling.

Eisenhower soon confronted another crisis in the Middle East. Gamal Abdel Nasser, who had seized power in Egypt in 1954, emerged as a forceful spokesman for Arab unity and nationalism. Fearing that Nasser would open the way for Soviet power in the region, John Foster Dulles withdrew an offer to aid the Egyptians. Nasser struck back by taking over the British- and French-owned Suez Canal in 1956. In retaliation, Britain and France, with Israel's cooperation, moved against Nasser. As Israeli troops entered

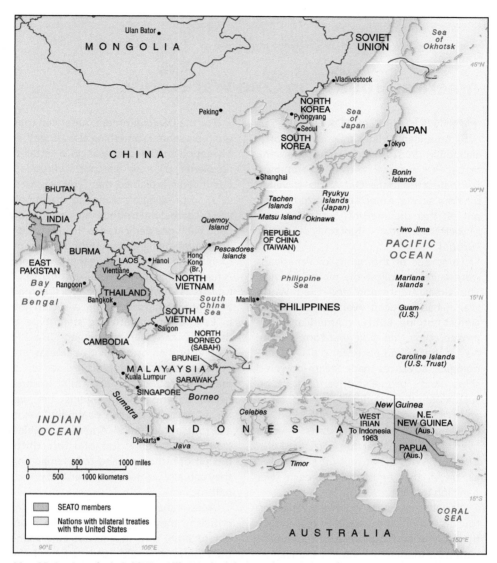

Map 25-1 America's Cold War Alliances in Asia Members of SEATO (the Southeast Asia Treaty Organization) and signers of other treaties with the United States. Through these pacts, the Eisenhower administration hoped to hold back the threat posed by Communist mainland China.

Egypt in October, Britain and France prepared to take back the Suez Canal. Eisenhower, fearing the invasion would give the Soviets an excuse to move into the Middle East, threatened the British, French, and Israelis—US allies—with economic sanctions. They soon withdrew.

The Suez crisis was a pivotal moment. Before a joint session of Congress in January 1957, Eisenhower promised that the United States would intervene to protect any Middle

AMERICA AND THE WORLD

American Tourists in Cold War Europe

"**T**HIS IS YOUR YEAR FOR EUROPE," an American Airlines magazine ad proclaimed in 1948. "Anyone with only a week or two—or even a few days—can enjoy a fascinating trip to the 'Old World,' traveling by time-saving American Flagship. Don't put off that dreamed-of-journey abroad. Make this your year—your family's year—for Europe!"

Hundreds of thousands of Americans were eager to follow the airline's advice. The Great Depression and then World War II had reduced overseas tourism to almost nothing. But now, Americans were prosperous again and war-torn Europe was at peace and eager for dollars. Technological advances made steam-powered ships and propeller-driven airplanes, such as American Airlines' Flagship, faster and more affordable than ever. In 1949, over half a million Americans traveled overseas; in 1955, that number soared past a million. With the advent of jet-powered air travel, that figure would reach over 2 million by 1961.

Various impulses spurred American tourists. Americans wanted to relax, enjoy themselves, and explore exotic places. A nation of immigrants, Americans wanted to see where their families originated. The consumerism and conformity of the 1950s drove tourism, too. As another American Airlines ad explained, a trip to Europe was "How to Keep up with the Joneses."

For the US government, American tourism represented something else altogether: a weapon in the cold war. In a letter to recipients of new passports, President Eisenhower explained that "you represent us all in bringing assurance to the people you meet that the United States is a friendly nation and one dedicated to the promotion of the well-being and security of the community of nations." Echoing that sentiment, Americans and foreigners alike spoke of US tourists as "unofficial ambassadors" abroad.

Those ambassadors did a mixed job. In Europe, an unflattering stereotype of the American tourist emerged. "He is a mobile human armed with cameras and broad-rimmed sunglasses, dressed-up in many-colored shirts and multi-colored neckties, who chewing-gums his way across an old and alien continent," wrote a European tour guide. American travelers were stereotyped as too loud, too critical, too unsophisticated, and too demanding: they actually wanted cold beer and private bathrooms!

Americans pushed back. Some of the criticism, they suggested, was the product of envy and insecurity: Europeans, their nations' wealth and power diminished, resented the triumphant rise of the United States. Admitting that too many Americans favored loud clothing, a New Yorker complained that "any slight misdemeanor committed by one of us

Eastern nation threatened by "power-hungry Communists." He implemented this "Eisenhower Doctrine" by sending troops to Lebanon the next year. In 1959, the United States joined with Turkey and Iran to create a Middle Eastern defense alliance known as the Central Treaty Organization (CENTO) for its geographical position between NATO on such a trip becomes magnified and is finally blamed on the United States as a whole."

American travelers developed another image, one rooted in the 1950s ideal of a democratic United States without social classes. "What the Italians like most about Americans is their free and easy manner," a journalist reported in 1957. "They consider Americans truly democratic, since they show not the slightest trace of class consciousness, and deal considerately and politely with one and all." Despite the reputation of some, the mass of travelers seemed to promote a positive understanding of their country, as US officials hoped. "Americans who are traveling abroad this Summer," said a Swiss teen in 1948, "are good ambassadors."

Travel also helped Americans get past some of their own stereotypes and prejudices. For instance, Americans who travelled to Moscow were in for a surprise. "Many American tourists here profess astonishment . . . that the Russians are people, that they smile and laugh and talk like people, that there are automobiles here. . . ," a writer noted in 1959. "Almost invariably, the Russians a tourist bumps into and talks with are friendly, helpful, deeply curious about the United States."

The encounters appeared to ease some of the cold war tensions and fears of the Soviets, too. "Some Russians who have met Americans," the writer added, "have adjusted some of their propaganda concepts of them as warmongers and imperialist exploiters scheming to blow up the Kremlin and enforce capitalism here."

American Airlines Advertisement

and SEATO (see Map 25–2). Eisenhower had helped to stabilize the Middle East and Southeast Asia temporarily, but he had also drawn the United States more deeply into these crisis-prone regions and increased the odds of future trouble. In the 1960s and 1970s, the United States would have to deal with this legacy.

Map 25-2   America's Cold War Alliances in the Middle East Located between the members of NATO and SEATO, the members of CENTO (the Central Treaty Organization) joined with the United States to deter the threat of international Communism sponsored by the Soviet Union to the north.

Challenges to the Consumer Society

Along with crises abroad, American society confronted challenges at home. In different ways, a rebellious youth culture, the alienated beat movement, a nascent environmental movement, and the divisive civil rights struggle upset the stability of the Eisenhower era. Consumerism had not solved all the nation's problems or won over all of its citizens. Moreover, despite prosperity, Americans worried about a crisis of power in the nation.

Rebellious Youth

"Never in our 180-year history," declared *Collier's* magazine in 1957, "has the United States been so aware of—or confused about—its teenagers." In the 1950s, the emergence of a distinct youth culture, built around rock and roll, cars, comic books, and premarital sex, troubled many adults. The youth culture culminated a trend apparent since the 1920s and 1930s. As more and more teenagers attended high school, they were segregated in their own world and developed their own values and practices. In the 1950s, young people claimed rock and roll as their music. They wore blue jeans; they read comic books and teen maga-zines. Expressing their individuality, boys modified cars into customized "hot rods." Teens were attracted to alienated and rebellious movie characters, such as the troubled son played by James Dean in *Rebel Without a Cause* (1955) and the motorcycle-gang leader played by Marlon Brando in *The Wild One* (1953). Adults worried about teenage defiance and juvenile delinquency.

Many young people were rebellious, but not nearly as much as adults feared. Juvenile delinquency did not actually increase after World War II, and neither did rates of sexual intercourse among teenagers. Girls never played a strongly visible role in male-dominated youth culture. Most young people never questioned the political system, and youth cul-ture exaggerated rather than rejected the values of the adult consumer society.

The early career of Elvis Presley illustrated the boundaries of youthful rebellion. Presley's appeal rested on an unsettling combination of rock-and-roll music and open sexuality. Presley's style—his sensual mouth, disheveled "duck's ass" haircut, and gyrating hips—amplified the music's sexuality.

Despite his appeal to teenagers, Presley was always polite, soft spoken, and devoted to his parents. Buying a pink Cadillac and other luxury cars, he was caught up in the consumer culture. Like millions of other Americans, Presley joined the suburban migration when he bought his house, Graceland, on the outskirts of Memphis. He was a new version of the old American dream of upward mobility.

Still, many adults blamed Presley, rock and roll, and mass media for the spread of violence, lust, and degeneration among young Americans. One popular television program showed Presley only from the waist up. To get rid of blue jeans and other teenage fashions, high schools imposed dress codes. There was a crusade against comic books, teen magazines, and movies. In well-publicized hearings from 1954 to 1956, the Senate's Subcommittee to Investigate Juvenile Delinquency focused attention on the corrupting power of the mass media.

The campaign against youth culture had little impact in a society of free speech and consumerism. Mass culture did not stop catering to teenagers with spending money. Many adults found youth culture appealing.

The Beat Movement

A smaller and older second group of rebels was much more critical of American society. The beat movement, which emerged in New York City in the 1940s, expressed a sense of both alienation and hope. The term "beat" referred to a feeling of exhaustion and also to a state of transcendence, the "beatific." Worn down by contemporary culture, the beats searched for a way beyond it.

Uptown at Columbia University and downtown in Greenwich Village, Allen Ginsberg, Jack Kerouac, John Clellon Holmes, William Burroughs, and others wanted, as one of them put it, "to emote, to soak up the world." Beats explored their sexuality, sampled mind-altering drugs, and pursued Eastern religions. In a society of bright colors, "beatniks" declared their alienation from consumerism by wearing black. Kerouac captured their spirit in his novel about a trip across America, *On the Road* (1957). In San Francisco, another center of beat culture, Allen Ginsberg published his long poem "Howl" (1956), which gave voice to alienation: "I saw the best minds of my generation destroyed by madness, starving hysterical naked. . . ."

Though few in number, the beats attracted a great deal of attention. Their movement signaled a new dissatisfaction with consumer society, conventional sexual mores, and politics as usual.

The Rebirth of Environmentalism

A rebirth of environmental consciousness was also evidence of concern about consumerism. By the late 1950s, Americans were more concerned about the environment than at any time since the beginning of the twentieth century. The environmental threat was obvious in the cities. A well-publicized pall of smog seemed to hang perpetually over car-choked Los Angeles. Americans could no longer ignore the fact that their automobiles, the symbol of the consumer society, were polluting the air.

The environmental threat was obvious in the countryside, too. Even as they filled new suburban developments built on old farms, some Americans lamented the disappearance of open land. They began to criticize society's attitude toward the natural world. In the mid-1950s, environmentalists, led by the Sierra Club and the Wilderness Society, blocked construction of the Echo Park Dam in the upper Colorado River because it would have flooded a national park, the Dinosaur National Monument. A new environmental movement to protect wilderness lands emerged from the battle.

The Struggle for Civil Rights

The African American struggle for civil rights also challenged the Eisenhower era. By the 1950s, segregation was under increasingly effective attack in the courts and on the streets. Focusing on public schools (see Map 25–3), the NAACP assaulted the discriminatory legacy of the Supreme Court's *Plessy v. Ferguson* ruling of 1896 (see Chapter 18). In 1951, the NAACP's special counsel, Thurgood Marshall, combined five school lawsuits, including Oliver Brown's challenge to the constitutionality of a Kansas state law that allowed cities to segregate their schools. Because of the law, Brown's eight-year-old daughter, Linda, had to ride a bus 21 blocks to a "colored-only" school, even though there was a "white-only" school just three blocks from home. When the Brown case reached the Supreme Court in December 1952, Marshall attacked the *Plessy* argument that justified "separate but equal" facilities for whites and African Americans. Because of segregation, Marshall argued, Linda Brown and other African Americans received both an inferior education and a feeling of inferiority. He concluded that segregation violated the citizenship rights guaranteed by the Fourteenth Amendment.

In May 1954, the Court, led by new Chief Justice Earl Warren, handed down its ruling in *Brown v. Board of Education, Topeka, Kansas*. Overturning *Plessy*, the justices ruled unanimously that public school segregation was unconstitutional under the Fourteenth Amendment.

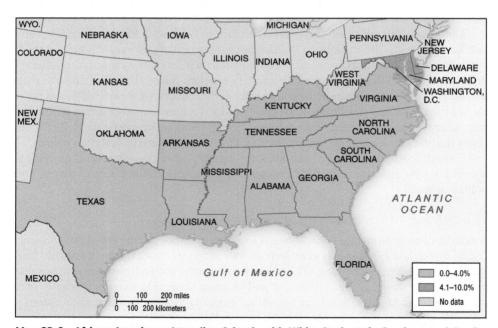

Map 25-3   African Americans Attending Schools with White Students in Southern and Border States, 1954 The small percentages indicate just how successfully segregation had separated the races before the Supreme Court ruled in *Brown v. Board of Education, Topeka, Kansas* in 1954.

"Separate but equal has no place," Warren announced. African Americans and white liberals were jubilant over what an African American newspaper called "a second emancipation proclamation." Marshall foresaw the end of school segregation before the close of the decade.

It did not work out that way. When the Supreme Court ruled on the enforcement of its decision in 1955, the justices turned to local school boards, dominated by whites, to carry out integration. Federal district courts were to oversee the process, which should occur with "all deliberate speed." School segregation would have to end, but not right away.

Taking heart from the enforcement ruling, many whites refused to give up Jim Crow. As one white southerner put it, a "reasonable time" for the end of segregation would be "one or two hundred years." In 1956, 101 congressmen signed a "Southern Manifesto" calling on their home states to reject the *Brown* ruling. Amid calls for massive resistance to desegregation, White Citizens' Councils formed to resist desegregation in southern states, some of which passed laws intended to stop school integration. There was violence, too. In October 1955, white Mississippians brutally killed Emmett Till, a 14-year-old black boy from Chicago, who had supposedly whistled at a white woman.

African Americans were ready to fight even harder against segregation. In Montgomery, Alabama, the NAACP wanted to test the state law that segregated the city's buses. On December 1, 1955, Rosa Parks, a 42-year-old African American tailor's assistant and NAACP official, boarded a bus. Local custom required her to give her seat to a white passenger and move to the back of the bus, but when the bus driver told her to move, Parks refused. As she said, "my feet hurt." More than that, she wanted to find out "once and for all what rights I had as a human being and a citizen." The angry driver thought she had none; he had Parks arrested.

Seizing on Parks's arrest, African Americans began to boycott the bus system. Twenty-six-year-old Martin Luther King Jr., pastor of the Dexter Avenue Baptist Church, agreed to lead the boycott. The son of a noted Atlanta preacher, King was already developing a brilliant oratorical style and a philosophy of nonviolent protest against segregation.

The boycott met immediate resistance. The city indicted the leaders, and African American homes and churches were bombed. In November 1956, however, the US Supreme Court ruled Alabama's bus-segregation law unconstitutional. By then, the boycott had cost the city dearly, and the white community had lost the will to resist. The city settled with the boycotters and agreed to integrate the buses. "We just rejoiced together," one of the boycotters remembered. "We had won self-respect."

Montgomery showed that a combination of local activism and federal intervention could overcome Jim Crow. It established a charismatic new leader with a powerful message and brought forward a new civil rights organization, the Southern Christian Leadership Conference. To one journalist, Montgomery "was the beginning of a flame that would go across America."

The flame did not travel easily. In 1957, the school board of Little Rock, Arkansas, accepted a federal court order to integrate Central High School, but in September the state's segregationist governor, Orval Faubus, called out National Guard troops to stop black students from enrolling. Even after meeting with Eisenhower, Faubus would not remove the troops. When he finally did, an angry mob of whites made it impossible for the African American students to stay. "Two, four, six, eight," cried the mob, "we ain't going to integrate."

Little Rock created a dilemma for the president. Not a believer in racial equality, Eisenhower wanted to avoid the divisive issue of civil rights. He privately opposed the *Brown* ruling and gave only mild support to the weak Civil Rights Act of 1957, which did not protect African Americans' right to vote. The president knew, however, that his government was being defied

Jubilation A packed crowd at First Baptist Church in Montgomery, Alabama, sings hymns and applauds the bus boycott in February 1956.

in Little Rock and humiliated around the world. So Eisenhower sent in troops of the army's 101st Airborne. With that protection, nine African American students went to Central High.

Like Montgomery, Little Rock demonstrated that a combination of federal action, however reluctant, and African American courage could triumph. The Central High crisis showed, too, how the cold war helped tip the balance against segregation. Competing with the Soviets for support from the multiracial third world, no president could afford the embarrassment of racial inequality at home. Segregation and discrimination were, the president concluded, "troublesome beyond imagination."

Time Line

▼**1947**
Levittown suburban
   development
Announcement of Truman
   Doctrine

▼**1948**
First McDonald's fast-food
   restaurant
Alfred Kinsey, *Sexual Behavior in
   the Human Male*

▼**1950**
Diners Club credit card

▼**1951**
UNIVAC 1 computer
Television premiere of *I Love Lucy*

▼**1952**
Dwight D. Eisenhower elected
   president

▼**1953**
Korean cease-fire

▼**1954**
"Baby boom" birthrate over 4
   million per year

Supreme Court school
   desegregation decision, *Brown
   v. Board of Education, Topeka,
   Kansas*
Creation of divided Vietnam in
   Geneva peace talks

▼**1955**
Formation of AFL-CIO
Disneyland opening

▼**1955–1956**
Montgomery, Alabama, bus
   boycott

The Crisis of "Misplaced Power"

Youth culture, the beat movement, the environmental movement, and the civil rights struggle contributed to an uneasy mood by the end of the 1950s. Many people, worrying that the consumer society was flawed, blamed the nature of power in post–World War II America.

To some observers, corporations had become too powerful. In his bestseller *The Hidden Persuaders* (1957), Vance Packard argued that advertisers manipulated Americans into buying corporate products. In 1958, the public got two object lessons in apparent corporate manipulation. That year, Americans learned about "payola," record companies' practice of paying disc jockeys to play particular records on the radio. Americans were shocked, too,

"The Helicopter Era" Cartoonist Herblock lampoons President Dwight Eisenhower's apparent lack of involvement in the nation's problems.

by revelations that contestants on popular TV quiz shows had secretly been given the answers to questions in advance.

Other observers believed that not only corporations, but large institutions generally, had too much power. Conservatives such as Republican senator Barry Goldwater of Arizona decried what they saw as the excessive activism of the federal government. Sociologist C. Wright

Mills argued in *The Power Elite* (1956) that an interlocking group of military, political, and economic managers ran the nation's institutions. In the age of nuclear weapons, still other Americans feared that scientists had too much power. Such movies as *The Day the Earth Stood Still* (1951) and *It Came from Beneath the Sea* (1955) exploited fears that scientific innovations would lead to disaster.

At the same time, Americans feared, too, that the nation might not be powerful enough. Such films as *The Deadly Mantis* (1957) and *Invasion of the Saucer Men* (1957) showed American science and technology unable to stop the destruction of the earth. There was also a sense in the age of conformity that ordinary Americans lacked the willpower to face the challenges of the twentieth century.

In October 1957, worries about American power went from science fiction fantasy to cold war reality. That month, the Soviet Union launched Sputnik, the world's first satellite, into orbit. The result was a wave of fear in the United States. If the Soviets could send up a satellite, they could be ahead in nuclear weapons and economic growth, too. Americans felt suddenly vulnerable.

Sputnik intensified concerns about American education. A diverse and growing student population and rising parental demands had strained the nation's schools. Now Americans worried that the schools were not preparing children to compete with the Soviets in science and technology. In 1958, Congress passed the National Defense Education Act. The measure promoted instruction in science, math, and foreign languages; supported construction of new schools; and offered loans and fellowships to students.

Sputnik forced Washington to accelerate the space program. The first US satellite launch collapsed in flames—Flopnik, the press called it. In January 1958, the government successfully launched its first satellite, Explorer 1. Later that year, Congress created the National Aeronautics and Space Administration (NASA) to coordinate space exploration. These initiatives did not completely wipe away Americans' worry that, as one magazine railed, "the whole kit and caboodle of our American way of life—missiles and toasters, our freedoms, fun, and foolishness—is about to go down the drain."

Eisenhower did little to calm the anxiety about American power. Slowed by poor health, he seemed old and out of ideas. In 1960, the president even created a Commission on National Goals to help figure out what the country should do. At the end of his term in January 1961, Eisenhower fed anxiety with a somber farewell address about the problem of "misplaced power" in the nation. Noting that cold war spending had built up the military and the defense industry, he warned against allowing this "military-industrial complex" to gain too much power or "endanger our liberties or democratic processes." Eisenhower also warned that universities, fueled by federal money for research, might become too powerful. The president's farewell was a stunning admission that the cold war could destroy rather than save democracy in America. The speech contributed to the sense of uncertainty: Was America too powerful, or not powerful enough?

Conclusion

Along with the cold war, the triumph of consumerism dramatically affected the United States in the 1950s. The booming consumer economy gave Americans a new sense of security and affluence during the unsettling confrontation with Communism. Breaking with the past, they moved to the suburbs, had record numbers of children, bought televisions, watched *I Love Lucy*, and defined life as the pursuit of material pleasures. Consumerism helped promote homogeneity and conformity and spurred the victory of Dwight Eisenhower and his moderate approach to government. For a moment, it seemed as if America had achieved stability and harmony in a dangerous world, but that feeling did not last. By the close of the 1950s, many Americans wanted more for themselves and their country. They worried that power was "misplaced." They questioned whether consumer society could provide prosperity, democracy, and security for all its citizens. The next decade would offer a dramatic answer.

Who, What, Where

Domino theory 792

Dulles, John Foster 790

Dynamic obsolescence 779

Echo Park Dam 798

Eisenhower, Dwight D. 786

Kinsey, Alfred C. 780

Levitt, William J. 777

Little Rock 799

Massive retaliation 790

Modern Republicanism 786

Nixon, Richard 787

Parks, Rosa 799

People's Republic of China 791

Suez Canal 792

Review Questions

1. What were the basic components of "the good life" in the 1950s?

2. What factors made American society more homogeneous in the 1950s? What factors kept the nation diverse?

3. What was Eisenhower and Dulles's strategy for fighting the cold war?

Critical-Thinking Questions

1. How did the emergence of consumer society affect democracy in the United States? Did the nation become more or less democratic during the 1950s?

2. Why did so many Americans believe there was a crisis of power by the end of the 1950s? Had the nation, in fact, become less powerful?

3. Was the United States winning the cold war in the 1950s?

Suggested Readings

Galambos, Louis. *Eisenhower: Becoming the Leader of the Free World*. Baltimore: Johns Hopkins University Press, 2017.

Klarman, Michael J. *Brown v. Board of Education and the Civil Rights Movement*. New York: Oxford University Press, 2007.

Packard, Vance. *The Hidden Persuaders*. New York: IG Publishing, 1957/2007.

For further review materials and resource information, please visit www.oup.com/us/oakes-mcgerr

CHAPTER 25: THE CONSUMER SOCIETY, 1945–1961
Primary Sources

25.1 GAEL GREENE, "THE BATTLE OF LEVITTOWN" (1957)

Largely because William J. Levitt sold only to whites, his second Levittown, northeast of Philadelphia, Pennsylvania, had no African American homeowners from its start in 1952. Then, in August 1957, a resident sold a ranch house at 43 Deepgreen Lane to a black refrigeration technician, William Myers, and his wife, Daisy. Some local residents tried to drive out the Myers family by marching in protest, crowding the street outside their house, and throwing rocks at the house's windows. As local police struggled to avert violence, Pennsylvania's governor, George Leader, sent in the state police. The *New York Post* sent in young reporter Gael Greene to write about the upheaval in suburbia. The Myerses won what the *Post* called "The Battle of Levittown": the black family stayed in the suburb until William got a new job in another city four years later.

Aug. 17. They look like folks gathered for a backyard barbecue. Housewives in Bermuda shorts. Shirt-sleeved men slapping each other on the back in greeting, Youngsters running under foot. Teenagers slouching self-consciously. . . . "*We don't want no mob violence.*" That is the rumbling, southern drawl of Jim Newell, 35, an electrician who came to Levittown from North Carolina because: "I understood this was a white settlement.'" Newell is chairman of the Levittown Betterment Committee, formed hurriedly Thursday night in honor of Myers' impending arrival. "We don't want no mob violence." He repeats his exhortation for the TV cameras as his audience applauds. "We want you all to respect the protection officers." . . . Voices in the crowd:

"*Tell Gov. Leader to get his Gestapo out of here.*" . . . "*Ask Gov. Leader how it feels to live next door to a Negro.*" . . . "The highest tribunal—the Supreme Court in Washington—has already spoken," Newell replies, using a rolled-up poster as a megaphone.

"*Well, what are we going to do?*" a dozen voices asked. "Ever hear of the old boycott trick?" Newell grinned. The crowd, 350 strong, claps and cheers. A man leaps to the platform. "Now I'm sure Jim didn't mean what he just said," he begins.

The crowd boos. "*Boycotts aren't legal. Jim wouldn't want to tell you to do anything illegal.*" "*I must have had the wrong phrase or wrong terminology,*" Jim agrees. He winks. . . . "*The jigs did it in [Montgomery],*" says a voice in the crowd. "*They stayed off the buses.*"

Joining Newell on the platform is Robert Camarote in a print sports shirt. "We have lost a happy home and a nice community," Camarote mourns. "Why, it's hard to get a decent meal because our wives are so upset. But we don't want a person's home blown up. We must demonstrate peaceably."

A voice: "They shouldn't stone him. They should string him up."

Now Newell takes over. He thrusts a massive arm into the air and quiets the restless crowd. "Let's go to church and pray to the good Lord that he carries us through the right way."

"*If the good Lord wanted us to live together he would have made us all one color,*" says a voice in the crowd.

Camarote again: "I hope the good Lord will help Myers make his decision. We are not radicals. We are God-fearing men." . . .

Voices: "I think the Communists are all behind this." "Me, too." "Why don't they stay with their own kind? You don't find whites trying to crash a nigger neighborhood." . . . "When Myers sees how many people don't want him we'll see if his heart is white enough to move out," Newell suggests. . . .

"Myers drives a '57 Mercury. It really makes you wonder where he's getting all this money."

"Do you people want to keep coming every night?" Newell asks the crowd. They answer with loud applause. . . .

"We don't want to set up him up as a martyr, this Mr. Myers," says Camarote. "Everything must be done peaceably." The meeting grinds to a close.

The state troopers reach instinctively to see if riot sticks are ready as the mob drifts toward the dusty-pink ranch-type home of Levittown's first Negro family.

The crowd decides to picket the house. Troopers head them off as they reach the sidewalk. They retreat, marching in a circle on the street. . . . They are the residents of what has been touted as a model town. . . .

Aug. 19. The homeowners of Deepgreen Lane spend long afternoons stationed on their lawn chairs—taking it all in, discussing their problem with neighbors, the egg salesman, the paper boy, and the out-of-town reporters who have flocked here.

"They ought to have a NAAWP," says a chubby youngster, parroting his parents. "A National Association for the Advancement of White People." *"It's true,"* said Mrs. Ruth Hughes of Deepgreen Lane. *"The colored people get more protection than we do."*

A man stops his car in front of Mrs. Hughes' home. "Got any idea where the meeting is?" he asks. He says he lives in another section of Levittown, refuses to give his name, but offers some advice. *"What we got to do is make them uncomfortable,"* he says. *"That Myers has got a lot of guts. It won't be easy."*

"I came here to get away from them," he explains. "I'm tired of running away. This time I'm making my stand. We'll freeze them out of here. Nobody sells out. Forbid your children to play with them. Sooner or later you'll get on their nerves and they'll leave."

"I won't deliver papers to them, even if it means losing my job," chimes in Mrs. Hughes' son, Dave.

The wife of a neighbor who befriended Myers drives by. "Nigger-lover, nigger-lover," kids chant after her.

"It makes me sick," [says] Mrs. John Trakimas. "It just makes me sick. If it had happened on another street I could go and sympathize with everybody and come home to sleep. But it's our own street, and we don't sleep at night anymore. It would be different if we had sons, but we have a daughter. Just think how my husband would feel if she brought one home and said this is my spouse."

"For God's sake!" cries a dissenter. "They don't want to be kissed by white people, they just want to be left alone."

***

Aug. 19. [Greene interviews with William Myers] "I want a good home for my children—that home is in Levittown. I won't give it up." The handsome, soft-spoken man spoke—not in stubborn defiance—but with calm matter-of-factness. "Nothing will make us leave Levittown. . . . It is difficult to explain why we are so determined to stick this out. . . Yes, it is partly the principle involved. But, I guess, it is something inside that drives a man to hold fast for that principle. . . . A few years ago we moved into a mixed neighborhood, in York, Pa.," Myers said. "Our home was only three blocks from my father's house, but it was on an all-white street. . . So you see, we have gone through something similar to this before—though in a mixed, rather than an all-white, neighborhood. We know what to expect.

"Having so many friends to support us will make it easier," he said with a glance toward the Levittown citizens seated at a long luncheon table waiting for Myers to join them. Many were members of the Friends Service Assn. which has dedicated its staff to the job of making Myers' entrance into the community of a peaceful one.

***

Aug. 23. The actions of the crowd have served only to stir new underdog sympathy for the Myerses. Hundreds have been sympathetic from the beginning. Some, being non-Levittowners, can only write—like former Dodger Jackie Robinson . . . "We've been hearing from people as far away as California who think there is blood running in the streets," Mrs. Myers said. "We'd like them to know how many good things have been done for us."

In a soft, tired voice, Mrs. Myers spoke of neighbors bringing groceries, friends bearing preserves and fresh fruit, the hundreds of phone calls and the mound of sympathetic mail. . . . Some excerpts: "We are 100 per cent behind you in your fight to live like free Americans . . ." "Don't judge all of this town by a few showoffs . . ." "Many of us are pleased we won't be a white island any longer . . ." . . .

"Neighbors have helped to mow the lawn," Mrs. Myers continued. "We've received many dinner invitations. Some local school teachers are hanging the curtains. Someone filled the re-frigerator with six quarts of milk one morning. And we want to commend the police for the wonderful cooperation and protection they have given us."

. . . Many townspeople have tried to assuage their own guilt by blaming teen-agers for being the real trouble makers. Bristol Township Police Chief John R. Stewart told the Post: "Juveniles have been the least of these mobs. The teen-agers are not to blame. They wouldn't have come here in the first place if their parents had not set an example."

Sources: "The Lawns of Levittown," *New York Post*, August 18, 1957, pp. 5 and 27; "The Battle of Levittown," *New York Post*, August 19, 1957, pp. 3 and 33; "Levittown: Dawn of Reason and Hope?" *New York Post*, August 23, 1957, pp. 3 and 41.

25.2 H. H. REMMERS AND D. H. RADLER, EXCERPTS FROM "TEENAGE ATTITUDES" (1958)

Despite alarms about rebellious beatniks, juvenile delinquents, and rock and rollers, adults worried that young Americans were actually conformists. The extent of adult concern became clear in this 1957 article by two social scientists reporting on their annual surveys of teenagers in high schools. According to H. H. Remmers and D. H. Radler, American teenagers wanted too much to be liked, failed to think independently, and did not ap-preciate scientists enough. Teens' abandonment of traditional American individualism, the social scientists concluded, threatened the future of democracy in the United States.

What is today's younger generation really like? What is its prevailing attitude; what is it thinking; how is it likely to handle its own and the world's problems when it grows up? . . . [O]n a statisti-cal basis we can paint something like a portrait of "the typical teenager." Scientific surveys of the nation's young people have made clear that their problems, beliefs and desires follow a charac-teristic pattern. . . .

Our samples of the younger generation have been drawn from the nation's high schools, which since the early 1940s have enrolled virtually all of the country's teenagers. Each sample consists of about 3,000 students, chosen to represent accurately all the high-school grades, the various sections of the country, rural and city dwellers and roughly the various family back-grounds. Aside from giving the correct statistical representation to these groupings, the samples are completely random. . . . The subjects' responses are recorded anonymously. . . .

The most significant place to start our examination of the results of these polls is to look at what U. S. teenagers list as their most common problems. . . . At the head of the list is the wist-ful plea: "Want people to like me more." And most of the things that 25 per cent or more of the teenagers list as problems express, in one form or another, the same sentiment. A majority of teenagers want to gain or lose weight or otherwise improve their appearance; they want more dates, more friends, more popularity; they get stage fright before a group, worry about their lack of self-confidence. Their overriding concern emerges again when they are asked direct questions about their feelings with respect to approval by others. More than half admit that they try very hard to do everything that will please their friends; 38 per cent declare that the worst of all calamities is to be considered an "oddball."

Naturally these feelings carry over into behavior. Nearly all the teenagers say they disapprove of high-school students drinking—but a quarter of them admit that they drink. More than three quarters disapprove of smoking—but 38 per cent smoke. The whole matter is summed up in the comment of a teenage girl: "It's hard for a teenager to say 'I don't care to' when all the rest of the gang are saying, 'Ah, come on.'"

. . . [W]hat should concern us much more is how the passion for popularity translates itself into an almost universal tendency to conformity among our younger generation. It runs through all social classes. American teenagers show substantial class differences in many aspects of their behavior, problems and aspirations, but in their desire for popularity and their conformist attitude they are as one: low-income or high-income, their highest concern is to be liked.

This is the most striking and most consistent fact that has emerged from our polls through the 17 years. Poll after poll among our youngsters has given statistical confirmation of the phenomenon of American life which David Riesman, in his book *The Lonely Crowd*, named "other-direction"—extreme sensitivity to the opinions of others, with a concomitant conformity. As a nation we seem to have a syndrome characterized by atrophy of the will, hypertrophy of the ego and dystrophy of the intellectual musculature.

This rather unpleasant portrait is an inescapable conclusion from the mass of data on the attitudes of the younger generation. More than half of our teenagers believe that censorship of books, magazines, newspapers, radio and television is all right. More than half believe that the Federal Bureau of Investigation and local police should be allowed to use wiretapping at will, that the police should be permitted to use the "third degree," that people who refuse to testify against themselves should be forced to do so. About half of our teenagers assert that most people aren't capable of deciding what's best for themselves; fully 75 per cent declare that obedience and respect for authority are the most important habits for children to learn. On practically all questions of social policy the youngsters lean strongly to stereotyped views.

Such answers may represent either unthinking responses or convinced and deliberate acceptance of an authoritarian point of view. In either case the picture is equally unhappy. The road to totalitarianism is the same length whether we walk down it consciously or merely drift down it. Unthinking conformity provides a setting which makes it possible for a demagogue to lead a nation into slavery.

As individuals our nation's young people consistently value others' opinions above their own. Fewer than half claim that they think things out for themselves and act on their own decisions. Only one fourth report that they often disagree with the group's opinion. No more than 18 per cent are willing to say that their tastes are quite different from those of their friends. Yet in spite of these admissions most teenagers declare that their freedom is not too limited.

Such soundings of the younger generation's attitudes uncover some of the roots of anti-intellectualism in the U.S. Almost three quarters of the high-school students believe that the most important thing they can learn in school is "how to get along with people." Only 14 per cent place academic learning first. In a recent poll of a representative sample of college students we found that the same attitude prevails at the university level: 60 per cent would rather be popular than brilliant; 51 per cent believe that students with low grades are more likely to be popular than those who get good marks; 72 per cent believe that development of a well-rounded personality is the main purpose of education; 71 per cent feel that personality counts more than grades when it comes to looking for a job.

The disdain for learning shows up most sharply and most dismayingly in the attitude of teenagers toward science and scientists. . . . More than a third find scientific work boring; 25 per cent think scientists as a group are "more than a little bit odd"; about 30 per cent believe that a scientist cannot enjoy life or raise a normal family. In a poll in October, 1957—the month of Sputnik 1—68 per cent of the teenagers said they would not like to be scientists. A majority asserted that scientists are likely to be radical, that they take no thought of the consequences of their work, that science should be restricted to physics and chemistry, that it is impossible to formulate scientific laws of human behavior. Most disquieting is the fact that views of this kind are just as common among students of high scientific aptitude as among those who have no interest in science. The climate of popular opinion among the nation's youth undoubtedly is keeping many able boys and girls out of science. . . .

A need and craving to be liked, drifting with the crowd, conformity, a kind of passive anti-intellectualism—these seem to be outstanding characteristics of the present-day younger generation as it has expressed itself in our polls. . . .

The present conformist spirit—demonstrably not confined to the younger generation—seems to us something new in American life. It reverses our history and the American ideal, which has been, above all, individualistic. The American tradition suggests that we have not been in the past a people who passively accepted dictation by the crowd or surrendered the exercise of our freedoms.

[Teenagers'] attitude derives in large part, of course, from their parents. . . . In recent decades we have seen the individual steadily depreciated even in intellectual pursuits. There is a rising admiration for "the power of the group mind." We have team research in science and "brainstorming" in industry. In every sphere group decision is replacing individual initiative.

In this light we must take a serious view of the tendency to conformity exhibited by the younger generation. In any circumstances it is always difficult for an adolescent to find himself. The teens are a time of transition, demanding adjustments to profound biological, emotional and social changes. Probably most parents today would testify from personal experience that the teenagers of our day are having an extraordinarily difficult time of growing up and finding themselves.

Ralph Waldo Emerson pointed out that the price of group agreement is descent to the least common denominator. As T. V. Smith and Eduard C. Lindeman remarked in their book *The Democratic Way of Life*, a democracy cannot afford to devalue "the finality of the individual," from whom "all things flow." In our view, the future of our democracy is not promising unless we restore a social climate which will reward independent thinking, personal morality and truly enlightened cooperation in place of going along with the crowd.

Source: H. H. Remmers and D. H. Radler, "Teenage Attitudes," *Scientific American* 198, no. 6 (June 1958): 25–29.

25.3 VISUAL DOCUMENTS: AUTOMOBILE ADVERTISEMENTS (1953–1955)

Advertising and automobiles were essential to the consumer culture of the 1950s. Here a trio of ads shows how car companies tried to persuade Americans to make very expensive purchases. How do these three car ads appeal to consumers? What do the advertisers argue that the 1953 Ford, the 1955 Packard Clipper, and the 1956 Buick Roadmaster will do for their drivers? Note how much the ads are rooted in some of Americans' basic concerns about conformity, individualism, and consumerism itself.

For those who desire individuality

CUSTOM CONSTELLATION
245 HORSEPOWER

The medium-priced car that makes it smart to be different

THE 1955 CLIPPER offers a distinctiveness . . . not confined by convention . . . unmatched by the commonplace. Here is a *smartness* that is *new* in its field . . . from sparkling exteriors to color-coordinated interiors. Two great V-8 engines, 225 and 245 horsepower, are the most powerful of all in the medium-price range. There is the new Twin Ultramatic — the industry's most advanced automatic transmission — actually two drives in one — offering the driver a finger-tip selection of super-smooth starts or jet-like getaways.

Small wonder people with a desire for individuality so warmly welcome this distinctive new car which sets both itself and its owner apart from the crowd. There's nothing uncertain in their approval . . . they are trying and buying the 1955 Clipper in unprecedented numbers. *One visit to your Packard dealer* will show you the reason for this tremendous reception . . . and will convince you the 1955 Clipper is the most individually distinctive car in the medium-price field. PACKARD DIVISION • STUDEBAKER-PACKARD CORP.

The 1955 Clipper

Built by Packard Craftsmen

Sources: J. Walter Thompson Company, Ford Motor Company. Courtesy Duke University Libraries, John W. Hartman Center for Sales, Advertising & Marketing History; The Studebaker National Museum Archives; Apic/Getty Images.

25.4 UNITED STATES OFFICE OF CIVIL AND DEFENSE MOBILIZATION, EXCERPTS FROM "SURVIVE NUCLEAR ATTACK" (1960)

As the United States and the Soviet Union rapidly built up their arsenals of nuclear weapons, Americans fearfully imagined what World War III would be like. A thermonuclear conflict was a frightening prospect—so frightening that the US government tried hard to persuade Americans that they could survive one. In this excerpt from a 1960 pamphlet, the federal Office of Civil and Defense Mobilization (OCDM) detailed the likely effects of a nuclear strike on the United States and listed the steps the American people could take to protect themselves. Would these recommendations, including building bomb shelters and stockpiling food, have worked in the event of a nuclear attack?

Axiom of Survival

If this country is attacked with nuclear weapons you can protect yourself. But, first, you must know what to do and how to do it.

Face These Facts

A 20-megaton explosion on the surface of the earth can kill most people and destroy most buildings within a 5-mile radius of ground zero, a total of about 80 square miles. The most likely targets are big cities—industrial areas—military centers.

However, you are not safe merely because you live far away from likely targets.

Distance protects you against heat and blast, but not against radioactive fallout which goes anywhere and can kill or injure the unprotected and the unprepared.

Without protection from fallout, millions would die who otherwise would survive. Put more positively, millions of Americans could save their lives by learning what to do—and doing it.

Knowledge Is Your Key to Survival

To protect yourself at the time of a nuclear explosion, you must understand NOW the hazards you would face.

You probably will be warned in advance by siren or radio that attack is coming. The Air Force, with its far-flung detection network, and the Office of Civil and Defense Mobilization are working together to do everything possible to warn you.

But surprise attack could come. You must know what to do if it does.

You Should Know the Three Main Destructive Effects of a Nuclear Explosion

Heat, Blast, Fallout

Heat

Dangers facing you: The bomb produces heat of several million degrees—a good deal hotter than the temperature on the surface of the sun. This heat travels at the speed of light. A megaton explosion could kill an unshielded man 8 miles from ground zero. A 20-megaton explosion could kill an unshielded man 20 miles away. It could blister and cripple the bodies of unsheltered people well beyond that.

What you should do: Beyond the 5-mile radius of total destruction, but still within range of the immediate killing power of the bomb, you would have split seconds to save your life.

You would have to act with instinctive speed to take cover behind whatever was at hand.

Blast

Dangers facing you: The shock waves of blast from a nuclear explosion travel about 900 miles an hour—nine times the force of a major hurricane!

Blast could destroy a brick building 9½ miles from ground zero.

What you should do: If caught unprotected beyond the 5-mile circle of total destruction you could save your life with an instantaneous dive for cover.

Cover is the same for both heat and blast.

In open country it might be a ditch or culvert. Lie face down and stay there until the heat and blast waves have passed.

In the city it might be a wall, a building, or even a truck.

Indoors it would be the floor (behind furniture or as close to an inside wall as possible).

The Main Idea—Get Behind Something

Fallout

Dangers facing you: The millions of tons of pulverized earth and debris sucked up as high as 15 miles by the fireball of a large nuclear explosion become a deadly radioactive fallout cloud. It spreads its lethal radioactivity over wide areas, hundreds of miles downwind from ground zero. Fallout radioactivity cannot be detected by taste or touch. Sometimes, but not always, the fine ash or dust carrying the radioactivity is visible. It fills the atmosphere, the air you breathe, and attacks the vital organs of your body with invisible radiation.

Protection from Fallout

The best protection against fallout radiation is a fallout shelter. Every family should have one. It can be an area in a building of such heavy construction as to afford the required shielding or a shelter designed to be a unit of a family dwelling. OCDM has designed several types of family fallout shelters which are described and illustrated in a new booklet entitled "The Family Fallout Shelter," MP-15. Copies may be obtained from your local civil defense director or from OCDM Operational Headquarters, Battle Creek, Mich.

Basement Concrete Block Shelter, designed as a do-it-yourself project. Solid concrete blocks are used to build it.

Preshaped Metal Shelter, built by placing preshaped corrugated metal sections on or close to the surface of the ground and mounding them over with earth.

Aboveground Double-Wall Shelter, which is a double-walled, concrete block structure with the walls built nearly 2 feet apart. The space between the walls is filled with earth. A roof is built of either poured concrete or wood and covered with earth.

How Will You Know If You Are in a Fallout Area?

Radiation from fallout cannot be detected by sight, taste, smell, hearing, or touch. If an unusual amount of dust is accumulating outside your house following a nuclear explosion you should assume it is radioactive. However, you should not depend on such an uncertain method of detection.

CONELRAD [short for Control of Electromagnetic Radiation] will be your main source of information on fallout and protective measures you might take. This is the national system of emergency broadcasting that goes into effect when the Commander of the North American Air Defense Command determines an air attack is imminent or under way. . . .

This is why you should have a battery-powered portable radio in your shelter. . . .

In rural sections or other localities where CONELRAD may not be operative, local officials may use different methods of communication. . . .

How Long Will You Have to Stay in Shelter?

[I]t is not possible to know in advance what the amount of fallout or dose rate would be in any given place. Therefore, the time you would have to remain in shelter can only be determined accurately by measuring the dose-rate of the fallout in your immediate vicinity. To this end local civil defense officials are required under the National Plan to be prepared to measure radiation levels and inform the public. The National Plan also calls on individual householders to store food for a minimum of 2 weeks.

. . . Where widespread and heavy fallout occurs local officials might decide to evacuate people to safer areas. You should keep tuned to CONELRAD for advice and guidance. . . .

A family in their fallout shelter.
Source: Photo by Dmitri Kessel/The
LIFE Picture Collection/Getty Images.

Prepare Now for Living in a Shelter

The National Plan calls on everyone to have a 14-day supply of food and water. Except for very brief departures from your shelter you could be pinned down longer than 2 weeks.

Two weeks after an attack State and local governments are responsible for supplying food for the next 4 weeks.

However, as in all planning for emergency, it is best to plan against the worst. It is possible that in instances local officials could not supply all of the people in their jurisdictions. There also might be instances of severe fallout from recurring attack that would keep people in their shelters for an extended period. A good plan would be to have 2 weeks' or more supply of food on hand at all times. . . .

Before Disaster Strikes You Should Have On Hand

1. Flashlight and extra batteries.
2. Battery-powered portable radio and extra batteries.
3. First-aid kits.
4. Stored water or other liquid—7 gallons per person for 2 weeks. Water in hot water tanks, in toilet tanks, and ice cubes in a refrigerator can be used as an additional source.
5. A 14-day supply of food, paper plates, and napkins.
6. Cooking and eating utensils, measuring cup, can and bottle openers, pocket knife, and matches.
7. Special foods for babies and invalids.
8. Large garbage can (20 gallons).
9. Smaller can for human wastes (10 gallons).
10. Covered pail for bathroom purposes.
11. Toilet tissue, paper towels, personal sanitary supplies, disposable diapers, and soap.
12. One blanket per person, rubber sheeting, and special equipment for the sick.
13. Grocery bags, and a week's accumulation of newspapers for wrapping garbage.
14. Two pints of household chlorine, and 1 quart of 5 percent DDT.
15. Wrench, screwdriver, and shovel; axe and crowbar to free yourself from debris, if necessary, or to help others to do so.
16. Waterproof gloves.

Source: United States Office of Civil and Defense Mobilization, excerpts, *Survive Nuclear Attack* (Washington, DC: US Government Printing Office, 1960).

"The Table of Democracy"

1960–1968

< Aerial View of "Missile Row" on Cape Canaveral

AMERICAN PORTRAIT

The A&T Four

Franklin McCain and Joseph McNeill were scared. On the afternoon of February 1, 1960, the two African American college students had done the unthinkable at the Woolworth's in Greensboro, North Carolina: they had sat down at the lunch counter and asked for donuts and coffee. When the white waitress refused to serve them, they persisted. By arrangement, two friends from North Carolina Agricultural and Technical College, Ezell Blair and David Richmond, joined them at the counter. All four waited to see what would happen to them for challenging segregation, the policy of the Woolworth's lunch counter and the basic principle of the twentieth-century South.

Some white customers insulted the four students; but other whites even encouraged them. A white policeman stood behind them, McCain recalled, "with his club in his hand, just sort of knocking it in his hand, and just looking mean and red and a little bit upset and a little bit disgusted." Were the four students about to get beaten? Then McCain realized with surprise that the policeman "didn't know what the hell to do." The four African Americans had effectively disarmed this representative of white authority. "You had the feeling that this is the first time that this big bad man with the gun and the club has been pushed in a corner, and he's got absolutely no defense, and the thing that's killing him more than anything else—he doesn't know what he can or what he cannot do," McCain observed. "He's defenseless."

McCain and his friends stayed at the lunch counter until closing time. They did not get service. But they did get something important. For months they had talked about the frustration and humiliation of segregation; for months they had debated what to do. Now, they had confronted injustice. "I felt," McCain admitted, "as though I had gained my manhood."

The A&T Four, as they became known, also made a critical discovery: they had power. A group of unarmed African Americans, polite and persistent, could challenge authority and get away with it. Their nonviolent protest, inspired mainly by Christianity and the example of the Indian activist Mohandas Gandhi, actually empowered them. "To me," Blair said, "we were sitting down at the table of democracy."

That night, back on campus, the discovery of the A&T Four inspired fellow students. The next day, Blair, McCain, McNeill, and Richmond returned to the Woolworth's. This time, more than 20 other black students went with them to contest segregation and to test the power of ordinary people.

The story of the A&T Four both inspired and reflected the experience of their country in the 1960s. In different ways, the crisis of "misplaced power" came to an end as many people, like the A&T Four, discovered that they and their society could confront the problems that plagued the nation. In the 1960s, Americans demanded to sit at "the table of democracy" and offer new solutions for the problems of consumerism, civil rights, and the cold war. In the process, the nation turned to a new form of liberalism that pledged to confront Communism abroad and reform life at home. The result was a decade of remarkable change and conflict, both at home and abroad.

New Approaches to Power

The discontents at the close of the 1950s created an opportunity for new ideas and new strategies at the start of the 1960s. In a nation worried by insufficient or "misplaced power," four groups, in particular, became energized and empowered. Across the political spectrum, civil rights activists, new liberals, new conservatives, and the New Left offered fresh approaches to domestic and international problems. All these groups were driven by the participation of young people. But the four had different and often conflicting views of power and democracy in America.

Grassroots Activism for Civil Rights

The A&T Four were part of a new generation of African Americans impatient with the slow "deliberate speed" of the desegregation ordered by the Supreme Court in *Brown v. Board of Education* (see Chapter 25). Young blacks were ready to go beyond court cases and boycotts to try new tactics. As the Greensboro protests continued, hundreds of African American students, along with some white students, besieged lunch counters. Under pressure, Woolworth's and other large stores agreed to serve African Americans.

The Greensboro sit-in, as it was called, quickly inspired grassroots civil rights activism in other communities in both the South and the North and the formation of a new national civil rights organization. There were wade-ins at whites-only beaches, kneel-ins at whites-only churches, and even paint-ins at whites-only art galleries. The demonstrations forced whites to open up facilities to black patrons and spawned the Student Nonviolent Coordinating Committee (SNCC). The SNCC (pronounced "Snick") brought together white and African American young people. Demonstrating that ordinary people could confront the powerful, the sit-ins energized the civil rights movement and inspired Americans to confront other problems.

The New Liberalism

Defeated by Eisenhower and the Republicans in the 1950s, liberal intellectuals and politicians, mostly Democrats, had been forced to reconsider their ideas and plans. By the 1960s, the liberals were offering a fresh agenda in response to the civil rights movement, consumerism, and the cold war confrontation with Communism.

Faith in economic growth drove the new liberalism. To meet its domestic and international challenges, the United States, liberals believed, had to expand its economy more rapidly. By manipulating its budget, the federal government could keep the economy growing. The right amount of taxes and expenditures would ensure full employment, strong consumer demand, and a rising gross national product.

Growth alone would not make America great, liberals cautioned. A society devoted mainly to piling up personal wealth and spending it on consumer goods was fundamentally flawed. As the liberal historian Arthur M. Schlesinger Jr. argued, the nation needed now to focus on the "quality" of life and on the broader "public interest." Economic growth should create a better life for all Americans. Because the private sector could not solve pressing problems, the federal government had to deal actively with poverty, racial inequality, pollution, housing, education, world Communism, and other problems. Unimpressed with warnings about the excessive power of big institutions, the new liberals believed that the solution to the nation's woes was a still more powerful federal government.

In this respect, 1960s liberalism was much like the New Deal liberalism of the 1930s and the Fair Deal liberalism of the 1940s (see Chapters 22 and 24), both of which argued that government could and should correct problems created or ignored by the private sector. Nevertheless, the new liberalism differed from the old in important ways. New Dealers had worried most of all about restoring prosperity in the Great Depression; the new liberals almost took prosperity for granted. The old liberals had feared big business and class conflict. Their successors generally saw racial divisions and civil rights as the country's greatest domestic problems.

The New Conservatism

As in the past, conservatives differed fundamentally with liberals over power: the conservatives believed the federal government was already too big and active. But the conservatives, like the liberals, had been unhappily out of power for quite a while. In the 1930s, Herbert Hoover's failure to halt the Great Depression had discredited the conservative faith in minimalist government; then Hitler's aggression had undercut the conservative belief in isolationism.

By 1950, conservative ideas had already begun a quiet resurgence. In 1951, conservative intellectual William F. Buckley's book *God and Man at Yale* attacked his alma mater for its liberalism and denial of individualism. Two years later, Russell Kirk published *The Conservative Mind* to prove that there was a living conservative tradition in America. In 1955, Buckley and Kirk founded the magazine *National Review* as a forum for conservative ideas, especially vigorous anti-Communism.

The leading conservative political hero was outspoken Republican senator Barry Goldwater of Arizona. With a Western belief in individual freedom and hostility to federal power, Goldwater was a blunt opponent of liberalism. A major general in the Air Force Reserve, he also advocated a more aggressive stance toward Communism.

By 1960, the growing conservative movement had its own younger generation of activists. That year, the Young Americans for Freedom gathered at Buckley's estate in Sharon, Connecticut, to adopt a manifesto. The Sharon Statement called for government to protect individual liberty by preserving economic freedom and maintaining a strong national defense.

The New Left

At the opposite end of the political spectrum, another young group, inspired by civil rights activism and troubled by life on campus, rejected both conservatism and liberalism. By the early 1960s, many students felt confined and oppressed in overcrowded and impersonal colleges and universities, where their lives were regulated by rules that governed eating in dining halls, drinking alcohol, keeping cars on campus, and socializing in dorm rooms. Female students were subject to particularly strict rules, including curfews.

Some of these youth formed the New Left, a radical movement that attempted to create a more democratic nation. The key organization of the New Left was Students for a Democratic Society (SDS), which emerged in 1960 to produce "radical alternatives to the inadequate society of today." During its national convention at Port Huron, Michigan, in 1962, SDS approved an "Agenda for a New Generation." An answer to the Sharon Statement, the Port Huron Statement argued that American society denied people real choice and real power in their lives. The answer, SDS claimed, was "participatory democracy." The members of SDS did not believe that liberalism would promote real democracy in America. SDS did not expect much help from the old Left of socialists and Communists, with their Marxist faith in the revolutionary power of the working class. Instead, students would lead the way by fighting for control of their schools. The message began to resonate: SDS membership rose from 2,500 to 10,000 in late 1965.

The Presidential Election of 1960

As so often in American politics, new ideas did not immediately transform mainstream politics. The presidential election of 1960 offered a choice between a vaguely liberal Democratic future and a moderate Republican status quo. The Democratic nominee, Senator John F. Kennedy of Massachusetts, was open to the liberals' agenda and shared their optimism. Only 42 when he announced his candidacy, Kennedy was energetic and charismatic. Although he had an undistinguished record in Congress, he exuded an enormous sense of promise.

Kennedy gave voice to that promise during the campaign. Americans, he explained, stood "on the edge of a New Frontier—the frontier of the 1960s—a frontier of unknown opportunities and paths, a frontier of unfulfilled hopes and threats." The United States needed to foster economic growth, rebuild slums, end poverty, improve education, and enhance retirement.

In contrast, Kennedy's Republican opponent, Vice President Richard Nixon of California, favored balanced budgets, limited government, and the qualified acceptance of New Deal programs that marked the Eisenhower administration's "Modern Republicanism." Nixon embraced neither the bold programs and dynamic economic growth of the new liberalism nor the soaring individualism and strident anti-Communism of the new conservatives.

Despite Kennedy's stirring rhetoric and apparent triumph in televised debates, the election was the closest in history. Kennedy managed to keep much of the Democratic New Deal coalition of liberals, workers, and African Americans together, but he won by fewer than 120,000 votes (see Map 26–1). However narrowly, the voters had turned to a Democrat, influenced by liberal ideas, who was eager to explore the New Frontier.

The New Frontier

As president, John F. Kennedy eloquently expressed the values of the New Frontier in his speeches and in his space program. But Kennedy's weak electoral mandate made him cautious about pursuing liberal policies too aggressively when it came to most domestic issues. It took sustained pressure from African American activists before he fully embraced the cause of civil rights. A committed cold warrior, the president did not need any pressure to support the containment of Communism. Putting in place a new defense strategy, the president faced crises around the world that decreased the chances for nuclear war but increased the odds of US military involvement in Vietnam.

Style and Substance

Kennedy voiced the confident liberal faith in America's unlimited power and responsibility. "Let every nation know," he declared in his inaugural address in January 1961, "that we shall pay any price, bear any burden, meet any hardship, support any friend,

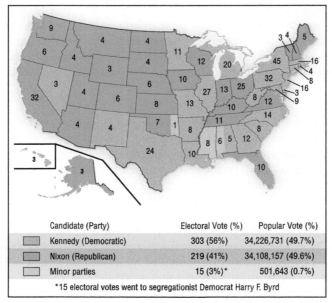

Candidate (Party)	Electoral Vote (%)	Popular Vote (%)
Kennedy (Democratic)	303 (56%)	34,226,731 (49.7%)
Nixon (Republican)	219 (41%)	34,108,157 (49.6%)
Minor parties	15 (3%)*	501,643 (0.7%)

*15 electoral votes went to segregationist Democrat Harry F. Byrd

Map 26-1 The Presidential Election, 1960 Democrat John F. Kennedy's clear margin in the electoral vote belies just how narrowly he outpolled Republican Richard M. Nixon in the popular vote.

oppose any foe to assure the survival and the success of liberty. This much we pledge— and more." He perfectly captured the optimistic spirit of the early 1960s.

So did the president's space program. The exploration of space, the ultimate frontier, seemed like an ideal occupation for confident Americans in the 1960s. Moreover, the space race allowed Kennedy to reject cautious Eisenhower policies and confront the Soviet challenge. In April 1961, the Soviet Union sent up the first astronaut to orbit Earth. The next month, NASA managed only to launch astronaut Alan Shepard for a brief, suborbital flight. Once again Americans feared "that the wave of the future is Russian."

Insistent on "beating the Soviets," the president boldly pledged to land "a man on the moon before the decade is out." Apollo, the moon project, got under way with 60,000 workers and billions of dollars. Meanwhile, in February 1962, astronaut John Glenn became the first American to orbit Earth. That year the United States launched Telstar, the first sophisticated communications satellite. The space program mixed practical achievements such as Telstar with more symbolic gestures such as manned space flights.

That mixture of style and substance epitomized the administration. The president maintained a dynamic image, but his administration, hampered by a weak mandate, did not venture too far out onto the liberal New Frontier.

For liberals, the persistence of poverty amid prosperity was a chief failure of the consumer society. Liberals argued that the government had to help the poor become productive workers; they contended that the battle against poverty should include improved housing, education, health, and job opportunities, as well as job training.

Kennedy supported some modest antipoverty measures. In 1961, he signed into law the Area Redevelopment Act to help revive depressed areas. He also signed the Omnibus Housing Act to clear slum housing and renew inner cities. But these measures were not enough to wipe out poverty.

Civil Rights

Grassroots activism for civil rights posed a critical challenge for the Kennedy administration. In one place after another, attempts to break down segregation and promote African American voting met with resistance.

After the Supreme Court outlawed the segregation of interstate bus terminals, a small group of African American and white "Freedom Riders" traveled south on buses to test the decision in the spring of 1961. The Freedom Riders met with beatings from white citizens and harassment from local authorities. Only then did the Kennedy administration send federal marshals to protect them.

In 1961, when SNCC started a voter-registration drive in Mississippi, white people struck back. SNCC workers were beaten and shot. When SNCC tried to register black voters in Albany, Georgia, members of this Albany Movement were beaten and arrested. Martin Luther King Jr., leader of the Southern Christian Leadership Conference (SCLC), came to Albany and was arrested, too, but segregation still ruled in the city.

SNCC activists resented the lack of presidential support. Kennedy understood that racial inequality damaged the United States' image abroad, but he also knew that the civil rights issue could split the Democratic Party.

The defiance of southern whites gradually pushed Kennedy toward action. In 1962, the governor of Mississippi, Ross Barnett, disregarded a federal court order by preventing a black student from enrolling at the University of Mississippi. When federal marshals escorted the student, James Meredith, to school, white students pelted them with rocks and Molotov cocktails. After the rioting killed two people and wounded more than 100 marshals, Kennedy called in federal troops to stop the violence and allow Meredith to enroll.

Two confrontations in Alabama forced the president's hand in 1963. In April, Martin Luther King Jr. and the SCLC tried to end segregation in Birmingham, perhaps the most segregated city in America. The city's public safety commissioner, Eugene "Bull" Connor, was a stereotypical racist white southern law enforcement officer. King and local allies planned to boycott department stores and overwhelm the jails with arrested protestors. In the next days, Connor's officers arrested demonstrators by the hundreds. Ignoring a judge's injunction against further protests, King ended up in solitary confinement. In a powerful statement, "Letter from Birmingham Jail," he rejected further patience: "We must come to see . . . that 'justice too long delayed is justice denied.'" Once King was out on bail, the SCLC pushed harder, with demonstrations by thousands of African American students.

Goaded by the new protests, Connor turned fire hoses on demonstrators, set dogs on them, and hit them with clubs. Shocking pictures of the scenes increased the pressure on the white leadership of Birmingham and on President Kennedy. The Justice Department arranged for a deal in which the SCLC gave up the demonstrations and local businesses gave up segregation and promised to hire African Americans. However, soon thereafter the Ku Klux Klan marched outside the city, and bombs went off at the home of King's brother and at SCLC headquarters. After African Americans rioted in the streets, Kennedy was forced to send federal troops to keep the peace.

"Spaceport USA"

There was no more famous place in the United States in the 1960s than a swath of Brevard County, Florida, along the Atlantic Ocean. No community so perfectly encapsulated Americans' hopes for the future as Cape Canaveral, home of US space launches. There, in what reporters called "Spaceport USA," the United States Air Force and the National Aeronautics and Space Administration (NASA) reached for both the glowing moon and the gleaming vision of a prosperous, peaceful, high-technology future.

For centuries, the cape lived in obscurity. It was, said a visitor, "a desolate arrowhead of land jutting into the ocean," a flat terrain of scrub brush and palmettos, full of alligators, snakes, armadillos, deer, and eagles. In the sixteenth century, the Spanish named this peninsula "Canaveral" after the sugar cane cultivated by Native Americans.

In 1949, the Air Force decided the temperate, sunny cape was ideal for shooting Snark, Vanguard, Atlas, Titan, and Thor missiles thousands of miles into the South Atlantic. The new military installation, cloaked in secrecy, was a product of the cold war; its purpose was to perfect these intermediate- and long-range weapons of mass destruction.

The development of the manned space program under President Eisenhower and then President Kennedy changed the cape's image. As NASA, a civilian agency, began testing rockets in preparation for space flights by astronauts, Cape Canaveral became a spaceport to a peaceful future of spirited, but not deadly, competition. Casting off cold war hypersecrecy, NASA welcomed visitors to its facility.

The cape also became a prime symbol of Kennedy's New Frontier. Outgrowing the original Air Force base, NASA took over more land on Cape Canaveral and Merritt Island, west of the Banana River. More and more missile gantries, launch pads, huge cranes, tall antennas, explosion-proof storage tanks, and igloo-shaped buildings overwhelmed beaches and orange groves.

"Spaceport USA" featured seemingly new people as well as new technologies. The more than 20,000 workers, a writer insisted, "have grown accustomed to living with one foot in the stars and one on earth." Despite the intensity of the competition with the

A second confrontation in Alabama drew the president still deeper into the civil rights struggle. The segregationist governor, George Wallace, defied federal officials and tried to stop two black students from enrolling at the University of Alabama. In an eloquent televised address, Kennedy finally admitted that there was "a moral crisis" and called for sweeping civil rights legislation.

On August 28, the March on Washington brought together a crowd of nearly 200,000 people, including 50,000 whites, at the Lincoln Memorial to commemorate the 100th anniversary of the Emancipation Proclamation and to demand "jobs and freedom." Demonstrators joined hands to sing the stirring civil rights anthem, "We Shall

Aerial View of "Missile Row" on Cape Canaveral

Soviet Union, Cape Canaveral's scientists, engineers, technicians, and astronauts supposedly subdued human emotion "under a bland blanket of professionalism." NASA seemingly subdued the emotions of racially divided America as well. Anticipating the integrated nation of the future, the space agency hired African Americans to work alongside whites in this corner of the segregated South.

Epitomizing the economic promise of the 1960s, the development of Cape Canaveral spurred the growth of surrounding Broward County. Houses went up for NASA employees and their families; the Astrocraft, the Sea Missile, and the Satellite motels went up for the tourists. Broward became the fastest growing county in the nation.

The conflicts and tragedies of the 1960s also left their mark on Cape Canaveral. In booming Cocoa, east of Merritt Island, African American space workers could not buy or rent the new houses. The assassination of President Kennedy, the space program's greatest booster, inspired Lyndon Johnson to rename the space installation "Cape Kennedy." In a characteristically sweeping expansion of federal power, Johnson also renamed the land itself "Cape Kennedy," even though he had no legal authority to do so.

In 1964, construction began on the Vehicle Assembly Building (VAB) that would house up to four of the huge Saturn rockets used to launch astronauts to the moon. More than 125 million cubic feet, the VAB would be the largest structure by volume in the world—bigger than the Great Pyramid of Cheops in Egypt and the Pentagon. The "atmosphere," said a reporter, "seems to be straight out of the twenty-first century."

Overcome." Martin Luther King Jr. moved the nation with his vision of racial harmony. "I have a dream," he said, "that one day . . . little black boys and black girls will be able to join with little white boys and white girls as sisters and brothers." King looked forward to "that day when . . . black men and white men, Jews and Gentiles, Protestants and Catholics, will be able to join hands and sing . . . 'Free at last! Free at last! Thank God Almighty, we are free at last!'"

Kennedy's address and the March on Washington marked a turning point. The surging grassroots movement for racial equality had created broad-based support for civil rights and finally forced the federal government to act.

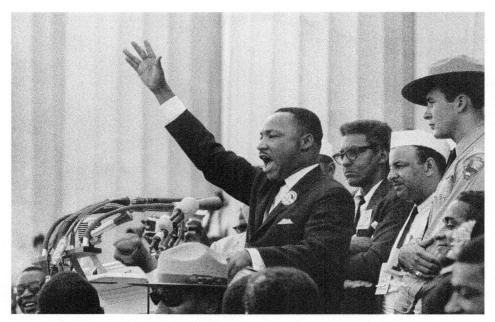

"I Have a Dream" Martin Luther King Jr. addresses the crowd at the Lincoln Memorial, Washington, DC, August 28, 1963.

Flexible Response and the Third World

Like Eisenhower, Kennedy supported the containment of Communism. The new president believed the nation could afford to increase military spending. He also abandoned the doctrine of massive retaliation, Eisenhower's threat to use nuclear weapons against any Soviet aggression. Kennedy preferred the strategy of flexible response—the threat of different military options, not just nuclear weapons, to counter the Soviets. While spending generously on nuclear weapons, the Kennedy administration also built up conventional ground forces and Special Forces—the highly trained troops, known as Green Berets, who could fight in guerilla wars.

Kennedy was more willing than Eisenhower to intervene in the third world. This was partly a reflection of Kennedy's confidence about American power and partly a response to Soviet actions. In January 1961, Nikita Khrushchev announced Soviet support for "wars of national liberation," insurgencies against established governments in Asia, Africa, and Latin America.

To counter the appeal of Communism, Kennedy supported modernization for Africa, Asia, and Latin America; that is, the development of capitalist, democratic, independent, and anti-Communist regimes along the lines of the United States. In 1961, his administration created the Peace Corps to send young volunteers to promote literacy, public health, and agriculture around the world. The Peace Corps reflected not only the importance of the young in the new movements of the 1960s but also the idealism, anti-Communism, and arrogant sense of superiority of the Kennedy years. Not surprisingly, the organization was not always welcomed by the people it was supposed to help. To promote the modernization of Latin America, Kennedy announced the formation of the Alliance for Progress in 1961. Over the next eight years, this venture provided $20 billion for housing, health, education, and economic development in the Western Hemisphere.

The Kennedy administration sometimes helped to thwart third-world independence and democracy in the name of anti-Communism by intervening in the domestic affairs of supposedly independent countries. In the Republic of the Congo, the CIA engineered the election of an anti-Communist leader, and it secretly tried to manipulate elections in Chile as well. The United States also backed antidemocratic, but anti-Communist, regimes in Argentina, Guatemala, Haiti, and Honduras.

Similarly, Kennedy wanted to bring down Fidel Castro, whose Cuban revolution was an example for the rest of Latin America. The president inherited a plan from the Eisenhower administration for a CIA-directed invasion of the island by anti-Communist Cuban exiles. To conceal US responsibility, Kennedy canceled air cover to protect the invaders. As a result, nearly all 1,500 exiles who landed at the Bay of Pigs in April 1961 were killed or captured. Embarrassed, Kennedy turned to the CIA, which launched "Operation Mongoose," an unsuccessful secret campaign to kill or depose Castro. The Cuban leader, aware of the plot, declared himself a Communist and turned to the Soviets for help.

Two Confrontations with the Soviets

Kennedy faced two direct confrontations with the Soviet Union. In 1961, Khrushchev threatened to stop Western traffic into West Berlin, which was surrounded by Soviet-dominated East Germany. In response, Kennedy called up reserve troops, asked Congress to increase defense spending, and hinted at a preemptive nuclear strike against the Soviets. Khrushchev backed down, but the East German government built a barbed-wire and concrete fence between East Berlin and West Berlin. By halting the embarrassing flight of East Germans to freedom in West Berlin, the Berlin Wall defused the crisis and became a symbol of cold war Europe, a visible "iron curtain" that separated Communists and non-Communists.

Trying to Laugh About Nuclear War President Kennedy and Soviet premier Khrushchev arm wrestle and threaten to push the buttons unleashing hydrogen bombs during the Cuban Missile Crisis, October 1962.

In 1962, Kennedy entered a more dangerous confrontation with the Soviet Union. On October 15, photos from a spy plane showed that the Soviets were building launch sites in Cuba for nuclear missiles that could strike the United States. On October 22, after tense secret meetings, Kennedy put ships in place to intercept Soviet vessels bound for Cuba. That night, a somber Kennedy told a television audience about the missiles and demanded their removal. Fearing a nuclear war, Americans waited for the Soviets' response. Khrushchev, unable to confront the United States in its own hemisphere, backed down. The Soviets withdrew the missiles in exchange for the removal of obsolete American missiles from Turkey.

The Cuban Missile Crisis both eased and intensified the cold war. Faced with a nuclear conflict, neither side found the prospect appealing. To ensure communication in a crisis, a teletype hotline was installed between the White House and the Kremlin. In 1963, the two powers also approved a Limited Test Ban Treaty halting aboveground tests of nuclear weapons, even as the Soviets and the Americans remained more determined to stand firm against each other.

Kennedy and Vietnam

Kennedy inherited a deteriorating situation in South Vietnam in 1961. Ngo Dinh Diem's anti-Communist government faced increasing attacks from the Viet Cong guerillas determined to overthrow his regime. Diem also faced the Viet Cong's new political organization, the National Liberation Front, which was trying to mobilize his Communist and non-Communist opponents. In addition, he faced the continuing hostility of Ho Chi Minh's Communist government in North Vietnam, which was secretly sending soldiers and supplies into South Vietnam.

Like Eisenhower, Kennedy tried to shore up the Diem government with financial aid and advisers. This included sending the Special Forces to train the South Vietnamese army. Before Kennedy took office, there were 900 American troops filling noncombat roles in South Vietnam. By late 1963, there were more than 16,000. Despite this support, Diem's regime spiraled downward. His army could not stop the Viet Cong. A cold, unpopular ruler, he alienated his people. Losing confidence in Diem, the Kennedy administration did nothing to stop a military coup that resulted in his murder in November.

What Kennedy would have done next will never be known. On a trip to Dallas, Texas, on November 22, 1963, the president was shot while riding in an open limousine at 12:33 p.m. Two bullets tore through Kennedy's throat and skull, and doctors pronounced him dead half an hour later. That afternoon, police arrested Lee Harvey Oswald for the shooting. A quiet former Marine, Oswald had spent time in the Soviet Union. Two days later, as police transferred him from a jail, Oswald was shot and killed by Jack Ruby, the troubled owner of a local nightclub.

Americans were shocked and numbed. Some could only believe the assassination was the product of a dark conspiracy, but there was never proof of such a plot. The presidency of John Kennedy, little more than 1,000 days long, left a sad sense of unfulfilled promise. To many Americans, Kennedy's White House seemed like "Camelot," the seat of the mythical English King Arthur. The reality was less magical. Kennedy gave voice to the new liberalism, but he seldom translated liberal ideas into action. Some wanted to believe that Kennedy, if he had lived, would not have escalated the Vietnam War. Yet there was no compelling evidence that he intended to withdraw American troops.

The Great Society

After Kennedy's death, Lyndon B. Johnson and the Democratic-controlled Congress carried out most of the liberal agenda. A flood of new laws addressed poverty, race relations, consumer and environmental protection, education, and health care. At the same time, the liberal majority on the Supreme Court afforded new protections for individual rights. By the mid-1960s, the principles of the new liberalism, turned into law, were transforming American government and society.

Lyndon Johnson's Mandate

The new president, Lyndon Johnson, seemed far different from his slain predecessor. Born to modest circumstances in rural Texas, he had made his fortune largely through political connections. Never an eloquent public speaker or a charismatic figure, he was an especially effective legislator who knew how to bully and cajole Senate colleagues into a deal.

Still, there were fundamental similarities between Johnson and Kennedy. Both were products of the Democratic Party that had engineered the New Deal, won World War II, and fought the cold war. Both shared the liberals' expansive sense of American might. "Hell, we're the richest country in the world, the most powerful," Johnson declared. "We can do it all."

Johnson stressed continuity with his predecessor. Yet the situation had changed: Kennedy's death left Americans more willing to accept innovation. The presidential election of 1964 strengthened Johnson's mandate. The contest offered voters a clear choice between competing visions. Embracing the new liberalism, Johnson stood for activist government, growth economics, and civil rights. His Republican opponent, Barry Goldwater, stood unequivocally for the new conservatism. "We have gotten where we are," he declared, "not because of government, but in spite of government."

It was no contest. Democrats painted Goldwater as a dangerous radical who would gut popular programs and perhaps start a war. Appearing as a statesman and man of peace, Johnson won 61.1 percent of the popular vote, 44 states, and 486 electoral votes. Moreover, the Democrats increased their majorities in the House and Senate. It was a greater victory than Johnson's hero, Franklin Roosevelt, had ever enjoyed.

"Success Without Squalor"

With his mandate, Johnson moved to enact a legislative program that rivaled Roosevelt's New Deal. In May 1964, he had called for the creation of the "Great Society"—"a society of success without squalor, beauty without barrenness, works of genius without the wretchedness of poverty." To create that society, his administration pushed through liberal laws to wipe out poverty, end segregation, and enhance the quality of life for all Americans.

Johnson, like many Americans, was disturbed by the persistence of poverty: nearly one in five Americans was poor. Declaring an "unconditional war on poverty," the administration won congressional approval in 1964 of the Economic Opportunity Act, which created an independent federal agency, the Office of Economic Opportunity (OEO), to spend nearly $1 billion on antipoverty programs. The OEO managed Volunteers in Service to America (VISTA), whose workers taught literacy and other skills in impoverished areas. It ran the Job Corps, which taught job skills to poor youth, and implemented Community Action Programs (CAPs), which encouraged the urban poor to organize themselves. By supporting the "maximum feasible participation" of the poor, the CAPs, unlike other poverty programs, had the potential to redistribute power away from local officials.

In 1965 and 1966, Congress continued the war on several fronts. It established an expanded food stamp program and created Head Start, which provided early schooling, meals, and medical exams for impoverished preschool-aged children. To protect the rights of the poor, the Legal Services Program brought lawyers into slums. To improve urban life, the Model Cities Program targeted 63 cities for slum clearance and redevelopment. Congress also created the Department of Housing and Urban Development in 1965 and the Transportation Department in 1966 partly to help manage antipoverty programs.

To improve the quality of life, the Great Society took a major step toward national health insurance when Congress created Medicare in 1965. This program provided the elderly with coverage for doctors' bills, surgery, and hospitalization. Congress also created Medicaid to help the states provide medical care to the nonworking poor.

The Johnson administration confronted the growing issue of consumer protection. In 1965, Ralph Nader published a disturbing book, *Unsafe at Any Speed*, charging that car manufacturers cared more about style and sales than about safety and that executives at General Motors had ignored safety defects in the Chevrolet Corvair. General Motors attempted to discredit Nader rather than promise to improve the Corvair. In response, Congress passed the National Traffic and Motor Vehicle Safety Act of 1966, which set the first federal safety standards for automobiles, and the Highway Safety Act, which required states to establish highway safety programs.

The president and Congress adopted the liberals' belief in using the federal government to support education. The Elementary and Secondary School Act of 1965 channeled $1.3 billion into school districts. The Higher Education Act of 1965 offered federally insured student loans.

The Great Society included programs for cultural enrichment. In 1965, Congress established the National Endowment for the Arts to fund the visual and performing arts and the National Endowment for the Humanities to support scholarly research. The Public Broadcasting Act of 1967 established the nonprofit Corporation for Public Broadcasting, which would support such commercial-free cultural and educational television shows as *Sesame Street*.

Protection of the environment was a natural issue for liberals. In 1962, the best-selling book *Silent Spring* sensitized Americans to the ecological threat posed by the consumer economy. The author, marine biologist Rachel Carson, warned that, like nuclear weapons, environmental contamination from pesticides threatened human survival.

During Johnson's presidency, more than 300 pieces of legislation led to the expenditure of more than $12 billion on environmental programs. In 1963, the Clean Air Act encouraged state and local governments to set up pollution control programs. Two years later, amendments established the first pollution emission standards for automobiles. The Air Quality Act of 1967 further strengthened federal authority to deal with air pollution. Meanwhile, the Water Quality Act of 1965 and the Clean Waters Restoration Act of 1966 enabled governments to fight water pollution. The Wilderness Act of 1964 created a system of lands protected from development.

Preserving Personal Freedom

The new liberalism contained a paradox: liberals wanted both to enhance the power of the federal government and to expand individual rights. Their concern for individual rights was apparent in their support for civil rights for African Americans and in a series of decisions by the Supreme Court, led by Chief Justice Earl Warren.

In *New York Times v. Sullivan* in 1964, the Supreme Court encouraged free speech by making it more difficult for public figures to sue news media for libel. In addition, two decisions protected the rights of people accused of crimes. In 1963, the court ruled in *Gideon v. Wainwright* that governments had to provide lawyers to poor felony defendants. Three years later, *Miranda v. Arizona* required police to inform individuals of their rights when they were arrested, including the right to remain silent and the right to an attorney.

The Warren Court also protected sexual and religious freedom. Throwing out a state law that banned the use of contraceptives in *Griswold v. Connecticut* in 1965, the court affirmed individuals' right to privacy and in effect kept government out of the bedroom. In *School District of Abington Township v. Schempp* (1963), the court prohibited state and local governments from requiring public school students to say the Lord's Prayer or read the Bible.

The Supreme Court's rulings were controversial. Some people charged that the Court was "driving God out" of the classroom. Others believed that the Court had gone too far to protect the rights of alleged criminals. Some conservatives demanded the impeachment of Chief Justice Warren. Through its rulings, the liberal majority on the court substantially increased individual freedom, but few people had yet thought much about the tension caused by expanding both individual rights and government power.

By 1967 the Great Society's programs added up to a major change in American democracy. Government claimed more authority than ever to manage many Americans' daily lives. The Great Society brought a massive expansion of the size, cost, and power of the federal government (see Table 26–1).

That expansion would be controversial for years to come. Some measures—Medicare in particular—proved to be enormously expensive. Conservatives did not welcome an enlarged federal government, and some corporations resented the regulation of business in the name of consumer protection. Despite these concerns, the attempts to improve the quality of life represented some of the major accomplishments of the new liberalism. The war on poverty was at least a partial success. Mainly because of an economic boom, the percentage

Table 26-1 Expanding the Federal Government, 1955–1970

Year	Civilian Employees (thousands)	Total Spending (millions)	Defense (millions)	Space (millions)	Health (millions)	Education and Manpower (millions)
1955	2,397	$68,509	$40,245	$74	$271	$573
1960	2,399	$92,223	$45,908	$401	$756	$1,060
1965	2,528	$118,430	$49,578	$5,091	$1,704	$1,284
1970	2,982	$196,588	$80,295	$3,749	$12,907	$1,289

Source: Historical Statistics of the United States (1976), vol. II, pp. 1102, 1116.

of people living in poverty decreased to 13 percent by 1970. But 25 million Americans were still poor. Moreover, poverty was unevenly distributed. About a third of African Americans and a quarter of Americans of Hispanic origin were impoverished as the 1970s began.

The Death of Jim Crow

Meanwhile, the battle for civil rights had become still more intense. In the 10 weeks after the Birmingham confrontation in 1963, 758 demonstrations led to 14,733 arrests across the United States. When a bomb killed four African American girls in a Baptist church in Birmingham in September, some African Americans rioted, and the police killed two more children.

The violence continued in 1964: CORE, SNCC, SCLC, and the NAACP had created the Council of Federated Organizations (COFO) to press for African American voting rights in Mississippi. Robert Moses, an African American schoolteacher, led the COFO crusade uniting young African American and white activists to register black voters and start "Freedom Schools" for African American children. The effort, known as Freedom Summer, met hostility from whites. Two white activists, Michael Schwerner and Andrew Goodman, and one African American activist, James Chaney, were found shot to death near Philadelphia, Mississippi. Eventually, a white deputy sheriff, a local Klan leader, and five other whites were convicted of "violating the rights" of Chaney, Goodman, and Schwerner. The violence continued in Mississippi throughout Freedom Summer. Homes and churches were burned, and three more COFO workers were killed.

Lyndon Johnson could not escape the events in Mississippi. In the summer of 1964, the Mississippi Freedom Democratic Party (MFDP) sent a full delegation to the Democratic National Convention in Atlantic City, New Jersey. The MFDP delegates, including the eloquent Fannie Lou Hamer, hoped at least to share Mississippi's convention seats with the whites-only delegation. Hamer, the daughter of sharecroppers, had been jailed and beaten for trying to register African American voters. Afraid of alienating white southerners, Johnson offered the delegates two seats in the convention. "We didn't come all this way for no two seats," Hamer retorted. The MFDP delegation went away empty-handed.

Johnson and the Democratic Party were clearly not ready to share power with African American activists, but they were ready to end legalized segregation. In July, Congress adopted the Civil Rights Act, which outlawed racial discrimination in public places and also set up an Equal Employment Opportunity Commission (EEOC) to stop discrimination in hiring and promotion. Even the schools gradually became integrated. In 1964, hardly any African American students attended integrated schools; by 1972, nearly half of African American children did.

However, across the South, most African Americans still could not vote. In January 1965, the SCLC and SNCC tried to force the voting rights issue with protests in Selma, Alabama. Predictably, the demonstrations produced violent opposition and helpful publicity. The sight of state troopers using tear gas, cattle prods, and clubs on peaceful marchers built support for voting rights.

Seizing the moment, Johnson called for the end of disfranchisement, and Congress passed the Voting Rights Act of 1965. This powerful measure forced southern states to give up literacy tests used to disfranchise black voters and empowered federal officials to make sure that African Americans could register to vote. In three years, Mississippi saw African American registration increase from 6 percent to 44 percent of eligible voters.

Together with the Civil Rights Act of 1964, the Voting Rights Act transformed the South. These twin achievements of the civil rights movement and the Great Society effectively doomed Jim Crow and laid a foundation for African American political power. However, the struggle for racial equality was far from over.

The American War in Vietnam

The war in Vietnam was the decisive event for the new liberalism and the nation in the 1960s. American participation in the conflict reflected the liberals' determined anti-Communism and their boundless sense of power and responsibility. Driven by these beliefs, Johnson made the fateful decision to send American troops into battle in 1965. When the war did not go according to plan, Americans divided passionately over the conflict, and the economy faltered. By the end of 1967, the war was destroying the Great Society.

Johnson's Decision for War

Like Kennedy, Johnson was a committed cold warrior with an optimistic view of American power. He kept flexible response in place and was equally willing to undermine the independence of third-world countries. In 1965, Johnson sent 22,000 troops to the Dominican Republic to stop an increasingly violent struggle for political power. He violated the sovereignty of this Caribbean nation without obtaining evidence of a Communist threat and without consulting Latin American countries as required by treaty.

At first, Johnson followed Kennedy's policy in Vietnam. The new president believed in the domino theory, the idea that the fall of one country to Communism would lead to the fall of others. The president also felt he could not turn his back on commitments made by Kennedy, Eisenhower, and Truman. As one weak government followed another, Johnson sent more aid and advisers to South Vietnam and stepped up covert action against the North.

This secret activity helped Johnson get congressional approval to act more aggressively. On August 2, 1964, a US destroyer, the *Maddox*, was cruising a few miles off the coast of North Vietnam in the Gulf of Tonkin. When three North Vietnamese torpedo boats unsuccessfully attacked the *Maddox*, the American ship sank two of the boats and damaged a third. Two days later, the *Maddox*, along with a second US destroyer, fired at a nonexistent North Vietnamese attack. Johnson ordered retaliatory air strikes and asked Congress for the power to protect American military personnel. With only two dissenting votes, Congress approved what became known as the Tonkin Gulf Resolution, which gave the president the authority, without a declaration of war, to use military force to safeguard South Vietnam. Even though Johnson knew there had been no real threat to the United States, he had misled Congress to obtain a "blank check" to fight in Southeast Asia.

He soon cashed it. After American soldiers were killed in a Viet Cong attack on a US base in February 1965, Johnson authorized air strikes against North Vietnam itself. In March, the United States began Operation Rolling Thunder, a series of bombing raids on military targets in North Vietnam.

When the raids failed, Johnson had a disagreeable but clear choice. If he wanted to save both South Vietnam and his reputation, he had to commit ground troops to battle;

otherwise, he would be blamed for the loss of South Vietnam to Communism. In July 1965, Johnson gave the order to send 180,000 soldiers to fight in South Vietnam without a declaration of war.

Johnson's decision was the ultimate expression of the new liberalism. The president went to war not only because he opposed Communism but also because he had faith that American wealth and wisdom could transform a weak, divided South Vietnam into a strong, united, modern nation. Although cautious about going to war, Johnson believed that the United States could afford to fight, and win, a war abroad and still build the Great Society at home. It was a fateful choice.

Fighting a Limited War

Johnson and his advisers believed the United States did not need all its power to save South Vietnam (see Map 26–2). Instead of another total war like World War II, Vietnam was to be a limited war in which the US forces, led by General William Westmoreland, would use conventional weapons against military targets. The goal was not to take over territory through "unconditional surrender" but rather to kill enough enemy soldiers to persuade the North Vietnamese and the Viet Cong to give up. Relying on superior technology, Westmoreland expected the United States to prevail by the end of 1967.

Westmoreland's strategy turned out to be poorly suited to the realities of Vietnam. As the United States discovered, the North Vietnamese and the Viet Cong usually escaped by hiding in tunnels, fleeing through the jungle, fighting mainly at night, or retreating into Cambodia, Laos, and North Vietnam. Their strategy was to live long enough for a frustrated US military to leave South Vietnam.

American troops fought well. Yet at the close of 1967, too many North Vietnamese and Viet Cong were still alive and committed to the overthrow of South Vietnam. Meanwhile, 9,000 US troops died in 1967 alone. Even with half a million troops in his command, Westmoreland had not won the war on schedule. He had not lost the war, either. But the United States was running out of time to win (see Table 26–2).

Table 26–2 The Escalating War in Vietnam, 1960-1968

Year	US Troops	US Battle Deaths	S. Vietnamese Battle Deaths	N. Vietnamese and Viet Cong Battle Deaths (estimated)
1961	3,164	11		12,000
1962	11,326	31	**(three-year total = 13,985)**	21,000
1963	16,263	78		21,000
1964	23,310	147	7,457	17,000
1965	184,000	1,369	11,403	35,382
1966	385,000	5,008	11,953	55,524
1967	486,000	9,378	12,716	88,104
1968	536,000	14,589	27,915	181,149

Sources: Michael Clodfelter, *Vietnam in Military Statistics,* pp. 46, 57, 209, 258; Fox Butterfield, ed., *Vietnam War Almanac,* pp. 50, 54, 57, 64, 102, 132, 158, 192; Shelby Stanton, ed., *Vietnam Order of Battle,* p. 333.

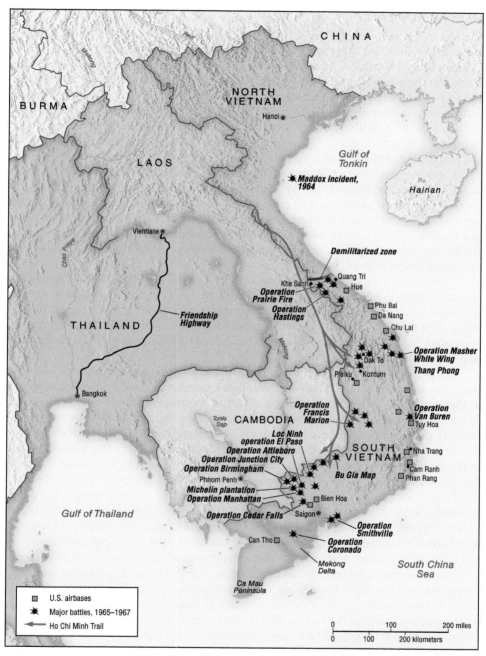

Map 26-2   America's War in Vietnam, 1965-1968 The many military bases suggest how much power the United States had to commit to South Vietnam; the many major battles show how hard American troops had to fight to protect the South Vietnamese regime from the Viet Cong and from the North Vietnamese soldiers who traveled the Ho Chi Minh Trail.

The War at Home

The war in Vietnam had a divisive impact back home. An impassioned antiwar movement, led by SDS and other student radicals, emerged to condemn American policy. Communism in Southeast Asia, they believed, did not pose a real threat to the United States. But the misguided cold war had led liberals to support an antidemocratic regime. The war also revealed how undemocratic America had become. Johnson, the New Left pointed out, had ignored the Constitution by sending troops into battle without a declaration of war. In addition, the selective service law was forcing a repugnant choice on young men: they could either fight this illegal war or obtain deferments to stay in school and prepare for empty lives as corporate employees in the consumer society.

A growing number of liberals and Democrats shared part of the radicals' analysis. These "doves" acknowledged that the United States was backing an antidemocratic government in a brutal and apparently unnecessary war. The conflict appeared to be a civil war rather than some plot to expand Soviet or Chinese influence. Meanwhile, the war had shattered many liberals' and Democrats' overconfident views of the Great Society. The United States, confessed Senator J. William Fulbright of Arkansas in 1966, was a "sick society" suffering from an "arrogance of power."

Some African Americans viewed the conflict as a painful illustration of American racism. A disproportionate number of poor African Americans, unable to go to college and avoid the draft, were being sent to kill nonwhites abroad on behalf of a racist United States. First the SNCC and then Martin Luther King Jr. condemned the war. Refusing to be drafted, boxer Muhammad Ali was sentenced to jail and stripped of his championship in 1967.

The growing opposition to the war produced large, angry demonstrations. In 1965, students and faculty staged "teach-ins" at college campuses to question American policy in Vietnam. In April, 20,000 people gathered at the Washington Monument to protest the war. Some young men risked jail by returning or burning their draft cards. On campuses, students protested the presence of recruiters for defense contractors. In October 1967, during Stop the Draft Week, radicals in Oakland, California, tried to shut down an army draft induction center, fought with police, and briefly took over a 25-square-block area of the city. Meanwhile, nearly 100,000 people rallied in Washington, DC, to protest the war.

Despite the protests, most Americans supported the war. To many people, the demonstrators were unpatriotic. "America—Love It or Leave It," read a popular bumper sticker. "Hawks," mostly conservative Republicans and Democrats, wanted Johnson to fight harder. Nevertheless, by October 1967, support for the war in one public opinion poll had fallen to 58 percent, while only 28 percent approved of Johnson's conduct of the war.

Bad economic news contributed to the public mood. Massive government spending for the war and the Great Society had overstimulated the economy. With jobs plentiful, strong consumer demand drove up prices, which in turn put upward pressure on wages. Anxious about inflation, the Federal Reserve shrank the money supply, making it harder for businesses to get loans. When interest rates reached their highest levels since the 1920s, there were fears of a financial panic.

By the end of 1967 the war had put enormous stress on the Great Society. It undermined liberals' commitment to anti-Communism and their confidence in American power and wisdom. By dividing the nation, the conflict also undermined support for the Great Society. By weakening the economy, furthermore, the Vietnam War made it harder to pay for the Great Society. The United States could not, as Johnson believed, "do it all." The new liberalism had reached its crisis.

The Great Society Comes Apart

Even as Congress enacted the liberals' agenda, many Americans were expressing new dissatisfactions that liberalism could not accommodate. New forms of activism—the Black Power movement, the youth rebellion, and a reborn women's movement—exposed the limits of the liberal vision. In 1968, the strain of new demands, the Vietnam War, and economic realities tore apart the Great Society and destroyed the fortunes of Lyndon Johnson, the Democratic Party, and the new liberalism.

The Emergence of Black Power

For many African Americans, the Great Society's response to racial inequality was too slow and weak. Even as the civil rights movement reached its climax, a wave of more than 300 race riots from 1964 to 1969 dramatized the gap between the promise of the Great Society and the reality of life in black America. When a white policeman shot a 15-year-old African American in Harlem in July 1964, angry African Americans burned and looted buildings. In August 1965, friction between white police and African American citizens touched off a riot in the poor Watts section of Los Angeles. In five days, more than 1,000 fires burned, and 34 people died. The wave of riots peaked in Detroit in July 1967 when 43 people died (see Map 26–3).

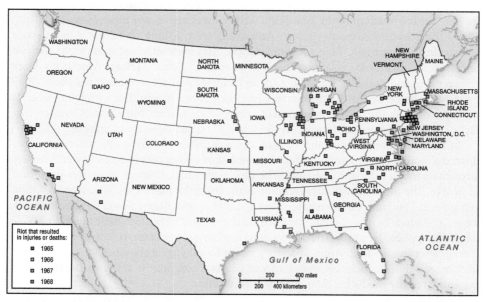

Map 26-3   Race Riots, 1965–1968 The clusters of riots in the Northeast, Midwest, and California emphasize that race was not just a southern issue in the 1960s.
Source: Mark C. Carnes et al., *Mapping America's Past* (New York: Henry Holt and Co., 1996), p. 217.

To many, the riots were, according to an official report on Watts, "senseless," but the disturbances flowed from real frustrations. Despite successful challenges to legalized segregation in the South, African Americans still lived with poverty and discrimination all across the country. Northern cities, the center of the riots, had been largely ignored by Martin Luther King Jr. and other civil rights leaders. The riots signaled that the civil rights movement and the new liberalism, for all their accomplishments, had not addressed some of the most difficult problems of racial inequality.

For years King and other activists had relied on nonviolent demonstrations and ties to white liberals to achieve integration, but that approach proved ineffective in the North. In 1965, King joined marches in Chicago protesting the de facto segregation of the city's schools. King faced the determined opposition of Mayor Richard Daley. Reluctant to challenge the powerful political boss, the Johnson administration did not give King real support. In 1966, King returned to lead the "Chicago Freedom movement" to wipe out slums and win access to better housing in white neighborhoods. "Go back to Africa," white demonstrators chanted. Daley accepted a compromise on fair housing but repudiated it as soon as King left town. Under the leadership of 24-year-old Jesse Jackson, Operation Breadbasket threatened demonstrations and boycotts against businesses that refused to hire African Americans. The project produced few results; King's nonviolent tactics had failed.

African Americans already had the example of a different approach to the problem of black-white relations. The Nation of Islam believed that whites were devils and African Americans were God's chosen people. The Black Muslims, as they were known, preached separation of the races and the self-reliance of African Americans. One of the Muslims' most powerful preachers was Malcolm X, a former pimp, drug pusher, and convict who angrily rejected integration and nonviolence. Malcolm X moderated his views before being gunned down, apparently by Muslims, in 1965. But he was best known for his militant call "for the freedom of the 22 million Afro-Americans by any means necessary."

By the mid-1960s, many African Americans were willing to follow at least some of Malcolm X's example. Rejecting integration, they now asserted a separate African American identity that declared, "Black is beautiful." Some African Americans wore African robes and dashikis, explored African language and art, and observed the holiday of Kwanzaa, based on an African harvest festival. Instead of working with white liberals and depending on the federal government, some African American activists insisted that blacks create their own institutions. In 1966, SNCC ousted its white members.

In rejecting nonviolence and integration, a number of African American activists adopted a more militant stance. "What we gonna start saying now is Black Power!" Stokely Carmichael told a rally in Mississippi. The new slogan had different meanings for different people. The most radical interpretation came from the Black Panthers, who were first organized in Oakland, California, by Huey P. Newton and Bobby Seale. Dressed in black clothes and black berets, the Panthers armed themselves to protect their neighborhoods from white police. Newton, admiringly described by an associate as "the baddest motherfucker ever to step foot inside of history," went to jail after a shootout with police. The Panthers also founded schools and promoted peaceful community activism, but they were best known in the media for their aura of violent militance.

Particularly because of the violent image of the Panthers, many people, African American and white, were hostile to the new slogan. For King and his allies, Black Power all too obviously meant repudiation of nonviolent integration. For many whites, Black

Power stirred fears of violence. For white leaders such as Richard Daley, Black Power meant giving up political authority to African Americans. For Lyndon Johnson, Black Power obviously meant a rejection of his Great Society.

The Youth Rebellion

The anti–Vietnam War movement was part of a broader rebellion against adult authority and expectations. The battle began at the University of California at Berkeley in 1964. That fall, the university's administration banned political speaking and organizing at the one street corner where it had been allowed. When a civil rights activist was arrested for defying the ban in October, hundreds of students sat down around the police cars, trapping the officers for 32 hours. After the standoff, students created the Free Speech movement (FSM) to pursue greater student involvement in the educational process. When the university refused to accept that demand, students took over the main administration building. Speaking that day, the student leader Mario Savio reflected the ideas of the New Left. "We have an autocracy which runs this university," he exclaimed. "[W]e're a bunch of raw material[s] that . . . don't mean to end up being bought by some clients of the University, be they the government, be they industry, be they organized labor, be they anyone! We're human beings!" The administration eventually succumbed to faculty protests and a student boycott of classes and agreed to new rules on free speech.

The New Left in Action, University of California at Berkeley, 1964 Student radical Mario Savio stands on top of a police car to address a crowd of protesting students while two policemen sit uncomfortably inside the vehicle.

Protest in the Schools

The civil rights movement, college protests, and other grassroots movements set a highly publicized example about the importance of rights and the impact of activism. By the mid-1960s, that example was even influencing students in high schools and middle schools around the country. Like many adults, secondary school pupils began confronting authority to demand more freedom and more democracy. Across the country, school dress codes—written or unwritten rules on clothes, hair, and grooming—became a flashpoint.

Several changes in fashion helped ignite controversy in schools. Long hair, sideburns, and moustaches for males and short "mini" skirts, long "maxi" skirts, pants, and pantsuits for females all conflicted with dress codes. So did blue jeans, untucked shirts, and supposedly excessive makeup. Fashion had come into conflict with dress codes before, but by the mid-1960s, students were more likely to ask teachers, administrators, and school boards to change the rules.

In some cases, those in authority agreed fairly readily to ease dress codes at least a bit and occasionally even eliminated them. But in many cases, the schools refused. Adults, including many parents, feared that students would become rebels unwilling to conform in school and then adapt to the adult world. According to social workers, there was a fear, too, that pants would make girls too masculine and that long hair would make boys too feminine.

The movement to change dress codes often involved more than fashion or comfort: it was about rights and democratic process. Administrators' refusal to listen to students' concerns about dress codes sparked new resentment. "The students . . . are puppets . . . being controlled so tightly by the administration, that they have no freedom of speech without getting in trouble," a female high schooler, calling herself "AN INDIVIDUAL," wrote to her local paper in Wausau, Wisconsin, in the fall of 1968. "We are held to such strict regulations that we are afraid to say what we really

Americans had never seen anything quite like the Berkeley protests. Here were privileged students condemning society, storming a building, and being dragged off by the police. Many people were infuriated; some younger Americans were inspired.

As campus activism flourished, young people were also creating the rebellious lifestyle that became known as the "counterculture." Less politically oriented than the New Left, the counterculture challenged conventional social values. By the mid-1960s, many younger Americans were condemning conformity, careerism, materialism, and sexual repression as they groped toward an alternative lifestyle.

The counterculture rested on the enjoyment of rock music, drugs, and sexual freedom. Beginning in 1964, the sudden popularity of the Beatles, the Rolling Stones, and other British bands brought back a rebellious note to rock and roll. The Beatles' irreverent feel inside. Is this democratic?" Increasingly, students bristled at the gap between their civics lessons and life in school. "We are taught democracy in class, but when we complain and there is no change we wonder if democracy is working," said Bruce Hollibaugh, a senior at Clinton High School in Decatur, Illinois, in January 1969. "There should be democracy in schools."

That argument didn't persuade many administrators and other adults. Pointing to the school football team and the US Army, Nicholas De Salvo, a vice principal in Dedham, Massachusetts, declared flatly, "This business of democracy in everything just doesn't work. In a training situation, much of democratic procedure must go out the window."

In response, students pressed their demands: they talked to principals and petitioned school boards. Sometimes students used the tactics of grassroots activism. In Lorain, Ohio, in October 1967, high schoolers staged a sit-in on the lawn to protest a ban on blue jeans. Locking them out of school, the principal required the students to bring a parent to gain access the next day. Elsewhere, students occupied administration offices indoors, struck, and marched and picketed outside.

Administrators suspended protesters and even had some arrested.

As on college campuses, secondary school protests typically involved a minority of students. Some favored the dress codes; others didn't care enough to take action. Meanwhile, the protests alienated some parents and other adults. "It is sinful," wrote a St. Albans, Vermont, newspaper editor, "when a group of local high school students begin acting like college students in other parts of the nation by plotting out-and-out disobedience just because they don't like the rules and regulations."

Nevertheless, parents and other adults often supported the movement against dress codes. Most important, teachers and administrators, caught in the middle, felt it was not worth the time and upheaval to try and enforce the unpopular regulations. By the early 1970s, public schools had largely eased or eliminated dress codes: long hair for boys, pants for girls were increasingly acceptable. Roman Catholic schools typically kept codes requiring uniforms, but other private schools watered down theirs. Reflecting students' push for democracy, many schools now allowed committees of students to help draw up and enforce dress and other policies.

attitude toward authority, symbolized by their long hair, helped create "Beatlemania" in the United States. Rock also became more socially and politically conscious in the 1960s. Bob Dylan, Simon and Garfunkel, and other musicians rooted in folk music sang about racism, nuclear weapons, and other issues.

Rock music often sang of the virtues of drugs and sex. The use of marijuana, the hallucinogen LSD, and other drugs increased during the 1960s as a way of flouting adult convention and escaping everyday reality for a more liberated consciousness. Sex offered a similar mix of pleasure and defiance. On campuses across the country, students demanded greater freedom, including the repeal of rules that restricted the mixing of male and female students in dorms. By the end of the decade, many students were living together before marriage.

Many young people hoped that the counterculture would weave sex, drugs, and rock into a new lifestyle. Novelist Ken Kesey joined with his followers, the Merry Pranksters, to set up a commune, complete with "Screw Shack," outside San Francisco. By 1965, Kesey had created the "acid test," which fused drugs, rock, and light shows into a multimedia experience and helped establish the popularity of "acid rock," the "San Francisco sound" of the Jefferson Airplane and the Grateful Dead.

The purest form of the countercultural lifestyle was created by the hippies, who appeared in the mid-1960s. Hippie culture centered in the Haight-Ashbury section of San Francisco. Rejecting materialism and consumerism, hippies celebrated free expression and free love. They wanted to replace capitalism, competition, and aggression with cooperation and community. One group of hippies, the Diggers, gave away clothes and food and staged the first "Human Be-In" at Golden Gate Park "to shower the country with waves of ecstasy and purification."

The power of youth rebellion was easy to exaggerate. There were not many full-time hippies. The countercultural lifestyle quickly became conformist consumerism, defined by the right clothes and records.

The counterculture also had roots in the orthodox culture it attacked. By the close of the 1950s, adults themselves had become ambivalent about consumerism, conventional morality, and institutional authority. Sexual freedom for youth was encouraged partly by the greater sexual openness of mainstream culture, the Supreme Court's *Griswold* decision, and the introduction of the oral contraceptive (the "pill") in 1960. Americans chafed at the authority of religious denominations. The "pop art" paintings of Andy Warhol and Roy Lichtenstein, the productions of the Living Theater, the essays of Susan Sontag, and the novels of Thomas Pynchon broke with formal, artistic conventions.

Nevertheless, the counterculture was a disruptive force in the 1960s. Like the Black Panthers, hippies deeply influenced young people and adults and encouraged Americans to question conventional values and authority and seek a freer way of life.

The Rebirth of the Women's Movement

By the 1960s, American women were reacting against the difficult social roles enforced on them after World War II. More women than ever went to college, but they were not expected to pursue long-term careers. More women than ever worked outside the home, but they were still expected to devote themselves to home and family. Women also had to put up with the continuing double standard of sexual behavior, which granted men more freedom to seek sexual gratification outside marriage. Women began to question their second-class status. In part, they were inspired by the example of the civil rights movement.

Two best-selling books reflected these complaints. In *The Feminine Mystique* (1963), Betty Friedan described "the problem that has no name," the growing frustration of educated, middle-class wives and mothers who had subordinated their own aspirations to the needs of men. Meanwhile, Helen Gurley Brown rejected unequal sexual opportunities in *Sex and the Single Girl* (1962). Neither Friedan nor Brown challenged male sexual ethics or male careerism. Instead, both wanted equal opportunity for women, in and out of marriage. Brown explained, coyly, that "nice, single girls do."

Women's complaints received attention but little action from men. In 1961, Kennedy appointed the Presidential Commission on the Status of Women, chaired by Eleanor Roosevelt. The commission's cautious report, *American Women*, documented gender discrimination but reaffirmed women's domestic role. In 1963, Congress passed the Equal Pay Act, which mandated the same pay for men and women who did the same work, but the measure, full of loopholes, had little impact. A year later, Title VII, a provision of the Civil Rights Act of 1964, prohibited employers from discriminating on the basis of sex in hiring and compensation. Yet the EEOC did little to enforce the law.

In 1966, Betty Friedan and a handful of other women, angry at the inaction of the EEOC, formed the National Organization for Women (NOW). Although frustrated with the Great Society, Friedan and the founders of NOW expressed essentially liberal values. They saw NOW as "a civil rights organization" and wrote a women's "Bill of Rights" that focused on government action to provide rights and opportunities. NOW also demanded access to contraception and abortion.

NOW's platform was too radical for many women and not radical enough for others. Some younger women, particularly activists in the civil rights movement and the New Left, wanted more than liberal solutions to their problems. By the fall of 1967, activists were forming new groups dedicated to "women's liberation." Influenced by the New Left, radical feminists blamed the capitalist system for the oppression of women, but a growing number of radicals saw men as the problem. Like African Americans in the Black Power movement, radical women talked less about rights and more about power. Their slogan was "Sisterhood Is Powerful!" Radical feminists also rejected collaboration with male liberal politicians.

Few in number, radical feminists nevertheless commanded public attention. In September 1968, New York Radical Women organized a protest against the annual Miss America pageant in Atlantic City, New Jersey. The pageant, they said, was an act of "thought control" intended "to make women oppressed and men oppressors; to enslave us all the more in high-heeled, low-status roles." The protestors threw bras, girdles, makeup, and other "women-garbage" into a "Freedom Trash Can." Then they crowned a sheep "Miss America." Not surprisingly, men and many women were generally uncomfortable with radical feminism. Onlookers at the Miss America protest called the women "lesbians" and "screwy, frustrated women."

Conservative Backlash

The rebellions against the Great Society strengthened the conservative movement. Just two years after humiliating defeat in the presidential election of 1964, conservatives won new national prominence. Two politicians became focal points for many Americans' resentment against feminism, civil rights and Black Power, the counterculture and the antiwar movement, and the new liberalism.

George Wallace, former governor of Alabama, increasingly combined his hostility to civil rights and federal power with a populist appeal to working-class and middle-class whites. In 1964, he ran for the Democratic presidential nomination, calling for "law and order." Encouraged by his success in northern primaries that year, Wallace prepared to mount an independent campaign aimed at the "average man—your taxi driver, your steel and textile worker" in 1968. Now he played on anger over the youth rebellion and the antiwar movement, as well as the civil rights movement. "If I ever get to be President and any of these demonstrators lay down in front of my car," Wallace vowed, "it'll be the last car they ever lay down in front of."

Meanwhile, former actor Ronald Reagan became a major conservative force in the Republican Party. A lifelong liberal Democrat, he had moved to the right and supported Goldwater in 1964. Two years later, Reagan ran for governor of California, vowing to "clean up the mess at Berkeley" with all its "Beatniks, radicals and filthy speech advocates" and its "sexual orgies so vile I cannot describe them." He opposed high taxes, Medicaid, and other liberal activism and favored escalation of the war in Vietnam.

1968: A Tumultuous Year

In 1968, the stresses and strains of the Great Society produced the most tumultuous year in the United States since World War II. In January, the Viet Cong and North Vietnamese launched bold, sometimes suicidal attacks all over South Vietnam on the first day of Tet, the Vietnamese New Year. Although US and South Vietnamese forces inflicted punishing losses on the attackers, the Tet Offensive shocked Americans. If the United States was winning the war, how could the North Vietnamese and the Viet Cong have struck so daringly? More Americans now began to believe the war was unwinnable.

The Tet Offensive doomed Johnson's increasingly troubled administration. The president needed to send reinforcements to Vietnam, but he knew public opinion would

Fighting in Vietnam A wary US soldier at a jungle camp.

Time Line

oppose the move. As it was, he could not even pay for more troops. The economy would no longer support both the war and the Great Society. The political situation was bad, too. On March 12, Senator Eugene McCarthy of Minnesota, a longshot antiwar candidate with little money, nearly beat Johnson in New Hampshire's primary. Four days later, Senator Robert Kennedy of New York, the younger brother of John Kennedy, announced his own candidacy for the nomination. The charismatic Kennedy, opposed to the war, would be a formidable opponent. Besieged by the war, the economy, and the campaign, Johnson went on television the night of March 31. He announced a halt to the bombing of much of North Vietnam and indicated his willingness to talk peace with the North Vietnamese. He then announced that he would not run again for president.

Johnson painfully accepted new limits to the Great Society. Despite liberal pressure, Johnson did not have the money or the clout for new welfare programs, new initiatives to improve race relations, or even much of the space program, that symbol of liberal dreams. The Great Society was coming back down to earth.

Meanwhile, upheaval and violence tore the nation. In the first six months of 1968, students demonstrated at 101 colleges and universities. On April 4, a white man assassinated Martin Luther King Jr. in Memphis, Tennessee, where he had gone to support striking sanitation workers. King's assassination set off riots in more than 100 cities. Forty-one African Americans and five whites died.

The violence soon spread to the presidential campaign. After winning the California Democratic primary on the evening of June 5, Robert Kennedy was shot in a Los Angeles hotel by Sirhan Sirhan, a troubled Palestinian. Kennedy's death the next morning left McCarthy to contest the nomination with Vice President Hubert Humphrey, who still supported the Vietnam War. Humphrey won the nomination at the Democratic convention in Chicago in August, but the party was deeply divided. Outside the convention hall, Mayor Daley's police battled in the streets with antiwar demonstrators.

The Republican Party nominated Richard Nixon, who had lost to John Kennedy in 1960. A critic of the Great Society, Nixon promised to end the war and unify the country. Like the more conservative Reagan and Wallace, Nixon tried to exploit social divisions with promises to speak for "the forgotten Americans, the nonshouters, the nondemonstrators."

Unlike 1960, Nixon won this time. Although Humphrey made it close by repudiating Johnson's Vietnam policy, the vice president could not overcome the troubles of the Great Society. Nixon, running strongly in every region, attracted 43.4 percent of the popular

▼**1964**

Civil Rights Act of 1964
Lyndon Johnson's "War on Poverty"
Free Speech movement
Tonkin Gulf incidents
Lyndon Johnson's landslide election as president

▼**1965**

US escalation of Vietnam War
Voting Rights Act of 1965
Water Quality Act
Watts race riot

▼**1966**

National Organization for Women (NOW)

▼**1967**

Air Quality Act
Stop the Draft Week

▼**1968**

Tet Offensive in Vietnam
Assassinations of Martin Luther King Jr. and Robert F. Kennedy
Richard Nixon elected president

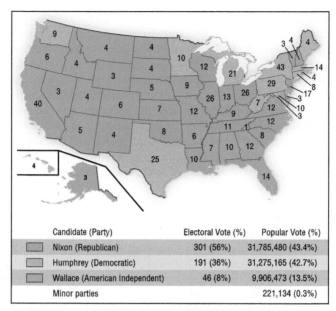

Candidate (Party)	Electoral Vote (%)	Popular Vote (%)
Nixon (Republican)	301 (56%)	31,785,480 (43.4%)
Humphrey (Democratic)	191 (36%)	31,275,165 (42.7%)
Wallace (American Independent)	46 (8%)	9,906,473 (13.5%)
Minor parties		221,134 (0.3%)

Map 26-4   The Presidential Election, 1968 Like the 1960 election, this was a close contest with widespread consequences. But this time, former Vice President Richard M. Nixon was the winner.

vote to Humphrey's 42.7 percent and Wallace's 13.5 percent (see Map 26–4). Although the Democrats retained control of Congress, the party's eight-year hold on the White House had been broken.

Conclusion

The upheavals of 1968 marked the end of illusions about limitless American power. John Kennedy's confident nation—able to "pay any price, bear any burden, meet any hardship, support any friend, oppose any foe"—had vanished. By 1968, the economy could no longer "pay any price." The United States could not support its friends in South Vietnam. The government could not extend the Great Society. Instead, generation, race, and gender deeply divided the nation. The assassinations of King and Robert Kennedy threatened democratic politics.

Nevertheless, the nation had changed in other ways in the 1960s. Americans did not enjoy unlimited power, but across the political spectrum they had found creative ways to change their nation. In critical respects, the United States was more democratic than ever before: African Americans and other Americans had new rights and new power. More people than ever sat, as Ezell Blair put it, at "the table of democracy." The New Frontier and the Great Society had established new protection for the poor, senior citizens, consumers, and the environment, as well as new precedents for supporting health and education.

So the 1960s fostered simultaneously a pessimistic sense of defeat and a triumphal claim to rights and empowerment. The nation would have difficulty coming to terms with these conflicting legacies.

Who, What, Where

Review Questions

1. What were the tactics of the civil rights movement in the 1960s?

2. What were the key programs of the Great Society?

3. What was the US strategy for winning the Vietnam War?

Critical-Thinking Questions

1. Why did the Great Society come apart? Was it a success or a failure?

2. Compare liberal and radical feminism. Were these movements incompatible with each other?

3. Did the struggles and changes of the 1960s make the United States more or less democratic?

Suggested Readings

Asselin, Pierre. *Vietnam's American War: A History.* New York: Cambridge University Press, 2018.

Cohen, Robert, ed. *Rebellion in Black and White: Southern Student Activism in the 1960s.* Baltimore: The Johns Hopkins University Press, 2013.

Rorabaugh, W. J. *American Hippies.* New York: Cambridge University Press, 2015.

For further review materials and resource information, please visit www.oup.com/us/oakes-mcgerr

CHAPTER 26: "THE TABLE OF DEMOCRACY," 1960–1968

Primary Sources

26.1 MARTIN LUTHER KING JR., "STATEMENT TO THE PRESS AT THE BEGINNING OF THE YOUTH LEADERSHIP CONFERENCE" (1960) AND STUDENT NONVIOLENT COORDINATING COMMITTEE, STATEMENT OF PURPOSE (1960)

In the spring of 1960, the wave of sit-ins for civil rights dramatically highlighted the power of nonviolent grassroots activism. Consequently, the first issue for the civil rights movement was how to organize that power. In a press release issued in April, Ella Baker and Martin Luther King Jr. laid out the issues for the young activists gathering for a conference at historically black Shaw University in Raleigh, North Carolina. The result was the formation of the Student Non-Violent Coordinating Committee (SNCC). In its Statement of Purpose, SNCC endorsed the principle of nonviolence rooted in the power of love.

"Statement to the Press at the Beginning of the Youth Leadership Conference": This is an era of offensive on the part of oppressed people. All peoples deprived of dignity and freedom are on the march on every continent throughout the world. The student sit-in movement represents just such an offensive in the history of the Negro peoples' struggle for freedom. The students have taken the struggle for justice into their own strong hands. In less than two months more Negro freedom fighters have revealed to the nation and the world their determination and courage than has occurred in many years. They have embraced a philosophy of mass direct nonviolent action. They are moving away from tactics which are suitable merely for gradual and long term change.

Today the leaders of the sit-in movement are assembled here from ten states and some forty communities to evaluate these recent sit-ins and to chart future goals. They realize that they must now evolve a strategy for victory. Some elements which suggest themselves for discussion are: (1) The need for some type of continuing organization. Those who oppose justice are well organized. To win out the student movement must be organized. (2) The students must consider calling for a nation-wide campaign of "selective buying." Such a program is a moral act. It is a moral necessity to select, to buy from these agencies, these stores, and businesses where one can buy with dignity and self-respect. It is immoral to spend one's money where one cannot be treated with respect. (3) The students must seriously consider training a group of volunteers who will willingly go to jail rather than pay bail or fines. This courageous willingness to go to jail may well be the thing to awaken the dozing conscience of many of our white brothers. We are in an era in which a prison term for a freedom struggle is a badge of honor. (4) The youth must take the freedom struggle into every community in the South without exception. The struggle must be spread into every nook and cranny. Inevitably this broadening of the struggle and the determination which it represents will arouse vocal and vigorous support and place pressures on the federal government that will compel its intervention. (5) The students will certainly want to delve deeper into the philosophy of nonviolence. It must be made palpably clear that resistance and nonviolence are not in themselves good. There is another element that must be present in our struggle that then makes our resistance and nonviolence truly meaningful. That element is reconciliation. Our ultimate end must be the creation of the beloved community. The tactics of nonviolence without the spirit of nonviolence may indeed become a new kind of violence.

SNCC Statement of Purpose: We affirm the philosophical or religious ideal of nonviolence as the foundation of our purpose, the pre-supposition of our faith, and the manner of our action. Nonviolence as it grows from Judaic-Christian traditions seeks a social order of justice permeated by love. Integration of human endeavor represents the crucial first step towards such a society.

Through nonviolence, courage displaces fear; love transforms hate. Acceptance dissipates prejudice; hope ends despair. Peace dominates war; faith reconciles doubt. Mutual regard cancels enmity. Justice for all overthrows injustice. The redemptive community supersedes systems of gross social immorality.

Love is the central motif of nonviolence. Love is the force by which God binds man to himself and man to man. Such love goes to the extreme; it remains loving and forgiving even in the midst of hostility. It matches the capacity of evil to inflict suffering with an even more enduring capacity to absorb evil, all the while persisting in love.

By appealing to conscience and standing on the moral nature of human existence, nonviolence nurtures the atmosphere in which reconciliation and justice become actual possibilities.

Sources: Martin Luther King Jr., "Statement to the Press at the Beginning of the Youth Leadership Conference," April 15, 1960. Student Non-Violent Coordinating Committee, Statement of Purpose, 1960. National Humanities Center.

26.2 JOHN F. KENNEDY, EXCERPTS FROM INAUGURAL ADDRESS (1961)

Taking the oath of office on a clear, cold day in January 1961, John F. Kennedy gave one of the best-known inaugural addresses in US history. The new president spoke squarely and eloquently about the paradox that characterized the United States during the cold war: Americans felt both a sense of great power and great vulnerability. Kennedy powerfully declared the nation's willingness to "pay any price, bear any burden" for the sake of liberty, but he was silent on many issues, including the African American struggle for civil rights.

. . . The world is very different now. For man holds in his mortal hands the power to abolish all forms of human poverty and all forms of human life. And yet the same revolutionary beliefs for which our forebears fought are still at issue around the globe—the belief that the rights of man come not from the generosity of the state but from the hand of God.

We dare not forget today that we are the heirs of that first revolution. Let the word go forth from this time and place, to friend and foe alike, that the torch has been passed to a new generation of Americans—born in this century, tempered by war, disciplined by a hard and bitter peace, proud of our ancient heritage—and unwilling to witness or permit the slow undoing of those human rights to which this nation has always been committed, and to which we are committed today at home and around the world.

Let every nation know, whether it wishes us well or ill, that we shall pay any price, bear any burden, meet any hardship, support any friend, oppose any foe to assure the survival and the success of liberty.

This much we pledge—and more. . . .

To those peoples in the huts and villages of half the globe struggling to break the bonds of mass misery, we pledge our best efforts to help them help themselves, for whatever period is required—not because the communists may be doing it, not because we seek their votes, but because it is right. If a free society cannot help the many who are poor, it cannot save the few who are rich. . . .

Finally, to those nations who would make themselves our adversary, we offer not a pledge but a request: that both sides begin anew the quest for peace, before the dark powers of destruction unleashed by science engulf all humanity in planned or accidental self-destruction.

We dare not tempt them with weakness. For only when our arms are sufficient beyond doubt can we be certain beyond doubt that they will never be employed.

But neither can two great and powerful groups of nations take comfort from our present course—both sides overburdened by the cost of modern weapons, both rightly alarmed by the steady spread of the deadly atom, yet both racing to alter that uncertain balance of terror that stays the hand of mankind's final war.

So let us begin anew—remembering on both sides that civility is not a sign of weakness, and sincerity is always subject to proof. Let us never negotiate out of fear. But let us never fear to negotiate. . . .

In your hands, my fellow citizens, more than mine, will rest the final success or failure of our course. Since this country was founded, each generation of Americans has been summoned to give testimony to its national loyalty. The graves of young Americans who answered the call to service surround the globe.

Now the trumpet summons us again—not as a call to bear arms, though arms we need— not as a call to battle, though embattled we are—but a call to bear the burden of a long twilight struggle, year in and year out, "rejoicing in hope, patient in tribulation"—a struggle against the common enemies of man: tyranny, poverty, disease and war itself. . . .

In the long history of the world, only a few generations have been granted the role of defending freedom in its hour of maximum danger. I do not shrink from this responsibility—I welcome it. I do not believe that any of us would exchange places with any other people or any other generation. The energy, the faith, the devotion which we bring to this endeavor will light our country and all who serve it—and the glow from that fire can truly light the world.

And so, my fellow Americans: ask not what your country can do for you—ask what you can do for your country.

My fellow citizens of the world: ask not what America will do for you, but what together we can do for the freedom of man. . . .

Source: John F. Kennedy, Inaugural Address, January 20, 1961.

26.3 TESTIMONY OF MARIAN WRIGHT, EXAMINATION OF THE WAR ON POVERTY; HEARINGS BEFORE THE SUBCOMMITTEE ON EMPLOYMENT, MANPOWER, AND POVERTY OF THE COMMITTEE ON LABOR AND PUBLIC WELFARE (1967)

For all its money and organization, the war on poverty faced daunting challenges. In 1967, Marian Wright, an African American lawyer, explained to a committee of the US Senate how the longtime disfranchisement of black voters, divisions among the white and black poor, and the power of middle- and upper-class whites combined to frustrate the Community Action Program and other elements of the war on poverty in Mississippi. As Senator Jacob Javits, a liberal Republican from New York reminded her, there was no obvious alternative.

Miss WRIGHT: [F]or many people the poverty program held out the largest hope. I think it has also held out the largest disappointment in many ways. I agree very much with most of the basic articulated goals of the poverty program and I am sure going to support the concept of community action. But in examining how these are actually functioning in Mississippi, one sees several trends.

One does not see CAP structures which are representative or democratic in any real way. One finds that the money in the CAP boards are going through the very same power structures that created or helped create the poverty problem in the first place. Too often I think there's been an assumption by the OEO that any Negro represents poor people and this is not true. Unless the concept of democratically elected representatives is implemented in the State of Mississippi we are going to continue to see middle-class Negroes picked by white boards of supervisors, put on CAP boards, many for their effectiveness in parroting the white community. There must be democratically elected boards which are representative of the poor and OEO's CAP boards are falling far below these standards today. . . .

[I]n those Delta counties which were once poor, where there is less organization, there is still a huge amount of fear, they are filled with a huge amount of economic dependence from the white power structure, the plantation owners, and are making very little inroad on the right to vote.

And again, the key to that is some kind of hope in terms of Federal programs which are going to feed people if they take the risk.

Secondly, there has to be much stronger action taken to protecting people once they exercise these rights. And in a large measure, that isn't yet being done, and we are not really getting the benefits of the civil rights acts, because there is no hope economically for these people in exercising these rights.

And again, under the community action structure I think that, as it applies to Mississippi, one has seen a trend rather than interest in eradicating poverty, but one has seen the trend of CAP board development more as a response to the few independent poverty programs that have come up and more out of desire to control the poverty funds that have come into that community rather than a commitment to poverty. I think the community action concept has been based on the assumption that there are many separate groups in the community who are interested in eradicating poverty, but I think that the whole experience of Mississippi defies that. You have two very distinct communities, white and Negro, who have been at loggerheads and some kind of processes must be designed to assure the CAP structures which are formulated do represent the entire community.

. . . Too often what we have seen is that the CAP structures . . . have already had their representatives chosen and people have had no involvement. As a result, many Negroes have refused to participate in these CAP structures because they felt they've not represented them and, too, they have seen those people on the CAP boards who have been their enemies traditional in past years. Let's take Sunflower County for example, where the sheriff of the county was sort of temporary chairman of the CAP board. This is the sheriff that we have been able to document and that the Civil Rights Commission reports documented who has traditionally been hostile to Negro citizens. . . .

Let's take one example, the work experience program of OEO where—unless it is assured that the mandate of the guidelines are going to be followed—I am afraid Mississippians are going to go on and continue to perpetuate the usual system. . . . Let us take Holmes County in

Mississippi, for example. You have a work training program where we have had Negroes in the work training program who have come in to complain they have been put to work on the white private school operated or being constructed by the White Citizens Council.

I hardly think this is a valid purpose of which a Federal program is going to finance labor to build white segregated private schools. . . .

Senator JAVITS: Miss Wright, have you faced the issue of rather having no program than having it this way because that is the problem we constantly face here; that if you don't want it this way you are not going to have it at all because you will have to deal through a governmental structure which is loaded against you. The OEO admits that. So the only thing you can do is deny them funds under title VI.

You cannot . . . install your own poverty administration in Mississippi of people from outside of Mississippi with a mixture also of those who are the poor themselves and who are being abused. Now, what is your attitude on that? Would you rather not have it at all? Let us face the stark issue that there can be no poverty program in Mississippi because it is rife with immorality and segregation.

Miss WRIGHT: . . . If the poverty program is going to function with the exception of the few independent programs that come into the State, as they have functioned so far, that has been just that much more money being given to the power structure to buy off that many more people, and it strengthens those forces which we are trying to get rid of. So unless there is going to be real implementation of guidelines—and one could make a strong argument on what is hard to defend—you are going to have additional poverty money come in for the use of the very same traditional people who kept Negroes down.

However, I see and have seen from our own experience in certain independent programs that the poverty program can work if a few people are willing to take enough of the risk to finance or help independent programs, either for single-purpose programs or through helping people at least get better and more democratic CAP structures in their communities. . . .

I would hate to say the poverty program should stop because it's our last hope in many ways of trying to build up the kind of community pride in the community organization that is going to get these people out of the very cycle they are in. We have got to do something for them. . . .

I think what one has gotten now is that the Negro community has seen they can run some few programs well. There is some hope, that if they get trained they can progress, and they do see now they can change their lives in certain fundamental ways. . . . They are not willing to give that up. . . .

Senator JAVITS: Miss Wright, is there also a poor white community in Mississippi?

Miss WRIGHT: Yes, there is.

Senator JAVITS: What happens to that?

Miss WRIGHT: In the Delta area, for instance, 75 percent of the population, white and Negro, fall into the poverty level, and I think that while I am talking about the poor Negro, the poor white has been more forgotten and while we are screaming about representation of poor Negroes on CAP boards, the poor white is almost nonrepresented anywhere and the poverty program, I feel, has almost not touched him.

Senator JAVITS: Is the poor white also a party to this hostility and resentment?

Miss WRIGHT: Well, he is the most hostile, Senator, because he is the guy who has to compete with the Negro, he thinks, for jobs. He has been taught that the only way he is going to be able to get anywhere in this society is to sort of keep the Negro down. As you find the largest amount of anti-Negro feeling among the poor whites where, traditionally one could really talk about economic issues. The need for us to build a new kind of coalition of poor whites and Negroes could be very valuable, but, unfortunately, these are the people, again, who are terribly poor but have no leadership and unfortunately have been used to perpetuate the status quo by the middle class, upper class whites. We don't know how to break that syndrome. . . .

Source: Testimony of Marian Wright, *Examination of the War on Poverty. Hearings Before the Subcommittee on Employment, Manpower, and Poverty of the Committee on Labor and Public Welfare.* United States Senate. Ninetieth Congress. First Session. Part 1. Washington, DC, March 13, 15, 16, and 17, 1967 (Washington, DC: US Government Printing Office, 1967), pp. 156–167.

26.4 LYNDON B. JOHNSON, EXCERPTS FROM ADDRESS AT JOHNS HOPKINS UNIVERSITY, "PEACE WITHOUT CONQUEST" (1965)

By the spring of 1965, the US-backed government of South Vietnam was in crisis. Realizing that he would have to increase the American military role in the struggle against North Vietnam and the Viet Cong, President Lyndon Johnson had to justify the war to the American people. In a speech at Johns Hopkins University in April, Johnson laid out a passionate case for American involvement in Vietnam. At the end of July, the president would order 44 more battalions of US troops into combat.

. . . Tonight Americans and Asians are dying for a world where each people may choose its own path to change.

This is the principle for which our ancestors fought in the valleys of Pennsylvania. It is the principle for which our sons fight tonight in the jungles of Viet-Nam.

Viet-Nam is far away from this quiet campus. We have no territory there, nor do we seek any. The war is dirty and brutal and difficult. And some 400 young men, born into an America that is bursting with opportunity and promise, have ended their lives on Viet-Nam's steaming soil.

Why must we take this painful road?

Why must this Nation hazard its ease, and its interest, and its power for the sake of a people so far away?

We fight because we must fight if we are to live in a world where every country can shape its own destiny. And only in such a world will our own freedom be finally secure.

This kind of world will never be built by bombs or bullets. Yet the infirmities of man are such that force must often precede reason, and the waste of war, the works of peace.

We wish that this were not so. But we must deal with the world as it is, if it is ever to be as we wish.

The world as it is in Asia is not a serene or peaceful place.

The first reality is that North Viet-Nam has attacked the independent nation of South Viet-Nam. Its object is total conquest.

Of course, some of the people of South Viet-Nam are participating in attack on their own government. But trained men and supplies, orders and arms, flow in a constant stream from north to south.

This support is the heartbeat of the war.

And it is a war of unparalleled brutality. Simple farmers are the targets of assassination and kidnapping. Women and children are strangled in the night because their men are loyal to their government. And helpless villages are ravaged by sneak attacks. Large-scale raids are conducted on towns, and terror strikes in the heart of cities.

The confused nature of this conflict cannot mask the fact that it is the new face of an old enemy.

Over this war—and all Asia—is another reality: the deepening shadow of Communist China. The rulers in Hanoi are urged on by Peking. This is a regime which has destroyed freedom in Tibet, which has attacked India, and has been condemned by the United Nations for aggression in Korea. It is a nation which is helping the forces of violence in almost every continent. The contest in Viet-Nam is part of a wider pattern of aggressive purposes.

Why are these realities our concern? Why are we in South Viet-Nam?

We are there because we have a promise to keep. Since 1954 every American President has offered support to the people of South Viet-Nam. We have helped to build, and we have helped to defend. Thus, over many years, we have made a national pledge to help South Viet-Nam defend its independence.

And I intend to keep that promise.

To dishonor that pledge, to abandon this small and brave nation to its enemies, and to the terror that must follow, would be an unforgivable wrong.

We are also there to strengthen world order. Around the globe, from Berlin to Thailand, are people whose well-being rests, in part, on the belief that they can count on us if they are attacked. To leave Viet-Nam to its fate would shake the confidence of all these people in the value of an American commitment and in the value of America's word. The result would be increased unrest and instability, and even wider war.

We are also there because there are great stakes in the balance. Let no one think for a moment that retreat from Viet-Nam would bring an end to conflict. The battle would be renewed in one country and then another. The central lesson of our time is that the appetite of aggression is never satisfied. To withdraw from one battlefield means only to prepare for the next. We must say in southeast Asia—as we did in Europe—in the words of the Bible: "Hitherto shalt thou come, but no further."

There are those who say that all our effort there will be futile—that China's power is such that it is bound to dominate all southeast Asia. But there is no end to that argument until all of the nations of Asia are swallowed up.

There are those who wonder why we have a responsibility there. Well, we have it there for the same reason that we have a responsibility for the defense of Europe. World War II was fought in both Europe and Asia, and when it ended we found ourselves with continued responsibility for the defense of freedom.

Our objective is the independence of South Viet-Nam, and its freedom from attack. We want nothing for ourselves—only that the people of South Viet-Nam be allowed to guide their own country in their own way.

We will do everything necessary to reach that objective. And we will do only what is absolutely necessary.

In recent months attacks on South Viet-Nam were stepped up. Thus, it became necessary for us to increase our response and to make attacks by air. This is not a change of purpose. It is a change in what we believe that purpose requires.

We do this in order to slow down aggression.

We do this to increase the confidence of the brave people of South Viet-Nam who have bravely borne this brutal battle for so many years with so many casualties.

And we do this to convince the leaders of North Viet-Nam—and all who seek to share their conquest—of a very simple fact: We will not be defeated. We will not grow tired.

We will not withdraw, either openly or under the cloak of a meaningless agreement.

We know that air attacks alone will not accomplish all of these purposes. But it is our best and prayerful judgment that they are a necessary part of the surest road to peace.

We hope that peace will come swiftly. But that is in the hands of others besides ourselves. And we must be prepared for a long continued conflict. It will require patience as well as bravery, the will to endure as well as the will to resist.

I wish it were possible to convince others with words of what we now find it necessary to say with guns and planes: Armed hostility is futile. Our resources are equal to any challenge. Because we fight for values and we fight for principles, rather than territory or colonies, our patience and our determination are unending.

Once this is clear, then it should also be clear that the only path for reasonable men is the path of peaceful settlement.

Such peace demands an independent South Viet-Nam—securely guaranteed and able to shape its own relationships to all others—free from outside interference—tied to no alliance—a military base for no other country.

These are the essentials of any final settlement.

We will never be second in the search for such a peaceful settlement in Viet-Nam.

There may be many ways to this kind of peace: in discussion or negotiation with the governments concerned; in large groups or in small ones; in the reaffirmation of old agreements or their strengthening with new ones.

We have stated this position over and over again, fifty times and more, to friend and foe alike. And we remain ready, with this purpose, for unconditional discussions.

And until that bright and necessary day of peace we will try to keep conflict from spreading. We have no desire to see thousands die in battle—Asians or Americans. We have no desire to devastate that which the people of North Viet-Nam have built with toil and sacrifice. We will use our power with restraint and with all the wisdom that we can command. But we will use it.

[W]e will always oppose the effort of one nation to conquer another nation.

We will do this because our own security is at stake.

But there is more to it than that. For our generation has a dream. It is a very old dream. But we have the power and now we have the opportunity to make that dream come true.

For centuries nations have struggled among each other. But we dream of a world where disputes are settled by law and reason. And we will try to make it so.

For most of history men have hated and killed one another in battle. But we dream of an end to war. And we will try to make it so.

. . . This generation of the world must choose: destroy or build, kill or aid, hate or understand. We can do all these things on a scale never dreamed of before.

Well, we will choose life. In so doing we will prevail over the enemies within man, and over the natural enemies of all mankind.

Source: Lyndon B. Johnson, Address at Johns Hopkins University, "Peace Without Conquest," April 7, 1965.

26.5 JOHN WILCOCK, "THE HUMAN BE-IN" AND "SAN FRANCISCO" (1967)

British-born journalist John Wilcock was a cofounder of New York's *East Village Other*, one of the many "underground" papers including the *Berkeley Barb* and San Francisco's *Oracle* that sprung up as part of the counterculture in the 1960s. Here, he reports on the first Human Be-In at Golden Gate Park in San Francisco in January 1967. After Wilcock conveys the color and excitement of this pivotal countercultural event and its San Francisco context, he describes the nearby hippie enclave Haight-Ashbury and the importance of the music scene. Strikingly, Wilcock details the differences and divisions emerging among the young of the San Francisco Bay area.

HUMAN BE-IN. Single most significant event of my stay in California (early December to late January) has been the "Human Be-In" which took place in Golden Gate Park under the auspices of the San Francisco *Oracle*. A beautiful day in which more than 20,000 hippies—many from L.A., 400 miles away—gathered with no other purpose than to celebrate life and the joy of being together. A fantastic scene: 20,000 young people whose only common link was the fact that they were heads.[1] Many of the current heroes spoke: poets Lenore Kandel (who was facing obscenity charges because of a poem called "To Fuck With Love," only just noticed by SF moral watchdogs after having been freely sold for a year), Allen Ginsberg, Lawrence Ferlinghetti, Gary Snyder, Michael McClure. . . . Most of the Berkeley people, particularly those associated with the militant *Berkeley Barb*, felt that the day's "celebration" was too much of a copout and that the crowd should have been motivated more politically. Undoubtedly the hero of the day was Tim Leary[2] who was treated as befitted the guru he has become for so many young people. Brilliantly planned by a brilliant newspaper (SF *Oracle*, 25¢ from 1542 Haight Street, SF), the celebration included bells, banners, balloons, bubbles, bare-backs, incense, most of SF's best known rock bands and even a parachutist who dropped dramatically out of an empty sky right into the park. Astonishingly enough there were virtually no police present and the smell of pot was everywhere.

SAN FRANCISCO. The kids in the San Francisco Bay area are more or less split into two camps. In Berkeley, most of the action centers around the campus protests at the university, the students having decided that in a university as big as theirs it is becoming necessary for them to help make their own environment and not be treated merely as so much material to be processed through the education machine.

The protests surface in many different ways (the pre-Xmas one centered over the right of Navy recruiters to operate on campus), but what they are basically fighting for is individual students' rights. Socio-political activists such as former student Mario Savio, Jerry Rubin and the editors of the *Berkeley Barb* publicize and encourage the protests as part of a larger battle against the Establishment and, specifically, the Vietnam war.

One of the protestors' problems is that a transient and ever-changing student population is very hard to keep interested in specific action and every semester the whole thing has to be started up all over again. The university has usually acted stupidly enough, however, to provide a new flashpoint for a fresh round of protests.

Over in SF's Haight-Ashbury district, once a semi-ghetto and now blossoming into a hipper North Beach (a similar relationship to NYC's Greenwich Village and East Village), most of the action centers around what can only be described as psychedelia. The long-haired beautiful people only want the right to BE (which includes being left alone). Dozens of stores, coffee houses, etc., provide resting places for the gypsy-like population which drifts in and out, sitting on the floor, studying the notices for parties or roommates on the numerous free signboards, wandering up the street to partake of the free food magically conjured up daily by the Provo-like Diggers.

The common meeting ground, however, for all the kids in the area is the decrepit, old Filmore Ballroom where every Friday and Saturday night SF's top groups (the Grateful Dead, Quicksilver Messenger Service, Country Joe and the Fish, the Jefferson Airplane, Big Brother &

---

[1] "Heads" was slang for young users, mainly of marijuana, and sometimes of LSD and other drugs.

[2] Timothy Leary was a former Harvard academic famous for his celebration of LSD's mind-altering properties.

the Holding Co.) play at the "light shows." The music is tremendous, as is the geniality of the crowds present (many people sit around on the floor painting words and images in luminous paint, which shines under the black light), but the light shows are not too imaginative. Warhol has been doing it so much better, using many more ingredients including film, which strangely is lacking at the Fillmore, and the nearby Avalon Ballroom which runs similar shows.

The main thing to come out of the light shows, in fact, has been an almost totally new art form: the beautiful series of posters, a combination of art nouveau and psychedelic, which are already collectors' items across the world. Each patron is given one free and, promises promoter Bill Graham, will continue to be. But whereas once only 2,000 posters were printed for each show now the press run is 25,000 and these are wholesaled at 60¢ apiece to sell for $1 in local stores and up to three or four bucks in the rest of the country.

Source: John Wilcock, "Human Be-In" and "San Francisco," *Other Scenes*, vol. 1, no. 1 (January 1, 1967), p. 6, from *Independent Voices: An Open Access Collection of an Alternative Press* (https://voices.revealdigital.com/).

27

Living with Less

1968–1980

< The South Bronx, 1979

"Fighting Shirley Chisholm"

At the end of the 1960s, Shirley Chisholm, an African American congresswoman from Brooklyn, New York, worried about her country. Amid the upheaval of the Great Society, the United States "sometimes seemed to be poised on the brink of racial and class war." Blacks, women, the poor, and the young demanded change, but the political system resisted. "Our representative democracy is not working," Chisholm declared. "It is ruled by a small group of old men."

It was not in Chisholm's nature to give in. Born to working-class West Indian immigrants, she had pushed her way to a master's degree and a career as an educator. Running as "Fighting Shirley Chisholm," she won election to Congress from a poor, mostly black and Puerto Rican district in 1968. In January 1972, she became the first black and first female candidate for the Democratic presidential nomination. "You've never had anyone looking like me running for President," Chisholm declared. "Other kinds of people can steer the ship of state besides white men."

Chisholm's campaign continued the 1960s battle for rights. She wanted to create a coalition of African Americans, women, and the young "to get their share of the American dream and participate in the decision-making process that governs our lives."

Chisholm campaigned hard in several primaries. But with little money and organization, she had little chance. She had to fight to win equal time on television. Black male politicians withheld their support, and black voters wondered whether an African American could really win. Her female and black supporters squabbled.

The campaign ended in defeat in California, but it enhanced her reputation. In November, she won reelection to Congress with a huge majority. An exhausted Chisholm did not regret her presidential bid. "I ran for the Presidency in order to crack a little more of the ice which has congealed to nearly immobilize our political system and demoralize people," she explained.

Shirley Chisholm's failed campaign was part of a collision between Americans' aspirations for equality and new political, economic, and cultural realities. As the struggle for rights and opportunities expanded in the 1970s, the nation's economy and global influence continued to weaken. The United States no longer seemed a land of unlimited possibilities. Americans worried whether the nation could afford to meet everyone's needs in an age of dwindling jobs and resources. As a magazine concluded, Americans were "learning to live with less."

The result was not the "racial and class war" that Chisholm feared. But neither did the liberal Great Society give way to a stable new order dominated by one party or ideology. Instead, workers, employers, politicians, and families struggled with the consequences of limited resources and power. While Americans puzzled over the relationship between the economy and government and between the nation and the world, the political system broke down in scandal and failure.

A New Crisis: Economic Decline

During the social, political, and military crises of the 1960s, Americans had largely taken the economy for granted. Prosperous and growing, the United States had seemed destined to remain the world's preeminent economic power. But the economy had faltered as the Great Society came apart. The failings of business, government, and economists, a shortage of oil, intensifying foreign competition, and the multinational strategies of giant corporations combined to weaken the foundations of prosperity. By the end of the 1970s, the United States seemed to be in critical economic decline.

Weakness at Home

Signs of economic weakness were almost everywhere in the 1970s. Although the economy continued to grow, corporate profits and workers' productivity fell off. Unemployment increased; inflation, which usually dropped when unemployment rose, also increased. At best, the economy seemed stagnant. The unprecedented combination of high unemployment and high inflation led to the coining of a new word—*stagflation*—to describe the nation's predicament (see Table 27–1).

Corporations were partially responsible for the weak economy. Corporate leaders had tended to maximize short-term profits at the cost of the long-term health of their companies. Some companies had not put enough of their earnings into research, development, and new equipment. As a result, some American products seemed less innovative and reliable. Detroit's automobiles, so attractive and advanced in the 1950s, now struck consumers as unglamorous, inefficient, and poorly made. Ford's new Pinto sedan had to be recalled because its fuel tank was prone to explode.

Table 27–1 Stagflation in the 1970s

Year	Inflation % Change	Unemployment % Change	Combined* % Change
1970	5.9	4.9	10.8
1971	4.3	5.9	10.2
1972	3.3	5.6	8.9
1973	6.2	4.9	11.1
1974	11.0	5.6	16.6
1975	9.1	8.5	17.6
1976	5.8	7.7	13.5
1977	6.5	7.1	13.6
1978	7.7	6.1	13.8
1979	11.3	5.8	17.1
1980	13.5	7.1	20.6

Source: Statistical Abstract of the United States (1984), pp. 375–376, 463; Tables 624–625, 760; 1971 inflation data from *Statistical Abstract* (1973), p. 348, Table 569.

*"Combined" means annual percentage changes of inflation and unemployment.

Long an emblem of security and stability, corporations now appeared as vulnerable as the Pinto. In 1970, the Penn Central Railroad became the largest corporation in American history to go bankrupt. That year, only federal aid saved Lockheed Aircraft from also going under. The federal government also played a part in the nation's predicament. Massive federal spending had stimulated the economy from the 1940s to the 1960s but did not have the same effect in the 1970s. Some analysts claimed that Washington had diverted too much of the nation's talent and resources from the private sector to military projects during the cold war. In addition, the government's huge expenditures for the Vietnam War promoted inflation.

Economists did not give federal policy makers much help. In the 1960s, liberal economists had been sure they understood the secret to prosperity. The new problem of stagflation left them baffled. "The rules of economics," admitted the chairman of the Federal Reserve, "are not working quite the way they used to."

The Energy Crisis

An emerging energy crisis intensified economic problems. By 1974, the nation had to import over a third of its oil, particularly from the Middle East. The energy needs of the United States and other western countries empowered the Organization of the Petroleum Exporting Countries (OPEC), a group of third-world nations that had joined together to get higher prices for their oil. In October 1973, war broke out between Israel and a coalition of Arab nations, including Egypt and Syria. Arab members of OPEC refused to send petroleum to the United States and other nations that supported Israel in the conflict. OPEC soon raised oil prices nearly 400 percent.

The Energy Crisis Motorists crowd around an open gas station, New York City, December 1973.

The effect of the oil shortage spread well beyond gas stations. In some states, truck drivers blockaded highways to protest the high cost of fuel and low speed limits. Lack of fuel grounded some airline flights. Heating oil for homes and businesses was in short supply. Some people could not afford to heat their homes. Although the Arabs ended the oil embargo in March 1974, the underlying energy problem remained.

Competition Abroad

Weakened by trouble at home, the United States was vulnerable to increasingly tough competition from abroad. Thanks to American aid after World War II, Japan and Western European countries rose to create efficient, up-to-date industries. By the 1970s, these nations rivaled the United States, even in the American market.

The rise of Japan was the most dramatic. For decades, Americans had derided Japanese goods. By the 1970s, Japan's modern factories turned out high-quality products. Japanese televisions and other electronic goods filled American homes. Japanese cars—small, well made, and fuel efficient—attracted American buyers worried about the high price of gas.

Because of such competition, the United States fell back in the global economic race. In 1950, the nation had accounted for 40 percent of the value of all the goods and services produced around the world. By 1970, that figure was down to 23 percent. By the end of the 1970s, the United States imported more manufactured goods than it exported.

The Multinationals

Multinational corporations—firms with factories and other operations in several nations—played a key role in the economic crisis. Taking advantage of new technologies and lower trade barriers, US and West European corporations had moved aggressively into global markets after World War II. Multinationals accounted for about 15 percent of the world's annual gross product, and the biggest had annual sales larger than the annual product of some countries.

US firms made up the majority of the largest multinationals in the 1970s. As Americans struggled, US multinationals still earned large profits because of their lucrative overseas units. Not surprisingly, these American firms rapidly expanded abroad. In 1957, just 9 percent of American investments went abroad; by 1972, the figure had reached 25 percent.

The multinationals' most controversial foreign investment was the transfer of manufacturing from the United States to nations with lower wages and less restrictive labor laws. As corporations shifted production to plants in Mexico or Asia, American plants closed, with stunning job losses. The combination of overseas production and foreign competition was devastating. In 1954, US companies had made 75 percent of the world's televisions. Twenty years later, they produced less than 25 percent—and almost all of that production took place in Mexico and overseas.

Multinational executives argued that investment abroad increased jobs and prosperity in the United States. Capital invested in Mexico and Asia came back home, they insisted, as dividends to stockholders and tax payments to the government.

The Impact of Decline

Economic decline began to reshape life in the United States in the 1970s. It seemed as if the Industrial Revolution were being reversed. As factories closed, Americans witnessed

The South Bronx

Along with the empty factories of the Rustbelt, the empty buildings and rubble-strewn lots of the South Bronx epitomized economic and social decline in the deindustrializing United States of the 1970s. In the 1940s and 1950s, the area, part of the borough of the Bronx in New York City, had flourished as a middle-class haven for upwardly mobile white ethnics. But as the city struggled, many of those residents fled to outlying suburbs. Working-class Puerto Ricans and African Americans moved in, but the population of the South Bronx dropped shockingly from 763,326 in 1970 to 459,777 in 1980. As landlords burned down apartment buildings for the insurance money, 30 percent of adult residents were unemployed and 40 percent were on welfare. One-fifth of the population had no running water; one-half had no heat most of

the time. Infant mortality, drug use, and crime soared.

Struggling to comprehend the community, residents and observers reached for comparisons. Photographs showed empty stores, burned-out buildings, and debris-covered lots, but no people. "It can only be compared to war," said a local Catholic priest and city councilman. The South Bronx conjured up images of Germany's bombed-out cities and Japan's atomic-incinerated Hiroshima and Nagasaki at the end of World War II.

Those who lived and worked in the South Bronx knew all too well that people lived and died there. For the doctor who founded a local medical center, the area was full of residents struggling and often failing to survive cold weather, malnutrition, drugs, and gang violence. "The South Bronx is a necropolis," he said, "a city of death."

the deindustrialization of their country. Huge steel plants, the symbol of American industrial might, stood empty. In the 1970s, most new jobs were in the sales and retail sectors, intensifying a 20-year trend toward a service-centered economy. America, a union official lamented, was turning into "a nation of hamburger stands."

For workers, the effects of deindustrialization were crushing. Heavy industry had been the stronghold of the labor movement. By the late 1970s, less than one in four workers belonged to a union, and organized labor lost power and influence.

The loss of unionized industrial jobs eroded workers' incomes. After rising from the 1950s into the 1960s, workers' spendable income began to drop. To keep up, more and more women took full-time jobs outside the home: the percentage of women in the workforce, 36 percent in 1960, rose to 50 percent in 1980—the highest level in American history to that time. Many Americans could not find work, however. As the huge baby boom generation came of age, the economy did not produce enough jobs. The unemployment rate, as low as 2.8 percent in 1969, jumped to a high of 9 percent in 1975.

Playing in the Rubble The South Bronx, 1979.

City officials feared the South Bronx was a breeding ground, a petri dish for disease. "A prime worry . . . is that the urban sickness shows signs of spreading to other parts of The Bronx," a reporter wrote in 1973. "If The Bronx goes under . . . there may be little hope for the rest of New York."

For the predominantly white police of the 41st Precinct, engaged in a seemingly constant battle with some of the surrounding nonwhite population, the area was "Fort Apache." The name for the precinct and its bullet-scarred headquarters was an evocation of the US Cavalry garrison in Arizona during the Apache Wars of the late nineteenth century. "Fort Apache was a racist name," recalled a resident. "It evokes images of savage people, uncontrollable people, people society gives up on."

Despite its image, the South Bronx, along with the rest of the borough, was a place of extraordinary creativity. In the 1970s, graffiti artists, break dancers, and the first rappers helped create the music and culture of hip-hop. In their 1982 single, "The Message," Grandmaster Flash and the Furious Five offered their own harrowing depiction: "It's like a jungle sometimes it makes me wonder/How I keep from going under."

Economic decline accelerated the transformation of America's regions. The energy crisis and deindustrialization sped up the shift of people and power from north to south and east to west (see Map 27–1). With its cold, snowy winters, the North was especially vulnerable to the oil embargo and higher energy prices. America's Snowbelt now seemed a less attractive place to live and do business. In the 1970s, empty, decaying factories made the Northeast and the Midwest America's "Rustbelt."

Fleeing deindustrialization and high prices, many northerners moved south to the band of states ranging from Florida to California. As this Sunbelt boomed, farms became suburbs, and cities such as Orlando, Houston, Phoenix, and San Diego boomed. Texas and the southwestern states, rich in oil and natural gas reserves, profited from the energy crisis. The Sunbelt was home to new high-technology businesses: aerospace firms, electronics companies, and defense contractors. The Sunbelt was also at the cutting edge of the service economy, which was focused on leisure and consumption. More retirees moved to Florida than to any other state. Tourists flocked to California's Disneyland and Florida's Disney World. They gambled their money in Las Vegas.

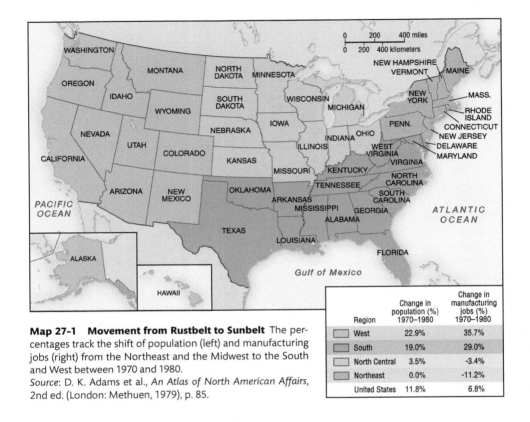

Map 27-1   Movement from Rustbelt to Sunbelt The percentages track the shift of population (left) and manufacturing jobs (right) from the Northeast and the Midwest to the South and West between 1970 and 1980.
Source: D. K. Adams et al., *An Atlas of North American Affairs*, 2nd ed. (London: Methuen, 1979), p. 85.

Region	Change in population (%) 1970–1980	Change in manufacturing jobs (%) 1970–1980
West	22.9%	35.7%
South	19.0%	29.0%
North Central	3.5%	-3.4%
Northeast	0.0%	-11.2%
United States	11.8%	6.8%

Confronting Decline: Nixon's Strategy

Richard Nixon was the first president to confront the decline of America's prosperity and power. He recognized that the failed war in Vietnam marked the end of America's cold war pretensions and that the American economy had weakened. Despite his long opposition to Communism and the New Deal, Nixon was a pragmatist, open to new realities and approaches.

A New Foreign Policy

The president and his national security adviser, Henry Kissinger, still regarded Communism as a menace and saw the cold war rivalry between the United States and the Soviet Union as the defining reality of the modern world. However, Nixon and Kissinger understood that the relative decline of American power dictated a new approach to the cold war.

The twin pillars of the new foreign policy were the Nixon Doctrine and détente. In July 1969, the president announced that the United States "cannot—and will not—conceive all the plans, design all the programs, execute all the decisions and undertake all the defense of the free nations of the world." America would continue to provide a nuclear umbrella, but its allies would have to defend themselves against insurgencies and invasions. This

Détente at the Great Wall of China, 1972 President Nixon, with his wife, Pat, became the first American president to visit mainland China.

Nixon Doctrine was a repudiation of the interventionist Truman Doctrine of 1947 (see Chapter 24).

The United States also pursued a new relationship with the Soviet Union and the People's Republic of China. Nixon and Kissinger wanted to lessen the cost of the rivalry with these two Communist nuclear powers. Separate agreements with the two nations might keep them from combining forces against the United States. Nixon and Kissinger therefore worked to establish détente, the relaxation of tensions.

At the start of Nixon's presidency, the United States had not recognized the legitimacy of the People's Republic of China. Instead, America supported the Communists' bitter foes, the Nationalist Chinese regime on Taiwan. In February 1972, Nixon became the first American president to go to mainland China. He gave the Chinese leaders what they most wanted—a promise that the United States would eventually withdraw its troops from Taiwan. The two sides also made clear they opposed any Soviet attempt to dominate Asia.

Nixon's trip brought American policy in line with the reality of the 1970s and underscored the gradual end of anti-Communist hysteria in America. By design, the trip also left the Soviets with the frightening possibility of a Chinese-American alliance.

Nixon did not want a confrontation with the Soviets, the only power that could destroy America with nuclear weapons. The United States no longer had clear military superiority. Instead, he sought détente. Above all, he wanted the Soviets to agree to limit their long-range or strategic nuclear arsenals. The Soviets also wished to reduce the cost and danger of the cold war and to counter Nixon's overture to the Chinese. Moreover, the Soviets needed American grain to feed their people.

The two sides began talks on the Strategic Arms Limitation Treaty (SALT I) in 1969. In May 1972, three months after his trip to China, Nixon became the first American president to travel to Moscow, where he signed the SALT treaty, limiting for five years the number of each nation's nuclear missiles. An Anti–Ballistic Missile (ABM) treaty sharply limited the number of defensive missiles the two sides could deploy. Although they did not stop the arms race, the treaties symbolized the American and Soviet agreement that "there is no alternative to . . . peaceful coexistence."

Ending the Vietnam War

Nixon and Kissinger sought better relations with the Soviet Union and the People's Republic of China in part to pressure the North Vietnamese to accept a peace agreement and end the Vietnam War. Nixon knew the United States could not win the war. Meanwhile, the war divided the American people and undermined American prestige and power around the world. But Nixon did not want the United States to look weak.

To appease public opinion, Nixon began to bring American soldiers home in 1969. With US forces reduced, Nixon needed a new strategy to persuade North Vietnam to accept the existence of South Vietnam. He turned to a policy known as "Vietnamization," in which the South Vietnamese were encouraged to defend themselves. But the South Vietnamese military alone could not beat back the Communists.

Accordingly, Nixon turned to US airpower to support South Vietnamese troops and intimidate the North Vietnamese. In March 1969, he authorized B-52 raids on North Vietnamese sanctuaries in Cambodia. Because bombing this neutral country might outrage American and world opinion, the raids were kept secret. Neither raids nor secret negotiations with North Vietnamese diplomats succeeded. Meanwhile, news of the secret bombings leaked out. In October, millions of Americans participated in Moratorium Day, a dramatic break from business as usual, to protest the war. In November, more than 250,000 people staged a "March Against Death" in Washington. That month, Americans learned about one of the most troubling episodes of the war. On March 16, 1968, US soldiers had killed between 200 and 500 unarmed South Vietnamese women, children, and old men in the hamlet of My Lai. This atrocity led to the 1970 court martial and eventual conviction of Lieutenant William Calley Jr. for mass murder.

Demonstrations did not stop the president from using violence to force a peace agreement. When General Lon Nol, the new pro-American leader of Cambodia, appealed for aid to stop a Communist insurgency, a joint United States–South Vietnamese force invaded Cambodia to look for North Vietnamese troops in April 1970. The Cambodian invasion sparked demonstrations on campuses across the country. On May 4, National Guard troops fired at unarmed protestors at Kent State University in Ohio. Four students died. Ten days later, state police killed two African American students at Jackson State College in Mississippi. These deaths intensified the outrage over Cambodia. Students went out on strike at about 450 campuses.

Some Americans, angered by these protests, mobilized in support of the president and the war. In New York City, construction workers attacked student demonstrators. "The country is virtually on the edge of a spiritual—and perhaps physical—breakdown," New York's mayor lamented.

As American troop withdrawals continued, the war and the peace negotiations dragged on. Meanwhile, the *New York Times* began publishing the so-called Pentagon Papers, a secret government history of American involvement in Vietnam. The documents, which revealed that the Johnson administration had misled the country, further undermined support for the war. The Nixon administration tried unsuccessfully to persuade the Supreme Court to block publication of the papers.

Nixon Under Pressure Across from the White House, a massive crowd protests the invasion of Cambodia in May 1970.

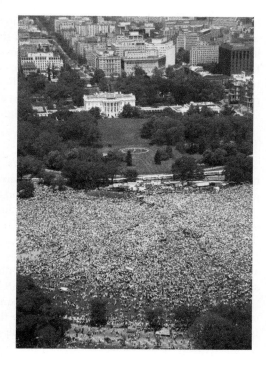

Unable to secure a peace agreement, Nixon pressed North Vietnam harder for a settlement. When the North Vietnamese army invaded South Vietnam in March 1972, the president ordered Operation Linebacker, an aerial attack on North Vietnam. When negotiations stalled in December, he ordered Linebacker II, the largest bombing mission since World War II, against the North. On January 27, 1973, negotiators signed a peace agreement in Paris. For the United States, at least, the Vietnam War was over.

Nixon had promised "peace with honor," but the agreement did not guarantee the survival of South Vietnam. The cease-fire came at a heavy cost. Twenty thousand Americans and more than 600,000 North and South Vietnamese soldiers had died since Nixon took office in 1969. The number of civilian casualties will never be known. Nixon had ended US participation in the Vietnam War, but his critics asked whether so flawed an agreement had been worth four years of fighting.

Chile and the Middle East

Détente, a practical accommodation with Soviet power, did not mean that the Nixon administration accepted the rise of potentially hostile regimes. To stop the spread of socialism and Communism, Nixon, like the presidents before him, was willing to subvert a democratically elected government and tolerate an authoritarian one. In 1970, he ordered the CIA to block the election of Salvador Allende, a Marxist, as president of Chile. Allende was elected anyway. "I don't see why we need to stand by and watch a country go communist due to the irresponsibility of its own people," Kissinger fumed. The CIA then helped destabilize Allende's regime by aiding right-wing parties, driving up the price of bread, and encouraging demonstrations. When a military coup deposed Allende in 1973, the United States denied responsibility and offered financial aid to the new military dictator, General Augusto Pinochet.

In the Middle East, the Nixon administration also displayed both its hostility to Communism and its inability to shape events decisively. In October 1973, on Yom Kippur, the holiest day of the Jewish calendar, Egypt and Syria attacked Israel in revenge for their defeat in the Six-Day War of 1967, when Israel occupied territory in Egypt, Syria, and

Jordan. After the United States sent critical supplies to Israel, Arab countries responded with the oil embargo. Meanwhile, the Soviets supplied the Arabs and pressed for a role in the region. Determined to keep out the Soviet Union, Nixon put American nuclear forces on alert. Kissinger mediated between the combatants, who agreed to pull back their troops in January 1974. The embargo ended, but American weakness was obvious. Supporting Israel, the United States still needed the Arabs' oil. Nixon and Kissinger held back the Soviets but could not bring peace to the Middle East.

Taming Big Government

The problem of decline, addressed in Nixon's foreign policy, proved more difficult to handle at home. Nixon took office with the conventional Republican goals of taming big government. He wanted a balanced budget and a reduction in federal power.

So Nixon cut spending for programs, including defense. The fate of the space program epitomized the new budgetary realities. On July 20, 1969, a landing module touched down on the moon. When astronaut Neil Armstrong set foot on the surface, the United States had beaten the Soviets to the moon, as President John F. Kennedy had vowed. There still seemed no limit to what Americans could do. There were, however, limits to what the space program could do. Congress slashed NASA's budget.

In 1969, Nixon called for a New Federalism, which would return "a greater share of control to state and local governments and to the people." Three years later, the administration persuaded Congress to pass a revenue-sharing plan that allowed state and local governments to spend funds collected by the federal government.

Nixon took the same pragmatic approach to domestic problems that he did to foreign affairs. He left popular New Deal and Great Society programs largely intact. Despite his budget cuts, the government kept spending vast amounts of money. By 1971, the cost of big government, combined with the unsettled economy, had produced a huge, un-Republican budget deficit.

The president did try to reform the federal welfare system put in place by the New Deal. Like many Republican conservatives, Nixon believed that welfare made the federal bureaucracy too large and the poor too dependent. His administration tried to replace the largest federal welfare program, Aid to Families with Dependent Children, with a controversial system inspired by presidential aide Daniel Patrick Moynihan, a Harvard sociologist. Moynihan's Family Assistance Plan would have provided poor families a guaranteed minimum annual income, but it also would have required the heads of poor households to accept any jobs available. Opposed by both liberals and conservatives, the program failed to pass Congress.

Meanwhile, the administration went along with several liberal initiatives expanding federal regulatory powers. By the 1970s, many Americans worried that corporations did not protect workers, consumers, or the environment. A grassroots environmental movement grew rapidly, particularly on college campuses, and on April 22, 1970, tens of millions of Americans celebrated the first Earth Day with teach-ins, demonstrations, and cleanup campaigns. Liberals in Congress responded to popular opinion with three new federal regulatory agencies: the Environmental Protection Agency (EPA), the Occupational Safety and Health Administration (OSHA), and the Consumer Product Safety Commission. These agencies enhanced the government's power over corporations, as did laws to safeguard coastlines and endangered species and limit strip-mining of coal, air and water pollution, and pesticide use.

An Uncertain Economic Policy

Nixon believed government should not interfere much in the economy. But high inflation, rising unemployment, and falling corporate profits tested his commitment to Republican orthodoxy. He was unable to persuade business to control price increases and organized labor to limit wage demands.

Meanwhile, the US dollar was in crisis. Since the Bretton Woods Conference (see Chapter 23), many nations had tied the value of their currencies to the dollar. The value of the dollar, in turn, had been supported by the US commitment to give an ounce of gold in return for $35. This commitment to the gold standard had stabilized the international financial system and helped spur global economic development for decades. But by the 1970s, the weakening US economy had undermined the dollar: strong European economies had too many dollars and too little confidence in the United States, and the US government didn't have enough gold. If other countries demanded gold for their dollars, Washington would be unable to pay, and panic would follow.

Confronting inflation, monetary crisis, and economic weakness, Nixon announced his New Economic Policy in August 1971. To prevent the breakdown of the monetary system, the president took the United States off the gold standard by ending the exchange of gold for dollars. To strengthen US producers against foreign competitors, Nixon lowered the value of the dollar and slapped new tariffs on imports; now American goods would sell more cheaply abroad and foreign goods would cost more in the United States. To slow inflation, he authorized a freeze on wages and prices.

The New Economic Policy did strengthen the international monetary system and help US producers. But wage and price controls did not solve the underlying problems that caused inflation. The cost of the Vietnam War and the Arab oil embargo continued to drive up prices. Deindustrialization continued, too.

Refusing to Settle for Less: Struggles for Rights

Despite the troubled economy, many Americans, like Shirley Chisholm, refused to settle for less. In the late 1960s and 1970s, African Americans and women continued their struggles for the rights and opportunities they had long been denied. Their example inspired other disadvantaged groups to demand recognition. Mexican Americans, Native Americans, and gays and lesbians organized and demonstrated for their causes. But other Americans, worried about preserving their own advantages in an era of limited resources, were often unwilling to support these new demands. At times, the result was almost the "racial and class war" that Chisholm dreaded.

African Americans' Struggle for Racial Justice

As the civil rights struggle continued, attention focused on two relatively new and controversial means of promoting racial equality—affirmative action and mandatory school busing. First ordered by the Johnson administration, affirmative action required businesses, universities, and other institutions receiving federal money to provide opportunities for women and nonwhites. Supporters viewed the policy as a way to make up for past and present discrimination. Opponents argued that affirmative action was itself a form of discrimination that reduced opportunities for whites, particularly white men.

STRUGGLES FOR DEMOCRACY

"ROAR"!

On Monday morning, September 9, 1974, 8,000 to 10,000 whites gathered in the barren red brick plaza flanked by two drab, hulking structures of concrete and glass—Boston City Hall and the John F. Kennedy Federal Building. The stark setting for a rally dramatized the equally stark divisions of race and class that defined democracy in 1970s America.

The crowd, mostly working-class and lower-middle-class "white ethnic" women, had come from Boston neighborhoods to protest the court-ordered busing due to start with the new school year in three days. As many as 1,500 protestors had come from South Boston, the predominantly Irish American center of opposition to the busing plan.

Crowd members were angry that their children would be bused to black-majority schools in Roxbury while black pupils would come into white-majority neighborhoods. Like the civil rights activists of the 1960s, these whites felt strongly that their own rights had been denied. The sponsor of the rally was the group Restore Our Alienated Rights (ROAR). "With Liberty and Justice for ALL?" one banner asked pointedly. Some protestors, evoking the Boston Tea Party of the Revolutionary era, threw teabags into the plaza's fountain and called for "the Second Revolution." "We're not ready to quit," insisted the moderator, Rita Graul of South Boston.

The protestors, most of them Democrats, were also angry at their own party and its leadership. They blamed the activist liberalism of the Democratic-sponsored Great Society for this intrusion of federal power into

Nixon, despite his commitment to limited government, generally supported affirmative action. His administration developed the Philadelphia Plan, which encouraged the construction industry to meet targets for hiring minority workers. In 1978, the Supreme Court offered qualified support for affirmative action with its decision in *Regents of the University of California v. Allan Bakke*. The justices ruled that the medical school of the University of California at Davis could not deny admission to Bakke, a white applicant with better grades and test scores than some minority applicants accepted by the school. Although the court barred schools from using fixed admissions quotas for different racial groups, it did allow race to be used as an admissions criterion. By the end of the 1970s, affirmative action had become an important means of increasing diversity in schools and other institutions.

School busing was more controversial than affirmative action. By the late 1960s, the Supreme Court had become impatient with delays in integrating the nation's schools. Even in the North, with no de jure, or legal, segregation, there was still extensive de facto segregation. In *Swann v. Charlotte-Mecklenburg Board of Education* in 1971, the court upheld their neighborhoods. The crowd's anger even extended to one of their own, Senator Ted Kennedy, who, despite his Irish American heritage and longtime family ties to Boston, supported civil rights and busing. There were "Impeach Kennedy" signs in the crowd. One of the speakers wore a chicken mask representing "the white chicken, Sen. Kennedy."

To everyone's surprise, the "white chicken" suddenly turned up on the platform. But the protestors would not let Kennedy speak. One of the organizers pulled the plug on his microphone. Some crowd members turned their backs on him. "Give us our rights back," the protestors demanded. "God Bless America," they sang. "You're a disgrace to the Irish," some people yelled. "Why don't you put your one-legged son on a bus for Roxbury," one crowd member called. "Yeah, let your daughter get bused there so she can get raped." A crowd member even shouted, "Why don't you let them shoot you like they shot your two brothers."

"Why won't they listen?" Kennedy asked. One of the organizers, Thomas O'Connell, answered that "maybe now he knew what it was like to be deprived of his rights—the way we've been deprived of our rights." Stone-faced, Kennedy left the platform and headed toward his office in the building named for his brother. Security held back angry protestors, who heckled him, turned thumbs down, and threw eggs and tomatoes. As he entered the building, crowd members banged on the big plate glass windows until one of them shattered.

Later, Kennedy told reporters, "They're not bigots." "We mourned President Kennedy," a woman declared outside the building. "We won't mourn this one." Three days later, whites began to boycott the schools. It was as if the 1960s had been reversed: now white protestors took up the tactics of civil rights activists. Ted Kennedy would win reelection to the Senate in the future, but his Democratic party no longer enjoyed the strong "white ethnic" support that had sustained the new liberalism of the 1960s.

the mandatory busing of thousands of children to desegregate schools in the Charlotte, North Carolina, area. But many Americans opposed busing, because they did not want integration or did not want children taken out of neighborhood schools.

Nixon sided with the opponents of busing. Privately ordering his aides to enforce busing less vigorously, he publicly called for a "moratorium" on new busing plans. Some communities implemented busing peacefully. Others faced protest and turmoil. In 1974, a federal court ordered busing in Boston. When the white-dominated local school committee refused to comply, a federal judge imposed a busing plan on the community. Working-class and lower-middle-class whites formed Restore Our Alienated Rights (ROAR) and other organizations to protest plans to bus students between the predominantly African American neighborhood of Roxbury and the largely Irish American neighborhood of South Boston. In "Southie," whites taunted and injured black students. Although violence spread through the fall, the busing plan went into effect. With busing and affirmative action, the civil rights movement seemed to have reached its limits: many Americans were unwilling to go any further to ensure racial equality.

Women's Liberation

By the 1970s, the movement for women's liberation was flourishing. Many women came together in "consciousness-raising" groups to discuss a broad range of issues in their lives. To commemorate the 50th anniversary of the women's suffrage amendment to the Constitution, thousands marched in the Women's Strike for Equality on August 26, 1970.

The women's liberation movement, like the struggle for African American equality, was diverse. Liberal feminist groups, such as the National Organization for Women (NOW), concentrated on equal public opportunities for women. Radical feminists focused on a broader range of private and public issues. Oppression, they insisted, took place in the bedroom and the kitchen, as well as the school and the workplace. Some radical feminists, influenced by the New Left, blamed women's plight on capitalism; others traced it to men. Cultural feminists insisted that women's culture was different from and superior to male culture and felt that women should create their own separate institutions. Some lesbian feminists went further to argue that women should avoid heterosexual relationships.

Linking the private and personal with the public and political, the women's movement fought on many fronts. More women who married decided to keep their own names rather than adopt their husbands'. Rather than identifying themselves by marital status, many women abandoned the forms of address "Miss" or "Mrs." for "Ms." Women's liberation made its mark on the media. In 1972, Gloria Steinem began the feminist magazine *Ms.* On television, popular sitcoms portrayed independent women.

In the 1970s, feminists focused especially on three public issues—access to abortion, equal treatment in schools and workplaces, and passage of the Equal Rights Amendment (ERA) to the Constitution. Long effectively outlawed, abortions were generally unavailable or unsafe. In *Roe v. Wade* in 1973, the Supreme Court ruled a Texas antiabortion law unconstitutional on the grounds that it violated the "right to privacy" guaranteed by the Ninth and Fourteenth Amendments. With this decision, abortion became legal and widely available.

Like the civil rights movement, the women's movement demanded equal treatment in schools and workplaces. At first reluctant, the Nixon administration opened up federal employment to women and pressed colleges and businesses to end discriminatory practices. In 1972, Congress approved Title IX of the Higher Education Act, which required schools and universities receiving federal funds to give equal opportunities to women and men in admissions, athletics, and other programs.

The women's movement also continued the struggle to enact the ERA. "Equality of rights under the law," the amendment read, "shall not be denied or abridged by the United States or by any State on account of sex." In 1972, Congress passed the ERA. If 38 states ratified the amendment within 7 years, it would become law. But after 28 states ratified within a year, the ERA met heavy opposition. To male critics, feminists were a "small band of braless bubbleheads." Fearing that equal rights would end their femininity and their protected legal status, conservative women, such as activist Phyllis Schlafly, campaigned effectively against the ERA. Although more states ratified the amendment, some rescinded their votes, and the ERA never became law (see Map 27–2).

The ERA's defeat underscored the challenges to the women's movement. Women still did not have full equality, but they had more control over their bodies, more access to education, and more opportunity in the workplace.

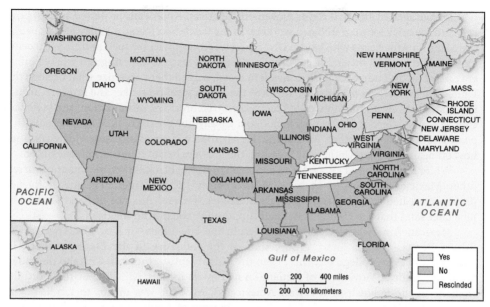

Map 27-2 The Equal Rights Amendment (ERA) Despite substantial support in state legislatures across the country, the ERA faced crippling opposition in the mountain West and the South.

Mexican Americans and "Brown Power"

In the 1960s and 1970s, Mexican Americans, the nation's second largest racial minority, developed a new self-consciousness. Proudly identifying themselves as Chicanos, they organized to protest poverty and discrimination.

Despite efforts to keep out Mexican immigrants, the Mexican American population grew rapidly. By 1980, at least 7 million Americans claimed Mexican heritage. The great majority lived in Arizona, California, Colorado, New Mexico, and Texas, most in urban areas and more than 1 million in Los Angeles. Winning more skilled and white-collar jobs, Mexican Americans still earned much less as a group than did Anglos (white Americans of non-Hispanic descent). One in four Mexican American families lived in poverty in the mid-1970s.

Stereotyped as lazy and shiftless, Mexican Americans faced racism and discrimination. Schools in their neighborhoods were underfunded. In some California schools, Mexican American children could not eat with Anglo children. California and Texas prohibited teaching in Spanish.

Gerrymandering diluted the political power of Mexican American voters. Despite its large Mexican American population, Los Angeles had no Hispanic city council member at the end of the 1960s. The justice system often treated Mexican Americans unfairly.

Poverty and discrimination marked Mexican American life. In cities, many Mexican Americans crowded into *barrios*, run-down neighborhoods. In the countryside, many lived without hot water or toilets. Infant mortality was high and life expectancy low. Nationwide, almost half the Mexican American population was functionally illiterate.

Encouraged by the civil rights movement, Mexican Americans protested against poverty and injustice for migrant farm workers. In the fertile San Joaquin Valley of California, the Mexican Americans who labored for powerful fruit growers earned as little as 10 cents an hour and lived in miserable conditions. César Chávez, a former migrant worker influenced by Martin Luther King Jr.'s nonviolent creed, helped them organize what became the United Farm Workers of America. In 1965, the union went on strike. The growers, accusing Chávez of Communist ties, called for police, strikebreakers, intimidation, and violence. Chávez's nonviolent tactics, which included a 25-day hunger strike in 1968, gradually appealed to liberals and other Americans. He also led a successful nationwide consumer boycott against grapes. Under this pressure, the growers began to settle with the union.

While King inspired Chávez, the nationalism of the Black Power movement spurred other Mexican Americans. In New Mexico, Reies López "Tiger" Tijerina, a former preacher, created the Alianza Federal de Mercedes (Federal Alliance of Land Grants) to take back land that the United States had supposedly stolen from Mexicans.

Mexican American activism flourished in the late 1960s. In East Los Angeles, the Brown Berets, a paramilitary group, showed the influence of the Black Panthers. In California in 1969, college students began the Movimiento Estudiantil Chicano de Aztlán (Chicano Student Movement of Aztlán, known by its initials, MEChA, or the word for "match" in the Spanish of Mexican Americans). MEChA was meant to kindle social change for Chicanos. In Crystal City, Texas, a boycott of Anglo businesses led to the formation of La Raza Unida ("The Unified Race"), a political party that won control of the local school board in 1970. These protests and organizations reflected a strong sense of pride and a powerful desire to preserve the Mexican American heritage. Activists asserted group identity by referring to Mexican Americans as "Chicanos." "A Chicano," said reporter Rubén Salazar, "is a Mexican-American with a non-Anglo image of himself."

Demanding bilingual education, Mexican American studies, equal opportunity, and affirmative action, activists fought for empowerment, for what some called "Brown Power." On the whole, white Americans paid less attention to Chicano activism than to African Americans' struggles. But Mexican American activists made important gains, including the end of state bans on teaching in Spanish.

Asian American Activism

Asian Americans also pressed for rights and recognition. Like Mexican Americans, they confronted a history of discrimination in the United States and faced denigrating stereotypes and hurtful epithets.

The small size of the Asian American population limited organization and protest, but the Immigration Act of 1965 made possible waves of new Asian immigration. By 1980, America was home to more than 3 million Asian immigrants, including 812,000 Chinese, 781,000 Filipinos, and 716,000 Japanese. Overall, there were 3.7 million Americans of Asian descent, mostly in the Pacific states and in cities.

Asian American activism followed the pattern of other minority movements. By the late 1960s, Asian Americans demonstrated a new ethnic self-consciousness and pride. Many Asian Americans saw themselves not only as Chinese or Japanese but also as members of a broader, pan-Asian group.

In 1968, the Asian American Political Alliance (AAPA) emerged on the campus of the University of California at Berkeley to unite Chinese, Japanese, and Filipino students.

In response to demands by Asian American students, colleges and universities established Asian studies courses and programs by the end of the 1970s. Beyond campuses, in 1974 protests forced the hiring of Chinese American workers to help build the Confucius Plaza housing complex in New York City's Chinatown. In San Francisco, activists brought suit against the public school system on behalf of 1,800 Chinese pupils. In *Lau v. Nichols* in 1974, the Supreme Court declared that school systems had to provide bilingual instruction for non-English-speaking students.

In the 1970s, Japanese groups demanded compensation for the US government's internment of Japanese Americans during World War II. In 1976, Washington rescinded Executive Order 9066, the 1942 directive that led to internment, but it did not make a more comprehensive settlement until 1988.

Asian Americans, like Chicanos, made only limited gains by 1980. However, with a new consciousness and new organizations, Asian Americans had also forced real social change.

The Struggle for Native American Rights

After many years of decline and stagnation, the Indian population had grown rapidly since World War II (see Map 27–3). By 1970, there were nearly 800,000 Native Americans, half of whom lived on reservations. Divided into about 175 tribes and other groups,

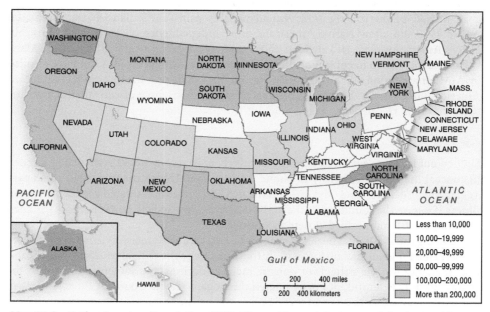

Map 27-3   Native American Population, 1980 After rapid growth in the years following World War II, the Native American population remained largest west of the Mississippi River and, above all, across the Southwest. But there were substantial numbers of Native Americans in every region.
Source: Data from *Statistical Abstract of the United States*, 1973 (Washington, DC: US Bureau of the Census, 1973), p. 348; and *Statistical Abstract of the United States*, 1984 (Washington, DC: US Bureau of the Census, 1984), pp. 375–376, 463, 760.

Native Americans were united by poverty and persistent discrimination. They had the lowest average family income of any ethnic group and faced high unemployment rates and substandard schools.

Native American life was shaped by the unique relationship with the federal government. Many resented the Bureau of Indian Affairs (BIA) for patronizing and exploiting tribes. Like African American and Mexican American separatists, some Native Americans saw themselves as a nation apart. Calling themselves "prisoners of war," they struck an aggressive stance, expressed in such slogans as "Custer Had It Coming" and "Red Power."

Beginning in the 1960s, a Native American movement emerged to protest federal policy, combat stereotypes, unite tribes, and perpetuate their cultures. Native Americans called for an end to employment discrimination and to the sale of Indian lands and resources to corporations. Activists staged "hunt-ins" and "fish-ins" to protest lost hunting and fishing rights. They also condemned the use of Indian symbols by schools and sports teams and demanded Indian-centered school curricula.

Some Native Americans favored more radical action. Copying the Black Panthers, a group of red-beret-clad Native Americans in Minneapolis formed an "Indian Patrol" to defend against the police. The patrol evolved into the American Indian movement (AIM), which spread to other cities. In 1969, AIM activists occupied the abandoned federal prison on Alcatraz Island in San Francisco Bay. They unsuccessfully offered the government "$24 in glass beads and cloth" for the prison, which they planned to convert into a Native American center. In 1972 and 1973, AIM took over BIA headquarters in Washington and the BIA office in Wounded Knee, South Dakota, where federal troops had massacred Indians in 1890.

The Native American rights movement made few gains. The Indian Self-Determination Act of 1975 did allow Native Americans more independence on the reservations, but Native Americans were still divided about their relationship to the government. Many tribal leaders wanted to continue selling off their lands through the BIA but were assailed by AIM for accepting bureau authority. Despite such divisions, the movement had forced Americans to confront the inequitable treatment of Indians more directly than at any time since the Great Depression.

Gay Power

Singled out for persecution in the McCarthy era, most gay men and women had learned to conceal their sexual identity in public. Mainstream American culture ridiculed gays as "faggots," "queers," and "dykes," and the medical profession treated gay identity as an illness. Despite the founding of the activist Mattachine Society in 1950, most gay men and women still maintained closeted identities.

During the 1960s, that began to change. In 1961, Frank Kameny, essentially fired from a federal job for being gay, unsuccessfully took his case to the federal courts. Another catalyst for change was the struggle of women, racial minorities, and students. Inspired by the chant "Black Is Beautiful," Kameny offered the slogan "Gay Is Good" in 1968. A decisive spur to the gay rights movement was a police raid on the Stonewall Inn, a gay bar in New York City's Greenwich Village, in June 1969. Such raids were commonplace, but this time gay men resisted. The next night, the police beat and arrested gay protestors, who yelled, "Gay Power!"

Stonewall became a rallying cry for gay activism. The Gay Liberation Front, the Student Homophile League, and other organizations appeared. Activists picketed companies that discriminated against gays, and gays socialized more openly. On the first anniversary of Stonewall, 10,000 gay men and lesbians paraded up New York's Sixth Avenue. "Two, four, six, eight!" marchers chanted. "Gay is just as good as straight!" The gay movement began to have an effect. In 1974, the American Psychiatric Association decided that gay identity was not a "mental disorder" and that gays deserved equal rights.

The emerging gay, Native American, and Chicano movements, along with the ongoing crusades of women and African Americans, made a deep impact on American society. Women, gays, African Americans, Native Americans, and Chicanos did not win full equality, but these groups made important gains despite the troubled economic climate.

Backlash: From Radical Action to Conservative Reaction

By the close of the 1960s, American society shook with demands for peace in Vietnam and equal rights at home. Some activists believed the United States would be torn apart and remade by the "racial and class war" that Shirley Chisholm feared, but the revolution never came. Radical movements fell apart. Many Americans abandoned activism for their private concerns; others angrily rejected protest movements. Encouraging this backlash, President Nixon won reelection in 1972.

"The Movement" and the "Me Decade"

By the end of the 1960s, women, minorities, student protestors, and antiwar activists seemed to be creating a single coalition, known simply as "the Movement." In August 1969, a crowd of nearly half a million mostly young people gathered for a music festival on a dairy farm near Woodstock in upstate New York. For three days, they created a temporary utopia dedicated to love, equality, and an end to the Vietnam War. What activist Abbie Hoffman called the "Woodstock Nation" briefly symbolized the possibility of a true mass-based coalition for radical change.

Nevertheless, the Movement stalled. "We had the dream and we are losing it," an activist lamented the same year. The different protest groups never merged and were often hostile to each other. Black activists, for instance, criticized white activists for neglecting poverty and other working-class problems.

In addition, Movement groups fell apart. Plagued by internal divisions, SDS held its last convention in 1969. The violent Weathermen called for "Days of Rage" in the "pig city" of Chicago in October 1969, but only a few hundred protestors showed up. Transient radical groups bombed or burned corporate headquarters and other "establishment" targets but succeeded only in giving the New Left and the Movement a bad name. The FBI infiltrated Black Panther chapters to discredit the organization. Panther leaders fled the country, went to jail, or died at the hands of police. Radical feminist groups also declined as women focused on liberal demands, such as the ERA.

Some protest movements lost their targets. After the demonstrations of 1970, the antiwar movement declined as the United States pulled out of Vietnam. The student movement declined as young people lost some of their grievances. In 1971, the voting age was lowered to 18, after ratification of the Twenty-sixth Amendment.

The revolution also failed because many people turned away from activism and political engagement. Some were disillusioned by the failure of the Great Society and the duplicity of the Johnson and Nixon administrations. Others were disappointed by radicalism's limited victories. Still others joined therapeutic and religious movements concerned with inner needs rather than political change.

To the writer Tom Wolfe, the 1970s were the "Me Decade," a time in which Americans had become self-absorbed and narcissistic. The cause, explained the historian and social critic Christopher Lasch, was the crisis of capitalism in "an age of diminishing expectations." Fears about the self-absorbed Me Decade were as exaggerated as hopes for the revolutionary Movement. People did not stop working for change, but in a time of economic decline and political disappointment, many Americans felt they could not afford the expansive liberal dreams of the 1960s. They had to look out for themselves.

The Plight of the White Ethnics

The "new American revolution" was a victim of anger, as well as apathy. Most lower-middle-class and working-class whites rejected the Movement. They decried radical feminism and resented the students and protestors who had avoided serving in Vietnam. They also rejected the new liberalism of the 1960s. Feeling threatened by urban renewal, welfare, and court-ordered busing, many whites believed the Great Society did too little for them and too much for minorities and young radicals. Most of all, they feared lost jobs and a lower living standard amid deindustrialization. "I work my ass off," said an ironworker. "But I can't make it."

The media painted an unflattering portrait of these Americans as frustrated racists and reactionaries. In reality, they were not all so racist or forlorn. They took renewed pride in the ethnic heritage that set them apart from other Americans. "White ethnics" were self-consciously German American or Irish American, like the opponents of busing in Boston. They were "PIGS"—Poles, Italians, Greeks, and Slavs.

White ethnics tapped their heritage to affirm an alternative set of values—their own counterculture. For them, ethnicity meant a grounding in family, neighborhood, and religion in place of the individualistic American dream and the centralizing federal government. In response, some colleges and universities created ethnic studies programs. In 1972, Congress passed the Ethnic Heritage Studies Act to "legitimatize ethnicity" and promote the study of immigrant cultures. Most important, white ethnics formed a large potential voting bloc, attractive to politicians.

The Republican Counterattack

Nixon tried to join white ethnics and white southerners in a Republican counterattack against radicalism, liberalism, and the Democratic Party. The president condemned protestors and demonstrations. "Anarchy," he said, "this is the way civilizations begin to die." Nixon ordered IRS investigations to harass liberal and antiwar figures. He used the FBI to infiltrate and disrupt the Black Power movement, the Brown Berets, and the New Left. He made illegal domestic use of the CIA against the antiwar movement.

Nixon also called for support from "the great silent majority of my fellow Americans." With his "southern strategy," the president reached out to Sunbelt voters by opposing busing, rapid integration, crime, and radicalism. He also tried to create a more conservative, less activist Supreme Court. In 1969, he named the cautious Warren Burger to succeed Earl Warren as chief justice. To fill another vacancy, Nixon nominated first a conservative South Carolina judge, Clement Haynsworth, who had angered civil rights and union leaders, and then Judge G. Harrold Carswell of Florida, a former avowed white supremacist. Both nominations failed, but Nixon had sent an unmistakable message to the "silent majority" and to white southerners.

The counterattack paid off in the 1972 presidential election. The Republican ticket of Nixon and Vice President Spiro Agnew benefited from unforeseen occurrences. Only George Wallace, the segregationist governor of Alabama, rivaled Nixon's appeal to the "silent majority." But Wallace's campaign for the Democratic nomination ended when a would-be assassin's bullet paralyzed him from the waist down. In addition, the Democratic vice-presidential nominee, Senator Thomas Eagleton of Missouri, had to withdraw after revelations about his treatment for depression.

Nixon did not really need good luck in 1972. The Democrats chose a strongly liberal senator, George McGovern of South Dakota, for president. McGovern's running mate was another liberal, Sargent Shriver, a brother-in-law of the Kennedys. The Democratic ticket—which endorsed busing and affirmative action and opposed the Vietnam War—alienated white ethnics, white southerners, and organized labor.

Nixon won 49 out of 50 states and nearly 61 percent of the popular vote, but the victory was deceptive: the Democrats still controlled both houses of Congress.

Nevertheless, the 1972 election was a sign that the traditional Democratic coalition was breaking up. Nixon's triumph, along with the failure of the Movement, the rise of the white ethnics, and the self-absorption of the Me Decade, showed that the glory days of liberalism and radicalism were over.

Political Crisis: Three Troubled Presidencies

Nixon's triumph turned out to be his undoing. The discovery of illegal activities in his campaign led to the revelation of other improprieties and, finally, to his resignation. Nixon's successors, Gerald Ford and Jimmy Carter, could not master the problems of a divided nation discovering the limits of its power. Unable to handle the conflicting issues of rights and economic decline, the three troubled presidencies of the 1970s intensified the sense of national crisis. At the decade's end, Americans wondered whether their democracy still worked.

Watergate: The Fall of Richard Nixon

Nixon's fall began when five men were caught breaking into the offices of the Democratic National Committee in the Watergate complex in Washington, DC, just before 2:00 a.m. on June 17, 1972. The five burglars had ties to Nixon's campaign organization, the Committee to Re-Elect the President (CREEP). They were attempting to repair an electronic eavesdropping device that had been planted in the Democrats' headquarters.

At first, Watergate had no impact on the president. He won reelection easily, but a disturbing story gradually emerged. Two reporters for the *Washington Post*, Bob Woodward and Carl Bernstein, revealed payments linking the five burglars to CREEP and to Nixon's White House staff. The burglars went on trial with two former CIA agents, who had directed the break-in for CREEP. Facing heavy sentences, the burglars admitted in March 1973 that "higher-ups" had planned the break-in and orchestrated a cover-up. One of those higher-ups, presidential counsel John Dean, revealed his role in the Watergate affair to a grand jury. By the end of April, the president had to accept the resignations of his most trusted aides, H. R. "Bob" Haldeman and John Ehrlichman. To investigate Watergate, Nixon named a special federal prosecutor, Archibald Cox.

In the end, the president was trapped by his own words. A Senate committee, chaired by Sam Ervin of North Carolina, began hearings on Watergate in May 1973. A White House aide told the committee that conversations in the president's Oval Office were routinely recorded on secret tapes. Claiming "executive privilege," Nixon refused to turn over tapes of his conversations after the break-in. When Archibald Cox pressed for the tapes, Nixon ordered him fired on Saturday, October 20, 1973. Attorney General Elliot Richardson and a top aide refused to carry out the order and resigned. A third official finally fired Cox. Nixon's "Saturday Night Massacre" set off a storm of public anger. Nixon had to name a new special prosecutor, Leon Jaworski. The Democratic-controlled House of Representatives began to consider impeachment against the president. "I am not a crook," Nixon insisted.

By 1974, it became clear that the Nixon administration had engaged in a shocking range of improper and illegal behavior. Infuriated by news leaks in 1969, Henry Kissinger had ordered wiretaps on the phones of newspaper reporters and his own staff. Two years later, the White House had created the "Plumbers," an inept group of operatives to combat leaks such as release of the Pentagon Papers. In 1972, Nixon's men had also engaged in dirty tricks to sabotage Democratic presidential aspirants. Nixon's personal lawyer had collected illegal political contributions, "laundered" the money to hide its source, and then transferred it to CREEP.

Nixon himself had ordered the secret and illegal bombing of Cambodia. He had impounded (refused to spend) money appropriated by Congress for programs he disliked. He had secretly approved the use of federal agencies to hurt "political enemies."

As a result of Watergate and other scandals, many of Nixon's associates had to leave office. No fewer than 26, including former attorney general John Mitchell, went to jail. Vice President Spiro Agnew was found to have accepted bribes as the governor of Maryland in the 1960s. In 1973, Agnew accepted a plea bargain deal and resigned. He was replaced by Republican congressman Gerald R. Ford of Michigan.

Under pressure to release his tapes, Nixon tried to get away with publishing edited selections. Revealing a vulgar, rambling, and inarticulate president, the transcripts only fed public disillusionment. In July 1974, the House Judiciary Committee voted to recommend to the full House of Representatives three articles of impeachment—obstruction of justice, abuse of power, and defiance of subpoenas.

Nixon wanted to fight the charges, but the Supreme Court ruled unanimously that he had to give his tapes to the special prosecutor. They showed that Nixon himself had participated in the Watergate cover-up as early as June 23, 1972. The president had conspired to obstruct justice and had lied repeatedly to the American people. Almost certain to be impeached, Nixon agreed to resign rather than face a trial in the Senate. On August 9, 1974, he left office in disgrace. "My fellow Americans, our long national nightmare is over," the new president, Gerald Ford, declared. "Our Constitution works."

Gerald Ford and a Skeptical Nation

At first, Gerald Ford was a welcome relief for a nation stunned by the misdeeds of Richard Nixon. Modest and good-humored, the new president seemed unlikely to abuse authority. But Ford also seemed stumbling and unimaginative in the face of declining prosperity and power. Moreover, he had no popular mandate. Ford was the first un-elected vice president to succeed to the presidency. His vice president, former New York governor Nelson Rockefeller, had not been elected, either.

Ford had to govern a nation skeptical about politicians. Johnson's deceitful conduct of the Vietnam War and Nixon's scandals raised fears that the presidency had grown too powerful. To reestablish its authority, Congress passed the War Powers Act of 1973, which allowed the president to send troops to hostilities overseas for no more than 60 days with-out congressional consent. In 1975, Congress held hearings on CIA secret operations. Amid revelations about the agency's improper roles in domestic spying and the assassina-tion of foreign leaders, Congress created permanent committees to oversee the agency. Ford had to ban the use of assassination in American foreign policy.

Soon after taking office, Ford himself fed the public's skepticism about the presidency by offering Nixon a full pardon for all crimes committed as president. Ford's popularity dropped immediately, and his presidency never fully recovered.

Ford's handling of economic issues did not help his popularity. A moderate Repub-lican, he preferred a less active federal role in managing the economy. But, like Nixon, he could not stop some liberal initiatives, as Congress strengthened the regulatory power of the Federal Trade Commission and extended the 1970 Clean Air Act.

Ford had no solutions for deindustrialization and stagflation. Believing inflation was the most serious problem, he did little to stop rising unemployment, which topped 9 percent. His anti-inflation program, known as WIN for "Whip Inflation Now," mainly encouraged Americans to control price increases voluntarily, but inflation continued.

In foreign affairs, Ford had to accept limits on American power. Despite the 1973 cease-fire, the fighting continued in Vietnam. Ford promised to protect South Vietnam, but Congress cut his requests for monetary aid to Saigon. Sending American troops back to South Vietnam was out of the question. When the North Vietnamese invaded early in 1975, panicked civilians fled southward. As Saigon was overrun, the last Americans evacuated in helicopters. Thousands of loyal South Vietnamese fled with them, but many more were left behind. On April 30, 1975, South Vietnam surrendered. There was nothing Ford could do to prevent the final, ignominious failure of America's 20-year-long Vietnam policy.

The president could also do nothing to save the pro-American government of Cambodia from Communist insurgents, the Khmer Rouge, in April 1975. Ford did act the next month when the Khmer Rouge captured an American merchant ship, the *Mayaguez*, off Cambodia. At the cost of 41 deaths, United States marines rescued the 39-man crew. Despite the rescue, the United States no longer wielded much power in Southeast Asia.

The policy of détente with the Soviet Union, meant to help America cope with its lim-ited power, was also in trouble. The United States and the Soviets failed to agree to a second Strategic Arms Limitation Treaty (SALT II). Critics of détente, including Democratic Senator Henry Jackson of Washington, claimed that the policy sapped American defenses and overlooked human rights violations by the Soviets. In 1974, Jackson added to a trade bill an amendment linking commerce to freedom for Soviet Jews to emigrate. The Jackson-Vanik Amendment helped sour the Soviets on détente. Ford further alienated conserva-tives when he signed an agreement in Helsinki, Finland, accepting the post–World War II boundaries of European nations.

Ford's troubles affected the polls. The Democrats made large gains in the 1974 con-gressional elections. Two years later, Ford won the Republican nomination for president,

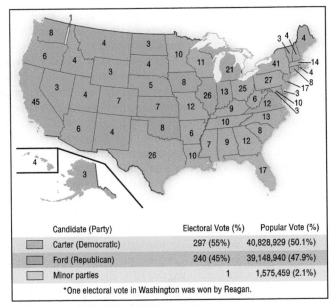

Candidate (Party)	Electoral Vote (%)	Popular Vote (%)
Carter (Democratic)	297 (55%)	40,828,929 (50.1%)
Ford (Republican)	240 (45%)	39,148,940 (47.9%)
Minor parties	1	1,575,459 (2.1%)

*One electoral vote in Washington was won by Reagan.

Map 27-4 The Presidential Election, 1976 Jimmy Carter managed to reestablish the Democratic Party's appeal to white southerners.

replacing Rockefeller with a more conservative vice-presidential nominee, Senator Robert Dole of Kansas. The Democrats chose former Georgia governor Jimmy Carter, a moderate promising efficiency rather than liberal reform.

With low turnout, Carter took 50.1 percent of the vote to Ford's 48 percent. The Democrat won an Electoral College majority by carrying the Northeast and taking back almost all the South from the Republicans (see Map 27–4). The outcome was less an endorsement of Carter than a rejection of Ford, who became the first sitting president to lose an election since Herbert Hoover during the Great Depression in 1932.

"Why Not the Best?": Jimmy Carter

As he took office in 1977, Jimmy Carter seemed capable and efficient. A graduate of the Naval Academy, he had served as an engineer in the nuclear submarine program and successfully managed his family's peanut farm before entering politics. Carter's perfectionism was captured in the title of his autobiography, *Why Not the Best?*

Carter responded more energetically and imaginatively than Ford to the nation's problems. But Carter came to be seen as a weak, uncertain leader. More important, he faced the same intractable problems that had bedeviled Ford.

Like his predecessor, Carter had trouble putting to rest the recent past. He met angry criticism when he pardoned Americans who had resisted the draft during the Vietnam War.

Carter also faced increasing popular resentment of government. Many Americans believed that regulation and taxation had gotten out of hand. When the Endangered Species Act of 1973 forced a halt to the construction of a Tennessee dam because it threatened the survival of the snail darter, a small local fish, it seemed as if the federal government worried more about fish than about people's need for electricity and recreation.

The West was the stronghold of antigovernment sentiment in the 1970s. Assailing Washington bureaucrats, the Sagebrush Rebellion demanded state control over federal lands in the West. Businessmen in the West also wanted more exploitation of oil, forests, and other resources on federal lands. Meanwhile, California became the center of an anti-tax movement in 1978. Angered by high taxes and local government spending, California voters passed Proposition 13, which sharply reduced property taxes.

As always, antigovernment sentiment was inconsistent. Many of the same people who attacked taxes and regulation expected aid and benefits from Washington. When Chrysler faced bankruptcy in 1979, the government saved the automaker with a $1.5 billion loan guarantee. When Carter moved to cancel federal water projects in the West in 1977, he faced protest from the heart of the Sagebrush Rebellion.

Carter was most successful when he moved to limit government. By the 1970s, some economists were advocating deregulation of businesses as a way to lower costs, increase competition, and improve services. In 1978, the government removed price controls on the airline industry. In the short run the move lowered fares, but in the long run it drove some airlines out of business.

Deregulation marked a changing balance of political power. Big business, under attack since the 1960s, now lobbied effectively against regulation, organized labor, and taxes. Liberals, meanwhile, failed to convince Congress to create the Consumer Protection Agency or to make labor organization easier. In 1978, Congress diluted the liberal Humphrey-Hawkins Bill asserting federal responsibility for full employment. When Carter tried to raise business taxes, Congress instead cut taxes on capital gains and added more tax loopholes.

Carter attempted, with mixed results, to adjust the economy to the realities of living with less. His voluntary wage and price controls did not stop soaring inflation. After fuel shortages forced schools and businesses to close in the harsh winter of 1976–1977, Carter addressed the energy crisis. The president told Americans that "the energy shortage is permanent" and urged them to conserve. His energy plan included a new Department of Energy, taxes on gas-guzzling automobiles and large consumers of oil, tax incentives to stimulate oil and gas production, and development of nuclear power. Conservatives complained that the program expanded government authority, whereas liberals and environmentalists objected to its support for nuclear power and oil-company profits. A weakened plan, passed in 1978, did encourage conservation.

Nuclear power, a key part of Carter's energy plan, lost much of its appeal. In March 1979, a nuclear reactor at Three Mile Island, Pennsylvania, nearly suffered a catastrophic meltdown. As 100,000 frightened residents fled their homes, the reactor had to be permanently closed. Around the country, utilities scrapped plans for new nuclear power plants.

Three Mile Island fed broader anxieties about the environmental damage of industrial capitalism. Americans wondered whether their neighborhoods would suffer the fate of Love Canal, near Niagara Falls, New York. There, hazardous waste buried by a chemical company caused so many cases of cancer, miscarriages, and other health problems that residents had to move away. Despite business hostility to regulation, Washington had to create a "Superfund" of $1.6 billion to clean up hazardous-waste sites. The administration also took control of 100 million acres of Alaska to prevent damage from economic development.

At first, Carter had success with foreign policy. Continuing Nixon's de-escalation of the cold war, Carter announced that "we are now free of the inordinate fear of Communism." Without abandoning détente, he focused on building harmony and supporting human rights and democracy around the world. In 1978, Carter won Senate approval of a treaty yielding ownership of the Panama Canal to Panama at the end of the century, representing a new, more respectful approach to Central and Latin America.

In 1978, Carter also mediated the first peace agreement between Israel and an Arab nation. Bringing together Israeli and Egyptian leaders at the Camp David presidential retreat, Carter helped forge a framework for peace that led to Israel's withdrawal from the Sinai Peninsula and the signing of an Israeli-Egyptian treaty. The agreement did not settle the fate of the Israeli-occupied Golan Heights and Gaza Strip or the future of the Palestinian people, but it did create a basis for future negotiations.

Carter viewed a commitment to human rights and democracy as America's way of recapturing the international respect lost during the Vietnam War. In practice, however, Carter supported authoritarian American allies, such as the rulers of Iran and the Philippines, who abused human rights in their own countries.

Carter's foreign policy suffered from the collapse of détente. The president did reach an agreement with the Soviets on the SALT II treaty, but the Senate was reluctant to ratify it. Then, in December 1979, the Soviet Union invaded its southern neighbor, Afghanistan. In response, Carter withdrew the SALT II treaty, stopped grain shipments to the Soviet Union, forbade American athletes to compete in the 1980 Olympics in Moscow, and increased military spending. These moves did not affect the Soviets' invasion, but détente was over, and the direction of American foreign policy was unclear.

By 1979, Carter was deeply unpopular. He had not stabilized the economy or forged a coherent foreign policy. After pondering the situation at Camp David for 11 days in July, he told a television audience that the nation was suffering a "crisis of the American spirit." The president offered proposals to deal with the energy crisis but spoke most strongly to the state of the nation. "All the legislation in the world can't fix what's wrong with America,"

Time Line

▼1968

Assassinations of Martin Luther King Jr. and Robert F. Kennedy
Election of Richard Nixon

▼1969

Secret bombing of Cambodia
Stonewall Riot in New York's Greenwich Village
Apollo 11 moon landing
Nixon Doctrine

▼1970

First Earth Day
Invasion of Cambodia

▼1971

United States off gold standard
Ratification of Twenty-sixth Amendment, lowering voting age to 18
Supreme Court busing decision, *Swann v. Charlotte-Mecklenburg Board of Education*

▼1972

President Nixon's trips to the People's Republic of China and the Soviet Union

Strategic Arms Limitation Treaty (SALT I) and Anti–Ballistic Missile (ABM) Treaty
Congressional passage of Equal Rights Amendment
Watergate burglary
Reelection of President Nixon

▼1973

Peace agreement to end Vietnam War
Supreme Court ruling to legalize abortion, *Roe v. Wade*

Disaster in the Iranian Desert, April 1980 The wreckage of this army helicopter, part of the failed attempt to free American hostages in Iran, symbolizes the weakness of the United States at the start of the 1980s.

Carter said. "What is lacking is confidence and a sense of community." The speech was popular, but the president failed to turn popular approval into effective legislation.

Carter became still more embattled when the Shah of Iran was overthrown by the followers of an Islamic leader, the Ayatollah Ruholla Khomeini, early in 1979. The Shah had

▼**1973–1974**
OPEC oil embargo

▼**1974**
Boston busing struggle
Resignation of President Nixon

▼**1975**
Surrender of South Vietnam to
    North Vietnam
Helsinki Agreement

▼**1976**
Announcement of the "Me
    Decade" by Tom Wolfe
Jimmy Carter elected president

▼**1977**
Carter's energy plan

▼**1978**
Camp David peace accords
Supreme Court affirmative
    action decision, *Regents of the*

University of California v. Allan
Bakke

▼**1979**
Accident at Three Mile Island
    nuclear power plant

▼**1979–1981**
Iranian hostage crisis

▼**1980**
Ronald Reagan elected president

long received lavish aid from the United States. Now, Iranian revolutionaries, eager to restore traditional Islamic values, condemned America for imposing the Shah and modern culture on their nation. In the wake of the revolution, oil prices rose. Americans had to contend again with gas lines and inflation.

The situation worsened when Khomeini condemned the United States for allowing the Shah to receive medical treatment in New York. On November 4, students loyal to Khomeini overran the United States embassy in Teheran, the Iranian capital, and took 60 Americans hostage. Carter froze Iranian assets in the United States but could not compel the release of the hostages. The United States seemed helpless. In the spring of 1980, a frustrated Carter ordered a secret military mission to rescue the hostages. On April 24, eight American helicopters headed for a desert rendezvous with six transport planes carrying troops and supplies. When two helicopters broke down and another became lost, the mission had to be aborted. An accident left eight soldiers dead. The hostages remained in captivity. And the limits of American power seemed more obvious than ever.

Conclusion

As the 1970s ended, Shirley Chisholm was still deeply worried about her nation. The congresswoman feared that "there was a real crisis . . . in this country. . . . Government was being conducted by crisis." The mixture of economic decline with movements for rights and opportunity had proved too much to handle. To Chisholm, even the changes of the liberal 1960s seemed at risk. "Lots happened in the '60s," she noted sadly. "What's happening today? Every gain has been eroded."

As always, Chisholm refused to give in to pessimism. "I will continue to do what I'm doing—fighting, fighting, fighting," she vowed, "because I realize that this country is moving to the right." As the 1980s would reveal, Chisholm was correct. After the political uncertainty of the 1970s, the nation would finally deal with economic decline and the other challenges of the decade by embracing a new conservatism. The future lay to the right.

Who, What, Where

Review Questions

1. What were the chief causes of American economic decline in the 1970s?

2. What were the main concerns of the white ethnics?

3. What were the key foreign policies of the Nixon administration?

Critical-Thinking Questions

1. Why did the demands of the African American civil rights movement become more controversial in the 1970s?

2. Did the upheavals of the 1970s strengthen or weaken democracy in America?

3. Analyze the troubled presidencies of Nixon, Ford, and Carter. Did these leaders create their own problems, or did they face impossible situations?

Suggested Readings

Bailey, Beth, and David Farber, eds. *America in the 1970s.* Lawrence: University Press of Kansas, 2003.

Borstelmann, Thomas. *The 1970s: A New Global History from Civil Rights to Inequality.* Princeton, NJ: Princeton University Press, 2012.

Cowie, Jefferson. *Stayin' Alive: The 1970s and the Last Days of the Working Class.* New York: The New Press, 2010.

For further review materials and resource information, please visit www.oup.com/us/oakes-mcgerr

CHAPTER 27: LIVING WITH LESS, 1968–1980
Primary Sources

27.1 TESTIMONY OF GERALD DICKEY, MERGERS AND INDUSTRIAL CONCENTRATION; HEARINGS BEFORE THE SUBCOMMITTEE ON ANTITRUST AND MONOPOLY OF THE COMMITTEE ON THE JUDICIARY (1978)

Deindustrialization was a complex, long-term process. But it also had stark, immediate consequences. On "Black Monday," September 19, 1977, most of the workers at the Ohio steel mill Youngstown Sheet & Tube suddenly lost their jobs. Testifying before a subcommittee of the US Senate, Gerald Dickey, a rigger for the company and an official of the steelworkers' union, traced the closure to a corporate takeover allowed by the federal government nearly a decade earlier. According to Dickey, the new management's ignorance and greed ensured that Youngstown Sheet & Tube failed to modernize and thus compete with efficient foreign rivals.

Youngstown Sheet & Tube was founded in 1900 by Youngstown industrialists. During the twenties the company acquired the Brier Hill Steel Co. in Youngstown, and a steel company in East Chicago, Ind. They bought interest in coal and iron ore mines and some steel finishing mills. Company owners were interested in making and selling steel. They were very successful at it.

Youngstown is a "company town." Years ago, when people migrated to Youngstown, they lived in company houses and bought from the company store. Today the company houses and stores are gone. But recently I heard a top manager say that Youngstown Sheet & Tube controls 1 out of 5 jobs in the Mahoning Valley. So, I guess you could say Youngstown is still a company town.

The people who work at Youngstown Sheet & Tube are second- or third-generation steel workers. Their fathers and grandfathers retired after working all their lives in the mill. To an outsider, a steel mill may not seem like a great place to work. But to us, it means a decent and honorable living. Youngstown steelworkers have always taken pride in their work. They are recognized as the finest labor force in the steel industry.

In 1969 something happened which changed the course of history in Youngstown. A small New Orleans–based shipping company called Lykes Bros. took over Youngstown Sheet & Tube. Lykes had $376 million in assets, while Youngstown Sheet & Tube had $1.026 billion. Something was wrong. Workers knew instinctively that something was wrong. Around the mill the talk was that "Lykes is going to milk this company dry, and let it go." The workers' fears were confirmed when a top Lykes executive . . . said that he would not hesitate to make use of Youngstown Sheet & Tube's $100 million annual cash flow to move into other fields "if our views on the future of steel should change."

Deterioration was slow at first; but before we knew it, we were so far downhill the road back seemed insurmountable. Strange things began to happen. We often had no spare parts to replace worn equipment. Sometimes we had to remove pieces from other machinery just to keep higher priority machines running. I recall an incident when Lyke formed their own trucking company to bring manganese to our open hearth. They replaced a local hauler. After waiting around all day, our supervisors discovered they had only one truck. Our open hearths came close to a standstill from lack of manganese before the supervisor found another trucking outfit.

I remember when hundreds of tons of steel plates were shipped to Lykes for new ship building. We were told that Lykes was taking advantage of our steel company. . . .

Other incidents took place that made us question the actions of our corporate executives. We overheard lower level management complain of irregularities in their purchasing department. Often the company had to purchase parts and equipment from a Lykes subsidiary at a higher price than they had previously paid a local firm. That practice made the subsidiary look good at the expense of the steel operations.

. . . Evidently the corporate leadership from the shipping firm did not understand, or cared to learn, how to maintain and operate a steel mill. . . .

Lower level management could not even purchase spare parts mandatory for operation. When they could get parts and equipment, the price was too high from the supplier, a Lykes subsidiary.

The words of a 40-year veteran of the mill best describe what happened. He said: "It's a crime that the place was allowed to go down so fast without any preventative maintenance."

The end came on September 19, 1977. Lykes Corp. announced they were closing 75 percent of their steelmaking facilities in Youngstown. That was just after workers in the open hearth department set production records during the intense heat of July and August. The months of July and August are, by far, the worst times to be employed in the steel industry because of the intense heat and often unbearable conditions.

In spite of the handicaps, those workers broke records. I suppose it really did not matter, they did not stand a chance. You see, they were competing against themselves and their own past production performance. Their real competitors were the newer, modern mills. Our workers were making steel in mills built before World War I. No matter how talented and dedicated they were, they could not match the performance of basic oxygen furnaces or electric furnaces. We lacked the technology and we did not have control. Lykes had control. By deciding not to invest the capital when it was available, by deciding not to modernize, they doomed our mill, annihilated our jobs and brought havoc to our community.

I'd like to add a special note here. When the shutdown was announced, Lykes blamed part of the reason on foreign imports. Recently we made quite a startling discovery. . . . We learned that the same banks . . . were denying additional credit and at the same time were investing in the Japanese steel industry. That leads us to ask who is really calling the shots?

A crime was committed against the people of Youngstown. Nobody was arrested, indicted, or convicted, or will they ever be. This is a moral crime. There are no laws against it.

If I may, I would like to recommend to this subcommittee that you change the law. Presently, when the U.S. Government makes decisions on mergers between corporations, they decide on the basis of the anti-trust laws. As I understand it, they look at competition within the industry to prevent monopoly. Something is missing. What about the workers? What about the communities?

I ask this subcommittee to consider legislation to require the U.S. Government to consider not only antitrust provisions, but also the impact on the workers and communities involved. Something like an "employment impact statement" would work. No merger should be allowed which would be detrimental to a community or the workers.

Source: Testimony of Gerald Dickey, *Mergers and Industrial Concentration. Hearings Before the Subcommittee on Antitrust and Monopoly of the Committee on the Judiciary. United States Senate. Ninety-Fifth Congress. Second Session on Acquisitions and Mergers by Conglomerates of Unrelated Businesses. May 12, July 27, 28, and September 21, 1978* (Washington, DC: US Government Printing Office, 1978), pp. 17–21.

27.2 NIXON DECIDES ON THE CHRISTMAS BOMBING (1972)

Thanks to the taping system he had installed in the Oval Office, Richard Nixon left an unequalled verbatim record of presidential decision making. These excerpts are from a meeting on December 14, 1972 in which Nixon, talking with National Security Advisor Henry Kissinger and Deputy National Security Advisor Alexander Haig Jr., made the controversial choice to intensify the bombing of North Vietnam. As a frustrated Kissinger reports, the North Vietnamese negotiators, representing their government in the city of Hanoi, had a "diabolical" way of avoiding an agreement to end the war. Note how concerned Nixon is about the state of public opinion in the United States, and his desire to avoid the bad publicity of an attack on Christmas. Despite his efforts, the raids, officially codenamed Linebacker II, became known as the Christmas bombings.

Kissinger: So, what they've done is quite diabolical. They've got the issue in a stage where, with one phone call to us, they can settle it in an hour. But they're always going to keep it just out of reach, and. . . . Now, [Secretary of Defense Melvin] Laird thinks we can just yield. We can't yield. . . .

Nixon: What is he suggesting? To yield?

Haig: Yeah. Oh, he called. I told you yesterday. He called me the night before and said, "We can't—we can't take military action. I'm going to send a memo over." Well, the memo got here yesterday morning and it just says we've got to settle. . . .

Nixon: What's new with him?

[laughter] . . .

Kissinger: There's the predominant possibility that there isn't enough pressure on them to make them settle. . . . I—that—what we are seeing now is their normal negotiating habit. They're shits, if I can use a—I mean, they are tawdry, miserable, filthy people. They make the Russians looks good.

Nixon: And the Russians make the Chinese look good, I know . . .

Nixon: All these assholes in the press said we were wrong. Now, at the present time, the press will say . . . "Peace has escaped da-da-da-da-da," and they're going to be wrong again. . . . My point is, you've got to remember who the enemy are. The enemy has never changed. The election didn't change it. The only friends we've got, Henry, are a few people of rather moderate education out in this country, and thank God, they're about 61 percent of the people, who support us. The left-wingers, most of your friends, and most—and many of mine—

Kissinger: Some friends of mine—

Nixon: —are against us.

. . .

Kissinger: Well, we are now in this position: as of today, we are caught between Hanoi and Saigon, both of them facing us down in a position of total impotence, in which Hanoi is just stringing us along, and Saigon is just ignoring us. Hanoi—I do not see why Hanoi would want to settle three weeks from now when they didn't settle this week. I do not see what additional factors are going to operate. I'm making a cold-blooded analysis . . .

Now, I would recommend that we leave open the possibility of this settlement, if the other side meets the very minimum conditions that we have indicated. I would then recommend that we start bombing the bejeezus out of them within 48 hours of having put the negotiating record out. And I would then recommend that after about two weeks of that, we offer withdrawal for prisoners, about the time that the Congress comes back—

Nixon: Yeah. . . .

Kissinger: I think there's a 50–50 chance if we give them a tremendous wallop, particularly not the sort of shit the Air Force likes to do, if I may use this word—

Nixon: I went over this with them—

Kissinger: —but if we did—

Nixon: It is shit.

Kissinger: If we got all their power plants in one day, so that the civilian population would be without light, knocked out all the docks in Haiphong, so that even if the harbor is cleared, they can't unload there for months to come, then they would know it's . . . We'd have to do it with smart bombs.

Nixon: Well, can then we knock out docks, then, without knocking out the ships? . . .

Kissinger: I'd frankly take my chance on the ships. Your great asset, Mr. President—

Nixon: All right. Take a chance on the ships. All right—

Kissinger: —is your unpredictability—

Nixon: Look, I'm going to do it. . . . Do you think they want to settle?

Kissinger: Mr. President, they are—

Nixon: Do you think they're going to?

Haig: Yes, if they get a good kick in the ass.

Kissinger: They are scared out of their minds that you'll resume bombing. . . .

Nixon: Now, the other point is: what about the [B–]52s? Can't they get in there now?

Kissinger: Yes.

Nixon: Well goddamnit, let's get them in. What's wrong with getting the '52s in—?

Kissinger: Well, we've done—

Nixon: Are we afraid they're going to be shot down?

Kissinger: Well, no. We've got the problem, Mr. President, let's face it: the Chief—the Chairman of the Chiefs [Admiral Thomas Moorer] is a Navy lobbyist; he's not a military commander. . . The Chiefs only give a damn about budget categories. . . . They didn't give one goddamn about the national interest. . . .

Nixon: Well, that's the point. They've got to get it done right, for a change. We cannot make these military decisions and take all the heat, and have them screw it up again. . . .

Kissinger: Thieu's behavior has also been totally unforgivable, Mr. President—

Nixon: Terrible. Never said a goddamn word of thanks for what we've done standing by him, and the rest. . . . I am fed up with him, totally, right up to the [unclear]—

Kissinger: He's been incompetent as a war leader. . .

Nixon: I don't give a goddamn what he accepts. . . . Now, Laird will bitch about the cost of this.

Haig: Right.

Nixon: Now, what is it? Sure, it's a problem. How much is the cost of this?

Kissinger: It's pretty high.

Haig: It—

Nixon: Bombing?

Haig: The real scrub will be about $3 billion, if it had to go through 'til—to June. If it stops short of that, we're talking about 1.5.

Kissinger: I think, Mr. President—

Nixon: You think 1.5—?

Kissinger: —these guys—

Nixon: The Defense Department is going to have to swallow it, anyway. . . .

Nixon: I don't want anybody flying over Christmas Day. People would not understand that. There's always been a truce; World War I, World War II, and so forth. All right, the main thing is for you to get rested and get ready for all this and go out there and just remember that when it's toughest, that's when we're the best. And remember, we're going to be around and outlive our enemies. And also, never forget, the press is the enemy.

Kissinger: On that, there's no question—

Nixon: The press is the enemy. The press is the enemy. The establishment is the enemy. The professors are the enemy. Professors are the enemy. Write that on the blackboard 100 times and never forget it.

Kissinger: I, on the professors—

Nixon: Always—

Kissinger: —I need no instruction at all.

Nixon: Always—

Kissinger: And on the press, I'm in complete agreement with you—

Nixon: It's the enemy . . . Yes, there are still a few patriots, but most of them are—they're very disappointed because we beat 'em in the election. They know they're out of touch with the country. It kills those bastards. They are the enemy, and we're just gonna continue to use them, and never let them think that we think they're the enemy. You see my point? But the press is the enemy. The press is the enemy. That's all.

Kissinger: Mr. President, if you don't do this—

Nixon: [laughs]

Kissinger: —you'll be—

Nixon: I'll do it.

Kissinger: —then you'll really be impotent, and you'll be caught between the liberals and the conservatives. You won't win the liberals. And—and, besides, we'll be totally finished by February. They'll be just be chopping the salami.

Source: Office of the Historian. *Foreign Relations of the United States, 1969–1976*, vol. IX, Vietnam, October 1972–January 1973. Document 175. "Conversation Among President Nixon, the President's Assistant for National Security Affairs (Kissinger), and the President's Deputy Assistant for National Security Affairs (Haig)." National Archives, Nixon Presidential Materials, White House Tapes, Oval Office, Conversation 823-1. No classification marking.

27.3 NEW YORK RADICAL WOMEN, *PRINCIPLES* (1968) AND PAT MAXWELL, "HOMOSEXUALS IN THE MOVEMENT" (1970)

Two documents authored by groups from New York City testify to the rising demands for women's rights and gay rights toward the end of the 1960s. In different ways, the pioneering feminist group, New York Radical Women, and the equally pioneering members of the Gay Liberation Front, convey a common sense of oppression, identity, and pride.

New York Radical Women, *Principles* (1968)

We take the woman's side in everything.

We ask not if something is "reformist," "radical," "revolutionary," or "moral." We ask: is it good for women or bad for women?

We ask not if something is "political." We ask: is it effective? Does it get us closest to what we really want in the fastest way?

We define the best interests of women as the best interests of the poorest, most insulted, most despised, most abused woman on earth. Her lot, her suffering and abuse is the threat that men use against all of us to keep us in line. She is what all women fear being called, fear being treated as and yet what we all really are in the eyes of men. She is Everywoman: ugly, dumb (dumb broad, dumb cunt), bitch, nag, hag, whore, fucking and breeding machine, mother of us all. Until Everywoman is free, no woman will be free. When her beauty and knowledge is revealed and seen, the new day will be at hand.

We are critical of all past ideology, literature and philosophy, products as they are of male supremacist culture. We are re-examining even our words, language itself.

We take as our source the hitherto unrecognized culture of women, a culture which from long experience of oppression developed an intense appreciation for life, a sensitivity to unspoken thoughts and the complexity of simple things, a powerful knowledge of human needs and feelings.

We regard our feelings as our most important source of political understanding.

We see the key to our liberation in our collective wisdom and our collective strength.

"Homosexuals in the Movement" (1970)

Bernard: I see the Gay Liberation Movement as a process which will help liberate gay people by making them fully part of the whole liberation movement. The movement for change in the system that will eventually annihilate any form of oppression. Before GLF I was active in these movements, but anonymously—nobody was conscious of the fact that I was homosexual. I think, the only way we can gain respect for ourselves and any of the help that we need from everyone else in overcoming our oppression is by showing that we participate even though they don't understand why we participate. I think even among a lot of our own people we have to fight for the right to participate as homosexuals.

Bob: I've always been active as a homosexual. Openly, but never publicly. In the past six or seven months I have suddenly found myself living the life of a public homosexual. I find resentment in many parts of the movement. When I find it, I confront it. This is very healthy for me; and it's very healthy for the movement. We can't hold the movement up as being any better or any worse than the rest of us. Gay Liberation to me is seeing 35 or 40 homosexuals marching as homosexuals in a vigil to free political prisoners. We have been political prisoners, and we will be political prisoners. Homosexuals are beginning to see themselves as an oppressed minority. I don't think homosexuality is a magic tie that binds us all but in a sense there is something. It's being proud of ourselves. And I think that's what liberation will help us find—a pride that we can just stand up and be proud of ourselves as human beings.

Bernard: I want to bring up the past in one way. When I was among young people, we had no way of expressing this. I never felt sick, although the attitude then was that we were a sickness. I could only fight this when I talked to individuals. We had no public way of fighting it. And it's exciting to be able to do it now, and the fight must be a very conscious fight.

Bob: Kay, do you have anything to say. Say something, we'll have Women's Liberation after us if you don't.

Kay: I'm very new in GLF and I don't have a great deal to say to people who want to know what it is. I see half of the gay liberation as a sort of attempt to try to change other people outside of ourselves—to try to make them stop oppressing us. But the half that interests me most now, at the beginning of my gay liberation, is self-liberation. I was never open or public. I always felt that I had to be a secret homosexual, and I was terrified. Indeed I am now. This article is the first time I have ever come out in a public way, and I find that a great deal of the oppression is built into myself—is built into us. So I still expect when I come out, people are going to dislike me because I am homosexual. People do dislike homosexuals. On the other hand, I myself have disliked my own homosexuality, so perhaps it's not going to be as bad as I thought.

Bernard: Although I haven't been a public homosexual, among my friends, it was always known. What interests me now is that, although I was completely loved, for me, being a homosexual,

I find that now that I'm getting active in GLF there's a resentment. People wonder why I have to work as a homosexual in the movement. Why I can't I take it up wherever I am in the movement. I don't think you can take it up wherever you are in the movement. It's only possible when we are working as a homosexual to take it up. I think that we should—those of us who can—be public as well as open.

Bob: I've been in the Village a long time, and I'm well known. There's a lunch room restaurant owned by a homosexual—not an open or public homosexual—but open to homosexuals. Since I've been in GLF, when I've walked into the restaurant, he announces in a very loud voice, "Well, here comes the Gay Liberation Front." I felt, Wow!, and heads turned, There I stood: Capt. Dum Dum, the Gay Liberation Front. I said something like, "Right on!," and sat down and ate. Nothing happened. Nothing at all. Much of our own oppression is in our own minds.

Pat: Well, it seems that as homosexuals in the movement, we have realized that just backing other causes won't liberate us in our particular oppression. Now we have a strange situation setting up where we find oppression in and out of the movement. In terms of homosexuality, the awareness of that oppression isn't anywhere except as that awareness develops in us.

Sources: Robin Morgan, *The Word of a Woman: Feminist Dispatches, 1968–1992* (New York: W. W. Norton & Company, 1992). Pat Maxwell, "Homosexuals in the Movement," *Come Out! A Liberation Forum for the Gay Community* 1, no. 3 (April/May 1970): 8–9.

27.4 STATEMENTS BY ROMAN PUCINSKI, ETHNIC HERITAGE STUDIES CENTERS; HEARINGS BEFORE THE GENERAL SUBCOMMITTEE ON EDUCATION OF THE COMMITTEE ON EDUCATION AND LABOR (1970)

In February 1970, a subcommittee of the House of Representatives held hearings over a bill to provide federal support for schoolchildren to learn about "cultural heritages of the major ethnic groups in the nation." In his remarks to witnesses, subcommittee chair Roman Pucinski, a Polish American Democrat from Chicago, revealed the pride and resentment that drove the "white ethnics," German, Irish, Polish, Italian, Greek, and Slavic Americans who took pride in the fact that their ethnic heritage set them apart from other Americans. For them, ethnicity meant a grounding in family, neighborhood, and religion. They rejected such ideas as the individualistic American dream, the new liberalism of the 1960s, and centralized government.

There is a growing sense of sameness permeating our existence—threatening to quiet the creative outpourings of the human soul and the gentle sensitivity of one man to the uniqueness and humanity of another.

Clearly, this sustained melancholia has touched all our lives. Perhaps most seriously afflicted by the deteriorating quality of human life are the young. The Nation's youth are engrossed in a restless, sometimes tumultuous, and often threatening search for identity. Our young people want to know who they are, where they belong, how they can remain distinctive: special individuals amidst the pervasive pressure for conformity.

[T]he basic problem in this country is that we have tried to deny our ethnicity . . . We have engaged in a noble experiment of trying to put 200 million human beings into a melting pot, and trying to make them something that they are not. We have never really tried to tell the American people anything about themselves. I am aware of the influence of the predominant white Anglo-Saxon Protestant ethos that has somewhat been imposed upon every person in this country, whether he wants it or not. . . .

You can go through this whole country and it is amazing how little material you can find about the Italian community, Americans of Italian descent; and, as you know, no group in this country has suffered a greater injustice in terms of outright distortion. You can go into the hustings of America and it is abominable what impressions the people have of an American citizen who happens, by circumstance or happenstance to have an Italian name, simply because of the films that they have seen or late movies on the TV that they have seen, or the kind of press they have seen.

. . . It is an interesting thing now. The Soviet Union is a nation of many states, many nationalities. They have the Georgians and various others, and interestingly enough, in the Soviet Union they encourage the cultural identity of each of these groups. But then, of course, they bring them into their single political structure or governmental structure or whatever you want to call it. They, as a matter of fact, encourage friendly competition among the various ethnic groups of the Soviet Union. This has brought about better understanding, friendly relationships among the various ethnic groups. . . .

We, on the other hand, in this country try to sweep them under the rug and deny it. And I think that a lot of these latent hostilities that we see in people generally, sometimes we think only in terms of problems between the races in America. I think that you have brought up a good point when you talked about the executive suite being closed to all but the chosen few in this country. I think this is a subject that is going to become more and more discussed in America.

Why is it that you can walk through some of the big corporations of this country and you look over the corporate structure and you find a predominance of one category of people? I don't mind telling you I have dinner very often with executives and presidents of the corporations, and they look at my name and they say, "Why, you have a Polish background."

I say, "Yes, I do." They say, "They are hard workers, they are the best workers we have in our plants."

I say, "I am very grateful to you for that, but how many of them are executives?" Then they kind of blush 14 different shades of red and they say, "I don't think we have any."

I say, "Why? If they are good workers, how come?"

Source: Statements by Roman Pucinski, *Ethnic Heritage Studies Centers. Hearings Before the General Subcommittee on Education of the Committee on Education and Labor. House of Representatives. Ninety-First Congress. Second Session on H.R. 14910. Hearings Held in Washington, D.C., February 1, 17, 18, 24, 26; March 4, 5, 19; and May 6, 1970* (Washington, DC: US Government Printing Office, 1970), pp. 1 and 256–259.

27.5 JIMMY CARTER, ADDRESS TO THE NATION ON ENERGY AND NATIONAL GOALS: "THE MALAISE SPEECH" (1979)

After 11 days of dialogue and contemplation at the presidential retreat Camp David, President Jimmy Carter addressed the nation on television the evening of July 15, 1979. With unusual candor for an American politician, the president laid out what he called the national "crisis of confidence" that had developed in the midst of energy and economic problems in the years after the Vietnam War. Carter's address became known as the "malaise" speech, even though he did not use the word. The address would be remembered as another unpopular act of a supposedly failed president, even though the national audience responded positively to it.

I know, of course, being President, that government actions and legislation can be very important. That's why I've worked hard to put my campaign promises into law—and I have to admit, with just mixed success. But after listening to the American people I have been reminded again that all the legislation in the world can't fix what's wrong with America. So, I want to speak to you first tonight about a subject even more serious than energy or inflation. I want to talk to you right now about a fundamental threat to American democracy.

I do not mean our political and civil liberties. They will endure. And I do not refer to the outward strength of America, a nation that is at peace tonight everywhere in the world, with unmatched economic power and military might.

The threat is nearly invisible in ordinary ways. It is a crisis of confidence. It is a crisis that strikes at the very heart and soul and spirit of our national will. We can see this crisis in the growing doubt about the meaning of our own lives and in the loss of a unity of purpose for our Nation.

The erosion of our confidence in the future is threatening to destroy the social and the political fabric of America.

The confidence that we have always had as a people is not simply some romantic dream or a proverb in a dusty book that we read just on the Fourth of July. It is the idea which founded our Nation and has guided our development as a people. Confidence in the future has supported everything else—public institutions and private enterprise, our own families, and the very Constitution of the United States. Confidence has defined our course and has served as a link between generations. We've always believed in something called progress. We've always had a faith that the days of our children would be better than our own.

Our people are losing that faith, not only in government itself but in the ability as citizens to serve as the ultimate rulers and shapers of our democracy. As a people we know our past and we are proud of it. Our progress has been part of the living history of America, even the world. We always believed that we were part of a great movement of humanity itself called democracy, involved in the search for freedom, and that belief has always strengthened us in our purpose. But just as we are losing our confidence in the future, we are also beginning to close the door on our past.

In a nation that was proud of hard work, strong families, close-knit communities, and our faith in God, too many of us now tend to worship self-indulgence and consumption. Human identity is no longer defined by what one does, but by what one owns. But we've discovered that owning things and consuming things does not satisfy our longing for meaning. We've learned that piling up material goods cannot fill the emptiness of lives which have no confidence or purpose.

The symptoms of this crisis of the American spirit are all around us. For the first time in the history of our country a majority of our people believe that the next 5 years will be worse than the past 5 years. Two-thirds of our people do not even vote. The productivity of American workers is actually dropping, and the willingness of Americans to save for the future has fallen below that of all other people in the Western world.

As you know, there is a growing disrespect for government and for churches and for schools, the news media, and other institutions. This is not a message of happiness or reassurance, but it is the truth and it is a warning.

These changes did not happen overnight. They've come upon us gradually over the last generation, years that were filled with shocks and tragedy.

We were sure that ours was a nation of the ballot, not the bullet, until the murders of John Kennedy and Robert Kennedy and Martin Luther King, Jr. We were taught that our armies were always invincible and our causes were always just, only to suffer the agony of Vietnam. We respected the Presidency as a place of honor until the shock of Watergate.

We remember when the phrase "sound as a dollar" was an expression of absolute dependability, until 10 years of inflation began to shrink our dollar and our savings. We believed that our Nation's resources were limitless until 1973, when we had to face a growing dependence on foreign oil.

These wounds are still very deep. They have never been healed.

Looking for a way out of this crisis, our people have turned to the Federal Government and found it isolated from the mainstream of our Nation's life. Washington, D.C., has become an island. The gap between our citizens and our Government has never been so wide. The people are looking for honest answers, not easy answers; clear leadership, not false claims and evasiveness and politics as usual.

What you see too often in Washington and elsewhere around the country is a system of government that seems incapable of action. You see a Congress twisted and pulled in every direction by hundreds of well-financed and powerful special interests. You see every extreme position defended to the last vote, almost to the last breath by one unyielding group or another. You often see a balanced and a fair approach that demands sacrifice, a little sacrifice from everyone, abandoned like an orphan without support and without friends.

Often you see paralysis and stagnation and drift. You don't like it, and neither do I. What can we do?

First of all, we must face the truth, and then we can change our course. We simply must have faith in each other, faith in our ability to govern ourselves, and faith in the future of this Nation. Restoring that faith and that confidence to America is now the most important task we face. It is a true challenge of this generation of Americans.

One of the visitors to Camp David last week put it this way: "We've got to stop crying and start sweating, stop talking and start walking, stop cursing and start praying. The strength we need will not come from the White House, but from every house in America."

We know the strength of America. We are strong. We can regain our unity. We can regain our confidence. We are the heirs of generations who survived threats much more powerful and awesome than those that challenge us now. Our fathers and mothers were strong men and women who shaped a new society during the Great Depression, who fought world wars, and who carved out a new charter of peace for the world.

We ourselves are the same Americans who just 10 years ago put a man on the Moon. We are the generation that dedicated our society to the pursuit of human rights and equality. And we are the generation that will win the war on the energy problem and in that process rebuild the unity and confidence of America.

We are at a turning point in our history. There are two paths to choose. One is a path I've warned about tonight, the path that leads to fragmentation and self-interest. Down that road lies a mistaken idea of freedom, the right to grasp for ourselves some advantage over others. That path would be one of constant conflict between narrow interests ending in chaos and immobility. It is a certain route to failure.

All the traditions of our past, all the lessons of our heritage, all the promises of our future point to another path, the path of common purpose and the restoration of American values. That path leads to true freedom for our Nation and ourselves. We can take the first steps down that path as we begin to solve our energy problem.

Source: Jimmy Carter, Address to the Nation on Energy and National Goals: "The Malaise Speech," July 15, 1979.

The Triumph of Conservatism

1980-1991

< The Fall of the Berlin Wall

869

AMERICAN PORTRAIT

Linda Chavez

"On Election Day 1980," Linda Chavez recalled, "I did something I had never imagined I could do: I voted for a Republican for president." A lifelong Democrat, she rejected her party's nominee, incumbent Jimmy Carter, and pulled the lever instead for the conservative Ronald Reagan. Chavez admitted that she made "an unlikely conservative." The daughter of an Anglo mother and a Mexican American father, Chavez had grown up in the Mexican American neighborhoods of Albuquerque and Denver. Her father, like most Mexican Americans, was a Democrat. Chavez herself was drawn to the party and its causes. As a girl in the early 1960s, she joined the civil rights organization CORE and demonstrated against racial discrimination. Chavez then worked for the Democratic National Committee, a liberal Democratic congressman, two liberal teachers unions, and the Carter administration.

Despite her partisan commitments, Chavez had been changing. As a student at the University of Colorado at Boulder in the late 1960s, Chavez discovered that she did not have to settle for her parents' working-class world. "For the first time," she said, "I realized that I could control my own destiny." Chavez also felt that the university's affirmative action programs shortchanged Mexican Americans by admitting unqualified students, allowing them to founder, teaching them to blame their problems on racism, and then leaving them to drop out.

Those realizations helped Chavez develop a new political outlook in the 1970s. She believed that individuals should take responsibility for their lives. She also rejected affirmative action programs, race-based hiring quotas, busing, and bilingual education as misguided liberal attempts to create equality.

Meanwhile, her stint in the Carter administration left her skeptical about another liberal article of faith. "The federal government was not at all what I expected," Chavez confessed. "Nothing—and almost no one—worked." She was troubled, too, that Carter and the Democrats did not support anti-Communism and a strong defense.

In some ways, Chavez felt that she was not the one who had changed. It was her party that had changed by adopting controversial solutions to racial and gender inequality and by abandoning its pledge to contain Communism. In 1976, Chavez stayed home rather than vote for Carter. By 1980, she was ready to vote for Reagan, another longtime Democrat who felt his party had changed.

Linda Chavez was an unusual figure: there were hardly any prominent Mexican American conservatives, male or female. But her change from liberal Democrat to conservative Republican typified a basic shift in the 1980s. Still dealing with economic and political decline, a new majority of Americans, including businesspeople, evangelical Christians, and "Reagan Democrats" like Chavez, adopted a conservative vision of the country. Rejecting the pessimism of the 1970s, they wanted to believe that individual and national success was still possible. The new conservative majority was open to materialism and to a government that left people free to succeed or fail.

The trend toward conservatism had many consequences. Eager to restore old values, Reagan cut taxes, reduced government regulation, and diminished union power to restore economic growth. The president also embraced a conservative social agenda, including attacks on affirmative action and abortion. His foreign policy was dedicated to confronting Communism. Despite scandals, setbacks, and compromises, Reagan and the new conservatism arrested fears of decline and altered America's politics and culture for a generation.

Creating a Conservative Majority

In the 1970s and 1980s, the conservative movement continued its rise to power. The New Right drew strength from the transformation of the economy, the changing reputation of big business, and the growth of evangelical Christianity. Conservative power became clear in the 1980 presidential election, when voters sent Ronald Reagan to the White House.

The New Economy

Conservatism benefited from the emergence of a postindustrial, computer-centered economy. As deindustrialization continued, technological change pointed the way to national economic revival. Along with other innovations, semiconductors—transistorized integrated circuits attached to small silicon crystals—allowed manufacturers to shrink the computer. By the late 1970s, they could put the power of a room-sized mainframe computer into a box that fit on a desktop. In 1981, IBM introduced its first personal computer, or PC. By the end of the 1980s, Americans were buying 7 million PCs a year (see Figure 28–1).

Computers seemed a way out of national economic decline. The microcomputer bolstered older companies such as IBM and created new firms such as Apple and Dell; it enriched new entrepreneurs such as Steve Jobs, a founder of Apple, and Bill Gates, a founder of Microsoft. Asian manufacturers built most consumer-electronics products, but American companies dominated computer hardware and software.

The growth of the computer industry inspired utopian dreams of a high-technology society built on the production of knowledge rather than things. Promoting literacy and education, the computer would lift up the poor and disadvantaged. Unlike the old industrial economy, a computerized economy would cut pollution and the consumption of raw materials. Enabling people to work at home, the microcomputer would eliminate commuting and relieve urban congestion.

The promise of the computer-driven economy helped conservatism. New industries, new companies, and new jobs seemed to confirm conservatives' faith in capitalist free enterprise, unaided by government. The new economy also benefited conservatism by stimulating the flow of people, jobs, and political power from the North and East to the South and West. Computing did revive parts of the Rustbelt. In Massachusetts, computer companies sprang up around Boston along Route 128 to replace long-gone textile mills and shoe factories. But computing most benefited the Sunbelt, birthplace of the new conservatism in the 1950s and 1960s. Dell's headquarters were in Texas. Apple was one of many computer firms clustered in the area called Silicon Valley, outside San Francisco.

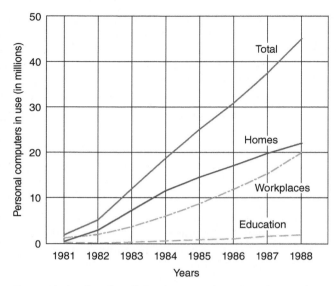

Figure 28-1 The Rise of the Personal Computer The rapid rise in the number of microcomputers in use in homes, workplaces, and schools in the 1980s inspired hopes that the nation's economic decline had ended.
Source: Statistical Abstract of the United States, 1989 (Washington, DC: US Bureau of the Census, 1990), p. 743; *Statistical Abstract, 1993* (Washington, DC: US Bureau of the Census, 1994), p. 761.

Rustbelt cities such as Pittsburgh and Detroit lost population, while some Sunbelt counties more than doubled in population. These regional shifts had direct political effects. Reapportionment in 1980 gave more congressional seats and electoral votes to the more conservative states of the Sunbelt.

The Rehabilitation of Business

While the 1980s pointed to a utopian future, the decade also recalled the cutthroat capitalism of the turn of the twentieth century. A wave of corporate takeovers and mergers swept the economy. Aggressive investment bankers and entrepreneurs such as Michael Milken and Ivan Boesky used junk bonds—high-risk, high-paying securities—and other techniques to finance takeovers. Executives took golden parachutes, huge payments for selling their companies and losing their jobs. Enormous deals merged some of the largest American corporations. In 1985, General Electric bought RCA for $6 billion. In 1986 alone, there were more than 4,000 mergers worth a total of $190 billion. The biggest deal came in 1988 when RJR Nabisco was sold for $25 billion, and the company's president and CEO received a $53 million golden parachute.

The takeover wave and the growth of the computer industry helped rehabilitate business and its values, under attack in the 1960s and 1970s. Although some observers criticized the concentration of so much economic power, others saw the takeovers as a sign of economic vitality. They argued that the mergers created larger, more efficient, more

Silicon Valley

It was, wrote a reporter, "an unlikely place to start a revolution." The Santa Clara Valley, south of San Francisco Bay, was a thin strip of lush orchards and conventional suburbs in the decades after World War II. Yet the region had long inspired a sense of promise and optimism. To farmers, it had been the "Valley of the Heart's Delight." By the 1980s, the area was the heart of "Silicon Valley," a much drier name, but just as full of promise and optimism. Silicon Valley, stretching from the mushrooming city of San Jose north through "intellectual boom-towns" on either side of San Francisco Bay, epitomized the hopes and accomplishments of the computer-centered new economy.

Like most revolutions, the rise of Silicon Valley was in fact the result of a long-term process. In the 1890s, the founding of Stanford University in Palo Alto established an engine for creativity and western economic development. In 1939, two Stanford graduates founded a pioneering electronics company, Hewlett-Packard, in Palo Alto. In the two decades after World War II, new companies sprang up, including National Semiconductor and Integrated Electronics Corporation (Intel). During the 1970s, computing took center stage. In 1971, Intel marketed the first commercial microprocessor, the 4004 chip. In 1976, Steve Jobs and Steve Wozniak started Apple Computing on a shoestring budget in Cupertino.

By the 1980s, Apple and other companies had created a distinctive regional culture of innovation and entrepreneurship. Hundreds of small start-up companies encouraged the unconventional. "Silicon Valley rewards people who don't fit in," said a businessman. "Steve Jobs would have been beaten into submission in the East." So Jobs and other entrepreneurs found riches in Silicon Valley. "This is the modern gold rush," declared a therapist in Palo Alto. "There is a strike-it-rich phenomenon, a feeling that 'I can do it as well as anybody else.'"

By the end of the decade, "Silicon Valley" meant even more than a cluster of companies and a culture. The term stood now for the whole range of computer-based technology business in the United States, just as "Detroit" stood for the nation's automobile business.

Silicon Valley was supposed to be an improvement over Detroit. The Michigan city's automobiles, typical of the smokestack-driven industrial economy, had helped pollute the American environment. Silicon Valley promised a less environmentally damaging future, but the reality was more complicated. Automobiles still transported the employees of Silicon Valley to and from work and contributed to pollution. In the 1980s, companies began moving their factories out of the valley to other nations, where still more pollution occurred.

The manufacturing shift did reflect a basic difference from Detroit. The Michigan city had remained affordable for the working class. For decades, the automobile industry had provided high-wage jobs and a middle-class standard of living for working-class Americans. Silicon Valley, in contrast, had become a crowded, expensive place that catered to the educated elite. The valley's manufacturing jobs increasingly benefited foreigners, not working-class Americans.

Perhaps Silicon Valley did not point to such a rosy economic and environmental future, after all. Could the region remain the "Valley of the Heart's Delight"?

competitive companies, and they praised takeover artists as models of energy and creativity. The media enthusiastically reported on Milken, Boesky, Jobs, and Gates. *Dallas, Dynasty*, and other popular television shows celebrated the fictional sagas of wealthy, freewheeling families. Business was more respectable than at any time since the 1950s.

So were materialism and the pursuit and enjoyment of wealth. "Everybody should be a little greedy," Boesky advised. "Thank goodness it's back," gushed the *New York Times*, "that lovely whipped cream of a word—luxury."

The baby boom generation reflected the new appeal of business. Former 1960s radicals such as Yippie (Youth Independent Party) leader Jerry Rubin took up business careers. By 1983, the media were talking about the emergence of yuppies, young urban professionals in their 20s and 30s. Uninterested in social reform, these optimistic, self-centered baby boomers were supposedly eager to make lots of money and then spend it on BMW cars, Perrier water, and other playthings. Although the transition from Yippies to yuppies was exaggerated, the yuppie stereotype underscored American aspirations to a more conservative, money-centered way of life.

The Rise of the Religious Right

As American culture celebrated materialism, many Americans still turned to spirituality to find meaning in their lives. Their choice of denominations reflected the trend to conservatism. Such mainline Protestant denominations as the United Methodist Church, the Episcopal Church, and the Presbyterian Church, USA, had been losing their share of church members since at least 1940. Meanwhile, evangelical churches boomed (see Map 28–1). By the 1980s, the Southern Baptist Convention was the largest American Protestant denomination. Such smaller evangelical bodies as the Assemblies of God more than doubled in size from the 1960s to the 1980s.

This changing denominational balance had social and political consequences. The mainline churches often took moderate or liberal positions on such issues as civil rights and abortion, but the evangelical churches more often supported conservative positions. Troubled by social change and emboldened by their own growth, evangelicals wanted to spread a conservative message across American culture and politics.

The emergence of "televangelists" was the most obvious result of this impulse. From 1978 to 1989, the number of Christian television ministries grew from 25 to 336. The most successful televangelists also had their own networks, colleges, political groups, and even an amusement park. Pat Robertson, a born-again Baptist from Virginia, hosted *The 700 Club* and ran the Christian Broadcast Network. Jerry Falwell, a fundamentalist who believed in the literal interpretation of the Bible, hosted the *Old Time Gospel Hour* and founded Liberty Baptist College in Virginia. He also organized the Moral Majority, a political pressure group. Deeply conservative, the televangelists condemned women's liberation, abortion, gay rights, and liberal Great Society programs. They wanted prayer in public schools. Earning millions of dollars, they praised low taxes, limited government, and financial success. Determined to win what Falwell called the "war against sin," the televangelists were the spearheads of a religious Right ready for politics.

The 1980 Presidential Election

The new conservative majority came together in the presidential election of 1980. Former California governor Ronald Reagan continued his political rise by winning the

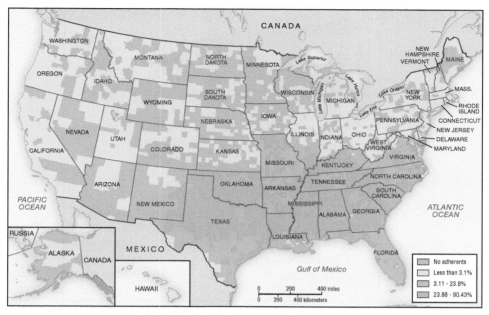

Map 28-1   The Growth of Evangelical Christianity The Southern Baptist Convention's share of the population, by county, reveals a gradual spread beyond its traditional base in the South by 1990.
Source: Peter L. Halvorson and William M. Newman, *Atlas of Religious Change in America, 1952–1990* (Cincinnati, OH: Glenmary Research Center, 1994), p. 120.

Republican nomination. Although he chose a moderate running mate, George H. W. Bush of Texas, Reagan ran a conservative campaign. His vision of less government, lower taxes, renewed military might, and traditional social values appealed to business and evangelicals. His genial optimism suggested that the political system could be made to work. As a former Democrat, Reagan reassured Democrats and independents that they too could find a home in the Republican Party.

Meanwhile, the Democratic nominee, incumbent president Jimmy Carter, struggled with a weak economy and the ongoing hostage crisis in Iran. His moderate, sometimes conservative policies had alienated liberal Democrats. His poor economic record had alienated the party's white ethnics. Moderate Republican congressman John Anderson of Illinois, who ran as an independent, drew voters away from Carter. Meanwhile, Reagan focused relentlessly on America's decline during Carter's presidency. In the last presidential debate before Election Day, Reagan told the audience, "I think . . . it might be well if you would ask yourself, are you better off than you were four years ago?"

Americans answered that question by giving Reagan the presidency. Reagan carried all but four states and the District of Columbia (see Map 28–2). He managed only 50.7 percent of the popular vote, but with Anderson's 6.6 percent, the tally suggested the extent of popular disaffection with Carter and the Democratic Party. The Democrats held on to the House of Representatives, but Republicans won the Senate for the first time since 1962. Sixteen years after the defeat of Barry Goldwater's conservative candidacy, the nation had turned sharply to the right.

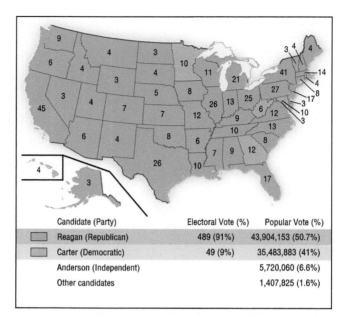

Candidate (Party)	Electoral Vote (%)	Popular Vote (%)
Reagan (Republican)	489 (91%)	43,904,153 (50.7%)
Carter (Democratic)	49 (9%)	35,483,883 (41%)
Anderson (Independent)		5,720,060 (6.6%)
Other candidates		1,407,825 (1.6%)

Map 28-2   The Presidential Election, 1980 As in other elections, a narrow victory in the popular vote translated into a landslide in the electoral college.

The Reagan Revolution at Home

Ronald Reagan shaped American life more decisively than any president since Franklin Roosevelt. Reagan's folksy optimism made him popular, but the Reagan years were more than a triumph of style. With some justice, his supporters believed that his "Reagan Revolution" spurred a sweeping conservative transformation of American economic and political life.

The Reagan Style

The Reagan Revolution was partly a matter of style. Despite the frustrations of the 1960s and 1970s, Reagan exuded optimism. Rather than ask Americans to live with less, he embraced luxury. Reagan's presidency signaled a confident, even opulent, new era. On Inauguration Day, as if to mark the end of the frustrating 1970s, the Iranian government finally released its American hostages. In his inaugural address, Reagan firmly rejected pessimism. "We are not," the new president declared, "doomed to an inevitable decline." The Reagan inaugural cost five times more than Jimmy Carter's had four years earlier.

Even while Ronald and Nancy Reagan lived lavishly in the White House, the president retained a popular, common touch. After his career in movies and television, he knew how to speak simply and effectively to the American people. He became known as the "Great Communicator."

Reagan also appeared to enjoy and master his job. Although he took office as America's oldest president at the age of 69, he projected vigor and energy. After the troubled presidencies of the 1970s, Reagan made the presidency—and democracy—seem workable again.

The president even managed to survive an assassination attempt. On March 30, 1981, John W. Hinckley, a troubled loner, shot and wounded Reagan, his press secretary, and a policeman. Reagan's chest wound was more serious than his spokesmen admitted, but he met the situation with good humor. "Honey," he told his wife, "I forgot to duck." The president's popularity soared.

Shrinking Government

Reagan offered a clear alternative to the New Deal and the Great Society. Above all, he denied that a large, activist federal government could deal with the challenges of American life in the 1980s. So Reagan vowed to reduce the government's size and power.

The president's efforts to shrink the federal government met with mixed success. In his 1982 State of the Union address, Reagan, like previous Republican president Richard Nixon, endorsed the New Federalism, a plan to transfer federal programs and tax revenues to the states. Reagan insisted the New Federalism would promote efficiency and economic growth, but governors worried that their states would be saddled with expensive responsibilities. In the end, only a few programs were transferred.

Congress also rebuffed administration plans to save money with tighter qualifications for government benefits and with a line-item veto permitting the president to reject specific spending programs.

Reagan had more success when he attacked social welfare programs. Like other conservatives, Reagan condemned antipoverty programs as a waste of federal resources that sapped the work ethic and the morals of the poor. He wanted reductions in food stamps, school meal programs, and aid to cities. In response, Congress cut funding for urban public housing and ended job training for the unemployed.

Reagan found it nearly impossible to touch Medicare and Social Security, two expensive and popular programs that benefited most Americans. By the 1980s, there was concern that workers' Social Security payments would eventually not be enough to cover the cost of benefits to retirees. After a long struggle, Congress produced the Social Security Reform Act of 1983, which raised the minimum age for full benefits from 65 to 67 and taxed some benefits. The measure did little to reduce program costs. By 1984, Reagan promised not to cut Social Security.

Although expenditures for welfare programs continued to rise, the Reagan administration managed to slow the growth of such spending. Benefits did not expand dramatically; there were no costly new programs. Reagan did not reduce the federal government overall, but he did shrink the relative size of some parts of it that he disliked.

Reaganomics

For Reagan and his followers, shrinking the government also meant decreasing Washington's role in the economy. As conservatives, they argued that the nation prospered most when Americans were left free to manage their own businesses and keep their own earnings. The Reagan administration worked to lower taxes, deregulate business, and cut federal support for unions.

"Reaganomics" drew on a new theory known as supply-side economics. In the 1970s, economist Arthur Laffer had offered an alternative to the liberal, Keynesian economics that had guided federal policy since the New Deal. While Keynesians believed that increased consumer demand would spur economic growth, Laffer contended that an increased supply of goods and services was the key to growth. He rejected the Keynesian idea that more government spending put more money in the hands of consumers. To promote prosperity, he believed government should cut, rather than raise, taxes. Leaving more money in the hands of businesses would allow them to produce more goods and services. The increase in supply would stimulate prosperity and increase, rather than decrease, tax revenues.

Supply-side economics was controversial. Liberal critics called it an excuse to let the rich keep more of their money. Even some Republicans doubted that a tax cut would produce more tax revenues. But the supply-side approach fit neatly with conservative dislike for high taxes and big government.

Following supply-side principles, Reagan asked Congress in 1981 to cut taxes dramatically. Impressed by Reagan's popularity and the electorate's conservatism, the Democratic-controlled House joined the Republican-dominated Senate to pass the Economic Recovery Act of 1981 (the Kemp-Roth Bill). An important victory for Reagan, it cut federal income taxes 5 percent the first year and 10 percent in each of the next two years. It benefited the wealthy by making the tax structure less progressive and by reducing the tax rates on the highest incomes and on large gifts and estates.

Like other conservatives, Reagan believed that federal regulations hamstrung American business and prevented economic growth. Accordingly, his administration stepped up the campaign for deregulation begun by Jimmy Carter. The budgets of such key regulatory agencies as the Environmental Protection Agency and the Occupational Safety and Health Administration were cut. The administration also made sure that officials did not strictly enforce regulatory rules and laws. In addition, the administration deregulated the telephone industry. In 1982, the giant American Telephone and Telegraph Company was broken into smaller regional companies, and new firms such as Sprint and MCI were allowed to compete for AT&T's long-distance business.

Reagan moved to lift environmental restrictions on business. His administration made it easier for timber and mining companies to exploit wilderness areas and for oil companies to drill off the Pacific coast. It also opposed environmentalists' demands for laws to protect against acid rain—industrial air pollution that harmed lakes, forests, and crops. Reaganomics also weakened organized labor, already suffering from deindustrialization. Ironically, Reagan, once the head of the Screen Actors Guild, was the first former union official to serve as president. Like most conservatives, Reagan believed that unions obstructed business and limited workers' freedom. He believed the federal government had done too much for organized labor since the New Deal.

Reagan took a strong antiunion stance during a strike by the Professional Air Traffic Controllers Organization (PATCO) in 1981. Despite a law banning strikes by federal workers, PATCO walked out to protest unsafe conditions in the air traffic control system. Reagan fired the striking controllers, refused to hire them back, and replaced them with nonunion workers. His action encouraged business to take a hard line with employees. By the end of the 1980s, unions were weaker than at any time since the Great Depression.

Reaganomics did not quite have the effect its supporters anticipated. Reagan's measures did not prevent a sharp recession, which began in the fall of 1981. As the Federal Reserve Bank fought inflation by raising interest rates, the economy slowed and unemployment increased. Reaganomics also increased the federal budget deficit. The supply-side theory that tax cuts would boost tax revenues and balance the budget proved incorrect.

By the spring of 1984, the recession had ended. Thanks largely to the Federal Reserve's monetary policy, "stagflation," the combination of stagnant economic growth and high inflation, was over. As employment increased, Reagan's supporters gave the president credit. His critics charged that the deficit, not Reaganomics, had produced the boom and that the deficit would ultimately hurt the economy. In the mid-1980s, however, Reaganomics seemed to be a success.

The 1984 Presidential Election

The changing impact of Reaganomics affected national politics. In the depths of the recession, the Republicans lost 26 House seats in the midterm elections of 1982. But with the return of prosperity, the president was easily renominated in 1984. Reagan ran against a liberal Democratic nominee, former vice president Walter Mondale of Minnesota. Against a popular incumbent, Mondale made bold moves. He chose the first female vice-presidential nominee of a major party, Representative Geraldine Ferraro of New York. To prove his honesty and openness, Mondale made the politically foolish announcement that he would raise taxes as president. The Democrat was also saddled with the record of the Carter administration and the alienation of white working- and middle-class Democrats.

Reagan ran an optimistic campaign emphasizing national renewal. "It's morning again in America," Reagan commercials announced. "And people have a sense of pride they never felt they'd feel again." Mondale would jeopardize all that, the Reagan campaign charged, with tax increases and favors to such "special interests" as labor unions, feminists, and civil rights groups.

Election Day revealed both the strength and the weakness of the Reagan Revolution. With his conservative message Reagan won 58.8 percent of the popular vote and lost only the District of Columbia and Mondale's home state of Minnesota. But his personal triumph did not translate into one for his party. Holding on to the Senate, the Republicans lost control of the House of Representatives.

The Reagan Revolution Abroad

Reagan's foreign policy, like his domestic policy, rested on old conservative values. The president rejected the main diplomatic approaches of the 1970s—Nixon's détente with the Soviet Union and Carter's support for international human rights. Instead, the Reagan Revolution revived the strident anti-Communism of the 1940s and 1950s. The president moved to restore the nation's military and economic power to challenge the Soviet Union and stop Communism in the Western Hemisphere. Communism, however, had little to do with such difficult international issues as conflict in the Middle East, terrorism, and global economic competition. Nevertheless, the Reagan Revolution refocused American policy on the cold war confrontation with Communism.

Restoring American Power

After losing the Vietnam War, the United States had reduced both its armed forces and its willingness to risk military confrontations abroad. Reagan set out to restore American power in the 1980s—and the will to use it.

Like most conservatives, the president did not believe that cutting government spending meant cutting the armed forces. Under Reagan, defense spending more than doubled, from $134 billion in 1980 to more than $300 billion by 1989. Reagan also ordered development of controversial weapons systems. Construction of the B-1 strategic bomber, stopped by Carter, resumed, while development of the B-2 Stealth bomber began. Reagan won congressional approval for the MX Peacekeeper, a nuclear missile with multiple warheads, and for work on the neutron bomb, a nuclear weapon. As he built up the military, Reagan faced a growing mass movement against nuclear weapons. In Europe and the United States, millions of people, frightened by nuclear war, called for a halt to new nuclear arms. In June 1982, a crowd of 700,000 in New York's Central Park demanded a nuclear freeze. The National Conference of Catholic Bishops supported the freeze and declared nuclear war immoral. But Reagan rejected the movement as naive and Communist-infiltrated. Peace, he believed, depended on developing more weapons.

The military buildup was also a matter of changing attitudes. In the wake of the Vietnam War, many Americans were reluctant to endorse intervention abroad. They feared becoming entrapped in another costly, losing, possibly immoral battle. This "Vietnam

Some of the 700,000 Demonstrators at the Nuclear Freeze Rally in New York City's Central Park, June 1982 For a time, the movement to halt new nuclear weapons challenged President Reagan's plans for an arms buildup.

syndrome" threatened Reagan's foreign policy. The president could not afford to let other countries think he would not back up his words with action. Accordingly, Reagan used his speeches to stir up patriotic emotion and to persuade Americans that the Vietnam War had been "a just cause" worth supporting.

By the mid-1980s, Reagan had restored much of America's military power. It remained to be seen, however, whether Americans were willing to use that power abroad.

Confronting the "Evil Empire"

The main purpose of the buildup was to contain the Soviet Union. Suspicion of the Soviets and their Communist ideology was the heart of Reagan's diplomacy. In the early 1980s, Reagan called the USSR the "evil empire" and insisted that failing economies and unpopular regimes doomed the Soviets and their Communist allies. Communism, he predicted, would end up "on the ash heap of history."

Reagan avoided cooperation with the Soviet Union and held no summit meetings during his first term. His administration openly supported the *mujahedeen*, the Afghan rebels who were resisting the Soviets. More important, he avoided arms-control agreements with the Soviets during his first term. Instead, he used the military buildup to pressure the USSR. Reagan refused to submit the second Strategic Arms Limitation Treaty, signed by Jimmy Carter, to the Senate for ratification. In response to the United States' deployment of new nuclear missiles in Western Europe, the Soviets walked out of arms-control talks in 1983.

That year, Reagan put even more pressure on the USSR by announcing plans for the Strategic Defense Initiative (SDI), a space-based defense system of lasers and other advanced technology designed to shoot down enemy missiles. Funded by Congress, SDI was such a long way from reality that critics, sure it was science fiction, called the plan "Star Wars," after the epic space movie.

SDI doubly threatened the Soviets. It seemingly made the USSR vulnerable to attack. Since the 1950s, the Americans and the Soviets had relied on the theory of mutual assured destruction as a deterrent to war: because a nuclear war would destroy both sides, there was no incentive for either to start one. Now SDI raised the possibility that because the United States could survive a nuclear attack, it might be willing to start a war with the Soviets. The Soviets would then need to develop their own SDI. There was the second threat: the USSR would have to divert scarce resources and perhaps weaken their economy in order to compete with the United States.

While the United States pressed the Soviets, Reagan wanted to avoid open confrontation with the major Communist powers. In 1983, a Soviet fighter plane shot down an unarmed Korean airliner, killing all 269 aboard. Although a US congressman was one of the victims, Reagan responded with restraint. A year later, Reagan traded visits with the premier of the People's Republic of China and encouraged stronger relations and a nuclear-weapons agreement.

The Reagan Doctrine in the Third World

The Reagan administration also changed American foreign policy toward the third world. Reagan and other conservatives had been impatient with the Carter administration's attempts to promote human rights abroad. The United States, they believed, needed to back anti-Communist, pro-American governments, whether or not they respected human rights. Jeane J. Kirkpatrick, who became Reagan's ambassador to the United Nations, distinguished between totalitarian regimes hostile to the United States and authoritarian governments friendly to American interests. Critics claimed this distinction was meaningless and insisted the nation not support antidemocratic governments. The administration adopted Kirkpatrick's view, which became known as the Reagan Doctrine.

The administration applied the Reagan Doctrine aggressively in Central America and the Caribbean (see Map 28–3). Determined to keep Communism out of the Western Hemisphere, the United States opposed the Marxist Sandinista government of Nicaragua and supported the repressive anti-Communist government of neighboring El Salvador.

Encouraged by the Carter administration, the Sandinistas had come to power in the late 1970s by overthrowing the dictatorship of Anastasio Somoza. The Reagan administration believed the Sandinistas were too friendly to the Soviet Union and to leftist rebels in El Salvador. Reagan halted aid to Nicaragua in April 1981 and directed the CIA to train, arm, and supply the Contra rebels, who opposed the Sandinistas. Many of the Contras had ties to the oppressive Somoza regime, but Reagan praised them as "freedom fighters." Meanwhile, the president strongly backed the right-wing military government of El Salvador, locked in a civil war with pro-Sandinista and pro-Cuban rebels. Employing infamous "death squads," the military government engaged in kidnapping, torture, and murder. Some 75,000 people died in the conflict. Still, Reagan did not want this brutal, undemocratic regime to fall. El Salvador, he explained, was "a textbook case of indirect armed aggression by Communist powers."

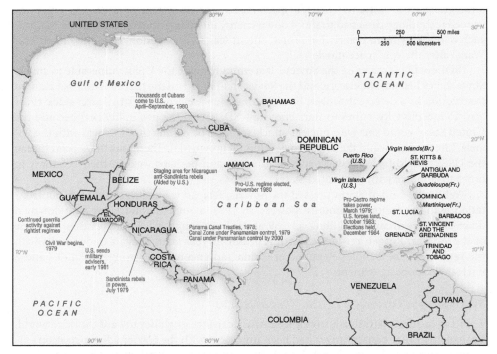

Map 28-3   The Reagan Doctrine in Central America and the Caribbean Events that shaped Reagan's anti-Communist initiative in the Western Hemisphere.

Reagan's Central American Policy The president holds up a T-shirt summing up his approach to the region: "STOP COMMUNISM CENTRAL AMERICA."

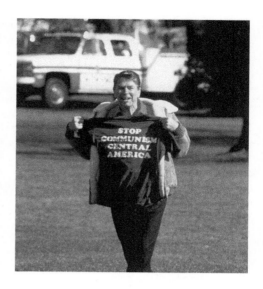

Despite such rhetoric, the administration could not persuade Congress to support its Central American policy. Congressional Democrats, like many Americans, did not want war in Central America. They were skeptical about the Communist threat and troubled by the antidemocratic character of the Salvadoran regime and the Contra rebels. In 1983, Congress approved Reagan's Caribbean Basin Initiative, an economic development package, but not military aid for the Salvadoran government. Instead, Congress passed the Boland Amendment, which restricted aid to the Contras and banned efforts to topple the Sandinista regime.

Reagan applied the Reagan Doctrine more successfully in the Caribbean. On October 25, 1983, US troops invaded the small island of Grenada, supposedly to protect about 1,000 Americans, mostly medical students, from a Marxist regime. Reagan feared Grenada would become a Cuban or Soviet base close to US shores. The invading force quickly secured the island and replaced the government with a pro-American regime. Critics charged that Reagan had violated the sovereignty of another state for an easy military victory. To his supporters, the invasion was a welcome demonstration of the Reagan Doctrine and an antidote to the Vietnam syndrome.

The president also applied the Reagan Doctrine in Africa. The Carter administration had condemned the long-standing policy of *apartheid*—racial separation—pursued by the white government of South Africa. Reagan, despite America's struggle with racial segregation, would not take such a strong stance. Rather than impose economic sanctions on South Africa, he endorsed mild diplomatic discussions known as "constructive engagement" while South Africa suffered violence and near civil war. Reagan held back because the South African regime was an ally against Communism in the region. During the 1980s, the United States supported South African military intervention in Angola, Mozambique, and Namibia against groups aided by Cuba and the Soviet Union. More than a million people died in these conflicts.

The Middle East and Terrorism

The Reagan Doctrine was not much help in dealing with the Middle East and the growing problem of terrorism. Communism and the Soviet Union had little impact on Middle Eastern issues in the 1980s. As before, the United States wanted to ensure its supply of oil and to support its longtime ally, Israel. There was no new Arab oil embargo during the Reagan years, but the administration could not bring peace to the Middle East or end the threat of terrorism.

The Ethiopian Famine

The devastating famine, brought on by drought, complicated by war, and worsened by government policies, began in the African nation of Ethiopia in 1983. Although foreshadowed for several years, the crisis in one of the poorest countries on earth evoked a surprisingly slow response from the United States and the rest of the world. The famine starkly illustrated America's diverse, uneven global connections in the age of the cold war.

As hundreds of thousands of Ethiopians died, most Americans knew little about the unfolding disaster. US television networks showed just over eight minutes' worth of stories on the famine in its first two years. Congressional hearings only briefly stirred public interest in 1983. As a result, American religious organizations, such as Catholic Relief Services, had a hard time raising money for Ethiopia.

The Reagan administration knew much more about the situation but was reluctant to aid a nation aligned with the Soviet Union. Mengistu Haile Mariam, leader of Ethiopia's Communist military junta, had nationalized US businesses and allowed in thousands of Soviet and Cuban military advisers. While the humanitarian crisis intensified, the Reagan administration even eliminated Ethiopian food aid from the budget for 1984. The USSR, federal officials suggested, ought to be providing help to its ally.

Then, a British film crew documented "the closest thing to hell on earth." Shown on more than 400 television stations around the world in October 1984, the film offered a stark, wrenching depiction of emaciated Ethiopians, a dying man, and dead children. In Britain, pop musicians, calling themselves Band Aid, quickly made a hit single, "Do They Know It's Christmas?," that raised money for famine relief. The combination of television coverage and musical celebrity dramatically changed popular awareness and response to the Ethiopian crisis.

In the United States, Americans made a flood of donations to charitable organizations. Church-related groups, including Roman Catholic, mainline and evangelical Protestant denominations, played a particularly important role in the response to

Reagan found it difficult to build on the Camp David Accords between Israel and Egypt, which were supposed to lead to self-government for the Palestinian Arabs living in the Israeli-occupied West Bank and Gaza Strip. Israel and the Palestine Liberation Organization (PLO), the official representative of the Palestinians, remained at odds. The PLO continued to threaten Israel from bases in neighboring Lebanon. In the spring of 1982, the Israelis invaded Lebanon, which was already convulsed by a civil war between Muslims and Christians.

To end the invasion and stabilize Lebanon, the United States sent marines to join an international peacekeeping force. On October 23, 1983, a terrorist bomb killed 241 Americans at marine headquarters in Beirut. The shocking attack marked a low point of Reagan's administration. The president did not retaliate. He did not want to reward terrorism by the famine. In Fort Myers, Florida, 60 teenagers from two Assembly of God churches fasted for 30 hours to raise money for World Vision International, an evangelical relief organiza-

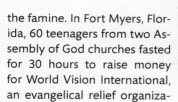

tion. The Church of Jesus Christ of Latter-Day Saints declared a special one-day fast that raised over $6 million from Mormons around the United States. Criticized for aiding a Communist government, the Mormon president answered "that where there is stark hunger, I will not let political considerations dull my sense of mercy or thwart my responsibility to the sons and daughters of God."

Inspired by their British counterparts, American pop musicians mobilized for the relief effort. Musicians of color, mindful of their African roots, played the lead role. Jamaican American folk musician and civil rights activist Harry Belafonte created United Support of Artists for Africa (USA for Africa). On behalf of the new

organization, African American pop stars Michael Jackson and Lionel Richie wrote "We Are the World," which was recorded by a mixed race group of musicians. "There comes a time when we heed a certain call," the song began. "When the world must come together as one." "We Are the World" quickly became a number-one hit in the United States and other countries.

Popular opinion, religious activism, and musical celebrity put enormous pressure on the Reagan administration to reverse course. The US government began providing hundreds of thousands of tons of food aid to Ethiopia. To make direct food donations legally easier, the administration even designated the Communist Mengistu regime a "friendly government"—a brief break from the cold war.

withdrawing from Lebanon. Nevertheless, he pulled out the soldiers in 1984, even though there was no peace in Lebanon and no agreement between the Israelis and the PLO.

The attack on the marine headquarters illustrated the growing threat of terrorism. Reagan vowed to make terrorists "pay for their actions," but terrorism proved hard to stop. Acts of terrorism by Palestinians and Libyans drew quick American reprisals in the 1980s. After Palestinians murdered an American passenger on a cruise ship in the Mediterranean in 1985, US planes forced down the Egyptian airliner carrying the escaping terrorists. The Reagan administration believed that Muammar Qaddafi, leader of the North African nation of Libya, supported terrorism. In 1982, US Navy fighter planes shot down two Libyan fighters. After American soldiers died in a terrorist bombing in West Germany in

1986, US jets bombed targets in Libya, among them military barracks and Qaddafi's personal residence, killing one of his daughters. Qaddafi seemed to become less critical of the United States, but the threat of terrorism did not go away.

Reagan also acted to safeguard America's oil supply. During a war between Iran and Iraq, the United States sent warships to protect oil tankers in the Persian Gulf. American intervention was costly. In May 1987, Iraqi missiles struck the US destroyer *Stark*, killing 37 of its crew. Unwilling to help Iran, Reagan accepted Iraq's apology. In July 1988, the US missile cruiser *Vincennes* accidentally shot down an Iranian airliner, killing 290 passengers. An American apology did not quell Iranian anger, but the Iran-Iraq war soon ended, and with it the threat to America's oil supply.

The United States and the World Economy

Middle Eastern oil was only one economic factor shaping Reagan's foreign policy. The president had to deal with strains on the world economy. Like presidents before him, Reagan believed strongly that free trade would boost national economies. He believed, too, that other nations would benefit from cutting taxes, government spending, and regulation. But after years of economic decline, the United States could not always impose its will on other nations.

Reagan did force his views on weak, debt-ridden, third-world countries. By the end of the 1980s, developing nations owed foreign banks more than $1.2 trillion. Mexico was more than $100 billion in debt. American banks would lose heavily if those nations defaulted on loans. American producers stood to lose if those countries could not afford to buy US goods. The Reagan administration refused to protect American banks from defaults, instead forcing debtor countries to adopt freer trade, deregulation of business, and austerity programs in return for new loans.

The Reagan administration had much less power to dictate trade policy with Japan. As Japanese exports flowed into the United States, Americans increasingly resented Japan's control of its home market. Congress, believing Japan discriminated against American goods, pushed for retaliation. Japan placed voluntary quotas on its export of steel and automobiles to the United States. Although the United States devalued the dollar to make American goods cheaper, the trade imbalance continued. In 1988, the president signed the Omnibus Trade and Competitiveness Act, which allowed the government to place high tariffs on Japanese goods if Japan discriminated against American goods. But as long as Americans wanted Japanese products, retaliation was unlikely. In 1989, a Japanese car, the Honda Accord, was the first international model to become the best-selling automobile in America.

Many Accords had been made in the United States. Even as the administration struggled to open Japanese markets to American goods, Japanese firms increased their direct investment in the United States. Honda built a new factory in Marysville, Ohio, to produce Accords for the American market. As Japanese companies built or took over other facilities, many Americans wondered whether the global expansion of trade really benefited their country after all.

The Battle over Conservative Social Values

For all of Ronald Reagan's success in the early 1980s, the new conservatism met with important opposition. The conservatives' social values were especially controversial. Angered by the changes of the 1960s, many conservatives, like Linda Chavez, wanted to restore supposedly traditional values and practices. The conservative agenda collided head-on with one of the chief legacies of the 1960s—disadvantaged groups' demands for equal rights and opportunities. Many Americans were also unwilling to abandon the social changes of the last generation. Faced with such opposition, conservatives failed to achieve much of their vision.

Attacking the Legacy of the 1960s

The new conservatism was driven by a desire to undo the liberal and radical legacies of the 1960s. Conservatives blamed federal courts for much of the social change over the last generation. In the 1960s and 1970s, liberal, activist justices had supported defendants' rights, civil rights, affirmative action, busing, and abortion while rejecting such conservative causes as school prayer.

Determined to take control of the courts, Reagan appointed many staunch, relatively young conservatives to the federal bench and the Supreme Court. In 1981, Sandra Day O'Connor, a fairly conservative judge from Arizona, became the Court's first woman justice. Reagan replaced retiring Chief Justice Warren Burger with conservative William Rehnquist. The appointments of two more conservatives, Antonin Scalia and Anthony Kennedy, seemed to push the Supreme Court away from liberalism.

It did not quite work out that way. In the 1980s, the Court followed conservative views in limiting the rights of defendants. Rulings in *United States v. Leon* and *Nix v. Williams* in 1984 made it easier for prosecutors to use evidence improperly obtained by police. However, on other issues, the Court took a moderate stance. In *Wallace v. Jaffree* in 1985, the Court invalidated an Alabama law that allowed schools to devote a minute each day to voluntary prayer or meditation.

Prayer was part of the conservatives' plan to reform public education. They believed that the federal government had played too large a role in the schools since the 1960s. Parents, meanwhile, had too little say in the education of their children. Preferring to use market forces rather than government to reform the schools, conservatives wanted to abolish the federal Department of Education. They also wanted to let parents choose the best schools—public or private—for their children and cover part of the cost with federally funded vouchers or tax credits.

Because many Americans worried about the quality of the schools, conservatives had a golden opportunity. But Congress refused to adopt vouchers or abolish the Department of Education.

Drug use was another issue conservatives linked to the 1960s. In the early 1980s, drugs again became a major concern with the spread of crack, a cheap, addictive form of cocaine. The sale and use of crack, especially in the cities, led to crime and violence. In 1986, the president and his wife, Nancy, announced a "national crusade" for a "drug-free" America. Their campaign encouraged young people to "Just Say No" to drugs, implemented drug testing for federal employees, and imposed mandatory minimum sentences for some drug use. The "war on drugs" was controversial. Critics called its rhetoric naive and ineffective. They also condemned new sentencing laws, which put millions in jail, as unfair to African Americans and expensive to taxpayers. Despite the crusade, drug use did not decrease appreciably.

Women's Rights and Abortion

One of the chief legacies of the 1960s was the women's rights movement. The new conservatism condemned feminism and deplored the changing role of women in America. Many conservatives, especially evangelical leaders, blamed feminists and liberal government for encouraging women to abandon their traditional family role for paid jobs. The conservative movement was especially determined to halt federal initiatives, such as affirmative action programs and the Equal Rights Amendment (ERA), that protected women's rights (see Chapter 27).

The conservative agenda on women's rights met with mixed results. The campaign for the ERA, lagging since the 1970s, ended unsuccessfully, but affirmative action programs to promote the hiring of women continued. So did women's push into the workplace and public life as more families needed two incomes. By 1983, women made up half of the paid workforce. As their economic role expanded, so did their political visibility. Ironically, Reagan gave women new public prominence by choosing Jeane J. Kirkpatrick and Sandra Day O'Connor for important offices.

Women still did not enjoy equality in America. They were generally paid less than men doing the same sort of work, and they had less opportunity to break through the "glass ceiling" and win managerial jobs. Commentators noted the feminization of poverty. Unmarried or divorced women, many with children, made up an increasing percentage of the poor. This unequal suffering, liberals and feminists argued, disproved the conservative claim that women did not need special protection.

For many conservatives, the right to abortion, guaranteed by the Supreme Court in *Roe v. Wade* in 1974, was the most troubling change in the status of women. A growing Right to Life movement passionately denounced abortion as the murder of the unborn, practiced by selfish women who rejected motherhood and family.

Conservatives failed to narrow abortion rights significantly in the 1980s (see Map 28–4). Reagan persuaded Congress to stop the use of federal funds to pay for

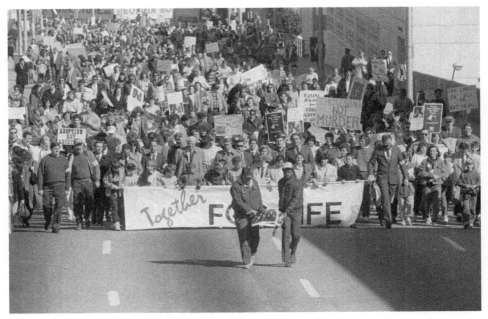

Pro-Life Protest Carrying a small coffin, a pro-life march protests the Supreme Court's *Roe v. Wade* decision in Atlanta, Georgia, in 1989.

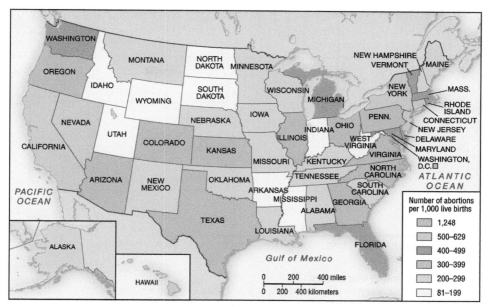

Map 28-4   Abortion in the 1980s The rate of abortions across the United States 14 years after the Supreme Court's decision legalizing abortion in *Roe v. Wade*.
Source: Timothy H. Fast and Cathy Carroll Fast, *The Women's Atlas of the United States, rev. ed.* (New York: Facts on File, 1995), p. 166.

abortions, but a constitutional amendment outlawing abortion stalled in the Senate. Supreme Court rulings in 1983 and 1986 upheld *Roe v. Wade*.

Gays and the AIDS Crisis

The gay rights movement was another legacy of the 1960s that troubled conservatives. Evangelical leaders such as Jerry Falwell condemned gays on religious grounds. Some people believed that equal rights for gay men and women would promote immorality and corrupt children. In 1977, Anita Bryant, a former Miss America, launched a national crusade, Save Our Children, to protest the passage of a gay rights ordinance in Florida. Voters soon repealed the measure. In San Francisco in 1978, Harvey Milk, the first avowedly gay member of the city's board of supervisors, was assassinated, along with the mayor, by a former supervisor. Many were shocked when the assassin received only a short jail sentence.

Despite such opposition, the gay rights movement made progress in the 1980s. In 1982, Wisconsin became the first state to pass a law protecting the rights of gay men and women. By the end of the decade, most states had repealed sodomy laws that criminalized gay sex. In *Bowers v. Hardwick* in 1986, however, the US Supreme Court dismissed a gay man's right to sexual privacy as "facetious."

The battle over gay rights took place against a tragic backdrop. In 1981, the Centers for Disease Control began reporting cases of acquired immune deficiency syndrome (AIDS), a disease that destroyed the body's immune system and left it unable to fight off infections and rare cancers. By the mid-1980s, researchers had traced AIDS to different forms of the

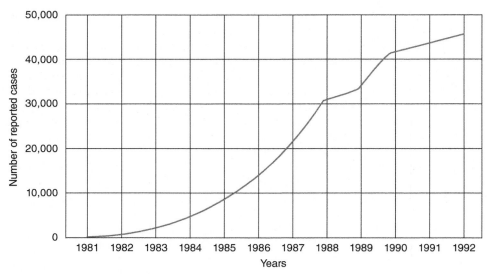

Figure 28–2   The Rapid Rise of AIDS
Source: Statistical Abstract of the United States, 1989, p. 111; Statistical Abstract, 1993, p. 203.

human immunodeficiency virus (HIV) that were transmitted in semen and blood. But no cure had been found. By 1990, there were nearly 100,000 recorded deaths from the AIDS epidemic in the United States (see Figure 28–2).

Because 75 percent of the first victims were gay men, Americans initially considered AIDS a gay disease. Some people, including evangelical leaders, believed this "gay cancer" was God's punishment for the alleged sin of same-sex love. It became clear, however, that AIDS could also be transmitted by heterosexual intercourse, by intravenous drug use with shared needles, and by tainted blood transfusions.

Although understanding of AIDS and HIV increased, the specter of "gay cancer" promoted homophobia and slowed the response to the disease. The AIDS Coalition to Unleash Power (ACT UP) and other organizations staged demonstrations and acts of civil disobedience to call attention to the crisis and push for government action. Nevertheless, the Reagan administration did not fund research on AIDS for several years, and the disease continued to spread.

The AIDS epidemic complicated the struggle over gay rights. For some Americans, the disease reinforced the conservative condemnation of gays. For others, the suffering of victims evoked sympathy and compassion. As the 1980s ended, the conservative backlash against gay rights had failed, but the epidemic continued.

African Americans and Racial Inequality

Conservatives were uneasy with another legacy of the 1960s, the expansion of African American civil rights and benefits guaranteed by the federal government. They believed that the liberal policies of the Great Society hurt, rather than helped, black people and argued that individual initiative, not government action, would promote racial equality. Reflecting these ideas, Reagan opposed renewal of the Voting Rights Act and condemned busing and affirmative action. Like many Republicans, he opposed the creation of a national holiday marking the birthday of Martin Luther King Jr.

The conservatives' tough stance came at a difficult time for racial equality. African Americans' crusade for justice and opportunity generally slowed in the 1970s and 1980s. Despite legal equality, African Americans faced persistent racism and discrimination. Disproportionately clustered in manual occupations, they were particularly hurt by deindustrialization and economic decline. After years of improvement, African Americans' economic status relative to whites stagnated or declined during the Reagan era. African Americans still made less money than whites did for comparable work and had much less chance to attain managerial positions. All African Americans were not affected equally. In the 1980s, the African American middle class continued to thrive. Among college-educated Americans, the incomes of black men rose faster than those of whites into the mid-1980s. Middle-class African Americans could afford to move to better housing, often in suburbs and integrated areas. Meanwhile, working-class African Americans found their wages stagnating or falling compared with those of white workers. In the 1970s and 1980s, poverty rates rose faster among African Americans than among whites. In 1985, 75 percent of poor African American children lived in families headed by a single female. Observers feared there was now a permanent African American underclass segregated in inner-city neighborhoods with poor schools and widespread crime.

As in the past, African American culture, driven by the distinctiveness of the black experience, was dynamic and controversial. In the poverty of the Bronx in New York City in the 1970s, young African Americans had begun to create a powerful new music, rap. Reflecting the city's diversity, pioneering rap artists such as Kool Herc, Afrika Bambaataa, and Grandmaster Flash drew on Caribbean musical styles and the popular dance music disco, as well as on African American expressive traditions. Rap typically featured spoken lyrics over a driving percussive "break" beat, often sampled from other music. Along with graffiti and break dancing, the new sound made up a loose African American cultural movement known as "hip-hop."

Rap was the first new musical form to rival the impact of jazz in the 1920s and rock and roll in the 1950s. Spreading rapidly, rap crossed boundaries of race, class, and nation to appeal to middle-class, white, and international audiences. Commercially successful, rap was also controversial for its often raw look at ghetto life. The subgenre of gangsta rap, with its celebrations of gang life, violence, and misogyny, was especially provocative to conservatives and other Americans. Rap also deeply influenced other genres of music—another instance of the powerful impact of African Americans on American culture.

African Americans also mobilized to fight for equality and opportunity. Across the nation, the number of African American elected officials increased markedly. The Reverend Jesse Jackson, a protégé of Martin Luther King Jr., won wide attention. Preaching self-esteem and economic self-help for African Americans, Jackson was the leader of Operation PUSH—People United to Save Humanity. In 1984, Jackson challenged Walter Mondale for the Democratic presidential nomination. His campaign suggested how far American society had come in accepting African American political participation.

African American activism and the persistence of inequality made it difficult to undo the civil rights revolution. Most Americans seemed to accept that some federal action was essential to redress the imbalance between races. Despite Reagan's opposition, in 1982 Congress voted to extend the Voting Rights Act for 25 years. In 1983, the Supreme Court ruled that Bob Jones University, an evangelical institution, could not retain its tax-exempt status while it prohibited interracial dating and practiced other forms of discrimination. The Court also rejected the Reagan administration's bid to set aside affirmative action programs.

The battles over the rights of African Americans, gays, and women underscored the limits of conservatism. Many Americans were not ready to undo the social and cultural legacies of the 1960s. New cultural expressions, such as rap, clashed with conservative values. The result was a stalemate. Disadvantaged groups made relatively little political progress in the 1980s, but conservatives also made little progress in their social and cultural agenda.

"The Decade of the Hispanic"

After the changes of the 1960s and 1970s, the Hispanic experience in the United States became quieter and more confident in the 1980s. Hispanics were not a homogeneous group but a diverse population defined by geographical, cultural, and even linguistic differences. In New York City, Puerto Ricans predominated; in South Florida, Cubans; and in the long arc from South Texas to Southern California, Mexican Americans. In 1980, Hispanics were the nation's fastest-growing minority group, with a birthrate 75 percent higher than the national average. Most immigrants to the United States were Hispanic, and demographers predicted that Hispanics would replace African Americans as the nation's largest minority group within a generation.

These growing numbers created a new sense in the 1980s that Hispanics mattered and could not be ignored. "We are," a Hispanic Roman Catholic priest declared, "the future."

In this consumer society, the increasing importance of the Hispanic population could be measured in goods and services. Hispanic culture affected the nation's foodways. From the 1970s into the 1980s, more and more Americans discovered "Tex-Mex," the distinctive cuisine of the Tejanos, the Mexican Americans of South Texas. By the 1990s, salsa had passed ketchup as the best-selling condiment in the United States.

Meanwhile, American business moved to attract Spanish-speaking consumers. The Coors brewery enthusiastically declared the 1980s "The Decade of the Hispanic." By 1983, Coors and other companies could advertise in the expanding Spanish-language media, including newspapers, magazines, and 67 television stations.

For politicians, the 1980s were also "The Decade of the Hispanic." Republicans, long unable to attract a majority of African Americans, hoped that Roman Catholic Hispanic voters, like Linda Chavez, would respond to the new conservatism's emphasis on values, family, and religion. Reagan's anti-Communism did attract Cuban Americans, so many of whom were refugees from the regime of Fidel Castro. However, most Hispanics, including Mexican Americans, emphasized economic issues. They continued to fight poverty and struggle for opportunity. Unlike Linda Chavez, the Hispanic majority preferred the more activist economic and educational policies of the Democrats.

The increasing importance of Hispanic voters also affected the response to the perhaps 3 million illegal immigrants who had crossed the border from Mexico into the United States. The Immigration Reform and Control Act of 1986, known as the Simpson-Mazzoli Act, penalized Americans who knowingly brought illegal aliens into the country and hired them. But the measure also reflected the sentiments of Mexican Americans and other Americans by offering amnesty to illegal aliens who had arrived since 1981.

From Scandal to Triumph

The stalemate over social values was not the only sign that there were limits to conservatism in the 1980s. Scandals plagued business and religious figures who had helped create the conservative agenda. Policy setbacks, economic woes, and scandals plagued the Reagan administration. For a time, the conservatives' triumph was in doubt, but then the cold war began to end.

Business and Religious Scandals

By the mid-1980s, the new conservatism was suffering a series of business and religious scandals. In 1986, Ivan Boesky, the swaggering Wall Street deal maker, was indicted for insider trading, the illegal use of secret financial information. Rather than go to trial, he agreed to give up stock trading, inform on other lawbreakers, spend two years in jail, and pay a $100 million fine. In 1987, Michael Milken, the junk bond king, was indicted on fraud and racketeering charges. His plea bargain agreement included a 10-year jail sentence and a $600 million fine, the largest judgment against an individual in American history.

Such scandals provoked second thoughts about the celebration of business and materialism. Critics pointed out that Boesky's and Milken's business methods had hurt the economy by saddling corporations with a great deal of debt and little cash to pay for it. Lavish lifestyles no longer seemed so attractive.

Scandal also touched religion. In 1987, Americans learned that televangelist Jim Bakker had defrauded investors in his theme park, Heritage USA, and paid hush money to hide an adulterous liaison with a church secretary. In 1988, Jerry Falwell had to resign from his Moral Majority. That year, televangelist Jimmy Swaggart admitted he "had sinned" with prostitutes.

Political Scandals

The Reagan administration had its own scandals. Before the end of the first term, more than 20 EPA officials resigned or were fired over charges of favoritism toward lobbyists and polluters. In 1985, Secretary of Labor Raymond Donovan resigned after becoming the first cabinet officer ever indicted. In 1988, Reagan's friend and attorney general, Edwin Meese III, resigned amid questions about his role in the corrupt awarding of government contracts. To critics, the administration's "sleaze factor" stemmed from the president's contemptuous attitude toward government and his eagerness to please business.

In his second term, Reagan faced much more damaging accusations. In October 1986, Sandinista soldiers in Nicaragua shot down a plane attempting to supply the Contra rebels. The plane had been part of a secret effort by the administration to violate the Boland Amendment's ban on aid to the Contras. Then, a Lebanese magazine reported that the United States had traded arms to Iran. Despite Reagan's denials, the government had sold arms to win the release of American hostages held by terrorists in Lebanon. The administration had broken the president's pledge not to negotiate with terrorists and had violated a ban on arms sales to Iran. The arms deal and the Nicaraguan plane crash were connected: the government had illegally used proceeds from the arms sale to pay for supplying the Contras.

The scandal that became known as the Iran-Contra affair had the potential to drive Reagan from office. If the president had ordered or known about the arms deal and the supply effort, he might have faced impeachment. Three separate investigations made clear the president's probable involvement in the Iran-Contra affair, but none turned up enough evidence to impeach him.

Nevertheless, Reagan's reputation was badly damaged. Several of his associates left office and faced jail sentences. Former national security adviser Robert "Bud" McFarlane pleaded guilty to withholding information from Congress. His successor, Rear Admiral John Poindexter, was allowed to resign. Poindexter's aide, Marine Lieutenant Colonel Oliver North, had to be fired. Meanwhile, the director of the CIA, William Casey, died in 1987, the day after he was implicated in the Contra affair. Much of the country concluded that Reagan must have known about his associates' dealings; his popularity dropped.

Setbacks for the Conservative Agenda

Amid the scandals, conservatives faced a series of policy setbacks. The Democratic-controlled House of Representatives was less cooperative during Reagan's second term. Democrats became even more combative after winning majorities in the House and Senate in the congressional elections of 1986.

As a result, Reagan had to compromise more with Congress. In 1985, he called for a Second American Revolution, a comprehensive overhaul of the income tax system. But the Tax Reform Act that Congress passed in 1986 did not lower and simplify income taxes nearly as much as the president had wanted.

Reagan also met outright defeat in Congress. In 1988, a coalition of Democrats and Republicans passed a bill compelling large companies to give workers 60 days' notice of plant closings and layoffs. Reagan opposed this liberal measure, but he allowed the bill to become law without his signature.

The president was often defeated on environmental policy at a time of growing concern about environmental hazards. In December 1984, the subsidiary of a US corporation accidentally allowed toxic gas to escape from a pesticide plant in Bhopal, India. The emission killed more than 2,500 people and injured 200,000. In April 1986, an explosion and fire released radioactive material from a nuclear power plant at Chernobyl in the Soviet Union. The accident killed more than 30 people, injured more than 200, and exposed countless others to radioactivity. Suddenly, Reagan's hostility to environmentalism was no longer so appealing. The president had to accept the 1986 extension of the federal Superfund program to clean up hazardous waste. The next year, Congress overrode his veto of a bill renewing the Water Quality Control Act. In 1988, the Reagan administration signed an international agreement setting limits on emissions linked to acid rain.

A Vulnerable Economy

Even the economy, the centerpiece of the Reagan Revolution, became a problem in the president's second term. During the 1980s, the gap between rich and poor widened sharply. From 1977 to 1980, the average family income of the highest-paid tenth of Americans rose 27 percent, whereas that of the poorest tenth fell 11 percent (see Figure 28–3). In the 1980s, only the rich earned more and kept more. Other Americans faced economic stagnation or decline.

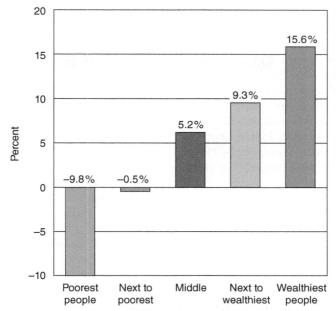

Figure 28-3   Changes in Families' Real Income, 1980–1990 The Reagan Revolution had very different consequences for the rich and the poor.
Source: Copyright © 1989 by the New York Times Co. Reprinted by permission.

In 1980, 29 million Americans lived below the poverty line. Ten years later, that figure had grown to almost 37 million. Despite Reaganomics, the United States had one of the highest poverty rates among industrialized nations.

One of the most visible consequences of poverty was homelessness. In the 1980s, the number of homeless Americans increased markedly. The sight of men and women sleeping on sidewalks was common during the Reagan years.

Homelessness, poverty, and inequality produced a spirited debate in the 1980s. Democrats and liberals blamed these problems on Reaganomics. The president, they charged, had done nothing to stop the erosion of high-paying factory jobs. His welfare, housing, and job-training cuts hurt the poor, while his tax cuts and deregulation helped the rich. Conservatives and Republicans maintained that activist, liberal government had hurt manufacturing and weakened the economy. Moreover, welfare programs caused poverty by destroying poor people's work ethic and making them dependent on handouts.

In reality, both liberal and conservative policies had produced flawed economic results. Lyndon Johnson's spending for the Great Society, along with the cost of the Vietnam War, had begun to undermine the economy in the 1960s. His antipoverty programs had been less effective than liberals wanted to admit, but the Reagan Revolution did not end poverty, either. Reaganomics did not reinvigorate manufacturing or boost middle-class incomes.

There were other signs of economic vulnerability by the mid-1980s. Despite Reaganomics, the federal budget deficit did not disappear. Instead, between 1981 and

1986, tax cuts and increased defense spending drove the deficit from $79 billion to $221 billion—a staggering new record.

Like poverty and inequality, the deficit was controversial. Some economists believed the deficit was a sign of great economic weakness; others believed it did not matter. Democrats and liberals blamed Reagan for the red ink. Reagan's supporters blamed Congress for failing to cut the budget.

In fact, both the president and Congress were to blame. Neither Republicans nor Democrats wanted to reduce Medicare and Social Security. Congress enacted the Balanced Budget and Emergency Deficit Control Act of 1985 (the Gramm-Rudman Act), which promised to balance the budget by 1990, but a Supreme Court ruling critically weakened the measure. During Reagan's last years in office, the national debt—the total amount owed by the federal government to its creditors—reached $2.6 trillion.

Along with burgeoning debt, the Reagan years produced a growing international trade deficit. In 1980, the annual value of imports was $25.4 billion greater than the value of the nation's exports. By 1986, that gap had grown to $145.1 billion, as American business lost out to foreign products both at home and abroad. Reaganomics had not solved the problem of America's relative decline in the world economy.

Doubts about Reagan's economic policy increased when the stock market fell unexpectedly on Monday, October 19, 1987, losing 508 points, or 23 percent of its value. It was the biggest one-day decline since "Black Tuesday" in October 1929. The market drop reflected underlying economic problems, including the federal budget deficit, the trade deficit, and deindustrialization, plus lax government regulation of Wall Street. The crash seemed to be a mortal blow to what a journalist called "the Reagan Illusion: the idea that there could be a defense buildup and tax cuts without a price, that the country could live beyond its means indefinitely."

Reagan's Comeback

Remarkably able to withstand defeat, Reagan began his comeback from scandals and economic troubles. Opponents dubbed him the "Teflon president" because nothing seemed to stick to him. That was a tribute to his political skills, as well as many Americans' real affection for him. After a series of disappointing presidencies, Americans seemed unwilling to let Reagan fail.

The economy also helped the president. The stock market crash did not, as feared, lead to depression or recession. The market soon recovered and the economy grew.

Reagan's comeback was probably helped most by the transformation of the Soviet Union. By the mid-1980s, the Soviets suffered from a weakening economy, an unpopular war in Afghanistan, and a costly arms race. Mikhail Gorbachev, dynamic and charismatic, became general secretary of the Communist Party and signaled a new era with a series of stunning reforms. At home, he called for restructuring the economy (*perestroika*) and tolerating more open discussion (*glasnost*). Abroad, he sought to ease tensions with the United States and the West.

Gorbachev's reforms gave the United States an opening to thaw cold war tensions. Reagan met with the Soviet leader in a series of summits beginning in November 1985. Visiting West Berlin in June 1987, the president challenged Gorbachev to "tear down" the Berlin Wall, which had symbolized the cold war division of Europe. Meanwhile, it became apparent that the Soviets were changing their foreign policy, as they withdrew their troops from Afghanistan and eased their control over Eastern Europe.

The United States and the Soviets also made real progress on arms control. In December 1987, Reagan and Gorbachev signed the Intermediate-Range Nuclear Forces Treaty (INF), promising to destroy more than 2,500 intermediate-range missiles. For the first time, the two powers had agreed to give up a weapon altogether.

The INF treaty permanently eased tensions. The cold war suddenly ended. Reagan's presidency ended in 1989; a year later, the United States and the Soviet Union agreed to end production of chemical weapons and reduce existing stockpiles. In 1991, the two

The Fall of the Berlin Wall Residents celebrate the fall of the Berlin Wall and the collapse of Communist rule in East Berlin and East Germany, November 1989.

STRUGGLES FOR DEMOCRACY

Reagan at the Berlin Wall

The history of democracy has not only been a tale of elections and legislation. Like other kinds of politics, it has also been a story of theater. American leaders have long tried to capture fundamental political ideas in a vivid moment, a memorable mixture of language and image. President Ronald Reagan, a veteran radio announcer, actor, and television host, was a master of the theater of democracy.

By the spring of 1987, Reagan had largely abandoned the rhetoric of the cold war as he moved cautiously toward working with Soviet leader Mikhail Gorbachev. Reagan's shift had yet to produce a dramatic easing of the cold war, but it had already disappointed some of his most ardent, anti-Communist supporters. In June, a trip to West Germany for the 750th anniversary of the city of Berlin offered the president an ideal opportunity to deal with both his domestic and foreign problems.

For four decades, the city—divided between communist, pro-Soviet East and capitalist, pro-American West—had epitomized the divisions of the cold war. For nearly three decades, the concrete-and-barbed-wire wall separating Berlin's two sections had perfectly symbolized the cold war's impact on the city, Europe, and the world.

On the drab afternoon of June 12, Reagan, dressed patriotically in a blue suit, white shirt, and red tie, stood on a temporary platform 25 yards in front of the Berlin Wall. His aides had set the stage with care. Looming behind the president and the wall, in East Berlin, was the great Brandenburg Gate. For nearly two centuries, the 12 pillars and crowning arch of the Gate had symbolized peace; now, blocked by the Berlin Wall, the Brandenburg Gate led nowhere. In front of Reagan, an invited crowd of 20,000 waved American and West German flags provided by the president's aides. On the other side of the wall, 200 East Germans could hear Reagan on loud speakers. Thanks to radio and television, many more East Germans and Soviets, as well as Americans, also heard the president's words.

Those words had been carefully drafted and redrafted by a young speechwriter, Paul Robinson. Inspired by his West German hostess at a dinner party, Robinson had written a line demanding

Time Line

▼**1979–1981**
Iranian hostage crisis

▼**1980**
Ronald Reagan elected president

▼**1981**
IBM personal computer

Air traffic controllers' strike
Economic Recovery Act

▼**1982**
Nuclear freeze rally in New York City
Boland Amendment

▼**1983**
Strategic Defense Initiative
US invasion of Grenada
Terrorist attack on US Marines in Lebanon

▼**1984**
Reelection of Ronald Reagan

that Gorbachev tear down the Berlin Wall. As Reagan's aides vetted the draft speech, the line had become the subject of a bureaucratic tug-of-war. The State Department and the National Security Council, anxious not to alienate the Soviet Union, had tried repeatedly to have the line removed or diluted. But the line reflected both Reagan's values and his political purposes. "The boys at State are going to kill me," Reagan wryly told an aide, "but it's the right thing to do." The line stayed.

"There is one sign the Soviets can make that would be unmistakable, that would advance dramatically the cause of freedom and peace," Reagan declared that afternoon. "General Secretary Gorbachev, if you seek peace, if you seek prosperity for the Soviet Union and Eastern Europe, if you seek liberalization, come here to this gate!" Then, with practiced, grave assurance, the president delivered Paul Robinson's line. "Mr. Gorbachev, open this gate!" Reagan demanded. "Mr. Gorbachev, tear down this wall!" And then, the president looked ahead to the future. "The wall," he predicted, "cannot withstand freedom."

Gorbachev did not immediately comply, but Reagan's speech served its purpose. Back in the United States, his conservative supporters were pleased by his tough, anti-Communist stance. Meanwhile, both the East Germans and their Soviet allies complained about Reagan's rhetoric. According to the official Soviet news agency, the speech was an "openly propagandistic speech couched in the spirit of the Cold War times." Nevertheless, Gorbachev continued to pursue diplomatic breakthroughs with the United States. Reagan's speech was almost forgotten.

On November 9, 1989, nearly two-and-a-half years after Reagan's demand, the East German authorities unexpectedly opened the Berlin Wall. Soon, the barrier came down as the cold war ended. "All of a sudden, within weeks after the wall came down, people were talking about the speech," an American diplomat recalled. "People were saying, 'Look at that. Ronald Reagan foresaw this. He was the one to give it its last push.'"

It was impossible to prove that words brought down the Berlin Wall, just as it was impossible to prove that Reagan ended the cold war. But the president's appearance in front of the wall suggested the importance of political theater. Mixing language and image, sound and picture, the president, with the help of his aides, had powerfully epitomized the value of freedom and used it as a democratic weapon. Two-and-a-half years later, Berliners who wanted more democracy naturally tore down the wall to make their point.

▼**1985**
General Electric purchase of RCA
Gramm-Rudman Act

▼**1986**
US bombing of Libya
Tax Reform Act

Revelation of Iran-Contra affair

▼**1987**
Stock market crash
Intermediate-Range Nuclear
 Forces Treaty

▼**1988**
Omnibus Trade and
 Competitiveness Act

▼**1991**
Collapse of the Soviet Union

nations signed the START (Strategic Arms Reduction Talks) Treaty, which called for each side to reduce its nuclear arsenals as much as 30 percent.

Meanwhile, the Soviet Union weakened. In 1989, Gorbachev could do nothing to stop the collapse of its repressive allies in Eastern Europe, as regimes toppled in Bulgaria, Czechoslovakia, Hungary, Poland, and Rumania. Most dramatically, a new East German government agreed in November to allow travel through the Berlin Wall. As jubilant Berliners dismantled it, the wall's fate epitomized the collapse of Communism. Accepting the transition to democracy, the Soviets withdrew their troops from Eastern Europe.

Powerless to save its allies, the Soviet leadership soon could not save itself. Despite Gorbachev's efforts, the low standard of living, Communist repression, and the unpopular war in Afghanistan made many unhappy. Estonia, Latvia, Lithuania, and other republics chafed under Russia's domination of the USSR. In 1990, Russia chose a charismatic president, Boris Yeltsin, who quit the Communist Party, supported independence for the republics, and challenged Gorbachev. The next year, Gorbachev resigned as party leader and president, and the Soviet parliament suspended the Communist Party. As one republic after another declared its independence, the USSR ceased to exist.

With the collapse of the Soviet Union, the United States and its allies had won the cold war. Conservatives insisted that Reagan's overpowering defense buildup had forced the Soviets to surrender. Democrats maintained that the buildup and the president's harsh rhetoric had actually slowed the thaw in US-Soviet relations and that America won the cold war because of its long-term strength and strategy. Typically modest, Reagan himself gave credit to American policies reaching back to the 1940s.

Meanwhile, Americans did not celebrate very much as the Berlin Wall came down and the Soviet Union collapsed. The cold war had cost a great deal in money and lives. Many Americans wondered whether Communism had posed a mortal danger to the United States in the first place.

Conclusion

Reagan left office with the highest popularity rating of any president since the beginning of modern polling in the 1930s. His comeback culminated the triumph of the new conservatism, but the nature of that triumph would be debated for years to come. The Reagan Revolution did not solve such basic economic problems as poverty and even worsened some problems, such as inequality and the budget deficit. Much of its conservative social agenda failed to take hold.

Nevertheless, Reagan successfully combated the sense of national decline that had pervaded America in the 1970s. After the troubled presidencies of that decade, Reagan's confident leadership made the democratic system seem viable again. His presidency reinvigorated faith in capitalist innovation, minimal government, and American military power. At the end of the 1980s, business values and evangelical religion claimed a more prominent place in American culture.

The accomplishments of the new conservatism, as Reagan's troubled second term indicated, were fragile. The nation's economic revival was shaky, and Americans were still worried about the future. "I think," a businessman concluded, "the '90s are going to be much trickier than the 1980s."

Who, What, Where

Review Questions

1. What were the main values and goals of the new conservatism in the 1980s? What role did business and religion play in the conservative movement?

2. What was the Reagan Revolution in domestic policy? How did Reagan's domestic programs reflect conservative values?

3. What were the aims of the Reagan Revolution abroad?

Critical-Thinking Questions

1. What groups resisted the conservative social agenda in the 1980s? Did the desire for equal rights and opportunities conflict with conservatism?

2. What factors limited the triumph of the new conservatism? Did conservatives really succeed in the 1980s?

3. How did the conservatism of the 1980s differ from earlier forms of conservatism in the twentieth century?

Suggested Readings

Berlin, Leslie. *Troublemakers: Silicon Valley's Coming of Age.* New York: Simon & Schuster, 2017.

McKevitt, Andrew C. *Consuming Japan: Popular Culture and the Globalizing of 1980s America.* Chapel Hill: North Carolina University Press, 2017.

Rossinow, Doug. *The Reagan Era: A History of the 1980s.* New York: Columbia University Press, 2016.

For further review materials and resource information, please visit www.oup.com/us/oakes-mcgerr

CHAPTER 28: THE TRIUMPH OF CONSERVATISM, 1980–1991
Primary Sources

28.1 VISUAL DOCUMENT: US CENTERS FOR DISEASE CONTROL, AIDS AWARENESS POSTER (1980s)

The AIDS epidemic tested Americans' openness about sex and sexuality. What does this poster from the US Centers for Disease Control seem to suggest is a major obstacle to stopping the spread of the disease? Note that the poster does not make clear the identity of Phillip's sexual partners. What else does it not reveal?

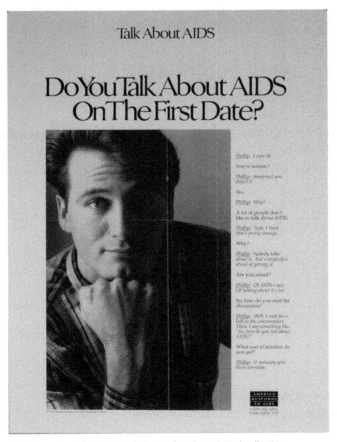

Source: US Centers for Disease Control, US National Library of Medicine Digital Collections.

28.2 JERRY FALWELL, EXCERPTS FROM *LISTEN, AMERICA!* (1980)

In his 1980 book, *Listen, America!* Reverend Jerry Falwell called on evangelical Protestants to go into politics in order to help solve the nation's problems. The televangelist traced America's decline to a wide variety of sources, including television, secular humanism, liberals, homosexuals, and the federal government. Falwell's brand of evangelical activism played a key role in building the Reagan coalition.

We must reverse the trend America finds herself in today. Young people between the ages of twenty-five and forty have been born and reared in a different world than Americans of years past. The television set has been their primary baby-sitter. From the television set they have learned situation ethics and immorality—they have learned a loss of respect for human life. They have learned to disrespect the family as God has established it. They have been educated in a public-school system that is permeated with secular humanism. They have been taught that the Bible is just another book of literature. They have been taught that there are no absolutes in our world today. They have been introduced to the drug culture. They have been reared by the family and the public school in a society that is greatly void of discipline and character-building. These same young people have been reared under the influence of a government that has taught them socialism and welfarism. They have been taught to believe that the world owes them a living whether they work or not.

I believe that America was built on integrity, on faith in God, and on hard work. I do not believe that anyone has ever been successful in life without being willing to add that last ingredient—diligence or hard work. We now have second- and third-generation welfare recipients. Welfare is not always wrong. There are those who do need welfare, but we have reared a generation that understands neither the dignity nor the importance of work.

Every American who looks at the facts must share a deep concern and burden for our country. We are not unduly concerned when we say that there are some very dark clouds on America's horizon. I am not a pessimist, but it is indeed a time for truth. If Americans will face the truth, our nation can be turned around and can be saved from the evils and the destruction that have fallen upon every other nation that has turned its back on God.

There is no excuse for what is happening in our country. We must, from the highest office in the land right down to the shoeshine boy in the airport, have a return to biblical basics. If the Congress of our United States will take its stand on that which is right and wrong, and if our President, our judiciary system, and our state and local leaders will take their stand on holy living, we can turn this country around.

I personally feel that the home and the family are still held in reverence by the vast majority of the American public. I believe there is still a vast number of Americans who love their country, are patriotic, and are willing to sacrifice for her. I remember the time when it was positive to be patriotic, and as far as I am concerned, it still is. I remember as a boy, when the flag was raised, everyone stood proudly and put his hand upon his heart and pledged allegiance with gratitude. I remember when the band struck up "The Stars and Stripes Forever," we stood and goose pimples would run all over me. I remember when I was in elementary school during World War II, when every report from the other shores meant something to us. We were not out demonstrating against our boys who were dying in Europe and Asia. We were praying for them and thanking God for them and buying war bonds to help pay for the materials and artillery they needed to fight and win and come back. . . .

My responsibility as a preacher of the Gospel is one of influence, not of control, and that is the responsibility of each individual citizen. Through the ballot box Americans must provide for strong moral leadership at every level. If our country will get back on the track in sensibility and moral sanity, the crises that I have herein mentioned will work out in the course of time and with God's blessings.

It is now time to take a stand on certain moral issues, and we can only stand if we have leaders. We must stand against the Equal Rights Amendment, the feminist revolution, and the homosexual revolution. We must have a revival in this country. . . .

As a preacher of the Gospel, I not only believe in prayer and preaching, I also believe in good citizenship. If a labor union in America has the right to organize and improve its working conditions, then I believe that the churches and the pastors, the priests, and the rabbis of America have a responsibility, not just the right, to see to it that the moral climate and conscience of Americans is such that this nation can be healed inwardly. If it is healed inwardly, then it will heal itself outwardly. . . .

We are not a perfect nation, but we are still a free nation because we have the blessing of God upon us. We must continue to follow in a path that will ensure that blessing. . . .

The hope of reversing the trends of decay in our republic now lies with the Christian public in America. We cannot expect help from the liberals. They certainly are not going to call our nation back to righteousness and neither are the pornographers, the smut peddlers, and those who are corrupting our youth. Moral Americans must be willing to put their reputations, their fortunes, and their very lives on the line for this great nation of ours. Would that we had the courage of our forefathers who knew the great responsibility that freedom carries with it. . . .

Our Founding Fathers separated church and state in function, but never intended to establish a government void of God. As is evidenced by our Constitution, good people in America must exert an influence and provide a conscience and climate of morality in which it is difficult to go wrong, not difficult for people to go right in America.

I am positive in my belief regarding the Constitution that God led in the development of that document, and as a result, we here in America have enjoyed 204 years of unparalleled freedom. . . .

Americans must no longer linger in ignorance and apathy. We cannot be silent about the sins that are destroying this nation. The choice is ours. We must turn America around or prepare for inevitable destruction. I am listening to the sounds that threaten to take away our liberties in America. And I have listened to God's admonitions and His direction—the only hopes of saving America. Are you listening too?

Source: Jerry Falwell, *Listen, America!* (Garden City, NY: Doubleday, 1980), pp. 17–23.

28.3 RONALD REAGAN, EXCERPTS FROM "ADDRESS TO THE NATION ON THE ECONOMY" (1981)

On February 5, 1981, President Ronald Reagan gave his first televised national address in which he discussed the troubled US economy. Although he described a difficult situation, Reagan was characteristically optimistic. The answer to the nation's fiscal issues, he insisted, was the set of economic policies, including cuts in federal taxes, spending, and regulation, that would become known as Reaganomics.

I'm speaking to you tonight to give you a report on the state of our Nation's economy. I regret to say that we're in the worst economic mess since the Great Depression.

A few days ago I was presented with a report I'd asked for, a comprehensive audit, if you will, of our economic condition. You won't like it. I didn't like it. But we have to face the truth and then go to work to turn things around. And make no mistake about it, we can turn them around. . . .

The Federal budget is out of control, and we face runaway deficits of almost $80 billion for this budget year that ends September 30th. That deficit is larger than the entire Federal budget in 1957, and so is the almost $80 billion we will pay in interest this year on the national debt.

Twenty years ago, in 1960, our Federal Government payroll was less than $13 billion. Today it is $75 billion. During these 20 years our population has only increased by 23.3 percent. The Federal budget has gone up 528 percent.

Now, we've just had 2 years of back-to-back double-digit inflation—13.3 percent in 1979, 12.4 percent last year. The last time this happened was in World War I.

In 1960 mortgage interest rates averaged about 6 percent. They're 2½ times as high now, 15.4 percent.

The percentage of your earnings the Federal Government took in taxes in 1960 has almost doubled.

And finally there are 7 million Americans caught up in the personal indignity and human tragedy of unemployment. If they stood in a line, allowing 3 feet for each person, the line would reach from the coast of Maine to California. . . .

We forgot or just overlooked the fact that government—any government—has a built-in tendency to grow. Now, we all had a hand in looking to government for benefits as if government had some source of revenue other than our earnings. Many if not most of the things we thought of or that government offered to us seemed attractive. . . .

Some government programs seemed so worthwhile that borrowing to fund them didn't bother us. . . .

We know now that inflation results from all that deficit spending. Government has only two ways of getting money other than raising taxes. It can go into the money market and borrow, competing with its own citizens and driving up interest rates, which it has done, or it can print money, and it's done that. Both methods are inflationary. . . .

Now, one way out would be to raise taxes so that government need not borrow or print money. But in all these years of government growth, we've reached, indeed surpassed, the limit of our people's tolerance or ability to bear an increase in the tax burden. Prior to World War II, taxes were such that on the average we only had to work just a little over 1 month each year to pay our total Federal, State, and local tax bill. Today we have to work 4 months to pay that bill.

Some say shift the tax burden to business and industry, but business doesn't pay taxes. Oh, don't get the wrong idea. Business is being taxed, so much so that we're being priced out of the world market. But business must pass its costs of operations—and that includes taxes—on to the customer in the price of the product. Only people pay taxes, all the taxes. Government just uses business in a kind of sneaky way to help collect the taxes. They're hidden in the price; we aren't aware of how much tax we actually pay.

Today this once great industrial giant of ours has the lowest rate of gain in productivity of virtually all the industrial nations with whom we must compete in the world market. We can't even hold our own market here in America against foreign automobiles, steel, and a number of other products. Japanese production of automobiles is almost twice as great per worker as it is in America. . . .

Now, this isn't because they're better workers. I'll match the American working man or woman against anyone in the world. But we have to give them the tools and equipment that workers in the other industrial nations have.

We invented the assembly line and mass production, but punitive tax policies and excessive and unnecessary regulations plus government borrowing have stifled our ability to update plant and equipment. When capital investment is made, it's too often for some unproductive alterations demanded by government to meet various of its regulations. Excessive taxation of individuals has robbed us of incentive and made overtime unprofitable. . . .

Over the past decades we've talked of curtailing government spending so that we can then lower the tax burden. . . . But there were always those who told us that taxes couldn't be cut until spending was reduced. Well, you know, we can lecture our children about extravagance until we run out of voice and breath. Or we can cure their extravagance by simply reducing their allowance. . . .

We must increase productivity. That means making it possible for industry to modernize and make use of the technology which we ourselves invented. That means putting Americans back to work. And that means above all bringing government spending back within government revenues, which is the only way, together with increased productivity, that we can reduce and, yes, eliminate inflation. . . .

[W]e cannot delay in implementing an economic program aimed at both reducing tax rates to stimulate productivity and reducing the growth in government spending to reduce unemployment and inflation. . . .

Source: Ronald Reagan, "Address to the Nation on the Economy," February 5, 1981.

28.4 NATIONAL CONFERENCE OF CATHOLIC BISHOPS, EXCERPTS FROM "THE CHALLENGE OF PEACE: GOD'S PROMISE AND OUR RESPONSE" (1983)

The Reagan administration's defense buildup helped spark a mass movement against nuclear weapons. One of the key antinuclear documents during this time was "The Challenge of Peace: God's Promise and Our Response," issued by the Roman Catholic Bishops of the United States in May 1983. Grounding opposition to nuclear armaments and nuclear war in the teachings of Jesus Christ, the bishops' pastoral letter posed a significant challenge to the Reagan administration's arms buildup.

[T]he crisis of the moment is embodied in the threat which nuclear weapons pose for the world and much that we hold dear in the world. We have seen and felt the effects of the crisis of the nuclear age in the lives of people we serve. Nuclear weaponry has drastically changed the nature of warfare, and the arms race poses a threat to human life and human civilization which is without precedent.

We write this letter from the perspective of Catholic faith. Faith does not insulate us from the daily challenges of life but intensifies our desire to address them precisely in light of the gospel which has come to us in the person of the risen Christ. Through the resources of faith and reason we desire in this letter to provide hope for people in our day and direction toward a world freed of the nuclear threat.

As Catholic bishops we write this letter as an exercise of our teaching ministry. . . . Catholic teaching has always understood peace in positive terms. In the words of Pope John Paul II: "Peace is not just the absence of war. . . . Like a cathedral, peace must be constructed patiently and with unshakable faith."

. . . Peace is the fruit of order. Order in human society must be shaped on the basis of respect for the transcendence of God and the unique dignity of each person, understood in terms of freedom, justice, truth and love. To avoid war in our day we must be intent on building peace in an increasingly interdependent world. . . .

A. On War

1. Catholic teaching begins in every case with a presumption against war and for peaceful settlement of disputes. In exceptional cases, determined by the moral principles of the just-war tradition, some uses of force are permitted.

2. Every nation has a right and duty to defend itself against unjust aggression.

3. Offensive war of any kind is not morally justifiable.

4. It is never permitted to direct nuclear or conventional weapons to "the indiscriminate destruction of whole cities or vast areas with their populations. . . ." The intentional killing of innocent civilians or non-combatants is always wrong.

5. Even defensive response to unjust attack can cause destruction which violates the principle of proportionality, going far beyond the limits of legitimate defense. This judgment is particularly important when assessing planned use of nuclear weapons. No defensive strategy, nuclear or conventional, which exceeds the limits of proportionity is morally permissible. . . .

C. The Arms Race and Disarmament

1. The arms race is one of the greatest curses on the human race; it is to be condemned as a danger, an act of aggression against the poor, and a folly which does not provide the security it promises. . . .

2. Negotiations must be pursued in every reasonable form possible; they should be governed by the "demand that the arms race should cease; that the stockpiles which exist in various countries should be reduced equally and simultaneously by the parties concerned; that nuclear weapons should be banned; and that a general agreement should eventually be reached about progressive disarmament and an effective method of control." (Pope John XXIII, *Peace on Earth*, #112)

II. Moral Principles and Policy Choices

As bishops in the United States, assessing the concrete circumstances of our society, we have made a number of observations and recommendations in the process of applying moral principles to specific policy choices.

A. On the Use of Nuclear Weapons

1. *Counter Population Use:* Under no circumstances may nuclear weapons or other instruments of mass slaughter be used for the purpose of destroying population centers or other predominantly civilian targets.

    Retaliatory action which would indiscriminately and disproportionately take many wholly innocent lives, lives of people who are in no way responsible for reckless actions of their government, must also be condemned.

2. *The Initiation of Nuclear War:* We do not perceive any situation in which the deliberate initiation of nuclear war, on however restricted a scale, can be morally justified. Nonnuclear attacks by another state must be resisted by other than nuclear means. Therefore, a serious moral obligation exists to develop non-nuclear defensive strategies as rapidly as possible. . . .

C. On Promoting Peace

1. We support immediate, bilateral verifiable agreements to halt the testing, production and deployment of new nuclear weapons systems. This recommendation is not to be identified with any specific political initiative.

2. We support efforts to achieve deep cuts in the arsenals of both superpowers; efforts should concentrate first on systems which threaten the retaliatory forces of either major power.

3. We support early and successful conclusion of negotiations of a comprehensive test ban treaty.

4. We urge new efforts to prevent the spread of nuclear weapons in the world, and to control the conventional arms race, particularly the conventional arms trade.

5. We support, in an increasingly interdependent word, political and economic policies designed to protect human dignity and to promote the human rights of every person, especially the least among us. In this regard, we call for the establishment of some form of global authority adequate to the needs of the international common good. . . .

What are we saying? Fundamentally, we are saying that the decisions about nuclear weapons are among the most pressing moral questions of our age. While these decisions have obvious military and political aspects, they involve fundamental moral choices. In simple terms, we are saying that good ends (defending one's country, protecting freedom, etc.) cannot justify immoral means (the use of weapons which kill indiscriminately and threaten whole societies). We fear that our world and nation are headed in the wrong direction. More weapons with greater destructive potential are produced every day. More and more nations are seeking to become nuclear powers. In our quest for more and more security we fear we are actually becoming less and less secure.

In the words of the Holy Father, we need a "moral about-face." The whole world must summon the moral courage and technical means to say no to nuclear conflict; no to weapons of mass destruction; no to an arms race which robs the poor and the vulnerable; and no to the moral danger of a nuclear age which places before humankind indefensible choices of constant terror or surrender. Peacemaking is not an optional commitment. It is a requirement of our faith. We are called to be peacemakers, not by some movement of the moment, but by our Lord Jesus. The content and context of our peacemaking is set not by some political agenda or ideological program, but by the teaching of his Church.

Ultimately, this letter is intended as an expression of Christian faith, affirming the confidence we have that the risen Lord remains with us precisely in moments of crisis. It is our belief in his presence and power among us which sustain us in confronting the awesome challenge of the nuclear age. We speak from faith to provide hope for all who recognize the challenge and are working to confront it with the resources of faith and reason. . . .

Source: National Conference of Catholic Bishops, "The Challenge of Peace: God's Promise and Our Response."

28.5 EXCERPTS FROM THE REPUBLICAN AND DEMOCRATIC PARTY PLATFORMS ON THE STATE OF THE AMERICAN FAMILY (1984)

By the 1984 presidential election, the state of the American family had become another battleground for the nation's two major political parties. The Democrats used the words "family" or "families" 27 times in their platform that year; the Republicans used the words no fewer than 78 times in theirs. As these excerpts from each party's platform make clear, the parties thought about the present and future state of the American family quite differently.

Republican platform: . . . America was built on the institutions of home, family, religion, and neighborhood. From these basic building blocks came self-reliant individuals, prepared to exercise both rights and responsibilities. . . .

Public policy long ignored these foundations of American life. Especially during the two decades preceding Ronald Reagan's election, the federal government eroded their authority, ignored their rights, and attempted to supplant their functions with programs at once intrusive and ineffectual. It thereby disrupted our traditional patterns of caring, sharing, and helping. . . .

Washington's governing elite . . . tried to build their brave new world by assaulting our basic values. They mocked the work ethic. They scorned frugality. They attacked the integrity of the family and parental rights. They ignored traditional morality. And they still do. . . .

Over the past two decades, welfare became a nightmare for the taxpayer and the poor alike. Fraud and abuse were rampant. The costs of public assistance are astronomical, in large part because resources often benefit the welfare industry rather than the poor. . . . This was a fantastic and unsustainable universalization of welfare.

Welfare's indirect effects were equally as bad. . . . Government created a hellish cycle of dependency. Family cohesion was shattered, both by providing economic incentives to set up maternal households and by usurping the breadwinner's economic role in intact families.

The cruelest result was the maternalization of poverty, worsened by the breakdown of the family and accelerated by destructive patterns of conduct too long tolerated by permissive liberals. We endorse programs to assist female-headed households to build self-sufficiency, such as efforts by localities to enable participants to achieve permanent employment.

Many health problems arise within the family and should be dealt with there. We affirm the right and responsibility of parents to participate in decisions about the treatment of children. We will not tolerate the use of federal funds, taxed away from parents, to abrogate their role in family health care. . . .

Republicans affirm the family as the natural and indispensable institution for human development. A society is only as strong as its families, for they nurture those qualities necessary to maintain and advance civilization.

Healthy families inculcate values—integrity, responsibility, concern for others—in our youth and build social cohesion. We give high priority to their well-being. During the 1970s, America's families were ravaged by worsening economic conditions and a Washington elite unconcerned with them.

We support the concept of creating Family Education Accounts which would allow tax-deferred savings for investment in America's most crucial asset, our children, to assist low- and middle-income families in becoming self-reliant in meeting the costs of higher education.

In addition, to further assist the young families of America in securing the dream of home-ownership, we would like to review the concept of Family Housing Accounts which would allow tax-exempt savings for a family's first home.

Preventing family dissolution, a leading cause of poverty, is vital. It has had a particularly tragic impact on the elderly, women, and minorities. Welfare programs have devastated low-income families and induced single parenthood among teens. We will review legislation and regulations to examine their impact on families and on parental rights and responsibilities. We seek to eliminate incentives for family break-up and to reverse the alarming rate of pregnancy outside

marriage. Meanwhile, the Republican Party believes that society must do all that is possible to guarantee those young parents the opportunity to achieve their full educational and parental potential.

The President's tax program . . . increased tax credits for child care expenses. We will encourage private sector initiatives to expand on-site child care facilities and options for working
parents.

The problem of physical and sexual abuse of children and spouses requires careful consideration of its causes. In particular, gratuitous sex and violence in entertainment media contribute
to this sad development. . . .

Democratic platform: . . . In Ronald Reagan's vision of America, there are no single parent
families, women only stay at home and care for children. Reagan's families do not worry about
the effects of unemployment on family stability: they do not worry about decent housing and
health care: they do not need child care. But in the real world, most Americans do. Providing
adequate child care for the millions of American children who need it, and for their parents,
is surely not a responsibility which belongs solely to the federal government. But, like the responsibility for decent housing and health care, it is one where federal leadership and support
are essential.

. . . Small businesses have closed: American families are suffering hunger and poor health,
as unemployment exceeds depression rates. Women continue to receive less than 60 percent of
the wages that men receive, with minority women receiving far less.

. . . Ronald Reagan's tax program gave huge breaks to wealthy individuals and to large corporations while shifting the burden to low and moderate income families. The Democratic Party
is pledged to reverse these unsound policies.

. . . There are . . . key goals that a Democratic program for educational excellence must address: . . . ensuring that all American families can send their children on to college or advanced
training.

. . . [E]ven in a growing economy, the pressures of competition and the pace of change
ensure that while jobs are being created, others are being destroyed. . . . We must make special
efforts to help families in economic transition who are faced with loss of homes, health benefits,
and pensions.

. . . More than one-third of all female-headed households are below the poverty line, and for
non-white families headed by women with more than one child, the figure is 70 percent.

But the numbers tell only part of the story; numbers do not convey the frustration and
suffering of women seeking a future for themselves and their children, with no support from
anyone; numbers do not recount the pain of growing numbers of homeless men and women
with no place to sleep, or of increasing infant mortality rates among children born to poor
mothers. Numbers do not convey the human effects of unemployment on a once stable and
strong family.

As Democrats, we call upon the American people to join with us in a renewed commitment
to combat the feminization of poverty in our nation so that every American can be a productive, contributing member of our society. In that effort, our goal is to strengthen families and
to reverse the existing incentives for their destruction. We therefore oppose laws requiring an
unemployed parent to leave the family or drop out of the work force in order to qualify for assistance and health care. We recognize the special need to increase the labor force participation
of minority males, and we are committed to expanding their opportunities through education
and training and to enforcing the laws which guarantee them equal opportunities. The plight of
young mothers must be separately addresses as well; they too need education and training and
quality child care must be available if they are to participate in such programs. Only through
a nation that cares and a government that acts can those Americans trapped in poverty move
toward meaningful independence.

. . . Since 1980, however, hunger has returned. High unemployment, coupled with deep cutbacks in food assistance and other basic support programs for poor families have led to conditions not seen in this country for years. Studies in hospitals and health departments document increases in numbers of malnourished children. Increasing numbers of homeless wander our cities streets in search of food and shelter. Religious organizations, charities and other agencies report record numbers of persons standing in line for food at soup kitchens and emergency food pantries.

Sources: "Republican Party Platform of 1984," August 20, 1984. "Democratic Party Platform of 1984," July 16, 1984.

The Globalized Nation

1989-2001

< The Democratic Ticket, 1992

AMERICAN PORTRAIT

James Sharlow

In his gray suit and red power tie, 51-year-old James E. Sharlow was the picture of middle-class success in 1996. He had a Mercedes and a large suburban ranch house in the San Fernando Valley of southern California. His life epitomized the American dream of upward mobility. The son of a working-class father in upstate New York, Jim had graduated from high school and started out as a machinist. Eventually earning a college degree, he became an office worker for the Eastman Kodak Company, famous for its photographic film, in the city of Rochester. "It just seemed like overnight he went from a closet full of work shirts to a closet full of white shirts," recalled his wife Gayle, herself the daughter of a carpenter. Like so many Americans after World War II, the Sharlows had migrated from the Snowbelt of the Northeast to the Sunbelt of the Southwest. Their move came in 1987, against the backdrop of the Reagan Revolution, when Kodak made Jim the plant manager of a sub-sidiary in Northridge, California. After many years with the corpo-ration, Jim was deeply loyal. "Kodak was everything," Gayle noted.

The picture of Jim Sharlow was deceptive. In reality, his mem-bership in the middle class was in grave jeopardy in 1996. Three years earlier, Kodak had closed down his plant. Just like that, Jim's job and his $130,000 salary were gone. He had been jobless ever since. His gray suit was old; his Mercedes had a bad transmission; and his house needed repairs. While he searched fruitlessly for an-other managerial position, Gayle took a low-paying job as a secretary to make ends meet. Even so, the Sharlows had to draw on savings that would eventually run out. Gayle stockpiled soap and paper towels in case she and Jim could not afford to buy more.

So the couple was, as Gayle put it, "Keeping up the front." Privately, the Sharlows' precari-ous position ate away at them. "How could my family not think less of me now?" Jim asked. "I failed my family." But his 26-year-old daughter Karen blamed Kodak and the ideal of cor-porate loyalty. "He gave them 26 years," she said bitterly, "and it meant nothing." Meanwhile, the uncertain future loomed. "I try not to lose hope," Gayle admitted, "but I'm afraid we will lose the house, everything. Gone." After sending out 2,205 resumes without success, Jim tried hard to hold onto hope, too. "I believe in the American dream," he insisted. "I feel it fading."

Jim Sharlow was not alone. He often competed with thousands of other people for just one job opening. Across America, many workers were caught in a wave of corporate layoffs known as downsizing. The firings reflected two fundamental trends that decisively shaped the United States in the 1990s: the rise of globalization and the information economy. During this decade, a complex web of economic, technological, social, and political ties bound the United States to the world in fresh ways, which became known as globalization. At the same time, an information economy, based on computers, high-speed communication, and other technologies, emerged as the old industrial economy declined. Globalization and the information economy posed complex challenges for American government and society. Still moving toward conservatism, American democracy struggled with the role of government in the economy, the increasing diversity of the nation's people, and the role of the United States in the post–cold war world.

The Age of Globalization

By the 1990s, Americans increasingly felt enmeshed in global forces. America, of course, had long been defined by its relationship to the world. But this global connection entered a new, more self-conscious phase in the 1980s. During the decade, the term *globalization* first came into use to describe the web of technological, economic, military, political, and cultural developments binding people and nations ever more tightly together. The cold war's end, technological advances, the spread of multinationals and other organizations, the creation of transnational economic alliances, and a new wave of immigration all drew the United States deeper into globalization.

The Cold War and Globalization

For two generations, the cold war had both facilitated and hindered globalization. In some ways, the confrontation between the United States and the Soviet Union linked the world more closely together. Each power had a host of ties to other nations. The United States had established regional military alliances around the world and helped rebuild Asian and European economies through lower trade barriers, the World Bank, and the International Monetary Fund.

Still, the cold war inhibited globalization, too. The United States and the Soviet Union had largely avoided trading with each other. Each power had discouraged its allies from ties with the other side. The collapse of the Soviet Union in 1991 opened the way to further globalization. Now nations and companies could forge new ties more freely across the old cold war divide.

New Communications Technologies

New communications technologies sped up the global flow of news, ideas, and money. The Internet, a product of the cold war, emerged from a Department of Defense search for a means of maintaining communications in the event of a nuclear attack. Aided by the development of the telephone modem and fiber-optic cable, the Internet spread quickly in the 1990s. At first, people used it to send and receive electronic messages, but by the middle of the 1990s, computer users also explored the World Wide Web, a rapidly expanding segment of the Internet that blended text, graphics, audio, and video. By 2000, some 304 million people from more than 40 nations already used the global "information superhighway" to do research, create and exhibit art, listen to music, share photographs and films, and buy and sell online.

Communications satellites also played a critical role in globalization. Following the US deployment of Telstar and other satellites in the 1960s, several other nations launched their own. In the 1990s, global satellite communications revolutionized the news business. Cable News Network (CNN), founded in 1979 by the entrepreneur Ted Turner, used satellite uplinks to provide live televised coverage of events around the world. Turner wanted CNN to be a "positive force in the world, to tie the world together." Satellite news organizations soon appeared in other countries.

Meanwhile, mobile and cellular telephones spread especially quickly in the United States and many other countries. In 1985, only 340,000 Americans subscribed to cell phone service using bulky phones over a primitive analog network. By 2000, more than half the population owned a cell phone. In relatively impoverished Africa, there were already more than 15 million cell telephone subscribers by the early 2000s.

Multinationals and NGOs

Connecting businesses across national borders, communications advances helped stimulate an astonishing increase in the number of multinational corporations. In 1990, there were 3,000 multinationals worldwide. By 2003, the number mushroomed to 63,000. With some 821,000 subsidiaries, multinationals employed about 90 million people and accounted for perhaps one-fourth of the world's economic output.

Long a leader in creating multinationals, the United States remained home to many of the largest and wealthiest. By the end of the century, Wal-Mart was Mexico's largest private-sector employer, with 100,000 workers. But America now faced intense competition from Japan, China, European nations, and others. In 1962, nearly 60 percent of the top 500 multinationals were American; by 1999, the percentage had declined to 36.

Along with multinational companies, private nongovernmental organizations (NGOs) also fostered globalization. Some NGOs, such as the International Red Cross, dated to the nineteenth century. The World Economic Forum, which brought leaders and experts together annually in Davos, Switzerland, was a product of the 1970s. So were the environmentalist Greenpeace and the humanitarian Doctors Without Borders. By the 2000s, there were more than 10,000 NGOs worldwide.

Expanding Trade

Along with peace and communication, the most basic necessity for globalization was the easy movement of goods, services, and capital across national boundaries. After the cold war, nations, eager to seize their share of the global market, aggressively removed barriers to trade and investment. America established economic relationships with the former republics of the USSR, the European countries of the Soviet bloc, the Socialist Republic of Vietnam, and the People's Republic of China. By 1996, Wal-Mart had a store in Beijing, and McDonald's had restaurants in Russia.

To spur international trade and investment, nations also created regional economic alliances that guaranteed member states trading and investment privileges and lowered or abolished tariffs. In 1991, the member states of the European Economic Community, a pioneering regional trade alliance, signed the Maastricht Treaty to create a single vast unit, the European Union (EU), with its own currency, the euro. With 6.4 percent of the global population, the EU produced a third of the world's goods and more than a third of its trade.

The 1990s also witnessed the transformation of the General Agreement on Tariffs and Trade (GATT). A US cold

Globalization Produced Unexpected Sights Sewing American flags in the People's Republic of China under the watchful eye of communist leader Mao Zedong.

war–era creation, GATT had drawn together over 100 nations. Its efforts to increase trade through agreements known as "rounds" culminated in 1993 when the Uruguay Round produced a dramatic victory for free-trade policies. GATT was then reborn as a more powerful global body, the World Trade Organization (WTO), whose decisions would be binding on member nations. The United States joined the WTO in 1995.

Moving People

The movement of human beings as well as goods was critical to globalization. Thanks to regional economic agreements and the end of the cold war, people could cross national borders more easily. Between 1990 and 1994, 4.5 million immigrants came to the United States. By 2000, the immigrant population had reached 26.3 million, about 11 percent of the national total population, the largest percentage since before World War II.

Travel also facilitated globalization by exposing people to other nations and cultures. Thanks to low-cost jet flights and improved living standards, tourism was possibly the largest single global industry by the 1990s.

Contesting Globalization

Despite their differences with one another, political leaders generally agreed with big business that globalization represented a triumph for American institutions and values, including capitalism, free trade, and democracy. Despite tough international economic competition, powerful Americans thought the nation was still better off than in a divided world without free trade.

In contrast, many middle- and working-class Americans questioned whether globalization made their lives better. As economists acknowledged, globalization promoted a kind of national economic specialization. Some American industries, such as information technology, agriculture, and entertainment, fared well in global competition, but others, such as steel and traditional manufacturing, did less well. The result was lower wages and lost jobs for many Americans.

The presence of several million illegal immigrants from Mexico angered many American citizens, particularly in Texas and California. Their argument was familiar: illegal aliens drove down wages and took jobs from native-born Americans who paid higher taxes to provide services and benefits to tax-evading immigrants. In 1994, California voters passed Proposition 187, a referendum denying illegal aliens access to public education and other benefits. Two years later, Congress increased efforts to stop the flow of illegal immigrants.

The anti-immigrant movement continued, but business generally welcomed immigration because it provided workers. Calculating the rapid growth of the Hispanic population, political leaders did not wish to antagonize an increasingly powerful group of voters. Many native-born Americans who were descendants of immigrants believed immigration would invigorate the economy and the culture.

International trade also provoked conflict. The US government, faced with the rapid-fire appearance of regional economic alliances, moved to create its own economic bloc. In 1992, the United States joined with Canada and Mexico in the North American Free Trade Agreement (NAFTA), which established the world's largest and richest low-tariff trading zone. Fearing more lost jobs, organized labor opposed the agreement. So did many environmentalists, who believed corporations would get around US environmental laws by

Titanic and the Globalization of Hollywood

In 1998, *Titanic* became the first Hollywood film to earn more than a billion dollars. That feat was the result of globalization: the cinematic tale of doomed, cross-social-class love, set against the tragic sinking of a huge trans-Atlantic ocean liner on its first voyage in 1912, earned nearly twice as much around the world as it did in the United States. *Titanic*'s enormous international success was unexpected but not unintended. From start to finish, the movie project about a failed attempt to connect nations at the beginning of the twentieth century epitomized the emerging web of global connections at the century's end.

Like the United States more broadly, Hollywood—both the place and the industry—had long interacted with the rest of the world. Immigrants, such as Hungarian-born William Fox, founder of Fox Film Corporation, helped create the business in the 1910s and 1920s. After World War I, Hollywood films found a wide audience in Europe. But the Great Depression and World War II hurt Hollywood's exports, just as those upheavals set back the larger processes of globalization. By the 1960s, new global forces transformed Hollywood. Studios were making "runaway films" abroad rather than in California. In the 1980s and 1990s, Hollywood was remade by global corporate takeovers.

News Corporation, a foreign firm dominated by Australian William Rupert Murdoch, took over Twentieth Century Fox, the successor to Fox Film Corporation.

Hollywood rebounded in the 1990s. As prosperity brought new movie screens around the world, the American industry successfully battled for global audiences. The success of films such as *Titanic* reflected old and new national advantages. *Titanic*'s writer, director, and producer was James Cameron, a Canadian immigrant who sold the project to Twentieth Century Fox, which shot much of the film in Mexico. In addition to new digital technologies, Cameron and his colleagues had the benefit of decades of Hollywood experience making films to appeal to the especially diverse US movie audience. *Titanic* "intentionally incorporates universals of human experience and emotions that are timeless—and familiar because they reflect our basic emotional fabric," Cameron explained. "By dealing in archetypes, the film touches people in all cultures and of all ages."

Along with universal emotions and special effects, *Titanic* reached foreign audiences because, paradoxically, it seemed distinctively American. Even moviegoers in nations at odds with the United States found themselves drawn to the film. In Iran, where many people condemned America

moving operations to Mexico. But the leadership of both major parties favored the agreement, and in 1993, the Senate ratified NAFTA.

Opposition to globalization flared again at a meeting of the WTO in Seattle, Washington, in 1999. Labor unions, environmentalists, consumer activists, women's groups, and other organizations staged parades, meetings, and street theater. Demonstrators charged that the

Titanic in China A woman buys a ticket to the Hollywood blockbuster in Beijing in 1998.

as the "Great Satan," a 28-year-old electrical engineer admitted that "American culture is very dominant." _Titanic_ seemed like a "cultural invasion," he said, but he loved it: "I've memorized every line."

In the communist People's Republic of China, the president speculated that _Titanic_ might be a "Trojan horse," full of cultural invaders from the capitalist, democratic United States. Even so, the president felt he had to let the film be shown. _Titanic_ proved as seductive in China as it did in Iran. "In China today, many people are disillusioned with the past and are searching for new values and new heroes," said a graduate student at Beijing University. "Watching 'Titanic' temporarily injects hope, romance, and fantasy back into some people's lives."

Titanic and the rest of globalized Hollywood seemed to increase the world power of the United States in the 1990s. "The American entertainment complex is one of the strongest forces in the world, and probably has greater global influence than the US military," insisted the dean of an American journalism school.

Other observers argued, however, that globalization had diluted the Americanness of the film business. "Hollywood is not an American industry," a former US ambassador maintained, "but, rather, an entertainment industry that is located in California and belongs to the world." Driven by the capitalist imperative for profit, Hollywood hired foreigners such as Cameron and made films that appealed to "world culture." "This is commerce at its best," the ambassador concluded, "not cultural imperialism."

The argument between the two sides would continue for years to come. In addition, there was a middle ground: because the United States was so diverse, so capitalist, and so open to global forces, the nation took particular advantage of globalization. Precisely because _Titanic_ so fully evoked universal hopes, dreams, and fantasies, the film was quintessentially American. Global and American values seemed to merge into a single widely accepted message and a billion-dollar film.

WTO favored corporations and developed nations, damaged the environment, allowed AIDS to spread, and destroyed indigenous cultures. Fears of protest and terrorism led to cancelation of the WTO meetings scheduled for 2001.

Globalization was hard to defeat. It would take more than isolated protests to halt the movement of people, ideas, technologies, goods, and capital in the twenty-first century.

A New Economy

Globalization combined with technological change to create a new, information-centered American economy. Like the industrial revolution of the nineteenth century, the information economy of the late twentieth century reorganized patterns of work and wealth. But it was unclear whether the new system was quite as revolutionary as the old. Like the Industrial Revolution, the globalized, information economy produced both new insecurity and new prosperity.

From Industry to Information

As global competition closed American factories, the nature of the postindustrial economy became clearer. By the 1990s, factories employed fewer production workers than in 1955; meanwhile, the service sector accounted for about 70 percent of America's economic activity. The rise of services using sophisticated communications, computing, and biomedical technology encouraged the belief that information would define the twenty-first-century economy.

From the 1990s into the next century, innovations in electronics continued to transform communications. High-speed fiber-optic cables, cell phone towers, and satellite dishes expanded the power and reach of telephone and television systems. By 1999, more than half of the nation's households had at least one computer. The new information economy spurred the hope that Americans would process data instead of coal and produce knowledge instead of steel.

Advances in genetics and medical technology further sparked hopes for an information-centered economy. At the close of the twentieth century, scientists made rapid advances in understanding animal and human genomes. Corporations soon began applying this genetic knowledge to agriculture, medicine, and other fields. The result was biomedical technology—the use of organisms and their products to alter health and the environment. By 2000, about one-third of the US corn, cotton, and soybean crops were products of genetic engineering. By then, over 125 genetically engineered drugs had been approved for the treatment of cancer and other diseases.

A Second Economic Revolution?

The information and industrial economies were quite different. Manual, blue-collar labor tended the machines of smokestack America; white-collar, well-educated labor tended the computers of information America. The industrial economy had eaten up fossil fuels, minerals, and other exhaustible resources and produced substantial pollution; the information economy promised less damage to the earth.

In some ways, the rise of the information economy repeated the Industrial Revolution. As in the late 1800s and early 1900s, technological change pushed new corporations to the forefront of American capitalism: e-commerce pioneers such as Amazon.com and eBay, the search engine giant Google, and, in the 2000s, the social-networking leader Facebook. Like the Industrial Revolution, the information revolution spurred a wave of corporate consolidation. In 1989, media company Time, Inc., merged with entertainment conglomerate Warner Communications; in 1995, Time Warner then gobbled Turner Broadcasting. During the 1990s, Microsoft took over 46 companies.

The information revolution also paralleled the Industrial Revolution by producing a wealthy elite. The most famous of the new multibillionaires was Bill Gates, cofounder of

Microsoft, who became the richest American since John D. Rockefeller, the cofounder of Standard Oil nearly a century before.

Just as the appearance of trains, planes, and machines stimulated artists and intellectuals in the nineteenth and twentieth centuries, so did the appearance of computers a century later. Digital technology made it easy to copy and manipulate text, images, and sounds, a development that encouraged collage and undermined linear narratives. More broadly, some thinkers believed a new, postmodern culture was replacing the modern culture inspired by industrialism. Hard to define, postmodern culture embraced a more skeptical view of accepted truths and dominant ideologies, and the techniques of hypertext and cut and paste.

Despite parallels to the Industrial Revolution, the information economy was not as potent a revolutionary force in critical ways. Machine tools, railroads, and electricity had greatly boosted workers' productivity in the industrial era. Computers, the Internet, and biotechnology did not do the same. Moreover, factories had generated the need for additional jobs in supporting businesses, such as mining and transportation. Information-centered businesses did not have the same effect. Despite the glamour of information and biotechnology, most service jobs required little education, used limited technology, and paid less than the best blue-collar jobs of the old economy. By the 2000s, the biggest employer in America was not an information company but rather a low-wage retail store, Wal-Mart.

Downsizing America

Like the Industrial Revolution, the information economy and global competition produced upheaval. Along with Jim Sharlow, millions of American workers found themselves victims of corporate downsizing. The cutbacks were remarkable for several reasons: they came during a period of relative prosperity, they involved some of the largest and seemingly most stable American companies, such as the computing firm IBM and the communications giant AT&T, and they affected many white-collar workers. Large corporations, typically quick to lay off assembly-line and other blue-collar employees, had traditionally been slow to cut loose white-collar workers. But now managers and professionals were vulnerable to unemployment as well.

Fundamentally, downsizing reflected corporate managers' imperative to cut costs and increase profits. Despite the general prosperity, management worried about remaining efficient and competitive in the global economy. The end of the cold war also affected American corporations. As the federal government downsized the military, defense contractors lost business, and they, too, had to downsize.

Downsizing dramatically affected American workers. Those who lost their jobs, like Jim Sharlow, faced an unsettling search for new employment. Many had to settle for lower-paying jobs and cope with a sense of failure and dislocation. Meanwhile, the remaining employees at downsized companies found themselves working harder than ever as they took over the responsibilities of laid-off coworkers. Realizing that they could lose their jobs at any moment, employees felt less loyalty to corporations. More broadly, downsizing suggested that the American middle class was not so stable and secure after all.

Not surprisingly, downsizing was controversial. Critics charged that downsizing actually made companies less efficient because the strategy left them short-handed and deprived them of experienced workers' know-how. Downsizing, the critics concluded, was just "dumbsizing." But corporations insisted that downsizing was necessary to restore efficiency, competitiveness, and profits. Rather than threaten the middle class, downsizing would assure its future by paving the way for better, high-paying jobs in new sectors of the globalized, information economy.

Boom and Insecurity

Despite—or because of—downsizing, globalization and the information revolution seemed to benefit the economy for most of the 1990s. Productive American workers and a vital service sector produced economic growth for nearly the entire decade, a record. Because of global competition, corporate cost cutting, and low oil prices, inflation was negligible. Interest rates stayed low; unemployment dropped to record lows. Excitement about information-related companies drove the stock market to one record high after another. After passing 3,000 for the first time ever in 1991, the Dow Jones industrial average soared past 11,000 in 1999. As memories of the 1987 market crash faded, many Americans no longer felt the need to live with less. Congress repealed the federal 55-mile-per-hour speed limit for interstate highways in 1995, and gas-guzzling sport utility vehicles (SUVs) became popular.

Nevertheless, Americans felt a continuing sense of insecurity about basic features of American life. From 1993 to 2004, the cost of tuition at four-year colleges increased about 50 percent above inflation. As a result, the debt burden on students and their families increased dramatically as well. The information economy depended on a highly educated workforce, but many Americans worried whether they could afford the education they needed.

The increasing costs of health care also troubled Americans. In the 1990s, the United States spent a greater proportion of its gross domestic product on health care than did other developed nations. Still, 14 percent of Americans had no health insurance in 2000. The United States, almost alone among developed nations, had no national health insurance plan for its citizens. As employers cut costs, they decreased medical benefits for employees. The need for costly medical care would only increase as life expectancy continued to rise and the huge baby boom generation aged.

Americans feared, too, that they could not afford retirement. With the aging of the baby boom generation, there were more Americans over 65 and eligible for Social Security benefits than ever before (see Map 29–1). Many people believed there would not be enough money to pay pensions in the twenty-first century. Private employers, meanwhile, reduced pension benefits for many retirees.

The Social Security, health care, and college issues, along with corporate downsizing, fostered an undertone of anxiety in the midst of prosperity. Even though the economy grew and the stock market flourished, Americans were unsure whether the future would be so prosperous. This uneasiness contributed to a broader uncertainty about the age of globalization.

Democratic Deadlock

The economic dynamism of the 1990s was often accompanied by political deadlock. After Ronald Reagan's presidency, his supporters hoped that conservative Republicans would continue to remake American politics. While conservative ideas continued to influence policy, Republicans and Democrats shared power in Washington, DC. Although party leaders generally agreed about globalization, they still differed over many other issues, such as taxes and government spending. Many Americans were unhappy with

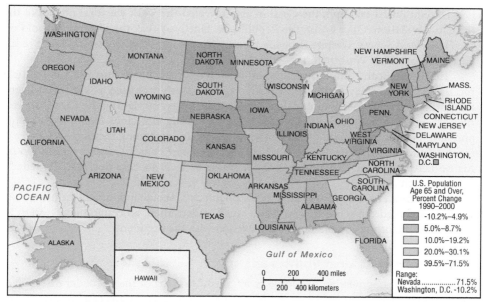

Map 29-1   Aging in America The increase in the percentage of the US population age 65 and over from 1980 to 2000 helped fuel worries about health care and Social Security.
Sources: US Census Bureau, *Population Estimates, July 1, 2000, to July 1*, 2006. He Wan, Manisha Sengupta, Victoria A. Velkoff, and Kimberly A. DeBarros, US Census Bureau, *Current Population Reports, P23-209, 65+ in the United States: 2005* (Washington, DC: US Government Printing Office, 2005).

politics as usual and some were angry enough with the government to resort to terrorism. Nevertheless, the political system remained largely unchanged and no party or philosophy seemed fully able to mold politics and government.

George H. W. Bush and the End of the Reagan Revolution

The natural choice for Reagan's successor, Vice President George H. W. Bush of Texas, was not a conservative but a moderate willing to make political compromises. Bush, the son of a Wall Street banker and US senator from Connecticut, had attended elite schools and become part of the upper-class "Establishment" that many conservatives distrusted. Nevertheless, Bush had loyally served Reagan through two terms. Bush had a broad background of government service, including stints as a congressman, ambassador to the United Nations, chair of the Republican Party, liaison to China, and director of the CIA.

Committing himself to Reagan's economic policy, Bush easily won the Republican presidential nomination in 1988. "Read my lips," he vowed: "No new taxes." At the same time, Bush softened the image of the new conservatism by emphasizing his support for education and the environment. He easily defeated the Democratic nominee, former Governor Michael Dukakis of Massachusetts, who ran a colorless, ineffective campaign calling for efficient government, civil rights, and little more. On election day, Bush polled 53 percent of the popular vote and carried 40 states for a total of 426 electoral votes.

Despite Bush's triumph, the election also revealed the weak electoral impact of the Reagan Revolution. Once again, the Republicans failed to break the Democrats' hold on the House and Senate. Despite Reagan's accomplishments, voters still would not give his party full control in Washington.

The Republicans' limited victory in 1988 reinforced Bush's instinct for political moderation. Downplaying the conservative agenda, Bush promised a "kinder and gentler" presidency. He disappointed conservatives, however, by signing the Clean Air Act of 1990, which attempted to reduce acid rain by cutting emissions from power plants and automobiles. He disappointed conservatives again by signing measures to increase federal funding for education. Above all, he alienated conservatives by abandoning his no-tax pledge and agreeing to a tax increase in 1990 to help decrease the federal budget deficit.

Bush's moderation did not ensure his popularity. The abandonment of his no-tax pledge reinforced the sense that he was a weak leader. Then, an economic recession in 1991–1992 intensified Americans' dissatisfaction with the president.

The Rebellion Against Politics as Usual

Americans' unhappiness with George H. W. Bush was part of their broader dissatisfaction with politicians and government. By the 1990s, there were signs of a brewing popular rebellion against politics as usual. Back in 1964, 76 percent of Americans had believed they could trust the government to do what was right always or most of the time. But Lyndon Johnson's "credibility gap" and Richard Nixon's lies and cover-ups had shaken Americans' faith in presidents and politicians in the 1960s and 1970s. Politics in the 1980s, including the Iran-Contra scandal, had done little to restore that faith. By 1994, only 19 percent of the American people felt they could trust government. Politicians, Americans believed, were unethical and out of touch with ordinary citizens.

That belief was reinforced by new ethical scandals that compelled the resignation of the Speaker of the House in 1989 and the reprimand of five senators in 1991. Americans were troubled by the feeling that politicians were ineffective as well as unethical. By the early 1990s, commentators bemoaned the "gridlock" in Washington. Like cars stuck in a massive traffic jam, legislation could not move past obstinate, squabbling politicians in Congress and the White House. During Bush's term, the president and Congress seemed unable to cooperate on critical issues. Bush vetoed legislation more than 40 times. Unable to agree on a budget with Congress, the president actually shut down "nonessential" government services over Columbus Day weekend in 1990. That episode epitomized many Americans' sense that the government no longer served their needs.

People grew still more frustrated because politicians seemed unwilling to reform. By the 1990s, there was widespread agreement that money played too large a role in elections. Politicians spent much of their time raising contributions for expensive campaigns. Americans feared that huge donations from special interest groups and wealthy individuals were corrupting politics. Although Congress and the president talked about the need for campaign finance reform, they could not bring themselves to change the system. Attempts to reform election spending failed repeatedly.

Americans tried other ways to reform Washington. There was considerable interest in passing laws that would limit the number of terms that officials could serve in Congress. But term limits, which could deny people the right to vote for the candidate of their choice, were too controversial. Instead, Americans settled for a more modest reform, the Twenty-seventh Amendment to the Constitution, which would keep a congressional pay increase from taking effect until after the next election. Known as the "Madison Amendment" for its originator, President James Madison, the measure ensured that members of a Congress had to face the voters before getting a raise. Amid the popular anger at Congress, the amendment, which was originally introduced in 1789, was finally ratified in 1992.

For a moment, it seemed as if popular disaffection was about to revolutionize American politics. Running a tired campaign for reelection in 1992, George H. W. Bush faced a sudden challenge from the strongest independent candidate in years, Ross Perot of Texas. A pugnacious, plainspoken billionaire businessman, Perot played to Americans' unhappiness with the political system by promising to end gridlock, balance the budget, and reform campaign finances.

When voters began to wonder whether the quirky Perot could be an effective president, it was the Democratic nominee, Governor Bill Clinton of Arkansas, and not President Bush, who seemed to embody hopes for change. Calling himself a "New Democrat," the charismatic Clinton polled 43 percent of the popular vote to Bush's 37 percent and Perot's surprisingly strong 19 percent. Clinton managed to assemble the kind of voting coalition that had put Franklin Roosevelt and Harry Truman in the White House. Holding on to black support, the Arkansas governor won back many white southerners and workers, the so-called Reagan Democrats. For the first time in 12 years, a Democrat occupied the White House. With the Democrats in control of the House and Senate as well, it seemed as if gridlock would come to an end.

The Democratic Ticket, 1992 Presidential nominee Bill Clinton (right) would be elected president in 1992 and 1996; Al Gore (left) would win the vice presidency twice before losing the presidential election of 2000.

Clinton's Compromise with Conservatism

In some ways, Clinton's election marked a shift in American political life. The first president born after World War II, Clinton was the first of the baby boom generation to become president. His marriage to fellow lawyer Hillary Rodham was another hint of change. The new first lady was the first presidential wife with her own professional career outside the home.

Clinton did act like a "New Democrat" by balancing traditional liberal activism with more conservative efforts to shrink government. In 1993, he won congressional approval for a national service plan that provided money for college to young people who performed community service. He signed the Family and Medical Leave Act of 1993, which allowed government workers and employees in most companies with 50 or more workers to take up to 12 weeks of unpaid leave to deal with birth, adoption, or family illness. Clinton was convinced that the federal government could not play an effective social role or maintain prosperity without balancing the budget. As part of a plan to "reinvent government," the president moved to cut the size of the federal workforce.

Nevertheless, Clinton lost his most important legislative battle, an attempt to achieve the longtime liberal goal of federally backed national health insurance. In the face of determined opposition from pharmaceutical companies, health insurers, and conservatives, the Health Security Act of 1993, which required employers to provide medical insurance for workers, was defeated.

Meanwhile, a series of scandals, involving allegations about a corrupt real estate deal in Arkansas, the misuse of confidential FBI files, the mistreatment of White House staff, the suicide of a longtime friend, and a lawsuit over an extramarital affair, threatened Clinton's reputation as a reformer. But a court-appointed special prosecutor, Kenneth Starr, did not indict Clinton on any of these matters. Even so, the president's reputation suffered.

As Clinton struggled, power flowed to the Republicans. In 1994, voters, disappointed by Clinton and the congressional Democrats, awarded control of the House of Representatives to Republicans for the first time in 40 years. Emboldened, the new Republican majority chose an outspoken conservative, Newt Gingrich of Georgia, as the Speaker of the House. The Republicans vowed to enact a conservative "Contract with America" that featured a balanced budget amendment to the Constitution, term limits, increased defense spending, welfare reform, and tax cuts. The Republicans, however, overplayed their hand. In 1995–1996, Gingrich and congressional Republicans forced two shutdowns of the federal government. Although the Republicans kept control of Congress for the remainder of the decade, the shutdowns hurt the popularity of the party, which failed to enact key provisions of its "Contract," including the balanced budget amendment and term limits.

The Republicans' miscalculation gave Clinton a second chance. To win back the public, the president compromised with conservatism. "The era of big Government is over," he declared in 1996. That year Clinton signed a welfare bill that significantly reduced federal support for the poor, especially children. Reflecting the conservative emphasis on individual responsibility, the measure tried to minimize the role of the federal government in people's lives. The welfare bill replaced Aid to Families with Dependent Children (AFDC), which had long guaranteed federal payments to the poor, with grants to the states for use as they saw fit. To discourage dependence on government handouts, the bill limited welfare recipients to five years of assistance over their lifetime and required heads of households on welfare to find work within two years. To discourage extramarital pregnancies that supposedly threatened "family values," the bill imposed restrictions on unwed teenage mothers receiving benefits and offered bonuses for states with declining rates of illegitimate childbirth. Many Democrats and liberals angrily claimed that the president had betrayed the poor.

Running for reelection in 1996, Clinton benefited from his compromise with conservatism, the strength of the economy, and the weakness of his opponents. Ross Perot had created a new organization, the Reform Party, but his presidential candidacy could not rekindle the enthusiasm of 1992. The Republicans turned to moderate Bob Dole of Kansas, the Senate Majority Leader, who seemed to epitomize the career Washington politician so many Americans distrusted. Never seriously threatened by Dole or Perot, Clinton won a clear victory with 49 percent of the popular vote. Dole attracted 41 percent of the popular vote and Perot only 8 percent.

Domestic Dissent and Terrorism

Beyond Washington, DC, another, more violent series of confrontations emerged over the role of the federal government in the lives of Americans. By the 1990s, a small number of Americans claimed the right, for religious or political reasons, to live free from governmental authority, which almost inevitably brought them into conflict with the federal government. The result was a series of deadly episodes that raised difficult questions about the way Washington used its power.

In 1992, Randy Weaver, a white separatist who wanted to keep his family away from other races and the government, failed to appear for a trial on weapons charges. As a result, federal agents converged on his remote cabin in Ruby Ridge, Idaho, but Weaver resisted arrest. An 11-day siege, punctuated by two gun battles, ended with the deaths of Weaver's wife, one of his sons, and a federal marshal. For some Americans, the Ruby Ridge confrontation demonstrated the arrogance and deceitfulness of the federal government. They felt vindicated in 1995 when Weaver was acquitted of assault, the US Justice Department agreed to pay him a $3.1 million settlement, five federal agents were suspended for misconduct, and one was convicted of obstruction of justice.

In 1993, another siege provoked more charges about the arrogance of federal power. David Koresh, the leader of the tiny Branch Davidian religious sect, had gathered about a hundred heavily armed followers in a compound outside Waco, Texas, to wait for the end of the world. When the federal Bureau of Alcohol, Tobacco, and Firearms (ATF) moved to arrest Koresh on weapons charges, a fierce gun battle killed four agents and at least five Branch Davidians. Hundreds of law enforcement officers, including FBI agents, then surrounded the compound. After an 11-day standoff, federal agents pumped tear gas into the compound and it burned down on April 19. At least 72 Branch Davidians, including Koresh and 17 children, died—some from bullets fired by members of the sect. Many Americans blamed Koresh for the horrifying fire, but others blamed the federal government. For critics of the FBI and the Clinton administration, Waco stood as a symbol of Washington's intolerance of personal and religious freedom.

After the Waco and Ruby Ridge incidents, right-wing paramilitary groups, known as "Patriots" and "civil militias," trained with weapons to protect themselves from a government that supposedly planned to take away Americans' guns and freedom. Other extremists denied that local, state, or national government had the right to tax American citizens.

"Temporarily Closed," 1995–1996

Arriving at the main gate of Everglades National Park in Florida, tourists eagerly expected to explore the nation's largest subtropical wilderness. Instead, they were brought up short by a sign that read "Temporarily Closed." The park wasn't the only federal site that failed to open as usual on November 14, 1995. Across the country, many offices of the US government were closed for business.

How could such a shutdown happen? It wasn't because of a revolution or a natural disaster; it was because of a lack of money. Even though the US Treasury still had plenty of revenues from taxes, fees, and bond sales, the Republican-controlled Congress and President Bill Clinton had been unable to agree on the budget law that would authorize the government to spend on salaries, goods, and services.

The disagreement reflected deep differences over the proper functions of government and the importance of a balanced federal budget. Congressional Republicans, led by Bob Dole of Kansas, the Senate Majority Leader, and Newt Gingrich of Georgia, the Speaker of the House, wanted

the annual budget deficit gradually reduced by cutting federal programs, such as Medicare, that Clinton and Democrats valued. When the Republicans sent the president a spending bill requiring him to commit to a balanced budget, Clinton vetoed the measure and the government of arguably the richest, most powerful nation on earth ran out of money.

The government had shut down briefly before. In the 1980s, budget disagreements sent federal workers home for less than a day three times; in 1990, a standoff between President George H. W. Bush and Democrats in Congress closed the government for three days over a holiday weekend. But 1995 was different. The federal government shut down five days in November and then, after a failed attempt to negotiate a budget, shut down again in December.

The government didn't close completely. By law, more than 2 million "essential" workers, including military personnel, had to stay on the job with the promise of getting paid when the budget was settled. But several hundred thousand

A handful of antigovernment extremists did more than train with guns and denounce Washington. On April 19, 1995—the second anniversary of the Waco tragedy—a car bomb exploded in front of a federal building in Oklahoma City, Oklahoma. Destroying much of the structure, the blast killed 169 people, including children in a day-care center. Americans were stunned that the worst terrorist attack in the nation's history at that time had occurred not in a metropolitan center like New York City or Los Angeles, but in the nation's heartland. People were even more surprised when they learned the terrorists were not foreigners but American-born critics of the federal government. In 1997, Timothy McVeigh, an Army veteran with ties to a right-wing militia group, was convicted "nonessential" personnel, including Park Service workers, were laid off. Many of these workers worried about how to make ends meet. Around the country, restaurants, parking lots, and other small businesses that served federal workers suffered. States feared the loss of federal money for unemployment programs, home loans, rent subsidies for the poor, payments to military veterans, and other programs. Despite the exceptions for "essential" workers, the shutdown underscored the many ways that the federal government affected the lives of Americans.

Nevertheless, the shutdown didn't badly disrupt the United States. Some Republicans cited the situation as proof that big government was not so important after all. Even so, a number of Republican congressmen wanted exceptions to the shutdown, such as keeping wildlife refuges open for hunting, in their districts. "Those guys didn't pass a budget and suddenly it comes home to them," said an Interior Department official. "It's sort of like the Republican rattlesnake eating its own tail."

The Republican Party suffered politically, too. Opinion polls suggested that more Americans blamed the shutdown on congressional Republicans than on President Clinton. The Republicans weren't helped when Speaker Gingrich revealed

that he had helped provoke the shutdown partly because Clinton hadn't given him a good seat or negotiated with him during a trip on Air Force One.

Clinton felt the heat as well. Finally accepting the Republicans' demand for a seven-year plan to balance the budget, the president came to an agreement with Gingrich and Dole to bring back federal workers on January 6, 1996. But Clinton's compromise with conservatism helped him win reelection by defeating Bob Dole in November that year.

In some respects, the two shutdowns of 1995–1996 were not epochal events. Arguably, the democratic system had worked: Clinton and congressional Republicans, driven by different understandings of government, had ultimately resolved their differences without a national collapse. Yet American leaders had been able to settle budget issues for decades without shutting down the government for 27 days. By using the shutdowns to fight their battles, the nation's elected officials also helped weaken democracy. Many Americans had one more reason not to trust politicians. "It just confirms how I felt about the political system in this country," declared elementary school teacher Marilyn Pina of Los Angeles. "It's no longer effective. It's just bogged down."

of murdering the victims of the bombing. Additionally, a friend of McVeigh's confessed to a role in planning the bombing, and another friend was convicted of conspiracy and manslaughter for his role.

The Oklahoma City bombing was followed by other incidents that raised fears of domestic terrorism. In July 1996, during the Olympic games in Atlanta, Georgia, a bomb went off in a crowded park, killing one person. That tragedy was followed by the bombings of an abortion clinic in an Atlanta suburb in January 1997, a lesbian bar in Atlanta in February that same year, and a reproductive services clinic in Birmingham, Alabama, in February 1998, which killed two people. The perpetrator in each of these incidents was Eric

Rudolph, an Army veteran vaguely tied to white supremacists and antigovernment militia, and an opponent of what he called "global socialism" and "the Washington government." Confessing to the bombings, Rudolph was sentenced to two consecutive life sentences.

The sudden spread of domestic terrorism emphasized how much the power of the federal government, along with such changes as legalized abortion and the increased rights of minorities and women since the 1960s, provoked discontent. Almost paradoxically, Americans such as Rudolph, who were troubled by the rights of others, wanted the right to live free from government.

Scandal

Despite his reelection, Clinton no longer seemed like an agent of political change. Then, in 1998, scandal engulfed his presidency. Independent counsel Kenneth Starr and a grand jury explored whether the president had obstructed justice by covering up a sexual relationship with a young White House intern, Monica Lewinsky. When the story broke, Clinton at first denied but then finally admitted "inappropriate intimate contact" with Lewinsky.

For a time, Clinton's presidency hung in the balance. In November 1998, he agreed to pay $500,000 to settle the lawsuit from a former extramarital lover. In December, the Republican-dominated House issued two articles of impeachment charging Clinton with perjury and obstruction of justice for his testimony about Lewinsky. The following month, he became only the second president to go on trial in the Senate. Because the Constitution required a two-thirds majority to convict, the Republicans needed to persuade some Democrats to vote against the president. But Republican and Democratic senators alike were well aware that Clinton remained surprisingly popular. Most Americans, whatever they thought of Clinton's relationship with Lewinsky, seemed willing to separate the private and public lives of the president. Approving of Clinton's handling of his public duties, including the economy, the majority of Americans did not want him removed from office. In February 1999, the Senate voted to acquit Clinton on both articles of impeachment.

Clinton held on to the presidency, but he lost the opportunity to make a major impact on public policy in his second term. Clinton's complicated legacy would rest on his management of the economy and the federal budget, his attempts to chart a course between liberalism and conservatism, and his private scandals. More broadly, the Clinton presidency reinforced the sense that politicians did not serve democracy well enough.

Republicans contributed to that sense, too. In 1999, after a House committee condemned Speaker Newt Gingrich's apparent violations of both House rules on personal finances and federal tax law, he resigned from Congress. Then his designated Republican successor admitted extramarital affairs and quit as well.

The Presidential Election of 2000

Against the backdrop of scandal, the Republicans nominated George W. Bush, then-governor of Texas, for president in 2000. The son of George H. W. Bush, the Republican nominee shared his father's moderation. Although critics questioned his experience and ability, the younger Bush benefited from the unity and enthusiasm of Republicans eager to reclaim the White House. He benefited, too, from the decision of the Democratic nominee, Vice President Al Gore of Tennessee, to distance himself from the record of the Clinton administration.

What was a dull campaign suddenly became riveting on election night when the contest between the two men turned out to be too close to call. As the vote counts stretched into days and then weeks without a clear result, there were fears of a constitutional crisis. The battle turned on the vote in Florida, where Bush held a fluctuating lead of a few hundred votes and Gore wanted a recount. Finally the justices of the United States Supreme Court, risking their credibility, settled the partisan battle with a controversial 5-to-4 ruling that effectively halted the recount Gore needed. Certified the victor in Florida, George W. Bush became the president-elect.

In one of the closest presidential elections in American history, Gore actually won the popular ballot with 550,000 more votes than Bush received, but Bush won the Electoral College, and therefore the election, with 271 votes to Gore's 266. The narrow margin of victory and the narrow differences between the two candidates emphasized the persistence of political gridlock. The uncertainty over the outcome also reinforced fears that American democracy was not working as well as it should.

Culture Wars

While quarrels over the economy and government pushed the nation somewhat toward conservatism, issues involving individual rights and social values moved America in the opposite direction. As the experience of African Americans underscored, race and rights remained explosive and divisive matters in the 1990s. Concern about rights also spurred a series of "culture wars" over family, sexual values, women, and the gay and lesbian community. Generally speaking, these struggles suggested that Americans were becoming more tolerant of social diversity and more willing to extend rights to disadvantaged groups.

African Americans in the Post-Civil Rights Era

For African Americans, life in the post–civil rights era had become a complex pattern of increasing gains and continuing inequities. Decades after the monumental *Brown v. Board of Education* decision in 1954, southern schools were largely desegregated, but thanks to white flight from inner cities, northern schools were more segregated than ever. On the plus side, however, graduation rates for African Americans increased significantly. In 1957, only 18 percent of black adults had graduated from high school. By 2002, 79 percent had graduated high school. Even so, the African American graduation rate lagged 10 percentage points behind the rate for whites.

Blacks had also made notable economic and political gains. The black middle class continued to grow at the turn of the twenty-first century. Yet high rates of unemployment and imprisonment meant that only about six out of every ten black men and women were in the paid workforce in 2002. The ranks of African American public officials also grew.

As notable as these "firsts" was the fact that so few whites objected. By the twenty-first century, in public at least, Americans were unwilling to contest the outcomes of the civil rights era. Many whites admired African American art such as rap music and the broader hip-hop culture. And whites idolized black athletes such as the professional basketball player Michael Jordan.

This acceptance did not mean the end of racial injustice and conflict in the United States. During the 1990s, three episodes, each involving the nation's legal system, dramatized the continuing unequal status of African Americans. In 1991, George H. W. Bush nominated a conservative African American judge, Clarence Thomas, to succeed Thurgood Marshall, the first African American justice on the Supreme Court. Thomas's Senate confirmation hearings included televised accusations of sexual harassment by a former subordinate, African American lawyer Anita Hill. Angrily denying her story, Thomas denounced the hearings as "a high-tech lynching for uppity blacks." The Senate shortly confirmed his nomination to the court, but Americans were left to wonder whether Thomas had been singled out for public embarrassment because of his race.

Also in 1991, white police in Los Angeles stopped an African American motorist, Rodney King, for drunk driving and then savagely beat him. Unknown to the officers, an onlooker had videotaped the beating. Despite this evidence, an all-white jury acquitted four of the policemen of all charges in April 1992. The stunning verdict set off rioting in the predominantly African American community of South Central Los Angeles, including the Watts section, which had been the center of rioting in 1965. Three days of violence left 51 people dead, 1,800 injured, and nearly 3,700 buildings burned. In the aftermath, Americans debated whether the legal system offered justice to African Americans while liberals and conservatives blamed each other for the poverty and despair of many black communities. Eventually a federal court convicted two of the police officers for depriving King of his civil rights and another court awarded $3.8 million in damages. But no one had concrete solutions to the problems of South Central Los Angeles.

Three years later, difficult questions about race and justice arose again when Los Angeles police charged O.J. Simpson, a popular African American actor, sports announcer, and former professional football player, with the murders of his white ex-wife and her male friend. During Simpson's criminal trial for the killings, his lawyers suggested that racist white police had lied and planted evidence to frame him. The mostly African American jury voted to acquit Simpson in October 1995, but in a civil trial in February 1997, a mostly white jury ordered Simpson to pay millions of dollars in damages to the families of the victims. The Simpson case laid bare deep differences in outlook between whites and African Americans. Most whites believed him guilty; most African Americans believed him innocent.

The Simpson case, the King beating, and the Thomas hearings provoked passionate debate but resulted in relatively little action. These episodes did help inspire the 1995 "Million Man March," a massive demonstration of 800,000 African American men at Washington, DC, organized by Minister Louis Farrakhan of the Nation of Islam, to dramatize their commitment to community, family, and personal responsibility. The march suggested the potential for mass action by African Americans, but that potential was largely unrealized in the 1990s.

Feeling less pressure from blacks, the federal government took few new steps to deal with racial inequality. In an age of popular pessimism about government activism, relatively few Americans seemed to believe that new

The Emotional Power of the Rodney King Case As a jury deliberated over the case against King's attackers, a woman prayed in church.

liberal programs, even on the scale of the Great Society of the 1960s, could secure equal conditions for African Americans. At the same time Americans did not want to undo the achievements of the past.

"Family Values"

The same concern about rights that affected issues of race also drove a cluster of controversies known as "culture wars." At the center of the culture wars was an intense debate over the family. By the end of the twentieth century, the ongoing transformation of the American family had become unmistakable. In the 1950s, two out of three families had a parent who stayed at home full time; by 2000, with so many mothers in the workforce, fewer than one in four families had a stay-at-home parent. The supposedly "traditional" nuclear family of father, mother, and children no longer predominated American households (see Table 29–1). Married couples with children, 40 percent of all households as late as 1970, made up only 25 percent by 1996. There were proportionally fewer families because more Americans were living alone: the percentage of single-person households rose from 17 percent in 1970 to 25 percent in 1996. Families themselves were also less likely to fit the traditional model romanticized in the situation comedies of 1950s television. By 1996, 27 percent of families with children contained one parent, usually a mother, rather than two.

A number of factors led to these changes in family structure. Americans were marrying later, having fewer children, and having them later in life. The divorce rate had doubled from 1960 to 1990. In the 1990s, about half of all marriages were ending in divorce. As women's wages gradually rose, more women could afford to live alone or to head families by themselves.

Many conservatives and Republicans blamed these developments on the nation's alleged moral decline. In their view, the counterculture of the 1960s, liberals, the media, feminists, gays, and others had undermined the nation's "family values." "It is a cultural war, as critical to the kind of nation we will one day be as was the Cold War itself," thundered the conservative commentator and presidential candidate Patrick Buchanan in a speech to the Republican national convention in 1992. He urged the delegates to "take back our culture, and take back our country." That year, George H. W. Bush's vice president, Dan Quayle,

Table 29-1 The Changing American Household, 1960–2000

Year	Households*	Families*	Married-Couple Families % of Total Households	Single-Parent Families % of Total Households	One-Person Households % of Total Households
1960	52,799	44,905	74.3%	10.7%	15.0%
1970	63,401	51,456	70.5%	10.6%	18.8%
1980*	80,776	59,550	60.8%	12.9%	26.3%
1990	93,347	66,090	56.0%	14.8%	29.2%
2000	104,705	72,025	52.8%	16.0%	31.2%

Source: US Census Bureau, *Current Population Survey, March and Annual Social and Economic Supplements, 2011 and Earlier,* http://www.census.gov/population/socdemo/hh-fam/hh1.xls.

*Numbers given in thousands.

**Revised using population controls based on the 1980 census.

attacked the TV sitcom *Murphy Brown* for supposedly denigrating fatherhood through its positive portrayal of the title character's decision to have a child out of wedlock. Some defenders of the family suggested that single mothers should receive fewer welfare benefits and that divorce should be made more difficult.

Liberals fought back by denying that conservatives spoke for real "family values." The conservatives, they claimed, failed to understand that the family was not dying but simply adapting to change as it always had. The different forms of the family, like social diversity in general, were supposedly a good thing. Whatever the merits of the liberal argument, conservatives found the cultural wars for "family values" almost impossible to win. *Murphy Brown* stayed on the air, but Quayle and George H. W. Bush lost their bid for reelection.

Multiculturalism

While liberals and conservatives quarreled over the family, they also fought over the state of culture in America. Since the 1960s, the authority of the Western literary, artistic, and philosophical heritage had been under attack from several directions. Literary critics and other advocates of "deconstruction" argued that cultural products possessed no inherent, objective value, that Western culture was revered not because of any intrinsic merit but because it reflected the interests of powerful Europeans and Americans. Other people, these critics felt, should be free to place a lesser value on Western culture.

Beginning in the 1960s, several groups did just that. As they demanded rights, feminists, African Americans, gays, lesbians, and other groups maintained that white heterosexual European men had not produced all important ideas and art. Society in general and schools in particular needed to recognize the cultural contributions of the disadvantaged and the oppressed. Instead of worshiping one culture, America needed to practice multiculturalism. At Stanford University in 1987, the Reverend Jesse Jackson joined students to protest a Western culture course that excluded the accomplishments of women and minorities. "Hey hey, ho ho," the crowd chanted, "Western culture's got to go!"

That cry horrified conservatives who believed that Western cultural values were vitally important for the well-being of American society. The conservatives charged that the multiculturalists were destroying the Western heritage. Further, the multiculturalists were destroying free speech by making it impossible for anyone to question their positions. This coercive "political correctness" or "PC" was actually promoting conformity instead of diversity. On some college campuses, the conservatives noted, PC speech codes punished students for using language that might offend others. The conservatives also attacked the National Endowment for the Humanities (NEH) and the National Endowment for the Arts (NEA), created by the liberal Great Society in the 1960s, for unfairly funding politically correct academic and artistic projects that flouted Western values.

Liberals, academics, artists, and others responded by defending the NEH, the NEA, campus speech codes, and multiculturalism. It was the conservatives, they asserted, who were trying to censor curricula and wipe out diversity.

In the end, the controversies over culture and the family did little to undermine the new diversity of American life. Although Congress cut the budgets of the NEH and the NEA, these agencies survived the conservative attack, states did little to make divorce more difficult, and the process of globalization continued to confront Americans with the diversity of world cultures. Meanwhile, the trends toward diverse households and multiculturalism continued.

Women in the Postfeminist Era

As the *Murphy Brown* controversy suggested, women, so often a focal point for fears about social change, were at the center of the culture wars. By the 1990s, women's place in society had changed dramatically since the feminist campaigns of the 1960s and 1970s. The percentage of adult women in the workforce had increased, along with the percentage of women in high-paying white-collar jobs. Women were also more visible in politics. After the 1992 elections, a record 53 women held seats in Congress. In 1993, Janet Reno became the first female attorney general, and Madeleine Albright became the first female secretary of state.

Nevertheless, women faced continuing discrimination. A woman was still likely to make less money than a man. She was also much more likely to live in poverty. Like African Americans, women were still underrepresented in Congress and other governmental bodies. Highly publicized incidents of the sexual harassment of women by a male US senator and by past and present male members of the US military provoked widespread public discussion about the nature of relationships between men and women. As the sexes differed over what constituted harassment, many women complained that men "just don't get it." The Clarence Thomas confirmation hearings were not only about race; they were also about gender. For many Americans, Thomas's alleged treatment of Anita Hill dramatized the widespread harassment of women in the workplace.

Despite such revelations, the organized feminist movement did not grow dramatically at the end of the twentieth century. Many Americans seemed to accept the expansion of women's rights but to reject feminism and feminists as too radical. Feminists often found themselves defending earlier accomplishments, such as affirmative-action programs, rather than pushing for new objectives.

Abortion provided a case in point. From the 1980s into the 1990s, the conservative Right to Life movement continued its passionate campaign against abortion. At the grassroots level, protestors picketed abortion clinics and tried to discourage pregnant women from having abortions. Some radicals, such as Eric Rudolph (discussed earlier in this chapter), resorted to violence, including the murder of clinic workers. Meanwhile, George H. W. Bush condemned abortion as "murder" and, like Reagan before him, named antiabortion judges to the federal courts.

In spite of this assault, the right and practice of abortion continued in the 1990s. The Supreme Court declined to overturn its decision in *Roe v. Wade*, acknowledging the constitutional right to abortion. In *Planned Parenthood v. Casey* in 1992, the Court did vote narrowly to uphold much of a Pennsylvania law limiting access to abortions. But the court also declared that a woman's right to choose an abortion was "a component of liberty we cannot renounce." Later that year, Bush's defeat at the hands of Clinton, a strongly prochoice Democrat, made abortion rights seem still more secure. Nevertheless, the struggle to shut down clinics and overturn *Roe v. Wade* continued.

Contesting Gay and Lesbian Rights

In a society struggling with issues concerning diversity, sexuality identity remained perhaps the most controversial difference of all. Like women and African Americans, gay men and lesbian women had made real gains since the 1960s. During the George H. W. Bush administration, the federal government committed more resources to AIDS research. As the disease spread more slowly among the gay population and heterosexuals contracted it, Americans were less likely to consider AIDS the "gay cancer" or God's punishment of gay men. Meanwhile, gays and lesbians became a more accepted presence in society. More television shows positively depicted gay identities. Two openly gay men served in Congress. Many businesses, including Disneyland, welcomed gay customers. Leading corporations, including General Motors and Ford, began providing benefits to the partners of gay employees.

Nevertheless, the public understanding of sexual identity lagged. During the 1990s, the term "Lesbian Gay Bisexual and Transgender" (LGBT) emerged as a more inclusive description of the range of identities beyond heterosexual. Even so, much of society continued to see a simple divide between heterosexuals and homosexuals.

Moreover, LGBT calls for equal rights met with substantial opposition. Although most Americans believed businesses should not discriminate on the basis of sexual identity, a majority still believed that LGBT identities were morally wrong. Every year, there were hundreds of documented instances of violence against gays and lesbians. In a notorious case in 1998, Matthew Shepherd, a gay student at the University of Wyoming in Laramie, was beaten, robbed, tied to a fence, pistol whipped, and left to die by two homophobic men who were later convicted of murder.

The resistance to gay rights was especially strong in the armed services. Officially barred from serving, gays and lesbians had long concealed their sexual orientation in order to remain in the military. By the 1990s, however, many people called on the armed forces to allow openly LGBT officers and enlisted personnel. Deeply committed to a heterosexual definition of masculinity, the military would not change its rules.

Then, in 1992 for the first time, a federal court ordered the navy to reinstate an openly gay petty officer who had been discharged. Campaigning for president that year, Bill Clinton promised to lift the ban on gays in the armed services. Once in office, however, he met stiff resistance from military leaders who argued that tolerance of gays would lower morale and hurt recruitment. Clinton compromised by instituting a "don't ask, don't tell" policy. The military would no longer ask recruits about their sexual identity, and gays and lesbians would continue to conceal it.

There was no compromise in the struggle over legal protection for LGBT rights in civilian life. In communities and states, activists demanded laws that would prevent businesses from discriminating on the basis of sexual identity. Conservatives, on the other hand, especially those concerned about the decline of "family values," moved to block gay and lesbian rights measures. In 1992, Colorado voters passed a state referendum forbidding communities to pass laws protecting gay rights, but the state's supreme court declared the referendum unconstitutional the next year. The issue, however, did not rest there. In 1996, Congress joined the battle by passing the Defense of Marriage Act, which declared that marriage was the "legal union between one man and one woman," denied federal benefits to same-sex couples living together, and allowed states to refuse to recognize same-sex marriages from other states. In 2000, the United States Supreme Court upheld the right of the Boy Scouts of America to dismiss a gay troop leader in New Jersey, despite the existence of a state gay rights law.

The battles over gay rights, women's rights, family values, and multiculturalism did little to alter the direction of social change in the United States. Despite the culture wars, Americans seemed willing to balance conservative economic policy with more liberal social attitudes and policies.

Redefining Foreign Policy in the Global Age

So long accustomed to the realities of the cold war, Americans had to rethink the foreign policy of the United States in the 1990s. Now that the United States no longer had to focus on the containment of Soviet power, questions remained as to what the nation's aims should be abroad. How much should the United States promote trade, freedom, and human rights? Could the country afford to spend less on military power? President George H. W. Bush believed strongly that the nation should play the role of an active international policeman in a "New World Order." However, many Americans were not so sure.

The New World Order

As Americans reconsidered the role of the United States in a changed world, some Republicans called for a new, less internationalist foreign policy. Echoing conservatives of the 1940s and 1950s, they insisted that the United States should no longer provide so much aid and military protection to other countries, especially in Europe. They felt that American soldiers should risk their lives to protect the United States, not other countries.

In contrast, a broad range of internationalists in both the Democratic and Republican Parties believed the United States could protect itself and advance its political and economic interests only by participating actively in world affairs. Even though the cold war was over, America still faced a variety of challenges abroad.

The most powerful internationalist was President George H. W. Bush. A naval aviator in World War II, Bush believed that American isolationism had encouraged fascist aggression in the 1930s and 1940s. American commitment to international freedom, the president understood, had won the war, preserved peace, and sustained the nation's economy for so many years. Now, Bush argued, the United States had to maintain its overseas commitments. With the help of other powerful countries, America should use foreign aid, military strength, NATO, and the United Nations to maintain a stable international system, a "New World Order." Bush wanted "a world in which democracy is the norm, in which private enterprise, free trade, and prosperity enrich every nation—a world in which the rule of law prevails." Much like Woodrow Wilson and Harry Truman before him, Bush mixed together idealism and self-interest in his vision of the international political economy: A free world would be good both for other nations and for the United States. However, the president believed only American leadership could preserve that world.

The New World Order was a broad, vague concept. Bush and other internationalists had a hard time explaining just what overseas commitments America needed to make. Did the United States need to intervene everywhere stability was threatened? It was also unclear whether the American people, still mindful of the costs of the Vietnam War, would endorse armed intervention abroad. Critics noted a tension between Bush's call for order and his support for democracy. Was the United States supposed to protect antidemocratic countries in the name of international stability and national prosperity?

There was also a tension between Bush's commitment to international cooperation and the long-standing tendency for the United States to act alone in its own hemisphere. While the president spoke of the New World Order, he intervened unilaterally in the Central American nation of Panama in 1989. By then Bush had grown frustrated with General Manuel Noriega, the Panamanian leader who engaged in drug sales to the United States and other illegal activities. After Noriega thwarted democratic elections, Bush did not try to handle the situation through joint action with the Organization of American States or the United Nations. Instead, he dispatched American troops, who captured Noriega and sent him to the United States for prosecution on drug charges. Bush's unilateral action, condemned by other Latin American countries, contradicted his rhetoric about international collaboration in the post–cold war world.

Finally, the New World Order would be expensive. Many Americans had looked forward to a "peace dividend" at the end of the cold war. They expected that money could now be saved on foreign aid and military expenditures and spent on domestic needs, but the New World Order abroad clearly jeopardized any "peace dividend" at home.

The Persian Gulf War

The test of the New World Order came soon enough. On August 2, 1990, Iraq, led by President Saddam Hussein, overran Kuwait, its wealthy but defenseless neighbor to the south. Entrenched in Kuwait, Iraq now threatened its much larger western neighbor, oil-producing Saudi Arabia. Hussein's actions clearly jeopardized America's oil supply and its Saudi Arabian ally. The Kuwaiti invasion also challenged Bush's calls for a stable New World Order of free nations.

The president reacted firmly. Comparing Hussein to Adolf Hitler, Bush created an international coalition opposing Iraq. By the end of 1990, more than half a million US troops had joined with forces from more than 30 nations in Operation Desert Shield to protect Saudi Arabia (see Map 29–2). Meanwhile, the United Nations imposed economic sanctions on Iraq. Convinced those sanctions were not enough to drive Hussein's soldiers

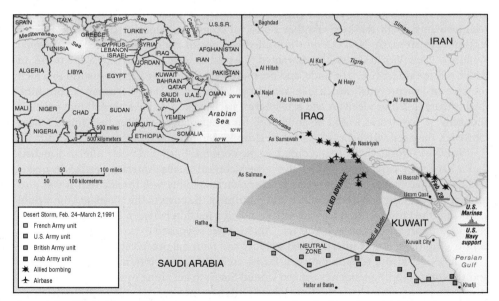

Map 29–2   The Persian Gulf War Operation Desert Storm, the allied attack on the forces of Iraq, tested President George H. W. Bush's vision of a "New World Order" in the oil-rich heart of the Middle East.
Source: Mark C. Carnes et al., *Mapping America's Past* (New York: Henry Holt, 1996), p. 267; *Hammond Atlas of the Twentieth Century* (New York: Times Books, 1996), p. 166.

The Gulf War Victory Parade in New York City In June 1991, the war against Saddam Hussein still seemed like an unqualified success.

out of Kuwait, the Bush administration successfully pressed the United Nations to authorize force if the Iraqis did not withdraw by January 15, 1991. The president also obtained congressional approval for the use of force.

When Hussein refused to pull back by the deadline, Operation Desert Shield became Operation Desert Storm. As television audiences watched around the world on the night of January 17, coalition forces began an intensive air attack against Iraq with planes and missiles. With Iraq's defenses weakened, coalition forces, led by US General Norman Schwarzkopf, began a ground attack against the Iraqi army on February 24. In just 100 hours, Schwarzkopf's soldiers swept into Kuwait, devastated the Iraqis, and pushed on into Iraq. Impressed by the results, Bush called a halt before the invasion reached the Iraqi capital of Baghdad and toppled Hussein.

At first, the Persian Gulf War seemed like a great victory for the United States and the New World Order. Coalition forces suffered only about 220 battle deaths and the United States lost only 148 troops. American technology appeared to work perfectly: US Stealth bombers evaded Iraqi radar and US Patriot missiles knocked Iraqi Scuds out of the sky. Bush's popularity soared. American leadership and American power had halted aggression and restored freedom abroad.

Americans' euphoria over the Gulf War did not last long, however. Studies showed that US weapons had not worked quite so well after all, and Gulf War veterans began to suffer health problems possibly caused by exposure to Iraqi chemical weapons. Saddam Hussein held on to power and hindered implementation of the agreement ending the war. His aircraft soon encroached on "no-fly" zones over northern and southern Iraq, where they had been forbidden to fly, and threatened Kurdish and Muslim minorities. The goals of the New World Order had not been completely achieved. Hussein remained a threat to his neighbors and to American interests in the new century.

Retreating from the New World Order

In the years after the Persian Gulf War, the United States retreated from Bush's vision of the New World Order. The American people were reluctant to accept the dangers of involvement abroad, especially where there was no obvious military or economic interest for the United States.

That reluctance was apparent when violence followed the collapse of Communist rule in Yugoslavia in 1990. As this Eastern European country broke apart in the early 1990s, three major ethnic groups—Muslim Slavs, Serbs, and Croatians—fought a bitter civil war in the newly independent province of Bosnia-Herzegovina. The remnants of the old Yugoslavia, under the harsh leadership of Slobodan Milosevic, aided the Serbs as they carried out "ethnic cleansing," the forcible expulsion of Muslims and Croats from their homes. Faced with the worst mass brutality in Europe since World War II, first Bush and then Clinton were unwilling to risk military involvement. Eventually, in 1994, American planes and missiles, operating in conjunction with NATO, began to attack Bosnian Serb forces from the air. The following year, the warring parties accepted a peace agreement brokered by the United States. The Clinton administration committed 20,000 troops to join a peacekeeping force, even though most Americans opposed the move.

Yugoslavia posed a challenge again when the Milosevic regime mistreated and attacked ethnic Albanians in the region of Kosovo. Humiliated by its inability to negotiate an end to the suffering in Kosovo, the Clinton administration finally supported a NATO air offensive against the Yugoslavian government in March 1999. The 78-day war that ended in June killed between 2,000 and 5,000 people, badly damaged Yugoslavia's infrastructure, and forced Milosevic to accept a multinational peacekeeping force. There were no NATO casualties, in part because Clinton and other NATO leaders were unwilling to risk them.

There were other costs for the United States, however. Clinton's unwillingness to commit ground troops to battle made it clear that America was hesitant to pay a human price to intervene around the world. Ultimately, the United States had helped restore some peace to the regions of the former Yugoslavia. Yet, critics charged, millions had suffered and thousands had died before a cautious America had been willing to employ even a minimum of force.

The New World Order depended on maintaining the American power built up during the cold war, but a reluctance to spend money and make international commitments diminished that power in the 1990s. As their budget declined, military leaders cut troops, closed bases, and reduced orders for new weapons. In 1993, the government officially abandoned the Strategic Defense Initiative or "Star Wars," Reagan's expensive project to create a space-based missile defense system. Meanwhile, the Central Intelligence Agency, the National Security Agency, and other intelligence operations struggled with tight budgets, low morale, and public criticism. With the Soviet confrontation over, many Americans no longer saw the need for so much spying. Additionally, the federal government's foreign aid budget stagnated in the 1990s and Washington failed to keep up its promised payments to support the work of the United Nations.

Time Line

▼**1988**
George H. W. Bush elected
  president

▼**1989**
Collapse of Communist regimes
  in Eastern Europe
Invasion of Panama

▼**1990**
Partial shutdown of federal
  government

▼**1991**
Persian Gulf War
Collapse of the Soviet Union
Dow Jones Industrial Average
  over 3,000 for first time

▼**1992**
Los Angeles riot after first
  Rodney King verdict
Bill Clinton elected president

▼**1993**
Terrorist truck bombing of World
  Trade Center, New York City
Ratification of North American
  Free Trade Agreement
  (NAFTA)

▼**1995**
Peace treaty in Bosnia-
  Herzegovina civil war

A New Threat

As the New World Order faded away, no single overarching principle emerged to direct the nation's diplomacy. After the cold war, anti-Communist passion no longer animated American foreign policy. For years, the United States had withheld diplomatic recognition of its former enemy, the Communist regime in the Socialist Republic of Vietnam, mainly because of the possibility that MIAs—American soldiers Missing in Action during the war—might still be held captive. However, by the 1990s, there was no evidence that MIAs remained alive in Southeast Asia. Eager for trade with Vietnam, President Clinton announced full diplomatic recognition of the Communist nation in 1995.

Economic interests helped shape policy toward another Asian Communist regime, the People's Republic of China. Although the Chinese leadership clearly violated the human rights of its people, both Presidents Bush and Clinton proved unwilling to disrupt developing economic ties with the world's most populous country. Despite evidence of China's growing nuclear arsenal and apparent spying on US weapons programs, the Clinton administration pressed Congress to ease trade relations with the Asian nation.

As Clinton's policy toward China suggested, the American commitment to human rights was fairly weak. In the 1990s, the US government professed support for human rights around the world, but Clinton never made that support the centerpiece of American diplomacy, as President Jimmy Carter had in the 1970s. During Clinton's first term, he offended human rights advocates by sending boatloads of refugees back to an uncertain future in Haiti. Despite his professed commitment to human rights, the president would not anger voters in Florida and other states who objected to the cost of caring for new immigrants.

While Americans failed to show much enthusiasm for human rights and the New World Order, the challenge of terrorism gradually forced them to reconsider the nation's foreign policy. In February 1993, a car bomb exploded in an underground garage of the World Trade Center in New York City. Six people were killed and more than a thousand injured in the first major international terrorist incident inside the United States. Investigators traced the attack to followers of a radical Islamic spiritual leader from Egypt, Sheikh Omar Abdel-Rahman, who lived in New Jersey. Rahman and over a dozen associates were

Opening of World Trade
Organization

▼1995–1996
Two federal government
shutdowns

▼1996
Federal welfare reform
First Wal-Mart in People's
Republic of China

Reelection of Bill Clinton as
president

▼1998
Terrorist truck bombings of
US embassies in Kenya and
Tanzania

▼1999
Acquittal of Bill Clinton in Senate
impeachment trial

NATO air war against
Yugoslavia
Dow Jones Industrial Average
over 10,000 for first time

▼2001
George W. Bush declared
president

convicted for the bombing and other plots. In 1996, another Muslim radical, charged with masterminding the attack, was convicted along with two other Muslims for plotting to blow up US airliners over the Pacific Ocean.

Surprisingly, most Americans paid little attention to terrorism in the aftermath of the attack. US authorities generally ignored the plotters' connections to a terrorist organization, Al Qaeda, led by a wealthy Saudi Arabian exile, Osama bin Laden. A veteran of the resistance to the Soviet invasion of Afghanistan, bin Laden had gradually made Al Qaeda—Arabic for "base" or "foundation"—into an anti-Western movement dedicated to restoring the supposedly lost glory of Islam. The terrorist financier particularly hated the United States for its support of Israel and its military presence in the Middle East.

Operating out of Sudan and then Afghanistan, Al Qaeda supported Muslim fighters in Bosnia and warlords in Somalia. In 1995 and 1996, the organization was involved in deadly terrorist attacks on US soldiers in Saudi Arabia. In 1996, bin Laden declared jihad—holy war—on the United States. In August 1998, bombs killed at least 190 people and wounded 5,000 at US embassies in the African nations of Kenya and Tanzania. Blaming the embassy attacks on bin Laden, the United States launched missile attacks on targets in Afghanistan and the Sudan linked to bin Laden's organization. Despite these incidents, Americans remained fairly unconcerned about international terrorism. To use James Woolsey's language, they believed the new threat was just one more "poisonous snake," not a big new "dragon." Time would soon change such feelings.

Conclusion

Globalization, information, and cultural change inexorably remade the United States in the 1990s. Facing such powerful forces, democratic institutions responded slowly and sometimes not at all with new domestic and foreign policies. The political stalemate troubled Americans, who seemed more conservative about economic issues and more liberal about social values. For all the uncertainty of change and the frustration of gridlock, many Americans enjoyed a period of prosperity.

As the United States came to terms with the globalized world, the information economy, the culture wars, and governmental gridlock, Jim Sharlow moved ahead. Having suffered the pain of "downsizing," he benefited from globalization when a multinational hired him to manage a factory in California. For him, as for the nation, perhaps the prosperous years would continue and the globalized new economy would work out well after all. Sharlow worried that he would lose this job, too, but he was happy again. He got his Mercedes fixed.

Who, What, Where

Review Questions

1. What innovations spurred globalization?
2. What were the main features of the information economy?
3. Why were Americans so often frustrated by the political system in the 1990s?

Critical-Thinking Questions

1. What made the globalization of the 1990s different from the earlier linkages between the United States and the rest of the world?
2. Considering both the expansion of rights and the rise of gridlock, did the United States become more or less democratic in the 1990s?
3. Did the information revolution affect American society as the Industrial Revolution did?

Suggested Readings

Engel, Jeffrey A. *When the World Seemed New: George H. W. Bush and the End of the Cold War.* Boston: Houghton, Mifflin, Harcourt, 2017.

Ngai, Mae. *Impossible Subjects: Illegal Aliens and the Making of Modern America, updated ed.* Princeton, NJ: Princeton University Press, 2014.

Troy, Gil. *The Age of Clinton: America in the 1990s.* New York: Thomas Dunne Books, 2015.

For further review materials and resource information, please visit www.oup.com/us/oakes-mcgerr

CHAPTER 29: THE GLOBALIZED NATION, 1989–2001

Primary Sources

29.1 KENICHI OHMAE, "DECLARATION OF INTERDEPENDENCE TOWARD THE WORLD—2005" (1990) AND HELENA NORBERG-HODGE, "BREAK UP THE MONOCULTURE" (1996)

The vast, complex process of globalization spawned both optimism and fear. On one hand, Japanese organizational theorist Kenichi Ohmae and his colleagues in a US consulting firm believed that increasing interconnections would make the world better in just about every way. Written in 1990, the "Declaration of Interdependence Toward the World" looked ahead to the year 2005, when a globalized near-utopia would have "no absolute losers" or "winners." On the other hand, Helena Norberg-Hodge, a Swedish-born, American-educated environmental and globalization activist, saw a much bleaker future for a homogenized world. Instead of globalization, the world, she argued, needed "localization."

Declaration of Interdependence Toward the World—2005

In recent decades we have watched the free flow of ideas, individuals, investments, and industries grow into an organic bond among developed economies. Not only are traditionally traded goods and securities freely exchanged in the interlinked economy, but so too are such crucial assets as land, companies, software, commercial rights (patents, memberships, and brands), art objects, and expertise.

Inevitably, the emergence of the interlinked economy brings with it an erosion of national sovereignty as the power of information directly touches local communities; academic, professional, and social institutions; corporations; and individuals. It is this borderless world that will give participating economies the capacity for boundless prosperity.

We avow that the security of humankind's social and economic institutions lies no longer in superpower deterrence but is rather to be found in the weave of economic and intellectual interdependence of nations.

As such, we believe that the interlinked economy

- Enhances the well-being of individuals and institutions.
- Stands open to all who wish to participate in it, mainly through deregulation of trade.
- Creates no absolute losers nor winners, as market mechanisms adjust participating nations' competitiveness rather fairly through currency exchange rates and employment.

Accordingly, the role of central governments must change, so as to

- Allow individuals access to the best and cheapest goods and services from anywhere in the world.
- Help corporations provide stable and rewarding jobs anywhere in the world regardless of the corporation's national identity.
- Coordinate activities with other governments to minimize conflicts arising from narrow interests.
- Avoid abrupt changes in economic and social fundamentals.

The leading nations must be united under this belief, so that they collectively can

- Enhance networking of individuals, institutions, and communities across the borders.
- Develop a new framework to deal collectively with traditionally parochial affairs, such as tax; standards and codes; and laws governing mobility of tradable goods, services, and assets.
- Induce developing, newly industrialized, and developed nations to actively participate in the global economy.
- Address and resolve issues that belong to the global community, such as:

    Enhancement of the earth's environment and conservation of natural resources.

    Underdeveloped nations.

    Human rights and dignity.

Break Up the Monoculture

The president of Nabisco once defined the goal of economic globalization as "a world of homogeneous consumption," in which people everywhere eat the same food, wear the same clothing and live in houses built from the same materials. It is a world in which every society employs the same technologies, depends on the same centrally managed economy, offers the same Western education for its children, speaks the same language, consumes the same media images, holds the same values and even thinks the same thoughts—monoculture. . . .

Although this sameness suits the needs of transnational corporations, which profit from the efficiencies of standardized production and standardized consumption, in the long term a homogenized planet is disastrous for all of us. It is leading to a breakdown of both biological and cultural diversity, erosion of our food security, an increase in conflict and violence, and devastation for the global biosphere. The myth of globalization is that we no longer need to be connected to a place on the earth. Our every need can be supplied by distant institutions and machines. Our contact with other people can be through electronic media. Globalization is creating a way of life that denies our natural instincts by severing our connection to others and to nature. And—because it is erasing both biological and cultural diversity—it is destined to fail.

Human societies have always been embedded in their local ecosystems, modifying and being modified by them. Cultural diversity has come to mirror the biological and geographic diversity of the planet. In arid environments, for example, pastoral or nomadic practices enable people to use more of the sparse resources of their region. . . .

There is still time to shift direction, restore diversity and begin moving toward sustainable, healthy societies and ecosystems. How to begin? In principle, the answer is straightforward: If globalization is the problem, the solution must lie in economic *localization*. This does not mean an end to all trade or intercultural communication, as some have unfairly charged. Nor does it mean that industrialized society must change from a culture of cities to villages.

However, the idea of localization runs counter to today's general belief that fast-paced urban areas are the locus of "real" culture, while small, local communities are isolated backwaters, relics of a past when small-mindedness and prejudice were the norm. The past is assumed to have been brutish, a time when exploitation was fierce, intolerance rampant, violence commonplace—a situation that the modem world has largely risen above.

These assumptions echo the elitist or racist belief that modernized people are superior—more highly evolved—than their underdeveloped rural counterparts. But most Westerners have a highly distorted notion of what life in small communities can be like. . . .

Efforts to rein in the runaway global economy need to be international—linking grassroots social and environmental movements from North and South in order to pressure governments to take back the power that has been handed over to corporations.

But long-term solutions to today's social and environmental problems will also require a range of small, local initiatives that are as diverse as the cultures and environments in which they take place. Promoting "small-scale on a large scale" would allow specific, on-the-ground initiatives to flourish—community banks, local currencies and trading systems, rediscovered traditional knowledge and more. Unlike halting the global economic steamroller, these small-scale steps require a slow pace and a deep and intimate understanding of local contexts, and will best be designed and implemented by local people themselves. Over time, such initiatives would inevitably foster a return to cultural and biological diversity and long-term sustainability.

Sources: Kenichi Ohmae, *The Borderless World: Power and Strategy in the Interlinked Economy* (New York: HarperBusiness, 1990), pp. 216–217. Helena Norberg-Hodge, "Break Up the Monoculture," *Nation*, July 15/22, 1996, pp. 20–23.

29.2 SOLOMON D. TRUJILLO, "OPPORTUNITY IN THE NEW INFORMATION ECONOMY" (1998)

Like globalization, the information economy simultaneously inspired optimism and fear. In this 1998 speech to the Latin Business Association in Los Angeles, Solomon D. Trujillo, the president of the telecommunications company U.S. West, considered the implications of high technology for the nation's Latinos. Trujillo was confident that the information economy was a democratizing force that would reward the talent of the Hispanic population. Yet he also feared that Latinos, mostly working-class people subject to discrimination and limited opportunity, might be left behind.

. . . Let's take a look into the future for a moment:

I'd now like to talk about a subject that is near and dear to my heart: what's happening in high-tech industries and around the Internet. I want to focus on it because Information Age industries can overcome traditional barriers that we've faced in the past, such as access to capital. That's why I believe that the greatest opportunity we have is in the emerging, high-tech industries. Indeed, we already have Latino success stories. . . . We can—and are—succeeding in the economy of the future.

The greatest opportunity in the future for Hispanics is in emerging, information-driven industries. It is the New Economy. And what's exciting about these industries is that "what you know is more important than who you are."

So I want to focus on Information Age industries for a moment, because technology is the great equalizer. It's the great equalizer because new technologies such as the Internet can overcome barriers common to small business such as access to capital, access to markets and access to information. It's the great equalizer because, over the Internet, small businesses can look big. Big businesses can look small or feel small if that's what they want. A business can customize. Or it can mass-market. It can lower the cost of doing business. It can expand to a global scope.

Today's telecommunications technology brings the whole world to anyone with a telephone and a modem. A friend of mine in the high-tech industry described it this way: "What I do is create products of the mind. I'm not limited by geography or anything else." Brain power is the natural resource of the Information Age. Brain power has no gender, no race, no religion, no ethnicity, no national origin. And brain power is something we have in abundance.

So the Information Age creates great new opportunities for small- to medium-sized businesses.

My last point tonight is that technology has the potential to create a dangerous world of "haves and have nots" in terms of cyberliteracy. Four centuries ago in the novel Don Quixote, Miguel de

Cervantes Saavedra warned us of a world of "haves and have nots." Technology has the potential either to enrich everyone's lives or to leave many of us behind. That's our choice.

To participate fully in the New Economy, all Americans—and that includes Latinos—need to acquire the knowledge to use technology to improve our lives. That means we all need to learn a second or third language. Not just English or Spanish, but the cyber language of Internet communications.

A recent study by the Tomas Rivera Policy Institute confirmed that the Internet, which has the potential to remove barriers and raise opportunities, also has the negative potential of becoming the basis of a new elite. How many people here own a home computer? The study found there's a 50 percent gap in home computer ownership between the general population and middle class Hispanics. Let me repeat—a 50 percent gap for middle class Hispanics in computer ownership. The gap grows even wider when we look at the least fortunate among us.

Compounding the computer access problem is the problem of high-speed access. Some companies that offer high-speed Information Age access are deciding to make a bee-line for high-yield business customers or high-income residential customers—in effect redlining the residential and small business markets. These trends are troublesome. . . .

Technological literacy is crucial if Hispanics are to avoid becoming the "have nots." And this is an area we can and must do something about. . . . If we don't want Hispanic communities to become the "have nots," we must continue to educate our people about technology and ensure that they have equal access.

And, we all need to continue to give back to our community, and to support each other through organizations like the Latin Business Association. There's a *dicho* that seems fitting: *Palabras sin obras, guitarras sin cuerdas*—words without deeds are like guitars without strings.

Source: Solomon D. Trujillo, "Opportunity in the New Information Economy," *Vital Speeches of the Day* 64, no. 16 (June 1998): 490–492.

29.3 VISUAL DOCUMENT: AZIZ + CUCHER, "MAN WITH COMPUTER" (1992)

In the 1990s, American artists both made use of information-age technology and explored its implications. Using digital photography, Anthony Aziz and Sammy Cucher created "visual metaphors for the increasing role that new technologies play in our lives and how they affect us politically, socially, and psychologically." Aziz and Cucher's 1992 digital photo, "Man with Computer," also considers the biological possibilities in the age of genetic engineering and biomedical innovation. Consider where "Man" is pointing and how he has been altered.

Source: Aziz + Cucher, "Man with Computer" (1992), Indianapolis Museum of Art.

29.4 EXCERPTS FROM NATIONAL DEFENSE AUTHORIZATION ACT OF 1994 (1993) AND DEFENSE OF MARRIAGE ACT (1996)

In the 1990s, two federal laws supported continued discrimination against the LGBT community. In 1993, Bill Clinton signed the National Defense Authorization Act for Fiscal Year 1994, which reaffirmed the long-standing refusal to allow gays and lesbians to serve openly in the military, effectively abandoning a campaign promise to support this right. The law, however, authorized a loophole: the military would not ask personnel about their sexual orientation; if gays and lesbians did not reveal their identities, they would be allowed to serve. Three years later, Clinton signed the Defense of Marriage Act, allowing states to refuse to recognize marriages entered into by same-sex couples in other jurisdictions.

Policy Concerning Homosexuality in the Armed Forces

(6) . . . Success in combat requires military units that are characterized by high morale, good order and discipline, and unit cohesion.

(7) One of the most critical elements in combat capability is unit cohesion, that is, the bonds of trust among individual service members that make the combat effectiveness of a military unit greater than the sum of the combat effectiveness of the individual unit members.

(8) Military life is fundamentally different from civilian life in that—

   (A) the extraordinary responsibilities of the armed forces, the unique conditions of military service, and the critical role of unit cohesion, require that the military community, while subject to civilian control, exist as a specialized society; and

   (B) the military society is characterized by its own laws, rules, customs, and traditions, including numerous restrictions on personal behavior, that would not be acceptable in civilian society.

(9) The standards of conduct for members of the armed forces regulate a member's life for 24 hours each day beginning at the moment the member enters military status and not ending until that person is discharged or otherwise separated from the armed forces.

(10) Those standards of conduct, including the Uniform Code of Military Justice, apply to a member of the armed forces at all times that the member has a military status, whether the member is on base or off base, and whether the member is on duty or off duty.

(11) The pervasive application of the standards of conduct is necessary because members of the armed forces must be ready at all times for worldwide deployment to a combat environment.

(12) The worldwide deployment of United States military forces, the international responsibilities of the United States, and the potential for involvement of the armed forces in actual combat routinely make it necessary for members of the armed forces involuntarily to accept living conditions and working conditions that are often spartan, primitive, and characterized by forced intimacy with little or no privacy.

(13) The prohibition against homosexual conduct is a long-standing element of military law that continues to be necessary in the unique circumstances of military service.

(14) The armed forces must maintain personnel policies that exclude persons whose presence in the armed forces would create an unacceptable risk to the armed forces' high standards

of morale, good order and discipline, and unit cohesion that are the essence of military capability.

(15) The presence in the armed forces of persons who demonstrate a propensity or intent to engage in homosexual acts would create an unacceptable risk to the high standards of morale, good order and discipline, and unit cohesion that are the essence of military capability.

(b) POLICY—A member of the armed forces shall be separated from the armed forces under regulations prescribed by the Secretary of Defense if one or more of the following findings is made and approved in accordance with procedures set forth in such regulations:

(1) That the member has engaged in, attempted to engage in, or solicited another to engage in a homosexual act or acts unless there are further findings, made and approved in accordance with procedures set forth in such regulations, that the member has demonstrated that

  (A) such conduct is a departure from the member's usual and customary behavior;

  (B) such conduct, under all the circumstances, is unlikely to recur;

  (C) such conduct was not accomplished by use of force, coercion, or intimidation;

  (D) under the particular circumstances of the case, the member's continued presence in the armed forces is consistent with the interests of the armed forces in proper discipline, good order, and morale; and

  (E) the member does not have a propensity or intent to engage in homosexual acts.

(2) That the member has stated that he or she is a homosexual or bisexual, or words to that effect, unless there is a further finding, made and approved in accordance with procedures set forth in the regulations, that the member has demonstrated that he or she is not a person who engages in, attempts to engage in, has a propensity to engage in, or intends to engage in homosexual acts.

(3) That the member has married or attempted to marry a person known to be of the same biological sex.

  . . . It is the sense of Congress that—

(1) the suspension of questioning concerning homosexuality as part of the processing of individuals for accession into the Armed Forces under the interim policy of January 29, 1993, should be continued, but the Secretary of Defense may reinstate that questioning with such questions or such revised questions as he considers appropriate if the Secretary determines that it is necessary to do so in order to effectuate the policy set forth in section 654 of title 10, United States Code. . . .

An Act

To define and protect the institution of marriage

Be it enacted by the Senate and House of Representatives of the United States of America in Congress assembled,

Sec. 1. Short Title

This Act may be cited as the "Defense of Marriage Act."

Sec. 2. Powers Reserved to the States

(a) IN GENERAL—Chapter 115 of title 28, United States Code, is amended by adding after section 1738B the following:

Sec. 1738C. Certain acts, records, and proceedings and the effect thereof

No State, territory, or possession of the United States, or Indian tribe, shall be required to give effect to any public act, record, or judicial proceeding of any other State, territory, possession, or tribe respecting a relationship between persons of the same sex that is treated as a marriage under the laws of such other State, territory, possession, or tribe, or a right or claim arising from such relationship. . . .

Sec. 3. Definition of Marriage

(a) IN GENERAL—Chapter 1 of title 1, United States Code, is amended by adding at the end the following:

Sec. 7. Definition of "Marriage" and "Spouse"

In determining the meaning of any Act of Congress, or of any ruling, regulation, or interpretation of the various administrative bureaus and agencies of the United States, the word "marriage" means only a legal union between one man and one woman as husband and wife, and the word "spouse" refers only to a person of the opposite sex who is a husband or a wife.

Sources: National Defense Authorization Act of 1994. H.R. 2401, 103rd Congress (1993). Defense of Marriage Act. H.R. 3396, 104th Congress (1996).

29.5 GEORGE H. W. BUSH, EXCERPTS FROM "ADDRESS BEFORE A JOINT SESSION OF THE CONGRESS ON THE CESSATION OF HOSTILITIES IN THE PERSIAN GULF CONFLICT" (1991)

On March 6, 1991, a week after the end of the Persian Gulf War, President George H. W. Bush addressed a joint session of Congress. Amid jubilation over the quick victory of the United States and its allies, Bush laid down the basic principles of the "New World Order" for the future. The president's argument for continuing American involvement abroad rested on his belief in international law and cooperation, the purity of American motives, and "the hard lessons of history."

Members of Congress, 5 short weeks ago I came to this House to speak to you about the state of the Union. We met then in time of war. Tonight, we meet in a world blessed by the promise of peace. . . .

This is a victory for every country in the coalition, for the United Nations. A victory for unprecedented international cooperation and diplomacy. . . . It is a victory for the rule of law and for what is right. . . .

Tonight, I come to this House to speak about the world—the world after war. The recent challenge could not have been clearer. Saddam Hussein was the villain; Kuwait, the victim. To the aid of this small country came nations from North America and Europe, from Asia and South America, from Africa and the Arab world, all united against aggression. Our uncommon coalition must now work in common purpose: to forge a future that should never again be held hostage to the darker side of human nature.

Tonight in Iraq, Saddam walks amidst ruin. His war machine is crushed. His ability to threaten mass destruction is itself destroyed. His people have been lied to, denied the truth. And when his defeated legions come home, all Iraqis will see and feel the havoc he has wrought. And this I promise you: For all that Saddam has done to his own people, to the Kuwaitis, and to the entire world, Saddam and those around him are accountable. . . .

All of us grieve for the victims of war, for the people of Kuwait and the suffering that scars the soul of that proud nation. We grieve for all our fallen soldiers and their families, for all the innocents caught up in this conflict. And, yes, we grieve for the people of Iraq, a people who have never been our enemy. My hope is that one day we will once again welcome them as friends into the community of nations. . . .

To all the challenges that confront this region of the world there is no single solution, no solely American answer. But we can make a difference. America will work tirelessly as a catalyst for positive change. . . .

The consequences of the conflict in the Gulf reach far beyond the confines of the Middle East. Twice before in this century, an entire world was convulsed by war. Twice this century, out of the horrors of war hope emerged for enduring peace. Twice before, those hopes proved to be a distant dream, beyond the grasp of man. Until now, the world we've known has been a world divided—a world of barbed wire and concrete block, conflict, and cold war.

Now, we can see a new world coming into view. A world in which there is the very real prospect of a new world order. In the words of Winston Churchill, a world order in which "the principles of justice and fair play protect the weak against the strong. . . ." A world where the United Nations, freed from cold war stalemate, is poised to fulfill the historic vision of its founders. A world in which freedom and respect for human rights find a home among all nations. The Gulf war put this new world to its first test. And my fellow Americans, we passed that test.

For the sake of our principles, for the sake of the Kuwaiti people, we stood our ground. Because the world would not look the other way, Ambassador al-Sabah, tonight Kuwait is free. And we're very happy about that.

Tonight, as our troops begin to come home, let us recognize that the hard work of freedom still calls us forward. We've learned the hard lessons of history. The victory over Iraq was not waged as "a war to end all wars." Even the new world order cannot guarantee an era of perpetual peace. But enduring peace must be our mission. Our success in the Gulf will shape not only the new world order we seek but our mission here at home. . . .

I'm sure that many of you saw on the television the unforgettable scene of four terrified Iraqi soldiers surrendering. They emerged from their bunker broken, tears streaming from their eyes, fearing the worst. And then there was an American soldier. Remember what he said? He said: "It's okay. You're all right now. You're all right now." That scene says a lot about America, a lot about who we are. Americans are a caring people. We are a good people, a generous people. Let us always be caring and good and generous in all we do. . . .

We went halfway around the world to do what is moral and just and right. We fought hard and, with others, we won the war. We lifted the yoke of aggression and tyranny from a small country that many Americans had never even heard of, and we ask nothing in return.

We're coming home now—proud, confident, heads high. There is much that we must do, at home and abroad. And we will do it. We are Americans.

May God bless this great nation, the United States of America. Thank you all very, very much.

Source: George H. W. Bush, "Address Before a Joint Session of the Congress on the Cessation of Hostilities in the Persian Gulf Conflict," March 6, 1991.

"A Nation Transformed"

The Twenty-First Century

< Prisoners at Guantánamo Bay, Cuba

AMERICAN PORTRAIT

Lt. Craig Mullaney

In 2003, Lieutenant Craig Mullaney of the 10th Mountain Division, like so many American soldiers before him, went overseas to serve his country. A year and a half earlier, the United States had invaded Afghanistan in retaliation for a devastating attack on American soil by the transnational terrorist group Al Qaeda on September 11, 2001. So Lt. Mullaney found himself in this rugged country at the crossroads of the Middle East and Asia to battle Al Qaeda fighters and their local Taliban protectors.

In critical respects, America's global war on terror was a product of globalization, as was Lt. Mullaney. A graduate of the US Military Academy, he had studied at Oxford University in England. His fiancée, a doctor, was the daughter of Indian immigrants.

Lt. Mullaney fought the war with the help of the advanced technology of the information economy. Satellite telephones and global positioning satellites, devices that also spurred globalization, allowed instant communication and sure navigation for Lt. Mullaney's squad around the ancient city of Gardez and then Shkin, the isolated spot his colonel called "the evilest place in Afghanistan." When under attack, they could quickly call for support from rocket-firing Apache helicopters and formidable A-10 attack planes. "I was energized by the power I commanded through the radio," Mullaney admitted. "It was like an incantation, like casting a spell, like summoning a demon."

The Americans also enjoyed the comforts of communications and information technology basic to globalization: computers, the Internet, DVDs, iPods, satellite television, and phone calls home. There was plenty of food and plenty of air conditioning, too.

Their enemies did not have such technological benefits. Yet for all their advantages, the Americans struggled. They did not have enough soldiers, vehicles, or heavy weapons. And they did not have enough armor on their vehicles to protect them from homemade bombs. "I felt as though I were riding in a death trap," Mullaney confessed. He and his men did not know enough of the Afghan language and culture. Driving through Gardez, he saw men raise their index fingers. Thinking it was "a number one gesture," he held out his index finger, too. "Yes, America is number one!" Afterward, his interpreter revealed that the men had been making an obscene gesture at the Americans.

Mullaney and his men inflicted far greater casualties than they suffered. He himself won promotion to captain. Yet the United States was not clearly triumphing. "We were never really sure whether we were winning," Mullaney admitted. "But we had been transformed."

His experience reflected American life in the first decades of the twenty-first century. As globalization and technological innovation continued to reshape American life, the nation struggled with the consequences. It was not clear that the economy was strong enough to enable Americans to live the good life at home and to project American power abroad. As the nation adjusted to increasing social and cultural diversity, American democracy seemed less able to confront economic dislocation and increasing inequality. Instead of feeling safer, the nation seemed to be perpetually at war. Echoing Lt. Craig Mullaney, the commission investigating the September 11, 2001, attacks agreed that Americans lived in "a nation transformed." But the outcome of that transformation, abroad and at home, was not clearly a victory.

Twin Crises

Two shocks bookended the presidency of George W. Bush and shaped America in the first decade of the twenty-first century. The terrorist attacks of September 11, 2001, led the United States into two wars abroad and into a substantial change in the relationship of the government and the people. Seven years later, as the wars dragged, the collapse of stock prices ushered in the most severe economic recession since the Great Depression of the 1930s. The dual crises of terrorism and recession sorely tested the nation.

Bush 43

George W. Bush, the 43rd president of the United States, took office during relative peace and prosperity in January 2001. "Bush 43," more conservative than his father, George H. W. Bush, the 41st president, pushed successfully for tax cuts, weaker regulation of the financial industry, and a limit on late-term "partial birth" abortions. Yet Bush also compromised with liberals in Congress to pass the No Child Left Behind Act of 2001, which combined the liberal goal of increased federal funding for public schools with the conservative demand for greater accountability for the schools, including annual standardized testing of students. The president also accepted a classic liberal initiative, an expensive drug benefit program for retired Americans.

In 2004, Bush faced another liberal Democrat, Senator John Kerry of Massachusetts, who tried to capitalize on worries over outsourcing, the sending of American jobs to other nations. Yet Bush prevailed with 50.7 percent of the popular vote and a solid electoral majority. Buoyed by his victory, the president promised new conservative initiatives, including a reform of the Social Security system. His plans went nowhere, particularly after the Democrats won control of both houses of Congress in 2006. Thanks to Bush's tax cuts, drug plan, and military expenditures, the federal government ran a budget deficit again— another disappointment to conservatives, who yearned for leaner government.

9/11

Despite Bush's accomplishments, two crises ultimately defined Bush's presidency. On the morning of September 11, 2001, the most ambitious Al Qaeda terrorist plot under the leadership of Osama bin Laden took place in a clear blue morning sky. Although Bush had received warning of Al Qaeda's intentions, the nation was unprepared. That day, 19 members of Al Qaeda from Saudi Arabia, the United Arab Emirates, Egypt, and Lebanon walked through security at East Coast airports and boarded four passenger jets. In flight, the terrorists, brandishing box cutters and Mace or pepper spray, overwhelmed flight attendants and passengers, killed or wounded pilots, took control, and redirected the planes.

At 8:46 a.m., American Airlines Flight 11 sped into the North Tower of the World Trade Center; 17 minutes later, United Airlines Flight 175 hit the World Trade Center's South Tower. At 9:37 a.m., American Airlines Flight 77 struck the west wall of the Pentagon, headquarters of the US Defense Department, outside Washington, DC. Aboard United Airlines Flight 93, there were indications of struggle, a voice shouted, "Allah is the greatest," and the jet crashed into an empty field in Shanksville, Pennsylvania, at 10:03 a.m. instead of hitting Washington, DC. By then, the North Tower of the World Trade Center had collapsed in a cloud of smoke and debris. The South Tower followed at 10:28 a.m.

The tragedy, which became known as "9/11," killed the 19 hijackers, 40 people in the crash at Shanksville, 184 at the Pentagon, and 2,753 at the World Trade Center. More Americans died on 9/11 than had died in the Japanese attack at Pearl Harbor on December 7, 1941. Only the Civil War battles of Antietam and Cold Harbor had been deadlier days.

The Global War on Terror

In the days after 9/11, stunned Americans felt the attacks had "changed everything." Much stayed the same, but the catastrophe did reshape American foreign and security policy—and arguably American democracy as well. Vowing privately on 9/11 "to kick some ass," President Bush declared publicly that evening, "We will make no distinction between the terrorists who committed these acts and those who harbor them." When Afghanistan's Islamic fundamentalist movement, the Taliban, refused to turn over bin Laden, the United States and other NATO countries responded in October by launching air strikes against Al Qaeda and Taliban targets and sending troops to hunt down bin Laden, destroy his camps, and drive out the Taliban. What the Bush administration called the "global war on terror" had begun.

Afghanistan, weak and impoverished, fell quickly, but bin Laden and many Al Qaeda and Taliban fighters escaped in the remote, mountainous terrain to continue their struggle. US and NATO forces remained to protect the new government and find bin Laden.

Meanwhile, the Bush administration reorganized the federal government to combat terror. Within a month of 9/11, Bush chose the first director of Homeland Security to protect US borders and infrastructure and to respond in the event of a terrorist strike. In 2002, Congress elevated the position to cabinet rank in a new Department of Homeland Security. Two years later, Congress answered harsh criticism of the CIA and FBI for failing to detect the 9/11 plot by transferring oversight of all US intelligence agencies from the head of the CIA to a new position, Director of National Intelligence.

More controversially, the Bush administration worked what Vice President Dick Cheney called "the dark side"—practices traditionally condemned by American law and culture. The government maintained a detention center at Guantánamo Bay, Cuba, where captured "enemy combatants" were denied trials and the protections of the Geneva Convention on prisoners of war and were, in some cases, tortured. In 2006 and 2008, the US Supreme Court asserted the rights of the Guantánamo detainees and reminded Bush that "a state of war is not a blank check for the president."

Bush also wanted the government to gather more information about its own citizens. In October 2001, the hastily passed USA Patriot Act made it easier for the federal government to spy on Americans and allowed the attorney general to imprison indefinitely, without trial, noncitizens considered threats to national security. Opponents condemned the Patriot Act as an unlawful deprivation of civil liberties. In 2004, a federal judge declared part of the measure an unconstitutional infringement on First Amendment rights. But the Bush administration secured the renewal and expansion of the act.

Bush also rethought the use of American military power. Previous presidents had rejected preemptive peacetime attacks on other nations. But Bush believed that terrorism, "a threat without precedent," might require the nation to strike even before a threat emerged. Bush further broke with cold war presidents, including his father, by calling for the United States to act alone when necessary rather than through alliances and the United Nations.

The Bush Doctrine of preemption and unilateral action risked isolating the United States and making it seem selfish, dangerous, and illegitimate. Yet Bush, confident of American power and virtue, was willing to go it alone.

The Iraq War

In January 2002, Bush declared that it was not enough to go after terrorist organizations. The United States must also "prevent regimes that sponsor terror from threatening America or our friends and allies with weapons of mass destruction." He identified Iran, Iraq, and North Korea as an "axis of evil," potentially able to arm terrorists with nuclear, chemical, or biological weapons that menaced the United States.

Iraq was Bush's primary focus. In his view, Hussein had plotted to assassinate the president's father, forced out United Nations weapons inspectors, resumed acquiring weapons of mass destruction (WMDs), and supported Al Qaeda. Bush was also influenced by Vice President Cheney and other advisers who advocated neoconservatism, the idea that the United States should unilaterally promote democracy abroad in order to make a better and more secure world. Replacing Hussein with a democratic regime would, these neoconservatives insisted, encourage the spread of democracy in the Middle East and make US ally Israel safer.

As Bush confronted Iraq, nearly all of America's European allies, as well as Russia, China, and Middle Eastern countries, opposed a unilateral US war. Bush did assemble a "coalition of the willing," but only Great Britain, Australia, and Poland joined the United States in committing troops.

On the night of March 19, 2003, Operation Iraqi Freedom began with a hail of Tomahawk cruise missiles aimed at Baghdad in an unsuccessful attempt to kill Hussein. On March 21, some 1,300 bombs and missiles rained down on Baghdad in a display of "shock and awe" meant to demoralize Iraqi leadership. Sweeping into Iraq, US troops occupied Baghdad and British forces seized a key port to the south. American technology, particularly missiles and smart bombs, worked well. Offering little resistance, much of the Iraqi army disappeared into the civilian population. Hussein disappeared, too. By mid-April, his statues were toppling.

Swift and short, like the Gulf War 12 years before, the Iraq war seemed everything that the Bush administration had hoped. Only 138 US soldiers had died. Standing before a banner declaring "Mission Accomplished" aboard an aircraft carrier in May, the president jubilantly announced, "Major combat operations in Iraq have ended." The United States seemed well on the way to winning the war on terror and reshaping the Middle East.

Iraq and Afghanistan in Turmoil

It was not that easy. The jubilation of "Mission Accomplished" gave way to sober realities in Iraq during 2003. WMDs, a chief justification of the war, were never found. Unable

The Fall of Saddam Hussein As the coalition invasion overthrew the Iraqi regime, jubilant Iraqis pulled down statues of Saddam Hussein, like this one, in the spring of 2003.

to prove Hussein's ties to Al Qaeda, the Bush administration faced charges of fighting a needless war in Iraq while bin Laden went free in Afghanistan. Meanwhile, the United States struggled to restart the Iraqi economy, train new police and military, and build a popular, democratic regime.

Soon, a violent insurgency, perhaps orchestrated by Hussein, tried to destabilize Iraq and drive out the United States. Although US forces captured Hussein in December 2003, his brutal execution and revelations of the humiliation and torture of Iraqis at a prison in Abu Ghraib embarrassed the United States. "Al Qaeda in Iraq," a new terrorist group loyal to bin Laden, joined the fight. Although the Bush administration handed over sovereignty to an American-chosen Iraqi government in 2004, over 100,000 US troops remained to keep the peace. Facing failure, Bush responded with a controversial "surge," a temporary troop increase that succeeded, along with changes in Iraqi politics, in decreasing the violence by mid-2008. But American public opinion had turned against the war.

Meanwhile, the Afghanistan conflict worsened. As the United States focused on Iraq, the Taliban, aided by foreign fighters, gradually regained strength and the pro–US government lost power. Osama bin Laden remained at large. By 2008, over 600 US soldiers and uncounted Afghans had died in seven years of fighting.

The wars in Afghanistan and Iraq cost the United States popularity and influence around the globe. Sympathetic to Americans after 9/11, many people no longer supported US military action in the Middle East. Critics argued that war, torture, and civilian casualties helped rather than hurt the terrorist cause. Moreover, the United States no longer seemed like an unstoppable military and economic superpower able to build democratic nations and reshape the world in its image.

Financial Crisis

Meanwhile, the second great crisis of the Bush years mushroomed. The economic boom of the 1990s and 2000s resembled the boom of the 1920s. In both periods, optimistic American consumers borrowed money to buy houses, cars, and stocks. All that buying spurred the economy and drove the stock market to record heights. But eventually all that borrowing reached its limits: unable to meet their debts, many Americans could not borrow any more. In both periods, business leaders and government officials paid too little attention to dangerous financial practices until it was too late.

By the early 2000s, the housing industry was developing a classic "bubble," an unrealistic inflation of prices. Some Americans bought houses they could not afford, and many used houses as collateral for loans. Banks made loans they should not have made, including risky subprime mortgages at high interest rates to people with poor credit. Moreover, financial institutions hid these bad loans by folding them into complex, risky financial instruments known as collateralized debt obligations (CDOs), which were sold around the world. Firms that bought CDOs, vulnerable to trouble in housing, did not understand the danger.

In 2005, US house prices began to fall. As the housing bubble burst, some homeowners, particularly those with subprime loans, had trouble making their payments; foreclosures—banks' repossession of homes for unpaid mortgages—increased. In consequence, the home-construction industry suffered, and consumers had trouble getting loans. Financial institutions suffered, too. In 2008, the federal government had to help firms involved in the mortgage business, and banking giant JPMorgan Chase took over failing investment bank Bear Stearns.

Developments linked to globalization also threatened the United States and other nations. Globalized free trade suffered when the World Trade Organization's round of trade talks in Doha, Qatar, ended without an agreement. Oil prices, driven by demand from the growing economies of China and India, hit record levels. Those prices drove up the cost of other goods and hurt the American auto industry, whose gas-guzzling SUVs became hard to sell. Felt worldwide, these events hit the United States as the global value of the dollar declined and American consumers lost confidence.

As the Dow Jones industrial average fell from a record high over 14,000 in October 2007 to the 8,000s in November 2008, the US financial industry nearly collapsed: investment firm Lehman Brothers became the most valuable American corporation ever to fail. As governments and financial institutions around the world scrambled to save banks and prop up stock markets, Americans feared a repeat of the great crash of 1929. A panicked Congress immediately approved the Emergency Economic Stabilization Act of 2008, a $700 billion financial package creating the Troubled Asset Relief Program (TARP) to bail out the US financial industry, ensure the availability of credit to borrowers, and save the nation from depression.

The near-collapse of the economy, along with the wars in Afghanistan and Iraq, cast a shadow over George W. Bush. Even though, unlike his father, he managed to win two presidential contests, Bush 43 was dogged by the sense that he should have been better prepared for the financial and terrorist threats. Although Bush had managed to rally the country after 9/11, his reputation was tarnished by the belief that his advisers had misrepresented the existence of Iraqi WMDs in order to force a perhaps unnecessary, unwinnable war.

Obama and the Promise of Change

Against the frightening backdrop of military and economic crises, Americans elected the first African American president in the fall of 2008. The groundbreaking choice of Barack Obama offered the promise of change after years of political gridlock. But change

AMERICAN LANDSCAPE

"Gitmo"

From the camera eye of a satellite miles above, Guantánamo Bay stood out from the rest of eastern Cuba. The inlet was a horseshoe of brown and gray amid the lush green of the island and the bright blue of the Atlantic. To the administration of George W. Bush, Guantánamo Bay was a gray area, too: one of the few places on earth that was American and yet not American, a drab anomaly perfect for one of the most controversial phases of the war on terror.

Guantánamo Bay, 520 miles from Miami, Florida, had been an anomaly for more than a century. After the Spanish-American War of 1898, the US government had taken the spot for a well-protected naval base. The Cuban-American Treaty of 1903 effectively gave America perpetual control over the base. For less than $4,000 a year, the United States could keep the facility until both Washington and Cuba agreed to end the arrangement.

Even when Fidel Castro came to power in 1959, the US base remained. Castro objected to the installation but did not try to drive out the United States. So Guantánamo Bay, or "Gitmo," as Americans called it, remained the oldest US overseas naval base and the only one in a Communist country.

Gitmo became less and less valuable over the years. As the cold war ended and the United States closed down military bases, there was no real need for a naval installation so close to the US mainland. Then the war on terror began. The Bush administration needed to put captured Taliban fighters and other "enemy combatants" somewhere safe. It was too risky to leave detainees in unstable Afghanistan or Iraq, but it was also too risky to bring them to the United States, where courts, Congress, and public opinion could interfere in their imprisonment. So the Bush administration looked, in the words of Secretary of Defense Donald Rumsfeld, for "the least worst place" to hold those captured in the war on terror.

They found it at Guantánamo Bay. The US military controlled the base, but US civil law did not apply. Gitmo, with its gray, pebbly beaches, was the perfect gray area for an administration determined to find a way around the law to prosecute the war on terror. Before 2001 was over, detainees began to arrive from Afghanistan. By the end of 2008, some 775 people had been

came slowly: it proved difficult to end the Iraq and Afghan wars and to get the economy growing strongly again, particularly amid fierce partisan differences.

The Presidential Election of 2008

The presidential election of 2008 featured a major-party candidate different from any of his predecessors. First-term senator Barack Obama of Illinois, the son of a black Kenyan

Gitmo Military police guarding new detainees in orange jumpsuits at one of the prison facilities at the US naval base at Guantánamo Bay, Cuba.

incarcerated at Gitmo. To accommodate them, the United States built no fewer than seven separate prison facilities; one of them, known only as "Camp 7," remained secret. Thousands of Americans streamed in to run Gitmo.

For a time, the base provided the Bush administration with the freedom it wanted and needed. CIA, FBI, and military interrogators, apparently copying Chinese Communist techniques from the 1950s, tortured some prisoners. According to detainees, their captors used sleep deprivation and beatings; they also mocked detainees' religious practices by defacing the Qur'an or flushing it down the toilet. Lacking the rights of captured military prisoners under the Geneva Convention, the detainees were deprived of the right to trial—a feature of justice in the United States. These conditions took a heavy toll on prisoners; an unknown number committed suicide.

As details of life at Gitmo leaked out, critics of the Bush administration argued

that the laws of the United States should apply to prisoners at the base; they deserved the protections of the Geneva Convention and the right to trial. They saw Gitmo as proof that the war on terror, like other wars, had eroded due process, human rights, and other features of democracy, all in the name of battling for democracy.

Ruling in 2006 and 2008 on the treatment of prisoners, the US Supreme Court seemed to agree that Gitmo was an assault on democratic values. Running for president in 2008, President Obama condemned torture and promised to close the facility. Reporting in 2014, a Senate subcommittee documented the torture that went on at Gitmo. Even so, the facility remained open—a swath of gray amid all the green and blue.

father and a white American mother, won the Democratic nomination on the promise of "change" for America and the end of the "stupid war" in Iraq. A symbol of the diverse, globalized nation, Obama became the first African American major-party presidential nominee. His Republican opponent, Senator John McCain of Arizona, reinforced a reputation as an independent "maverick" by choosing the second female major-party candidate for the vice presidency, Governor Sarah Palin of Alaska. But the 72-year-old McCain, a generation older than Obama, seemed more like a defender of the status quo,

"Change We Can Believe In" Democratic nominee Barack Obama campaigns for the presidency in 2008.

including Bush's policies, and Palin seemed unprepared for national office. On November 4, 2008, voters did what still appeared unthinkable: they elected an African American to the presidency of the United States. Obama won a clear victory with 52.8 percent of the popular vote, the highest in 20 years, and 365 electoral votes. The Democrat seemed to have his mandate for "change."

Confronting Economic Crisis

Before the celebration of Obama's history-making victory ended, the economic crisis deepened. In mid-November, the stock market lurched below 8,000. With American automakers heading toward bankruptcy, President Bush provided $13 billion in TARP funds to the troubled automakers. As consumer spending fell and unemployment rose, the nation was in the grip of what became known as the Great Recession.

Taking office amid hardship and war in January 2009, Obama optimistically promised a new politics. "We have chosen hope over fear, unity of purpose over conflict and discord," he declared. "We come to proclaim an end to the petty grievances and false promises, the recriminations and worn-out dogmas that for far too long have strangled our politics."

To restore prosperity, Obama pushed successfully for the sort of deficit spending that liberals had long advocated to stimulate economic growth. The American Recovery and Reinvestment Act of 2009, known as the stimulus package, appropriated three-quarters of a trillion dollars including tax incentives and money for housing, health care, educational programs, food stamps, retirees, scientific research, highways, and other infrastructure. Some liberals believed the stimulus spent too little, while conservatives charged that the act spent far too much and irresponsibly increased federal power and the national debt.

To save Chrysler and General Motors (GM) in 2009, the US government stepped in to support quick bankruptcies for the two manufacturers, which reemerged as new, restructured companies with less debt and new ownership. To Republicans' dismay, the US Treasury temporarily became the majority owner of GM. Despite this controversial "socialism," the bailout worked: the American automakers survived, and the federal government sold off its ownership of GM.

Rather than punish financial leaders for their role in the economic crisis, Obama focused on protecting consumers and regulating banks and insurance companies. In 2009, Congress passed new rules for credit card companies. The next year, the president signed the Wall Street Reform and Consumer Protection Act, known as Dodd-Frank, perhaps the most significant overhaul of federal financial regulation since the 1930s.

As the stock market climbed again and the danger of depression receded, Obama concentrated on winning the longtime liberal goal of national health care. After a lengthy congressional battle, the president signed the Patient Protection and Affordable Health Care Act of 2010 and the Health Care and Educational Reconciliation Act of 2010. The two measures helped uninsured and self-employed Americans buy health insurance, made more poor people eligible for Medicaid, allowed parents' health insurance to cover their children for longer, prevented insurance companies from denying coverage because of preexisting conditions, and encouraged large employers to provide health care plans. Through Medicare taxes and benefit cuts, the measures would reduce the federal budget deficit. Finally, a controversial "individual mandate" required all adults to obtain health insurance beginning in 2014 or pay a penalty.

Obama's landmark reform was difficult to explain, passionately attacked by conservatives as "socialism," criticized by some liberals as less than full government-subsidized health care, and limited by a Supreme Court decision. Nevertheless, Obama had achieved the system of national health insurance that Democratic presidents such as Harry Truman and Bill Clinton had failed to win. The measures that became known as "Obamacare," like Lyndon Johnson's Medicare in the 1960s and Franklin Roosevelt's Social Security in the 1930s, marked a basic change in the relationship between government and the American people.

Ending the Wars in Afghanistan and Iraq

Like every president since World War II, Obama believed the United States should engage with the world primarily through the United Nations, military alliances such as NATO, and trade agreements such as NAFTA and the WTO. He did not care for George W. Bush's experiments in unilateral US action, the threat of preemptive warfare, and neoconservative nation building abroad.

Determined to stop terrorist threats, Obama nevertheless believed the nation should be able to end its wars in Afghanistan and Iraq. To terminate the Afghan conflict, the president sent 30,000 more troops to battle the Taliban and Al Qaeda in 2009. Despite the troop increase, American forces faced the same difficult battle that Lieutenant Craig Mullaney had fought to defeat the enemy and win over the Afghan people. As the fighting continued into 2010, Afghanistan surpassed Vietnam as the longest war in American history.

Meanwhile, the Obama administration aggressively used other means to pursue terrorists and their supporters. Controversially, the CIA increased the use of unmanned, rocket-firing drones to kill suspected terrorists and their leaders inside Pakistan and Yemen. The president also ordered the CIA and Special Forces to go after terrorist leaders. On May 1, 2011, nearly a decade after 9/11, a daring helicopter raid conducted by Special Forces inside Pakistan killed Osama bin Laden—a turning point in the war on terror.

Following bin Laden's death, Obama announced the beginning of American troop withdrawals from Afghanistan and shifted the US effort to training the Afghan military and police. Despite uncertainty that the Afghan government could hold off the Taliban, Obama announced in 2014 that a much smaller US military contingent would remain to help Afghan security forces in 2016.

Observers also doubted that the Iraqi government could defend its country with US-trained soldiers and police. Despite this concern, Obama brought the Iraq War to a close. In October 2011, he declared that American troops would leave by the end of the year.

The Politics of Frustration

Obama's foreign policy successes earned him little credit because the economy did not recover as strongly as he and his advisers had expected. The Great Recession, more severe than economists had first recognized, continued to strain American society. Although unemployment gradually declined, the economy grew slowly and wages lagged.

Against this backdrop of hardship and frustration, the president's optimistic call for a new politics went unheeded. Obama found himself whipsawed by an often nasty debate. On one hand, he disappointed supporters who had expected more aggressive domestic leadership, a better economy, and more "change" generally. Many liberal Democrats and independents, who called themselves "progressives," felt that Obama should have punished Wall Street, expanded federal regulation and spending still further, taxed the rich more heavily, and implemented federally subsidized "single-payer" health care covering all Americans. On the other hand, conservatives were horrified by Obama's accomplishments, including health care reform and the stimulus.

Two new movements reflected conservative and progressive discontent. In 2009, the Tea Party movement, evoking the spirit of the Boston Tea Party of 1773 before the American Revolution, voiced conservative anger at federal activism and deficits. Composed mostly of white, older Americans, the movement served primarily as a pressure group within the Republican Party pushing more conservative candidates and policies. While the Tea Party blamed the federal government for the nation's woes, a new movement on the left blamed financial elites and the rich. Beginning in 2011, the Occupy movement, also known as Occupy Wall Street, staged demonstrations in Wall Street in New York City and around the world on behalf of the "99 percent" against the wealthiest "1 percent."

Although most Americans endorsed neither movement, there was considerable disappointment with Obama's presidency. In the 2010 midterm elections, Republicans recaptured the House of Representatives. Once again the United States had divided partisan control of the federal government, and once again the result was legislative gridlock. Pressured by the Tea Party, Republican leaders wanted to repeal Obamacare, cut taxes and lower domestic spending; refusing, Obama and the Democrats wanted more economic stimulus. In 2011, the president and the parties finally made a modest bargain to cut the deficit, but not before the United States, for the first time in its history, nearly failed to meet its financial obligations. Many Americans criticized Obama as a weak leader who did not care enough about the nation's financial plight. But they condemned Congress and Republicans even more.

A Second Term

As George W. Bush demonstrated, incumbent presidents were hard to defeat for re-election. Despite the criticism of Obama, Republicans struggled to come up with a strong alternative in 2012. The party, divided by the Tea Party movement, chose Mitt Romney, a wealthy Mormon and moderate former governor of Massachusetts, as its presidential nominee. Obama's supporters, their hopes for change diminished, were not as passionate this time. But Romney suffered from the perception that he was a rich man out of touch with ordinary Americans. The Republican nominee also had trouble explaining his opposition to Obamacare, which borrowed features from the Massachusetts health insurance system that Romney had signed into law as governor. In November, Obama received a smaller percentage of the popular vote (51.1) and a smaller number of electoral votes (332) than four years earlier, but he won reelection.

Once again, Obama faced a divided Congress with a Republican-controlled House and a Democratic-controlled Senate. That combination produced more gridlock. In 2013, the nation endured another temporary shutdown of the federal government when Republicans and Democrats could not agree on budgets, spending, and the funding of Obamacare.

Unable to win legislation from Congress, Obama increasingly relied on the executive power of the presidency. Controversially, his administration issued over 560 major regulations covering health care, financial institutions, industrial pollution, civil rights, and worker and consumer protection—twice as many as the George W. Bush administration. Obama officials raised the value of a human life from $6.6 million to $9.4 million—a key figure used to calculate the impact of regulations and other federal action. Although they had seldom criticized Bush's use of executive power, conservatives and Republicans now condemned the cost and intrusiveness of Obama's regulations.

Climate Change

President Obama used his executive power in response to the problem of climate change. As early as the 1950s, scientists had begun to predict and then explore a gradual increase in surface temperatures around the world. By the 2010s, scientific consensus argued that human activity—in particular, the industrial use of coal, oil, and other fossil fuels producing greenhouse gasses such as carbon dioxide—was heavily responsible for long-term global warming. According to scientists, the effects of climate change included melting glaciers, rising sea levels, shifting seasons, spreading deserts, and increasing extreme weather events. In the United States, devastating, deadly hurricanes—Katrina along the Gulf Coast in 2005, "Super Storm" Sandy along the Atlantic Coast in 2012, and Harvey along the south coast of Texas, Irma on the south coast of Florida, and Maria in Puerto Rico in 2017—dramatically underscored the possibilities of climate change. Accordingly, environmental activists urged America to reduce greenhouse gas emissions by decreasing the use of fossil fuels and to join other nations in seeking solutions.

Worried that climate change measures would hurt the fossil fuel industry, George W. Bush had declined to support ratification of a key international treaty, the Kyoto Protocol. In contrast, Barack Obama pushed to develop solar and wind power as alternatives to coal and oil. In 2015, the president implemented his Clean Power Plan, which aimed to reduce carbon dioxide emissions by placing restrictive regulations on coal-burning power plants. That year, the United States joined 195 nations in adopting the path-breaking Paris Agreement. To limit global warming, each party to the agreement set its own voluntary targets for reducing greenhouse gases.

Unending War?

The Paris Agreement reflected Obama's strong belief that the United States should engage with other nations to promote its interests and avoid war. Unable to end conflict in Afghanistan and Iraq, his administration also could not unilaterally or collectively stop Russian expansion in Europe. Moreover, events in the Middle East threatened to draw America into new conflicts abroad. Additionally, terrorist acts in the United States made it seem as though the nation was caught in unending war.

In the twenty-first century, Vladimir Putin, serving alternately as president and prime minister, wanted to restore the power and influence that Russia had enjoyed as part of the Soviet Union during the cold war. The communist leader particularly resented the decision of the United States and its European allies to enlarge the North Atlantic Treaty Organization to include Central and Eastern European nations bordering Russia. In 2008, Putin sent troops across Russia's southern border to ensure that two regions of the neighboring country of Georgia could break free from the Georgian government. In 2014, as troops repeatedly crossed Russia's eastern border into Ukraine, Russia annexed the Ukrainian territory of Crimea. In response, the United States and its allies imposed strong economic sanctions against Russian officials and companies. Damaging Russia's economy, the sanctions slowed Putin's aggression in Ukraine but did not stop the annexation of Crimea.

In the Middle East and Africa in 2011, the "Arab Spring" saw popular uprisings against repressive leaders in nations including Tunisia, Egypt, Libya, and Syria. Facing criticism for doing either too little or too much, President Obama partnered with NATO and used airpower, without an American military casualty, to help overthrow Libya's Muammar Qaddafi, who had supported terrorism against the United States. In Syria, President Bashar Hafez al-Assad's ruthless repression of the Arab Spring led to civil war. Under pressure to intervene on the side of the anti-Assad rebels, Obama held back. In 2012, the president declared that Assad would cross "a red line" if he used chemical weapons against his own people. But when Assad did just that, Congress refused to authorize retaliatory air strikes.

Meanwhile, one of Assad's opponents created new problems for the United States. The Islamic State in Iraq and Syria (ISIS), a jihadist group that had split from Al Qaeda, aimed to establish a caliphate—an Islamic state—in the Middle East. Amid the chaos of civil war, ISIS fighters took over territory in Syria and, with the aid of former supporters of Saddam Hussein, spread across Iraq. After ISIS murdered Iraqis and beheaded two American hostages, Obama authorized air drops of humanitarian aid to besieged Iraqis and air strikes against ISIS fighters in the summer of 2014. With the fate of Iraq hanging in the balance, Obama found it impossible to leave the country after all. Americans faced the prospect that the nation would remain on a war footing for years to come (see Map 30–1).

The Obama administration did manage to use collective action to deal with key challenges in the Middle East and Asia. In 2015, the United States joined European nations, Russia, and the People's Republic of China in a deal to prevent Iran from developing nuclear weapons that would have further destabilized the Middle East. As China grew economically and militarily powerful and as North Korea experimented with nuclear weapons, the president tried to contain these developments through diplomacy and alliances. The Obama administration joined negotiations with South Korea, Japan, Vietnam, Australia, Canada, Mexico, Peru, and various Pacific nations that led to the Trans-Pacific Partnership (TPP), a vast new trade agreement, in 2016.

Meanwhile, Obama encountered difficulty at home scaling back the Bush administration's post-9/11 national security measures. Disappointing his supporters, the president could not close the Guantánamo Bay detention center, as he had promised. In 2013, computer specialist and former National Security Agency contractor Edward Snowden leaked classified documents detailing the federal government's extensive surveillance programs around the world and inside the United States. Snowden fled to Hong Kong and then Russia to avoid prosecution, while Americans debated whether the government should be able to collect data about their lives. But the programs, like US involvement in conflicts abroad, continued.

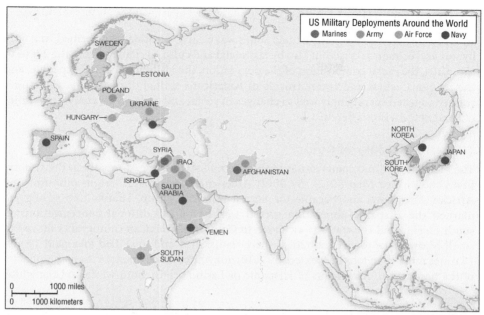

Map 30-1   US Military Deployments in the Age of Terror Location of Air Force, Army, Marines, and Navy units, totaling over 450,000 people, outside the United States in 2017.
Source: Daniel Brown and Skye Gould, "The US has 1.3 million troops stationed around the world— here are the major hotspots," *Business Insider*, August 31, 2017. http://www.businessinsider.com/ us-military-deployments-may-2017-5

They continued, too, because terrorism endured in the United States. As the fortunes of ISIS declined, the group urged followers not to come to the Middle East but instead to stay home and conduct attacks. In addition to attacks in Queens, New York; Garland, Texas; Chattanooga, Tennessee; and Columbus, Ohio, three acts of terrorism commanded national attention. In April 2013, two Chechen brothers, seeking revenge for the US wars in Afghanistan and Iraq, set off bombs that killed three and injured hundreds at the annual marathon in Boston, Massachusetts. During a subsequent manhunt in which a policeman was killed and another mortally wounded, the brothers were captured: one died from his wounds; the other was sentenced to death. In December 2015, a Chicago-born man and his Pakistan-born wife shot and killed 14 people at a holiday party in San Bernardino, California. According to the FBI, the couple were "homegrown violent extremists . . . inspired by foreign terrorist organizations." In June 2016, American-born Omar Mateen, who called himself an "Islamic soldier" and apparently pledged allegiance to ISIS, shot and killed 49 people at Pulse, a gay nightclub in Orlando, Florida. The deadliest act of terrorism on US soil since 9/11, the murders were also the bloodiest anti-LGBTQ violence in American history. Meanwhile, a wave of deadly attacks occurred in Australia, Canada, and Europe, as well as the Middle East. The battle with terror was far from over.

Against the sobering backdrop of war and terrorism, the US economy gradually improved during Obama's second term. As the stock market reached record heights, the unemployment rate dropped under 5 percent for the first time since the financial crisis. His administration free from scandal, Obama regained public approval.

Diversity and Division

In the twenty-first century, the United States was clearly "a nation transformed" not only by war and economic crisis but also by fast social and cultural change. From the 2000s to the 2010s, the racial composition of the population, the visibility of LGBTQ people, and the religious beliefs and commitments of Americans shifted dramatically. Sometimes society adjusted surprisingly well to changes in social and cultural diversity; sometimes old and new divisions flared.

A Diverse Society of Color

The racial and ethnic composition of the United States changed rapidly in the twenty-first century (see Map 30–2). By 2001, Americans of Hispanic origin outnumbered African Americans and became the largest minority group. Thanks to a strong job market, the Hispanic population spread well beyond traditional concentrations in south Florida and the states from Texas to California. Mexican immigrants moved to small Midwestern towns and cities where semiskilled and unskilled jobs paid 10 and 15 times more than jobs in Mexico. By 2010, nonwhites made up more than one-quarter of the population. Americans of Hispanic or Latino origin, both white and nonwhite,

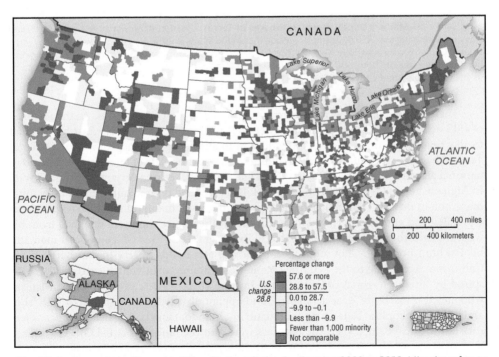

Map 30-2   Percentage Change in Minority Population by County: 2000 to 2010 Minority refers to people who reported their ethnicity and race as something other than non-Hispanic white alone in the decennial census. (Counties with a minority population of at least 1,000 are included in the map.)
Sources: US Census Bureau, *Census 2000 Redistricting Data (Public Law 94–171) Summary File*, Tables PL1 and PL2; and *2010 Census Redistricting Data (Public Law 94–171) Summary File*, Tables P1 and P2.

numbered more than 50 million—just over 16 percent of the population. Expecting the number of Hispanics and Asians to triple in the next 50 years, the Census Bureau predicted that the United States would become a diverse society of color, with a nonwhite majority. Already in 2014, non-Hispanic whites made up a minority of the children who went to school that fall.

As the population changed, the concept of race became more complicated. To many Americans, race was largely a divide between black and white. But the growth of the Hispanic population confounded this simple division. Moreover, many Americans, especially younger ones, felt that mixed racial background was a basic and distinctive part of their identity. In 2000, the Census Bureau let people choose more than one race to describe themselves. Hispanics, epitomizing the complications of race, were allowed to identify themselves both as Hispanic and as members of any race. Although officially labeled Hispanic, many Americans increasingly considered themselves Latinos or Latinas.

Tolerance and Intolerance

In some ways, greater diversity brought greater tolerance. In the immediate aftermath of 9/11, American Muslims did not face the discrimination that German Americans confronted during World War I or that Japanese Americans suffered during World War II. As the first Mormon major party candidate for president, Mitt Romney met no significant criticism of his religion.

Nevertheless, social diversity brought division and discrimination. In 2008, Obama's election occasioned optimism that America was becoming a "postracial" society in which racial differences did not matter. But many Obama supporters believed that racism played a role in the determined opposition to his administration, including unfounded claims by so-called birthers that he was an illegal president who had not actually been born in the United States. Decades after the African American civil rights movement, black men remained disproportionately likely to be unemployed and imprisoned.

Due in part to new technology, the Obama years saw the raw reemergence of an old racial concern—the justice system's treatment of African Americans. Just as analog videotape footage of the Rodney King beating spurred protest in the 1990s, digital cell phone video of the controversial deaths of unarmed black men spurred nationwide protests in the 2010s. After a Florida jury acquitted George Zimmerman of murder in the shooting death of Trayvon Martin in 2013, community activists launched an online protest movement with the hashtag "Black Lives Matter." In 2014, the police killings of Eric Garner in New York City and Michael Brown in Ferguson, Missouri, led to nationwide, nonviolent Black Lives Matter protests. In turn, both violence against police and the rise of Black Lives Matter inspired the creation of Blue Lives Matter—a hashtag reflecting the typically blue uniforms of police officers. A White Lives Matter movement also appeared. While Black Lives Matter demanded equal treatment of different races under the law, White Lives Matter often insisted on white supremacy.

The 2010s saw a revival of white supremacist groups and violence. In 2012, a neo-Nazi shot and killed six Sikhs at their temple in Cudahy, Wisconsin. In 2015, a white supremacist obsessed with the Confederacy shot and killed nine African American members of a Bible study group at the Emanuel African Methodist Episcopal Church in Charleston, South Carolina. Afterward, the state government removed the Confederate flag, raised in the 1960s in protest against the civil rights movement, from the statehouse grounds.

Meanwhile, the nation's inability to resolve the status of illegal immigrants from Mexico and Central America indicated continuing uneasiness about the increase of the Latino population. After the Great Recession, about 11 million foreign-born people, around half of them Mexican, lived without legal approval in the United States. While many Americans called for more rigorous enforcement of immigration laws, employers relied on undocumented workers, who made up about 5 percent of the nation's labor force. Public debate focused particularly on the fate of the "Dreamers," brought illegally as children to the United States, typically by their parents. In 2012, the Obama administration's Deferred Action for Childhood Arrivals program (DACA) allowed eligible Dreamers to pay a fee to study, work, and postpone deportation. Like other Obama executive actions, DACA met resistance from both anti-immigration activists and opponents of presidential power.

Despite progress toward greater equality, Americans became more pessimistic about racial issues toward the end of Obama's presidency. Majorities of whites, blacks, and Latinos all believed that race relations were "bad."

LGBTQ Rights

In the twenty-first century, Americans increasingly celebrated or at least accepted sexual diversity. After centuries of hostility and discrimination, the shift in attitudes and policies toward the lesbian, gay, bisexual, transgender, and queer or questioning communities came with stunning speed. Despite conservatives' crusade for family values in the 1990s, Americans' social attitudes became more liberal. To a great extent, the change was the result of activists' courage in beginning to come out in the late 1960s and become a more visible presence in American society and culture. The change also reflected the rise of a younger generation of Americans for whom sexual equality was as important as racial equality had been for young Americans during the civil rights era. But many older, powerful Americans, including judges, proved open to change, too.

Ruling in *Lawrence v. Texas* in 2003, the US Supreme Court struck down state antisodomy laws and effectively legalized gay sexual behavior. In 2004, the mayor of San Francisco, flouting state law, issued marriage licenses to same-sex couples. Liberal Massachusetts became the first state to legalize same-sex marriages, and couples flocked there to be married. Supported by conservatives and George W. Bush, a constitutional amendment banning gay marriage failed to pass that year. But in 2008, a majority of California voters passed Proposition Eight, a referendum imposing a ban on same-sex marriages.

Despite such setbacks, public opinion increasingly favored LGBTQ rights. In 2010–2011, Obama and Congress ended the military's "don't ask, don't tell" policy. Ruling in *Hollingsworth v. Perry* in June 2013, the US Supreme Court upheld a lower court's decision that California's Proposition Eight was unconstitutional. The same day, in *United States v. Windsor*, the Supreme Court invalidated Section 3 of the Defense of Marriage Act of 1996, which had denied federal recognition of same-sex unions. In 2015, the Supreme Court settled the issue nationwide by ruling same-sex marriage bans unconstitutional in *Obergefell v. Hodges*.

As opinion shifted on LGBTQ rights, Americans became more aware and somewhat more accepting of the transgender population and queer or questioning—as many as 1.4 million by 2016. One sign was the increasing addition of Q to the original term LGBT. In 2016, the Obama administration lifted the formal ban on transgender people serving openly in the military. But that year North Carolina passed the Public Facilities Privacy & Security Act requiring people to use restrooms and changing facilities corresponding to the biological sex on their birth certificates in all government buildings. Intended to keep transgender people from using the facilities of their choice, the "bathroom bill" met opposition, including boycotts, from corporations, musicians, sports leagues, and other states. The US government and North Carolina sued each other. Succumbing to intense pressure, the state legislature repealed the facilities provision in 2017.

Shifting Religious Beliefs and Practices

As the presence of a Sikh temple in Wisconsin suggested, American religious practices became more diverse in the twenty-first century. Non-Christian faiths, including Buddhists, Hindus, and Muslims, increased from 5 to 6 percent of the population between 2007 and 2014. Most Americans still considered themselves Christians, but the percentage fell from 78 to 71 percent. Even the largest Christian religious grouping, Evangelical Protestants, saw a slight decline to 25 percent. Most strikingly, the percentage of Americans unaffiliated with any religious denomination jumped from 16 to 23 percent during these years—a larger group than Roman Catholics and mainline Protestants. Like the growth of the nonwhite population, the number of the religiously unaffiliated seemed likely to increase: Americans born after the 1980s were less likely to pray daily, attend religious services, and consider religion very important to their lives than their elders were.

Although the United States still led industrialized nations in the percentage of the population who believed in God and attended Christian churches, some Americans worried that Christianity was under attack. Conservative commentators condemned the "War on Christmas" allegedly led by liberals and progressives. Too many people and businesses, conservatives argued, said "Happy Holidays" instead of the more Christian "Merry Christmas"; too many local governments were afraid to display Christian symbols such as crosses, Christmas trees, and nativity scenes. In short, the United States was supposedly losing its identity as a Christian nation.

Economic Change and a Divided Nation

As so often in American history, anxieties about religion, race, and gender partly reflected anxieties about economic change. In the twenty-first century, the implications of deindustrialization, digitization, and globalization became increasingly clear. Despite the recovery from the Great Recession, the economy seemed to divide Americans into unequal groups: the rich and everyone else; men and women; old and young; urban and rural.

Jobs and Growth

By the 2010s, some optimistic forecasts about the information revolution and globalization were not coming true. New technologies and freer trade turned out to be more disruptive than expected. While observers anticipated that globalization would threaten some American manufacturing, they were unprepared for the sharp decline in the twenty-first century. Instead of increasing, jobs in manufacturing dropped 20 percent

A Robotic Car Assembly Line in Delaware Where are the workers?

from 2000 to 2007, dropped again during the Great Recession, and then made only a partial recovery. In 1980, about one in five American workers had labored in factories; in 2016, less than one in ten did. Meanwhile, the ranks of coal miners, who had helped power the Industrial Revolution, continued a long-term decline to just 50,000 in 2016. Thanks to new extraction techniques and competitive prices, jobs in the fossil fuel industry—oil and natural gas—grew in the twenty-first century but did not reach the highs of the 1980s.

The service sector, which had grown in the late twentieth century as manufacturing declined, faced upheaval, too. As online shopping became more popular in the twenty-first century, Amazon and other e-commerce companies built new distribution centers and hired more workers. But towns and small cities, which had counted on retail to make up for lost factories, saw local stores shed workers and go out of business.

An intense debate enveloped changes in employment. As advocates of globalization contended, trade agreements indeed benefited many American workers and offered American consumers a wider selection of goods at lower prices. But freer trade, including the "China Shock"—the admission of the People's Republic of China, with its vast economy of low-wage workers, to the World Trade Organization in 2001—led to the loss of some American factories and jobs. Unexpectedly, technological change proved an even bigger factor in job losses, not only in manufacturing but also in the service sector. Much as the horse gave way to the internal combustion engine, human workers increasingly gave way to robots in factories, warehouses, stores, and even fast food restaurants in the 2010s. "They're always polite," the head of a restaurant company explained happily, "they always upsell, they never take a vacation, they never show up late, there's never a slip-and-fall, or an age, sex or race discrimination case."

All these changes had a dramatic effect on the American economy; some observers believed they added up to a new technological and economic revolution. Politicians, economists, and corporate executives had predicted that new technologies and freer trade would drive the economy to new heights. Instead, national economic growth tapered off. From 1948 to 2000, the United States had grown an average of 2.3 percent per year; from 2001 to 2016, the average growth rate fell to just 1.1 percent.

The Rich, the Poor, and the Middle Class

By 2000, the United States, the richest country in the world, also had the largest gap between rich and poor. That gap grew larger in the twenty-first century. On one hand, the bottom 20 percent of American workers received only 3 percent of national income in 2016. On the other, the top 20 percent of American earners received 51 percent of national income that year. In 2012, the top 400 American earners had an average annual income of $336 million, more than four times the inflation-adjusted value of their earnings 30 years before. After the financial crisis of 2008, the stock market soared again to one record level after another—a windfall for the bare majority of Americans who owned corporate shares. The tax cuts of the Reagan and Bush administrations, only partially moderated by Obama-era tax increases, allowed the rich to keep more of their gains. The richest 5 percent of households owned nearly two-thirds of all the nation's wealth. By 2017, the number of American billionaires had grown to 565—more than a quarter of the world's billionaires.

Meanwhile, the middle class—households earning between $35,000 and $100,000 a year—shrank. After decades of downsizing, outsourcing, and deindustrialization, the average weekly earnings of American workers in 2014, allowing for inflation, were less than in 1970. The decline of manufacturing meant the loss of relatively high-paying blue-collar jobs that paid for a middle-class lifestyle. Although workers continued to become more efficient and productive, employers held down the growth of wages and salaries (see Figure 30–1). For decades, American families had made up lost economic ground by having both spouses or partners work. But in the 2010s, that was no longer necessarily enough to

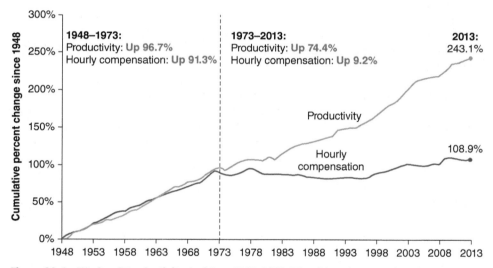

Figure 30-1 Workers' Productivity and Pay, 1948-2013 Why did workers stop benefiting so much from their increasing productivity after 1970?

Note: Data are for compensation (wages and benefits) of production/nonsupervisory workers in the private sector and net productivity of the total economy. "Net productivity" is the growth of output of goods and services less depreciation per hour worked.

Source: Lawrence Mishel, Elise Gould, and Josh Bivens, "Wage Stagnation in Nine Charts," Economic Policy Institute, January 6, 2015. http://www.epi.org/publication/charting-wage-stagnation/

Data: EPI analysis of unpublished Total Economy Productivity data from Bureau of Labor Statistics (BLS) Labor Productivity and Costs program, wage data from the BLS Current Employment Statistics, BLS Employment Cost Trends, BLS Consumer Price Index, and Bureau of Economic Analysis National Income and Product Accounts. Updated from Figure A in *Raising America's Pay: Why It's Our Central Economic Policy Challenge*, by Josh Bivens, Elise Gould, Lawrence Mishel, and Heidi Shierholz, Economic Policy Institute, 2014.

maintain a middle-class lifestyle. In the 2000s, 60 percent of adult Americans considered themselves middle class; by 2016, only 51 percent did. Since the 1950s, Americans and their leaders had proudly claimed that the United States was a middle-class country. That claim was harder to maintain in the 2010s.

Official figures hid the extent of some Americans' economic challenges. According to federal statistics, the unemployment rate was a very low 4.3 percent at one point in 2017. However, the government only counted people actually working or looking for jobs; in addition to the retired, the statistics omitted discouraged or ill people who had given up looking. Male participation in the labor force had been declining since the mid-1950s to 69 percent in 2017; surprisingly, female labor force participation had peaked at 60 percent in 2000 and only stood at 57 percent in 2017. Among the factors keeping both men and women from work was a stunning increase in physical disability and in opioid addiction. Almost incredibly, for such a rich country, the life expectancy of middle-aged whites, typically rising for decades, began to fall in 2015.

Women and Men

The changing economy reshaped the relative status of women and men. Female workers continued to face discrimination in the twenty-first century. Despite long, slow progress, women earned 85 percent as much as men did in 2015. Just 6 percent of America's 500 largest companies had female chief executive officers. Only about one in three American billionaires was female. Meanwhile, on average, mothers spent about twice as much time per week doing childcare and housework as fathers did. These domestic commitments, as well as caring for parents, were reasons why the percentage of women in the labor force fell.

Even so, women fared better than men in important ways. In an economy that demanded well-educated workers, women were more likely to have a college degree than men were for the first time in history. As high-school-educated men found fewer high-paying jobs in heavy industry, the rapidly growing health care sector eagerly sought the social and professional skills of women. As a result, women, who held about 25 percent of middle-income jobs in 1985, held 44 percent of them in 2015.

Women also protested another form of inequality. While the well-publicized examples of male sexual harassment and assault of women had produced little change in the 1990s, more women and gay men spoke out forcefully against these practices in the 2010s. A new openness, demonstrated by the Me Too and Time's Up movements, led to the resignations of powerful men in Hollywood, media, business, and government in 2017–2018.

Baby Boomers and Millennials

Long-term economic change affected generations differently, too. The vast generation of baby boomers, born in the affluent years from 1946 to 1964, lived comparatively well in the twenty-first century. In retirement, they enjoyed Social Security and Medicare benefits, paid partly by the taxes of younger generations. Meanwhile, the Millennials, born between the 1980s and the early 2000s, struggled with student debt, stagnating wages, and a difficult job market. In 2013, the median household headed by people age 65 and older was worth $203,000; the median household headed by people 35 and under was worth $7,000.

Millennials were often negatively stereotyped as thin-skinned, cautious, "entitled whiners" who postponed marriage and adulthood. Supposedly made dependent by constant praise and support from their parents, Millennials were more likely to live at home as young adults than the preceding generation had been. "Millennials," said one commentator, "need to put away the juice boxes and grow up." Yet other observers noted that Millennials lived at home and put off marriage for practical, financial reasons. The Millennial generation, defenders argued, was resilient and less materialistic—good preparation for lives that might well be less financially prosperous than those of their parents.

Urban and Rural

Economic transformation also helped power an increasing divide between urban and rural areas. Continuing a trend since the end of World War II, the suburban population, part of urban American, increased the largest percentage in the twenty-first century. Particularly in the South and West, less-populated suburbs around large cities—for instance, Kendal and Cosmal Counties, north of San Antonio, Texas—grew especially rapidly. Although the growth of cities slowed, the population of Sunbelt metropolitan areas such as Cape Coral–Fort Myers, Florida, boomed. Some older cities, such as Milwaukee, after decades of deindustrialization, experienced a revival by attracting college-educated Millennials and wealthy, well-educated older people. In turn, corporations, eager for college-educated, tech-savvy workers, moved their headquarters from suburbs to the cities.

In contrast, rural America, made up of small towns and countryside, lost population. By 2016, only 14 percent of Americans lived in the enormous territory outside of metropolitan areas. The rural Midwest and Northeast faced particularly large decreases. In addition to the decline of manufacturing and retail, rural America suffered from the rise of worldwide competition in farming. Brazil, for example, surpassed the United States as the largest producer of soybeans. "You keep pinching and pinching," said a fifth-generation Kansas farmer, "and pretty soon there's nothing left to pinch."

Economic change reinforced social and cultural differences among the regions. In 2017, 40 percent of urban Americans felt rural people had different values while 70 percent of rural people felt urbanites had different values. "It's like two worlds now," said a Virginian.

Democracy Under Stress

The accumulation of economic, social, and cultural differences fueled intense political division and further strained American democracy. So did massive election spending, changing technology and media, and new political boundaries. In 2016, the tumultuous, unprecedented presidential election laid bare the differences over the changes transforming the nation. Donald Trump, an unconventional president, faced daunting challenges in living up to his promise to "Make America Great Again."

Money and Politics

Growing wealth inequality intensified the long-term problem of spending on political campaigns. By the twenty-first century, the 1970s Watergate reforms regulating the role of money in elections had weakened. The Federal Election Commission allowed donors to give unlimited amounts of "soft money"—contributions not directed to specific candidates—to political parties and political action committees (PACs), which could use the funds freely, even for candidate-related advertising. As wealthy donors poured more money into elections, Congress passed the Bipartisan Campaign Reform Act of 2002, known as McCain-Feingold after its chief sponsors, Senators John McCain (R-AZ) and Russ Feingold (D-WI). The measure strictly limited expenditures of soft money and barred corporations, unions, and other groups from funding campaign-related communications 60 days before an election.

Contracting the role of money in politics, McCain-Feingold was inevitably divisive. Critics condemned the law as an unconstitutional interference with freedom and free speech. In a series of decisions, the Supreme Court agreed and effectively gutted McCain-Feingold. The last ruling, *Citizens United v. Federal Election Commission* (2010), invoked free speech rights to invalidate the prohibitions on groups' spending and pre-election campaign communications. The result was still more expenditures on elections, particularly through so-called Super PACs, independent political action committees that could spend unlimited funds on a campaign so long as they had no direct communication with the candidate. Critics worried that the rich now had still more influence over the political system.

Polarized Politics

Twenty-first-century politics became increasingly polarized, much like the intense partisanship of the nineteenth century. For decades after World War II, Americans had mostly gotten their news from the same sources: the three major television networks, officially nonpartisan; and newspapers, either Democratic, Republican, or independent in affiliation, but claiming to offer objective reporting. Believing that the networks and the press had a liberal bias, new conservative media figures such as the outspoken talk radio host Rush Limbaugh emerged in the 1980s and 1990s. When cable television and the Internet destroyed the dominance of the television networks and newspapers in the 1990s and 2000s, Americans increasingly got their news from quite different sources. On cable television, CNN, heir to the ideal of nonpartisan objectivity, competed with right-leaning Fox News and left-leaning MSNBC. With the rise of social media in the 2000s and 2010s, many people got most of their news from feeds specially tailored to their preferences. By then, Americans were less often forced to confront opposing ideas and were increasingly unlikely even to agree about a shared set of facts. Republicans were far more likely than Democrats to believe that Barack Obama was born in Kenya, rather than the United States.

The nation's political geography also became more polarized. State legislatures redrew electoral boundaries to favor one major party or the other. As more state legislative districts and federal congressional districts became safely Republican or Democratic, each party chose candidates who did not have to appeal to the other side. Once in office, they were less likely to compromise, which made gridlock still more likely in state capitals and Washington, DC.

Living in a kind of political isolation, Americans tended to have a more negative view of their partisan opponents. In 1994, 16 percent of Democrats and 17 percent of Republicans had a "very unfavorable" view of the opposition party; by 2014, 38 percent of Democrats and 43 percent of Republicans felt that way. Similarly, growing percentages of Americans wanted their friends to share their own political views.

Four Political Approaches

Political debate, long a battle between conservatism and liberalism, became more complex in the 2010s with the emergence of four contending political approaches. On the right, a nationalistic populism, like earlier populist movements, resented the increasing diversity of the United States. Fearing the deindustrialization and de-Christianization of America, these conservatives were nostalgic for the generation or so after World War II when, seemingly, the United States was dominant abroad and white men were dominant at home. Although the new populists were somewhat hostile to Wall Street, they were angrier with liberal elites in the media, Hollywood, and higher education and with immigration, LGBTQ rights, and African American activism. More worried about domestic problems, right-wing populism was dismayed by the ill effects of globalization and trade agreements, the human and financial cost of the war on terror and democratic nation building abroad, and the danger of still more wars.

Strongest among whites and evangelical Protestants in the South, Midwest, and rural areas, the new populism challenged the small-government conservatism that had long dominated the Republican Party. Much less critical of Wall Street, this mainstream Republicanism did not oppose some of the populist agenda. But this political approach was most concerned with cutting federal spending, regulations, and corporate and individual taxes and with repealing Obamacare. Mainstream Republicanism advocated globalization and trade agreements and still supported an activist foreign policy. Strongest among wealthy and well-to-do whites, this Republican approach struggled to hold onto Tea Party members disappointed with the short list of conservative accomplishments in Congress.

The Democratic Party faced a similar challenge. A left-of-center populism condemned big banks, trade agreements, deindustrialization, and wars overseas. Unlike conservative populism, this political approach did not condemn social and cultural change but focused more on economic issues, including demands for single-payer health care, higher taxes on the "1 percent," and more stringent regulation of banks and other corporations. Reflected in the Occupy movement, this left-wing populism was strongest among young Democrats and independents, the well-educated, and trade unions.

Like the conservative populists, left-wing populists opposed a major party establishment: the liberal Democratic mainstream. More than any other major political group, the establishment Democrats celebrated demographic, social, and cultural change, including racial and ethnic diversity, immigration and the Dreamers, women's empowerment, LGBTQ rights, and civil rights generally. This political approach favored greater economic equality but did not share the left populists' harsher critique of globalization, corporations, and the rich. Mainstream Democratic ideas appealed strongly to minority groups and women, particularly in urban areas.

These four approaches overlapped in sometimes confusing ways. There were self-described populists on both the left and right. Many mainstream Republicans and right-wing populists considered themselves conservatives; many mainstream Democrats and left-wing populists called themselves progressives. But underneath common names were four sets of conflicting ideas about the state of America.

The Presidential Election of 2016

The 2016 contest for the presidency became a referendum on these different approaches. The battle for the Republican nomination featured a parade of mostly

"Make America Great Again"
Donald Trump rallies his supporters during the 2016 presidential
campaign.

conservative, mainstream Republicans, but to the surprise
of nearly everyone, they all
lost to the brash real estate
mogul and reality television
star, Donald J. Trump, of New
York, a former Democrat who
now spoke for right-wing populism. Vowing to "Make America Great Again," Trump
criticized globalization, immigrants, and liberal elites and promised to "drain the
swamp" of lobbyists and corruption in Washington, build a wall on the US border
with Mexico, ban Muslim immigration temporarily, renegotiate trade agreements,
replace Obamacare with a better health care system, and bring back jobs in manufacturing and coal.

Meanwhile, US Senator Bernie Sanders, a socialist independent from Vermont, advocated left-wing populism as he fought for the Democratic nomination. His main opponent
was Hillary Clinton, the former First Lady and US senator from New York who had served
as Obama's secretary of state. Defending the mainstream Democratic approach, Clinton
held off the populist challenge and became the first woman ever nominated for president
by a major political party.

Already remarkable, the presidential contest between Clinton and Trump became a
clamorous, rancorous faceoff. Clinton struggled with accusations of mishandling her State
Department email by using a private email server, and earning large sums for speeches
to Wall Street bankers. Trump faced reports of discriminating against African American
tenants, defrauding contractors and customers, and sexually assaulting women. Unlike
all major party presidential candidates since the 1970s, Trump refused to divulge his tax
returns. The contest became even more charged with stunning revelations of Russian
attempts to influence the outcome of the election. Russian-related groups placed anti-
Clinton ads on social media and stole and publicized the emails of Clinton's campaign
manager and the Democratic National Committee.

Still, Clinton seemed likely to win until the FBI briefly reopened its investigation of
her email just before Election Day. Even then, Clinton won the popular vote, but Trump
won the electoral vote and the presidency. Eking out narrow victories in supposedly safe
Democratic territory, Trump carried whites, evangelical Christians, and rural and small-
town residents. While Clinton ran strongest among minority groups and the poor, Trump's
populist message attracted Republicans and just enough Obama voters. "I feel like the
American people are at the point where they've had it, and this was the last chance," a
steelworker from Indiana explained. With the Republican Party carrying the White House
and both houses of Congress, the chance seemed good.

"Make America Great Again"

A controversial nominee, Donald Trump made a controversial president from the start. His inaugural address, which painted a dark picture of "American carnage," offered a populist promise: "The forgotten men and women of our country will be forgotten no longer." The day after his inauguration, massive women's marches protested in the nation's capital and around the country. Using Twitter to speak his mind in short bursts, the president freely attacked the media, Obama, Democrats, and even fellow Republicans and accused them all of misdeeds. Americans differed over whether Trump's behavior was "presidential" or not as he tried to redeem his pledge to "Make America Great Again."

Despite controlling both Congress and the White House, Trump and Republicans had a hard time enacting their agenda during the president's first year in office. Trump, torn between the two Republican approaches, seemed most determined to undo Obama's legacy. Trump and his cabinet rescinded Obama executive orders on the environment, DACA, and the status of transgender people in the military. The president withdrew the United States from both the Paris Agreement and the TPP. But Trump and the Republicans failed to repeal Obama's signature and increasingly popular legislation, the Affordable Care Act, partly because the measure benefited many of Trump's own voters. The president and his congressional allies did manage to pass the Tax Cuts and Jobs Act of 2017, which drastically lowered taxes on corporations and offered important benefits to wealthy Americans while giving much less financial relief to the "forgotten." However, the president faced major challenges in carrying out the rest of his domestic agenda. While federal courts slowed Trump's attempts to ban Muslims from the United States, Congress refused to fund his border wall.

The president also faced challenges carrying out his agenda abroad. Like Obama, Trump found it impossible to withdraw from foreign conflicts. His administration increased troop levels and military activity in Afghanistan and Syria. As North Korea made rapid progress on nuclear missiles that could strike the United States, Trump raised the possibility of a preemptive American strike. His treatment of America's traditional friends and adversaries produced more controversy. Criticizing close US allies such as Australia, Germany, and South Korea, Trump held off on promised economic reprisals against China and remained surprisingly friendly to Russia.

Trump also became a lightning rod for controversy at home. After a neo-Nazi demonstration in Charlottesville, Virginia, left a counterprotester dead, the president seemed unwilling to condemn Nazism and white supremacy. The specter of Russian involvement in the 2016 election cast a pall over Trump's administration. After the election, US intelligence agencies revealed that Vladimir Putin, who detested Clinton, had tried to elect Trump. As Congress and the Federal Bureau of Investigation explored whether Trump's campaign had illegally colluded with Russians, the president fired FBI Director James Comey. That move triggered the appointment of a special counsel within the Department of Justice to investigate the whole matter, including the president's possible ties to Russia and obstruction of justice. In a matter of months, the special counsel had obtained guilty pleas from Trump's former national security adviser and a campaign member and had indicted two campaign officials.

Although the stock market soared, unemployment modestly decreased, and Trump still commanded fervent support from his populist base, his overall popularity plummeted

The Russian Attack on Democracy

It was a strange, almost paradoxical aspect of democracy: the simple, even boring act of standing in line and then checking a box or pulling a lever could have a dramatic impact on the future of the richest, most powerful country in the world. For all the attention given to who had the right to vote, Americans seldom devoted much thought to the mechanism of casting a ballot. After states and localities took firm control of the voting process from political parties around the turn of the twentieth century, fears of fraud decreased. With increased federal oversight of elections during and after the civil rights movement, those fears largely vanished.

Then, during the 2016 presidential election, strange, unsettling events occurred. In June, some voters turned up at the polls for California's primary only to find that they were mysteriously no longer registered. Hackers had gotten into the official computer system and altered their voting records. Similar break-ins happened in at least 20 more places around the country before the end of voting in November.

Meanwhile, US intelligence agencies revealed that the Russian government was behind the hacking and release of the emails of Hillary Clinton's campaign manager and the Democratic National Committee. The agencies also disclosed that Russia had used social media to spread false stories in another effort to affect the election. Despite these revelations, President Obama avoided public retaliation against Russia: he did not want to seem to be helping Clinton, who looked likely to win anyway. Instead, the president privately warned Russia's president, Vladimir Putin, not to interfere further.

After Donald Trump's surprising victory, Obama finally took public action. Late in 2016, the United States sanctioned Russian

Time Line

▼**2001**
George W. Bush declared president
9/11 attacks
Invasion of Afghanistan

▼**2002**
Creation of Department of Homeland Security

▼**2003**
US Supreme Court gay rights ruling, *Lawrence v. Texas*

"Operation Iraqi Freedom," coalition invasion of Iraq

▼**2004**
George W. Bush reelected

▼**2007**
US military "surge" in Iraq

▼**2008**
Collapse of Doha world trade talks

US financial crisis
Barack Obama elected president

▼**2009**
American Recovery and Reinvestment Act (stimulus package)
Tea Party founded

▼**2010**
Patient Protection and Affordable Health Care Act

individuals and groups, seized two Russian compounds in the United States, and ordered 35 Russian diplomatic personnel to leave the country. "Russia's cyber activities were intended to influence the election, erode faith in US democratic institutions, sow doubt about the integrity of our electoral process, and undermine confidence in the institutions of the US government," the White House explained. "These actions are unacceptable and will not be tolerated."

Even so, it was unclear how the United States could stop further Russian activity. It was unclear, too, how to protect the sprawling machinery of elections, much of it computer based, controlled by so many states and communities.

Moreover, Americans were divided about Russian hacking, as they were about so many things in the 2010s. Putin had not only wanted to make Americans lose faith that elections were genuine. The Russian president, who loathed Hillary Clinton for her strong opposition to his country's foreign policy, had also wanted to elect Donald Trump. For Trump and his supporters, stories of Russian hacking and manipulation of social media seemed like an attempt by Democratic sore losers to undermine his legitimacy. But other Americans believed the government should aggressively pursue the Russian campaign. Suspicious of Trump's refusal to criticize Putin or fully acknowledge the Russian hacking, some people believed that the Trump campaign had colluded with Russians to get him elected.

As the nation awaited reports by Congress and the special counsel, information about Russian activity continued to emerge. Facebook admitted that starting the month Trump announced his candidacy in 2015, the company had unknowingly let Russian "troll farms" run fake, divisive advertisements, sometimes pro-Trump, on the social media site. Another Russian source bought ads on Google's Gmail and YouTube platforms.

Americans were left wondering about a distinctively twenty-first century problem: whether a foreign government could use technology to influence voters, keep some from casting ballots, elect a president, and undermine confidence in democracy itself.

Health Care and Educational
    Reconciliation Act
*Citizens United v. Federal Election
    Commission*

▼2011
Death of Osama bin Laden
End of Iraq War

▼2012
Barack Obama reelected
    president

▼2013
US Supreme Court same-sex
    marriage ruling, *US v. Windsor*
Boston marathon bombing

▼2014
US air strikes against the Islamic
    State of Iraq and Syria

▼2015
Paris Agreement

▼2016
Trans-Pacific Partnership (TPP)
Pulse nightclub attack, Orlando,
    Florida
Donald Trump elected president

▼2017
US withdrawal from Paris
    Agreement and TPP
Tax Cuts and Jobs Act of 2017
Special counsel investigation of
    Russian election interference

in his first year in office. Much like Richard Nixon in the 1970s and Bill Clinton in the 1990s, Trump had to govern amid scandal as he attempted to "Make America Great Again."

Conclusion

In the first two decades of the twenty-first century, the United States continued its bumpy transformation into a globalized, information-based, diverse nation. Confronting terrorism, the nation seemed perpetually at war. Economic, social, and cultural change, along with the war on terror, all strained the democratic political system. More than 150 years after Abraham Lincoln spoke on the battlefield at Gettysburg, Americans still faced the challenge of creating a government and a nation "of the people."

Who, What, Where

Bipartisan Campaign Reform Act of 2002 (McCain-Feingold) 958

Bush, George W. ("Bush 43") 937

Charleston 951

Charlottesville 961

Citizens United v. Federal Election Commission (2010) 958

Crimea 948

Deferred Action for Childhood Arrivals (DACA) 952

Islamic State in Iraq and Syria (ISIS) 948

"Make America Great Again" 957

Neoconservatism 939

North Korea 939

Obama, Barack 941

Paris Agreement 947

Patient Protection and Affordable Health Care Act of 2010 (Obamacare) 945

Political action committee (PAC) 958

Populism 959

Pulse nightclub 949

Subprime mortgages 941

Syria 948

Tea Party 946

Trump, Donald J. 957

World Trade Center 938

Review Questions

1. Why did the United States go to war in Afghanistan and Iraq?
2. Why did the US economy fall into recession in 2008?
3. What factors led to Donald Trump's election as president in 2016?

Critical-Thinking Questions

1. Did the global war on terror change American life in a fundamental way?
2. Why did income and wealth inequality matter to the United States?
3. Did Americans become more or less tolerant of one another in the twenty-first century?

Suggested Readings

Sorkin, Andrew Ross. *Too Big to Fail: The Inside Story of How Wall Street and Washington Fought to Save the Financial System—and Themselves.* New York: Penguin Books, 2010.

Vance, J. D. *Hillbilly Elegy: A Memoir of a Family and Culture in Crisis.* New York: HarperCollins, 2016.

Wright, Lawrence. *The Looming Tower: Al-Qaeda and the Road to 9/11.* New York: Knopf, 2007.

For further review materials and resource information, please visit www.oup.com/us/oakes-mcgerr

CHAPTER 30: "A NATION TRANSFORMED": THE TWENTY-FIRST CENTURY
Primary Sources

30.1 GEORGE W. BUSH, EXCERPTS FROM "ADDRESS BEFORE A JOINT SESSION OF THE CONGRESS ON THE UNITED STATES RESPONSE TO THE TERRORIST ATTACKS OF SEPTEMBER 11" (2001)

Nine days after the 9/11 attacks, President George W. Bush addressed a joint session of Congress. In the emotional aftermath of Al Qaeda's strike, he compared the terrorists to earlier enemies such as the Nazis and vowed to destroy them. But the president also warned the nation to prepare for a long war, different from past conflicts. Calling the war a fight for freedom, Bush insisted that Americans respected the Muslim faith.

...On September 11th, enemies of freedom committed an act of war against our country. Americans have known wars, but for the past 136 years, they have been wars on foreign soil, except for one Sunday in 1941. Americans have known the casualties of war, but not at the center of a great city on a peaceful morning. Americans have known surprise attacks, but never before on thousands of civilians. All of this was brought upon us in a single day, and night fell on a different world, a world where freedom itself is under attack. . . .

Al Qaida is to terror what the Mafia is to crime. But its goal is not making money. Its goal is remaking the world and imposing its radical beliefs on people everywhere.

The terrorists practice a fringe form of Islamic extremism that has been rejected by Muslim scholars and the vast majority of Muslim clerics, a fringe movement that perverts the peaceful teachings of Islam. The terrorists' directive commands them to kill Christians and Jews, to kill all Americans, and make no distinctions among military and civilians, including women and children. . . .

The leadership of Al Qaida has great influence in Afghanistan and supports the Taliban regime in controlling most of that country. . . .

The United States respects the people of Afghanistan—after all, we are currently its largest source of humanitarian aid—but we condemn the Taliban regime. It is not only repressing its own people; it is threatening people everywhere by sponsoring and sheltering and supplying terrorists. By aiding and abetting murder, the Taliban regime is committing murder.

And tonight the United States of America makes the following demands on the Taliban: . . . Close immediately and permanently every terrorist training camp in Afghanistan, and hand over every terrorist and every person in their support structure to appropriate authorities. Give the United States full access to terrorist training camps, so we can make sure they are no longer operating.

These demands are not open to negotiation or discussion. The Taliban must act and act immediately. They will hand over the terrorists, or they will share in their fate.

I also want to speak tonight directly to Muslims throughout the world. We respect your faith. It's practiced freely by many millions of Americans and by millions more in countries that America counts as friends. Its teachings are good and peaceful, and those who commit evil in the name of Allah blaspheme the name of Allah. The terrorists are traitors to their own faith, trying, in effect, to hijack Islam itself. The enemy of America is not our many Muslim friends; it is not our many Arab friends. Our enemy is a radical network of terrorists and every government that supports them.

Our war on terror begins with Al Qaida, but it does not end there. It will not end until every terrorist group of global reach has been found, stopped, and defeated. . . .

They hate our freedoms—our freedom of religion, our freedom of speech, our freedom to vote and assemble and disagree with each other.

These terrorists kill not merely to end lives but to disrupt and end a way of life. With every atrocity, they hope that America grows fearful, retreating from the world and forsaking our friends. They stand against us, because we stand in their way.

We are not deceived by their pretenses to piety. We have seen their kind before. They are the heirs of all the murderous ideologies of the 20th century. By sacrificing human life to serve their radical visions, by abandoning every value except the will to power, they follow in the path of fascism and Nazism and totalitarianism. And they will follow that path all the way, to where it ends, in history's unmarked grave of discarded lies. . . .

Americans should not expect one battle but a lengthy campaign, unlike any other we have ever seen. It may include dramatic strikes, visible on TV, and covert operations, secret even in success. We will starve terrorists of funding, turn them one against another, drive them from place to place, until there is no refuge or no rest. And we will pursue nations that provide aid or safe haven to terrorism. Every nation, in every region, now has a decision to make: Either you are with us, or you are with the terrorists. From this day forward, any nation that continues to harbor or support terrorism will be regarded by the United States as a hostile regime.

Our Nation has been put on notice: We are not immune from attack. We will take defensive measures against terrorism to protect Americans. Today dozens of Federal departments and agencies, as well as State and local governments, have responsibilities affecting homeland security. These efforts must be coordinated at the highest level.

So tonight I announce the creation of a Cabinet-level position reporting directly to me, the Office of Homeland Security. . . .

This is not, however, just America's fight, and what is at stake is not just America's freedom. This is the world's fight. This is civilization's fight. This is the fight of all who believe in progress and pluralism, tolerance and freedom.

We ask every nation to join us. . . .

Americans are asking, what is expected of us? I ask you to live your lives and hug your children. I know many citizens have fears tonight, and I ask you to be calm and resolute, even in the face of a continuing threat.

I ask you to uphold the values of America and remember why so many have come here. We are in a fight for our principles, and our first responsibility is to live by them. No one should be singled out for unfair treatment or unkind words because of their ethnic background or religious faith. . . .

After all that has just passed, all the lives taken and all the possibilities and hopes that died with them, it is natural to wonder if America's future is one of fear. Some speak of an age of terror. I know there are struggles ahead and dangers to face. But this country will define our times, not be defined by them. As long as the United States of America is determined and strong, this will not be an age of terror; this will be an age of liberty, here and across the world. . . . . .

Source: George W. Bush, "Address Before a Joint Session of the Congress on the United States Response to the Terrorist Attacks of September 11," September 20, 2001.

30.2 BARACK OBAMA, KEYNOTE ADDRESS, DEMOCRATIC PARTY CONVENTION (2004)

In 2004, then-Senator Barack Obama of Illinois emerged as a national figure with this soaring address to the Democratic National Convention in Boston, Massachusetts. Note how the future president invokes the diversity of America while insisting on the nation's fundamental unity.

. . . . Tonight, we gather to affirm the greatness of our nation, not because of the height of our skyscrapers, or the power of our military, or the size of our economy. Our pride is based on a very simple premise, summed up in a declaration made over two hundred years ago, "We hold these truths to be self-evident, that all men are created equal. That they are endowed by their Creator with certain inalienable rights. That among these are life, liberty and the pursuit of happiness."

That is the true genius of America, a faith in the simple dreams of its people, the insistence on small miracles. That we can tuck in our children at night and know they are fed and clothed and safe from harm. That we can say what we think, write what we think, without hearing a sudden knock on the door. That we can have an idea and start our own business without paying a bribe or hiring somebody's son. That we can participate in the political process without fear of retribution, and that our votes will he counted—or at least, most of the time.

This year, in this election, we are called to reaffirm our values and commitments, to hold them against a hard reality and see how we are measuring up, to the legacy of our forbears, and the promise of future generations. And fellow Americans—Democrats, Republicans, Independents—I say to you tonight: we have more work to do. More to do for the workers I met in Galesburg, Illinois, who are losing their union jobs at the Maytag plant that's moving to Mexico, and now are having to compete with their own children for jobs that pay seven bucks an hour. More to do for the father I met who was losing his job and choking back tears, wondering how he would pay $4,500 a month for the drugs his son needs without the health benefits he counted on. More to do for the young woman in East St. Louis, and thousands more like her, who has the grades, has the drive, has the will, but doesn't have the money to go to college.

Don't get me wrong. The people I meet in small towns and big cities, in diners and office parks, they don't expect government to solve all their problems. They know they have to work hard to get ahead and they want to. . . . But they sense, deep in their bones, that with just a change in priorities, we can make sure that every child in America has a decent shot at life, and that the doors of opportunity remain open to all. They know we can do better. And they want that choice. For alongside our famous individualism, there's another ingredient in the American saga.

A belief that we are connected as one people. If there's a child on the south side of Chicago who can't read, that matters to me, even if it's not my child. If there's a senior citizen somewhere who can't pay for her prescription and has to choose between medicine and the rent, that makes my life poorer, even if it's not my grandmother. If there's an Arab American family being rounded up without benefit of an attorney or due process, that threatens my civil liberties. It's that fundamental belief—I am my brother's keeper, I am my sister's keeper—that makes this country work. It's what allows us to pursue our individual dreams, yet still come together as a single American family. "E pluribus unum." Out of many, one.

Yet even as we speak, there are those who are preparing to divide us, the spin masters and negative ad peddlers who embrace the politics of anything goes. Well, I say to them tonight, there's not a liberal America and a conservative America—there's the United States of America. There's not a black America and white America and Latino America and Asian America; there's the United States of America. The pundits like to slice-and-dice our country into Red States and Blue States; Red States for Republicans, Blue States for Democrats. But I've got news for them, too. We worship an awesome God in the Blue States, and we don't like federal agents poking around our libraries in the Red States. We coach Little League in the Blue States and have gay friends in the Red States. There are patriots who opposed the war in Iraq and patriots who supported it. We are one people, all of us pledging allegiance to the stars and stripes, all of us defending the United States of America.

In the end, that's what this election is about. Do we participate in a politics of cynicism or a politics of hope? . . . I'm not talking about blind optimism here—the almost willful ignorance that thinks unemployment will go away if we just don't talk about it, or the health care crisis will solve itself if we just ignore it. No, I'm talking about something more substantial. It's the hope of slaves sitting around a fire singing freedom songs; the hope of immigrants setting out for distant shores; . . . the hope of a skinny kid with a funny name who believes that America has a place for him, too. The audacity of hope!

In the end, that is God's greatest gift to us, the bedrock of this nation; the belief in things not seen; the belief that there are better days ahead. I believe we can give our middle class relief and provide working families with a road to opportunity. I believe we can provide jobs to the jobless, homes to the homeless, and reclaim young people in cities across America from violence and despair. I believe that as we stand on the crossroads of history, we can make the right choices, and meet the challenges that face us. America!

Source: Barack Obama, "Keynote Address at the 2004 Democratic National Convention," July 27, 2004.

30.3 DEBATE IN THE HOUSE OF REPRESENTATIVES ON A RESOLUTION "THAT SYMBOLS AND TRADITIONS OF CHRISTMAS SHOULD BE PROTECTED" (2005)

On December 14, 2005, conservative representative Jo Ann Davis (R-VA), an evangelical Protestant, spoke in favor of House Resolution 579, a statement protesting "attempts to ban references to Christmas" and supporting the "symbols and traditions, for those who celebrate Christmas." How does Davis defend public displays and mentions of Christmas, and whom does she blame for the attacks on the Christian holiday? In reply, two liberal representatives—Gary L. Ackerman (D-NY), a Jew, and Lynn C. Woolsey (D-CA), a mainline Protestant—questioned the purpose of the resolution. The next day, the House adopted the resolution by a vote of 401–22.

Mrs. JO ANN DAVIS of Virginia. This measure simply states congressional support for traditional references to Christmas that I believe are being eradicated from the public dialogue. . . .

Christmas has been declared politically incorrect. Any sign or even mention of Christmas in public can lead to complaints, litigation, protest, and threats. America's favorite holiday is being twisted beyond recognition. The push towards a neutered "holiday" season is stronger than ever so that no one can be even the slightest bit offended. . . .

When did wishing someone a Merry Christmas show insensitivity? According to a recent poll, 96 percent of Americans celebrate Christmas. In an effort to create a generic holiday starting at Thanksgiving and ending at New Year's, what are we exactly celebrating?

The purpose of celebrating the Fourth of July is to celebrate our Nation's independence. Why is it not reasonable to say that celebrating Christmas is a celebration of Christ's birth?

This is a selective assault on religious free speech which is a fundamental right. The Founders did not view celebrating Christmas as an issue of church versus State. It is celebrating a holiday that has for thousands of years been celebrated. The framers intended that the first amendment to the Constitution of the United States would prohibit the establishment of religion, not prohibit any mention of religion or reference to God in civic dialogue.

From Madison Avenue to Wall Street, from activists and lawyers to politicians, educators and the media, a culture is being created that shames people for saying Merry Christmas. . . .

The attack on Christmas, while not new, has now shifted its focus from overtly religious symbols, like the nativity, to symbols regarded by most Americans, including the Supreme Court, to be secular symbols of Christmas, a federally recognized holiday. Now these innocent secular symbols are causing concerns of insensitivity. Santa Claus, Christmas trees, candy canes, Christmas carols, even the colors red and green, they have been place on the endangered list.

They say to boil a frog you have to do it gradually because if you throw it into boiling water, it will jump out; but if you put the frog in cold water and gradually turn up the heat, the frog will never know he is being boiled until it is too late, and I am afraid that is what is happening to us with our Christmas holiday.

[T]he transition to replace Christmas with this vague "holiday season" is a gradual process that over the past few years has reached a new crescendo. Let us protect the symbols and traditions of Christmas for those who celebrate Christmas, or before we know it, we will be looking at a holiday season that represents nothing and celebrates anything.

I for one do not want to surrender and let retailers, overzealous civil liberty lawyers, and the media make me feel guilty for wishing someone a Merry Christmas. For generations, Christmas has been a public expression of the celebration of the birth of Christ. I hope we can say that for many more years to come.

Mr. ACKERMAN. . . . There are people around who need an enemy at all times to try to separate us one from the other as Americans in order to advance their own agenda. I do not think we should be playing into their hands. Nobody is attacking Christmas or its symbols. . . .

I like Christmas. I like the message of Christmas. I like helping the needy and the poor and the least among us. But I did not come here to protect the symbols.

Did something happen when I was not looking? Did somebody mug Santa Claus? Is somebody engaging in elf tossing? . . . What silliness we engage in, protecting symbols.

If you wanted to protect the message of Christmas, come to the floor with real bills with substance. Where is your bill to house the homeless? Where is your bill to feed the needy? Where is your bill to clothe the naked? Where is your bill to protect senior citizens who will not be able to heat their homes this winter? Where is the substance? Why are we engaging, in this terrible time in which we are in, in symbolism?

. . . I think we could be doing so much more instead of feeding the flames that divide us instead of bringing us together.

I wish the gentlewoman a merry Christmas. I have no compunction about doing that. But I do not want my government to engage in the foolishness of deciding for people what their symbols should or have to be. . . .

Ms. WOOLSEY. [N]obody enjoys Christmas more than I. But today we have roughly 160,000 men and women in Iraq putting their lives on the line for an immoral, senseless war. Here at home many of our vulnerable citizens will face a cold, bitter winter because they do not have home energy assistance from the Federal Government. Many others will not get the health care or education they need because of harsh cuts in Medicaid and student loans.

Naturally, the majority does not want to talk about this, and one can always tell when the right wing is in political trouble. They invariably cook up some divisive culture war that has nothing to do with our real challenges in this country.

What American families really want is the ability to afford more gifts for their children this season regardless of whether there is a wreath in the local department store.

Meanwhile, how many casualties have there been in the so-called "war on Christmas"? Here is a hint: several thousand less than in the war on Iraq.

Source: *Congressional Record* (109th Congress, 1st Session) 151, no. 160, p. H11596.

30.4 HARRY M. REID, "THE KOCH BROTHERS" (2015)

For Democrats and left-wing populists, the conservative billionaire brothers Charles and David Koch epitomize the threatening power of the "1 percent" in the age of wealth inequality and *Citizens United*. The Kochs, enriched by their ownership of a huge multinational corporation, spent heavily to create a right-wing network of political action committees (PACs), think tanks, and donors. In this speech from 2015, Harry M. Reid (D-NV), Majority Leader of the US Senate, describes the Kochs' power. What does Reid think the Kochs want, and who does he think can stop them?

[O]ver the last several months, the Koch brothers have been on a public relations campaign. This Koch propaganda campaign has accelerated over the past few weeks. Charles and David Koch have been going to great lengths to convince the American people that they are not just a couple of billionaires who are trying to dismantle Social Security. . . .

The Kochs want everyone to believe they are not the ones rigging the system to benefit themselves and their wealthy friends. The Koch brothers are spending their vast wealth holding newspaper and television interviews on their propaganda campaign. In spite of all their efforts, this Koch media tour has failed to bury the one simple truth: The Koch brothers are trying to buy America.

During an interview yesterday, the scales fell away once again and revealed the Koch brothers' true intentions. In justifying his and his brother's efforts to inject hundreds of millions of dollars into conservative political campaigns, Charles Koch said: "I expect something in return."

The Koch brothers are getting plenty in return. So far they have bought a Republican House, a Republican Senate, a government shutdown, an ousted Speaker of the House, . . . and a Republican Presidential field where nearly every candidate kowtows to these billionaires. But that is not all. The Kochs have procured a media that is intimidated by their billions—too intimidated to hold them accountable.

Consider yesterday's interview on MSNBC's "Morning Joe" show. This is classic. Here are some of the questions that Joe and Mika asked the Koch brothers.

Joe Scarborough asked: "It's hard to find people in New York, liberals, we were talking about this before, liberals or conservative alike, who haven't been touched by your graciousness, whether it is towards the arts or cancer research. Do you think you got that instinct from your mom?"

Mika asked: "Sitting here in your childhood home"—they were doing this interview in Topeka, KS—"we have the Koch brothers. Which was the good brother?" That was another tough question.

Joe then asked: "You guys both play rugby together, right?"

Sometimes—most of the time—they weren't even questions; they were just compliments.

At one point, here is what he said: "You sound like my dad. That's very diplomatic. That's very good."

Wow. Those were some really tough questions asked by the host of "Morning Joe." . . . Those questions are so easy; they may even qualify them to moderate the next Republican Presidential debate.

It seems that some journalists are determined not to get on the wrong side of the Koch brothers and their billions. After all, we have seen how the Koch empire targets people, cities, and States that do anything that conflicts with the Koch brothers' radical agenda. When the media rolls over for these modern-day robber barons, as it is doing now, our country is in trouble.

As Charles Koch himself said, he and his brother are not spending this money for altruistic reasons; they are doing it for one reason and one reason only—for the profits of themselves and fellow billionaires who have rigged the system against the middle class. They said it themselves. They want something in return, and what they want is profit for their corporations. Their own publicist once explained why the Koch brothers are trying to buy a new government: "It's because we can make more profit, OK?"

That is what this is all about for Charles and David Koch: bigger profits, more money because $100 billion or more isn't enough for them.

By their own admission, the Kochs will spend and spend and spend until they get the government they want—a government—a government that lets Koch Industries do what it wants, a government whose sole goal is to make these billionaires even richer.

Unfortunately for the United States, the Supreme Court has constructed a political system that allows them to do just that. The Citizens United case, decided in January 2010, has effectively put the U.S. Government up for sale to the highest bidder, and right now the Koch brothers are the highest bidder. Right now our country has no real restrictions on how much money a billionaire or a millionaire can spend to buy the government they want. All the power is with the wealthy, and that puts middle-class Americans at a significant disadvantage.

So we can't stand idly by while the government sits on an auction block and neither should any American sit idly by. Instead, we should be working to rid the system of the Koch brothers' dark money, but this cannot and will not happen if reporters and journalists refuse to ask Charles and David Koch questions-maybe even probing questions. Otherwise no one is holding these two oil barons accountable for their nefarious actions.

Source: Congressional Record (114th Congress, 1st Session) 161, no. 164, p. S7734.

30.5 STEVE A. KING, "ILLEGAL IMMIGRATION," HOUSE OF REPRESENTATIVES (2007)

Congressman Steve A. King (R-IA), a conservative right-wing populist, and Senator Harry M. Reid (D-NV) were political opponents. But the two elected officials shared concerns about the power of the rich and the weakening of the middle class. In this 2007 speech in the House of Representatives, King offers a striking argument about the impact of illegal immigration on inequality in the United States. How, according to King, does illegal immigration help the political "left" as well as the rich?

Well, first of all, the Federal Government has failed to enforce adequately our immigration laws. And as we got more and more illegal immigrants into the United States, it became a magnet for more and more to follow. . . .

Secondly, employers took advantage of that because they could hire illegal labor cheaper than they could local labor. And capital is always rational. Capital is going to do the smart thing. Capital is going to follow the path of least resistance like electricity. . . .

So you hire them cheaper, maybe at $8 an hour, compared to a $15 an hour legal person. . . . Then that magnetized and brought more and more into this country. . . .

Well, one thing that has happened . . . we have seen the unskilled purchasing power drop by 12 percent over the last 10 years, that is because there is a flood of cheap labor on the market. And it should go the other way. We want a broad middle-class. We want an ever more prosperous middle-class. Instead, the pressure that is coming here is those that are making money off of the cheap labor are becoming an aristocracy. They are part of nouveau rich in the United States of America. And our upper-middle class, or upper class, for that matter, is growing, and so is our lower class growing, because we are importing it, and that is putting a squeeze on middle America.

One of the principles of a free society is you need to have a broad and prosperous middle-class. We have been growing and broadening that middle-class for generations and becoming a stronger Nation because of it. But this last generation it is going the other way. . . . This last generation, we are growing the aristocracy and we are growing the lower class, importing a lower class, all at the expense of the middle class, which is being squeezed in between the two. . . .

In the middle is the real America that understands truth, justice, the American way, the merits of hard work, the American dream. They have a tremendous work ethic, a sense of family and community. They are being squeezed . . . by the interests on the upper levels of our society and by the thunderous herds that are coming across particularly our southern border, on the lower end of our society, at the expense of our middle-class.

I would point out that if you envision this society like a barbell, and the middle-class would be the bar, and the weights on each end would be the bells, on one side you have the weight on the right side of that barbell, that is the business elitists that sit in that category too. And they are clamoring for more cheap labor because they make money doing it, and they are not threatened, nor do they believe their children will ever be threatened by the competition in the labor market that takes place down in the lower end of the spectrum.

The people on the right side of that, the business side of that barbell, that interest, they will send their children to Ivy League schools, upper crust universities, they will get an education. They won't ever have to compete, probably, with the lower income people that don't have that kind of education, that kind of culture, that gives them a path to professionalism.

So they will end up living in their ivory towers and end up living in their gated communities and getting rich off the cheaper labor, and their children will be wired into that same kind of thing. And that is how you grow an aristocracy. That is how you grow a ruling class. That is how you grow an arrogance, that they have a birthright to a servant class, which they are creating.

That servant class that they are creating is the other end of this barbell, and that is this massive number of people who give especially the left a lot of political power. Even those who are in this country illegally give political power to many Members here in this Congress because we count people rather than citizens when we redistrict in America.

As we count people, that means we count illegal immigrant in these districts. So illegal immigrants give political power to the Members of Congress who are here because they don't have to get their vote. They only have to compete. . . .

I am not here to say that they are all bad people. No, the vast majority of them are very good people looking for a better life for their families. But they have a higher percentage of violence among them, even as good people, than the average American that is here, and we are paying a price of about 12 Americans a day who lose their life as victims of murder to criminal aliens, about 13 a day who die at the hands of negligent homicide, mostly the victims of drunk drivers, not the drunks themselves.

Source: *Congressional Record* (110th Congress, 1st Session) 153, no. 42, pp. H2432–44.

30.6 DONALD TRUMP, EXTRACT OF REMARKS AT A "MAKE AMERICA GREAT AGAIN" RALLY IN HARRISBURG, PENNSYLVANIA (2017)

After his election as president, Donald Trump continued holding campaign-style rallies for his supporters around the country. Feeding off the energy of the crowd, Trump articulated his right-wing populist message in the Rustbelt community of Harrisburg, Pennsylvania. Whom does he blame for the condition of the country?

As you may know, there's another big gathering taking place tonight in Washington, D.C. Did you hear about it?

AUDIENCE: Booo—

THE PRESIDENT: A large group of Hollywood actors and Washington media are consoling each other in a hotel ballroom in our nation's capital right now. (Applause.) They are gathered together for the White House Correspondents Dinner—without the President. (Applause.) And I could not possibly be more thrilled than to be more than 100 miles away from Washington Swamp—(applause)—spending my evening with all of you, and with a much, much larger crowd and much better people. Right? (Applause.) Right?

AUDIENCE: U-S-A! U-S-A!

THE PRESIDENT: And look at the media back there. . . .

AUDIENCE: Booo—

THE PRESIDENT: That's right.

AUDIENCE: CNN Sucks! CNN Sucks!

THE PRESIDENT: Media outlets like CNN and MSNBC are fake news. Fake news . . .

The truth is, there is no place I'd rather be than right here in Pennsylvania to celebrate our 100-day milestone to reflect on an incredible journey together, and to get ready for the great, great battles to come, and that we will win in every case, okay? We will win. (Applause.) Because make no mistake, we are just beginning in our fight to make America great again. (Applause.)

Now, before we talk about my first 100 days, which has been very exciting and very productive, let's rate the media's 100 days. Should we do that? Should we do it? Because, as you know, they are a disgrace. . . .

So just as an example of media, take the totally failing New York Times.

AUDIENCE: Booo—

THE PRESIDENT: But that's what we have. They're incompetent, dishonest people. . . .

So here's the story. If the media's job is to be honest and tell the truth, then I think we would all agree the media deserves a very, very, big fat failing grade.

AUDIENCE: Booo—

THE PRESIDENT: Very dishonest people. And not all of them. You know, we call it the "fake news." Not all of them. . . . By contrast, for the last 100 days, my administration has been delivering every single day for the great citizens of our country—whether it's putting our coal miners back to work, protecting America's steel and aluminum workers—we love that steel and aluminum—or eliminating job-killing regulations, we are keeping one promise after another. And, frankly, the people are really happy about it. They see what's happening. (Applause.)

But to understand the historic progress that we've made, we must speak honestly about the situation that we and I inherited. Because believe me, the previous administration gave us a mess.

AUDIENCE: Booo—

THE PRESIDENT: For decades, our country has lived through the greatest jobs theft in the history of the world. You people know it better than anybody, in Pennsylvania. Our factories were shuttered, our steel mills closed down, and our jobs were stolen away and shipped far away to other countries, some of which you've never even heard of. Politicians sent troops to protect the borders of foreign nations, but left America's borders wide open for all to violate.

We've spent billions and billions of dollars on one global project after another, and yet, as gangs flooded into our country, we couldn't even provide safety for our own people.

Our government rushed to join international agreements where the United States pays the costs and bears the burdens, while other countries get the benefit and pay nothing.

AUDIENCE: Booo—

THE PRESIDENT: This includes deals like the one-sided Paris Climate Accord, where the United States pays billions of dollars while China, Russia and India have contributed and will contribute nothing.

AUDIENCE: Booo—

THE PRESIDENT: Does that remind you of the Iran deal? How about that beauty, right? . . .

Those are the facts, whether we like them or not. The dishonest media won't print them, won't report them, because the Washington media is part of the problem: their priorities are not my priorities and they're not your priorities, believe me. (Applause.) Their agenda is not your agenda. . . .

But they're all part of a broken system that has profited from this global theft and plunder of American wealth at the expense of the American worker. We are not going to let other countries take advantage of us anymore. Because, from now on, it's going to be America first. (Applause.) . . .

AUDIENCE: U-S-A! U-S-A! . . .

To protect our jobs and our economic freedom, I immediately withdrew the United States from the horrible, disastrous . . . Trans-Pacific Partnership. (Applause.) . . . That was a total hoax. (Applause.) . . .

Perhaps in no area have past governments sold out to special interests and foreign lobbyists more than on the issue of immigration. Year after year, you pleaded for Washington to enforce our laws as illegal immigration surged, refugees flooded in, and lax vetting threatened your family's safety and security.

Your pleas have finally been—

AUDIENCE MEMBER: Build the wall!

THE PRESIDENT: Oh, don't worry, we're going to have the wall. Don't worry about it. (Applause.)

AUDIENCE: Build the wall! Build the wall! . . .

THE PRESIDENT: We are operating on a very simple principle: that our immigration system should put the needs of American workers, American families, American companies, and American citizens first. (Applause.) . . .

And we are also working around the clock to keep our nation safe from terrorism. (Applause.) My administration has taken historic steps to improve screening and vetting for those seeking visas to enter the United States. We have seen the attacks, from 9/11 to Boston to San Bernardino. We have seen the bloodshed overseas. . . .

We already have enough problems to worry about in the United States, which we love so much. We don't need to be admitting people who want to oppress, hurt or kill innocent Americans. They're not coming in. (Applause.)

So let me state this as clearly as I possibly can: We are going to keep radical Islamic terrorists the hell out of our country. (Applause.)

AUDIENCE: U-S-A! U-S-A!

THE PRESIDENT: So I have a question for you. You've been to a lot of countries, you've seen a lot of rallies. First of all, is there any place like a Trump rally? In all fairness. Right? (Applause.). . .

Source: Donald J. Trump, Remarks at a "Make America Great Again Rally," Harrisburg, Pennsylvania, April 29, 2017.

Historical Documents

The Declaration of Independence

When in the course of human events, it becomes necessary for one people to dissolve the political bands which have connected them with another, and to assume, among the powers of the earth, the separate and equal station to which the Laws of Nature and of Nature's God entitle them, a decent respect to the opinions of mankind requires that they should declare the causes which impel them to the separation.

We hold these truths to be self-evident, that all men are created equal, that they are endowed by their Creator with certain unalienable Rights, that among these are life, liberty and the pursuit of happiness. That to secure these rights, governments are instituted among men, deriving their just powers from the consent of the governed; that whenever any form of government becomes destructive of these ends, it is the right of the people to alter or to abolish it, and to institute new Government, laying its foundation on such principles and organizing its powers in such form, as to them shall seem most likely to effect their safety and happiness. Prudence, indeed, will dictate that Governments long established should not be changed for light and transient causes; and, accordingly, all experience hath shown, that mankind are more disposed to suffer, while evils are sufferable, than to right themselves by abolishing the forms to which they are accustomed. But when a long train of abuses and usurpations, pursuing invariably the same object evinces a design to reduce them under absolute despotism, it is their right, it is their duty, to throw off such government, and to provide new guards for their future security. Such has been the patient sufferance of these colonies; and such is now the necessity which constrains them to alter their former systems of government. The history of the present King of Great Britain is a history of repeated injuries and usurpations, all having in direct object the establishment of an absolute tyranny over these States. To prove this, let facts be submitted to a candid world:

He has refused his assent to laws, the most wholesome and necessary for the public good.

He has forbidden his governors to pass laws of immediate and pressing importance, unless suspended in their operation till his assent should be obtained; and, when so suspended, he has utterly neglected to attend to them.

He has refused to pass other laws for the accommodation of large districts of people, unless those people would relinquish the right of representation in the legislature, a right inestimable to them and formidable to tyrants only.

He has called together legislative bodies at places unusual, uncomfortable, and distant from the depository of their public records, for the sole purpose of fatiguing them into compliance with his measures.

He has dissolved representative houses repeatedly, for opposing with manly firmness his invasions on the rights of the people.

He has refused for a long time, after such dissolutions, to cause others to be elected; whereby the legislative powers, incapable of annihilation, have returned to the People at large for their exercise; the State remaining in the mean time exposed to all the dangers of invasion from without, and convulsions within.

He has endeavored to prevent the population of these States; for that purpose obstructing the laws for naturalization of foreigners; refusing to pass others to encourage their migrations hither, and raising the conditions of new appropriations of lands.

He has obstructed the administration of justice, by refusing his assent to laws for establishing judiciary powers.

He has made judges dependent on his will alone, for the tenure of their offices, and the amount and payment of their salaries.

He has erected a multitude of new offices, and sent hither swarms of officers to harass our people, and eat out their substance.

He has kept among us, in times of peace, standing armies without the consent of our legislatures.

He has affected to render the Military independent of, and superior to, the civil power.

He has combined with others to subject us to a jurisdiction foreign to our constitution and unacknowledged by our laws; giving his assent to their acts of pretended legislation:

For quartering large bodies of armed troops among us;

For protecting them, by a mock trial, from punishment for any murders which they should commit on the inhabitants of these States;

For cutting off our trade with all parts of the world;

For imposing taxes on us without our Consent;

For depriving us, in many cases, of the benefits of Trial by Jury;

For transporting us beyond Seas to be tried for pretended offences;

For abolishing the free System of English Laws in a neighbouring Province, establishing therein an Arbitrary government, and enlarging its Boundaries so as to render it at once an example and fit instrument for introducing the same absolute rule into these colonies;

For taking away our charters, abolishing our most valuable laws, and altering fundamentally the forms of our governments;

For suspending our own legislatures, and declaring themselves invested with power to legislate for us in all cases whatsoever.

He has abdicated government here, by declaring us out of his protection and waging war against us.

He has plundered our seas, ravaged our coasts, burnt our towns, and destroyed the lives of our people.

He is at this time transporting large armies of foreign mercenaries to complete the works of death, desolation and tyranny, already begun with circumstances of cruelty and perfidy scarcely paralleled in the most barbarous ages, and totally unworthy the head of a civilized nation.

He has constrained our fellow citizens taken captive on the high seas to bear arms against their country, to become the executioners of their friends and brethren, or to fall themselves by their hands.

He has excited domestic insurrections amongst us, and has endeavored to bring on the inhabitants of our frontiers, the merciless Indian savages, whose known rule of warfare, is an undistinguished destruction of all ages, sexes and conditions.

In every stage of these oppressions we have petitioned for redress in the most humble terms; our repeated petitions have been answered only by repeated injury. A prince whose character is thus marked by every act which may define a tyrant, is unfit to be the ruler of a free people.

Nor have we been wanting in attentions to our British brethren. We have warned them from time to time of attempts by their legislature to extend an unwarrantable jurisdiction over us. We have reminded them of the circumstances of our emigration and settlement here. We have appealed to their native justice and magnanimity, and we have conjured them by the ties of our common kindred to disavow these usurpations, which, would inevitably interrupt our connections and correspondence. They, too, have been deaf to the voice of justice and of consanguinity. We must, therefore, acquiesce in the necessity, which denounces our separation, and hold them, as we hold the rest of mankind, enemies in war, in peace friends.

We, therefore, the representatives of the United States of America, in general Congress, assembled, appealing to the Supreme Judge of the world for the rectitude of our intentions, do, in the name, and by the authority of the good people of these colonies, solemnly publish and declare, that these united colonies are, and of right ought to be free and independent states; that they are absolved from all allegiance to the British Crown, and that all political connection between them and the state of Great Britain, is and ought to be totally dissolved; and that, as free and independent states, they have full power to levy war, conclude peace, contract alliances, establish commerce, and to do all other acts and things which independent states may of right do. And for the support of this declaration, with a firm reliance on the protection of Divine Providence, we mutually pledge to each other our lives, our fortunes and our sacred honor.

The Constitution of the United States of America

We the People of the United States, in Order to form a more perfect Union, establish Justice, insure domestic Tranquility, provide for the common defence, promote the general Welfare, and secure the Blessings of Liberty to ourselves and our Posterity, do ordain and establish this Constitution for the United States of America.

Article I
Section 1

All legislative Powers herein granted shall be vested in a Congress of the United States, which shall consist of a Senate and House of Representatives.

Section 2

The House of Representatives shall be composed of Members chosen every second Year by the People of the several States, and the Electors in each State shall have the Qualifications requisite for Electors of the most numerous Branch of the State Legislature.

No Person shall be a Representative who shall not have attained to the Age of twenty five Years, and been seven Years a Citizen of the United States, and who shall not, when elected, be an Inhabitant of that State in which he shall be chosen.

Representatives and direct Taxes shall be apportioned among the several States which may be included within this Union, according to their respective Numbers, which shall be determined by adding to the whole Number of free Persons, including those bound to Service for a Term of Years, and excluding Indians not taxed, three fifths of all other Persons. The actual Enumeration shall be made within three Years after the first Meeting of the Congress of the United States, and within every subsequent Term of ten Years, in such Manner as they shall by Law direct. The Number of Representatives shall not exceed one for every thirty Thousand, but each State shall have at Least one Representative; and until such enumeration shall be made, the State of New Hampshire shall be entitled to choose three, Massachusetts eight, Rhode-Island and Providence Plantations one, Connecticut five, New York six, New Jersey four, Pennsylvania eight, Delaware one, Maryland six, Virginia ten, North Carolina five, South Carolina five, and Georgia three.

When vacancies happen in the Representation from any State, the Executive Authority thereof shall issue Writs of Election to fill such Vacancies.

The House of Representatives shall choose their Speaker and other Officers; and shall have the sole Power of Impeachment.

Section 3

The Senate of the United States shall be composed of two Senators from each State, chosen by the Legislature thereof for six Years; and each Senator shall have one Vote.

Immediately after they shall be assembled in Consequence of the first Election, they shall be divided as equally as may be into three Classes. The Seats of the Senators of the first Class shall be vacated at the Expiration of the second Year, of the second Class at the Expiration of the fourth Year, and of the third Class at the Expiration of the sixth Year, so that one third may be chosen every second Year; and if Vacancies happen by Resignation, or otherwise, during the Recess of the Legislature of any State, the Executive thereof may make temporary Appointments until the next Meeting of the Legislature, which shall then fill such Vacancies.

No Person shall be a Senator who shall not have attained to the Age of thirty Years, and been nine Years a Citizen of the United States, and who shall not, when elected, be an Inhabitant of that State for which he shall be chosen.

The Vice President of the United States shall be President of the Senate, but shall have no Vote, unless they be equally divided.

The Senate shall choose their other Officers, and also a President pro tempore, in the Absence of the Vice President, or when he shall exercise the Office of President of the United States.

The Senate shall have the sole Power to try all Impeachments. When sitting for that Purpose, they shall be on Oath or Affirmation. When the President of the United States is tried, the Chief Justice shall preside: And no Person shall be convicted without the Concurrence of two thirds of the Members present.

Judgment in Cases of Impeachment shall not extend further than to removal from Office, and disqualification to hold and enjoy any Office of honor, Trust or Profit under the United States: but the Party convicted shall nevertheless be liable and subject to Indictment, Trial, Judgment and Punishment, according to Law.

Section 4

The Times, Places and Manner of holding Elections for Senators and Representatives, shall be prescribed in each State by the Legislature thereof; but the Congress may at any time by Law make or alter such Regulations, except as to the Places of chusing Senators.

The Congress shall assemble at least once in every Year, and such Meeting shall be on the first Monday in December, unless they shall by Law appoint a different Day.

Section 5

Each House shall be the Judge of the Elections, Returns and Qualifications of its own Members, and a Majority of each shall constitute a Quorum to do Business; but a smaller Number may adjourn from day to day, and may be authorized to compel the Attendance of absent Members, in such Manner, and under such Penalties as each House may provide.

Each House may determine the Rules of its Proceedings, punish its Members for disorderly Behaviour, and, with the Concurrence of two thirds, expel a Member.

Each House shall keep a Journal of its Proceedings, and from time to time publish the same, excepting such Parts as may in their Judgment require Secrecy; and the Yeas and Nays of the Members of either House on any question shall, at the Desire of one fifth of those Present, be entered on the Journal.

Neither House, during the Session of Congress, shall, without the Consent of the other, adjourn for more than three days, nor to any other Place than that in which the two Houses shall be sitting.

Section 6

The Senators and Representatives shall receive a Compensation for their Services, to be ascertained by Law, and paid out of the Treasury of the United States. They shall in all Cases, except Treason, Felony and Breach of the Peace, be privileged from Arrest during their Attendance at the Session of their respective Houses, and in going to and returning from the same; and for any Speech or Debate in either House, they shall not be questioned in any other Place.

No Senator or Representative shall, during the Time for which he was elected, be appointed to any civil Office under the Authority of the United States, which shall have been created, or the Emoluments whereof shall have been increased during such time; and no Person holding any Office under the United States, shall be a Member of either House during his Continuance in Office.

Section 7

All Bills for raising Revenue shall originate in the House of Representatives; but the Senate may propose or concur with Amendments as on other Bills.

Every Bill which shall have passed the House of Representatives and the Senate, shall, before it become a Law, be presented to the President of the United States: If he approve he shall sign it, but if not he shall return it, with his Objections to that House in which it shall have originated, who shall enter the Objections at large on their Journal, and proceed to reconsider it. If after such Reconsideration two thirds of that House shall agree to pass the Bill, it shall be sent, together with the Objections, to the other House, by which it shall likewise be reconsidered, and if approved by two thirds of that House, it shall become a Law. But in all such Cases the Votes of both Houses shall be determined by yeas and Nays, and the Names of the Persons voting for and against the Bill shall be entered on the Journal of each House respectively. If any Bill shall not be returned by the President within ten Days (Sundays excepted) after it shall have been presented to him, the Same shall be a Law, in like Manner as if he had signed it, unless the Congress by their Adjournment prevent its Return, in which Case it shall not be a Law.

Every Order, Resolution, or Vote to which the Concurrence of the Senate and House of Representatives may be necessary (except on a question of Adjournment) shall be presented to the President of the United States; and before the Same shall take Effect, shall be approved by him, or being disapproved by him, shall be repassed by two thirds of the Senate and House of Representatives, according to the Rules and Limitations prescribed in the Case of a Bill.

Section 8

The Congress shall have Power

To lay and collect Taxes, Duties, Imposts and Excises, to pay the Debts and provide for the common Defence and general Welfare of the United States; but all Duties, Imposts and Excises shall be uniform throughout the United States;

To borrow Money on the credit of the United States;

To regulate Commerce with foreign Nations, and among the several States, and with the Indian Tribes;

To establish an uniform Rule of Naturalization, and uniform Laws on the subject of Bankruptcies throughout the United States;

To coin Money, regulate the Value thereof, and of foreign Coin, and fix the Standard of Weights and Measures;

To provide for the Punishment of counterfeiting the Securities and current Coin of the United States;

To establish Post Offices and post Roads;

To promote the Progress of Science and useful Arts, by securing for limited Times to Authors and Inventors the exclusive Right to their respective Writings and Discoveries;

To constitute Tribunals inferior to the supreme Court;

To define and punish Piracies and Felonies committed on the high Seas, and Offences against the Law of Nations;

To declare War, grant Letters of Marque and Reprisal, and make Rules concerning Captures on Land and Water;

To raise and support Armies, but no Appropriation of Money to that Use shall be for a longer Term than two Years;

To provide and maintain a Navy;

To make Rules for the Government and Regulation of the land and naval Forces;

To provide for calling forth the Militia to execute the Laws of the Union, suppress Insurrections and repel Invasions;

To provide for organizing, arming, and disciplining the Militia, and for governing such Part of them as may be employed in the Service of the United States, reserving to the States respectively, the Appointment of the Officers, and the Authority of training the Militia according to the discipline prescribed by Congress;

To exercise exclusive Legislation in all Cases whatsoever, over such District (not exceeding ten Miles square) as may, by Cession of particular States, and the Acceptance of

Congress, become the Seat of the Government of the United States, and to exercise like Authority over all Places purchased by the Consent of the Legislature of the State in which the Same shall be, for the Erection of Forts, Magazines, Arsenals, dock-Yards, and other needful Buildings;—And

To make all Laws which shall be necessary and proper for carrying into Execution the foregoing Powers, and all other Powers vested by this Constitution in the Government of the United States, or in any Department or Officer thereof.

Section 9

The Migration or Importation of such Persons as any of the States now existing shall think proper to admit, shall not be prohibited by the Congress prior to the Year one thousand eight hundred and eight, but a Tax or duty may be imposed on such Importation, not exceeding ten dollars for each Person.

The Privilege of the Writ of Habeas Corpus shall not be suspended, unless when in Cases of Rebellion or Invasion the public Safety may require it.

No Bill of Attainder or ex post facto Law shall be passed.

No Capitation, or other direct, Tax shall be laid, unless in Proportion to the Census or enumeration herein before directed to be taken.

No Tax or Duty shall be laid on Articles exported from any State.

No Preference shall be given by any Regulation of Commerce or Revenue to the Ports of one State over those of another; nor shall Vessels bound to, or from, one State, be obliged to enter, clear, or pay Duties in another.

No Money shall be drawn from the Treasury, but in Consequence of Appropriations made by Law; and a regular Statement and Account of the Receipts and Expenditures of all public Money shall be published from time to time.

No Title of Nobility shall be granted by the United States: And no Person holding any Office of Profit or Trust under them, shall, without the Consent of the Congress, accept of any present, Emolument, Office, or Title, of any kind whatever, from any King, Prince, or foreign State.

Section 10

No State shall enter into any Treaty, Alliance, or Confederation; grant Letters of Marque and Reprisal; coin Money; emit Bills of Credit; make any Thing but gold and silver Coin a Tender in Payment of Debts; pass any Bill of Attainder, ex post facto Law, or Law impairing the Obligation of Contracts, or grant any Title of Nobility.

No State shall, without the Consent of the Congress, lay any Imposts or Duties on Imports or Exports, except what may be absolutely necessary for executing it's inspection Laws: and the net Produce of all Duties and Imposts, laid by any State on Imports or Exports, shall be for the Use of the Treasury of the United States; and all such Laws shall be subject to the Revision and Control of the Congress.

No State shall, without the Consent of Congress, lay any Duty of Tonnage, keep Troops, or Ships of War in time of Peace, enter into any Agreement or Compact with another State, or with a foreign Power, or engage in War, unless actually invaded, or in such imminent Danger as will not admit of delay.

Article II
Section 1

The executive Power shall be vested in a President of the United States of America. He shall hold his Office during the Term of four Years, and, together with the Vice President, chosen for the same Term, be elected, as follows:

Each State shall appoint, in such Manner as the Legislature thereof may direct, a Number of Electors, equal to the whole Number of Senators and Representatives to which the State may be entitled in the Congress: but no Senator or Representative, or Person holding an Office of Trust or Profit under the United States, shall be appointed an Elector.

The Electors shall meet in their respective States, and vote by Ballot for two Persons, of whom one at least shall not be an Inhabitant of the same State with themselves. And they shall make a List of all the Persons voted for, and of the Number of Votes for each; which List they shall sign and certify, and transmit sealed to the Seat of the Government of the United States, directed to the President of the Senate. The President of the Senate shall, in the Presence of the Senate and House of Representatives, open all the Certificates, and the Votes shall then be counted. The Person having the greatest Number of Votes shall be the President, if such Number be a Majority of the whole Number of Electors appointed; and if there be more than one who have such Majority, and have an equal Number of Votes, then the House of Representatives shall immediately choose by Ballot one of them for President; and if no Person have a Majority, then from the five highest on the List the said House shall in like Manner choose the President. But in choosing the President, the Votes shall be taken by States, the Representation from each State having one Vote; A quorum for this purpose shall consist of a Member or Members from two thirds of the States, and a Majority of all the States shall be necessary to a Choice. In every Case, after the Choice of the President, the Person having the greatest Number of Votes of the Electors shall be the Vice President. But if there should remain two or more who have equal Votes, the Senate shall choose from them by Ballot the Vice President.

The Congress may determine the Time of choosing the Electors, and the Day on which they shall give their Votes; which Day shall be the same throughout the United States.

No Person except a natural born Citizen, or a Citizen of the United States, at the time of the Adoption of this Constitution, shall be eligible to the Office of President; neither shall any Person be eligible to that Office who shall not have attained to the Age of thirty five Years, and been fourteen Years a Resident within the United States.

In Case of the Removal of the President from Office, or of his Death, Resignation, or Inability to discharge the Powers and Duties of the said Office, the Same shall devolve on the Vice President, and the Congress may by Law provide for the Case of Removal, Death, Resignation or Inability, both of the President and Vice President, declaring what Officer shall then act as President, and such Officer shall act accordingly, until the Disability be removed, or a President shall be elected.

The President shall, at stated Times, receive for his Services, a Compensation, which shall neither be increased nor diminished during the Period for which he shall have been elected, and he shall not receive within that Period any other Emolument from the United States, or any of them.

Before he enter on the Execution of his Office, he shall take the following Oath or Affirmation:—"I do solemnly swear (or affirm) that I will faithfully execute the Office of President of the United States, and will to the best of my Ability, preserve, protect and defend the Constitution of the United States."

Section 2

The President shall be Commander in Chief of the Army and Navy of the United States, and of the Militia of the several States, when called into the actual Service of the United States; he may require the Opinion, in writing, of the principal Officer in each of the executive Departments, upon any Subject relating to the Duties of their respective Offices, and he shall have Power to grant Reprieves and Pardons for Offences against the United States, except in Cases of Impeachment.

He shall have Power, by and with the Advice and Consent of the Senate, to make Treaties, provided two thirds of the Senators present concur; and he shall nominate, and by and with the Advice and Consent of the Senate, shall appoint Ambassadors, other public Ministers and Consuls, Judges of the supreme Court, and all other Officers of the United States, whose Appointments are not herein otherwise provided for, and which shall be established by Law: but the Congress may by Law vest the Appointment of such inferior Officers, as they think proper, in the President alone, in the Courts of Law, or in the Heads of Departments.

The President shall have Power to fill up all Vacancies that may happen during the Recess of the Senate, by granting Commissions which shall expire at the End of their next Session.

Section 3

He shall from time to time give to the Congress Information of the State of the Union, and recommend to their Consideration such Measures as he shall judge necessary and expedient; he may, on extraordinary Occasions, convene both Houses, or either of them, and in Case of Disagreement between them, with Respect to the Time of Adjournment, he may adjourn them to such Time as he shall think proper; he shall receive Ambassadors and other public Ministers; he shall take Care that the Laws be faithfully executed, and shall Commission all the Officers of the United States.

Section 4

The President, Vice President and all civil Officers of the United States, shall be removed from Office on Impeachment for, and Conviction of, Treason, Bribery, or other high Crimes and Misdemeanors.

Article III
Section 1

The judicial Power of the United States shall be vested in one supreme Court, and in such inferior Courts as the Congress may from time to time ordain and establish. The Judges, both of the supreme and inferior Courts, shall hold their Offices during good Behaviour, and shall, at stated Times, receive for their Services a Compensation, which shall not be diminished during their Continuance in Office.

Section 2

The judicial Power shall extend to all Cases, in Law and Equity, arising under this Constitution, the Laws of the United States, and Treaties made, or which shall be made, under their Authority;—to all Cases affecting Ambassadors, other public Ministers and Consuls;—to all Cases of admiralty and maritime Jurisdiction;—to Controversies to which the United States shall be a Party;—to Controversies between two or more States;—between a State and Citizens of another State;—between Citizens of different States;—between Citizens of the same State claiming Lands under Grants of different States, and between a State, or the Citizens thereof, and foreign States, Citizens or Subjects.

In all Cases affecting Ambassadors, other public Ministers and Consuls, and those in which a State shall be Party, the supreme Court shall have original Jurisdiction. In all the other Cases before mentioned, the supreme Court shall have appellate Jurisdiction, both as to Law and Fact, with such Exceptions, and under such Regulations as the Congress shall make.

The Trial of all Crimes, except in Cases of Impeachment, shall be by Jury; and such Trial shall be held in the State where the said Crimes shall have been committed; but when not committed within any State, the Trial shall be at such Place or Places as the Congress may by Law have directed.

Section 3

Treason against the United States, shall consist only in levying War against them, or in adhering to their Enemies, giving them Aid and Comfort. No Person shall be convicted of Treason unless on the Testimony of two Witnesses to the same overt Act, or on Confession in open Court.

The Congress shall have Power to declare the Punishment of Treason, but no Attainder of Treason shall work Corruption of Blood, or Forfeiture except during the Life of the Person attainted.

Article IV
Section 1

Full Faith and Credit shall be given in each State to the public Acts, Records, and judicial Proceedings of every other State. And the Congress may by general Laws prescribe the Manner in which such Acts, Records and Proceedings shall be proved, and the Effect thereof.

Section 2

The Citizens of each State shall be entitled to all Privileges and Immunities of Citizens in the several States.

A Person charged in any State with Treason, Felony, or other Crime, who shall flee from Justice, and be found in another State, shall on Demand of the executive Authority of the State from which he fled, be delivered up, to be removed to the State having Jurisdiction of the Crime.

No Person held to Service or Labour in one State, under the Laws thereof, escaping into another, shall, in Consequence of any Law or Regulation therein, be discharged from such Service or Labour, but shall be delivered up on Claim of the Party to whom such Service or Labour may be due.

Section 3

New States may be admitted by the Congress into this Union; but no new State shall be formed or erected within the Jurisdiction of any other State; nor any State be formed by the Junction of two or more States, or Parts of States, without the Consent of the Legislatures of the States concerned as well as of the Congress.

The Congress shall have Power to dispose of and make all needful Rules and Regulations respecting the Territory or other Property belonging to the United States; and nothing in this Constitution shall be so construed as to Prejudice any Claims of the United States, or of any particular State.

Section 4

The United States shall guarantee to every State in this Union a Republican Form of Government, and shall protect each of them against Invasion; and on Application of the Legislature, or of the Executive (when the Legislature cannot be convened), against domestic Violence.

Article V

The Congress, whenever two thirds of both Houses shall deem it necessary, shall propose Amendments to this Constitution, or, on the Application of the Legislatures of two thirds of the several States, shall call a Convention for proposing Amendments, which, in either Case, shall be valid to all Intents and Purposes, as Part of this Constitution, when ratified by the Legislatures of three fourths of the several States, or by Conventions in three fourths thereof, as the one or the other Mode of Ratification may be proposed by the Congress; Provided that no Amendment which may be made prior to the Year One thousand eight hundred and eight shall in any Manner affect the first and fourth Clauses in the Ninth Section of the first Article; and that no State, without its Consent, shall be deprived of its equal Suffrage in the Senate.

Article VI

All Debts contracted and Engagements entered into, before the Adoption of this Constitution, shall be as valid against the United States under this Constitution, as under the Confederation.

This Constitution, and the Laws of the United States which shall be made in Pursuance thereof; and all Treaties made, or which shall be made, under the Authority of the United States, shall be the supreme Law of the Land; and the Judges in every State shall be bound thereby, any Thing in the Constitution or Laws of any State to the Contrary notwithstanding.

The Senators and Representatives before mentioned, and the Members of the several State Legislatures, and all executive and judicial Officers, both of the United States and of the several States, shall be bound by Oath or Affirmation, to support this Constitution; but no religious Test shall ever be required as a Qualification to any Office or public Trust under the United States.

Article VII

The Ratification of the Conventions of nine States, shall be sufficient for the Establishment of this Constitution between the States so ratifying the Same.

The Word, "the," being interlined between the seventh and eighth Lines of the first Page, the Word "Thirty" being partly written on an Erazure in the fifteenth Line of the first Page, The Words "is tried" being interlined between the thirty second and thirty third Lines of the first Page and the Word "the" being interlined between the forty third and forty fourth Lines of the second Page.

Attest William Jackson Secretary

Done in Convention by the Unanimous Consent of the States present the Seventeenth Day of September in the Year of our Lord one thousand seven hundred and Eighty seven and of the Independence of the United States of America the Twelfth In witness whereof We have hereunto subscribed our Names,

G°. Washington
Presidt and deputy from Virginia

Delaware
Geo: Read
Gunning Bedford jun
John Dickinson
Richard Bassett
Jaco: Broom

Maryland
James McHenry
Dan of St Thos. Jenifer
Danl. Carroll

Virginia
John Blair
James Madison Jr.

North Carolina
Wm. Blount
Richd. Dobbs Spaight
Hu Williamson

South Carolina
J. Rutledge
Charles Cotesworth Pinckney
Charles Pinckney
Pierce Butler

Georgia
William Few
Abr Baldwin

New Hampshire
John Langdon
Nicholas Gilman

Massachusetts
Nathaniel Gorham
Rufus King

Connecticut
Wm. Saml. Johnson
Roger Sherman

New York
Alexander Hamilton

New Jersey
Wil: Livingston
David Brearley
Wm. Paterson
Jona: Dayton

Pennsylvania
B Franklin
Thomas Mifflin
Robt. Morris
Geo. Clymer
Thos. FitzSimons
Jared Ingersoll
James Wilson
Gouv Morris

Articles

In addition to, and Amendment of the Constitution of the United States of America, proposed by Congress, and ratified by the Legislatures of the several States, pursuant to the fifth Article of the original Constitution.

(The first ten amendments to the U.S. Constitution were ratified December 15, 1791, and form what is known as the "Bill of Rights.")

AMENDMENT I

Congress shall make no law respecting an establishment of religion, or prohibiting the free exercise thereof; or abridging the freedom of speech, or of the press; or the right of the people peaceably to assemble, and to petition the Government for a redress of grievances.

AMENDMENT II

A well regulated Militia, being necessary to the security of a free State, the right of the people to keep and bear Arms, shall not be infringed.

AMENDMENT III

No Soldier shall, in time of peace be quartered in any house, without the consent of the Owner, nor in time of war, but in a manner to be prescribed by law.

AMENDMENT IV

The right of the people to be secure in their persons, houses, papers, and effects, against unreasonable searches and seizures, shall not be violated, and no Warrants shall issue, but upon probable cause, supported by Oath or affirmation, and particularly describing the place to be searched, and the persons or things to be seized.

AMENDMENT V

No person shall be held to answer for a capital, or otherwise infamous crime, unless on a presentment or indictment of a Grand Jury, except in cases arising in the land or naval forces, or in the Militia, when in actual service in time of War or public danger; nor shall any person be subject for the same offence to be twice put in jeopardy of life or limb; nor shall be compelled in any criminal case to be a witness against himself, nor be deprived of life, liberty, or property, without due process of law; nor shall private property be taken for public use, without just compensation.

AMENDMENT VI

In all criminal prosecutions, the accused shall enjoy the right to a speedy and public trial, by an impartial jury of the State and district wherein the crime shall have been committed, which district shall have been previously ascertained by law, and to be informed of the nature and cause of the accusation; to be confronted with the witnesses against him; to have compulsory process for obtaining witnesses in his favor, and to have the Assistance of Counsel for his defence.

AMENDMENT VII

In Suits at common law, where the value in controversy shall exceed twenty dollars, the right of trial by jury shall be preserved, and no fact tried by a jury, shall be otherwise re-examined in any Court of the United States, than according to the rules of the common law.

AMENDMENT VIII

Excessive bail shall not be required, nor excessive fines imposed, nor cruel and unusual punishments inflicted.

AMENDMENT IX

The enumeration in the Constitution, of certain rights, shall not be construed to deny or disparage others retained by the people.

AMENDMENT X

The powers not delegated to the United States by the Constitution, nor prohibited by it to the States, are reserved to the States respectively, or to the people.

AMENDMENT XI

Passed by Congress March 4, 1794. Ratified February 7, 1795.

Note: Article III, Section 2, of the Constitution was modified by Amendment XI.

The Judicial power of the United States shall not be construed to extend to any suit in law or equity, commenced or prosecuted against one of the United States by Citizens of another State, or by Citizens or Subjects of any Foreign State.

AMENDMENT XII

Passed by Congress December 9, 1803. Ratified June 15, 1804.

Note: A portion of Article II, Section 1, of the Constitution was superseded by the Twelfth Amendment.

The Electors shall meet in their respective states and vote by ballot for President and Vice-President, one of whom, at least, shall not be an inhabitant of the same state with themselves; they shall name in their ballots the person voted for as President, and in distinct ballots the person voted for as Vice-President, and they shall make distinct lists of all persons voted for as President, and of all persons voted for as Vice-President, and of the number of votes for each, which lists they shall sign and certify, and transmit sealed to the seat of the government of the United States, directed to the President of the Senate;— the President of the Senate shall, in the presence of the Senate and House of Representatives, open all the certificates and the votes shall then be counted;—The person having the greatest number of votes for President, shall be the President, if such number be a majority of the whole number of Electors appointed; and if no person have such majority, then from the persons having the highest numbers not exceeding three on the list of those voted for as President, the House of Representatives shall choose immediately, by ballot, the President. But in choosing the President, the votes shall be taken by states, the representation from each state having one vote; a quorum for this purpose shall consist of a member or members from two-thirds of the states, and a majority of all the states shall be necessary to a choice. [And if the House of Representatives shall not choose a President whenever the right of choice shall devolve upon them, before the fourth day of March next following, then the Vice-President shall act as President, as in case of the death or other constitutional disability of the President.—]* The person having the greatest number of votes as Vice-President, shall be the Vice-President, if such number be a majority of the whole number of Electors appointed, and if no person have a majority, then from the two highest numbers on the list, the Senate shall choose the Vice-President; a quorum for the purpose shall consist of two-thirds of the whole number of Senators, and a majority of the whole number shall be necessary to a choice. But no person constitutionally ineligible to the office of President shall be eligible to that of Vice-President of the United States.

*Superseded by Section 3 of the Twentieth Amendment.

AMENDMENT XIII

Passed by Congress January 31, 1865. Ratified December 6, 1865.

Note: A portion of Article IV, Section 2, of the Constitution was superseded by the Thirteenth Amendment.

Section 1

Neither slavery nor involuntary servitude, except as a punishment for crime whereof the party shall have been duly convicted, shall exist within the United States, or any place subject to their jurisdiction.

Section 2

Congress shall have power to enforce this article by appropriate legislation.

AMENDMENT XIV

Passed by Congress June 13, 1866. Ratified July 9, 1868.

Note: Article I, Section 2, of the Constitution was modified by Section 2 of the Fourteenth Amendment.

Section 1

All persons born or naturalized in the United States, and subject to the jurisdiction thereof, are citizens of the United States and of the State wherein they reside. No State shall make or enforce any law which shall abridge the privileges or immunities of citizens of the United States; nor shall any State deprive any person of life, liberty, or property, without due process of law; nor deny to any person within its jurisdiction the equal protection of the laws.

Section 2

Representatives shall be apportioned among the several States according to their respective numbers, counting the whole number of persons in each State, excluding Indians not taxed. But when the right to vote at any election for the choice of electors for President and Vice-President of the United States, Representatives in Congress, the Executive and Judicial officers of a State, or the members of the Legislature thereof, is denied to any of the male inhabitants of such State, being twenty-one years of age,* and citizens of the United States, or in any way abridged, except for participation in rebellion, or other crime, the basis of representation therein shall be reduced in the proportion which the number of such male citizens shall bear to the whole number of male citizens twenty-one years of age in such State.

Section 3

No person shall be a Senator or Representative in Congress, or elector of President and Vice-President, or hold any office, civil or military, under the United States, or under any State, who, having previously taken an oath, as a member of Congress, or as an officer of the United States, or as a member of any State legislature, or as an executive or judicial officer of any State, to support the Constitution of the United States, shall have engaged in insurrection or rebellion against the same, or given aid or comfort to the enemies thereof. But Congress may by a vote of two-thirds of each House, remove such disability.

Section 4

The validity of the public debt of the United States, authorized by law, including debts incurred for payment of pensions and bounties for services in suppressing insurrection or rebellion, shall not be questioned. But neither the United States nor any State shall assume or pay any debt or obligation incurred in aid of insurrection or rebellion against the United States, or any claim for the loss or emancipation of any slave; but all such debts, obligations and claims shall be held illegal and void.

Section 5

The Congress shall have the power to enforce, by appropriate legislation, the provisions of this article.

*Changed by Section 1 of the Twenty-sixth Amendment.

AMENDMENT XV

Passed by Congress February 26, 1869. Ratified February 3, 1870.

Section 1

The right of citizens of the United States to vote shall not be denied or abridged by the United States or by any State on account of race, color, or previous condition of servitude.

Section 2

The Congress shall have the power to enforce this article by appropriate legislation.

AMENDMENT XVI

Passed by Congress July 2, 1909. Ratified February 3, 1913.

Note: Article I, Section 9, of the Constitution was modified by Amendment XVI.

The Congress shall have power to lay and collect taxes on incomes, from whatever source derived, without apportionment among the several States, and without regard to any census or enumeration.

AMENDMENT XVII

Passed by Congress May 13, 1912. Ratified April 8, 1913.

Note: Article I, Section 3, of the Constitution was modified by the Seventeenth Amendment.

The Senate of the United States shall be composed of two Senators from each State, elected by the people thereof, for six years; and each Senator shall have one vote. The electors in each State shall have the qualifications requisite for electors of the most numerous branch of the State legislatures.

When vacancies happen in the representation of any State in the Senate, the executive authority of such State shall issue writs of election to fill such vacancies: Provided, That the legislature of any State may empower the executive thereof to make temporary appointments until the people fill the vacancies by election as the legislature may direct.

This amendment shall not be so construed as to affect the election or term of any Senator chosen before it becomes valid as part of the Constitution.

AMENDMENT XVIII

Passed by Congress December 18, 1917. Ratified January 16, 1919. Repealed by Amendment XXI.

Section 1

After one year from the ratification of this article the manufacture, sale, or transportation of intoxicating liquors within, the importation thereof into, or the exportation thereof from the United States and all territory subject to the jurisdiction thereof for beverage purposes is hereby prohibited.

Section 2

The Congress and the several States shall have concurrent power to enforce this article by appropriate legislation.

Section 3

This article shall be inoperative unless it shall have been ratified as an amendment to the Constitution by the legislatures of the several States, as provided in the Constitution, within seven years from the date of the submission hereof to the States by the Congress.

AMENDMENT XIX

Passed by Congress June 4, 1919. Ratified August 18, 1920.

The right of citizens of the United States to vote shall not be denied or abridged by the United States or by any State on account of sex.
    Congress shall have power to enforce this article by appropriate legislation.

AMENDMENT XX

Passed by Congress March 2, 1932. Ratified January 23, 1933.

Note: Article I, Section 4, of the Constitution was modified by Section 2 of this amendment. In addition, a portion of the Twelfth Amendment was superseded by Section 3.

Section 1

The terms of the President and the Vice President shall end at noon on the 20th day of January, and the terms of Senators and Representatives at noon on the 3d day of January, of the years in which such terms would have ended if this article had not been ratified; and the terms of their successors shall then begin.

Section 2

The Congress shall assemble at least once in every year, and such meeting shall begin at noon on the 3d day of January, unless they shall by law appoint a different day.

Section 3

If, at the time fixed for the beginning of the term of the President, the President elect shall have died, the Vice President elect shall become President. If a President shall not have been chosen before the time fixed for the beginning of his term, or if the President elect shall have failed to qualify, then the Vice President elect shall act as President until a President shall have qualified; and the Congress may by law provide for the case wherein neither a President elect nor a Vice President shall have qualified, declaring who shall then act as President, or the manner in which one who is to act shall be selected, and such person shall act accordingly until a President or Vice President shall have qualified.

Section 4

The Congress may by law provide for the case of the death of any of the persons from whom the House of Representatives may choose a President whenever the right of choice shall have devolved upon them, and for the case of the death of any of the persons from whom the Senate may choose a Vice President whenever the right of choice shall have devolved upon them.

Section 5

Sections 1 and 2 shall take effect on the 15th day of October following the ratification of this article.

Section 6

This article shall be inoperative unless it shall have been ratified as an amendment to the Constitution by the legislatures of three-fourths of the several States within seven years from the date of its submission.

AMENDMENT XXI

Passed by Congress February 20, 1933. Ratified December 5, 1933.

Section 1

The eighteenth article of amendment to the Constitution of the United States is hereby repealed.

Section 2

The transportation or importation into any State, Territory, or Possession of the United States for delivery or use therein of intoxicating liquors, in violation of the laws thereof, is hereby prohibited.

Section 3

This article shall be inoperative unless it shall have been ratified as an amendment to the Constitution by conventions in the several States, as provided in the Constitution, within seven years from the date of the submission hereof to the States by the Congress.

AMENDMENT XXII

Passed by Congress March 21, 1947. Ratified February 27, 1951.

Section 1

No person shall be elected to the office of the President more than twice, and no person who has held the office of President, or acted as President, for more than two years of a term to which some other person was elected President shall be elected to the office of President more than once. But this Article shall not apply to any person holding the office of President when this Article was proposed by Congress, and shall not prevent any person who may be holding the office of President, or acting as President, during the term within which this Article becomes operative from holding the office of President or acting as President during the remainder of such term.

Section 2

This article shall be inoperative unless it shall have been ratified as an amendment to the Constitution by the legislatures of three-fourths of the several States within seven years from the date of its submission to the States by the Congress.

AMENDMENT XXIII

Passed by Congress June 16, 1960. Ratified March 29, 1961.

Section 1

The District constituting the seat of Government of the United States shall appoint in such manner as Congress may direct:

A number of electors of President and Vice President equal to the whole number of Senators and Representatives in Congress to which the District would be entitled if it were a State, but in no event more than the least populous State; they shall be in addition to those appointed by the States, but they shall be considered, for the purposes of the election of President and Vice President, to be electors appointed by a State; and they shall meet in the District and perform such duties as provided by the twelfth article of amendment.

Section 2

The Congress shall have power to enforce this article by appropriate legislation.

AMENDMENT XXIV

Passed by Congress August 27, 1962. Ratified January 23, 1964.

Section 1

The right of citizens of the United States to vote in any primary or other election for President or Vice President, for electors for President or Vice President, or for Senator or Representative in Congress, shall not be denied or abridged by the United States or any State by reason of failure to pay poll tax or other tax.

Section 2

The Congress shall have power to enforce this article by appropriate legislation.

AMENDMENT XXV

Passed by Congress July 6, 1965. Ratified February 10, 1967.

Note: Article II, Section 1, of the Constitution was affected by the Twenty-fifth Amendment.

Section 1

In case of the removal of the President from office or of his death or resignation, the Vice President shall become President.

Section 2

Whenever there is a vacancy in the office of the Vice President, the President shall nominate a Vice President who shall take office upon confirmation by a majority vote of both Houses of Congress.

Section 3

Whenever the President transmits to the President pro tempore of the Senate and the Speaker of the House of Representatives his written declaration that he is unable to discharge the powers and duties of his office, and until he transmits to them a written declaration to the contrary, such powers and duties shall be discharged by the Vice President as Acting President.

Section 4

Whenever the Vice President and a majority of either the principal officers of the executive departments or of such other body as Congress may by law provide, transmit to the President pro tempore of the Senate and the Speaker of the House of Representatives their written declaration that the President is unable to discharge the powers and duties of his office, the Vice President shall immediately assume the powers and duties of the office as Acting President.

Thereafter, when the President transmits to the President pro tempore of the Senate and the Speaker of the House of Representatives his written declaration that no inability exists, he shall resume the powers and duties of his office unless the Vice President and a majority of either the principal officers of the executive department or of such other body as Congress may by law provide, transmit within four days to the President pro tempore of the Senate and the Speaker of the House of Representatives their written declaration that the President is unable to discharge the powers and duties of his office. Thereupon Congress shall decide the issue, assembling within forty-eight hours for that purpose if not in session. If the Congress, within twenty-one days after receipt of the latter written declaration, or, if Congress is not in session, within twenty-one days after Congress is required to assemble, determines by two-thirds vote of both Houses that the President is unable to discharge the powers and duties of his office, the Vice President shall continue to discharge the same as Acting President; otherwise, the President shall resume the powers and duties of his office.

AMENDMENT XXVI

Passed by Congress March 23, 1971. Ratified July 1, 1971.

Note: Amendment XIV, Section 2, of the Constitution was modified by Section 1 of the Twenty-sixth Amendment.

Section 1

The right of citizens of the United States, who are eighteen years of age or older, to vote shall not be denied or abridged by the United States or by any State on account of age.

Section 2

The Congress shall have power to enforce this article by appropriate legislation.

AMENDMENT XXVII

Originally proposed Sept. 25, 1789. Ratified May 7, 1992.

No law, varying the compensation for the services of the Senators and Representatives, shall take effect, until an election of representatives shall have intervened.

Lincoln's Gettysburg Address

Four score and seven years ago our fathers brought forth on this continent, a new nation, conceived in Liberty, and dedicated to the proposition that all men are created equal.

Now we are engaged in a great civil war, testing whether that nation, or any nation so conceived and so dedicated, can long endure. We are met on a great battle-field of that war. We have come to dedicate a portion of that field, as a final resting place for those who here gave their lives that that nation might live. It is altogether fitting and proper that we should do this.

But, in a larger sense, we can not dedicate—we can not consecrate—we can not hallow—this ground. The brave men, living and dead, who struggled here, have consecrated it, far above our poor power to add or detract. The world will little note, nor long remember what we say here, but it can never forget what they did here. It is for us the living, rather, to be dedicated here to the unfinished work which they who fought here have thus far so nobly advanced. It is rather for us to be here dedicated to the great task remaining before us—that from these honored dead we take increased devotion to that cause for which they gave the last full measure of devotion—that we here highly resolve that these dead shall not have died in vain—that this nation, under God, shall have a new birth of freedom—and that government of the people, by the people, for the people, shall not perish from the earth.

Appendix B

Historical Facts and Data
US Presidents and Vice Presidents

Table App B-1 Presidents and Vice Presidents

	President	Vice President	Political Party	Term
1	George Washington	John Adams	No Party Designation	1789–1797
2	John Adams	Thomas Jefferson	Federalist	1797–1801
3	Thomas Jefferson	Aaron Burr George Clinton	Democratic Republican	1801–1809
4	James Madison	George Clinton Elbridge Gerry	Democratic Republican	1809–1817
5	James Monroe	Daniel D. Tompkins	Democratic Republican	1817–1825
6	John Quincy Adams	John C. Calhoun	Democratic Republican	1825–1829
7	Andrew Jackson	John C. Calhoun Martin Van Buren	Democratic	1829–1837
8	Martin Van Buren	Richard M. Johnson	Democratic	1837–1841
9	William Henry Harrison	John Tyler	Whig	1841
10	John Tyler	None	Whig	1841–1845
11	James Knox Polk	George M. Dallas	Democratic	1845–1849
12	Zachary Taylor	Millard Fillmore	Whig	1849–1850
13	Millard Fillmore	None	Whig	1850–1853
14	Franklin Pierce	William R. King	Democratic	1853–1857
15	James Buchanan	John C. Breckinridge	Democratic	1857–1861
16	Abraham Lincoln	Hannibal Hamlin Andrew Johnson	Union	1861–1865
17	Andrew Johnson	None	Union	1865–1869
18	Ulysses Simpson Grant	Schuyler Colfax Henry Wilson	Republican	1869–1877
19	Rutherford Birchard Hayes	William A. Wheeler	Republican	1877–1881
20	James Abram Garfield	Chester Alan Arthur	Republican	1881
21	Chester Alan Arthur	None	Republican	1881–1885
22	Stephen Grover Cleveland	Thomas Hendricks	Democratic	1885–1889
23	Benjamin Harrison	Levi P. Morton	Republican	1889–1893

(continued)

Table App B-1 *continued*

	President	Vice President	Political Party	Term
24	Stephen Grover Cleveland	Adlai E. Stevenson	Democratic	1893–1897
25	William McKinley	Garret A. Hobart Theodore Roosevelt	Republican	1897–1901
26	Theodore Roosevelt	Charles W. Fairbanks	Republican	1901–1909
27	William Howard Taft	James S. Sherman	Republican	1909–1913
28	Woodrow Wilson	Thomas R. Marshall	Democratic	1913–1921
29	Warren Gamaliel Harding	Calvin Coolidge	Republican	1921–1923
30	Calvin Coolidge	Charles G. Dawes	Republican	1923–1929
31	Herbert Clark Hoover	Charles Curtis	Republican	1929–1933
32	Franklin Delano Roosevelt	John Nance Garner Henry A. Wallace Harry S. Truman	Democratic	1933–1945
33	Harry S. Truman	Alben W. Barkley	Democratic	1945–1953
34	Dwight David Eisenhower	Richard Milhous Nixon	Republican	1953–1961
35	John Fitzgerald Kennedy	Lyndon Baines Johnson	Democratic	1961–1963
36	Lyndon Baines Johnson	Hubert Horatio Humphrey	Democratic	1963–1969
37	Richard Milhous Nixon	Spiro T. Agnew Gerald Rudolph Ford	Republican	1969–1974
38	Gerald Rudolph Ford	Nelson Rockefeller	Republican	1974–1977
39	James Earl Carter Jr.	Walter Mondale	Democratic	1977–1981
40	Ronald Wilson Reagan	George Herbert Walker Bush	Republican	1981–1989
41	George Herbert Walker Bush	J. Danforth Quayle	Republican	1989–1993
42	William Jefferson Clinton	Albert Gore Jr.	Democratic	1993–2001
43	George Walker Bush	Richard Cheney	Republican	2001–2009
44	Barack Hussein Obama	Joseph Biden	Democratic	2009–2016
45	Donald J. Trump	Michael R. Pence	Republican	2017–

Admission of States into the Union

Table App B-2 Admission of States into the Union

	State	Date of Admission		State	Date of Admission
1	Delaware	December 7, 1787	26	Michigan	January 26, 1837
2	Pennsylvania	December 12, 1787	27	Florida	March 3, 1845
3	New Jersey	December 18, 1787	28	Texas	December 29, 1845
4	Georgia	January 2, 1788	29	Iowa	December 28, 1846
5	Connecticut	January 9, 1788	30	Wisconsin	May 29, 1848
6	Massachusetts	February 6, 1788	31	California	September 9, 1850
7	Maryland	April 28, 1788	32	Minnesota	May 11, 1858
8	South Carolina	May 23, 1788	33	Oregon	February 14, 1859
9	New Hampshire	June 21, 1788	34	Kansas	January 29, 1861
10	Virginia	June 25, 1788	35	West Virginia	June 20, 1863
11	New York	July 26, 1788	36	Nevada	October 31, 1864
12	North Carolina	November 21, 1789	37	Nebraska	March 1, 1867
13	Rhode Island	May 29, 1790	38	Colorado	August 1, 1876
14	Vermont	March 4, 1791	39	North Dakota	November 2, 1889
15	Kentucky	June 1, 1792	40	South Dakota	November 2, 1889
16	Tennessee	June 1, 1796	41	Montana	November 8, 1889
17	Ohio	March 1, 1803	42	Washington	November 11, 1889
18	Louisiana	April 30, 1812	43	Idaho	July 3, 1890
19	Indiana	December 11, 1816	44	Wyoming	July 10, 1890
20	Mississippi	December 10, 1817	45	Utah	January 4, 1896
21	Illinois	December 3, 1818	46	Oklahoma	November 16, 1907
22	Alabama	December 14, 1819	47	New Mexico	January 6, 1912
23	Maine	March 15, 1820	48	Arizona	February 14, 1912
24	Missouri	August 10, 1821	49	Alaska	January 3, 1959
25	Arkansas	June 15, 1836	50	Hawaii	August 21, 1959

Glossary

Affirmative action   A federal policy, begun in the Johnson administration in the 1960s, that required businesses, universities, and other recipients of federal funds to provide opportunities for women and people of color. Intended to make up for past and present discrimination, affirmative action remained a controversial practice, subject to political and legal challenge into the twenty-first century.

Antifederalists   People who were against the idea of strengthening the national government at the expense of local authority.

Antinomianism   The belief that moral law was not binding on true Christians. The opposite of Arminianism, antinomianism held that good works would not count in the afterlife. Justification, or entrance to heaven, was by faith alone. *See also* Calvinism.

Arminianism   Religious doctrine developed by the Dutch theologian Jacobus Arminius that argued that men and women had free will and would earn their way into heaven by good works.

Armistice   A cessation of hostilities by agreement among the opposing sides; a cease-fire.

Associationalism   President Herbert Hoover's preferred method of responding to the Great Depression. Rather than have the government directly involve itself in the economy, Hoover hoped to use the government to encourage associations of businessmen to cooperate voluntarily to meet the crisis.

Atomic bomb   A nuclear weapon that causes tremendous damage via heat, blast, and radioactivity. The United States, which developed the weapon via the Manhattan Project, dropped the first atomic bomb on Hiroshima on August 6, 1945, and the second on Nagaski on August 9, 1945. On August 15, Japan surrendered.

Autarky   At the height of the world depression, industrial powers sought to isolate their economies within self-contained spheres, generally governed by national (or imperial) economic planning. Japan's Co-Prosperity Sphere, the Soviet Union, and the British Empire each comprised a more or less closed economic unit.

Benevolent Empire   The loosely affiliated network of charitable reform associations that emerged (especially in urban areas) in response to the widespread revivalism of the early nineteenth century.

Bessemer process   Method invented by Henry Bessemer for removing the impurities from molten pig iron by blasting air through it and readying it to make a stronger steel.

Black Codes   Southern state laws passed just after the Civil War to define the limits of black freedom, restrict African Americans' right to testify in court, and to mete out distinctive punishments for offenses committed. Their passage helped convince Congress that a federal law protecting civil rights was needed.

Blockade   A military tactic used in both land and naval warfare by which a location is sealed off to prevent goods or people from entering or leaving.

Budget deficit   The failure of tax revenues to pay for annual federal spending on military, welfare, and other programs. The resulting budget deficits forced Washington to borrow money to cover its costs. The growing budget deficits were controversial, in part because the government's borrowing increased both its long-term debt and the amount of money it had to spend each year to pay for the interest on loans.

Busing   The controversial court-ordered practice of sending children by bus to public schools outside their neighborhoods in order to promote racial integration in the schools.

Calvinism   Religious doctrine developed by the theologian John Calvin that argued that God alone determines who will receive salvation and, hence, men and women cannot earn their own salvation or even be certain about their final destinies.

Carpetbagger   A derogatory term referring to northern whites who moved to the South after the Civil War. Stereotyped as corrupt and unprincipled, "carpetbaggers" were in fact a diverse group motivated by a variety of interests and beliefs.

Central Intelligence Agency (CIA)   Federal agency created in 1947 to investigate and advise the president on political and military threats to the United States. The CIA's mission expanded in the 1950s to include clandestine activities abroad.

Charter colony   Settlement established by a trading company or other group of private entrepreneurs who received from the king a grant of land and the right to govern it. The charter colonies included Virginia, Plymouth, Massachusetts Bay, Rhode Island, and Connecticut.

Chisholm Trail   Named for Jesse Chisholm, a route blazed after the Civil War to move cattle from Texas to railroad termini in Kansas. Also known as the Abilene Trail.

City busting   As late as the 1930s, President Roosevelt and most Americans regarded attacking civilians from the air as an atrocity, but during World War II cities became a primary target for US warplanes. The inaccuracy of bombing, combined with racism and the belief that Japanese and German actions justified retaliation, led American air commanders to follow a policy of systematically destroying urban areas, particularly in Japan.

City-commission plan   A government overseen by appointed officials who ran a city with an eye to economy and efficiency, as though running a business. Designed as an alternative to the political machines of the late nineteenth century.

Civilian Conservation Corps (CCC)   Early New Deal program that provided young men with food, shelter, and employment. Working at camps throughout the country, the men participated in conservation efforts and the building of American infrastructure.

Common Sense   The title of a well-loved pamphlet written by Thomas Paine at a low point in the American Revolutionary War. The phrase alluded to the idea that human beings have certain natural rights that we all instinctively recognize.

Communist   Member of the Communist Party or follower of the doctrines of Karl Marx. The term (or accusation) was applied more broadly in the twentieth century to brand labor unionists, progressives, civil rights workers, and other reformers as agents of a foreign ideology.

Communitarians   Individuals who supported and/or took up residence in separate communities created to embody improved plans of social, religious, and/or economic life.

Commutation   The controversial policy of allowing potential draftees to pay for a replacement to serve in the army. The policy was adopted by both the Union and Confederate governments during the Civil War, and in both cases opposition to commutation was so intense that the policy was abandoned.

Compromise of 1850   A set of measures proposed by Henry Clay and much revised, to settle all the key issues over slavery: its expansion into the West, the admission of a free state of California, the boundary disputes between Texas and New Mexico, and the slave trade in the District of Columbia.

Conscription   The compulsory drafting of men into the army, imposed by both sides during the Civil War.

Consent   One of the key principles of liberalism, which held that people could not be subject to laws to which they had not given their consent. This principle is reflected in both the Declaration of Independence and the preamble to the Constitution, which begins with the famous words "We the people of the United States, in order to form a more perfect union."

Conspiracy theory   A belief that history is shaped intentionally by unseen powers. Conspiracy theory lay behind the McCarthy anti-Communism hearings, which assumed that American society and government had been infiltrated by countless Communist spies.

Constitutionalism   A loose body of thought that developed in Britain and the colonies and was used by the colonists to justify the Revolution by claiming that it was in accord with the principles of the British Constitution. Constitutionalism had two main elements. One was the rule of law, and the other the principle of consent, that one cannot be subject to laws or taxation except by duly elected representatives. Both were rights that had been won through struggle with the monarch. Constitutionalism also refers to the tendency in American politics, particularly in the early nineteenth century, to transpose all political questions into constitutional ones.

Consumer revolution   A slow and steady increase over the course of the eighteenth century in the demand for, and purchase of, consumer goods. The consumer revolution of the eighteenth century was closely related to the Industrial Revolution.

Consumerism   An ideology that defined the purchase of goods and services as both an expression of individual identity and essential to the national economy. Increasingly powerful by the 1920s and dominant by the 1950s, consumerism urged people to find happiness in the pursuit of leisure and pleasure more than in the work ethic.

Containment   The basic US strategy for fighting the cold war. As used by diplomat George Kennan in a 1947 magazine essay, "containment" referred to the combination of diplomatic, economic, and military programs necessary to hold back Soviet expansionism after World War II.

Contraband of war   In its general sense, contraband of war was property seized from an enemy. But early in the Civil War the term was applied to slaves running to Union lines as a way of preventing owners from reclaiming them. The policy effectively nullified the fugitive slave clause of the US Constitution. It was a first critical step in a process that would lead to a federal emancipation policy the following year.

Cooperationists   Those southerners who opposed immediate secession after the election of Abraham Lincoln in 1860. Cooperationists argued instead that secessionists should wait to see if the new president was willing to "cooperate" with the South's demands.

Copperhead   A northerner who sympathized with the South during the Civil War.

Cost-plus contract   This style of contract provides manufacturers with a guarantee of costs of research and production and a profit. During World War I, to incentivize wartime industry, the United States government offered cost-plus contracts to industries that switched to production of wartime goods.

Coverture   A legal principle according to which a married woman's rights and even identity are subsumed under those of her husband.

Crop lien The first right to the proceeds of a harvested crop, given by farmers to their creditors. At the beginning of the growing season, farmers paid on credit for seeds, supplies, and food to get them through the year. They repaid these debts when the crop was sold.

Deindustrialization The reverse of industrialization, as factory shutdowns decreased the size of the manufacturing sector. Plant closings began to plague the American economy in the 1970s, prompting fears that the nation would lose its industrial base.

Democratic Republicans One of the two parties to make up the first American party system. Following the fiscal and political views of Jefferson and Madison, Democratic Republicans generally advocated a weak federal government and opposed federal intervention in the economy of the nation.

Détente This French term for the relaxation of tensions was used to describe the central foreign policy innovation of the Nixon administration—a new, less confrontational relationship with Communism. In addition to opening a dialogue with the People's Republic of China, Nixon sought a more stable, less confrontational relationship with the Soviet Union.

Disfranchisement The act of depriving a person or group of voting rights. In the nineteenth century the right to vote was popularly known as the franchise. The Fourteenth Amendment of the Constitution affirmed the right of adult male citizens to vote, but state-imposed restrictions and taxes deprived large numbers of Americans—particularly African Americans—of the vote from the 1890s until the passage of the Voting Rights Act of 1965.

Domino theory The idea that the fall of one country to Communism would lead to the fall of others. The theory was one of the chief justifications for US intervention in Vietnam in the 1950s and 1960s.

Downsizing American corporations' layoffs of both blue- and white-collar workers in an attempt to become more efficient and competitive. Downsizing was one of the factors that made Americans uneasy about the economy in the 1990s, despite the impressive surge in the stock market.

Draft riots Uprisings in New York City, Buffalo, and elsewhere in 1863 in protest of conscription.

Dred Scott decision An 1857 Supreme Court decision that declared the Missouri Compromise or any Congressional ban on slavery in the territories unconstitutional and denied African Americans from becoming citizens of the United States.

Dust Bowl Across much of the Great Plains, decades of wasteful farming practices combined with several years of drought in the early 1930s to produce a series of massive dust storms that blew the topsoil across hundreds of miles. The area in Texas and Oklahoma affected by these storms became known as the Dust Bowl.

E-commerce Short for "electronic commerce," this was the term for the Internet-based buying and selling that was one of the key hopes for the computer-driven postindustrial economy. The promise of e-commerce was still unfulfilled by the start of the twenty-first century.

Encomienda A system of labor developed by the Spanish in the New World in which Spanish settlers (*encomenderos*) compelled groups of Native Americans to work for them. The encomendero owned neither the land nor the Indians who worked for him, but he had the unlimited right to compel a particular group of Indians to work for him. This system was unique to the New World; nothing precisely like it had existed in Europe or elsewhere.

Enlightenment   A shift in thinking that occurred in the eighteenth century valuing the natural rights of individuals over traditional hierarchy, and scientific rationalism over faith. The term is much debated today for a number of reasons, among them the fact that men who considered themselves proponents of the Enlightenment often remained slaveholders.

"Establishment"   The elite of mainly Ivy League–educated, Anglo-Saxon, Protestant, male, liberal northeasterners that supposedly dominated Wall Street and Washington after World War II. The Establishment's support for corporations, activist government, and containment engendered hostility from opposite poles of the political spectrum—from conservatives and Republicans like Richard Nixon at one end and from the New Left and the Movement at the other. Although many of the post–World War II leaders of the United States did tend to share common origins and ideologies, this elite was never as powerful, self-conscious, or unified as its opponents believed.

Eugenics   The practice of attempting to solve social problems through the control of human reproduction. Drawing on the authority of evolutionary biology, eugenists enjoyed considerable influence in the United States, especially on issues of corrections and public health, from the turn of the century through World War II. Applications of this pseudoscience included the identification of "born" criminals by physical characteristics and "better baby" contests at county fairs.

"Family values"   Rallying cry for conservatives and Republicans in the 1990s and after who believed that gay and women's rights, changing family structures, and popular culture were undermining traditional morality.

Farmers' Alliance   A group organized in the late nineteenth century to help farmers pool their knowledge and resources. By 1890, it had entered politics, endorsing candidates and building the political connections in the South and West that would lead to the Populist Party.

Federalists   One of the two political parties to make up the first American party system. Following the fiscal and political policies proposed by Alexander Hamilton, Federalists generally advocated the importance of a strong federal government, including federal intervention in the economy of the new nation.

Feminism   An ideology insisting on the fundamental equality of women and men. The feminists of the 1960s differed over how to achieve that equality: while liberal feminists mostly demanded equal rights for women in the workplace and in politics, radical feminists more thoroughly condemned the capitalist system and male oppression and demanded equality in both private and public life.

Feudalism   A social and political system that developed in Europe in the Middle Ages under which powerful lords offered less powerful noblemen protection in return for their loyalty. Feudalism also included the economic system of manorialism, under which dependent serfs worked on the manors controlled by those lords.

Fifteenth Amendment   An 1870 constitutional amendment forbidding discrimination in voting on the basis of race, color, or previous condition of servitude.

Fire-eaters   Militant southerners who pushed for secession in the 1850s.

Flexible response   The defense doctrine of the Kennedy and Johnson administrations. Abandoning the Eisenhower administration's heavy emphasis on nuclear weapons, flexible response stressed the buildup of the nation's conventional and special forces so that the president had a range of military options in response to Communist aggression.

Fordism   A system of mass production that relied on mass consumption, pioneered by and named for Henry Ford.

Fourteenth Amendment   An 1868 constitutional amendment defining national citizenship, mandating equal justice before the law, guaranteeing essential civil rights, redefining the basis on which seats in the House of Representatives would be apportioned, declaring the national debt inviolate, and disqualifying some Confederate leaders from holding office until Congress had removed their disabilities.

Freedmen's Bureau   The Bureau of Refugees, Freedmen, and Abandoned Lands, a government agency formed in 1865 and administered by the army, that afforded aid and protection to former slaves, among others.

Front   Early twentieth-century mechanized wars were fought along a battle line or "front" separating opposing sides. By World War II, tactical innovations—blitzkrieg, parachute troops, gliders, and amphibious landings—complicated warfare by breaking through, disrupting, or bypassing the front. The front thus became a more fluid boundary than the fortified trench lines of World War I. The term also acquired a political meaning, particularly for labor and the left. A coalition of parties supporting (or opposing) an agreed-upon line could be called a "popular front."

Fugitive Slave Act   A widely protested 1850 law that increased federal powers to capture people accused of being runaway slaves and to convict them without a jury trial or the right to testify on their own behalf.

Fundamentalism   A conservative Christian doctrine that subscribed to the literal truths of the Bible. Uneasy with the changes of the 1920s, Fundamentalists rejected modern culture and instead advocated a dedication to traditional authority and religious beliefs.

Galveston Plan   A system of municipal government by appointed commissioners, each with responsibility for a utility or service. After a hurricane devastated Galveston, Texas, in 1900, unelected commissioners temporarily took charge to oversee relief and rebuilding efforts.

Gentility   A term without precise meaning that represented all that was polite, civilized, refined, and fashionable. It was everything that vulgarity was not. Because the term had no precise meaning, it was always subject to negotiation, striving, and anxiety as Americans, beginning in the eighteenth century, tried to show others that they were genteel through their manners, their appearance, and their styles of life.

Glass ceiling   The invisible barrier of discrimination that prevented female white-collar workers from rising to top executive positions in corporations.

Globalization   This term first came into use during the 1980s to describe the web of technological, economic, military, political, and cultural developments binding people and nations ever more tightly together. America had been defined by its relationship to the world for centuries, but the coining of the term *globalization* reflected the emergence of closer international ties.

Gold standard   The practice by which gold served as backing for all national currency.

Great Awakening   A period in which a large proportion of the populace becomes invested in evangelical revivalism. In American history, there have been a number of such periods, but the term is most often applied to the years of the 1730s through 1750s, and the 1820s and 1830s.

Great Society   President Lyndon Johnson's ambitious legislative program embodying the vision of the activist new liberalism of the 1960s. Enacted from 1965 to 1968, the Great Society sought to wipe out poverty, end segregation, and enhance the quality of life for all Americans.

Greenbackers   Those who advocated currency inflation by keeping the type of money printed during the Civil War, known as "greenbacks," in circulation.

Gridlock   The political traffic jam that tied up the federal government in the late 1980s and the 1990s. Gridlock developed from the inability of either major party to control both the presidency and Congress for any extended period of time. More fundamentally, gridlock reflected the inability of any party or president to win a popular mandate for a bold legislative program.

Half-Way Covenant   A policy solution developed by Puritan New England congregations in the second half of the seventeenth century which allowed the children and grandchildren of people who had not had a conversion experience to become partial members of the church.

Hard war   A term used to describe the Civil War's transformation into a conflict in which cities and civilians, not just armies, became targets as a means of hastening victory.

Headright   The system whereby a white male European settler was offered a certain number of acres of land for every family member or servant he brought with him to the New World.

Homestead Act   An 1862 law giving 160 acres of public land without cost to heads of households who would agree to settle and cultivate it for five years.

Homestead Steel Works   Andrew Carnegie's modernized Pennsylvania steel plant, which served as the site of an 1892 conflict between management and labor.

Hoovervilles   Makeshift settlements created on the outskirts of cities by those left homeless as a result of the Great Depression. Named for President Herbert Hoover, who many Americans believed to be indifferent to their suffering.

Horizontal integration   More commonly known as "monopoly." An industry was "horizontally integrated" when a single company took control of virtually the entire market for a specific product. John D. Rockefeller's Standard Oil came close to doing this.

Hudson River school   A movement among mid-nineteenth-century landscape painters. These artists were influenced by romanticism and sought inspiration in the idea of the sublime as embodied in America's natural terrain.

Hull House   After visiting Toynbee Hall in London, Jane Addams opened this settlement house in 1889 with the intent of providing aid to the impoverished population of Chicago's Near West Side.

Immediatism   The variant antislavery sentiment that demanded immediate (as opposed to gradual) personal and federal action against the institution of slavery. This approach was most closely associated with William Lloyd Garrison and is dated from the publication of Garrison's newspaper, *The Liberator*, in January 1831.

Imperialism   A process of extending dominion over territories beyond the national boundaries of a state. In the eighteenth century, Britain extended imperial control over North America through settlement, but in the 1890s, imperial influence was generally exercised through indirect rule. Subject peoples generally retained some local autonomy while the imperial power controlled commerce and defense. Few Americans went to the Philippines as settlers, but many passed through as tourists, missionaries, traders, and soldiers.

Indentured servants   People who promised to work for a term of years (usually between two and seven) in exchange for passage to the New World.

Individualism   The social and political philosophy celebrating the central importance of the individual human being in society. Insisting on the rights of the individual in relationship to the group, individualism was one of the intellectual bases of capitalism and democracy. The resurgent individualism of the 1920s, with its emphasis on each American's freedom and fulfillment, was a critical element of the decade's emergent consumerism and Republican dominance.

Industrious revolution   Beginning in the late seventeenth century in western Europe and extending to the North American colonies in the eighteenth century, a fundamental change in the way people worked, as they worked harder and organized their households to produce goods that could be sold, so they could have money to pay for the new consumer goods they wanted.

Information economy   The postindustrial economy, gradually emerging in the mid- and late twentieth century, in which sophisticated communications, computing, biomedical technology, and services took the place of manufacturing.

Initiative, recall, and referendum   First proposed by the People's Party's Omaha Platform (1892), along with the direct election of senators and the secret ballot, as measures to subject corporate capitalism to democratic controls. Progressives, chiefly in western and midwestern states, favored them as a check on the power of state officials. The initiative allows legislation to be proposed by petition. The recall allows voters to remove public officials, and the referendum places new laws or constitutional amendments on the ballot for the direct approval of the voters.

Interest group   An association whose members organize to exert political pressure on officials or the public. Unlike political parties, whose platforms and slates cover nearly every issue and office, an interest group focuses on a narrower list of concerns reflecting the shared outlook of its members. With the decline of popular politics around the turn of the twentieth century, business, religious, agricultural, women's, professional, neighborhood, and reform associations created a new form of political participation.

Internment   Imprisonment, without trial, inspired by political justifications. During World War II, the United States government seized the property of, relocated, and imprisoned both Japanese immigrants and natural-born Japanese-Americans based on the presumed threat this population posed to the nation.

Isolationist   Between World War I and World War II, the United States refused to join the League of Nations, scaled back its military commitments abroad, and sought to maintain its independence of action in foreign affairs. These policies were called isolationist, although some historians prefer the term "independent internationalist," in recognition of the United States' continuing global influence. In the late 1930s, isolationists favored policies aimed at distancing the United States from European affairs and building a national defense based on air power and hemispheric security.

Jim Crow laws   Statutes discriminating against nonwhite Americans, particularly in the South. The term specifically refers to regulations excluding blacks from public facilities or compelling them to use ones separate from those allotted to whites.

Joint-stock company   A form of business organization that was a forerunner to the modern corporation. The joint-stock company was used to raise both capital and labor for New World ventures. Shareholders contributed either capital or their labor for a period of years.

Jones Mixer   Developed by Captain William R. Jones, a massive machine used for keeping molten iron hot, until it could be used with other ingredients to make steel.

Keynesian economics   The theory, named after the English economist John Maynard Keynes, that advocated the use of "countercyclical" fiscal policy. This meant that during good times the government should pay down the debt, so that during bad times, it could afford to stimulate the economy with deficit spending.

King Cotton diplomacy   Confederate efforts to use European dependence on cotton exports to win recognition as an independent nation.

Knights of Labor   The first national federation of trade unions, led by Terence V. Powderly. The Knights grew to its fullest size in the mid-1880s before a steep decline. The federation was based on the premise of a common interest of all producers (for example, farmers and industrial workers), and it supported reform as well as united action by workers.

Liberalism   A body of political thought that traces its origins to John Locke and whose chief principles are consent, freedom of conscience, and property. Liberalism held that people could not be governed except by their own consent and that the purpose of government was to protect people as well as their property.

Limited war   In the age of total war in the mid-twentieth century, limited war became a useful term to describe armed conflicts such as the Korean, Vietnam, Iraq, and Afghan wars in which a country did not fully mobilize its population, persistently attack civilians, and use its full arsenal, including nuclear weapons.

Linked economic development   A form of economic development that ties together a variety of enterprises so that development in one stimulates development in others, for example, those that provide raw materials, parts, or transportation.

Longhorn cattle   Rangy, tough, resourceful cattle found on the southern Great Plains. They were ideal for long cattle drives like those along the Abilene Trail.

Loyalists   Those who remained devoted to the British monarchical government during the Revolutionary War.

Lyceum movement   A voluntary adult-education movement that swept New England and the mid-Atlantic states in the early and mid-nineteenth century, credited in large part to the efforts of Josiah Holbrook. Lyceum organizations hosted educational lectures in towns and cities. Lecturers included such prominent speakers as Ralph Waldo Emerson, Mark Twain, and Abraham Lincoln.

Manifest destiny   A term first coined in 1845 by journalist John O'Sullivan to express the belief, widespread among antebellum Americans, that the United States was destined to expand across the North American continent to the Pacific and had an irrefutable right to the lands absorbed in this expansion. This belief was frequently justified on the grounds of claims to political and racial superiority.

Market revolution   The term used to designate the period of the early nineteenth century, roughly 1815–1830, during which internal dependence on cash markets and wages became widespread.

Mass production   A system of efficient, high-volume manufacturing based on division of labor into repetitive tasks, simplification, and standardization of parts, increasing use of specialized machinery, and careful supervision. Emerging since the nineteenth century, mass production reached a critical stage of development with Henry Ford's introduction of the moving assembly line at his Highland Park automobile factory. Mass production drove the prosperity of the 1920s and helped make consumerism possible.

Massive resistance   The rallying cry of southern segregationists who pledged to oppose the integration of the schools ordered by the Supreme Court in *Brown v. Board of Education* in 1954. The tactics of massive resistance included legislation, demonstrations, and violence.

Massive retaliation   The defense doctrine of the Eisenhower administration which promised "instant, massive retaliation" with nuclear weapons in response to Soviet aggression.

McCarthyism   The hunt for Communist subversion in the United States in the first years of the cold war. Democrats, in particular, used the term, a reference to the sometimes disreputable tactics of Republican Senator Joseph R. McCarthy of Wisconsin, in order to question the legitimacy of the conservative anti-Communist crusade.

Mercantilism   An economic theory developed in early-modern Europe to explain and guide the growth of European nation-states. Its goal was to strengthen the state by making the economy serve its interests. According to the theory of mercantilism, the world's wealth, measured in gold and silver, was fixed; that is, it could never be increased. As a result, each nation's chief economic objective must be to secure as much of the world's wealth as possible. One nation's gain was necessarily another's loss. Colonies played an important part in the theory of mercantilism. Their role was to serve as sources of raw materials and as markets for manufactured goods for the mother country alone.

Millennialism   A strain of Protestant belief that holds that history will end with the thousand-year reign of Christ (the millennium). Some Americans saw the Great Awakening, the French and Indian War, and the Revolution as signs that the millennium was about to begin in America, and this belief infused Revolutionary thought with an element of optimism. Millennialism was also one aspect of a broad drive for social perfection in nineteenth-century America.

Minstrel show   Form of popular entertainment in the nineteenth century, with black performers or white ones pretending to be black. Minstrel shows included music, comedy acts, and drama.

Modern Republicanism   President Dwight Eisenhower's middle-of-the-road legislative program of the 1950s. Reflecting traditional Republican faith in limited government and balanced budgets, Modern Republicanism still left alone such liberal programs as Social Security and farm subsidies.

Modernization   The process by which developing countries in the third world were to become more like the United States—that is, capitalist, independent, and anti-Communist. Confidence about the prospects for modernization was one of the cornerstones of liberal foreign policy in the 1960s.

Moral suasion   The strategy of using persuasion (as opposed to legal coercion) to convince individuals to alter their behavior. In the antebellum years, moral suasion generally implied an appeal to religious values.

Mugwump   Name applied to liberal reformers in the late nineteenth century. Unattached to either major party, Mugwumps would endorse any candidate supportive of civil service reform, a secret ballot, and honest government.

Multinationals   Corporations with factories and other operations in several nations that did not necessarily see themselves as citizens of any one country in particular. Originating in the nineteenth century, multinationals became controversial in the 1970s as the deindustrializing United States lost factory jobs to other countries.

Mutual aid societies   Organizations through which people of relatively meager means pooled their resources for emergencies. Usually, individuals paid small amounts in dues and were able to borrow large amounts in times of need. In the early nineteenth century, mutual aid societies were especially common among workers in free African American communities.

National Labor Union   The first federation of trade unions, founded in 1866, and the forerunner of the Knights of Labor and the American Federation of Labor.

National Republicanism   Over the first 20 years of the nineteenth century, the Republican Party gradually abandoned its Jeffersonian animosity toward an activist federal government and industrial development and became a strong proponent of both of these positions. Embodied in the American system, these new views were fully captured in the party's designation of itself as National Republicans by 1824.

Nationalist Clubs   Associations formed in the 1880s to further the social planning ideas of Edward Bellamy.

Nativism   A bias against anyone not born in the United States and in favor of native-born Americans. This attitude assumes the superior culture and political virtue of white Americans of Anglo-Saxon descent, or of individuals assumed to have that lineage. During the period 1820–1850, Irish immigrants became the particular targets of nativist attitudes.

Navigation Acts   A series of laws passed by the British Parliament in the seventeenth century to govern trade with the colonies so as to maximize profits for the mother country.

Neoconservatism   Form of conservative ideology that advocated the aggressive promotion of democracy abroad by the United States in order to make a better and more secure world. Emerging in the 1970s and 1980s, neoconservative ideas influenced the foreign policy of President George W. Bush.

Neutrality   A practice by which a nation remains impartial and refuses to support either side in a conflict. The United States responded to each of the world wars with an initial policy of neutrality.

New conservatism   The resurgent conservative ideology of the 1950s and 1960s reiterated the old conservatism's faith in individual freedom and liberal government and added an aggressive, anti-Communist defense policy.

New Deal   Name for government programs created during Franklin D. Roosevelt's administration intended to end the Great Depression. Shifting in focus across the Depression-era years, the New Deal aimed, at varying times, to regulate, reform, and stimulate the American economy.

New Era   A term, like "the Roaring Twenties," used to describe the social, political, and economic changes of the decade, many of which celebrated the individual.

New Federalism   Conservative policy of President Richard Nixon intended to limit the federal government by returning revenue and control to state and local government.

New Left   The radical student movement that emerged in opposition to the new liberalism in the 1960s. The New Left condemned the cold war and corporate power and called for the creation of a true "participatory democracy" in the United States. Placing its faith in the radical potential of young, middle-class students, the New Left differed from the "old left" of the late nineteenth and early twentieth centuries, which believed workers would lead the way to socialism.

New Negro   A term used to describe African Americans, many of whom had left the rural South during the first decades of the twentieth century, who challenged racial inequality and expressed racial pride.

New Right   The conservative movement that swept Ronald Reagan into power in 1980 and sustained his presidency. The New Right was much like the new conservatism of the 1950s and 1960s, but with greater emphasis on social issues such as abortion.

New Woman   A term used to describe women of the late nineteenth century who advocated on behalf of their rights to equal educational, economic, and political opportunities. In the 1920s, this figure became increasingly linked to sexual liberation and the culture of fun.

New World Order   With the end of the cold war, President George H. W. Bush called for the United States to help ensure a world dominated by democracy, free trade, and peace.

Nongovernmental organizations (NGOs)   Private, nongovernmental, noncommercial organizations. NGOs such as Greenpeace, the International Red Cross, and the World Economic Forum played key roles in globalization in the late twentieth and early twenty-first centuries.

NSC-68   A secret document issued by President Truman's National Security Council that detailed US strategy, including the development of thermonuclear weapons, to counter the Soviet Union.

Omaha Platform   The Populist Party's program endorsed at the party's national convention in Omaha in 1892. Among its planks were government ownership of railroads and telegraph lines, the direct election of senators, a subtreasury system, and an expansion of the money supply.

Open Door   The turn-of-the-twentieth-century American ideal for China, in which the country remained open to international trade. This model would allow the United States to expand its global economic reach without the responsibilities of maintaining an empire.

Ostend Manifesto   An 1854 declaration justifying the United States' need to buy Cuba, indicating a readiness to take it by force if Spain would not agree to sell it.

Overland Trail   The trail from the Missouri River to Oregon and California, begun in the early 1840s and only replaced with the completion of a transcontinental railroad in 1869.

Panama Canal   The waterway, constructed between 1903 and 1914, after the United States supported the Panamanian overthrow of the Columbian government, which cuts through Central America and serves as a means of connecting the Atlantic and Pacific Oceans. Represents technological innovation and American imperial endeavors.

Participatory democracy   Believing that the American political system did not heed the will of the people in the 1960s, Students for a Democratic Society called for a more truly participatory democratic politics that would empower ordinary Americans.

Patriotism   Love of country. Ways of declaring and displaying national devotion underwent a change from the nineteenth to the twentieth centuries. Whereas politicians were once unblushingly called patriotic, after World War I the title was appropriated to describe the sacrifices of war veterans. Patriotic spectacle in the form of public oration and electoral rallies gave way to military-style commemorations of Armistice Day and the nation's martial heritage.

Patronage   *See* spoils system.

Pendleton Civil Service Act   1883 legislation that set up a merit system for hiring and promoting federal workers, and protecting them from forced political contributions. Covering only a small fraction of all government employees at first, its range expanded with each presidency.

Political action committees (PACs)   Dating to the 1940s, organizations, not part of political parties, that have had greater and lesser freedom from the federal government to accept and spend unlimited donations on issues and candidates.

Political economy   Traditionally, the study of the connections between economics and politics. In this text, political economy refers to the relationships between the economy, politics, and the daily lives of ordinary people. Use of the term underscores the importance of the economy in shaping American life and the importance of politics in shaping the economy. However, the economy and politics did not simply shape, but were in turn shaped by, the lives and cultural values of ordinary men and women.

Political machine   An organization controlling a party, usually dominated by a "boss" and held together by loyalty and the distribution of rewards to those who had done the organization service.

Popular sovereignty   A solution to the slavery controversy espoused by leading northern Democrats in the 1850s. It held that the inhabitants of western territories should be free to decide for themselves whether or not they wanted to have slavery. In principle, popular sovereignty would prevent Congress from either enforcing or restricting slavery's expansion into the western territories.

Populism   The ideology of the People's (Populist) party in the 1890s, opposing the eastern economic elites and favoring government action to help producers in general and farmers in particular.

Postindustrial economy   The service- and computer-based economy that was succeeding the industrial economy at the end of the twentieth century.

Principle of judicial review   The principle of law that recognizes in the judiciary the power to review and rule on the constitutionality of laws. First established in *Marbury v. Madison* (1803) under Chief Justice John Marshall.

Privateering   Piratical ventures authorized by a European government. A colonizing power might provide financial backing to captains who used their ships to attack the galleons or New World settlements belonging to a different colonial power.

Producers ideology   The belief that all those who lived by producing goods shared a common political identity in opposition to those who lived off financial speculation, rent, or interest.

Propaganda   Information used to promote a particular cause or point of view. During the twentieth century, the United States' government attempted to persuade the American people to support various national efforts via text, image, radio, and film.

Proprietary colony   Colony established by a royal grant to an individual or family. The proprietary colonies included Maryland, New York, New Jersey, Pennsylvania, and the Carolinas.

Public opinion   Not quite democracy or consent, public opinion was a way of understanding the influence of the citizenry on political calculations. It emerged in the eighteenth century, when it was defined as a crucial source of a government's legitimacy. It was associated with the emergence of a press and a literate public free to discuss, and to question, government policy. In the twentieth century, Freudian psychology and the new mass media encouraged a view of the public as both fickle and powerful. Whereas the popular will (a nineteenth-century concept) was steady and rooted in national traditions, public opinion was variable and based on attitudes that could be aroused or manipulated by advertising.

Reagan Doctrine   Rejecting the Carter administration's emphasis on promoting human rights around the world in the 1970s, President Ronald Reagan contended in the 1980s that the United States should support authoritarian, antidemocratic regimes friendly to the United States.

Reaganomics   *See* supply-side economics.

Reconquista   Literally "reconquest." Between the eleventh and the fifteenth centuries, Christian nobles in Spain and Portugal fought to eject Muslim conquerors who had come from North Africa in the seventh and eighth centuries. In 1492, Ferdinand and Isabel defeated the last remaining Muslim ruler.

Reconversion   The economic and social transition from the war effort to peacetime. Americans feared that reconversion might bring a return to the depression conditions of the 1930s.

Red Scare   The fear of a communist takeover of the United States following the Bolshevik Revolution of 1917. After World War I, the American government attempted to limit radicalism by suppressing the voices of communists, socialists, anarchists, and organized labor.

Redemption   A term used by southern Democrats for the undoing of Radical Reconstruction and the replacement of biracial regimes with conservative, white-dominated ones.

Redemptioners   People who sold themselves into indentured servitude. At the end of the voyage to America, they were to be "redeemed" by those who paid the cost of their passage.

Religious Right   Conservative political movement by evangelical Protestants against abortion and for the Republican Party prominent in the 1980s and after.

Republicanism   A set of doctrines rooted in classical antiquity that held that power is always grasping and dangerous and presents a threat to liberty. Republicanism supplied constitutionalism with a motive by explaining how a balanced constitution could be transformed into a tyranny as grasping men used their power to encroach on the liberty of citizens. In addition, republicanism held that people achieved fulfillment only through participation in public life, as citizens in a republic. Republicanism required the individual to display virtue by sacrificing his (or her) private interest for the good of the republic.

Requerimiento **(the Requirement)**   A document issued by the Spanish Crown in 1513 in order to clarify the legal bases for the enslavement of hostile Indians. Each conquistador was required to read a copy of the *Requerimiento* to each group of Indians he encountered. The *Requerimiento* promised friendship to all Indians who accepted Christianity, but threatened war and enslavement for all those who resisted.

Reservations   Lands that the federal government reserved for Native American tribes as their homelands, either through limiting the domain that a tribe had claimed originally or through forcible relocation from the place where it already lived.

Revivals   Large gatherings of people who come to hear evangelical preachers. Many experience their own Christian conversion and testify before the multitude.

Royal colony   A colony owned and managed by the Crown (as opposed to a proprietary colony owned and managed by individual investors).

Safety-valve theory   An argument commonly made in the nineteenth century that the abundance of western land spared the United States from the social upheavals common to capitalist societies in Europe. In theory, as long as eastern workers had the option of migrating west and becoming independent farmers, they could not be subject to European levels of exploitation. Thus, the West was said to provide a "safety valve" against the pressures caused by capitalist development.

Scab   Slang term for a worker employed during a strike; a strike-breaker.

Scalawag   A derogatory term referring to southern whites who sympathized with the Republicans during Reconstruction.

Secession   A state's act in dissolving its allegiance to the United States government, as 11 southern states did in 1860 and 1861. The question of its legality formed the essential issue of the Civil War.

Separate but equal   In 1896, *Plessy v. Ferguson* declared segregation was constitutional as long as the different accommodations provided for blacks and whites were equivalent. The doctrine of "separate but equal" would allow legalized segregation throughout the South until the Supreme Court overturned the edict in 1954 with *Brown v. Board of Education.*

Separation of powers   One of the chief innovations of the Constitution and a distinguishing mark of the American form of democracy, in which the executive, legislative, and judicial branches of government are separated so that they can check and balance each other.

Sharecropping   The practice of a tenant farming the landlord's ground for a share of the crop, sold when the harvest came in. This became a common form of employment for former slaves in the post–Civil War South.

Sherman Anti-Trust Act   An 1890 law forbidding business combinations in restraint of trade, which gave the government power to break monopolies.

Sit-in   An important tactic of grassroots, nonviolent civil disobedience, a sit-in is the occupation of a public place in order to protest and to demand change. The 1960 sit-in by the A&T Four to protest segregation at the Woolworth's lunch counter in Greensboro, North Carolina, popularized the tactic, which spread to the African American freedom struggle and inspired other protest movements for decades to come.

Slave power   In the 1850s, northern Republicans explained the continued economic and political strength of slavery by claiming that a "slave power" had taken control of the federal government and used its authority to keep slavery alive artificially.

Slave society   A society in which slavery is central to the economy and political structure, in contrast to a society with slaves, in which the presence of slaves does not alter the fundamental structures of the society.

Slavery   A system of extreme social inequality distinguished by the definition of a human being as property, or chattel, and thus, in principle, totally subordinated to the slave owner.

Social Darwinism   Darwin's theory of natural selection transferred from biological evolution to human history. Social Darwinists argued that some individuals and groups, particularly racial groups, were better able to survive in the "race of life."

Social Security   Social insurance plan established in 1935 that required contributions from both employers and employees. The original legislation, though limited, provided Americans with workers' compensation, unemployment insurance, family aid, and old-age pensions.

Spoils system   The practice of politicians rewarding their friends with offices and contracts.

Stagflation   The unusual combination of stagnant growth and high inflation that plagued the American economy in the 1970s.

Strict constructionism   The view that the Constitution has a fixed, explicit meaning which can be altered only through formal amendment. Loose constructionism is the view that the Constitution is a broad framework within which various interpretations and applications are possible without formal amendment.

Subtreasury   A government-run bank in which farmers could get low-interest loans using their crops as collateral. The creation of subtreasuries formed a key plank in the Populist platform.

Suburbanization   The spread of suburban housing developments and communities and, more broadly, of the suburban ideal.

Suffrage   The right to vote in political elections. Women advocated for the right to vote from the mid-nineteenth century on and eventually secured the franchise via the Nineteenth Amendment in 1920.

Supply-side economics   The controversial theory, associated with economist Arthur Laffer, that drove "Reaganomics," the conservative economic policy of the Reagan administration. In contrast to liberal economic theory, supply-side economics emphasized that producers—the "supply side" of the economic equation—drove economic growth, rather than consumers—the "demand side." To encourage producers to invest more in new production, Laffer and other supply-siders called for massive tax cuts.

Tammany Hall   A fraternal organization in New York City that developed into a Democratic political machine, electing officials, mobilizing voters, and allotting contracts. Its enemies saw it as a symbol of corrupt, selfish, and incompetent government.

Tariff   A tax on goods moving across an international boundary. Because the Constitution allows tariffs only on imports, as a political issue the tariff question has chiefly concerned the protection of domestic manufacturing from foreign competition. Industries producing mainly for American consumers have preferred a higher tariff, while farmers and industries aimed at global markets have typically favored reduced tariffs. Prior to the Civil War, the tariff was a symbol of diverging political economies in North and South. The North advocated high tariffs to protect growing domestic manufacturing ("protective tariffs"), and the South opposed high tariffs on the grounds that they increased the cost of imported manufactured goods.

Taylorism   A method for maximizing industrial efficiency by systematically reducing the time and motion involved in each step of the production process. The "scientific" system was designed by Frederick Taylor and explained in his book *The Principles of Scientific Management* (1911).

Temperance   Moderation, or the use of something with restraint. In the Gilded Age, the temperance movement opposed the use of alcohol.

Ten Percent Plan   Abraham Lincoln's 1863 proposal for reconstructing former Confederate states, based on the creation of governments after 10 percent of the eligible voters had taken an oath of loyalty to the United States.

Tenement   A multiapartment building in major cities, generally inhabited by the poor, often under the most squalid conditions.

Tennessee Valley Authority (TVA)   New Deal program that attempted to modernize the rural area along the Tennessee River via environmental control, the introduction of electricity, and the establishment of modern manufacturing.

Tenure of Office Act   Passed by Congress in 1867, the act forbade a president from removing any officer that he had appointed, without the consent of the Senate. Its violation became the central charge in Andrew Johnson's impeachment proceedings.

Total War   Armed conflict that involves the complete mobilization of a nation's resources and population and that targets civilians as well as soldiers. A comparatively modern development, total war began in the United States with the Civil War, expanded in World War I with the introduction of bombers, submarines, and poison gas, and grew again in World War II with the strategic bombing of cities, the Holocaust, and the dropping of the first atomic bombs.

Trusts   Corporate arrangements to unify action in production and distribution among different firms. Shareholders handed over control of their stock to a board that held the shares in trust and operated the combined concerns.

Universalism   Enlightenment belief that all people are by their nature essentially the same.

Vertical integration   The practice of taking control of every aspect of the production, distribution, and sale of a commodity. For example, Andrew Carnegie vertically integrated his steel operations by purchasing the mines that produced the ore, the railroads that carried the ore to the steel mills, the mills themselves, and the distribution system that carried the finished steel to consumers.

Virtual representation   British doctrine that said that all Britons, even those who did not vote, were represented by Parliament, if not "actually," by representatives they had chosen, then "virtually," because each member of parliament was supposed to act on behalf of the entire realm, not only his constituents or even those who had voted for him.

Voluntarism   A style of political activism that took place largely outside of electoral politics. Voluntarism emerged in the nineteenth century, particularly among those Americans who were not allowed to vote. Thus, women formed voluntary associations that pressed for social and political reforms, even though women were excluded from electoral politics.

Wagner Act   1935 legislation that guaranteed workers' rights to bargain collectively with their employers, prohibited the firing of workers after a strike, and restricted other antiunion measures.

Waltham system   Named after the system used in early textile mills in Waltham, Massachusetts, the term refers to the practice of bringing all elements of production together in a single factory setting with the application of non-human-powered machinery.

Wampum   Shell beads used by Indians of the Eastern Woodlands to make jewelry and to memorialize political agreements; later used as currency in the trade networks established between Europeans and Indians.

War on Poverty   Declared by President Johnson in 1964, the war on poverty became the catch-all term for the Economic Opportunity Act of 1964 and the antipoverty legislation of the Democrats' Great Society.

Watergate   The name of the Washington, DC, office and condominium complex where five men with ties to the presidential campaign of Richard Nixon were caught breaking into the headquarters of the Democratic National Committee in June 1972. "Watergate" became the catch-all term for the wide range of illegal practices of Nixon and his followers that were uncovered in the aftermath of the break-in.

The Wealth of Nations   The title of the most famous work of the renowned economist and philosopher, Adam Smith. Today the phrase is often used to short-handedly refer to the core principles of classical economics.

Western front   The main theater of action during World War I, traveling through France from the North Sea coast of Belgium to the Swiss border. Stretching approximately 440 miles, much of the front was comprised of an intricate system of trenches.

Whig Party   The political party founded by Henry Clay in the mid-1830s. The name derived from the seventeenth- and eighteenth-century British antimonarchical position and was intended to suggest that the Jacksonian Democrats (and Jackson in particular) sought despotic powers. In many ways the heirs of National Republicans, the Whigs supported economic expansion, but they also believed in a strong federal government to control the dynamism of the market. The Whig Party attracted many moral reformers.

Wilmot Proviso   An amendment to a military appropriations bill proposed in 1846 to keep slavery out of all territories taken in the Mexican War. Although it never passed, it excited four years of bitter sectional controversy.

Women's Christian Temperance Union (WCTU)   Women's reform organization founded in 1873 to discourage drinking and close down saloons, if possible by prohibition of the sale or manufacture of alcohol.

Women's rights movement   The antebellum organizing efforts of women on their own behalf, in the attempt to secure a broad range of social, civic, and political rights. This movement is generally dated from the convention of Seneca Falls in 1848. Only after the Civil War would women's rights activism begin to confine its efforts to suffrage.

Photo Credits

Antiquarian Society copy the gift of Armstrong Hunter, 1991, 265; Kean Collection/Getty Images, 273; Catlin, George (1796–1872) Ten-squat-a-way, The Open Door, Known as The Prophet, Brother of Tecumseh. Shawnee. 1830. Oil on canvas. 29 × 24 in. (73.7 × 60.9 cm) Location: Smithsonian American Art Museum, Washington, DC, U. Photo Credit: Smithsonian American Art Museum, Washington, DC/Art Resource, NY, 280; Image located in Robert Stuart Sanders, Presbyterianism in Paris and Bourbon County, Kentucky, 1786–1961 (First Presbyterian Church, 1961), p. 209, 282.

Chapter 10: Granger–All rights reserved, 288–289, 308; McKenney and Hall (19th CE) John Ross, A Cherokee Chief. From History of the Indian Tribes of North America. ca. 1843. Hand-colored lithograph on paper. 19 5/8 × 13 3/8 in. (49.9 × 34 cm). Smithsonian American Art Museum, Washington, DC/Art Resource, NY National Portrait Gallery, Smithsonian Institution, gift of Betty A. and Lloyd G. Schermer, 290; Granger–All rights reserved, 292; Granger–All rights reserved, 299; Page 041, in the Manigault Family Papers #484, Southern Historical Collection, Wilson Library, University of North Carolina at Chapel Hill, 305; Courtesy of the Library of Congress, 320; Gilcrease Museum, Tulsa, OK, 322; Courtesy of the Library of Congress, S10-4.

Chapter 11: Geoffrey Clements/Getty Images, 330–331, 345; Courtesy of the Library of Congress, 332; Courtesy of the Library of Congress, 333; Granger–All rights reserved, 335; Photo by: Universal History Archive/UIG via Getty Images, 339; Granger–All rights reserved, 350; Granger–All rights reserved, 354.

Chapter 12: Photo by Herbert Orth/The LIFE Images Collection/Getty Images, 360-361, 381; Granger–All rights reserved, 362; Courtesy of the Library of Congress, 365; Apic/RETIRED/Getty Images, 373; George Catlin (1796–1872) [Buffalo Hunt, with Wolf-Skin Mask.], 1844. Toned lithograph with applied watercolor. Amon Carter Museum of American Art, Fort Worth, Texas, 376; Los Angeles Public Library, 386; Thomas Cole, Landscape, 1825 oil on canvas 23 ¾ × 31 ½ in. Minneapolis Institute of Art 15.299 Bequest of Mrs. Kate L. Dunwoody, S12-3; Granger–All rights reserved, S12-4; Louis Rémy Mignot Landscape in Ecuador, 1859 24 × 39 ½ in. (61.0 × 100.3 cm) Oil on canvas. Purchased with funds from gifts by the American Credit Corporation in memory of Guy T. Carswell, and various donors, by exchange 91.2, S12-4.

Chapter 13: Granger–All rights reserved, 388–389, 415; Frederick Douglass. ca. 1855.

Daguerreotype, 7.0 × 5.6 cm (2 ¾ × 2 3/16 in.). The Rubel Collection, Partial and Promised Gift of William Rubel, 2001 (2001.756). Image copyright © The Metropolitan Museum of Art. Image source: Art Resource, NY, 390; Outward Bound, The Quay of Dubli . . . Nicol, J (19th century) (after). Collection of the New York Historical Society, USA/Bridgeman Images, 393; Granger–All rights reserved, 399; Granger–All rights reserved, 407; Courtesy of the Library of Congress, 411.

Chapter 14: Granger–All rights reserved, 420–421, 446; Penn School Papers, Southern Historical Collection, University of North Carolina at Chapel Hill, 422; Granger–All rights reserved, 431; Granger–All rights reserved, 441; Courtesy of the Library of Congress, 445; David Gilmour Blythe (American, 1815–1865), Lincoln Crushing the Dragon of Rebellion, 1862 oil on canvas 45.72 × 55.88 cm. Museum of Fine Arts Boston 48.413 Bequest of Martha C. Karolik for the M. and M. Karolik Collection of American Paintings, 1815–1865. Photograph © 2018 Museum of Fine Arts, Boston, 451; Culver Pictures/The Art Archive/Art Resource, NY, 453.

Chapter 15: Photo by MPI/Getty Images, 458–459, 489; Courtesy of the Library of Congress, 460; Courtesy of the Library of Congress, 468; Courtesy of the Library of Congress, 473; Bettmann/Getty Images, 480; Granger–All rights reserved, 482; Courtesy of the Library of Congress, 486.

Chapter 16: The Granger Collection, 496–497, 510; The Granger Collection, 498; The Granger Collection, 505; Curt Teich Postcard Archives Collection (Newberry Library) DPC79785, 507; California History, Vol. 64, No. 3, Summer 1985, page 174 (University of California Press and California Historical Society), 515; The Granger Collection, 522; Courtesy of the Library of Congress, S16-2.

Chapter 17: Courtesy of the Ohio History Connection, 524–525, 541; Nebraska State Historical Society, 526; Photo by PhotoQuest/Getty Images, 529; The Granger Collection, 534; Bettmann/Getty Images, 535; Weir, John Ferguson (1841–1926) Forging the Shaft. 1874–77. Oil on canvas, 52 × 73 ¼ in. (132.1 × 186.1 cm). Purchase, Lyman G. Bloomingdale Gift, 1901 (01.7.1). Location: The Metropolitan Museum of Art, New York, NY, USA Photo Credit: Image copyright © The Metropolitan Museum of Art. Image source: Art Resource, NY, 550; Kansas State Historical Society, 553; The Granger Collection, S17-5; Courtesy of the Library of Congress, S17-7; Courtesy of the Library of Congress, S17-7.

Index

Croly, Herbert, 606, 612
Cromwell, Oliver, 92
Crop liens, 567
"Cross of Gold" speech, 565, 567
Crow, P., *Letters from Polly Crow to Her Husband during World War II* (1944), S24–7–9(d)
Crow Indians, 373, 480, 481
Crusade, The (against alcohol), 540–41
Crusades, 11
Cuba, 582, 882, 883, 942
  American gunrunners to, 547
  annexation issue, 578
  Bay of Pigs incident, 815
  independence achieved, 580
  missile crisis, 816
  Ostend Manifesto and, 406
  revolution in, 578
  under Spain, 25, 575
  Wilson administration and, 622
Cuban-American Treaty of 1903, 942
Cuban Americans, 892
Cucher, Sammy, S29–3(v)
Cullen, Countee, 669
Cultural feminism, 852
Culture
  of American Republic, 240–42
  of industrial America: immigration and, 531–35
  manifest destiny in, 367–68
  postmodern, 911
  See also Modern culture; Urban culture
Culture wars, 921–26
Cumberland River, 274
Cummins, Sarah, 371
Currency
  in American Republic, 229, 271, 286
  in Civil War, 434, 541–42
  in colonial era, 171
  Confederate, 434
  Continental, depreciation of (1770-1781), 208(figure)
  greenbacks, 434, 484, 541–42, 551, 565
  "In God We Trust" added to, 781
  in industrial era, 541–42, 543, 551
  Jackson's policy, 317–18
  in modern economy, 565–67
  panic of 1893 and, 558
  in post-revolution era, 207, 208, 215
  Van Buren's policy, 365
Currency Act of 1764, 171, 182, 183(table)
Cushing, John Perkins, 366
Custer, George Armstrong, 481–82
Cvetic, Matt, 769

CWA (*See* Civil Works Administration)
Czechoslovakia
  communism collapse in, 900
  World War II and, 713
Czolgosz, Leon, 605

D-Day, 734–35
DACA (*see* Deferred Action for Childhood Arrivals program (DACA))
Daily Record, 572, 573
Daley, Richard, 826, 827, 833
Dallas (television program), 874
Dalrymple, Louis, *School Begins* (1899), S18–6–7(d)
Daly, Marcus, 504
Dams, 277, 691, 694(map), 725, 798, 862
Danbury Hatters case, 574
Dardanelles, 749
Darrow, Clarence, 666
Dartmouth College, 154, 278
Dartmouth v. Woodward, 278
Darwin, Charles, 517
Daughters of Bilitis, 783
Davenport, James, 153
Davenport, John, 83
Davidson, Donald, 665
Davis, Benjamin O., 720
Davis, Henry Winter, 462
Davis, Jefferson, 424, 426, 436, 451, 461, 462
  criticism of, 449
  on Emancipation Proclamation, 442
Davis, Jo Ann, S30–2–3(d)
Davis, John W., 672
Dawes, William, 191
Dawes Severalty Act of 1887, 483, 544
Day care, 727
Day The Earth Stood Still, The (film), 802
Dayan, Moshe, 719
Days of Rage, 857
Dayton, Jonathan, 252
De Feria, P., *Letter from Fray Pedro de Feria to Phillip II, King of Spain about Paquiquineo* (1563), S2–0–1(d)
De La Warr, Lord, 66
De Salvo, Nicholas, 829
De Soto, Hernando, 23
Deadly Mantis, The (film), 802
Dean, James, 796
Dean, John, 859
Debate in the House of Representatives on a Resolution "That Symbols and Traditions of Christmas Should be Protected" (2005), S30–3–4(d)

Debs, Eugene V., 563, 575, 628–29
  Canton, Ohio Speech (1918), S20–1–3(d)
  imperialism opposed by, 581
  imprisonment of, 628–29, S20–1
  presidential candidacy of, 595, 613, 629
Debtors' prisons, 146, 286, 473
Decade of the Hispanic, 892
Declaration of a Pueblo Indian Captured by the Spaniards (1680), S4–4–5(d)
Declaration of Independence, 193–95, 200, 247, 250, 404
Declaration of Interdependence toward the World--2005 (Ohmae, K., 1990), S29–0–2(d)
Declaration of Rights, 186
Declaration of Rights and Sentiments, 355, 358
Declaration of the Causes and Necessities of Taking Up Arms, 193
Declaration of the Rights of Man and of the Citizen, 247
Declaratory Act of 1766, 177, 183(table)
Deconstruction, 924
Deepwater Port Commission, 568–69
Defense Department, 905
Defense of Marriage Act of 1996, 926, 952, S29–4, S29–4–6(d)
Deferred Action for Childhood Arrivals program (DACA), 952
Deficit spending, 705, 724
Deflation, 543, 551
Deganawidah, 10
Deindustrialization, 842–44, 849, 871, 890
Del Monte Company, 533
Delaware
  in colonial era, 141
  Constitutional ratification and, 218
  emancipation resisted in, 455
  secession resisted by, 426
  slavery in, 211, 238, 455
Delaware Indians, 165, 408–9
Delaware River, 46, 69, 93
  Washington's crossing of, 197–98
Dell Computer, 871
Democracy
  abolitionism and, 324–25
  Adams (John Q.) presidency and, 296–97
  the Barstow family trip and, 788–89
  Boston Massacre and, 180–81
  Bush (George H. W.) and, 927

Sunday, Billy, 634
Sunday School movement, 337
Sunday School Union, 281
Super PACs, 958
Super Storm Sandy, 947
Superfund, 863, 894
Superiority of the Anglo-Saxon Race, The (Strong, J., 1885) (excerpts), S17–4–6(d)
Supply-side economics, 878, 879
Supreme Court
  on abortion legality, 852, 888, 925
  on affirmative action, 849
  in American Republic, 228
  on antisodomy laws, 889
  on the Bank of the United States, 278, 286, 317
  on bilingual education, 854
  on Bush-Gore election, 920–21
  Civil War impact on influence in, 455
  cold war legislation and, 767
  creation of, 217
  Debs' conviction upheld by, 629
  Democratic Republicans and, 261–62
  on gay rights issues, 925–26
  on Gramm-Rudman Act, 896
  and Guantánamo Bay detention center, 938
  on Japanese American internment, 730–31
  on labor union activities, 641, 654
  on Mexican land claims in California, 386
  "midnight appointees" of, 261–62
  on military trials, 435
  on Native American land rights, 319, 320, 362
  New Deal legislation and, 696, 698, 700, 701–2
  Nixon appointees, 858
  on Nixon tapes, 860
  Pentagon Papers and, 846
  on personal freedom, 819
  on racial discrimination, 488–89, 570, 571, 729, 759, 760, 799, 891
  Reagan appointees, 887
  on school busing, 849–51
  on school segregation, 798–99, 807
  on sexual material, 780
  Sherman Anti-Trust Act and, 545, 548, 606
  on slavery issues, 410–12
  on strikes, 575
  support for market economy, 277–78
  on voting rights, 485, 602, 729, 759

Survive Nuclear Attack, Office of Civil and Defense Mobilization (1960) (excerpts), S25–6–9(d)
Susquehanna River, 163
Susquehannock Indians, 49, 69, 101
Sutter, John, 504
Sutter's mill, 504
Swaggart, Jimmy, 893
Swann v. Charlotte-Mecklenburg Board of Education, 850
Swansea, 105
Sweatshops, 514–16
Swift, Gustavus, 501, 510, 511
Symes, Lillian, 660
Syngman Rhee, 754
Syria, 840, 847, 948

Taft, Robert, 714, 762
Taft, William H., 609–15, 621, 673
Taft-Hartley Act of 1947, 758, 762
Tailoresses, 346
Tailors, 353–54
Taino Indians, 15, 16
Taiping Rebellion, 518
Taiwan, 754
  Eisenhower and, 792
  Nixon and, 846
Takagi, Takeo, 718
Taliban, 936, 938, 940, 945
Talleyrand, Charles, 251
Tallmadge, James, 294
Tammany Hall, 486, 536, 548, 549, 615, S17–0, S17–1
Tammany Times, And Reform Moves On (November 18, 1895), S17–1–2(d)
Tanacharison, 163
Taney, Roger, 317, 410–13
Tanzania, U.S. embassy attack in, 932
Tappan, Arthur, 357
Tappan, Lewis, 357
Tarawa, 736
Tarbell, Ida, 597
Tariff Act of 1789, 229
Tariffs
  of 1816, 297, 323
  of 1824, 297
  of 1832, 326, 327
  of 1833, 327
  of 1846, 384
  of abominations (1828), 323, 327
  in American Republic, 229
  Dingley Tariff Act, 567
  Fordney-McCumber, 672
  globalization and, 906
  Hawley-Smoot, 686, 712
  in industrial America, 544–45
  in late 19th century, 561, 567
  McKinley, 545, 561, 578, 580

Morrill "War Tariff," 433–34
Payne-Aldrich, 611
Reagan administration and, 886
Tariff Act of 1789, 229
Underwood-Simmons, 615
Tarleton, Banastre, 203
TARP (*See* Troubled Asset Relief Program)
Task system in slavery, 135, 145, 305, 309
Tate, Allen, 665
Taverns, 141, 232, 241
Tax Cuts and Jobs Act of 2017, 961
Tax Reform Act of 1986, 894
Taxes, 946
  in American Republic, 246, 251, 262, 264
  Antifederalists on, 221
  and Barack Obama, 955
  Bush (George H. W.) and, 913, 914
  capital gains, 863
  in colonial America, 92, 100, 160, 166–67, 175–77, 182, 185
  estate, 878
  excise, 246
  income, 434, 604, 609, 613, 696–97, 878, 894
  Reagan and, 878, 879, 894
  Roosevelt (Franklin) and, 696–97
  single, 550
  Taft and, 609
Taylor, Frederick Winslow, 562, 653
Taylor, J., *Account of the Murders of Joseph and Hyrum Smith* (1844), S11–5–7(d)
Taylor, Paul, 680
Taylor, Zachary
  death of, 399
  Mexican War and, 380, 382, 383
  presidency of, 397, 398, 400
Taylorism, 562, 656
Tea
  colonial era demand for, 138
  tax on, 182
Tea Act of 1773, 179, 182, 183(table)
Tea Party movement, 946
Teach-ins, 824
Teapot Dome scandal, 672
Technology
  communications, 905
  economic impact of, 871–72
  and employment, 953
  in war, 936
Tecumseh, 246, 258, 268, 279, 377
Teenage Attitudes (Remmers, H. H., and Radler, D. H., 1958) (excerpts), S25–2–4(d)
Teenagers (*See* Youth)
Tejanos, 369, 786, 892